THE HISTORY
OF ENGLAND

VOLUME VI

THE HISTORY
OF ENGLAND

from the Invasion of Julius Caesar

to The Revolution in 1688

IN SIX VOLUMES

BY DAVID HUME, ESQ.

VOLUME VI

Based on the Edition of 1778, with the Author's

Last Corrections and Improvements

LibertyClassics

Liberty*Classics* is a publishing imprint of Liberty Fund, Inc., a foundation established to encourage study of the ideal of a society of free and responsible individuals.

The cuneiform inscription that serves as the design motif for our end-papers is the earliest-known written appearance of the word "freedom" (*ama-gi*), or "liberty." It is taken from a clay document written about 2300 B.C. in the Sumerian city-state of Lagash.

This Liberty*Classics* edition is based on the edition of 1778, containing the author's last corrections and improvements. The only two recorded sets of that edition in the United States were consulted. One is a complete set at the Humanities Research Center of the University of Texas at Austin. The other is an incomplete set in the Boston Public Library. The publisher acknowledges with thanks the cooperation of both institutions as well as the advice of Professors William B. Todd and David Levy.

Design by Martin Lubin/Betty Binns Graphics, New York, New York.
Editorial services provided by Harkavy Publishing Service, New York, New York.

Library of Congress Cataloging in Publication Data

Hume, David, 1711–1776.
    The history of England.

    "Based on the edition of 1778, with the author's last corrections and improvements."
    Reprint. Originally published: London: T. Cadell, 1778. With new foreword.
    1. Great Britain—History—To 1485. 2. Great Britain—History—Tudors, 1485–1603. 3. Great Britain—History—Stuarts, 1603–1714. I. Title.
DA30.H9 1985   942   82–25868
ISBN 0–86597–019–X (series)
ISBN 0–86597–020–3 (pbk. series)
ISBN 0–86597–034–3 (Volume VI)
ISBN 0–86597–035–1 (Volume VI pbk.)

10 9 8 7 6 5 4 3 2 1

CONTENTS

OF THE SIXTH VOLUME

Parliament – Prelacy restored –
Insurrection of the Millenarians – Affairs of Scotland –
Conference at the Savoy – Arguments for
and against a comprehension – A new parliament –
Bishops' seats restored – Corporation act –
Act of uniformity – King's marriage –
Trial of Vane – And execution –
Presbyterian clergy ejected – Dunkirk
sold to the French – Declaration of
indulgence – Decline of
Clarendon's credit

PAGE 155

LXIV

A new session – Rupture with
Holland – A new session – Victory of the
English – Rupture with France – Rupture
with Denmark – New session – Five-mile act – Sea-fight
of four days – Victory of the English – Fire of London –
Advances towards peace – Disgrace at Chatham – Peace
of Breda – Clarendon's fall – and banishment –
State of France – Character of Lewis XIV. –
French invasion of the Low Countries –
Negociations – Triple league – Treaty
of Aix-la-Chapelle – Affairs of
Scotland – and of Ireland

PAGE 190

LXV

A parliament – The cabal – Their characters –
Their counsels – Alliance with France – A parliament –
Coventry act – Blood's crimes – Duke declares himself
catholic – Exchequer shut – Declaration of indulgence –
Attack of the Smyrna fleet – War declared with
Holland – Weakness of the States – Battle
of Solebay – Sandwich killed – Progress of the French –
Consternation of the Dutch – Prince of Orange
Stadtholder – Massacre of the de Wits –
Good conduct of the prince – A parliament –
Declaration of indulgence recalled – Sea-fight – Another
sea-fight – Another sea-fight – Congress of Cologne –
A parliament – Peace with Holland

PAGE 233

LXVI

Schemes of the cabal – Remonstrances
of Sir William Temple – Campaign of 1674 –
A Parliament – Passive obedience – A Parliament –
Campaign of 1675 – Congress of Nimeguen – Campaign
of 1676 – Uncertain conduct of the King – A Parliament –
Campaign of 1677 – Parliament's distrust of the King –
Marriage of the Prince of Orange with the Lady Mary –
Plan of peace – Negociations – Campaign of 1678 –
Negociations – Peace of Nimeguen –
State of affairs in Scotland

PAGE 284

LXVII

LXVIII

LXIX

LXX

JAMES II

LXXI

INDEX
TO THE SIX VOLUMES

THE HISTORY
OF ENGLAND

VOLUME VI

LX

THE COMMONWEALTH

State of England – Of Scotland –
Of Ireland – Levellers suppressed –
Siege of Dublin raised – Tredah stormed –
Covenanters – Montrose taken prisoner –
Executed – Covenanters – Battle of
Dunbar – Of Worcester – King's escape –
The commonwealth – Dutch war –
Dissolution of the parliament

THE CONFUSIONS, which overspread England after the murder of Charles I. proceeded as well from the spirit of refinement and innovation, which agitated the ruling party, as from the dissolution of all that authority, both civil and ecclesiastical, by which the nation had ever been accustomed to be governed. Every man had framed the model of a republic; and, however new it was, or fantastical, he was eager in recommending it to his fellow citizens, or even imposing it by force upon them. Every man had adjusted a system of religion, which, being derived from no traditional authority, was peculiar to himself; and being founded on supposed inspiration, not on any principles of human reason, had no means, besides cant and low rhetoric, by which it could recommend itself to others. The levellers insisted on an equal distribution of power and property, and disclaimed all dependance and subordination.

1649.
State of
England.

3

The millenarians or fifth-monarchy-men required, that government itself should be abolished, and all human powers be laid in the dust, in order to pave the way for the dominion of Christ, whose second coming they suddenly expected. The Antinomians even insisted, that the obligations of morality and natural law were suspended, and that the elect, guided by an internal principle, more perfect and divine, were superior to the *beggarly elements* of justice and humanity. A considerable party declaimed against tythes and hireling priesthood, and were resolved, that the magistrate should not support by power or revenue any ecclesiastical establishment. Another party inveighed against the law and its professors; and on pretence of rendering more simple the distribution of justice, were desirous of abolishing the whole system of English jurisprudence, which seemed interwoven with monarchical government. Even those among the republicans, who adopted not such extravagancies, were so intoxicated with their saintly character, that they supposed themselves possessed of peculiar privileges; and all professions, oaths, laws, and engagements had, in a great measure, lost their influence over them. The bands of society were every where loosened; and the irregular passions of men were encouraged by speculative principles, still more unsocial and irregular.

The royalists, consisting of the nobles and more considerable gentry, being degraded from their authority and plundered of their property, were inflamed with the highest resentment and indignation against those ignoble adversaries, who had reduced them to subjection. The presbyterians, whose credit had first supported the arms of the parliament, were enraged to find, that, by the treachery or superior cunning of their associates, the fruits of all their successful labours were ravished from them. The former party, from inclination and principle, zealously attached themselves to the son of their unfortunate monarch, whose memory they respected, and whose tragical death they deplored. The latter cast their eye towards the same object; but they had still many prejudices to overcome, many fears and jealousies to be allayed, ere they could cordially entertain thoughts of restoring the family, which they had so grievously offended, and whose principles they regarded with such violent abhorrence.

CHAPTER LX

The only solid support of the republican independent faction, which, though it formed so small a part of the nation, had violently usurped the government of the whole, was a numerous army of near fifty thousand men. But this army, formidable from its discipline and courage, as well as its numbers, was actuated by a spirit, that rendered it dangerous to the assembly, which had assumed the command over it. Accustomed to indulge every chimera in politics, every frenzy in religion, the soldiers knew little of the subordination of citizens, and had only learned, from apparent necessity, some maxims of military obedience. And while they still maintained, that all those enormous violations of law and equity, of which they had been guilty, were justified by the success, with which providence had blessed them; they were ready to break out into any new disorder, wherever they had the prospect of a like sanction and authority.

What alone gave some stability to all these unsettled humours, was the great influence, both civil and military, acquired by Oliver Cromwel. This man, suited to the age in which he lived, and to that alone, was equally qualified to gain the affection and confidence of men, by what was mean, vulgar, and ridiculous in his character; as to command their obedience by what was great, daring, and enterprizing. Familiar even to buffoonery with the meanest centinel, he never lost his authority: Transported to a degree of madness with religious extasies, he never forgot the political purposes, to which they might serve. Hating monarchy, while a subject; despising liberty, while a citizen; though he retained for a time all orders of men under a seeming obedience to the parliament; he was secretly paving the way, by artifice and courage, to his own unlimited authority.

The parliament, for so we must henceforth call a small and inconsiderable part of the house of commons, having murdered their sovereign with so many appearing circumstances of solemnity and justice, and so much real violence and even fury, began to assume more the air of a civil, legal power, and to enlarge a little the narrow bottom upon which they stood. They admitted a few of the excluded and absent members, such as were liable to least exception; but on condition, that these members should sign an approbation of whatever had been done in their absence with regard to the king's trial: And some of them were willing to acquire a share of power on such terms: The greater part disdained to lend their authority to such apparent usurpations. They issued some writs for new elections, in places where they hoped to have interest enough to bring in their own friends and dependants. They named a council of state, thirty-eight in number, to whom all addresses were made, who gave orders to all generals and admirals, who executed the laws, and who digested all business before it was introduced into parliament.[a] They pretended to employ themselves entirely in adjusting the laws, forms, and plan of a new representative; and as soon as they should have settled the nation, they professed their intention of restoring the power to the people, from whom, they acknowledged, they had entirely derived it.

The commonwealth found every thing in England composed into a seeming tranquillity by the terror of their arms. Foreign powers, occupied in wars among themselves, had no leisure or inclination to interpose in the domestic dissensions of this island. The young king, poor and neglected, living sometimes in Holland, sometimes in France, sometimes in Jersey, comforted himself, amidst his present distresses, with the hopes of better fortune. The situation alone of Scotland and Ireland gave any immediate inquietude to the new republic.

Of Scotland. After the successive defeats of Montrose and Hamilton, and the ruin of their parties, the whole authority in Scotland fell into the hands of Argyle and the rigid churchmen, that party which was most averse to the interests of the royal family. Their enmity, however, against the independents, who had prevented the settlement of presbyterian discipline in England, carried them to embrace opposite maxims in their political conduct. Though invited by the English parliament to model their government into a republican form, they resolved still to adhere to monarchy, which had ever prevailed in their country, and which, by the express terms of their covenant, they had engaged to defend. They consid-

[a] Their names were, the earls of Denbigh, Mulgrave, Pembroke, Salisbury, lords Grey and Fairfax, Lisle, Rolles, St. John, Wilde, Bradshaw, Cromwel, Skippon, Pickering, Massam, Haselrig, Harrington, Vane jun, Danvers, Armine, Mildmay, Constable, Pennington, Wilson, Whitlocke, Martin, Ludlow, Stapleton, Hevingham, Wallop, Hutchinson, Bond, Popham, Valentine, Walton, Scot, Purefoy, Jones.

CHAPTER LX

ered besides, that as the property of the kingdom lay mostly in the hands of great families, it would be difficult to establish a commonwealth, or without some chief magistrate, invested with royal authority, to preserve peace or justice in the community. The execution, therefore, of the king, against which they had always protested, having occasioned a vacancy of the throne, they immediately proclaimed his son and successor, Charles II.; but upon condition "of his good behaviour and strict observance of the covenant, and his entertaining no other persons about him but such as were godly men and faithful to that obligation." These unusual clauses, inserted in the very first acknowledgement of their prince, sufficiently shewed their intention of limiting extremely his authority. And the English commonwealth, having no pretence to interpose in the affairs of that kingdom, allowed the Scots, for the present, to take their own measures in settling their government.

The dominion, which England claimed over Ireland, demanded more immediately their efforts for subduing that country. *Of Ireland.* In order to convey a just notion of Irish affairs, it will be necessary to look backwards some years, and to relate briefly those transactions, which had past during the memorable revolutions in England. When the late king agreed to that cessation of arms with the Popish rebels,[b] which was become so requisite, as well for the security of the Irish protestants as for promoting his interests in England, the parliament, in order to blacken his conduct, reproached him with favouring that odious rebellion, and exclaimed loudly against the terms of the cessation. They even went so far as to declare it entirely null and invalid, because finished without their consent; and to this declaration the Scots in Ulster, and the earl of Inchiquin, a nobleman of great authority in Munster, professed to adhere. By their means, the war was still kept alive; but as the dangerous distractions in England hindered the parliament from sending any considerable assistance to their allies in Ireland, the marquess of Ormond, lord lieutenant, being a native of Ireland, and a person endowed with great prudence and virtue, formed a scheme for composing the disorders of his country, and for engaging the rebel Irish to support the cause of his royal master. There were many circumstances which strongly invited the natives of

[b] 1643.

Ireland to embrace the king's party. The maxims of that prince had always led him to give a reasonable indulgence to the catholics throughout all his dominions; and one principal ground of that enmity, which the puritans professed against him, was this tacit toleration. The parliament, on the contrary, even when un-provoked, had ever menaced the papists with the most rigid re-straint, if not a total extirpation; and immediately after the com-mencement of the Irish rebellion, they put to sale all the estates of the rebels, and had engaged the public faith for transferring them to the adventurers, who had already advanced money upon that security. The success, therefore, which the arms of the parliament met with at Naseby, struck a just terror into the Irish; and engaged the council of Kilkenny, composed of deputies from all the catholic counties and cities, to conclude a peace with the marquess of Or-mond.[c] They professed to return to their duty and allegiance, engaged to furnish ten thousand men for the support of the king's authority in England, and were content with stipulating, in return, indemnity for their rebellion and toleration of their religion.

Ormond not doubting but a peace, so advantageous and even necessary to the Irish, would be strictly observed, advanced with a small body of troops to Kilkenny, in order to concert measures for common defence with his new allies. The pope had sent over to Ireland a nuncio, Rinuccini, an Italian; and this man, whose com-mission empowered him to direct the spiritual concerns of the Irish, was emboldened, by their ignorance and bigotry, to assume the chief authority in the civil government. Foreseeing that a gen-eral submission to the lord-lieutenant would put an end to his own influence, he conspired with Owen Oneal, who commanded the native Irish in Ulster, and who bore a great jealousy to Preston, the general chiefly trusted by the council of Kilkenny. By concert, these two malcontents secretly drew forces together, and were ready to fall on Ormond, who remained in security, trusting to the pacification so lately concluded with the rebels. He received intel-ligence of their treachery, made his retreat with celerity and con-duct, and sheltered his small army in Dublin and the other fortified towns, which still remained in the hands of the protestants.

[c] 1646.

CHAPTER LX

The nuncio, full of arrogance, levity, and ambition, was not contented with this violation of treaty. He summoned an assembly of the clergy at Waterford, and engaged them to declare against that pacification, which the civil council had concluded with their sovereign. He even thundered out a sentence of excommunication against all who should adhere to a peace, so prejudicial, as he pretended, to the catholic religion; and the deluded Irish, terrified with his spiritual menaces, ranged themselves every where on his side, and submitted to his authority. Without scruple, he carried on war against the lord-lieutenant, and threatened with a siege the protestant garrisons, which were, all of them, very ill provided for defence.

Meanwhile, the unfortunate king was necessitated to take shelter in the Scottish army; and being there reduced to close confinement, and secluded from all commerce with his friends, despaired, that his authority, or even his liberty, would ever be restored to him. He sent orders to Ormond, if he could not defend himself, rather to submit to the English than to the Irish rebels; and accordingly the lord-lieutenant, being reduced to extremities, delivered up Dublin, Tredah, Dundalk, and other garrisons to colonel Michael Jones, who took possession of them in the name of the English parliament. Ormond himself went over to England, was admitted into the king's presence, received a grateful acknowledgment for his past services, and during some time lived in tranquillity near London. But being banished, with the other royalists, to a distance from that city, and seeing every event turn out unfortunately for his royal master, and threaten him with a catastrophe still more direful, he thought proper to retire into France, where he joined the queen and the prince of Wales.

In Ireland, during these transactions, the authority of the nuncio prevailed without controul among all the catholics; and that prelate, by his indiscretion and insolence, soon made them repent of the power, with which they had entrusted him. Prudent men likewise were sensible of the total destruction, which was hanging over the nation from the English parliament, and saw no resource or safety but in giving support to the declining authority of the king. The earl of Clanricarde, a nobleman of an ancient family, a person too of merit, who had ever preserved his loyalty, was sensi-

ble of the ruin which threatened his countrymen, and was resolved, if possible, to prevent it. He secretly formed a combination
among the catholics; he entered into a correspondence with Inchiquin, who preserved great authority over the protestants in Munster; he attacked the nuncio, whom he chaced out of the island;
and he sent to Paris a deputation, inviting the lord-lieutenant to
return and take possession of his government.

Ormond, on his arrival in Ireland, found the kingdom divided
into many factions, among which either open war or secret enmity
prevailed. The authority of the English parliament was established
in Dublin, and the other towns, which he himself had delivered
into their hands. Oneal maintained his credit in Ulster; and having
entered into a secret correspondence with the parliamentary generals, was more intent on schemes for his own personal safety than
anxious for the preservation of his country or religion. The other
Irish, divided between their clergy, who were averse to Ormond,
and their nobility, who were attached to him, were very uncertain
in their motions and feeble in their measures. The Scots in the
north, enraged, as well as their other countrymen, against the
usurpations of the sectarian army, professed their adherence to
the king; but were still hindered by many prejudices from entering
into a cordial union with his lieutenant. All these distracted councils and contrary humours checked the progress of Ormond, and
enabled the parliamentary forces in Ireland to maintain their
ground against him. The republican faction, meanwhile, in England, employed in subduing the revolted royalists, in reducing the
parliament to subjection, in the trial, condemnation, and execution of their sovereign, totally neglected the supplying of Ireland, and allowed Jones and the forces in Dublin to remain in the
utmost weakness and necessity. The lord lieutenant, though surrounded with difficulties, neglected not the favourable opportunity of promoting the royal cause. Having at last assembled an
army of 16,000 men, he advanced upon the parliamentary garrisons. Dundalk, where Monk commanded, was delivered up by the
troops, who mutinied against their governor. Tredah, Neury, and
other forts were taken. Dublin was threatened with a siege; and the
affairs of the lieutenant appeared in so prosperous a condition,
that the young king entertained thoughts of coming in person into
Ireland.

CHAPTER LX

When the English commonwealth was brought to some tolerable settlement, men began to cast their eyes towards the neighbouring island. During the contest of the two parties, the government of Ireland had remained a great object of intrigue; and the
presbyterians endeavoured to obtain the lieutenancy for Waller,
the independents for Lambert. After the execution of the king,
Cromwel himself began to aspire to a command, where so much
glory, he saw, might be won, and so much authority acquired. In
his absence, he took care to have his name proposed to the council *15th*
of state; and both friends and enemies concurred immediately to *March.*
vote him into that important office: The former suspected, that
the matter had not been proposed merely by chance, without his
own concurrence; the latter desired to remove him to a distance,
and hoped, during his absence, to gain the ascendant over Fairfax,
whom he had so long blinded by his hypocritical professions.
Cromwel himself, when informed of his election, feigned surprize,
and pretended at first to hesitate with regard to the acceptance of
the command. And Lambert, either deceived by his dissimulation,
or in his turn, feigning to be deceived, still continued, notwithstanding this disappointment, his friendship and connexions with
Cromwel.

The new lieutenant immediately applied himself with his
wonted vigilance to make preparations for his expedition. Many
disorders in England it behoved him previously to compose. All
places were full of danger and inquietude. Though men, astonished with the successes of the army, remained in seeming tranquillity, symptoms of the greatest discontent every where appeared. The English, long accustomed to a mild administration,
and unacquainted with dissimulation, could not conform their
speech and countenance to the present necessity, or pretend attachment to a form of government, which they generally regarded
with such violent abhorrence. It was requisite to change the magistracy of London, and to degrade, as well as punish, the mayor
and some of the aldermen, before the proclamation for the abolition of monarchy could be published in the city. An engagement
being framed to support the commonwealth without king or house
of peers, the army was with some difficulty brought to subscribe it;
but though it was imposed upon the rest of the nation under severe
penalties, no less than putting all who refused out of the protec-

tion of law; such obstinate reluctance was observed in the people, that even the imperious parliament was obliged to desist from it. The spirit of fanaticism, by which that assembly had at first been strongly supported, was now turned, in a great measure, against them. The pulpits, being chiefly filled with presbyterians, or disguised royalists, and having long been the scene of news and politics, could by no penalties be restrained from declarations, unfavourable to the established government. Numberless were the extravagances, which broke out among the people. Everard, a disbanded soldier, having preached that the time was now come when the community of goods would be renewed among christians, led out his followers to take possession of the land; and being carried before the general, he refused to salute him; because he was but his fellow creature.[d] What seemed more dangerous: The army itself was infected with like humours.[e] Though the levellers had for a time been suppressed by the audacious spirit of Cromwel, they still continued to propagate their doctrines among the private men and inferior officers, who pretended a right to be consulted, as before, in the administration of the commonwealth. They now practised against their officers the same lesson, which they had been taught against the parliament. They framed a remonstrance, and sent five agitators to present it to the general and council of war: These were cashiered with ignominy by sentence of a court martial. One Lockier, having carried his sedition farther, was sentenced to death; but this punishment was so far from quelling the mutinous spirit, that above a thousand of his companions showed their adherence to him, by attending his funeral, and *Levellers* wearing in their hats black and sea-green ribbons by way of fa*suppressed.* vours. About four thousand assembled at Burford, under the command of Thomson, a man formerly condemned for sedition by a court-martial, but pardoned by the general. Colonel Reynolds, and *May.* afterwards Fairfax and Cromwel, fell upon them, while unprepared for defence, and seduced by the appearance of a treaty. Four hundred were taken prisoners: Some of them capitally punished: The rest pardoned: And this tumultuous spirit, though it still lurked in the army, and broke out from time to time, seemed for the present to be suppressed.

[d] Whitlocke. [e] See note [A] at the end of the volume.

CHAPTER LX

Petitions, framed in the same spirit of opposition, were presented to the parliament by lieutenant-colonel Lilburn, the person who, for dispersing seditious libels, had formerly been treated with such severity by the star-chamber. His liberty was at this time as ill relished by the parliament, and he was thrown into prison, as a promoter of sedition and disorder in the common-wealth. The women applied by petition for his release; but were now desired to mind their houshold affairs, and leave the government of the state to the men. From all quarters, the parliament was harassed with petitions of a very free nature, which strongly spoke the sense of the nation, and proved how ardently all men longed for the restoration of their laws and liberties. Even in a feast, which the city gave to the parliament and council of state, it was deemed a requisite precaution, if we may credit Walker and Dugdale, to swear all the cooks, that they would serve nothing but wholesome food to them.

The parliament judged it necessary to enlarge the laws of high-treason beyond those narrow bounds, within which they had been confined during the monarchy. They even comprehended verbal offences, nay intentions, though they had never appeared in any overt-act against the state. To affirm the present government to be an usurpation, to assert that the parliament or council of state were tyrannical or illegal, to endeavour subverting their authority or stirring up sedition against them; these offences were declared to be high-treason. The power of imprisonment, of which the petition of right had bereaved the king, it was now found necessary to restore to the council of state; and all the jails in England were filled with men whom the jealousies and fears of the ruling party had represented as dangerous.[f] The taxes, continued by the new government, and which, being unusual, were esteemed heavy, encreased the general ill will, under which it laboured. Besides the customs and excise, ninety thousand pounds a month were levied on land for the subsistance of the army. The sequestrations and compositions of the royalists, the sale of the crown lands, and of the dean and chapter lands, though they yielded great sums, were not sufficient to support the vast expences, and, as was suspected, the great depredations, of the parliament and of their creatures.[g]

[f] History of Independency, part II.   [g] Parl. History, vol. xix. p. 136, 176.

Amidst all these difficulties and disturbances, the steddy mind of Cromwel, without confusion or embarrassment, still pursued its purpose. While he was collecting an army of twelve thousand men in the west of England, he sent to Ireland, under Reynolds and Venables, a reinforcement of four thousand horse and foot, in order to strengthen Jones, and enable him to defend himself against the marquess of Ormond, who lay at Finglass, and was making preparations for the attack of Dublin. Inchiquin, who had now made a treaty with the king's lieutenant, having, with a separate body, taken Tredah and Dundalk, gave a defeat to Offarrell who served under Oneal, and to young Coot who commanded some parliamentary forces. After he had joined his troops to the main army, with whom, for some time, he remained united, Ormond passed the river Liffy, and took post at Rathmines, two miles from Dublin; with a view of commencing the siege of that city. In order to cut off all farther supply from Jones, he had begun the reparation of an old fort, which lay at the gates of Dublin; and being exhausted with continual fatigue for some days, he had retired to rest, after leaving orders to keep his forces under arms.

2d August.

He was suddenly awaked with the noise of firing; and starting from his bed, saw every thing already in tumult and confusion. Jones, an excellent officer, formerly a lawyer, had sallied out with the reinforcement newly arrived; and attacking the party employed in repairing the fort, he totally routed them, pursued the advantage, and fell in with the army, which had neglected Ormond's orders. These he soon threw into disorder; put them to flight, in spite of all the efforts of the lord lieutenant; chaced them off the field;

Siege of Dublin raised.

seized all their tents, baggage, ammunition; and returned victorious to Dublin, after killing a thousand men, and taking above two thousand prisoners.[h]

This loss, which threw some blemish on the military character of Ormond, was irreparable to the royal cause. That numerous army, which, with so much pains and difficulty, the lord lieutenant had been collecting for more than a year, was dispersed in a moment. Cromwel soon after arrived in Dublin, where he was welcomed with shouts and rejoicings. He hastened to Tredah. That

15th August.

[h] Parl. Hist. vol. xix. p. 165.

town was well fortified: Ormond had thrown into it a good garrison of three thousand men, under Sir Arthur Aston, an officer of reputation. He expected that Tredah, lying in the neighbourhood of Dublin, would first be attempted by Cromwel, and he was desirous to employ the enemy some time in that siege, while he himself should repair his broken forces. But Cromwel knew the importance of dispatch. Having made a breach, he ordered a general assault. Though twice repulsed with loss, he renewed the attack, and himself, along with Ireton, led on his men. All opposition was overborne by the furious valour of the troops. The town was taken sword in hand; and orders being issued to give no quarter, a cruel slaughter was made of the garrison. Even a few, who were saved by the soldiers, satiated with blood, were next day miserably butchered by orders from the general. One person alone of the garrison escaped to be a messenger of this universal havoc and destruction. *September. Tredah stormed.*

Cromwel pretended to retaliate by this severe execution the cruelty of the Irish massacre: But he well knew, that almost the whole garrison was English; and his justice was only a barbarous policy, in order to terrify all other garrisons from resistance. His policy, however, had the desired effect. Having led the army without delay to Wexford, he began to batter the town. The garrison after a slight defence offered to capitulate; but before they obtained a cessation, they imprudently neglected their guards; and the English army rushed in upon them. The same severity was exercised as at Tredah.

Every town, before which Cromwel presented himself, now opened its gates without resistance. Ross, though strongly garrisoned, was surrendered by lord Taffe. Having taken Estionage; Cromwel threw a bridge over the Barrow, and made himself master of Passage and Carric. The English had no farther difficulties to encounter than what arose from fatigue and the advanced season. Fluxes and contagious distempers creeped in among the soldiers, who perished in great numbers. Jones himself, the brave governor of Dublin, died at Wexford. And Cromwel had so far advanced with his decayed army, that he began to find it difficult, either to subsist in the enemies country, or retreat to his own garrisons. But while he was in these straits, Corke, Kinsale, and all *October.*

the English garrisons in Munster deserted to him, and opening their gates resolved to share the fortunes of their victorious countrymen.

This desertion of the English put an end to Ormond's authority, which was already much diminished by the misfortunes at Dublin, Tredah, and Wexford. The Irish, actuated by national and religious prejudices, could no longer be kept in obedience by a protestant governor, who was so unsuccessful in all his enterprizes. The clergy renewed their excommunications against him and his adherents, and added the terrors of superstition to those which arose from a victorious enemy. Cromwel having received a reinforcement from England, again took the field early in the spring. He made himself master of Kilkenny and Clonmel, the only places where he met with any vigorous resistance. The whole frame of the Irish union being in a manner dissolved, Ormond, soon after, left the island, and delegated his authority to Clanricarde, who found affairs so desperate as to admit of no remedy. The Irish were glad to embrace banishment as a refuge. Above 40,000 men passed into foreign service; and Cromwel, well-pleased to free the island from enemies, who never could be cordially reconciled to the English, gave them full liberty and leisure for their embarkation.

While Cromwel proceeded with such uninterrupted success in Ireland, which in the space of nine months he had almost entirely subdued, fortune was preparing for him a new scene of victory and triumph in Scotland. Charles was at the Hague, when Sir Joseph Douglas brought him intelligence, that he was proclaimed king by the Scottish parliament. At the same time, Douglas informed him of the hard conditions annexed to the proclamation, and extremely damped that joy, which might arise from his being recognized sovereign in one of his kingdoms. Charles too considered, that those who pretended to acknowledge his title, were at that very time in actual rebellion against his family, and would be sure to intrust very little authority in his hands, and scarcely would afford him personal liberty and security. As the prospect of affairs in Ireland was at that time not unpromising, he intended rather to try his fortune in that kingdom, from which he expected more dutiful submission and obedience.

Meanwhile he found it expedient to depart from Holland. The people in the United Provinces were much attached to his interests. Besides his connexion with the family of Orange, which was extremely beloved by the populace, all men regarded with compassion his helpless condition, and expressed the greatest abhorrence against the murder of his father; a deed, to which nothing, they thought, but the rage of fanaticism and faction could have impelled the parliament. But though the public in general bore great favour to the king, the States were uneasy at his presence. They dreaded the parliament, so formidable by their power, and so prosperous in all their enterprizes. They apprehended the most precipitate resolutions from men of such violent and haughty dispositions. And after the murder of Dorislaus, they found it still more necessary to satisfy the English commonwealth, by removing the king to a distance from them.

Dorislaus, though a native of Holland, had lived long in England; and being employed as assistant to the high court of justice, which condemned the late king, he had risen to great credit and favour with the ruling party. They sent him envoy to Holland; but no sooner had he arrived at the Hague, than he was set upon by some royalists, chiefly retainers to Montrose. They rushed into the room, where he was sitting with some company; dragged him from the table; put him to death as the first victim to their murdered sovereign; very leisurely and peaceably separated themselves; and though orders were issued by the magistrates to arrest them, these were executed with such slowness and reluctance, that the criminals had, all of them, the opportunity of making their escape.

1650.

Charles, having passed some time at Paris, where no assistance was given him, and even few civilities were paid him, made his retreat into Jersey, where his authority was still acknowledged. Here, Winram, laird of Liberton, came to him as deputy from the committee of estates in Scotland, and informed him of the conditions, to which he must necessarily submit before he could be admitted to the exercise of his authority. Conditions more severe were never imposed by subjects upon their sovereign; but as the affairs of Ireland began to decline, and the king found it no longer safe to venture himself in that island, he gave a civil answer to Winram, and desired commissioners to meet him at Breda, in order to enter into a treaty with regard to these conditions.

The earls of Cassilis and Lothian, lord Burley, the laird of Liberton and other commissioners arrived at Breda; but without

Covenant-ers.

any power of treating: The king must submit without reserve to the terms imposed upon him. The terms were, that he should issue a proclamation, banishing from court all excommunicated persons, that is, all those, who, either under Hamilton or Montrose, had ventured their lives for his family; that no English subject, who had served against the parliament, should be allowed to approach him; that he should bind himself by his royal promise to take the covenant; that he should ratify all acts of parliament, by which presbyterian government, the directory of worship, the confession of faith, and the catechism were established; and that in civil affairs he should entirely conform himself to the direction of parliament, and in ecclesiastical to that of the assembly. These proposals, the commissioners, after passing some time in sermons and prayers, in order to express the more determined resolution, very solemnly delivered to the king.

The king's friends were divided with regard to the part, which he should act in this critical conjuncture. Most of his English counsellors dissuaded him from accepting conditions, so disadvantageous and dishonourable. They said, that the men, who now governed Scotland, were the most furious and bigotted of that party, which, notwithstanding his gentle government, had first excited a rebellion against the late king; after the most unlimited concessions, had renewed their rebellion, and stopped the progress of his victories in England; and after he had entrusted his person to them in his uttermost distress, had basely sold him, together with their own honour, to his barbarous enemies: That they had as yet shown no marks of repentance, and even in the terms, which they now proposed, displayed the same antimonarchical principles, and the same jealousy of their sovereign, by which they had ever been actuated: That nothing could be more dishonourable, than that the king, in his first enterprize, should sacrifice, merely for the empty name of royalty, those principles, for which his father had died a martyr, and in which he himself had been strictly educated: That by this hypocrisy he might lose the royalists, who alone were sincerely attached to him; but never would gain the presbyterians, who were averse to his family and his cause, and would ascribe his compliance merely to policy and necessity: That the Scots had refused to give him any assurances of their intending to restore him to the throne of England; and could they even be brought to make such an attempt, it had sufficiently appeared, by the event of Hamilton's engagement, how unequal their force was to so great an enterprize: That on the first check, which they should receive, Argyle and his partizans would lay hold of the quickest expedient for reconciling themselves to the English parliament, and would betray the king, as they had done his father, into the hands of his enemies: And that, however desperate the royal cause, it must still be regarded as highly imprudent in the king to make a sacrifice of his honour; where the sole purchase was to endanger his life or liberty.

The earl of Laneric, now duke of Hamilton, the earl of Lauderdale, and others of that party, who had been banished their country for the late engagement, were then with the king; and being desirous of returning home in his retinue, they joined the opinion of the young duke of Buckingham, and earnestly pressed him to submit to the conditions required of him. It was urged, that nothing would more gratify the king's enemies than to see him fall into the snare laid for him, and by so scrupulous a nicety, leave the possession of his dominions to those who desired but a pretence for excluding him: That Argyle, not daring so far to oppose the bent of the nation as to throw off all allegiance to his sovereign, had embraced this expedient, by which he hoped to make Charles dethrone himself, and refuse a kingdom, which was offered him: That it was not to be doubted, but the same national spirit, assisted by Hamilton and his party, would rise still higher in favour of their prince after he had entrusted himself to their fidelity, and would much abate the rigour of the conditions, now imposed upon him: That whatever might be the present intentions of the ruling party, they must unavoidably be engaged in a war with England, and must accept the assistance of the king's friends of all parties, in order to support themselves against a power, so much superior: That how much soever a steddy, uniform conduct might have been suitable to the advanced age, and strict engagements of the late king, no one would throw any blame on a young prince for complying with conditions, which necessity had extorted from him: That even the rigour of those principles, professed by his father, though with some it had exalted his character, had been extremely prejudicial to his interests; nor could any thing be more serviceable to the royal cause than to give all parties room to hope for more equal and more indulgent maxims of government: And that where affairs were reduced to so desperate a situation, dangers ought little to be regarded; and the king's honour lay rather in showing some early symptoms of courage and activity, than in choosing strictly a party among theological controversies, with which, it might be supposed, he was, as yet, very little acquainted.

These arguments, seconded by the advice of the queen mother and of the prince of Orange, the king's brother in law, who both of them thought it ridiculous to refuse a kingdom merely from regard to episcopacy, had great influence on Charles. But what chiefly determined him to comply was the account brought him of the fate of Montrose, who, with all the circumstances of rage and contumely, had been put to death by his zealous countrymen. Though in this instance the king saw more evidently the furious spirit, by which the Scots were actuated, he had now no farther resource, and was obliged to grant whatever was demanded of him.

Montrose, having laid down his arms at the command of the late king, had retired into France, and, contrary to his natural disposition, had lived for some time unactive at Paris. He there became acquainted with the famous cardinal de Retz; and that penetrating judge celebrates him in his memoirs as one of those heroes, of whom there are no longer any remains in the world, and who are only to be met with in Plutarch. Desirous of improving his martial genius, he took a journey to Germany, was caressed by the emperor, received the rank of mareschal, and proposed to levy a regiment for the imperial service. While employed for that purpose in the Low Countries, he heard of the tragical death of the king; and at the same time received from his young master a renewal of his commission of captain general in Scotland.[i] His ardent and daring spirit needed but this authority to put him in action. He gathered followers in Holland and the north of Germany, whom his great reputation allured to him. The king of Denmark and duke of Holstein sent him some small supply of money: The queen of Sweden furnished him with arms: The prince of Orange with ships: And Montrose, hastening his enterprize, lest the king's agreement with the Scots should make him

[i] Burnet, Clarendon.

revoke his commission, set out for the Orkneys with about 500 men, most of them Germans. These were all the preparations, which he could make against a kingdom, settled in domestic peace, supported by a disciplined army, fully apprized of his enterprize, and prepared against him. Some of his retainers having told him of a prophesy, that *to him and him alone it was reserved to restore the king's authority in all his dominions;* he lent a willing ear to suggestions, which, however ill grounded or improbable, were so conformable to his own daring character.

He armed several of the inhabitants of the Orkneys, though an unwarlike people, and carried them over with him to Caithness; hoping, that the general affection to the king's service, and the fame of his former exploits, would make the Highlanders flock to his standard. But all men were now harassed and fatigued with wars and disorders: Many of those, who formerly adhered to him, had been severely punished by the covenanters: And no prospect of success was entertained in opposition to so great a force as was drawn together against him. But however weak Montrose's army, the memory of past events struck a great terror into the committee of estates. They immediately ordered Lesley and Holborne to march against him with an army of 4000 men. Strahan was sent before with a body of cavalry to check his progress. He fell unexpectedly on Montrose, who had no horse to bring him intelligence. The royalists were put to flight; all of them either killed or taken prisoners; and Montrose himself, having put on the disguise of a peasant, was perfidiously delivered into the hands of his enemies, by a friend, to whom he had entrusted his person.

Montrose taken prisoner.

All the insolence, which success can produce in ungenerous minds, was exercised by the covenanters against Montrose, whom they so much hated and so much dreaded. Theological antipathy farther encreased their indignities towards a person, whom they regarded as impious on account of the excommunication, which had been pronounced against him. Lesley led him about for several days in the same low habit, under which he had disguised himself. The vulgar, wherever he passed, were instigated to reproach and vilify him. When he came to Edinburgh, every circumstance of elaborate rage and insult was put in practice by order of the parliament. At the gate of the city, he was met by the magistrates, and put into a new cart, purposely made with a high chair or bench, where he was placed, that the people might have a full view of him. He was bound with a cord, drawn over his breast and shoulders, and fastened through holes made in the cart. The hangman then took off the hat of the noble prisoner, and rode himself before the cart in his livery, and with his bonnet on; the other officers, who were taken prisoners with the marquess, walking two and two before them.

The populace, more generous and humane, when they saw so mighty a change of fortune in this great man, so lately their dread and terror, into whose hands the magistrates, a few years before, had delivered on their knees the keys of the city, were struck with compassion, and viewed him with silent tears and admiration. The preachers, next Sunday, exclaimed against this movement of rebel nature, as they termed it; and reproached the people with their profane tenderness towards the capital enemy of piety and religion.

When he was carried before the parliament, which was then sitting, Loudon, the chancellor, in a violent declamation, reproached him with the breach of the national covenant, which he had subscribed; his rebellion against God, the king, and the kingdom; and the many horrible murders, treasons, and impieties, for which he was now to be brought to condign punishment. Montrose in his answer maintained the same superiority above his enemies, to which, by his fame and great actions, as well as by the consciousness of a good cause, he was justly entitled. He told the parliament, that, since the king, as he was informed, had so far avowed their authority as to enter into treaty with them, he now appeared uncovered before their tribunal; a respect, which, while they stood in open defiance to their sovereign, they would in vain have required of him. That he acknowledged, with infinite shame and remorse, the errors of his early conduct, when their plausible pretences had seduced him to tread with them the paths of rebellion, and bear arms against his prince and country. That his following services, he hoped, had sufficiently testified his repentance; and his death would now atone for that guilt, the only one with which he could justly reproach himself. That in all his warlike enterprizes he was warranted by that commission, which he had received from his and their master, against whose lawful authority they had erected their standard. That to venture his life for his sovereign was the least part of his merit: He had even thrown down his arms in obedience to the sacred commands of the king; and had resigned to them the victory, which, in defiance of all their efforts, he was still enabled to dispute with them. That no blood had ever been shed by him but in the field of battle; and many persons were now in his eye, many now dared to pronounce sentence of death upon him, whose life, forfeited by the laws of war, he had formerly saved from the fury of the soldiers. That he was sorry to find no better testimony of their return to allegiance than the murder of so faithful a subject, in whose death the king's commission must be, at once, so highly injured and affronted. That as to himself, they had in vain endeavoured to vilify and degrade him by all their studied indignities: The justice of his cause, he knew, would ennoble any fortune; nor had he other affliction than to see the authority of his prince, with which he was invested, treated with so much ignominy. And that he now joyfully followed, by a like unjust sentence, his late sovereign; and should be happy, if, in his future destiny, he could follow him to the same blissful mansions, where his piety and humane virtues had already, without doubt, secured him an eternal recompence.

Montrose's sentence was next pronounced against him, "That he, James Graham" (for this was the only name they vouchsafed to give him) "should next day be carried to Edinburgh cross, and there be hanged on a gibbet, thirty feet high, for the space of three hours: Then be taken down, his head be cut off upon a scaffold, and affixed to the prison: His legs and arms be stuck up on the four chief towns of the kingdom: His body be buried in the place appropriated for common malefactors; except the church, upon his repentance, should take off his excommunication."

The clergy, hoping, that the terrors of immediate death had now given them an advantage over their enemy, flocked about him, and insulted over his fallen fortunes. They pronounced his damnation, and assured him, that the judgment, which he was so soon to suffer, would prove but an easy prologue to that which he must undergo hereafter. They next offered to pray with him: But he was too well acquainted with those forms of imprecation, which they called prayers. "Lord, vouchsafe yet to touch the obdurate heart of this proud incorrigible sinner; this wicked, perjured, traiterous, and profane person, who refuses to hearken to the voice of thy church." Such were the petitions, which, he expected, they would, according to custom, offer up for him. He told them, that they were a miserably deluded and deluding people; and would shortly bring their country under the most insupportable servitude, to which any nation had ever been reduced. "For my part," added he, "I am much prouder to have my head affixed to the place, where it is sentenced to stand, than to have my picture hang in the king's bed-chamber. So far from being sorry, that my quarters are to be sent to four cities of the kingdom; I wish I had limbs enow to be dispersed into all the cities of Christendom, there to remain as testimonies in favour of the cause, for which I suffer." This sentiment, that very evening, while in prison, he threw into verse. The poem remains; a signal monument of his heroic spirit, and no despicable proof of his poetical genius.

21st May.

Now was led forth, amidst the insults of his enemies and the tears of the people, this man of illustrious birth and of the greatest renown in the nation, to suffer, for his adhering to the laws of his country, and the rights of his sovereign, the ignominious death destined to the meanest malefactor. Every attempt, which the insolence of the governing party had made to subdue his spirit, had hitherto proved fruitless: They made yet one effort more, in this last and melancholy scene, when all enmity, arising from motives merely human, is commonly softened and disarmed. The executioner brought that book, which had been published in elegant Latin of his great military actions, and tied it by a cord about his neck. Montrose smiled at this new instance of their malice. He thanked them, however, for their officious zeal; and said, that he bore this testimony of his bravery and loyalty with more pride than he had ever worn the garter. Having asked, whether they had any more indignities to put upon him, and renewing some devout

Executed.

ejaculations, he patiently endured the last act of the executioner.

Thus perished, in the thirty-eighth year of his age, the gallant marquess of Montrose; the man whose military genius, both by valour and conduct, had shone forth beyond any, which, during these civil disorders, had appeared in the three kingdoms. The finer arts too, he had, in his youth, successfully cultivated; and whatever was sublime, elegant, or noble touched his great soul. Nor was he insensible to the pleasures either of society or of love. Something, however, of the *vast* and *unbounded* characterized his

CHAPTER LX

actions and deportment; and it was merely by an heroic effort of duty, that he brought his mind, impatient of superiority, and even of equality, to pay such unlimited submission to the will of his sovereign.

The vengeance of the covenanters was not satisfied with Montrose's execution. Urrey, whose inconstancy now led him to take part with the king, suffered about the same time: Spotiswood of Daersie, a youth of eighteen, Sir Francis Hay of Dalgetie, and colonel Sibbald, all of them of birth and character, underwent a like fate. These were taken prisoners with Montrose. The Marquess of Huntley, about a year before, had also fallen a victim to the severity of the covenanters.

The past scene displays in a full light the barbarity of this theological faction: The sequel will sufficiently display their absurdity.

The king, in consequence of his agreement with the commissioners of Scotland, set sail for that country; and being escorted by seven Dutch ships of war, who were sent to guard the herring fishery, he arrived in the frith of Cromarty. Before he was permitted to land, he was required to sign the covenant; and many sermons and lectures were made him, exhorting him to persevere in that holy confederacy.[k] Hamilton, Lauderdale, Dumfermling, and other noblemen of that party whom they called Engagers, were immediately separated from him, and obliged to retire to their houses, where they lived in a private manner, without trust or authority. None of his English friends, who had served his father, were allowed to remain in the kingdom. The king himself found, that he was considered as a mere pageant of state, and that the few remains of royalty, which he possessed, served only to draw on him the greater indignities. One of the quarters of Montrose, his faithful servant, who had borne his commission, had been sent to Aberdeen, and was still allowed to hang over the gates when he passed by that place.[l] The general assembly, and afterwards the committee of estates and the army, who were entirely governed by the assembly, set forth a public declaration, in which they protested, "that they did not espouse any malignant quarrel or party, but

23d June.

Covenanters.

---

[k] Sir Edward Walker's Historical Discourses, p. 159. [l] Sir Edward Walker's Historical Discourses, p. 160.

fought merely on their former grounds or principles; that they disclaimed all the sins and guilt of the king, and of his house; nor would they own him or his interest, otherwise than with a subordination to God, and so far as he owned and prosecuted the cause of God, and acknowledged the sins of his house, and of his former ways."[m]

16th
Aug.

The king, lying entirely at mercy, and having no assurance of life or liberty, farther than was agreeable to the fancy of these austere zealots, was constrained to embrace a measure, which nothing but the necessity of his affairs, and his great youth and inexperience could excuse. He issued a declaration, such as they required of him.[n] He there gave thanks for the merciful dispensations of providence, by which he was recovered from the snare of evil counsel, had attained a full persuasion of the righteousness of the covenant, and was induced to cast himself and his interests wholly upon God. He desired to be deeply humbled and afflicted in spirit, because of his father's following wicked measures, opposing the covenant and the work of reformation, and shedding the blood of God's people throughout all his dominions. He lamented the idolatry of his mother and the toleration of it in his father's house; a matter of great offence, he said, to all the protestant churches, and a great provocation to him who is a jealous God, visiting the sins of the father upon the children. He professed, that he would have no enemies but the enemies of the covenant; and that he detested all popery, superstition, prelacy, heresy, schism, and profaneness; and was resolved not to tolerate; much less to countenance, any of them in any of his dominions. He declared, that he should never love or favour those who had so little conscience as to follow his interests, in preference to the gospel and the kingdom of Jesus Christ. And he expressed his hope, that, whatever ill success his former guilt might have drawn upon his cause, yet now, having obtained mercy to be on God's side, and to acknowledge his own cause subordinate to that of God, divine providence would crown his arms with victory.

Still the covenanters and the clergy were dissident of the king's sincerity. The facility, which he discovered in yielding whatever was required of him, made them suspect, that he regarded all his

[m] Ibid. p. 166, 167.   [n] Ibid. p. 170.

CHAPTER LX

concessions merely as ridiculous farces, to which he must of necessity submit. They had another trial prepared for him. Instead of the solemnity of his coronation, which was delayed, they were resolved, that he should pass through a public humiliation, and do penance before the whole people. They sent him twelve articles of repentance, which he was to acknowledge; and the king had agreed, that he would submit to this indignity. The various transgressions of his father and grandfather, together with the idolatry of his mother, are again enumerated and aggravated in these articles; and farther declarations were insisted on, that he sought the restoration of his rights, for the sole advancement of religion, and in subordination to the kingdom of Christ.[o] In short, having exalted the altar above the throne, and brought royalty under their feet, the clergy were resolved to trample on it and vilify it, by every instance of contumely, which their present influence enabled them to impose upon their unhappy prince.

Charles in the mean time found his authority entirely annihilated, as well as his character degraded. He was consulted in no public measure. He was not called to assist at any councils. His favour was sufficient to discredit any pretender to office or advancement. All efforts, which he made to unite the opposite parties, encreased the suspicion, which the covenanters had entertained of him, as if he were not entirely their own. Argyle, who, by subtilties and compliances, partly led and partly was governed by this wild faction, still turned a deaf ear to all advances, which the king made to enter into confidence with him. *Malignants* and *Engagers* continued to be the objects of general hatred and persecution; and whoever was obnoxious to the clergy, failed not to have one or other of these epithets affixed to him. The fanaticism, which prevailed, being so full of sour and angry principles, and so overcharged with various antipathies, had acquired a new object of abhorrence: These were the *Sorcerers*. So prevalent was the opinion of witchcraft, that great numbers, accused of that crime, were burnt by sentence of the magistrates throughout all parts of Scotland. In a village near Berwic, which contained only fourteen houses, fourteen persons were punished by fire; [p] and it became a

[o] Sir Edward Walker's Historical Discourses, p. 178.   [p] Whitlocke, p. 434, 408.

science, every where much studied and cultivated, to distinguish a true witch by proper trials and symptoms.[q]

The advance of the English army under Cromwel was not able to appease or soften the animosities among the parties in Scotland. The clergy were still resolute to exclude all but their most zealous adherents. As soon as the English parliament found, that the treaty between the king and the Scots would probably terminate in an accommodation, they made preparations for a war, which, they saw, would, in the end, prove inevitable. Cromwel, having broken the force and courage of the Irish, was sent for; and he left the command of Ireland to Ireton, who governed that kingdom in the character of deputy, and with vigilance and industry persevered in the work of subduing and expelling the natives.

It was expected, that Fairfax, who still retained the name of general, would continue to act against Scotland, and appear at the head of the forces; a station for which he was well qualified, and where alone he made any figure. But Fairfax, though he had allowed the army to make use of his name in murdering their sovereign, and offering violence to the parliament, had entertained unsurmountable scruples against invading the Scots, whom he considered as zealous presbyterians, and united to England by the sacred bands of the covenant. He was farther disgusted at the extremities, into which he had already been hurried; and was confirmed in his repugnance by the exhortations of his wife, who had great influence over him, and was herself much governed by the presbyterian clergy. A committee of parliament was sent to reason with him; and Cromwel was of the number. In vain did they urge, that the Scots had first broken the covenant by their invasion of England under Hamilton; and that they would surely renew their hostile attempts, if not prevented by the vigorous measures of the commonwealth. Cromwel, who knew the rigid inflexibility of Fairfax, in every thing, which he regarded as matter of principle, ventured to solicit him with the utmost earnestness; and he went so far as to shed tears of grief and vexation on the occasion. No one could suspect any ambition in the man, who laboured so zealously to retain his general in that high office, which, he knew, he himself was alone entitled to fill. The same warmth of temper,

[q] Ibid. p. 396, 418.

CHAPTER LX

which made Cromwel a frantic enthusiast, rendered him the most dangerous of hypocrites; and it was to this turn of mind, as much as to his courage and capacity, that he owed all his wonderful successes. By the contagious ferment of his zeal, he engaged every one to co-operate with him in his measures; and entering easily and affectionately into every part, which he was disposed to act, he was enabled, even after multiplied deceits, to cover, under a tempest of passion, all his crooked schemes and profound artifices.

Fairfax having resigned his commission, it was bestowed on Cromwel, who was declared captain-general of all the forces in England. This command, in a commonwealth, which stood entirely by arms, was of the utmost importance; and was the chief step, which this ambitious politician had yet made towards sovereign power. He immediately marched his forces, and entered Scotland with an army of 16,000 men.

The command of the Scottish army was given to Lesley, an experienced officer, who formed a very proper plan of defence. He entrenched himself in a fortified camp between Edinburgh and Leith, and took care to remove from the counties of Merse and the Lothians every thing which could serve to the subsistance of the English army. Cromwel advanced to the Scotch camp, and endeavoured, by every expedient, to bring Lesley to a battle: The prudent Scotchman knew, that, though superior in numbers, his army was much inferior in discipline to the English; and he carefully kept himself within his entrenchments. By skirmishes and small rencounters he tried to confirm the spirits of his soldiers; and he was successful in these enterprizes. His army daily encreased both in numbers and courage. The king came to the camp; and having exerted himself in an action, gained on the affections of the soldiery, who were more desirous of serving under a young prince of spirit and vivacity than under a committee of talking gown-men. The clergy were alarmed. They ordered Charles immediately to leave the camp. They also purged it carefully of about 4000 *Malignants* and *Engagers,* whose zeal had led them to attend the king, and who were the soldiers of chief credit and experience in the nation.[r] They then concluded, that they had an army composed entirely of saints, and could not be beaten. They murmured extremely, not

[r] Sir Edw. Walker, p. 165.

only against their prudent general, but also against the Lord, on account of his delays in giving them deliverance;[s] and they plainly told him, that, if he would not save them from the English sectaries, he should no longer be their God.[t] An advantage having offered itself on a Sunday, they hindered the general from making use of it, lest he should involve the nation in the guilt of sabbath-breaking.

Cromwel found himself in a very bad situation. He had no provisions but what he received by sea. He had not had the precaution to bring these in sufficient quantities; and his army was reduced to difficulties. He retired to Dunbar. Lesley followed him and encamped on the heights of Lammermure, which overlook that town. There lay many difficult passes between Dunbar and Berwic, and of these Lesley had taken possession. The English general was reduced to extremities. He had even embraced a resolution of sending by sea all his foot and artillery to England, and of breaking through, at all hazards, with his cavalry. The madness of the Scottish ecclesiastics saved him from this loss and dishonour.

Night and day the ministers had been wrestling with the Lord in prayer, as they termed it; and they fancied, that they had at last obtained the victory. Revelations, they said, were made them, that the sectarian and heretical army, together with Agag, meaning Cromwel, was delivered into their hands. Upon the faith of these visions, they forced their general, in spite of his remonstrances, to *Battle of* descend into the plain, with a view of attacking the English in their *Dunbar.* retreat. Cromwel, looking through a glass, saw the enemy's camp in motion; and foretold, without the help of revelations, that the Lord had delivered them into *his* hands. He gave orders immedi-*3d* ately for an attack. In this battle it was easily observed, that noth-*Septemb.* ing, in military actions, can supply the place of discipline and experience; and that, in the presence of real danger, where men are not accustomed to it, the fumes of enthusiasm presently dissipate, and lose their influence. The Scots, though double in number to the English, were soon put to flight, and pursued with great slaughter. The chief, if not only resistance was made by one regiment of Highlanders, that part of the army, which was the least infected with fanaticism. No victory could be more complete than

[s] Id. p. 168. [t] Whitlocke, p. 449.

this which was obtained by Cromwel. About 3000 of the enemy were slain, and 9000 taken prisoners. Cromwel pursued his advantage, and took possession of Edinburgh and Leith. The remnant of the Scottish army fled to Sterling. The approach of the winter season, and an ague, which seized Cromwel, kept him from pushing the victory any farther.

The clergy made great lamentations, and told the Lord, that to them it was little to sacrifice their lives and estates, but to him it was a great loss to suffer his elect to be destroyed.[u] They published a declaration, containing the cause of their late misfortunes. These visitations they ascribed to the manifold provocations of the king's house, of which, they feared, he had not yet thoroughly repented; the secret intrusion of malignants into the king's family and even into the camp; the leaving of a most malignant and profane guard of horse, who, being sent for to be purged, came two days before the defeat, and were allowed to fight with the army; the owning of the king's quarrel by many without subordination to religion and liberty; and the carnal self-seeking of some, together with the neglect of family prayers by others.

Cromwel, having been so successful in the war of the sword, took up the pen against the Scottish ecclesiastics. He wrote them some polemical letters, in which he maintained the chief points of the independent theology. He took care likewise to retort on them their favourite argument of providence; and asked them, whether the Lord had not declared against them. But the ministers thought, that the same events, which to their enemies were judgements, to them were trials; and they replied, that the Lord had only hid his face, for a time, from Jacob. But Cromwel insisted, that the appeal had been made to God in the most express and solemn manner, and that, in the fields of Dunbar, an irrevocable decision had been awarded in favour of the English army.[w]

---

[u] Sir Edward Walker.   [w] This is the best of Cromwel's wretched compositions that remains, and we shall here extract a passage out of it. "You say you have not so learned Christ as to hang the equity of your cause upon events. We could wish that blindness had not been upon your eyes to all those marvellous dispensations, which God hath wrought lately in England. But did not you solemnly appeal and pray? Did not we do so too? And ought not we and you to think, with fear and trembling, of the hand of the great God, in this mighty and strange appearance of his, but can slightly call

The defeat of the Scots was regarded by the king as a fortunate event. The armies, which fought on both sides, were almost equally his enemies; and the vanquished were now obliged to give him some more authority, and apply to him for support. The parliament was summoned to meet at St. Johnstone's. Hamilton, Lauderdale and all the Engagers were admitted into court and camp, on condition of doing public pennance, and expressing repentance for their late transgressions. Some Malignants also creeped in under various pretences. The intended humiliation or pennance of the king was changed into the ceremony of his coro-

nation, which was performed at Scone with great pomp and solemnity. But amidst all this appearance of respect, Charles remained in the hands of the most rigid Covenanters: And though treated with civility and courtesy by Argyle, a man of parts and address, he was little better than a prisoner, and was still exposed to all the rudeness and pedantry of the ecclesiastics.

This young prince was in a situation, which very ill suited his temper and disposition. All those good qualities which he possessed, his affability, his wit, his gaiety, his gentleman-like, disengaged behaviour, were here so many vices; and his love of ease, liberty, and pleasure was regarded as the highest enormity. Though artful in the practice of courtly dissimulation, the sanctified style was utterly unknown to him; and he never could mould his deportment into that starched grimace, which the covenanters required as an infallible mark of conversion. The duke of Buckingham was the only English courtier allowed to attend him; and by his ingenious talent for ridicule, he had rendered himself extremely agreeable to his master. While so many objects of derision surrounded them, it was difficult to be altogether insensible to the

---

it an event? Were not both your and our expectations renewed from time to time, while we waited on God, to see which way he would manifest himself upon our appeals? And shall we, after all these our prayers, fastings, tears, expectations and solemn appeals, call these mere events? The Lord pity you. Surely we fear, because it has been a merciful and a gracious deliverance to us.

"I beseech you in the bowels of Christ, search after the mind of the Lord in it towards you, and we shall help you by our prayers that you may find it. For yet, if we know our heart at all, our bowels do in Christ yearn after the godly in Scotland." Thurloe, vol. i. p. 158.

CHAPTER LX

temptation, and wholly to suppress the laugh. Obliged to attend from morning to night at prayers and sermons, they betrayed evident symptoms of weariness or contempt. The clergy never could esteem the king sufficiently regenerated: And by continual exhortations, remonstrances, and reprimands, they still endeavoured to bring him to a juster sense of his spiritual duty.

The king's passion for the fair could not altogether be restrained. He had once been observed using some familiarities with a young woman; and a committee of ministers was appointed to reprove him for a behaviour so unbecoming a covenanted monarch. The spokesman of the committee, one Douglass, began with a severe aspect, informed the king that great scandal had been given to the godly, enlarged on the heinous nature of sin, and concluded with exhorting his majesty, whenever he was disposed to amuse himself, to be more careful, for the future, in shutting the windows. This delicacy, so unusual to the place and to the character of the man, was remarked by the king; and he never forgot the obligation.

The king, shocked at all the indignities, and perhaps, still more tired with all the formalities, to which he was obliged to submit, made an attempt to regain his liberty. General Middleton, at the head of some royalists, being proscribed by the covenanters, kept in the mountains, expecting some opportunity of serving his master. The king resolved to join this body. He secretly made his escape from Argyle, and fled towards the Highlands. Colonel Montgomery, with a troop of horse, was sent in pursuit of him. He overtook the king, and persuaded him to return. The royalists being too weak to support him, Charles was the more easily induced to comply. This incident procured him afterwards better treatment and more authority; the covenanters being afraid of driving him, by their rigours, to some desperate resolution. Argyle renewed his courtship to the king, and the king, with equal dissimulation, pretended to repose great confidence in Argyle. He even went so far as to drop hints of his intention to marry that nobleman's daughter: But he had to do with a man too wise to be seduced by such gross artifices.

As soon as the season would permit, the Scottish army was assembled under Hamilton and Lesley; and the king was allowed to join the camp. The forces of the western counties, notwithstanding the imminent danger, which threatened their country, were resolute not to unite their cause with that of an army, which admitted any engagers or malignants among them; and they kept in a body apart under Ker. They called themselves the *Protesters;* and their frantic clergy declaimed equally against the king and against Cromwel. The other party were denominated *Resolutioners;* and these distinctions continued long after to divide and agitate the kingdom.

Charles encamped at the Torwood; and his generals resolved to conduct themselves by the same cautious maxims, which, so long as they were embraced, had been successful during the former campaign. The town of Stirling lay at his back, and the whole north supplied him with provisions. Strong entrenchments defended his front; and it was in vain that Cromwel made every attempt to bring him to an engagement. After losing much time, the English general sent Lambert over the frith into Fife, with an intention of cutting off the provisions of the enemy. Lambert fell upon Holborne and Brown, who commanded a party of the Scots, and put them to rout with great slaughter. Cromwel also passed over with his whole army; and lying at the back of the king, made it impossible for him to keep his post any longer.

Charles, reduced to despair, embraced a resolution worthy of a young prince contending for empire. Having the way open, he resolved immediately to march into England; where he expected, that all his friends, and all those who were discontented with the present government, would flock to his standard. He persuaded the generals to enter into the same views; and with one consent the army, to the number of 14,000 men, rose from their camp, and advanced by great journies towards the south.

Cromwel was surprized at this movement of the royal army. Wholly intent on offending his enemy, he had exposed his friends to imminent danger, and saw the king with numerous forces marching into England; where his presence, from the general hatred which prevailed against the parliament, was capable of producing some great revolution. But if this conduct was an oversight in Cromwel, he quickly repaired it by his vigilance and activity. He dispatched letters to the parliament, exhorting them not to be dismayed at the approach of the Scots: He sent orders every where for assembling forces to oppose the king: He ordered Lam-

CHAPTER LX

bert with a body of cavalry to hang upon the rear of the royal army, and infest their march: And he himself, leaving Monk with 7000 men to complete the reduction of Scotland, followed the king with all the expedition possible.

Charles found himself disappointed in his expectations of en-creasing his army. The Scots, terrified at the prospect of so haz-ardous an enterprize, fell off in great numbers. The English pres-byterians, having no warning given them of the king's approach, were not prepared to join him. To the royalists, this measure was equally unexpected; and they were farther deterred from joining the Scottish army by the orders, which the committee of ministers had issued, not to admit any, even in this desperate extremity, who would not subscribe the covenant. The earl of Derby, leaving the isle of Man, where he had hitherto maintained his independance, was employed in levying forces in Cheshire and Lancashire; but was soon suppressed by a party of the parliamentary army. And the king, when he arrived at Worcester, found, that his forces, extremely harassed by a hasty and fatiguing march, were not more numerous, than when he rose from his camp in the Torwood.

Such is the influence of established government, that the com-monwealth, though founded in usurpation the most unjust and unpopular, had authority sufficient to raise every where the militia of the counties; and these, united with the regular forces, bent all their efforts against the king. With an army of about 30,000 men, *3d Sept.* Cromwel fell upon Worcester; and attacking it on all sides, and meeting with little resistance except from duke Hamilton and gen-eral Middleton, broke in upon the disordered royalists. The streets of the city were strowed with dead: Hamilton, a nobleman of brav- *Battle of* ery and honour, was mortally wounded; Massey wounded and *Worcester.* taken prisoner; the king himself, having given many proofs of personal valour, was obliged to fly. The whole Scottish army was either killed or taken prisoners. The country people, inflamed with national antipathy, put to death the few that escaped from the field of battle.

The king left Worcester at six o'clock in the afternoon, and *The* without halting, travelled about twenty-six miles, in company with *king's* fifty or sixty of his friends. To provide for his safety, he thought it *escape.* best to separate himself from his companions; and he left them without communicating his intentions to any of them. By the earl of Derby's directions, he went to Boscobel, a lone house in the borders of Staffordshire, inhabited by one Penderell, a farmer. To this man Charles entrusted himself. The man had dignity of sentiments much above his condition; and though death was denounced against all who concealed the king, and a great reward promised to any one who should betray him, he professed and maintained unshaken fidelity. He took the assistance of his four brothers, equally honourable with himself; and having cloathed the king in a garb like their own, they led him into the neighbouring wood, put a bill into his hand, and pretended to employ themselves in cutting faggots. Some nights he lay upon straw in the house, and fed on such homely fare as it afforded. For a better concealment, he mounted upon an oak, where he sheltered himself among the leaves and branches for twenty-four hours. He saw several soldiers pass bye. All of them were intent in search of the king; and some expressed in his hearing their earnest wishes of seizing him. This tree was afterwards denominated the *Royal Oak;* and for many years was regarded by the neighbourhood with great veneration.

Charles was in the middle of the kingdom, and could neither stay in his retreat, nor stir a step from it, without the most imminent danger. Fears, hopes, and party zeal interested multitudes to discover him; and even the smallest indiscretion of his friends might prove fatal. Having joined lord Wilmot, who was skulking in the neighbourhood, they agreed to put themselves into the hands of colonel Lane, a zealous royalist, who lived at Bentley, not many miles distant. The king's feet were so hurt by walking about in heavy boots or countrymen's shoes which did not fit him, that he was obliged to mount on horseback; and he travelled in this situation to Bentley, attended by the Penderels, who had been so faithful to him. Lane formed a scheme for his journey to Bristol, where, it was hoped, he would find a ship, in which he might transport himself. He had a near kinswoman, Mrs. Norton, who lived within three miles of that city, and was with child, very near the time of her delivery. He obtained a pass (for during those times of confusion this precaution was requisite) for his sister Jane Lane and a servant, to travel towards Bristol, under pretence of visiting and attending her relation. The king rode before the lady, and personated the servant.

CHAPTER LX

When they arrived at Norton's, Mrs. Lane pretended that she had brought along as her servant, a poor lad, a neighbouring farmer's son, who was ill of an ague; and she begged a private room for him, where he might be quiet. Though Charles kept himself retired in this chamber, the butler, one Pope, soon knew him: The king was alarmed, but made the butler promise that he would keep the secret from every mortal, even from his master; and he was faithful to his engagement.

No ship, it was found, would, for a month, set sail from Bristol, either for France or Spain; and the king was obliged to go elsewhere for a passage. He entrusted himself to colonel Windham of Dorsetshire, an affectionate partizan of the royal family. The natural effect of the long civil wars and of the furious rage, to which all men were wrought up in their different factions, was, that every one's inclinations and affections were thoroughly known, and even the courage and fidelity of most men, by the variety of incidents, had been put to trial. The royalists too had, many of them, been obliged to make concealments in their houses for themselves, their friends, or more valuable effects; and the arts of eluding the enemy had been frequently practised. All these circumstances proved favourable to the king in the present exigency. As he often passed through the hands of catholics, the *Priest's hole,* as they called it, the place, where they were obliged to conceal their persecuted priests, was sometimes employed for sheltering their distressed sovereign.

Windham, before he received the king, asked leave to entrust the important secret to his mother, his wife, and four servants, on whose fidelity he could rely. Of all these, no one proved wanting either in honour or discretion. The venerable old matron, on the reception of her royal guest, expressed the utmost joy, that having lost, without regret, three sons and one grandchild in defence of his father, she was now reserved, in her declining years, to be instrumental in the preservation of himself. Windham told the king, that Sir Thomas, his father, in the year 1636, a few days before his death, called to him his five sons. "My children," said he, "we have hitherto seen serene and quiet times under our three last sovereigns: But I must now warn you to prepare for clouds and storms. Factions arise on every side, and threaten the tranquillity of your native country. But whatever happen, do you faithfully honour and obey your prince, and adhere to the crown. I charge you never to forsake the crown, though it should hang upon a bush." "These last words," added Windham, "made such impressions on all our breasts, that the many afflictions of these sad times could never efface their indelible characters." From innumerable instances it appears how deep rooted in the minds of the English gentry of that age was the principle of loyalty to their sovereign; that noble and generous principle, inferior only in excellence to the more enlarged and more enlightened affection towards a legal constitution. But during those times of military usurpation, these passions were the same.

The king continued several days in Windham's house; and all his friends in Britain and in every part of Europe, remained in the most anxious suspence with regard to his fortunes: No one could conjecture whether he were dead or alive; and the report of his death, being generally believed, happily relaxed the vigilant search of his enemies. Trials were made to procure a vessel for his escape; but he still met with disappointments. Having left Windham's house, he was obliged again to return to it. He passed through many other adventures; assumed different disguises; in every step was exposed to imminent perils; and received daily proofs of uncorrupted fidelity and attachment. The sagacity of a smith, who remarked, that his horses' shoes had been made in the north, not in the west, as he pretended, once detected him; and he narrowly escaped. At Shoreham in Sussex a vessel was at last found, in which he embarked. He had been known to so many, that if he had not set sail in that critical moment, it had been impossible for him to escape. After one and forty days concealment, he arrived safely at Fescamp in Normandy. No less than forty men and women had at different times been privy to his concealment and escape.[x]

The battle of Worcester afforded Cromwel what he called his *crowning mercy*.[y] So elated was he, that he intended to have knighted in the field two of his generals, Lambert and Fleetwood; but was dissuaded by his friends from exerting this act of regal authority. His power and ambition were too great to brook submission to the empty name of a republic, which stood chiefly by his influence, and was supported by his victories. How early he enter-

---

[x] Heathe's Chronicle, p. 301.   [y] Parl. Hist. vol. xx. p. 47.

CHAPTER LX

tained thoughts of taking into his hand the reins of government is uncertain. We are only assured, that he now discovered to his intimate friends these aspiring views; and even expressed a desire of assuming the rank of king, which he had contributed, with such seeming zeal, to abolish.[z]

The little popularity and credit, acquired by the republicans, farther stimulated the ambition of this enterprizing politician. These men had not that large thought, nor those comprehensive views, which might qualify them for acting the part of legislators: Selfish aims and bigotry chiefly engrossed their attention. They carried their rigid austerity so far as to enact a law, declaring fornication, after the first act, to be felony, without benefit of clergy.[a] They made small progress in that important work, which they professed to have so much at heart, the settling of a new model of representation, and fixing a plan of government. The nation began to apprehend, that they intended to establish themselves as a perpetual legislature, and to confine the whole power to 60 or 70 persons, who called themselves the parliament of the commonwealth of England. And while they pretended to bestow new liberties upon the nation, they found themselves obliged to infringe even the most valuable of those, which, through time immemorial, had been transmitted from their ancestors. Not daring to entrust the trials of treason to juries, who, being chosen indifferently from among the people, would have been little favourable to the commonwealth, and would have formed their verdict upon the ancient laws, they eluded that noble institution, by which the government of this island has ever been so much distinguished. They had evidently seen in the trial of Lilburn what they could expect from juries. This man, the most turbulent, but the most upright and courageous of human kind, was tried for a transgression of the new statute of treasons: But though he was plainly guilty, he was acquitted, to the great joy of the people. Westminster-hall, nay the whole city, rang with shouts and acclamations. Never did any established power receive so strong a declaration of its usurpation and invalidity; and from no institu-

The common-wealth.

---

[z] Whitlocke, p. 523.   [a] Scobel, p. 121. A bill was introduced into the house against painting, patches, and other immodest dress of women; but it did not pass. Parl. Hist. vol. xix. p. 263.

tion, besides the admirable one of juries, could be expected this magnanimous effort.

That they might not for the future be exposed to affronts, which so much lessened their authority, the parliament erected a high court of justice, which was to receive indictments from the council of state. This court was composed of men, devoted to the ruling party, without name or character, determined to sacrifice every thing to their own safety or ambition. Colonel Eusebius Andrews, and colonel Walter Slingsby were tried by this court for conspiracies, and condemned to death. They were royalists, and refused to plead before so illegal a jurisdiction. Love, Gibbons, and other presbyterians, having entered into a plot against the republic, were also tried, condemned, and executed. The earl of Derby, Sir Timothy Featherstone, Bemboe, being taken prisoners after the battle of Worcester, were put to death by sentence of a court martial: A method of proceeding declared illegal by that very petition of right, for which a former parliament had so strenuously contended, and which, after great efforts, they had extorted from the king.

Excepting their principles of toleration, the maxims, by which the republicans regulated ecclesiastical affairs, no more prognosticated any durable settlement, than those by which they conducted their civil concerns. The presbyterian model of congregation, classes, and assemblies, was not allowed to be finished: It seemed even the intention of many leaders in the parliament to admit of no established church, and to leave every one, without any guidance of the magistrate, to embrace whatever sect, and to support whatever clergy, were most agreeable to him.

The parliament went so far as to make some approaches in one province, to their independant model. Almost all the clergy of Wales being ejected as malignants, itinerant preachers with small salaries were settled, not above four or five in each county; and these, being furnished with horses at the public expence, hurried from place to place, and carried, as they expressed themselves, the glad tidings of the gospel.[b] They were all of them men of the lowest birth and education, who had deserted mechanical trades, in order

[b] Dr. John Walker's attempt, p. 147, & seq.

CHAPTER LX

to follow this new profession. And in this particular, as well as in their wandering life, they pretended to be more truly apostolical.

The republicans, both by the turn of their disposition, and by the nature of the instruments, which they employed, were better qualified for acts of force and vigour than for the slow and deliberate work of legislation. Notwithstanding the late wars and bloodshed, and the present factions, the power of England had never, in any period, appeared so formidable to the neighbouring kingdoms as it did at this time, in the hands of the commonwealth. A numerous army served equally to retain every one in implicit subjection to established authority, and to strike a terror into foreign nations. The power of peace and war was lodged in the same hands with that of imposing taxes; and no difference of views, among the several members of the legislature, could any longer be apprehended. The present impositions, though much superior to what had ever formerly been experienced, were in reality moderate, and what a nation, so opulent, could easily bear. The military genius of the people had, by the civil contests, been rouzed from its former lethargy; and excellent officers were formed in every branch of service. The confusion, into which all things had been thrown, had given opportunity to men of low stations to break through their obscurity, and to raise themselves by their courage to commands, which they were well qualified to exercise, but to which their birth could never have entitled them. And while so great a power was lodged in such active hands, no wonder the republic was successful in all its enterprizes.

Blake, a man of great courage and a generous disposition, the same person who had defended Lyme and Taunton with such unshaken obstinacy against the late king, was made an admiral; and though he had hitherto been accustomed only to land service, into which too he had not entered till past fifty years of age, he soon raised the naval glory of the nation to a greater height than it had ever attained in any former period. A fleet was put under his command, and he received orders to pursue prince Rupert, to whom the king had entrusted that squadron, which had deserted to him. Rupert took shelter in Kinsale; and escaping thence, fled towards the coast of Portugal. Blake pursued, and chased him into the Tagus, where he intended to make an attack upon him. But the king of Portugal, moved by the favour, which, throughout all Europe, attended the royal cause, refused Blake admittance, and aided prince Rupert in making his escape. To be revenged of this partiality, the English admiral made prize of twenty Portuguese ships richly laden; and he threatened still farther vengeance. The king of Portugal, dreading so dangerous a foe to his newly acquired dominion, and sensible of the unequal contest, in which he was engaged, made all possible submissions to the haughty republic, and was at last admitted to negociate the renewal of his alliance with England. Prince Rupert, having lost a great part of his squadron on the coast of Spain, made sail towards the West Indies. His brother, prince Maurice, was there ship-wrecked in a hurricane. Every where, this squadron subsisted by privateering, sometimes on English, sometimes on Spanish vessels. And Rupert at last returned to France, where he disposed of the remnants of his fleet, together with his prizes.

All the settlements in America, except New England, which had been planted entirely by the puritans, adhered to the royal party, even after the settlement of the republic; and Sir George Ayscue was sent with a squadron to reduce them. Bermudas, Antigua, Virginia were soon subdued. Barbadoes, commanded by lord Willoughby of Parham, made some resistance; but was at last obliged to submit.

With equal ease were Jersey, Guernsey, Scilly, and the isle of Man brought under subjection to the republic; and the sea, which had been much infested by privateers from these islands, was rendered safe to the English commerce. The countess of Derby defended the isle of Man; and with great reluctance yielded to the necessity of surrendering to the enemy. This lady, a daughter of the illustrious house of Trimoille in France, had, during the civil war, displayed a manly courage by her obstinate defence of Latham-House against the parliamentary forces; and she retained the glory of being the last person in the three kingdoms and in all their dependant dominions, who submitted to the victorious commonwealth.[c]

Ireland and Scotland were now entirely subjected and reduced to tranquillity. Ireton, the new deputy of Ireland, at the head of a

[c] See note [B] at the end of the volume.

CHAPTER LX

numerous army 30,000 strong, prosecuted the work of subduing the revolted Irish; and he defeated them in many rencounters, which, though of themselves of no great moment, proved fatal to their declining cause. He punished without mercy all the prisoners who had any hand in the massacres. Sir Phelim Oneale, among the rest, was, some time after, brought to the gibbet, and suffered an ignominious death, which he had so well merited by his inhuman cruelties. Limeric, a considerable town, still remained in the hands of the Irish; and Ireton, after a vigorous siege, made himself master of it. He was here infected with the plague, and shortly after died; a memorable personage, much celebrated for his vigilance, industry, capacity, even for the strict execution of justice in that unlimited command, which he possessed in Ireland. He was observed to be inflexible in all his purposes; and it was believed by many, that he was animated with a sincere and passionate love of liberty, and never could have been induced by any motive, to submit to the smallest appearance of regal government. Cromwel appeared to be much affected by his death; and the republicans, who reposed great confidence in him, were inconsoleable. To shew their regard for his merit and services, they bestowed an estate of two thousand pounds a year on his family, and honoured him with a magnificent funeral at the public charge. Though the established government was but the mere shadow of a commonwealth, yet was it beginning by proper arts to encourage that public spirit, which no other species of civil polity is ever able fully to inspire.

The command of the army in Ireland devolved on lieutenant-general Ludlow. The civil government of the island was entrusted to commissioners. Ludlow continued to push the advantages against the Irish, and every where obtained an easy victory. That unhappy people, disgusted with the king on account of those violent declarations against them and their religion, which had been extorted by the Scots, applied to the king of Spain, to the duke of Lorraine; and found assistance no where. Clanricarde, unable to assist the prevailing power, made submissions to the parliament, and retired into England, where he soon after died. He was a steady catholic; but a man much respected by all parties.

The successes, which attended Monk in Scotland, were no less decisive. That able general laid siege to Stirling castle; and though it was well provided for defence, it was soon surrendered to him.

He there became master of all the records of the kingdom; and he sent them to England. The earl of Leven, the earl of Crawford, lord Ogilvy, and other noblemen, having met near Perth, in order to concert measures for raising a new army, were suddenly set upon by colonel Alured, and most of them taken prisoners. Sir Philip Musgrave, with some Scots, being engaged at Dumfries in a like enterprize, met with a like fate. Dundee was a town well fortified, supplied with a good garrison under Lumisden, and full of all the rich furniture, the plate, and money of the kingdom, which had been sent thither as to a place of safety. Monk appeared before it; and having made a breach, gave a general assault. He carried the town; and following the example and instructions of Cromwel, put all the inhabitants to the sword, in order to strike a general terror into the kingdom. Warned by this example, Aberdeen, St. Andrew's, Inverness, and other towns and forts yielded, of their own accord, to the enemy. Argyle made his submissions to the English commonwealth; and excepting a few royalists, who remained some time in the mountains, under the earl of Glencairn, lord Balcarras, and general Middleton, that kingdom, which had hitherto, through all ages, by means of its situation, poverty, and valour, maintained its independance, was reduced to total subjection.

The English parliament sent Sir Harry Vane, St. John, and other commissioners to settle Scotland. These men, who possessed little of the true spirit of liberty, knew how to maintain the appearance of it; and they required the voluntary consent of all the counties and towns of this conquered kingdom, before they would unite them into the same commonwealth with England. The clergy protested; because, they said, this incorporating union would draw along with it a subordination of the church to the state in the things of Christ.[d] English judges, joined to some Scottish, were appointed to determine all causes; justice was strictly administered; order and peace maintained; and the Scots, freed from the tyranny of the ecclesiastics, were not much dissatisfied with the present government.[e] The prudent conduct of Monk, a man who possessed a

---

[d] Whitlocke, p. 496. Heathe's chronicle, p. 307.   [e] See note [C] at the end of the volume.

capacity for the arts both of peace and war, served much to reconcile the minds of men, and to allay their prejudices.

By the total reduction and pacification of the British dominions, the parliament had leisure to look abroad, and to exert their
vigour in foreign enterprizes. The Dutch were the first that felt the
weight of their arms.

*1652.
Dutch
war.*

During the life of Frederic Henry, prince of Orange, the Dutch
republic had maintained a neutrality in the civil wars of England,
and had never interposed, except by her good offices, between the
contending parties. When William, who had married an English
princess, succeeded to his father's commands and authority,[f] the
states, both before and after the execution of the late king, were
accused of taking steps more favourable to the royal cause, and of
betraying a great prejudice against that of the parliament. It was
long before the envoy of the English commonwealth could obtain
an audience of the states general. The murderers of Dorislaus
were not pursued with such vigour as the parliament expected.
And much regard had been payed to the king, and many good
offices performed to him, both by the public, and by men of all
ranks, in the united provinces.

After the death of William, prince of Orange,[g] which was attended with the depression of his party and the triumph of the
Dutch republicans, the parliament thought, that the time was now
favourable for cementing a closer confederacy with the states. St.
John, chief justice, who was sent over to the Hague, had entertained the idea of forming a kind of coalition between the two
republics, which would have rendered their interests totally inseparable; but fearing that so extraordinary a project would not be
relished, he contented himself with dropping some hints of it, and
openly went no farther than to propose a strict defensive alliance
between England and the united provinces, such as has now, for
near seventy years, taken place between these friendly powers.[h]
But the states, who were unwilling to form a nearer confederacy
with a government, whose measures were so obnoxious, and whose
situation seemed so precarious, offered only to renew the former
alliances with England. And the haughty St. John, disgusted with

[f] 1647.   [g] In October 17, 1650.   [h] Thurloe, vol. i. p. 182.

this disappointment, as well as incensed at many affronts, which had been offered him with impunity, by the retainers of the Palatine and Orange families, and indeed by the populace in general, returned into England, and endeavoured to foment a quarrel between the republics.

The movements of great states are often directed by as slender springs as those of individuals. Though war with so considerable a naval power as the Dutch, who were in peace with all their other neighbours, might seem dangerous to the yet unsettled commonwealth, there were several motives, which at this time induced the English parliament to embrace hostile measures. Many of the members thought that a foreign war would serve as a pretence for continuing the same parliament, and delaying the new model of a representative, with which the nation had so long been flattered. Others hoped, that the war would furnish a reason for maintaining, some time longer, that numerous standing army, which was so much complained of.[i] On the other hand, some, who dreaded the encreasing power of Cromwel, expected, that the great expence of naval armaments, would prove a motive for diminishing the military establishment. To divert the attention of the public from domestic quarrels towards foreign transactions, seemed, in the present disposition of men's minds, to be good policy. The superior power of the English commonwealth, together with its advantages of situation, promised success; and the parliamentary leaders hoped to gain many rich prizes from the Dutch, to distress and sink their flourishing commerce, and by victories to throw a lustre on their own establishment, which was so new and unpopular. All these views, enforced by the violent spirit of St. John, who had great influence over Cromwel, determined the parliament to change the purposed alliance into a furious war against the united provinces.

To cover these hostile intentions, the parliament, under pretence of providing for the interests of commerce, embraced such measures as, they knew, would give disgust to the states. They framed the famous act of navigation; which prohibited all nations

---

[i] We are told in the life of Sir Harry Vane, that that famous republican opposed the Dutch war, and that it was the military gentlemen chiefly who supported that measure.

CHAPTER LX

from importing into England in their bottoms any commodity, which was not the growth and manufacture of their own country. By this law, though the terms, in which it was conceived, were general, the Dutch were principally affected; because their country produces few commodities, and they subsist chiefly by being the general carriers and factors of Europe. Letters of reprisal were granted to several merchants, who complained of injuries, which, they pretended, they had received from the states; and above eighty Dutch ships fell into their hands, and were made prizes. The cruelties committed on the English at Amboyna, which were certainly enormous, but which seemed to be buried in oblivion by a thirty years' silence, were again made the ground of complaint. And the allowing the murderers of Dorislaus to escape, and the conniving at the insults to which St. John had been exposed, were represented as symptoms of an unfriendly, if not a hostile disposition, in the states.

The states, alarmed at all these steps, sent orders to their ambassadors to endeavour the renewal of the treaty of alliance, which had been broken off by the abrupt departure of St. John. Not to be unprepared, they equipped a fleet of a hundred and fifty sail, and took care, by their ministers at London, to inform the council of state of that armament. This intelligence instead of striking terror into the English republic, was considered as a menace, and farther confirmed the parliament in their hostile resolutions. The minds of men in both states were, every day, more irritated against each other; and it was not long before these humours broke forth into action.

Tromp, an admiral of great renown, received from the states the command of a fleet of forty-two sail, in order to protect the Dutch navigation against the privateers of the English. He was forced by stress of weather, as he alledged, to take shelter in the road of Dover, where he met with Blake, who commanded an English fleet much inferior in number. Who was the aggressor in the action, which ensued between these two admirals, both of them men of such prompt and fiery dispositions, it is not easy to determine; since each of them sent to his own state a relation totally opposite in all its circumstances to that of the other, and yet supported by the testimony of every captain in his fleet. Blake pretended, that, having given a signal to the Dutch admiral to strike,

Tromp, instead of complying, fired a broad-side at him. Tromp asserted, that he was preparing to strike, and that the English admiral, nevertheless, began hostilities. It is certain that the admiralty of Holland, who are distinct from the council of state, had given Tromp no orders to strike, but had left him to his own discretion, with regard to that vain but much contested ceremonial. They seemed willing to introduce the claim of an equality with the new commonwealth, and to interpret the former respect payed the English flag, as a deference due only to the monarchy. This circumstance forms a strong presumption against the narrative of the Dutch admiral. The whole Orange party, it must be remarked, to which Tromp was suspected to adhere, were desirous of a war with England.

Blake, though his squadron consisted only of fifteen vessels, re-inforced, after the battle began, by eight under captain Bourne, maintained the fight with bravery for five hours, and sunk one ship of the enemy, and took another. Night parted the combatants, and the Dutch fleet retired towards the coast of Holland. The populace of London were enraged, and would have insulted the Dutch ambassadors, who lived at Chelsea, had not the council of state sent guards to protect them.

When the states heard of this action, of which the consequences were easily foreseen, they were in the utmost consternation. They immediately dispatched Paw, Pensionary of Holland, as their ambassador extraordinary to London, and ordered him to lay before the parliament the narrative, which Tromp had sent of the late rencounter. They entreated them, by all the bands of their common religion, and common liberties, not to precipitate themselves into hostile measures, but to appoint commissioners who should examine every circumstance of the action, and clear up the truth, which lay in obscurity. And they pretended, that they had given no orders to their admiral to offer any violence to the English, but would severely punish him, if they found, upon enquiry, that he had been guilty of an action, which they so much disapproved. The imperious parliament would hearken to none of these reasons or remonstrances. Elated by the numerous successes, which they had obtained over their domestic enemies, they thought that every thing must yield to their fortunate arms; and they gladly seized the opportunity, which they sought, of making war upon the states.

CHAPTER LX

They demanded, that, without any farther delay or enquiry, reparation should be made for all the damages, which the English had sustained. And when this demand was not complied with, they dispatched orders for commencing war against the united provinces.

Blake sailed northwards with a numerous fleet, and fell upon the herring busses, which were escorted by twelve men of war. All these he either took or dispersed. Tromp followed him with a fleet of above a hundred sail. When these two admirals were within sight of each other, and preparing for battle, a furious storm attacked them. Blake took shelter in the English harbours. The Dutch fleet was dispersed and received great damage.

Sir George Ayscue, though he commanded only forty ships, according to the English accounts, engaged near Plymouth the famous de Ruiter, who had under him fifty ships of war, with thirty merchant-men. The Dutch ships were indeed of inferior force to the English. De Ruiter, the only admiral in Europe, who has attained a renown equal to that of the greatest general, defended himself so well, that Ayscue gained no advantage over him. Night parted them in the greatest heat of the action. De Ruiter next day sailed off with his convoy. The English fleet had been so shattered in the fight, that it was not able to pursue. *16th Aug.*

Near the coast of Kent, Blake, seconded by Bourne and Pen, met a Dutch squadron, nearly equal in numbers, commanded by de Witte and de Ruiter. A battle was fought much to the disadvantage of the Dutch. Their rear-admiral was boarded and taken. Two other vessels were sunk, and one blown up. The Dutch next day made sail towards Holland. *28th Oct.*

The English were not so successful in the Mediterranean. Van Galen with much superior force attacked captain Badily and defeated him. He bought, however, his victory with the loss of his life.

Sea-fights are seldom so decisive as to disable the vanquished from making head in a little time against the victors. Tromp, seconded by de Ruiter, met near the Goodwins, with Blake, whose fleet was inferior to the Dutch, but who resolved not to decline the combat. A furious battle commenced, where the admirals on both sides, as well as the inferior officers and seamen, exerted great bravery. In this action the Dutch had the advantage. Blake himself was wounded. The Garland and Bonaventure were taken. Two *29th Nov.*

ships were burned, and one sunk; and night came opportunely to save the English fleet. After this victory, Tromp in a bravado fixed a broom to his main-mast; as if he were resolved to sweep the sea entirely of all English vessels.

Great preparations were made in England, in order to wipe off this disgrace. A gallant fleet of eighty sail was fitted out. Blake commanded, and Dean under him, together with Monk, who had been sent for from Scotland. When the English lay off Portland, they descried near break of day a Dutch fleet of seventy-six vessels, sailing up the channel, along with a convoy of 300 merchantmen, who had received orders to wait at the isle of Rhé, till the fleet should arrive to escorte them. Tromp, and, under him, de Ruiter, commanded the Dutch. This battle was the most furious that had yet been fought between these warlike and rival nations. Three days was the combat continued with the utmost rage and obstinacy; and Blake, who was victor, gained not more honour than Tromp, who was vanquished. The Dutch admiral made a skilful retreat, and saved all the merchant ships, except thirty. He lost however eleven ships of war, had 2000 men slain, and near 1500 taken prisoners. The English, though many of their ships were extremely shattered, had but one sunk. Their slain were not much inferior in number to those of the enemy.

All these successes of the English were chiefly owing to the superior size of their vessels; an advantage which all the skill and bravery of the Dutch admirals could not compensate. By means of ship-money, an imposition, which had been so much complained of, and in some respects with reason, the late king had put the navy into a situation, which it had never attained in any former reign; and he ventured to build ships of a size, which was then unusual. But the misfortunes, which the Dutch met with in battle, were small in comparison of those, which their trade sustained from the English. Their whole commerce by the channel was cut off: Even that to the Baltic was much infested by English privateers. Their fisheries were totally suspended. A great number of their ships, above 1600, had fallen into the hands of the enemy. And all this distress they suffered, not for any national interests or necessity; but from vain points of honour and personal resentments, of which it was difficult to give a satisfactory account to the public. They resolved therefore to gratify the pride of the parliament, and to make some advances towards peace. They met not, however, with a favourable reception; and it was not without pleasure, that they learned the dissolution of that haughty assembly by the violence of Cromwel, an event from which they expected a more prosperous turn to their affairs.

The zealous republicans in the parliament had not been the chief or first promoters of the war; but when it was once entered upon, they endeavoured to draw from it every possible advantage. On all occasions they set up the fleet in opposition to the army, and celebrated the glory and successes of their naval armaments. They insisted on the intolerable expence, to which the nation was subjected, and urged the necessity of diminishing it by a reduction of the land forces. They had ordered some regiments to serve on board the fleet in the quality of marines. And Cromwel, by the whole train of their proceedings, evidently saw, that they had entertained a jealousy of his power and ambition, and were resolved to bring him to a subordination under their authority. Without scruple or delay he resolved to prevent them. *Dissolution of the parliament.*

On such firm foundations was built the credit of this extraordinary man, that though a great master of fraud and dissimulation, he judged it superfluous to employ any disguise in conducting this bold enterprize. He summoned a general council of officers; and immediately found, that they were disposed to receive whatever impressions he was pleased to give them. Most of them were his creatures, had owed their advancement to his favour, and relied entirely upon him for their future preferment. The breach being already made between the military and civil powers, when the late king was seized at Holdenby; the general officers regarded the parliament as at once their creature and their rival; and thought, that they themselves were entitled to share among them those offices and riches, of which its members had so long kept possession. Harrison, Rich, Overton, and a few others, who retained some principle, were guided by notions so extravagant, that they were easily deluded into measures the most violent and most criminal. And the whole army had already been guilty of such illegal and atrocious actions, that they could entertain no farther scruple with regard to any enterprize, which might serve their selfish or fanatical purposes.

In the council of officers it was presently voted to frame a remonstrance to the parliament. After complaining of the arrears, due to the army, they there desired the parliament to reflect how many years they had sitten, and what professions they had formerly made of their intentions to new model the representative, and establish successive parliaments, who might bear the burthen of national affairs, from which they themselves would gladly, after so much danger and fatigue, be at last relieved. They confessed that the parliament had atchieved great enterprizes, and had surmounted mighty difficulties; yet was it an injury, they said, to the rest of the nation to be excluded from bearing any part in the service of their country. It was now full time for them to give place to others; and they therefore desired them, after settling a council, who might execute the laws during the interval, to summon a new parliament, and establish that free and equal government, which they had so long promised to the people.

The parliament took this remonstrance in ill part, and made a sharp reply to the council of officers. The officers insisted on their advice; and by mutual altercation and opposition the breach became still wider between the army and the commonwealth. Cromwel, finding matters ripe for his purpose, called a council of officers, in order to come to a determination with regard to the public settlement. As he had here many friends, so had he also some opponents. Harrison having assured the council, that the general sought only to pave the way for the government of Jesus and his saints, major Streater briskly replied, that Jesus ought then to come quickly: For if he delayed it till after Christmas, he would come too late; he would find his place occupied. While the officers were in debate, colonel Ingoldsby informed Cromwel, that the parliament was sitting, and had come to a resolution not to dissolve themselves, but to fill up the house by new elections; and was at that very time engaged in deliberations with regard to this expedient. Cromwel in a rage immediately hastened to the house, and carried a body of 300 soldiers along with him. Some of them he placed at the door, some in the lobby, some on the stairs. He first addressed himself to his friend St. John, and told him, that he had come with a purpose of doing what grieved him to the very soul, and what he had earnestly with tears besought the Lord not to impose upon him: But there was a necessity, in order to the glory of God and good of the nation. He sat down for some time, and heard the debate. He beckoned Harrison, and told him, that he now judged the parliament ripe for a dissolution. "Sir," said Har-

10th April.

CHAPTER LX

rison, "the work is very great and dangerous: I desire you seriously to consider, before you engage in it." "You say well," replied the general; and thereupon sat still about a quarter of an hour. When the question was ready to be put, he said again to Harrison, "This is the time: I must do it." And suddenly starting up, he loaded the parliament with the vilest reproaches, for their tyranny, ambition, oppression, and robbery of the public. Then stamping with his foot, which was a signal for the soldiers to enter, "For shame," said he to the parliament, "get you gone: give place to honester men; to those who will more faithfully discharge their trust. You are no longer a parliament: I tell you, you are no longer a parliament. The Lord has done with you; He has chosen other instruments for carrying on his work." Sir Harry Vane exclaiming against this proceeding, he cried with a loud voice, "O! Sir Harry Vane, Sir Harry Vane! The Lord deliver me from Sir Harry Vane!" Taking hold of Martin by the cloke, "Thou art a whore master," said he. To another, "Thou art an adulterer." To a third, "Thou art a drunkard and a glutton:" "And thou an extortioner," to a fourth. He commanded a soldier to seize the mace. "What shall we do with this bauble? Here take it away. It is you," said he, addressing himself to the house, "that have forced me upon this. I have sought the Lord night and day, that he would rather slay me than put me upon this work." Having commanded the soldiers to clear the hall, he himself went out the last, and ordering the doors to be locked, departed to his lodgings in Whitehall.

In this furious manner, which so well denotes his genuine character, did Cromwel, without the least opposition, or even murmur, annihilate that famous assembly, which had filled all Europe with the renown of its actions, and with astonishment at its crimes, and whose commencement was not more ardently desired by the people than was its final dissolution. All parties now reaped successively the melancholy pleasure of seeing the injuries, which they had suffered, revenged on their enemies; and that too by the same arts, which had been practised against them. The king had, in some instances, stretched his prerogative beyond its just bounds; and aided by the church, had well nigh put an end to all the liberties and privileges of the nation. The presbyterians checked the progress of the court and clergy, and excited, by cant and hypocrisy, the populace first to tumults, then to war, against the king, the peers, and all the royalists. No sooner had they reached the pinnacle of grandeur, than the independents, under the appearance of still greater sanctity, instigated the army against them, and reduced them to subjection. The independents, amidst their empty dreams of liberty, or rather of dominion, were oppressed by the rebellion of their own servants, and found themselves at once exposed to the insults of power and hatred of the people. By recent, as well as all ancient example, it was become evident, that illegal violence, with whatever pretences it may be covered, and whatever object it may pursue, must inevitably end at last in the arbitrary and despotic government of a single person.

LXI

Cromwel's birth and private life –
Barebone's parliament – Cromwel made protector –
Peace with Holland – A new parliament –
Insurrection of the royalists – State of Europe –
War with Spain – Jamaica conquered –
Success and death of admiral Blake –
Domestic administration of Cromwel –
Humble Petition and Advice – Dunkirk
taken – Sickness of the protector –
His death – And character

O LIVER CROMWEL, in whose hands the dissolution of the parliament had left the whole power, civil and military, of three
kingdoms, was born at Huntingdon, the last year of the former
century, of a good family; though he himself, being the son of a
second brother, inherited but a small estate from his father. In the
course of his education he had been sent to the university; but his
genius was found little fitted for the calm and elegant occupations
of learning; and he made small proficiencies in his studies. He
even threw himself into a dissolute and disorderly course of life;
and he consumed, in gaming, drinking, debauchery, and country
riots, the more early years of his youth, and dissipated part of his
patrimony. All of a sudden, the spirit of reformation seized him;
he married, affected a grave and composed behaviour, entered

Cromwel's
birth and
private
life.

into all the zeal and rigour of the puritanical party, and offered to restore to every one whatever sums he had formerly gained by gaming. The same vehemence of temper, which had transported him into the extremes of pleasure, now distinguished his religious habits. His house was the resort of all the zealous clergy of the party; and his hospitality, as well as his liberalities to the silenced and deprived ministers, proved as chargeable as his former debaucheries. Though he had acquired a tolerable fortune by a maternal uncle, he found his affairs so injured by his expences, that he was obliged to take a farm at St. Ives, and apply himself, for some years, to agriculture as a profession. But this expedient served rather to involve him in farther debts and difficulties. The long prayers, which he said to his family in the morning, and again in the afternoon, consumed his own time and that of his ploughmen; and he reserved no leisure for the care of his temporal affairs. His active mind, superior to the low occupations, to which he was condemned, preyed upon itself; and he indulged his imagination in visions, illuminations, revelations; the great nourishment of that hypocondriacal temper, to which he was ever subject. Urged by his wants and his piety, he had made a party with Hambden, his near kinsman, who was pressed only by the latter motive, to transport himself into New England, now become the retreat of the more zealous among the puritanical party; and it was an order of council, which obliged them to disembark and remain in England. The earl of Bedford, who possessed a large estate in the Fen Country, near the isle of Ely, having undertaken to drain these morasses, was obliged to apply to the king; and by the powers of the prerogative, he got commissioners appointed, who conducted that work, and divided the new acquired land among the several proprietors. He met with opposition from many, among whom Cromwel distinguished himself; and this was the first public opportunity, which he had met with, of discovering the factious zeal and obstinacy of his character.

From accident and intrigue he was chosen by the town of Cambridge member of the long parliament. His domestic affairs were then in great disorder; and he seemed not to possess any talents, which could qualify him to rise in that public sphere, into which he was now at last entered. His person was ungraceful, his dress

CHAPTER LXI

slovenly, his voice untunable, his elocution homely, tedious, obscure, and embarrassed. The fervor of his spirit frequently
prompted him to rise in the house; but he was not heard with
attention: His name, for above two years, is not to be found oftner
than twice in any committee; and those committees, into which he
was admitted, were chosen for affairs, which would more interest
the zealots than the men of business. In comparison of the eloquent speakers and fine gentlemen of the house, he was entirely
overlooked; and his friend Hambden alone was acquainted with
the depth of his genius, and foretold, that, if a civil war should
ensue, he would soon rise to eminence and distinction.

Cromwel himself seems to have been conscious where his
strength lay; and partly from that motive, partly from the uncon-
trolable fury of his zeal, he always joined that party, which pushed
every thing to extremities against the king. He was active in promoting the famous remonstrance, which was the signal for all the
ensuing commotions; and when, after a long debate, it was carried
by a small majority, he told lord Falkland, that, if the question had
been lost, he was resolved next day to have converted into ready
money the remains of his fortune, and immediately to have left the
kingdom. Nor was this resolution, he said, peculiar to himself:
Many others of his party he knew to be equally determined.

He was no less than forty-three years of age, when he first
embraced the military profession; and by force of genius, without
any master, he soon became an excellent officer; though perhaps
he never reached the fame of a consummate commander. He
raised a troop of horse; fixed his quarters in Cambridge; exerted
great severity towards that university, which zealously adhered to
the royal party; and showed himself a man who would go all
lengths in favour of that cause, which he had espoused. He would
not allow his soldiers to perplex their heads with those subtilties,
of fighting by the king's authority against his person, and of obeying his majesty's commands signified by both houses of parliament: He plainly told them, that, if he met the king in battle, he
would fire a pistol in his face as readily as against any other man.
His troop of horse he soon augmented to a regiment; and he first
instituted that discipline and inspired that spirit, which rendered
the parliamentary armies in the end victorious. "Your troops," said

he to Hambden, according to his own account,[k] "are most of them old decayed serving men and tapsters, and such kind of fellows; the king's forces are composed of gentlemen's younger sons and persons of good quality. And do you think, that the mean spirits of such base and low fellows as ours will ever be able to encounter gentlemen, that have honour and courage and resolution in them? You must get men of spirit, and take it not ill that I say, of a spirit, that is likely to go as far as gentlemen will go, or else I am sure you will still be beaten, as you have hitherto been, in every encounter." He did as he proposed. He enlisted the sons of freeholders and farmers. He carefully invited into his regiment all the zealous fanatics throughout England. When they were collected in a body, their enthusiastic spirit still rose to a higher pitch. Their colonel, from his own natural character, as well as from policy, was sufficiently inclined to encrease the flame. He preached, he prayed, he fought, he punished, he rewarded. The wild enthusiasm, together with valour and discipline, still propagated itself; and all men cast their eyes on so pious and so successful a leader. From low commands he rose with great rapidity to be really the first, though in appearance only the second, in the army. By fraud and violence, he soon rendered himself the first in the state. In proportion to the encrease of his authority, his talents always seemed to expand themselves; and he displayed every day new abilities, which had lain dormant, till the very emergence, by which they were called forth into action. All Europe stood astonished to see a nation, so turbulent and unruly, who, for some doubtful encroachments on their privileges, had dethroned and murdered an excellent prince, descended from a long line of monarchs, now at last subdued and reduced to slavery by one, who, a few years before, was no better than a private gentleman, whose name was not known in the nation, and who was little regarded even in that low sphere, to which he had always been confined.

The indignation, entertained by the people, against an authority, founded on such manifest usurpation, was not so violent as might naturally be expected. Congratulatory addresses, the first of the kind, were made to Cromwel by the fleet, by the army, even by many of the chief corporations and counties of England; but espe-

[k] Conference held at Whitehall.

CHAPTER LXI

cially by the several congregations of saints, dispersed throughout the kingdom.[1] The royalists, though they could not love the man, who had embrued his hands in the blood of their sovereign, expected more lenity from him, than from the jealous and imperious republicans, who had hitherto governed. The presbyterians were pleased to see those men, by whom they had been outwitted and expelled, now in their turn expelled and outwitted by their own servant; and they applauded him, for this last act of violence upon the parliament. These two parties composed the bulk of the nation, and kept the people in some tolerable temper. All men, likewise, harassed with wars and factions, were glad to see any prospect of settlement. And they deemed it less ignominious to submit to a person of such admirable talents and capacity than to a few ignoble enthusiastic hypocrites, who under the name of a republic, had reduced them to a cruel subjection.

The republicans, being dethroned by Cromwel, were the party whose resentment he had the greatest reason to apprehend. That party, besides the independents, contained two sets of men, who are seemingly of the most opposite principles, but who were then united by a similitude of genius and of character. The first and most numerous were the millenarians, or fifth monarchy men, who insisted, that, dominion being founded in grace, all distinction in magistracy must be abolished, except what arose from piety and holiness; who expected suddenly the second coming of Christ upon earth; and who pretended, that the saints in the mean while, that is, themselves, were alone entitled to govern. The second were the deists, who had no other object than political liberty, who denied entirely the truth of revelation, and insinuated, that all the various sects, so heated against each other, were alike founded in folly and in error. Men of such daring geniuses were not contented with the antient and legal forms of civil government; but challenged a degree of freedom beyond what they expected ever to enjoy under any monarchy. Martin, Challoner, Harrington, Sidney, Wildman, Nevil, were esteemed the heads of this small division.

The deists were perfectly hated by Cromwel, because he had no hold of enthusiasm, by which he could govern or over-reach them;

[1] See Milton's State Papers.

he therefore treated them with great rigour and disdain, and usually denominated them the *heathens*. As the millenarians had a great interest in the army, it was much more important for him to gain their confidence; and their size of understanding afforded him great facility in deceiving them. Of late years, it had been so usual a topic of conversation to discourse of parliaments and councils and senates, and the soldiers themselves had been so much accustomed to enter into that spirit, that Cromwel thought it requisite to establish something which might bear the face of a commonwealth. He supposed, that God, in his providence, had thrown the whole right, as well as power, of government into his hands; and without any more ceremony, by the advice of his council of officers, he sent summons to a hundred and twenty-eight persons of different towns and counties of England, to five of Scotland, to six of Ireland. He pretended, by his sole act and deed, to devolve

Barebone's parliament.

upon these the whole authority of the state. This legislative power they were to exercise during fifteen months; and they were afterwards to choose the same number of persons, who might succeed them in that high and important office.

There were great numbers at that time, who made it a principle always to adhere to any power, which was uppermost, and to support the established government. This maxim is not peculiar to the people of that age; but what may be esteemed peculiar to them, is, that there prevailed a hypocritical phrase for expressing so prudential a conduct: It was called a waiting upon providence. When providence, therefore, was so kind as to bestow on these men, now assembled together, the supreme authority, they must have been very ungrateful, if, in their turn, they had been wanting

4th July.

in complaisance towards her. They immediately voted themselves a parliament; and having their own consent, as well as that of Oliver Cromwel, for their legislative authority, they now proceeded very gravely to the exercise of it.

In this notable assembly were some persons of the rank of gentlemen; but the far greater part were low mechanics; fifth monarchy men, anabaptists, antinomians, independents; the very dregs of the fanatics. They began with seeking God by prayer: This office was performed by eight or ten *gifted* men of the assembly; and with so much success, that according to the confession of all, they had never before, in any of their devotional exercises, enjoyed

CHAPTER LXI

so much of the holy spirit as was then communicated to them.[m] Their hearts were, no doubt, dilated when they considered the high dignity, to which they supposed themselves exalted. They had been told by Cromwel in his first discourse, that he never looked to see such a day, when Christ should be so owned.[n] They thought it, therefore, their duty to proceed to a thorough reformation, and to pave the way for the reign of the Redeemer, and for that great work, which, it was expected, the Lord was to bring forth among them. All fanatics, being consecrated by their own fond imaginations, naturally bear an antipathy to the ecclesiastics, who claim a peculiar sanctity, derived merely from their office and priestly character. This parliament took into consideration the abolition of the clerical function, as favouring of popery; and the taking away of tythes, which they called a relict of Judaism. Learning also and the universities were deemed heathenish and unnecessary: The common law was denominated a badge of the conquest and of Norman slavery; and they threatened the lawyers with a total abrogation of their profession. Some steps were even taken towards an abolition of the chancery,[o] the highest court of judicature in the kingdom; and the Mosaical law was intended to be established as the sole system of English jurisprudence.[p]

[m] Parl. Hist. vol. xx. p. 182.   [n] These are his expressions. "Indeed, I have but one word more to say to you, though in that perhaps I shall show my weakness: It is by way of encouragement to you in this work; give me leave to begin thus: I confess I never looked to have seen such a day as this, it may be nor you neither, when Jesus Christ should be so owned as he is at this day and in this work. Jesus Christ is owned this day by your call, and you own him by your willingness to appear for him, and you manifest this (as far as poor creatures can do) to be a day of the power of Christ. I know you will remember that scripture, *he makes his people willing in the day of his power.* God manifests it to be the day of the power of Christ, having thro' so much blood and so much tryal as has been upon this nation, he makes this one of the greatest mercies, next to his own son, to have his people called to the supreme authority. God hath owned his son, and hath owned you, and hath made you to own him. I confess, I never looked to have seen such a day: I did not." I suppose at this passage he cried: For he was very much given to weeping, and could at any time shed abundance of tears. The rest of the speech may be seen among Milton's State Papers, page 106. It is very curious, and full of the same obscurity, confusion, embarrassment, and absurdity, which appear in almost all Oliver's productions.   [o] Whitlocke, p. 543, 548.   [p] Conference held at Whitehall.

Of all the extraordinary schemes, adopted by these legislators, they had not leisure to finish any, except that which established the legal solemnization of marriage by the civil magistrate alone, without the interposition of the clergy. They found themselves exposed to the derision of the public. Among the fanatics of the house, there was an active member, much noted for his long prayers, sermons, and harangues. He was a leather-seller in London: His name *Praise-god Barebone*. This ridiculous name, which seems to have been chosen by some poet or allegorist to suit so ridiculous a personage, struck the fancy of the people; and they commonly affixed to this assembly the appellation of Barebone's parliament.*q*

The Dutch ambassadors endeavoured to enter into negotiation with this parliament; but though protestants and even presby-

---

q It was usual for the pretended saints at that time to change their names from Henry, Edward, Anthony, William, which they regarded as heathenish, into others more sanctified and godly: Even the New Testament names, James, Andrew, John, Peter, were not held in such regard as those which were borrowed from the Old Testament, Hezekiah, Habbakuk, Joshua, Zerobabel. Sometimes a whole godly sentence was adopted as a name. Here are the names of a jury said to be enclosed in the county of Sussex about that time.

Accepted, Trevor of Northam.	Return, Spelman of Watling.
Redeemed, Compton of Battle.	Be Faithful, Joiner of Britling.
Faint not, Hewit of Heathfield.	Fly Debate, Roberts of the same.
Make Peace, Heaton of Hare.	Fight the good Fight of Faith, White of Emer.
God Reward, Smart of Fivehurst.	
Standfast on High, Stringer of Crowhurst.	More Fruit, Fowler of East Hadley.
	Hope for, Bending of the same.
Earth, Adams of Warbleton.	Graceful, Harding of Lewes.
Called, Lower of the same.	Weep not, Biling of the same.
Kill Sin, Pimple of Witham.	Meek, Brewer of Okeham.

See Brome's Travels into England, p. 279. "Cromwell," says Cleveland, "hath beat up his drums clean through the Old Testament. You may learn the genealogy of our Saviour by the names of his regiment. The mustermaster has no other list, than the first chapter of St. Matthew." The brother of this Praise-god Barebone had for name, *If Christ had not died for you, you had been damned Barebone.* But the people, tired of this long name, retained only the last word, and commonly gave him the appellation of *Damn'd Barebone.*

terians, they met with a bad reception from those who pretended to a sanctity so much superior. The Hollanders were regarded as worldly minded men, intent only on commerce and industry; whom it was fitting the saints should first extirpate, ere they undertook that great work, to which they believed themselves destined by providence, of subduing Antichrist, the man of sin, and extending to the uttermost bounds of the earth the kingdom of the Redeemer.[r] The ambassadors finding themselves proscribed, not as enemies of England, but of Christ, remained in astonishment, and knew not which was most to be admired, the implacable spirit or egregious folly of these pretended saints.

Cromwel began to be ashamed of his legislature. If he ever had any design in summoning so preposterous an assembly beyond amusing the populace and the army; he had intended to alarm the clergy and lawyers; and he had so far succeeded as to make them desire any other government, which might secure their professions, now brought in danger by these desperate fanatics. Cromwel himself was dissatisfied, that the parliament, though they had derived all their authority from him, began to pretend power from the Lord,[s] and to insist already on their divine commission. He had been careful to summon in his writs several persons entirely devoted to him. By concert, these met early; and it was mentioned by some among them, that the sitting of this parliament any longer would be of no service to the nation. They hastened, therefore, to Cromwel, along with Rouse, their speaker; and by a formal deed or assignment, restored into his hands that supreme authority, which they had so lately received from him. General Harrison and about twenty more remained in the house; and that they might prevent the reign of the saints from coming to an untimely end, they placed one Moyer in the chair, and began to draw up protests. They were soon interrupted by colonel White, with a party of soldiers. He asked them what they did there. "We are seeking the Lord," said they. "Then you may go elsewhere," replied he: "For to my certain knowledge, he has not been here these many years."

12th of December.

The military being now, in appearance, as well as in reality, the sole power which prevailed in the nation, Cromwel thought fit to

[r] Thurloe, vol. i. p. 273, 591. Also Stubbe, p. 91, 92.   [s] Thurloe, vol. i. p. 393.

indulge a new fancy: For he seems not to have had any deliberate plan in all these alterations. Lambert, his creature, who, under the appearance of obsequiousness to him, indulged an unbounded ambition, proposed in a council of officers to adopt another scheme of government, and to temper the liberty of a commonwealth by the authority of a single person, who should be known by the appellation of protector. Without delay, he prepared what was called *the instrument of government,* containing the plan of this new legislature; and as it was supposed to be agreeable to the general, it was immediately voted by the council of officers. Cromwel was declared protector; and with great solemnity installed in that high office.

Cromwel made protector.

So little were these men endowed with the spirit of legislation, that they confessed, or rather boasted, that they had employed only four days in drawing this instrument, by which the whole government of three kingdoms was pretended to be regulated and adjusted to all succeeding generations. There appears no difficulty in believing them; when it is considered how crude and undigested a system of civil polity they endeavoured to establish. The chief articles of the instrument are these: A council was appointed, which was not to exceed twenty-one, nor be less than thirteen persons. These were to enjoy their office during life or good behaviour; and in case of a vacancy, the remaining members named three, of whom the protector chose one. The protector was appointed supreme magistrate of the commonwealth: In his name was all justice to be administered; from him were all magistracy and honours derived; he had the power of pardoning all crimes, excepting murder and treason; to him the benefit of all forfeitures devolved. The right of peace, war, and alliance, rested in him; but in these particulars he was to act by the advice and with the consent of his council. The power of the sword was vested in the protector, jointly with the parliament, while it was sitting, or with the council of state in the intervals. He was obliged to summon a parliament every three years, and allow them to sit five months, without adjournment, prorogation, or dissolution. The bills, which they passed, were to be presented to the protector for his assent; but if within twenty days it were not obtained, they were to become laws by the authority alone of parliament. A standing army for Great Britain and Ireland was established, of 20,000 foot and 10,000

CHAPTER LXI

horse; and funds were assigned for their support. These were not to be diminished without consent of the protector; and in this article alone he assumed a negative. During the intervals of parliament, the protector and council had the power of enacting laws, which were to be valid till the next meeting of parliament. The chancellor, treasurer, admiral, chief governors of Ireland and Scotland, and the chief justices of both the benches must be chosen with the approbation of parliament; and in the intervals, with the approbation of the council, to be afterwards ratified by parliament. The protector was to enjoy his office during life; and on his death, the place was immediately to be supplied by the council. This was the instrument of government enacted by the council of officers, and solemnly sworn to by Oliver Cromwel. The council of state, named by the instrument, were fifteen; men entirely devoted to the protector, and by reason of the opposition among themselves in party and principles, not likely ever to combine against him.

Cromwel said, that he accepted the dignity of protector, merely that he might exert the duty of a constable, and preserve peace in the nation. Affairs indeed were brought to that pass, by the furious animosities of the several factions, that the extensive authority and even arbitrary power of some first magistrate was become a necessary evil, in order to keep the people from relapsing into blood and confusion. The independents were too small a party ever to establish a popular government, or entrust the nation, where they had so little interest, with the free choice of its representatives. The presbyterians had adopted the violent maxims of persecution; incompatible at all times with the peace of society, much more with the wild zeal of those numerous sects, which prevailed among the people. The royalists were so much enraged by the injuries, which they had suffered, that the other prevailing parties would never submit to them, who, they knew were enabled, merely by the execution of the ancient laws, to take severe vengeance upon them. Had Cromwel been guilty of no crime but this temporary usurpation, the plea of necessity and public good, which he alledged, might be allowed, in every view, a reasonable excuse for his conduct.

During the variety of ridiculous and distracted scenes, which the civil government exhibited in England, the military force was exerted with vigor, conduct, and unanimity; and never did the kingdom appear more formidable to all foreign nations. The English fleet, consisting of a hundred sail, and commanded by Monk and Dean, and under them by Pen and Lauson, met, near the coast of Flanders, with the Dutch fleet, equally numerous, and commanded by Tromp. The two republics were not inflamed by any national antipathy, and their interests very little interfered: Yet few battles have been disputed with more fierce and obstinate courage than were those many naval combats, which were fought during this short, but violent war. The desire of remaining sole lords of the ocean animated these states to an honourable emulation against each other. After a battle of two days, in the first of which Dean was killed, the Dutch, inferior in the size of their ships, were obliged, with great loss, to retire into their harbours. Blake, towards the end of the fight, joined his countrymen with eighteen sail. The English fleet lay off the coast of Holland, and totally interrupted the commerce of that republic.

The ambassadors, whom the Dutch had sent over to England, gave them hopes of peace. But as they could obtain no cessation of hostilities, the states, unwilling to suffer any longer the loss and dishonour of being blockaded by the enemy, made the utmost efforts to recover their injured honour. Never on any occasion did the power and vigour of that republic appear in a more conspicuous light. In a few weeks, they had repaired and manned their fleet; and they equipped some ships of a larger size, than any which they had hitherto sent to sea. Tromp issued out, determined again to fight the victors, and to die rather than to yield the contest. He met with the enemy, commanded by Monk; and both sides immediately rushed into the combat. Tromp, gallantly animating his men, with his sword drawn, was shot through the heart with a musquet ball. This event alone decided the battle in favour of the English. Though near thirty ships of the Dutch were sunk and taken, they little regarded this loss compared with that of their brave admiral.

29th July.

Meanwhile the negotiations of peace were continually advancing. The states, overwhelmed with the expence of the war, terrified by their losses, and mortified by their defeats, were extremely desirous of an accommodation with an enemy whom they found, by experience, too powerful for them. The king having shown an inclination to serve on board their fleet; though they expressed their sense of the honour intended them, they declined an offer, which might inflame the quarrel with the English commonwealth. The great obstacle to the peace was found not to be any animosity on the part of the English; but on the contrary a desire too earnest of union and confederacy. Cromwel had revived the chimerical scheme of a coalition with the united provinces; a total conjunction of government, privileges, interests, and councils. This project appeared so wild to the states, that they wondered any man of sense could ever entertain it; and they refused to enter into conferences with regard to a proposal, which could serve only to delay any practicable scheme of accommodation. The peace was at last signed by Cromwel, now invested with the dignity of protector; and it proves sufficiently, that the war had been impolitic, since, after the most signal victories, no terms more advantageous could be obtained. A defensive league was made between the two republics. They agreed, each of them, to banish the enemies of the other; those who had been concerned in the massacre of Amboyna were to be punished, if any remained alive; the honour of the flag was yielded to the English; eighty-five thousand pounds were stipulated to be paid by the Dutch East India company for losses, which the English company had sustained; and the island of Polerone in the East Indies was promised to be ceded to the latter.

1654.

15th April.

Peace with Holland.

Cromwel, jealous of the connexions between the royal family and that of Orange, insisted on a separate article; that neither the young prince nor any of his family should ever be invested with the dignity of stadholder. The province of Holland, strongly prejudiced against that office, which they esteemed dangerous to liberty, secretly ratified this article. The protector, knowing that the other provinces would not be induced to make such a concession, was satisfied with this security.

The Dutch war, being successful, and the peace reasonable, brought credit to Cromwel's administration. An act of justice, which he exercised at home, gave likewise satisfaction to the people; though the regularity of it may perhaps appear somewhat doubtful. Don Pantaleon Sa, brother to the Portuguese ambassador, and joined with him in the same commission,[t] fancying himself to be insulted, came upon the exchange, armed and attended

[t] Thurloe, vol. ii. p. 429.

by several servants. By mistake, he fell on a gentleman, whom he took for the person that had given him the offence; and having butchered him with many wounds, he and all his attendants took shelter in the house of the Portuguese ambassador, who had connived at this base enterprize.^u The populace surrounded the house, and threatened to set fire to it. Cromwel sent a guard, who seized all the criminals. They were brought to trial: And notwithstanding the opposition of the ambassador, who pleaded the privileges of his office, Don Pantaleon was executed on Tower-hill. The laws of nations were here plainly violated: But the crime committed by the Portuguese gentleman was to the last degree atrocious; and the vigorous chastisement of it, suiting so well the undaunted character of Cromwel, was universally approved of at home and admired among foreign nations. The situation of Portugal obliged that court to acquiesce; and the ambassador soon after signed with the protector a treaty of peace and alliance, which was very advantageous to the English commerce.

Another act of severity, but necessary in his situation, was, at the very same time, exercised by the protector, in the capital punishment of Gerard and Vowel, two royalists, who were accused of conspiring against his life. He had erected a high court of justice for their trial; an infringement of the ancient laws, which at this time was become familiar, but one to which no custom or precedent could reconcile the nation. Juries were found altogether unmanageable. The restless Lilburn, for new offences, had been brought to a new trial; and had been acquitted with new triumph and exultation. If no other method of conviction had been devised during this illegal and unpopular government, all its enemies were assured of entire impunity.

3d of September. A new parliament. The protector had occasion to observe the prejudices entertained against his government, by the disposition of the parliament, which he summoned on the third of September, that day of the year, on which he gained his two great victories of Dunbar and Worcester, and which he always regarded as fortunate for him. It must be confessed, that, if we are left to gather Cromwel's intentions from his instrument of government, it is such a motley piece, that we cannot easily conjecture, whether he seriously

^u Ibid. vol. i. p. 616.

meant to establish a tyranny or a republic. On one hand, a first magistrate, in so extensive a government, seemed necessary both for the dignity and tranquillity of the state; and the authority, which he assumed as protector, was, in some respects, inferior to the prerogatives, which the laws entrusted and still entrust to the king. On the other hand, the legislative power, which he reserved to himself and council, together with so great an army, independant of the parliament, were bad prognostics of his intention to submit to a civil and legal constitution. But if this were not his intention, the method, in which he distributed and conducted the elections, being so favourable to liberty, form an inconsistency which is not easily accounted for. He deprived of their right of election all the small burroughs, places the most exposed to influence and corruption. Of 400 members, which represented England, 270 were chosen by the counties. The rest were elected by London, and the more considerable corporations. The lower populace too, so easily guided or deceived, were excluded from the elections: An estate of 200 pounds value was necessary to entitle any one to a vote. The elections of this parliament were conducted with perfect freedom; and, excepting that such of the royalists as had borne arms against the parliament and all their sons were excluded, a more fair representation of the people could not be desired or expected. Thirty members were returned from Scotland; as many from Ireland.

The protector seems to have been disappointed, when he found, that all these precautions, which were probably nothing but covers to his ambition, had not procured him the confidence of the public. Though Cromwel's administration was less odious to every party than that of any other party, yet was it entirely acceptable to none. The royalists had been instructed by the king to remain quiet, and to cover themselves under the appearance of republicans; and they found in this latter faction such inveterate hatred against the protector, that they could not wish for more zealous adversaries to his authority. It was maintained by them, that the pretence of liberty and a popular election was but a new artifice of this great deceiver, in order to lay asleep the deluded nation, and give himself leisure to rivet their chains more securely upon them: That in the instrument of government he openly declared his intention of still retaining the same mercenary army, by whose assistance he had subdued the ancient, established government, and who would with less scruple obey him, in overturning, whenever he should please to order them, that new system, which he himself had been pleased to model: That being sensible of the danger and uncertainty of all military government, he endeavoured to intermix some appearance, and but an appearance, of civil administration, and to balance the army by a seeming consent of the people: That the absurd trial, which he had made, of a parliament, elected by himself, appointed perpetually to elect their successors, plainly proved, that he aimed at nothing but temporary expedients, was totally averse to a free republican government, and possessed not that mature and deliberate reflection, which could qualify him to act the part of a legislator: That his imperious character, which had betrayed itself in so many incidents, could never seriously submit to legal limitations; nor would the very image of popular government be longer upheld than while conformable to his arbitrary will and pleasure: And that the best policy was to oblige him to take off the mask at once; and either submit entirely to that parliament which he had summoned, or by totally rejecting its authority, leave himself no resource but in his seditious and enthusiastic army.

In prosecution of these views, the parliament, having heard the protector's speech, three hours long,[w] and having chosen Lenthal for their speaker, immediately entered into a discussion of the pretended instrument of government, and of that authority, which Cromwel, by the title of protector, had assumed over the nation. The greatest liberty was used in arraigning this new dignity; and even the personal character and conduct of Cromwel escaped not without censure. The utmost, that could be obtained by the officers and by the court party, for so they were called, was to protract the debate by arguments and long speeches, and prevent the decision of a question, which, they were sensible, would be carried against them by a great majority. The protector, surprised and enraged at this refractory spirit in the parliament, which however he had so much reason to expect, sent for them to the painted chamber, and with an air of great authority inveighed against their conduct. He told them, that nothing could be more absurd than

[w] Thurloe, vol. ii. p. 588.

for them to dispute his title; since the same instrument of government, which made them a parliament, had invested him with the protectorship; that some points in the new constitution were supposed to be fundamentals, and were not, on any pretence, to be altered or disputed; that among these were the government of the nation by a single person and a parliament, their joint authority over the army and militia, the succession of new parliaments, and liberty of conscience; and that, with regard to these particulars, there was reserved to him a negative voice, to which, in the other circumstances of government, he confessed himself no wise intitled.

The protector now found the necessity of exacting a security, which, had he foreseen the spirit of the house, he would with better grace have required at their first meeting.[x] He obliged the members to sign a recognition of his authority, and an engagement not to propose or consent to any alteration in the government, as it was settled in a single person and a parliament; and he placed guards at the door of the house, who allowed none but subscribers to enter. Most of the members, after some hesitation, submitted to this condition; but retained the same refractory spirit, which they had discovered in their first debates. The instrument of government was taken in pieces, and examined, article by article, with the most scrupulous accuracy: Very free topics were advanced with the general approbation of the house: And during the whole course of their proceedings, they neither sent up one bill to the protector, nor took any notice of him. Being informed, that conspiracies were entered into between the members and some malcontents officers; he hastened to the dissolution of so dangerous an assembly. By the instrument of government, to which he had sworn, no parliament could be dissolved, till it had sitten five months; but Cromwel pretended, that a month contained only twenty-eight days, according to the method of computation practised in paying the fleet and army. The full time, therefore, according to this reckoning, being elapsed; the parliament was ordered to attend the protector, who made them a tedious, confused, angry harangue, and dismissed them. Were we to judge of Cromwel's capacity by this, and indeed by all his other compositions, we

1655.
22d of
Jan.

---

[x] Thurloe, vol. ii. p. 620.

should be apt to entertain no very favourable idea of it. But in the great variety of human geniuses, there are some, which, though they see their object clearly and distinctly in general; yet, when they come to unfold its parts by discourse or writing, lose that luminous conception, which they had before attained. All accounts agree in ascribing to Cromwel a tiresome, dark, unintelligible elocution, even when he had no intention to disguise his meaning: Yet no man's actions were ever, in such a variety of difficult incidents, more decisive and judicious.

The electing of a discontented parliament is a proof of a discontented nation: The angry and abrupt dissolution of that parliament is always sure to encrease the general discontent. The members of this assembly, returning to their counties, propagated that spirit of mutiny, which they had exerted in the house. Sir Harry Vane and the old republicans, who maintained the indissoluble authority of the long parliament, encouraged the murmurs against the present usurpation; though they acted so cautiously as to give the protector no handle against them. Wildman and some others of that party carried still farther their conspiracies against the protector's authority. The royalists, observing this general ill will towards the establishment, could no longer be retained in subjection; but fancied, that every one, who was dissatisfied like them, had also embraced the same views and inclinations. They did not consider, that the old parliamentary party, though many of them were displeased with Cromwel, who had dispossessed them of their power, were still more apprehensive of any success to the royal cause; whence, besides a certain prospect of the same consequence, they had so much reason to dread the severest vengeance for their past transgressions.

Insurrection of the royalists. In concert with the king a conspiracy was entered into by the royalists throughout England, and a day of general rising appointed. Information of this design was conveyed to Cromwel. The protector's administration was extremely vigilant. Thurloe, his secretary, had spies every where. Manning, who had access to the king's family, kept a regular correspondence with him. And it was not difficult to obtain intelligence of a confederacy, so generally diffused among a party, who valued themselves more on zeal and courage, than on secrecy and sobriety. Many of the royalists

CHAPTER LXI

were thrown into prison. Others, on the approach of the day, were terrified with the danger of the undertaking, and remained at home. In one place alone the conspiracy broke into action. Penruddoc, Groves, Jones, and other gentlemen of the west, entered Salisbury with about 200 horse; at the very time when the sheriff and judges were holding the assizes. These they made prisoners; and they proclaimed the king. Contrary to their expectations, they received no accession of force; so prevalent was the terror of the established government. Having in vain wandered about for some time, they were totally discouraged; and one troop of horse was able at last to suppress them. The leaders of the conspiracy, being taken prisoners, were capitally punished. The rest were sold for slaves, and transported to Barbadoes. *11th of March.*

The easy subduing of this insurrection, which, by the boldness of the undertaking, struck at first a great terror into the nation, was a singular felicity to the protector; who could not, without danger, have brought together any considerable body of his mutinous army, in order to suppress it. The very insurrection itself he regarded as a fortunate event; since it proved the reality of those conspiracies, which his enemies, on every occasion, represented as mere fictions, invented to colour his tyrannical severities. He resolved to keep no longer any terms with the royalists, who, though they were not perhaps the most implacable of his enemies, were those whom he could oppress under the most plausible pretences, and who met with least countenance and protection from his adherents. He issued an edict with the consent of his council, for exacting the tenth penny from that whole party; in order, as he pretended, to make them pay the expences, to which their mutinous disposition continually exposed the public. Without regard to compositions, articles of capitulation, or acts of indemnity, all the royalists, however harassed with former oppressions, were obliged anew to redeem themselves by great sums of money; and many of them were reduced by these multiplied disasters to extreme poverty. Whoever was known to be disaffected, or even lay under any suspicion, though no guilt could be proved against him, was exposed to the new exaction.

In order to raise this imposition, which commonly passed by the name of decimation, the protector instituted twelve major-generals; and divided the whole kingdom of England into so many military jurisdictions.[y] These men, assisted by commissioners, had power to subject whom they pleased to decimation, to levy all the taxes imposed by the protector and his council, and to imprison any person who should be exposed to their jealousy or suspicion; nor was there any appeal from them but to the protector himself and his council. Under colour of these powers, which were sufficiently exorbitant, the major-generals exercised an authority still more arbitrary, and acted as if absolute masters of the property and person of every subject. All reasonable men now concluded, that the very masque of liberty was thrown aside, and that the nation was for ever subjected to military and despotic government, exercised not in the legal manner of European nations, but according to the maxims of eastern tyranny. Not only the supreme magistrate owed his authority to illegal force and usurpation: He had parcelled out the people into so many subdivisions of slavery, and had delegated to his inferior ministers the same unlimited authority, which he himself had so violently assumed.

A government, totally military and despotic, is almost sure, after some time, to fall into impotence and languor: But when it immediately succeeds a legal constitution, it may, at first, to foreign nations appear very vigorous and active, and may exert with more unanimity that power, spirit, and riches, which had been acquired under a better form. It seems now proper, after so long an interval, to look abroad to the general state of Europe, and to consider the measures, which England, at this time, embraced in its negotiations with the neighbouring princes. The moderate temper and unwarlike genius of the two last princes, the extreme difficulties under which they laboured at home, and the great security which they enjoyed from foreign enemies, had rendered them negligent of the transactions on the continent; and England, during their reigns, had been, in a manner, overlooked in the general system of Europe. The bold and restless genius of the protector led him to extend his alliances and enterprizes to every part of Christendom; and partly from the ascendant of his magnanimous spirit, partly from the situation of foreign kingdoms, the weight of England, even under its most legal and bravest princes,

State of Europe.

---

[y] Parl. Hist. vol. xx. p. 433.

CHAPTER LXI

was never more sensibly felt than during this unjust and violent usurpation.

A war of thirty years, the most signal and most destructive that had appeared in modern annals, was at last finished in Germany; [z] and by the treaty of Westphalia, were composed those fatal quarrels, which had been excited by the palatine's precipitate acceptance of the crown of Bohemia. The young palatine was restored to part of his dignities and of his dominions.[a] The rights, privileges, and authority of the several members of the Germanic body were fixed and ascertained: Sovereign princes and free states were in some degree reduced to obedience under laws: And by the valour of the heroic Gustavus, the enterprizes of the active Richelieu, the intrigues of the artful Mazarine, was in part effected, after an infinite expence of blood and treasure, what had been fondly expected and loudly demanded from the feeble efforts of the pacific James, seconded by the scanty supplies of his jealous parliaments.

Sweden, which had acquired by conquest large dominions in the north of Germany, was engaged in enterprizes, which promised her, from her success and valour, still more extensive acquisitions on the side both of Poland and of Denmark. Charles X. who had mounted the throne of that kingdom after the voluntary resignation of Christina, being stimulated by the fame of Gustavus as well as by his own martial disposition, carried his conquering arms to the south of the Baltic, and gained the celebrated battle of Warsaw, which had been obstinately disputed during the space of three days. The protector, at the time his alliance was courted by every power in Europe, anxiously courted the alliance of Sweden; and he was fond of forming a confederacy with a protestant power of such renown, even though it threatened the whole north with conquest and subjection.

The transactions of the parliament and protector with France had been various and complicated. The emissaries of Richelieu had furnished fuel to the flame of rebellion, when it first broke out in Scotland; but after the conflagration had diffused itself, the

---

[z] In 1648.　[a] This prince, during the civil wars, had much neglected his uncle and payed court to the parliament: He accepted of a pension of 8000 l. a year from them, and took a place in their assembly of divines.

French court, observing the materials to be of themselves sufficiently combustible, found it unnecessary any longer to animate
the British malcontents to an opposition of their sovereign. On the
contrary, they offered their mediation for composing these intestine disorders; and their ambassadors, from decency, pretended to
act in concert with the court of England, and to receive directions
from a prince, with whom their master was connected with so near
an affinity. Meanwhile, Richelieu died, and soon after him, the
French king, Louis XIII. leaving his son an infant four years old,
and his widow, Anne of Austria, regent of the kingdom. Cardinal
Mazarine succeeded Richelieu in the ministry; and the same general plan of policy, though by men of such opposite characters, was
still continued in the French counsels. The establishment of royal
authority, the reduction of the Austrian family, were pursued with
ardor and success; and every year brought an accession of force
and grandeur to the French monarchy. Not only battles were won,
towns and fortresses taken; the genius too of the nation seemed
gradually to improve, and to compose itself to the spirit of dutiful
obedience and of steddy enterprize. A Condé, a Turenne were
formed; and the troops, animated by their valour, and guided by
their discipline, acquired every day a greater ascendant over the
Spaniards. All of a sudden, from some intrigues of the court, and
some discontents in the courts of judicature, intestine commotions
were excited, and every thing relapsed into confusion. But these
rebellions of the French, neither ennobled by the spirit of liberty,
nor disgraced by the fanatical extravagances, which distinguished
the British civil wars, were conducted with little bloodshed, and
made but a small impression on the minds of the people. Though
seconded by the force of Spain, and conducted by the prince of
Condé, the malcontents, in a little time, were either expelled or
subdued; and the French monarchy, having lost a few of its conquests, returned, with fresh vigour, to the acquisition of new dominion.

The queen of England and her son, Charles, during these commotions, passed most of their time at Paris; and notwithstanding
their near connexion of blood, received but few civilities, and still
less support, from the French court. Had the queen regent been
ever so much inclined to assist the English prince, the disorders of
her own affairs, would, for a long time, have rendered such in-

CHAPTER LXI

tentions impracticable. The banished queen had a moderate pension assigned her; but it was so ill payed, and her credit ran so low, that, one morning, when the cardinal de Retz waited on her, she informed him, that her daughter, the princess Henrietta, was obliged to lie abed, for want of a fire to warm her. To such a condition was reduced, in the midst of Paris, a queen of England, and daughter of Henry IV. of France!

The English parliament, however, having assumed the sovereignty of the state, resented the countenance, cold as it was, which the French court gave to the unfortunate monarch. On pretence of injuries, of which the English merchants complained, they issued letters of reprisal upon the French; and Blake went so far as to attack and seize a whole squadron of ships, which were carrying supplies to Dunkirk, then closely besieged by the Spaniards. That town, disappointed of these supplies, fell into the hands of the enemy. The French ministers soon found it necessary to change their measures. They treated Charles with such affected indifference, that he thought it more decent to withdraw, and prevent the indignity of being desired to leave the kingdom. He went first to Spaw, thence he retired to Cologne; where he lived two years, on a small pension, about 6000 pounds a year, payed him by the court of France, and on some contributions sent him by his friends in England. In the management of his family, he discovered a disposition to order and economy; and his temper, cheerful, careless, and sociable, was more than a sufficient compensation for that empire, of which his enemies had bereaved him. Sir Edward Hyde, created lord-chancellor, and the marquess of Ormond, were his chief friends and confidents.

If the French ministry had thought it prudent to bend under the English parliament, they deemed it still more necessary to pay deference to the protector, when he assumed the reins of government. Cardinal Mazarine, by whom all the councils of France were directed, was artful and vigilant, supple and patient, false and intriguing; desirous rather to prevail by dexterity than violence, and placing his honour more in the final success of his measures than in the splendor and magnanimity of the means, which he employed. Cromwel, by his imperious character, rather than by the advantage of his situation, acquired an ascendant over this man; and every proposal made by the protector, however unreasonable in itself and urged with whatever insolence, met with a ready compliance from the politic and timid cardinal. Bourdeaux was sent over to England as minister; and all circumstances of respect were payed to the daring usurper, who had imbrued his hands in the blood of his sovereign, a prince so nearly related to the royal family of France. With indefatigable patience did Bourdeaux conduct this negotiation, which Cromwel seemed entirely to neglect; and though privateers with English commissions committed daily depredations on the French commerce, Mazarine was content, in hopes of a fortunate issue, still to submit to these indignities.[b]

The court of Spain, less connected with the unfortunate royal family, and reduced to greater distress than the French monarchy, had been still more forward in her advances to the prosperous parliament and protector. Don Alonzo de Cardenas, the Spanish envoy, was the first public minister, who recognized the authority of the new republic; and in return for this civility, Ascham was sent envoy into Spain by the parliament. No sooner had this minister arrived in Madrid, than some of the banished royalists, inflamed by that inveterate hatred, which animated the English factions, broke into his chamber, and murdered him together with his secretary. Immediately, they took sanctuary in the churches; and, assisted by the general favour, which every where attended the royal cause, were enabled, most of them, to make their escape. Only one of the criminals suffered death; and the parliament seemed to rest satisfied with this atonement.

Spain, at this time, assailed every where by vigorous enemies from without, and labouring under many internal disorders, retained nothing of her former grandeur, except the haughty pride of her counsels, and the hatred and jealousy of her neighbours. Portugal had rebelled, and established her monarchy in the house of Braganza: Catalonia, complaining of violated privileges, had revolted to France: Naples was shaken with popular convulsions:

[b] Thurloe, vol. iii. p. 103, 619, 653. In the treaty, which was signed after long negociation, the protector's name was inserted before the French king's in that copy which remained in England. Thurloe, vol. vi. p. 116. See farther, vol. vii. p. 178.

CHAPTER LXI

The Low Countries were invaded with superior forces, and seemed ready to change their master: The Spanish infantry, anciently so formidable, had been annihilated by Condé in the fields of Rocroy: And though the same prince, banished France, sustained by his activity and valour, the falling fortunes of Spain, he could only hope to protract, not prevent, the ruin, with which that monarchy was visibly threatened.

Had Cromwel understood and regarded the interests of his country, he would have supported the declining condition of Spain against the dangerous ambition of France, and preserved that balance of power, on which the greatness and security of England so much depend. Had he studied only his own interests, he would have maintained an exact neutrality between those great monarchies; nor would he have hazarded his ill-acquired and unsettled power, by provoking foreign enemies, who might lend assistance to domestic faction, and overturn his tottering throne. But his magnanimity undervalued danger: His active disposition and avidity of extensive glory, made him incapable of repose: And as the policy of men is continually warped by their temper, no sooner was peace made with Holland, than he began to deliberate what new enemy he should invade with his victorious arms.

The extensive empire and yet extreme weakness of Spain in the West Indies; the vigorous courage and great naval power of England; were circumstances, which, when compared, excited the ambition of the enterprizing protector, and made him hope, that he might, by some gainful conquest, render for ever illustrious that dominion, which he had assumed over his country. Should he fail of these durable acquisitions, the Indian treasures, which must every year cross the ocean to reach Spain, were, he thought, a sure prey to the English navy, and would support his military force, without his laying new burthens on the discontented people. From France a vigorous resistance must be expected: No plunder, no conquests could be hoped for: The progress of his arms, even if attended with success, must there be slow and gradual: And the advantages acquired, however real, would be less striking to the multitude, whom it was his interest to allure. The royal family, so closely connected with the French monarch, might receive great assistance from that neighbouring kingdom; and an army of

War with Spain.

French protestants, landed in England, would be able, he dreaded, to unite the most opposite factions against the present usurpation.[c]

These motives of policy were probably seconded by his bigotted prejudices; as no human mind ever contained so strange a mixture of sagacity and absurdity as that of this extraordinary personage. The Swedish alliance, though much contrary to the interests of England, he had contracted, merely from his zeal for protestantism; [d] and Sweden being closely connected with France, he could not hope to maintain that confederacy, in which he so much prided himself, should a rupture ensue between England and this latter kingdom.[e] The Hugonots, he expected, would meet with better treatment, while he engaged in a close union with their sovereign.[f] And as the Spaniards were much more papists than the French, were much more exposed to the old puritanical hatred,[g] and had even erected the bloody tribunal of the inquisition, whose rigours they had refused to mitigate on Cromwel's solicitation; [h] he hoped that a holy and meritorious war with such idolaters could not fail of protection from heaven.[i] A preacher likewise, inspired, as was supposed, by a prophetic spirit, bid him *go and prosper;* calling him *a stone cut out of the mountains without hands, that would break the pride of the Spaniard, crush Antichrist, and make way for the purity of the Gospel over the whole world.*[k]

Actuated equally by these bigotted, these ambitious, and these interested motives, the protector equipped two considerable squadrons; and while he was making those preparations, the neighbouring states, ignorant of his intentions, remained in suspence, and looked with anxious expectation on what side the storm should discharge itself. One of these squadrons, consisting of thirty capital ships, was sent into the Mediterranean under Blake, whose fame was now spread over Europe. No English fleet, except

[c] See the account of the negociations with France and Spain by Thurloe, vol. i. p. 759. [d] He proposed to Sweden a general league and confederacy of all the protestants. Whitlocke, p. 620. Thurloe, vol. vii. p. 1. In order to judge of the maxims, by which he conducted his foreign politics, see farther Thurloe, vol. iv. p. 295, 343, 443, vol. vii. p. 174. [e] Thurloe, vol. i. p. 759. [f] Thurloe, vol. i. p. 759. [g] Id. ibid. [h] Id. ibid. Don Alonzo said, that the Indian trade and the inquisition were his master's two eyes, and the protector insisted upon the putting out both of them at once. [i] Carrington, p. 191. [k] Bates.

during the Crusades, had ever before sailed in those seas; and from one extremity to the other, there was no naval force, Christian or Mahometan, able to resist them. The Roman pontiff, whose weakness and whose pride equally provoke attacks, dreaded invasion from a power, which professed the most inveterate enmity against him, and which so little regulated its movements by the usual motives of interest and prudence. Blake, casting anchor before Leghorn, demanded and obtained from the duke of Tuscany reparation for some losses, which the English commerce had formerly sustained from him. He next sailed to Algiers, and compelled the dey to make peace, and to restrain his pyratical subjects from farther violences on the English. He presented himself before Tunis; and having there made the same demands, the dey of that republic bade him look to the castles of Porto-Farino and Goletta, and do his utmost. Blake needed not to be rouzed by such a bravado: He drew his ships close up to the castles, and tore them in pieces with his artillery. He sent a numerous detachment of sailors in their long boats into the harbour, and burned every ship which lay there. This bold action, which its very temerity, perhaps, rendered safe, was executed with little loss, and filled all that part of the world with the renown of English valour.

The other squadron was not equally successful. It was commanded by Pen, and carried on board 4000 men, under the command of Venables. About 5000 more joined them from Barbadoes and St. Christopher's. Both these officers were inclined to the king's service; [l] and it is pretended, that Cromwel was obliged to hurry the soldiers on board, in order to prevent the execution of a conspiracy which had been formed among them, in favour of the exiled family.[m] The ill success of this enterprize may justly be ascribed, as much to the injudicious schemes of the protector, who planned it, as to the bad execution of the officers, by whom it was conducted. The soldiers were the refuse of the whole army: The forces, inlisted in the West Indies, were the most profligate of mankind: Pen and Venables were of incompatible tempers: The troops were not furnished with arms fit for such an expedition: Their provisions were defective both in quantity and quality: All hopes of pillage, the best incentive to valour among such men,

Jamaica conquered.

---

[l] Clarendon.   [m] Vita D. Berwici, p. 124.

HISTORY OF ENGLAND

were refused the soldiers and seamen: No directions or intelligence were given to conduct the officers in their enterprize: And at the same time, they were tied down to follow the advice of commissioners, who disconcerted them in all their projects.[n]

*13th
April.*
It was agreed by the admiral and general to attempt St. Domingo, the only place of strength in the island of Hispaniola. On the approach of the English the Spaniards in a fright deserted their houses, and fled into the woods. Contrary to the opinion of Venables, the soldiers were disembarked without guides ten leagues distant from the town. They wandered four days through the woods without provisions, and what was still more intolerable in that sultry climate, without water. The Spaniards recovered spirit, and attacked them. The English, discouraged with the bad conduct of their officers, and scarcely alive from hunger, thirst, and fatigue, were unable to resist. An inconsiderable number of the enemy put the whole army to rout, killed 600 of them, and chased the rest on board their vessels.

The English commanders, in order to atone, as much as possible, for this unprosperous attempt, bent their course to Jamaica, which was surrendered to them without a blow. Pen and Venables returned to England, and were both of them sent to the Tower by the protector, who, though commonly master of his fiery temper, was thrown into a violent passion at this disappointment. He had made a conquest of greater importance, than he was himself at that time aware of; yet was it much inferior to the vast projects, which he had formed. He gave orders, however, to support it by men and money; and that island has ever since remained in the hands of the English; the chief acquisition which they owe to the enterprizing spirit of Cromwel.

1656.
As soon as the news of this expedition, which was an unwarrantable violation of treaty, arrived in Europe, the Spaniards declared war against England, and seized all the ships and goods of English merchants, of which they could make themselves masters. The commerce with Spain, so profitable to the English, was cut off; and near 1500 vessels, it is computed,[o] fell in a few years

---

[n] Burchet's Naval History. See also Carte's Collection, vol. ii. p. 46, 47. Thurloe, vol. iii. p. 505.   [o] Thurloe, vol. iv. p. 135. World's Mistake in Oliver Cromwel, in the Harl. Miscel. vol. i.

into the hands of the enemy. Blake, to whom Montague was now joined in command, after receiving new orders, prepared himself for hostilities against the Spaniards.

Several sea officers, having entertained scruples of conscience with regard to the justice of the Spanish war, threw up their commissions, and retired.[p] No commands, they thought, of their superiors could justify a war, which was contrary to the principles of natural equity, and which the civil magistrate had no right to order. Individuals, they maintained, in resigning to the public their natural liberty, could bestow on it only what they themselves were possessed of, a right of performing lawful actions, and could invest it with no authority of commanding what is contrary to the decrees of heaven. Such maxims, though they seem reasonable, are perhaps too perfect for human nature; and must be regarded as one effect, though of the most innocent and even honourable kind, of that spirit, partly fanatical, partly republican, which predominated in England.

Blake lay some time off Cadiz, in expectation of intercepting the plate fleet, but was at last obliged, for want of water, to make sail towards Portugal. Captain Stayner, whom he had left on the coast with a squadron of seven vessels, came in sight of the galleons, and immediately set sail to pursue them. The Spanish admiral ran his ship ashore: Two others followed his example: The English took two ships valued at near two millions of pieces of eight. Two galleons were set on fire; and the marquess of Badajox, viceroy of Peru, with his wife and his daughter, betrothed to the young duke of Medina Celi, were destroyed in them. The marquess himself might have escaped; but seeing these unfortunate women, astonished with the danger, fall in a swoon, and perish in the flames, he rather chose to die with them than drag out a life, embittered with the remembrance of such dismal scenes.[q] When the treasures, gained by this enterprize, arrived at Portsmouth, the protector, from a spirit of ostentation, ordered them to be transported by land to London.

Success.

September.

The next action against the Spaniards was more honourable, though less profitable, to the nation. Blake, having heard that a Spanish fleet of sixteen ships, much richer than the former, had

---

[p] Thurloe, vol. iv. p. 570, 589.   [q] Thurloe, vol. v. p. 433.

taken shelter in the Canaries, immediately made sail towards them. He found them in the bay of Santa Cruz, disposed in a formidable posture. The bay was secured with a strong castle, well provided with cannon, besides seven forts in several parts of it, all united by a line of communication, manned with musqueteers. Don Diego Diagues, the Spanish admiral, ordered all his smaller vessels to moor close to the shore, and posted the larger galleons farther off, at anchor, with their broadsides to the sea.

Blake was rather animated than daunted with this appearance. The wind seconded his courage, and blowing full into the bay, in a moment brought him among the thickest of his enemies. After a resistance of four hours, the Spaniards yielded to English valour, and abandoned their ships, which were set on fire, and consumed with all their treasure. The greatest danger still remained to the English. They lay under the fire of the castles and all the forts, which must, in a little time, have torn them in pieces. But the wind, suddenly shifting, carried them out of the bay; where they left the Spaniards in astonishment at the happy temerity of their audacious victors.

And death of admiral Blake. This was the last and greatest action of the gallant Blake. He was consumed with a dropsy and scurvy, and hastened home, that he might yield up his breath in his native country, which he had so much adorned by his valour. As he came within sight of land, he expired.[r] Never man, so zealous for a faction, was so much respected and esteemed even by the opposite factions. He was by principle an inflexible republican; and the late usurpations, amidst all the trust and caresses, which he received from the ruling powers, were thought to be very little grateful to him. *It is still our duty,* he said to the seamen, *to fight for our country, into what hands so ever the government may fall.* Disinterested, generous, liberal; ambitious only of true glory, dreadful only to his avowed enemies; he forms one of the most perfect characters of the age, and the least stained with those errors and violences, which were then so predominant. The protector ordered him a pompous funeral at the public charge: But the tears of his countrymen were the most honourable panegyric on his memory.

[r] 20th of April, 1657.

CHAPTER LXI

The conduct of the protector in foreign affairs, though imprudent and impolitic, was full of vigour and enterprize, and drew a
consideration to his country, which, since the reign of Elizabeth, it
seemed to have totally lost. The great mind of this successful
usurper was intent on spreading the renown of the English nation;
and while he struck mankind with astonishment at his extraordinary fortune, he seemed to ennoble, instead of debasing, that
people, whom he had reduced to subjection. It was his boast, that
he would render the name of an Englishman as much feared and
revered as ever was that of a Roman; and as his countrymen found
some reality in these pretensions, their national vanity, being gratified, made them bear with more patience all the indignities and
calamities, under which they laboured.

It must also be acknowledged, that the protector, in his civil and *Domestic*
domestic administration, displayed as great regard both to justice *administra-*
and clemency, as his usurped authority, derived from no law, and *tion of*
founded only on the sword, could possibly permit. All the chief *Cromwel.*
offices in the courts of judicature were filled with men of integrity:
Amidst the virulence of faction, the decrees of the judges were
upright and impartial: And to every man but himself, and to himself, except where necessity required the contrary, the law was the
great rule of conduct and behaviour. Vane and Lilburn, whose
credit with the republicans and levellers he dreaded, were indeed
for some time confined to prison: Cony, who refused to pay illegal
taxes, was obliged by menaces to depart from his obstinacy: High
courts of justice were erected to try those who had engaged in
conspiracies and insurrections against the protector's authority,
and whom he could not safely commit to the verdict of juries. But
these irregularities were deemed inevitable consequences of his
illegal authority. And though often urged by his officers, as is
pretended,[s] to attempt a general massacre of the royalists, he always with horror rejected such sanguinary counsels.

In the army was laid the sole basis of the protector's power; and
in managing it consisted the chief art and delicacy of his government. The soldiers were held in exact discipline; a policy, which
both accustomed them to obedience, and made them less hateful

[s] Clarendon, Life of Dr. Berwick, &c.

and burthensome to the people. He augmented their pay; though
the public necessities some times obliged him to run in arrears to
them. Their interests, they were sensible, were closely connected
with those of their general and protector. And he entirely commanded their affectionate regard, by his abilities and success in
almost every enterprize, which he had hitherto undertaken. But all
military government is precarious; much more where it stands in
opposition to civil establishments; and still more, where it encoun-
ters religious prejudices. By the wild fanaticism, which he had
nourished in the soldiers, he had seduced them into measures, for
which, if openly proposed to them, they would have entertained
the utmost aversion. But this same spirit rendered them more
difficult to be governed, and made their caprices terrible even to
that hand, which directed their movements. So often taught, that
the office of king was an usurpation upon Christ, they were apt to
suspect a protector not to be altogether compatible with that divine
authority. Harrison, though raised to the highest dignity, and possessed of Cromwel's confidence, became his most inveterate enemy as soon as the authority of a single person was established,
against which that usurper had always made such violent protestations. Overton, Rich, Okey, officers of rank in the army, were
actuated with like principles, and Cromwel was obliged to deprive
them of their commissions. Their influence, which was before
thought unbounded among the troops, seemed from that moment
to be totally annihilated.

The more effectually to curb the enthusiastic and seditious
spirit of the troops, Cromwel established a kind of militia in the
several counties. Companies of infantry and cavalry were enlisted
under proper officers, regular pay distributed among them, and a
resource by that means provided both against the insurrections of
the royalists, and mutiny of the army.

Religion can never be deemed a point of small consequence in
civil government: But during this period, it may be regarded as the
great spring of men's actions and determinations. Though transported, himself, with the most frantic whimsies, Cromwel had
adopted a scheme for regulating this principle in others, which was
sagacious and political. Being resolved to maintain a national
church, yet determined neither to admit episcopacy nor presbytery, he established a number of commissioners, under the name

of *tryers*, partly laymen, partly ecclesiastics, some presbyterians, some independents. These presented to all livings, which were formerly in the gift of the crown; they examined and admitted such persons as received holy orders; and they inspected the lives, doctrine, and behaviour of the clergy. Instead of supporting that union between learning and theology, which has so long been attempted in Europe, these tryers embraced the latter principle in its full purity, and made it the sole object of their examination. The candidates were no more perplexed with questions concerning their progress in Greek and Roman erudition; concerning their talent for profane arts and sciences: The chief object of scrutiny regarded their advances in grace, and fixing the critical moment of their conversion.

With the pretended saints of all denominations Cromwel was familiar and easy. Laying aside the state of protector, which, on other occasions, he well knew how to maintain, he insinuated to them, that nothing but necessity could ever oblige him to invest himself with it. He talked spiritually to them; he sighed, he weeped, he canted, he prayed. He even entered with them into an emulation of ghostly gifts; and these men, instead of grieving to be out done in their own way, were proud, that his highness, by his princely example, had dignified those practices, in which they themselves were daily occupied.[*]

If Cromwel might be said to adhere to any particular form of religion, they were the independents who could chiefly boast of his favour; and it may be affirmed, that such pastors of that sect, as were not passionately addicted to civil liberty, were all of them devoted to him. The presbyterian clergy also, saved from the ravages of the anabaptists and millenarians, and enjoying their establishments and tythes, were not averse to his government; though

---

[*] Cromwel followed, though but in part, the advice which he received from general Harrison, at the time when the intimacy and endearment most strongly subsisted betwixt them. "Let the waiting upon Jehovah," said that military saint, "be the greatest and most considerable business you have every day: Reckon it so, more than to eat, sleep, and council together. Run aside sometimes from your company, and get a word with the Lord. Why should not you have three or four precious souls always standing at your elbow, with whom you might now and then turn into a corner; I have found refreshment and mercy in such a way." Milton's state papers, p. 12.

he still entertained a great jealousy of that ambitious and restless spirit, by which they were actuated. He granted an unbounded liberty of conscience, to all but catholics and prelatists; and by that means, he both attached the wild sectaries to his person, and employed them in curbing the domineering spirit of the presbyterians. "I am the only man," he was often heard to say, "who has known how to subdue that insolent sect, which can suffer none but itself."

The protestant zeal, which possessed the presbyterians and independents, was highly gratified by the haughty manner, in which the protector so successfully supported the persecuted protestants throughout all Europe. Even the duke of Savoy, so remote a power, and so little exposed to the naval force of England, was obliged, by the authority of France, to comply with his mediation, and to tolerate the protestants of the vallies, against whom that prince had commenced a furious persecution. France itself was constrained to bear, not only with the religion, but even, in some instances, with the seditious insolence of the Hugonots; and when the French court applied for a reciprocal toleration of the catholic religion in England, the protector, who arrogated in every thing the superiority, would hearken to no such proposal. He had entertained a project of instituting a college in imitation of that at Rome, for the propagation of the faith; and his apostles, in zeal, though not in unanimity, had certainly been a full match for the catholics.

Cromwel retained the church of England in constraint; though he permitted its clergy a little more liberty than the republican parliament had formerly allowed. He was pleased, that the superior lenity of his administration should in every thing be remarked. He bridled the royalists, both by the army which he retained, and by those secret spies, which he found means to intermix in all their counsels. Manning being detected and punished with death, he corrupted Sir Richard Willis, who was much trusted by chancellor Hyde and all the royalists; and by means of this man he was let into every design and conspiracy of the party. He could disconcert any project, by confining the persons who were to be the actors in it; and as he restored them afterwards to liberty, his severity passed only for the result of general jealousy and suspicion. The secret source of his intelligence remained still unknown and unsuspected.

CHAPTER LXI

Conspiracies for an assassination he was chiefly afraid of; these being designs, which no prudence or vigilance could evade. Colonel Titus, under the name of Allen, had written a spirited discourse, exhorting every one to embrace this method of vengeance; and Cromwel knew, that the inflamed minds of the royal party were sufficiently disposed to put the doctrine in practice against him. He openly told them, that assassinations were base and odious, and he never would commence hostilities by so shameful an expedient; but if the first attempt or provocation came from them, he would retaliate to the uttermost. He had instruments, he said, whom he could employ; and he never would desist, till he had totally exterminated the royal family. This menace, more than all his guards, contributed to the security of his person.[u]

There was no point about which the protector was more solicitous than to procure intelligence. This article alone, it is said, cost him sixty thousand pounds a year. Postmasters, both at home and abroad, were in his pay: Carriers were searched or bribed: Secretaries and clerks were corrupted: The greatest zealots in all parties were often those who conveyed private information to him: And nothing could escape his vigilant enquiry. Such at least is the representation made by historians of Cromwel's administration: But it must be confessed, that, if we may judge by those volumes of Thurloe's papers, which have been lately published, this affair, like many others, has been greatly magnified. We scarcely find by that collection, that any secret counsels of foreign states, except those of Holland, which are not expected to be concealed, were known to the protector.

The general behaviour and deportment of this man, who had been raised from a very private station, who had passed most of his youth in the country, and who was still constrained so much to frequent bad company, was such as might befit the greatest monarch. He maintained a dignity without either affectation or ostentation; and supported with all strangers that high idea, with which his great exploits and prodigious fortune had impressed them. Among his ancient friends, he could relax himself; and by trifling and amusement, jesting and making verses, he feared not exposing himself to their most familiar approaches.[w] With others, he

---

[u] See note [D] at the end of the volume.   [w] Whitlocke, p. 647.

sometimes pushed matters to the length of rustic buffoonery; and he would amuse himself by putting burning coals into the boots and hose of the officers, who attended him.[x] Before the king's trial, a meeting was agreed on between the chiefs of the republican party and the general officers, in order to concert the model of that free government, which they were to substitute, in the room of the monarchical constitution, now totally subverted. After debates on this subject, the most important, that could fall under the discussion of human creatures, Ludlow tells us, that Cromwel, by way of frolic, threw a cushion at his head; and when Ludlow took up another cushion, in order to return the compliment, the general ran down stairs, and had almost fallen in the hurry. When the high court of justice was signing the warrant for the execution of the king, a matter, if possible, still more serious; Cromwel, taking the pen in his hand, before he subscribed his name, bedaubed with ink the face of Martin, who sat next him. And the pen being delivered to Martin, he practised the same frolic upon Cromwel.[y] He frequently gave feasts to his inferior officers; and when the meat was set upon the table, a signal was given; the soldiers rushed in upon them; and with much noise, tumult, and confusion, ran away with all the dishes, and disappointed the guests of their expected meal.[z]

That vein of frolic and pleasantry, which made a part, however inconsistent, of Cromwel's character, was apt sometimes to betray him into other inconsistencies, and to discover itself even where religion might seem to be a little concerned. It is a tradition, that, one day, sitting at table, the protector had a bottle of wine brought him, of a kind which he valued so highly, that he must needs open the bottle himself: But in attempting it, the corkscrew dropt from his hand. Immediately his courtiers and generals flung themselves on the floor to recover it. Cromwel burst out a laughing. *Should any fool*, said he, *put in his head at the door, he would fancy, from your posture, that you were seeking the Lord; and you are only seeking a cork screw.*

Amidst all the unguarded play and buffoonery of this singular personage, he took the opportunity of remarking the characters, designs, and weaknesses of men; and he would sometimes push them, by an indulgence in wine, to open to him the most secret

[x] Bates.　[y] Trial of the regicides.　[z] Bates.

recesses of their bosom. Great regularity, however, and even, austerity of manners were always maintained in his court; and he was
careful never by any liberties to give offence to the most rigid of
the godly. Some state was upheld; but with little expence, and
without any splendor. The nobility, though courted by him, kept
at a distance, and disdained to intermix with those mean persons,
who were the instruments of his government. Without departing
from œconomy, he was generous to those who served him; and he
knew how to find out and engage in his interests every man possessed of those talents, which any particular employment demanded. His generals, his admirals, his judges, his ambassadors,
were persons, who contributed, all of them, in their several
spheres, to the security of the protector, and to the honour and
interest of the nation.

Under pretence of uniting Scotland and Ireland in one commonwealth with England, Cromwell had reduced those kingdoms
to a total subjection; and he treated them entirely as conquered
provinces. The civil administration of Scotland was placed in a
council, consisting mostly of English, of which lord Broghil was
president. Justice was administered by seven judges, four of whom
were English. In order to curb the tyrannical nobility, he both
abolished all vassalage *a* and revived the office of justice of peace,
which king James had introduced, but was not able to support.*b* A
long line of forts and garrisons was maintained throughout the
kingdom. An army of 10,000 men *c* kept every thing in peace and
obedience; and neither the banditti of the mountains nor the bigots of the low countries could indulge their inclination to turbulence and disorder. He courted the presbyterian clergy; though
he nourished that intestine enmity which prevailed between the
resolutioners and protesters; and he found, that very little policy
was requisite to foment quarrels among theologians. He permitted
no church assemblies; being sensible that from thence had proceeded many of the past disorders. And in the main, the Scots were
obliged to acknowledge, that never before, while they enjoyed
their irregular, factious liberty, had they attained so much happiness as at present, when reduced to subjection under a foreign
nation.

---

a Whitlocke, p. 570.   *b* Thurloe, vol. iv. p. 57.   *c* Thurloe, vol. vi. p. 557.

The protector's administration of Ireland was more severe and violent. The government of that island was first entrusted to Fleetwood, a notorious fanatic, who had married Ireton's widow; then to Henry Cromwel, second son of the protector, a young man of an amiable mild disposition, and not destitute of vigor and capacity. Above five millions of acres, forfeited either by the popish rebels or by the adherents of the king, were divided, partly among the adventurers, who had advanced money to the parliament, partly among the English soldiers, who had arrears due to them. Examples of a more sudden and violent change of property are scarcely to be found in any history. An order was even issued to confine all the native Irish to the province of Connaught, where they would be shut up by rivers, lakes, and mountains, and could not, it was hoped, be any longer dangerous to the English government: But this barbarous and absurd policy, which, from an impatience of attaining immediate security, must have depopulated all the other provinces, and rendered the English estates of no value, was soon abandoned as impracticable.

New parliament.

Cromwel began to hope, that, by his administration, attended with so much lustre and success abroad, so much order and tranquillity at home, he had now acquired such authority as would enable him to meet the representatives of the nation, and would assure him of their dutiful compliance with his government. He summoned a parliament; but not trusting altogether to the good will of the people, he used every art, which his new model of representation allowed him to employ, in order to influence the elections and fill the house with his own creatures. Ireland, being entirely in the hands of the army, chose few but such officers as were most acceptable to him. Scotland showed a like compliance; and as the nobility and gentry of that kingdom regarded their attendance on English parliaments as an ignominious badge of slavery, it was, on that account, more easy for the officers to prevail in the elections. Notwithstanding all these precautions, the protector still found, that the majority would not be favourable to him.

17th of September.

He set guards, therefore, on the door, who permitted none to enter but such as produced a warrant from his council; and the council rejected about a hundred, who either refused a recognition of the protector's government, or were on other accounts obnoxious to him. These protested against so egregious a violence, subversive of all liberty; but every application for redress was neglected both by the council and the parliament.

The majority of the parliament, by means of these arts and violences, was now at last either friendly to the protector, or resolved, by their compliance, to adjust, if possible, this military government to their laws and liberties. They voted a renunciation of all title in Charles Stuart or any of his family; and this was the first act, dignified with the appearance of national consent, which had ever had that tendency. Colonel Jephson, in order to sound the inclinations of the house, ventured to move, that the parliament should bestow the crown on Cromwel; and no surprize or reluctance was discovered on the occasion. When Cromwel afterwards asked Jephson what induced him to make such a motion, "As long," said Jephson, "as I have the honour to sit in parliament, I must follow the dictates of my own conscience, whatever offence I may be so unfortunate as to give you." "Get thee gone," said Cromwel, giving him a gentle blow on the shoulder, "get thee gone, for a mad fellow as thou art."

In order to pave the way to this advancement, for which he so ardently longed, Cromwel resolved to sacrifice his major-generals, whom he knew to be extremely odious to the nation. That measure was also become necessary for his own security. All government, purely military, fluctuates perpetually between a despotic monarchy and a despotic aristocracy, according as the authority of the chief commander prevails, or that of the officers next him in rank and dignity. The major-generals, being possessed of so much distinct jurisdiction, began to establish a separate title to power, and had rendered themselves formidable to the protector himself; and for this inconvenience, though he had not foreseen it, he well knew, before it was too late, to provide a proper remedy. Claypole, his son-in-law, who possessed his confidence, abandoned them to the pleasure of the house; and though the name was still retained, it was agreed to abridge, or rather entirely annihilate, the power of the major-generals.

At length, a motion in form was made by alderman Pack, one of the city members, for investing the protector with the dignity of king. This motion, at first, excited great disorder, and divided the whole house into parties. The chief opposition came from the usual adherents of the protector, the major-generals and such officers as depended on them. Lambert, a man of deep intrigue and of great interest in the army, had long entertained the ambition of succeeding Cromwel in the protectorship; and he foresaw, that, if the monarchy were restored, hereditary right would also be established, and the crown be transmitted to the posterity of the prince first elected. He pleaded, therefore, conscience; and rouzing all those civil and religious jealousies against kingly government, which had been so industriously encouraged among the soldiers, and which served them as a pretence for so many violences, he raised a numerous, and still more formidable party against the motion.

On the other hand, the motion was supported by every one, who was more particularly devoted to the protector, and who hoped, by so acceptable a measure, to pay court to the prevailing authority. Many persons also, attached to their country, despaired of ever being able to subvert the present illegal establishment, and were desirous, by fixing it on ancient foundations, to induce the protector, from views of his own safety, to pay a regard to the ancient laws and liberties of the kingdom. Even the royalists imprudently joined in the measure; and hoped, that, when the question regarded only persons, not forms of government, no one would any longer balance between the ancient royal family, and an ignoble usurper, who, by blood, treason, and perfidy, had made his way to the throne. The bill was voted by a considerable majority; and a committee was appointed to reason with the protector, and to overcome those scruples, which he pretended against accepting so liberal an offer.

1657.
Crown
offered to
Cromwel.

9th April. The conference lasted for several days. The committee urged, that all the statutes and customs of England were founded on the supposition of regal authority, and could not, without extreme violence, be adjusted to any other form of government: That a protector, except during the minority of a king, was a name utterly unknown to the laws; and no man was acquainted with the extent or limits of his authority: That if it were attempted to define every part of his jurisdiction, many years, if not ages, would be required for the execution of so complicated a work; if the whole power of the king were at once transferred to him, the question was plainly about a name, and the preference was undisputably due to the ancient title: That the English constitution was more anxious concerning the form of government than concerning the birthright of the first magistrate, and had provided, by an express law of Henry VII. for the security of those who act in defence of the king in being, by whatever means he might have acquired possession: That it was extremely the interest of all his Highness's friends to seek the shelter of this statute; and even the people in general were desirous of such a settlement, and in all juries were with great difficulty induced to give their verdict in favour of a protector: That the great source of all the late commotions had been the jealousy of liberty; and that a republic, together with a protector, had been established in order to provide farther securities for the freedom of the constitution; but that by experience the remedy had been found insufficient, even dangerous and pernicious; since every undeterminate power, such as that of a protector, must be arbitrary; and the more arbitrary, as it was contrary to the genius and inclination of the people.

The difficulty consisted not in perswading Cromwel. He was sufficiently convinced of the solidity of these reasons; and his inclination, as well as judgment, was entirely on the side of the committee. But how to bring over the soldiers to the same way of thinking was the question. The office of king had been painted to them in such horrible colours, that there were no hopes of reconciling them suddenly to it, even though bestowed upon their general, to whom they were so much devoted. A contradiction, open and direct, to all past professions would make them pass, in the eyes of the whole nation, for the most shameless hypocrites, inlisted, by no other than mercenary motives, in the cause of the most perfidious traitor. Principles, such as they were, had been encouraged in them by every consideration, human and divine; and though it was easy, where interest concurred, to deceive them by the thinnest disguises, it might be found dangerous at once to pull off the masque, and to show them in a full light the whole crime and deformity of their conduct. Suspended between these fears and his own most ardent desires, Cromwel protracted the time, and seemed still to oppose the reasonings of the committee; in hopes, that by artifice he might be able to reconcile the refractory minds of the soldiers to his new dignity.

While the protector argued so much in contradiction both to his judgment and inclination, it is no wonder, that his elocution, always confused, embarrassed, and unintelligible, should be involved in tenfold darkness, and discover no glimmering of common sense or reason. An exact account of this conference remains, and may be regarded as a great curiosity. The members of the committee, in their reasonings, discover judgment, knowledge, elocution: Lord Broghill in particular exerts himself on this memorable occasion. But what a contrast, when we pass to the protector's replies! After so singular a manner does nature distribute her talents, that, in a nation abounding with sense and learning, a man, who, by superior personal merit alone, had made his way to supreme dignity, and had even obliged the parliament to make him a tender of the crown, was yet incapable of expressing himself on this occasion, but in a manner which a peasant of the most ordinary capacity would justly be ashamed of.[d]

[d] We shall produce any passage at random: For his discourse is all of a piece. "I confess, for it behoves me to deal plainly with you, I must confess, I would say, I hope, I may be understood in this, for indeed I must be tender what I say to such an audience as this; I say, I would be understood, that in this argument I do not make parallel betwixt men of a different mind and a parliament, which shall have their desires. I know there is no comparison, nor can it be urged upon me, that my words have the least colour that way, because the parliament seems to give liberty to me to say anything to you; as that, that is a tender of my humble reasons and judgement and opinion to them; and if I think they are such and will be such to them, and are faithful servants, and will be so to the supreme authority, and the legislative wheresoever it is: If, I say, I should not tell you, knowing their minds to be so, I should not be faithful, if I should not tell you so, to the end you may report it to the parliament: I shall say something for myself, for my own mind, I do profess it, I am not a man scrupulous about words or names of such things I have not: But as I have the word of God, and I hope I shall ever have it, for the rule of my conscience, for my informations; so truly men that have been led in dark paths, through the providence and dispensation of God; why surely it is not to be objected to a man; for who can love to walk in the dark? But providence does so dispose. And though a man may impute his own folly and blindness to providence sinfully, yet it must be at my peril; the case may be that it is the providence of God, that doth lead men in darkness: I must need say, that I have had a great deal of experience of providence, and though it is no rule without or against the word, yet it is a very good expositor of the word in many cases." *Conference at Whitehall.* The great defect in Oliver's speeches consists not in his want of elocution, but in his want of ideas. The sagacity of his actions, and the absurdity of his discourse, form the most prodigious

CHAPTER LXI

The opposition, which Cromwel dreaded, was not that which came from Lambert and his adherents, whom he now regarded as capital enemies, and whom he was resolved, on the first occasion, to deprive of all power and authority: It was that which he met with in his own family, and from men, who, by interest as well as inclination, were the most devoted to him. Fleetwood had married his daughter: Desborow his sister: Yet these men, actuated by principle alone, could, by no persuasion, artifice, or entreaty, be induced to consent, that their friend and patron should be invested with regal dignity. They told him, that, if he accepted of the crown, they would instantly throw up their commissions, and never afterwards should have it in their power to serve him.ᵉ Colonel Pride procured a petition against the office of king, signed by a majority of the officers, who were in London and the neighbourhood. Several persons, it is said, had entered into an engagement to murder the protector within a few hours after he should have accepted the offer of the parliament. Some sudden mutiny in the army was justly dreaded. And upon the whole, Cromwel, after the agony and perplexity of long doubt, was at last obliged to refuse that crown, which the representatives of the nation, in the most solemn manner, had tendered to him. Most historians are inclined to blame his choice; but he must be allowed the best judge of his own situation. And in such complicated subjects, the alteration of a very minute circumstance, unknown to the spectator, will often be sufficient to cast the balance, and render a determination, which, in itself, may be uneligible, very prudent, or even absolutely necessary to the actor.

He rejects it.

A dream or prophecy, lord Clarendon mentions, which he affirms (and he must have known the truth), was universally talked of almost from the beginning of the civil wars, and long before Cromwel was so considerable a person as to bestow upon it any degree of probability. In this prophecy it was foretold, that Cromwel should be the greatest man in England, and would nearly, but never would fully, mount the throne. Such a prepossession proba-

---

contrast that ever was known. The collection of all his speeches, letters, sermons (for he also wrote sermons) would make a great curiosity, and with a few exceptions might justly pass for one of the most nonsensical books in the world.   ᵉ Thurloe, vol. vi. p. 261.

bly arose from the heated imagination either of himself or of his followers; and as it might be one cause of the great progress, which he had already made, it is not an unlikely reason, which may be assigned, for his refusing at this time any farther elevation.

The parliament, when the regal dignity was rejected by Cromwel, found themselves obliged to retain the name of a commonwealth and protector; and as the government was hitherto a manifest usurpation, it was thought proper to sanctify it by a seeming choice of the people and their representatives. Instead of the *instrument of government,* which was the work of the general officers alone, *a humble petition and advice* was framed, and offered to the protector by the parliament. This was represented as the great basis of the republican establishment, regulating and limiting the powers of each member of the constitution, and securing the liberty of the people to the most remote posterity. By this deed, the authority of protector was in some particulars enlarged: In others, it was considerably diminished. He had the power of nominating his successor; he had a perpetual revenue assigned him, a million a year for the pay of the fleet and army, three hundred thousand pounds for the support of civil government; and he had authority to name another house, who should enjoy their seats during life, and exercise some functions of the former house of peers. But he abandoned the power assumed in the intervals of parliament, of framing laws with the consent of his council; and he agreed, that no members of either house should be excluded but by the consent of that house, of which they were members. The other articles were in the main the same as in the instrument of government. The instrument of government Cromwel had formerly extolled as the most perfect work of human invention: He now represented it as a rotten plank, upon which no man could trust himself without sinking. Even the humble petition and advice, which he extolled in its turn, appeared so lame and imperfect, that it was found requisite, this very session, to mend it by a supplement; and after all, it may be regarded as a crude and undigested model of government. It was, however, accepted for the voluntary deed of the whole people in the three united nations; and Cromwel, as if his power had just commenced from this popular consent, was anew inaugurated in Westminster Hall, after the most solemn and most pompous manner.

Humble petition and advice.

CHAPTER LXI

The parliament having adjourned itself, the protector deprived *26th June.* Lambert of all his commissions; but still allowed him a considerable pension, of 2000 pounds a year, as a bribe for his future peaceable deportment. Lambert's authority in the army, to the surprise of every body, was found immediately to expire with the loss of his commission. Packer and some other officers, whom Cromwel suspected, were also displaced.

Richard, eldest son of the protector, was brought to court, introduced into public business, and thenceforth regarded by many as his heir in the protectorship: though Cromwel sometimes employed the gross artifice of flattering others with hopes of the succession. Richard was a person possessed of the most peaceable, inoffensive, unambitious character; and had hitherto lived contentedly in the country on a small estate, which his wife had brought him. All the activity, which he discovered, and which never was great, was however exerted to beneficent purposes: At the time of the king's trial, he had fallen on his knees before his father, and had conjured him, by every tye of duty and humanity, to spare the life of that monarch. Cromwel had two daughters unmarried: One of them he now gave in marriage to the grandson and heir of his great friend, the earl of Warwic, with whom he had, in every fortune, preserved an uninterrupted intimacy and good correspondence. The other, he married to the viscount Fauconberg, of a family, formerly devoted to the royal party. He was ambitious of forming connexions with the nobility; and it was one chief motive for his desiring the title of king, that he might replace every thing in its natural order, and restore, to the ancient families, the trust and honour, of which he now found himself obliged, for his own safety, to deprive them.

The parliament was again assembled; consisting, as in the times *1658.* of monarchy, of two houses, the commons and the other house. *20th Jan.* Cromwel, during the interval, had sent writs to his house of peers, which consisted of sixty members. They were composed of five or six ancient peers, of several gentlemen of fortune and distinction, and of some officers who had risen from the meanest stations. None of the ancient peers, however, though summoned by writ, would deign to accept of a seat, which they must share with such companions as were assigned them. The protector endeavoured at first to maintain the appearance of a legal magistrate. He placed no guard at the door of either house: But soon found how incompatible liberty is with military usurpations. By bringing so great a number of his friends and adherents into the other house, he had lost the majority among the national representatives. In consequence of a clause in the humble petition and advice, the commons assumed a power of re-admitting those members, whom the council had formerly excluded. Sir Arthur Hazelrig and some others, whom Cromwel had created lords, rather chose to take their seat with the commons. An incontestible majority now declared themselves against the protector; and they refused to acknowledge the jurisdiction of that other house, which he had established. Even the validity of the humble petition and advice was questioned; as being voted by a parliament, which lay under force, and which was deprived by military violence of a considerable number of its members. The protector, dreading combinations between the parliament and the malcontents in the army, resolved to allow no leisure for forming any conspiracy against him; and *4th Feb.* with expressions of great displeasure, he dissolved the parliament. When urged by Fleetwood and others of his friends not to precipitate himself into this rash measure, he swore by the living God, that they should not sit a moment longer.

These distractions at home were not able to take off the protector's attention from foreign affairs; and in all his measures he proceeded with the same vigour and enterprize, as if secure of the duty and attachment of the three kingdoms. His alliance with Sweden he still supported; and he endeavoured to assist that crown in its successful enterprizes, for reducing all its neighbours to subjection, and rendering itself absolute master of the Baltic. As soon as Spain declared war against him, he concluded a peace and an alliance with France, and united himself in all his counsels with that potent and ambitious kingdom. Spain, having long courted in vain the friendship of the successful usurper, was reduced at last to apply to the unfortunate prince. Charles formed a league with Philip, removed his small court to Bruges in the Low Countries, and raised four regiments of his own subjects, whom he employed in the Spanish service. The duke of York, who had, with applause, served some campaigns in the French army, and who had merited the particular esteem of marshal Turenne, now joined his brother,

CHAPTER LXI

and continued to seek military experience under Don John of Austria and the prince of Condé.

The scheme of foreign politics, adopted by the protector, was highly imprudent, but was suitable to that magnanimity and enterprize, with which he was so signally endowed. He was particularly desirous of conquest and dominion on the continent; [f] and he sent over into Flanders six thousand men under Reynolds, who joined the French army commanded by Turenne. In the former campaign, Mardyke was taken, and put into the hands of the English. Early this campaign, siege was laid to Dunkirk; and when the Spanish army advanced to relieve it, the combined armies of France and England marched out of their trenches, and fought the battle of the Dunes, where the Spaniards were totally defeated. [g] The valour of the English was much remarked on this occasion. Dunkirk, being soon after surrendered, was by agreement delivered to Cromwel. He committed the government of that important place to Lockhart, a Scotchman of abilities, who had married his niece, and was his ambassador at the court of France.

Dunkirk taken.

This acquisition was regarded by the protector as the means only of obtaining farther advantages. He was resolved to concert

---

[f] He aspired to get possession of Elsinore and the passage of the Sound. See *World's Mistake in Oliver Cromwel.* He also endeavoured to get possession of Bremen. Thurloe, vol. vi. p. 478.   [g] It was remarked by the saints of that time, that the battle was fought on a day which was held for a fast in London, so that as Fleetwood said (Thurloe, vol. vii. p. 159,) while we were praying, they were fighting; and the Lord hath given a signal answer. The Lord has not only owned us in our work there, but in our waiting upon him in a way of prayer, which is indeed our old experienced approved way in all streights and difficulties. Cromwel's letter to Blake and Montague, his brave admirals, is remarkable for the same spirit. Thurloe, vol. iv. p. 744. You have, says he, as I verily believe and am persuaded, a plentiful stock of prayers going for you daily, sent up by the soberest and most approved ministers and christians in this nation, and, notwithstanding some discouragements, very much wrestling of faith for you, which are to us, and I trust will be to you, matter of great encouragement. But notwithstanding all this, it will be good for you and us to deliver up ourselves and all our affairs to the disposition of our all-wise Father, who not only out of prerogative, but because of his goodness, wisdom and truth, ought to be resigned unto by his creatures, especially those who are children of his begetting through the spirit, &c.

measures with the French court for the final conquest and partition of the Low Countries.[h] Had he lived much longer, and maintained his authority in England, so chimerical or rather so dangerous a project, would certainly have been carried into execution. And this first and principal step towards more extensive conquest, which France, during a whole century, has never yet been able, by an infinite expence of blood and treasure, fully to attain, had at once been accomplished by the enterprizing, though unskilful politics of Cromwel.

During these transactions, great demonstrations of mutual friendship and regard passed between the French king and the protector. Lord Fauconberg, Cromwel's son-in-law, was dispatched to Louis, then in the camp before Dunkirk; and was received with the regard, usually payed to foreign princes by the French court.[i] Mazarine sent to London his nephew Mancini, along with the duke of Crequi; and expressed his regret, that his urgent affairs should deprive him of the honour, which he had long wished for, of paying, in person, his respects to the greatest man in the world.[k]

The protector reaped little satisfaction from the success of his arms abroad: The situation, in which he stood at home, kept him in perpetual uneasiness and inquietude. His administration, so expensive both by military enterprizes and secret intelligence, had exhausted his revenue, and involved him in a considerable debt. The royalists, he heard, had renewed their conspiracies, for a general insurrection; and Ormond was secretly come over with a view of concerting measures for the execution of this project. Lord Fairfax, Sir William Waller, and many heads of the presbyterians, had secretly entered into the engagement. Even the army was infected with the general spirit of discontent; and some sudden and dangerous eruption was every moment to be dreaded from it. No hopes remained, after his violent breach with the last parliament, that he should ever be able to establish, with general consent, a legal settlement, or temper the military with any mixture of

[h] Thurloe, vol. i. p. 762.   [i] Ibid. vol. vii. p. 151, 158.   [k] In reality the cardinal had not entertained so high an idea of Cromwel. He used to say, that he was a fortunate madman. Vie de Cromwel par Raguenet. See also Carte's Collection, vol. ii. p. 81. Gumble's Life of Monk, p. 93. World's Mistake in O. Cromwel.

CHAPTER LXI

civil authority. All his arts and policy were exhausted; and having so often, by fraud and false pretences, deceived every party, and almost every individual, he could no longer hope, by repeating the same professions, to meet with equal confidence and regard.

However zealous the royalists, their conspiracy took not effect: Willis discovered the whole to the protector. Ormond was obliged to fly, and he deemed himself fortunate to have escaped so vigilant an administration. Great numbers were thrown into prison. A high court of justice was anew erected for the trial of those criminals, whose guilt was most apparent. Notwithstanding the recognition of his authority by the last parliament, the protector could not, as yet, trust to an unbyassed jury. Sir Henry Slingsby, and Dr. Huet were condemned and beheaded. Mordaunt, brother to the earl of Peterborow, narrowly escaped. The numbers for his condemnation and his acquittal were equal; and just as the sentence was pronounced in his favour, colonel Pride, who was resolved to condemn him, came into court. Ashton, Storey, and Bestley were hanged in different streets of the city.

The conspiracy of the Millenarians in the army struck Cromwel with still greater apprehensions. Harrison and the other discarded officers of that party could not remain at rest. Stimulated equally by revenge, by ambition, and by conscience, they still harboured in their breast some desperate project; and there wanted not officers in the army, who, from like motives, were disposed to second all their undertakings. The levellers and agitators had been encouraged by Cromwel to interpose with their advice in all political deliberations; and he had even pretended to honour many of them with his intimate friendship, while he conducted his daring enterprizes against the king and the parliament. It was a usual practice with him, in order to familiarize himself the more with the agitators, who were commonly corporals or serjeants, to take them to bed with him, and there, after prayers and exhortations, to discuss together their projects and principles, political as well as religious. Having assumed the dignity of protector, he excluded them from all his councils, and had neither leisure nor inclination to indulge them any farther in their wonted familiarities. Among those who were enraged at this treatment was Sexby; an active agitator, who now employed against him all that restless industry, which had formerly been exerted in his favour. He even went so far as to enter into a correspondence with Spain; and Cromwel, who knew the distempers of the army, was justly afraid of some mutiny, to which a day, an hour, an instant, might provide leaders.

Of assassinations likewise he was apprehensive, from the zealous spirit, which actuated the soldiers. Sindercome had undertaken to murder him; and, by the most unaccountable accidents, had often been prevented from executing his bloody purpose. His design was discovered; but the protector could never find the bottom of the enterprize, nor detect any of his accomplices. He was tried by a jury; and notwithstanding the general odium attending that crime, notwithstanding the clear and full proof of his guilt, so little conviction prevailed of the protector's right to the supreme government, it was with the utmost difficulty [l] that this conspirator was condemned. When every thing was prepared for his execution, he was found dead; from poison, as is supposed, which he had voluntarily taken.

The protector might better have supported those fears and apprehensions, which the public distempers occasioned, had he enjoyed any domestic satisfaction, or possessed any cordial friend of his own family, in whose bosom he could safely have unloaded his anxious and corroding cares. But Fleetwood, his son-in-law, actuated by the wildest zeal, began to estrange himself from him; and was enraged to discover, that Cromwel, in all his enterprizes, had entertained views of promoting his own grandeur, more than of encouraging piety and religion, of which he made such fervent professions. His eldest daughter, married to Fleetwood, had adopted republican principles so vehement, that she could not with patience behold power lodged in a single person, even in her indulgent father. His other daughters were no less prejudiced in favour of the royal cause, and regretted the violences and iniquities, into which, they thought, their family had so unhappily been transported. Above all, the sickness of Mrs. Claypole, his peculiar favourite, a lady endued with many humane virtues, and amiable accomplishments, depressed his anxious mind, and poisoned all his enjoyments. She had entertained a high regard for Dr. Huet, lately executed; and being refused his pardon, the melancholy of her temper, encreased by her distempered body, had prompted

---

[l] Thurloe, vol. vi. p. 53.

CHAPTER LXI

her to lament to her father all his sanguinary measures, and urge him to compunction for those heinous crimes, into which his fatal ambition had betrayed him. Her death, which followed soon after, gave new edge to every word, which she had uttered.

All composure of mind was now for ever fled from the protector: He felt, that the grandeur, which he had attained with so much guilt and courage, could not ensure him that tranquillity, which it belongs to virtue alone, and moderation fully to ascertain. Overwhelmed with the load of public affairs, dreading perpetually some fatal accident in his distempered government, seeing nothing around him but treacherous friends or enraged enemies, possessing the confidence of no party, resting his title on no principle, civil or religious, he found his power to depend on so delicate a poize of factions and interests, as the smallest event was able, without any preparation, in a moment to overturn. Death too, which, with such signal intrepidity, he had braved in the field, being incessantly threatened by the poniards of fanatical or interested assassins, was ever present to his terrified apprehension, and haunted him in every scene of business or repose. Each action of his life betrayed the terrors under which he laboured. The aspect of strangers was uneasy to him: With a piercing and anxious eye he surveyed every face, to which he was not daily accustomed. He never moved a step without strong guards attending him: He wore armour under his cloaths, and farther secured himself by offensive weapons, a sword, falchion, and pistols, which he always carried about him. He returned from no place by the direct road, or by the same way which he went. Every journey he performed with hurry and precipitation. Seldom he slept above three nights together in the same chamber: And he never let it be known beforehand what chamber he intended to choose, nor entrusted himself in any, which was not provided with back-doors, at which sentinels were carefully placed. Society terrified him, while he reflected on his numerous, unknown, and implacable enemies: Solitude astonished him, by withdrawing that protection, which he found so necessary for his security.

His body also, from the contagion of his anxious mind, began to be affected; and his health seemed sensibly to decline. He was seized with a slow fever, which changed into a tertian ague. For the space of a week, no dangerous symptoms appeared; and in the

Sickness of the protector.

intervals of the fits he was able to walk abroad. At length, the fever encreased, and he himself began to entertain some thoughts of death, and to cast his eye towards that future existence, whose idea had once been intimately present to him; though since, in the hurry of affairs, and in the shock of wars and factions, it had, no doubt, been considerably obliterated. He asked Goodwin, one of his preachers, if the doctrine were true, that the elect could never fall or suffer a final reprobation. "Nothing more certain," replied the preacher. "Then am I safe," said the protector: "For I am sure that once I was in a state of grace."

His physicians were sensible of the perilous condition, to which his distemper had reduced him: But his chaplains, by their prayers, visions, and revelations, so buoyed up his hopes, that he began to believe his life out of all danger. A favourable answer, it was pretended, had been returned by heaven to the petitions of all the godly; and he relied on their asseverations much more than on the opinion of the most experienced physicians. "I tell you," he cried with confidence to the latter, "I tell you, I shall not die of this distemper: I am well assured of my recovery. It is promised by the Lord, not only to my supplications, but to those of men who hold a stricter commerce and more intimate correspondence with him. Ye may have skill in your profession; but nature can do more than all the physicians in the world, and God is far above nature." [m] Nay, to such a degree of madness did their enthusiastic assurances mount, that, upon a fast day, which was observed, on his account, both at Hampton Court and at White-hall, they did not so much pray for his health, as give thanks for the undoubted pledges, which they had received of his recovery. He himself was overheard offering up his addresses to heaven; and so far had the illusions of fanaticism prevailed over the plainest dictates of natural morality, that he assumed more the character of a mediator, in interceding for his people, than that of a criminal, whose atrocious violation of social duty had, from every tribunal, human and divine, merited the severest vengeance.

Meanwhile all the symptoms began to wear a more fatal aspect; and the physicians were obliged to break silence, and to declare that the protector could not survive the next fit, with which he

[m] Bates: See also Thurloe, vol. vii. p. 355, 416.

CHAPTER LXI

was threatened. The council was alarmed. A deputation was sent to know his will with regard to his successor. His senses were gone, and he could not now express his intentions. They asked him whether he did not mean, that his eldest son, Richard, should succeed him in the protectorship. A simple affirmative was, or seemed to be extorted from him. Soon after, on the 3d of September, that very day, which he had always considered as the most fortunate for him, he expired. A violent tempest, which im- *His death,* mediately succeeded his death, served as a subject of discourse to the vulgar. His partizans, as well as his enemies, were fond of remarking this event; and each of them endeavoured, by forced inferences, to interpret it as a confirmation of their particular prejudices.

The writers, attached to the memory of this wonderful person, *and* make his character, with regard to abilities, bear the air of the most *character.* extravagant panegyric: His enemies form such a representation of his moral qualities as resembles the most virulent invective. Both of them, it must be confessed, are supported by such striking circumstances in his conduct and fortune as bestow on their repre- sentation a great air of probability. "What can be more extraor- dinary," it is said,[n] "than that a person, of private birth and edu- cation, no fortune, no eminent qualities of body, which have sometimes, nor shining talents of mind, which have often raised men to the highest dignities, should have the courage to attempt and the abilities to execute so great a design as the subverting one of the most ancient and best established monarchies in the world? That he should have the power and boldness to put his prince and master to an open and infamous death? Should banish that numer- ous and strongly allied family? Cover all these temerities under a seeming obedience to a parliament, in whose service he pretended to be retained? Trample too upon that parliament in their turn, and scornfully expel them as soon as they gave him ground of dissatisfaction? Erect in their place the dominion of the saints, and give reality to the most visionary idea, which the heated imag- ination of any fanatic was ever able to entertain? Suppress again that monster in its infancy, and openly set up himself above all

[n] Cowley's Discourses: This passage is altered in some particulars from the original.

things that ever were called sovereign in England? Overcome first all his enemies by arms, and all his friends afterwards by artifice? Serve all parties patiently for a while, and command them victoriously at last? Over-run each corner of the three nations, and subdue with equal facility, both the riches of the south, and the poverty of the north? Be feared and courted by all foreign princes, and be adopted a brother to the gods of the earth? Call together parliaments with a word of his pen, and scatter them again with the breath of his mouth? Reduce to subjection a warlike and discontented nation, by means of a mutinous army? Command a mutinous army by means of seditious and factious officers? Be humbly and daily petitioned, that he would be pleased, at the rate of millions a year, to be hired as master of those who had hired him before to be their servant? Have the estates and lives of three nations as much at his disposal as was once the little inheritance of his father, and be as noble and liberal in the spending of them? And lastly (for there is no end of enumerating every particular of his glory) with one word bequeath all this power and splendor to his posterity? Die possessed of peace at home and triumph abroad? Be buried among kings, and with more than regal solemnity; and leave a name behind him not to be extinguished but with the whole world; which as it was too little for his praise, so might it have been for his conquests, if the short line of his mortal life could have stretched out the extent of his immortal designs?"

My intention is not to disfigure this picture, drawn by so masterly a hand: I shall only endeavour to remove from it somewhat of the marvellous; a circumstance which, on all occasions, gives much ground for doubt and suspicion. It seems to me, that the circumstance of Cromwel's life, in which his abilities are principally discovered, is his rising, from a private station, in opposition to so many rivals, so much advanced before him, to a high command and authority in the army. His great courage, his signal military talents, his eminent dexterity and address, were all requisite for this important acquisition. Yet will not this promotion appear the effect of supernatural abilities, when we consider, that Fairfax himself, a private gentleman, who had not the advantage of a seat in parliament, had, through the same steps, attained even a superior rank, and, if endued with common capacity and penetration, had been able to retain it. To incite such an army to rebellion against the parliament, required no uncommon art or

CHAPTER LXI

industry: To have kept them in obedience had been the more difficult enterprize. When the breach was once formed between the military and civil powers, a supreme and absolute authority, from that moment, is devolved on the general; and if he be afterwards pleased to employ artifice or policy, it may be regarded, on most occasions, as great condescension, if not as superfluous caution. That Cromwel was ever able really to blind or over-reach, either the king or the republicans, does not appear: As they possessed no means of resisting the force under his command, they were glad to temporize with him, and, by seeming to be deceived, wait for opportunities of freeing themselves from his dominion. If he seduced the military fanatics, it is to be considered, that their interests and his evidently concurred, that their ignorance and low education exposed them to the grossest imposition, and that he himself was at bottom as frantic an enthusiast as the worst of them, and, in order to obtain their confidence, needed but to display those vulgar and ridiculous habits, which he had early acquired, and on which he set so high a value. An army is so forcible, and at the same time so coarse a weapon, that any hand, which wields it, may, without much dexterity, perform any operation, and attain any ascendant, in human society.

The domestic administration of Cromwel, though it discovers great abilities, was conducted without any plan either of liberty or arbitrary power: Perhaps, his difficult situation admitted of neither. His foreign enterprizes, though full of intrepidity, were pernicious to national interest, and seem more the result of impetuous fury or narrow prejudices, than of cool foresight and deliberation. An eminent personage, however, he was in many respects, and even a superior genius; but unequal and irregular in his operations. And though not defective in any talent, except that of elocution, the abilities, which in him were most admirable, and which most contributed to his marvellous success, were the magnanimous resolution of his enterprizes, and his peculiar dexterity in discovering the characters, and practising on the weaknesses of mankind.

If we survey the moral character of Cromwel with that indulgence, which is due to the blindness and infirmities of the human species, we shall not be inclined to load his memory with such violent reproaches as those which his enemies usually throw upon it. Amidst the passions and prejudices of that period, that he should prefer the parliamentary to the royal cause, will not appear extraordinary; since, even at present, some men of sense and knowledge are disposed to think, that the question, with regard to the justice of the quarrel, may be regarded as doubtful and uncertain. The murder of the king, the most atrocious of all his actions, was to him covered under a mighty cloud of republican and fanatical illusions; and it is not impossible, but he might believe it, as many others did, the most meritorious action, that he could perform. His subsequent usurpation was the effect of necessity, as well as of ambition; nor is it easy to see, how the various factions could at that time have been restrained, without a mixture of military and arbitrary authority. The private deportment of Cromwel, as a son, a husband, a father, a friend, is exposed to no considerable censure, if it does not rather merit praise. And upon the whole, his character does not appear more extraordinary and unusual by the mixture of so much absurdity with so much penetration, than by his tempering such violent ambition and such enraged fanaticism with so much regard to justice and humanity.

Cromwel was in the fifty-ninth year of his age when he died. He was of a robust frame of body, and of a manly, though not of an agreeable aspect. He left only two sons, Richard and Henry; and three daughters; one married to general Fleetwood, another to Lord Fauconberg, a third to lord Rich. His father died when he was young. His mother lived till after he was protector; and, contrary to her orders, he buried her with great pomp in Westminster Abbey. She could not be persuaded, that his power or person was ever in safety. At every noise, which she heard, she exclaimed, that her son was murdered; and was never satisfied that he was alive, if she did not receive frequent visits from him. She was a decent woman; and by her frugality and industry had raised and educated a numerous family upon a small fortune. She had even been obliged to set up a brewery at Huntingdon, which she managed to good advantage. Hence Cromwel, in the invectives of that age, is often stigmatized with the name of the brewer. Ludlow, by way of insult, mentions the great accession, which he would receive to his royal revenues upon his mother's death, who possessed a jointure of sixty pounds a year upon his estate. She was of a good family, of the name of Stuart; remotely allied, as is by some supposed, to the royal family.

LXII

Richard acknowledged protector –
A parliament – Cabal of Wallingford House –
Richard deposed – Long parliament or
Rump restored – Conspiracy
of the royalists – Insurrection – Suppressed –
Parliament expelled – Committee of safety –
Foreign affairs – General Monk –
Monk declares for the parliament – Parliament
restored – Monk enters London, declares
for a free parliament – Secluded members
restored – Long parliament dissolved –
New parliament – The Restoration –
Manners and arts

ALL THE ARTS of Cromwel's policy had been so often practised, that they began to lose their effect; and his power, instead of being confirmed by time and success, seemed every day to become more uncertain and precarious. His friends the most closely connected with him, and his counsellors the most trusted, were entering into cabals against his authority; and with all his penetration into the characters of men, he could not find any ministers, on whom he could rely. Men of probity and honour, he knew, would not submit to be the instruments of an usurpation, violent and

1658.

illegal: Those, who were free from the restraint of principle, might betray, from interest, that cause, in which, from no better motives, they had inlisted themselves. Even those, on whom he conferred any favour, never deemed the recompence an equivalent for the sacrifices, which they made to obtain it: Whoever was refused any demand, justified his anger by the specious colours of conscience and of duty. Such difficulties surrounded the protector, that his dying at so critical a time, is esteemed by many the most fortunate circumstance that ever attended him; and it was thought, that all his courage and dexterity could not much longer have extended his usurped administration.

But when that potent hand was removed, which conducted the government, every one expected a sudden dissolution of the unwieldy and ill-jointed fabric. Richard, a young man of no experience, educated in the country, accustomed to a retired life, unacquainted with the officers and unknown to them, recommended by no military exploits, endeared by no familiarities, could not long, it was thought, maintain that authority, which his father had acquired by so many valorous atchievements, and such signal successes. And when it was observed, that he possessed only the virtues of private life, which in his situation were so many vices; that indolence, incapacity, irresolution attended his facility and good nature; the various hopes of men were excited by the expectation of some great event or revolution. For some time, however, the public was disappointed in this opinion. The council recognized the succession of Richard: Fleetwood, in whose favour, it was supposed, Cromwel had formerly made a will, renounced all claim or pretension to the protectorship: Henry, Richard's brother, who governed Ireland with popularity, ensured him the obedience of that kingdom: Monk, whose authority was well established in Scotland, being much attached to the family of Cromwel, immediately proclaimed the new protector: The army, every where, the fleet, acknowledged his title: Above ninety addresses, from the counties and most considerable corporations, congratulated him on his accession, in all the terms of dutiful allegiance: Foreign ministers were forward in paying him the usual compliments: And Richard, whose moderate, unambitious character, never would have led him to contend for empire, was tempted to accept of so rich an inheritance, which seemed to be tendered to him, by the consent of all mankind.

Richard acknowledged protector.

CHAPTER LXII

It was found necessary to call a parliament, in order to furnish supplies, both for the ordinary administration, and for fulfilling those engagements with foreign princes, particularly Sweden, into which the late protector had entered. In hopes of obtaining greater influence in elections, the ancient right was restored to all the small burroughs; and the counties were allowed no more than their usual members. The house of peers or the other house consisted of the same persons, that had been appointed by Oliver.

A parliament.

1659.

All the commons, at first, signed without hesitation an engagement not to alter the present government. They next proceeded to examine *the humble petition and advice;* and after great opposition and many vehement debates, it was, at length, with much difficulty, carried by the court-party to confirm it. An acknowledgment too of the authority of the other house was extorted from them; though it was resolved not to treat this house of peers with any greater respect than they should return to the commons. A declaration was also made, that the establishment of the other house should no wise prejudice the right of such of the ancient peers as had, from the beginning of the war, adhered to the parliament. But in all these proceedings, the opposition among the commons was so considerable, and the debates were so much prolonged, that all business was retarded, and great alarm given to the partizans of the young protector.

7th of January.

But there was another quarter from which greater dangers were justly apprehended. The most considerable officers of the army, and even Fleetwood, brother-in-law to the protector, were entering into cabals against him. No character in human society is more dangerous than that of the fanatic; because, if attended with weak judgment, he is exposed to the suggestions of others; if supported by more discernment, he is entirely governed by his own illusions, which sanctify his most selfish views and passions. Fleetwood was of the former species; and as he was extremely addicted to a republic, and even to the fifth monarchy or dominion of the saints, it was easy for those, who had insinuated themselves into his confidence, to instil disgusts against the dignity of protector. The whole republican party in the army, which was still considerable, Fitz, Mason, Moss, Farley, united themselves to that general. The officers too of the same party, whom Cromwel had discarded, Overton, Ludlow, Rich, Okey, Alured, began to appear, and to recover that authority, which had been only for a time suspended. A party likewise, who found themselves eclipsed in Richard's favour, Sydenham, Kelsey, Berry, Haines, joined the cabal of the others. Even Desborow, the protector's uncle, lent his authority to that faction. But above all, the intrigues of Lambert, who was now rouzed from his retreat, inflamed all those dangerous humours, and threatened the nation with some great convulsion. The discontented officers established their meetings in Fleetwood's apartments; and because he dwelt in Wallingford-house, the party received a denomination from that place.

Cabal of Walling-ford-house.

Richard, who possessed neither resolution nor penetration, was prevailed on to give an unguarded consent for calling a general council of officers, who might make him proposals, as they pretended, for the good of the army. No sooner were they assembled than they voted a remonstrance. They there lamented, that *the good old cause,* as they termed it, that is, the cause, for which they had engaged against the late king, was entirely neglected; and they proposed as a remedy, that the whole military power should be entrusted to some person, in whom they might all confide. The city militia, influenced by two aldermen, Tichburn and Ireton, expressed the same resolution of adhering to *the good old cause.*

The protector was justly alarmed at those movements among the officers. The persons, in whom he chiefly confided, were, all of them, excepting Broghill, men of civil characters and professions; Fiennes, Thurloe, Whitlocke, Wolseley; who could only assist him with their advice and opinion. He possessed none of those arts, which were proper to gain an enthusiastic army. Murmurs being thrown out against some promotions, which he had made, *Would you have me,* said he, *prefer none but the godly? Here is Dick Ingoldsby,* continued he, *who can neither pray nor preach; yet will I trust him before ye all.*[o] This imprudence gave great offence to the pretended saints. The other qualities of the protector were correspondent to these sentiments: He was of a gentle, humane, and generous disposition. Some of his party offering to put an end to those intrigues by the death of Lambert, he declared, that he would not purchase power or dominion by such sanguinary measures.

The parliament was no less alarmed at the military cabals. They voted, that there should be no meeting or general council of offi-

[o] Ludlow.

cers, except with the protector's consent, or by his orders. This vote brought affairs immediately to a rupture. The officers hastened to Richard, and demanded of him the dissolution of the parliament. Desborow, a man of a clownish and brutal nature, threatened him, if he should refuse compliance. The protector wanted the resolution to deny, and possessed little ability to resist. The parliament was dissolved; and by the same act, the protector was, by every one, considered as effectually dethroned. Soon after, he signed his demission in form.

22d April.
Richard
deposed.

Henry, the deputy of Ireland, was endowed with the same moderate disposition as Richard; but as he possessed more vigour and capacity, it was apprehended, that he might make resistance. His popularity in Ireland was great; and even his personal authority, notwithstanding his youth, was considerable. Had his ambition been very eager, he had, no doubt, been able to create disturbance: But being threatened by Sir Hardress Waller, colonel John Jones, and other officers, he very quietly resigned his command, and retired to England. He had once entertained thoughts, which he had not resolution to execute, of proclaiming the king in Dublin.*p*

Thus fell, suddenly and from an enormous height, but, by a rare fortune, without any hurt or injury, the family of the Cromwels. Richard continued to possess an estate, which was moderate, and burthened too with a large debt, which he had contracted for the interment of his father. After the restoration, though he remained unmolested, he thought proper to travel for some years; and at Pezenas in Languedoc he was introduced under a borrowed name to the prince of Conti. That prince, talking of English affairs, broke out into admiration of Cromwel's courage and capacity. "But as for that poor pitiful fellow, Richard," said he, "what has become of him? How could he be such a blockhead as to reap no greater benefit from all his father's crimes and successes?" Richard extended his peaceful and quiet life to an extreme old age, and died not till the latter end of queen Anne's reign. His social virtues, more valuable than the greatest capacity, met with a recompence, more precious than noisy fame and more suitable, contentment and tranquillity.

The council of officers, now possessed of supreme authority,

---

p Carte's collections, vol. ii. p. 243.

deliberated what form of government they should establish. Many of them seemed inclined to exercise the power of the sword in the most open manner; but as it was apprehended, that the people would with great difficulty be induced to pay taxes, levied by arbitrary will and pleasure; it was agreed to preserve the shadow of civil administration, and to revive the long parliament, which had been expelled by Cromwel. That assembly could not be dissolved, it was asserted, but by their own consent; and violence had interrupted, but was not able to destroy, their right to government. The officers also expected, that, as these members had sufficiently felt their own weakness, they would be contented to act in subordination to the military commanders, and would thenceforth allow all the authority to remain, where the power was so visibly vested.

The officers applied to Lenthal, the speaker, and proposed to him, that the parliament should resume their seats. Lenthal was of a low, timid spirit; and being uncertain what issue might attend these measures, was desirous of evading the proposal. He replied, that he could by no means comply with the desire of the officers; being engaged in a business of far greater importance to himself, which he could not omit on any account, because it concerned the salvation of his own soul. The officers pressed him to tell what it might be. He was preparing, he said, to participate of the Lord's supper, which he resolved to take next sabbath. They insisted, that mercy was preferable to sacrifice, and that he could not better prepare himself for that great duty, than by contributing to the public service. All their remonstrances had no effect. However, on the appointed day, the speaker, being informed, that a quorum of the house was likely to meet, thought proper, notwithstanding the salvation of his soul, as Ludlow observes, to join them; and the house immediately proceeded upon business. The secluded members attempted, but in vain, to resume their seats among them.

Long parliament or rump restored. The numbers of this parliament were small, little exceeding seventy members: Their authority in the nation, ever since they had been purged by the army, was extremely diminished; and after their expulsion, had been totally annihilated: But being all of them men of violent ambition; some of them men of experience and capacity; they were resolved, since they enjoyed the title of the supreme authority, and observed, that some appearance of a parliament was requisite for the purposes of the army, not to act a

CHAPTER LXII

subordinate part to those who acknowledged themselves their servants. They chose a council, in which they took care that the officers of Wallingford-house should not be the majority: They appointed Fleetwood lieutenant-general, but inserted in his commission, that it should only continue during the pleasure of the house: They chose seven persons, who should nominate to such commands as became vacant: And they voted, that all commissions should be received from the speaker, and be assigned by him in the name of the house. These precautions, the tendency of which was visible, gave great disgust to the general officers; and their discontent would immediately have broken out into some resolution, fatal to the parliament, had it not been checked by the apprehensions of danger from the common enemy.

The bulk of the nation consisted of royalists and presbyterians; and to both these parties the dominion of the pretended parliament had ever been to the last degree odious. When that assembly was expelled by Cromwel, contempt had succeeded to hatred; and no reserve had been used in expressing the utmost derision against the impotent ambition of these usurpers. Seeing them reinstated in authority, all orders of men felt the highest indignation; together with apprehensions, lest such tyrannical rulers should exert their power by taking vengeance upon their enemies, who had so openly insulted them. A secret reconciliation, therefore, was made between the rival parties; and it was agreed, that, burying former enmities in oblivion, all efforts should be used for the overthrow of the rump; so they called the parliament, in allusion to that part of the animal body. The presbyterians, sensible from experience, that their passion for liberty, however laudable, had carried them into unwarrantable excesses, were willing to lay aside ancient jealousies, and, at all hazards, to restore the royal family. The nobility, the gentry bent their passionate endeavours to the same enterprize, by which alone they could be redeemed from slavery. And no man was so remote from party, so indifferent to public good, as not to feel the most ardent wishes, for the dissolution of that tyranny, which, whether the civil or the military part of it were considered, appeared equally oppressive and ruinous to the nation.

Mordaunt, who had so narrowly escaped on his trial, before the high-court of justice, seemed rather animated than daunted with past danger; and having, by his resolute behaviour, obtained the highest confidence of the royal party, he was now become the centre of all their conspiracies. In many counties, a resolution was taken to rise in arms. Lord Willoughby of Parham and Sir Horatio Townshend undertook to secure Lynne: General Massey engaged to seize Glocester: Lord Newport, Littleton, and other gentlemen conspired to take possession of Shrewsbury; Sir George Booth of Chester; Sir Thomas Middleton of North-Wales; Arundel, Pollar, Granville, Trelawney, of Plymouth and Exeter. A day was appointed for the execution of all these enterprizes. And the king, attended by the duke of York, had secretly arrived at Calais, with a resolution of putting himself at the head of his loyal subjects. The French court had promised to supply him with a small body of forces, in order to countenance the insurrections of the English.

This combination was disconcerted by the infidelity of Sir Richard Willis. That traitor continued with the parliament the same correspondence, which he had begun with Cromwel. He had engaged to reveal all conspiracies, so far as to destroy their effect; but reserved to himself, if he pleased, the power of concealing the conspirators. He took care never to name any of the old, genuine cavaliers, who had zealously adhered, and were resolved still to adhere, to the royal cause in every fortune. These men he esteemed; these he even loved. He betrayed only the new converts among the presbyterians, or such lukewarm royalists, as, discouraged with their disappointments, were resolved to expose themselves to no more hazards. A lively proof, how impossible it is, even for the most corrupted minds, to divest themselves of all regard to morality and social duty!

July. Many of the conspirators in the different counties were thrown into prison: Others, astonished at such symptoms of secret treachery, left their houses or remained quiet: The most tempestuous weather prevailed during the whole time appointed for the rendezvouses; insomuch that some found it impossible to join their friends, and others were dismayed with fear and superstition at an incident so unusual during the summer season. Of all the projects, the only one which took effect, was that of Sir George Booth for the seizing of Chester. The earl of Derby, lord Herbert of Cherbury, Mr. Lee, colonel Morgan entered into this enterprize. Sir William Middleton joined Booth with some troops from North

CHAPTER LXII

Wales; and the malcontents were powerful enough to subdue all in that neighbourhood, who ventured to oppose them. In their declaration they made no mention of the king: They only demanded a free and full parliament.

The parliament was justly alarmed. How combustible the materials they well knew; and the fire was now fallen among them. Booth was of a family eminently presbyterian; and his conjunction with the royalists they regarded as a dangerous symptom. They had many officers, whose fidelity they could more depend on than that of Lambert: But there was no one in whose vigilance and capacity they reposed such confidence. They commissioned him to suppress the rebels. He made incredible haste. Booth imprudently ventured himself out of the walls of Chester, and exposed, in the open field, his raw troops against these hardy veterans. He was soon routed and taken prisoner. His whole army was dispersed. *Suppressed.* And the parliament had no farther occupation than to fill all the jails with their open or secret enemies. Designs were even entertained of transporting the loyal families to Barbadoes, Jamaica, and the other colonies; lest they should propagate in England children of the same malignant affections with themselves.

This success hastened the ruin of the parliament, Lambert, at the head of a body of troops, was no less dangerous to them than Booth. A thousand pounds, which they sent him to buy a jewel, were employed by him in liberalities to his officers. At his instigation they drew up a petition, and transmitted it to Fleetwood, a weak man, and an honest, if sincerity in folly deserve that honourable name. The import of this petition was, that Fleetwood should be made commander in chief, Lambert major general, Desborow lieutenant-general of the horse, Monk major-general of the foot. To which a demand was added, that no officer should be dismissed from his command but by a court-martial.

The parliament, alarmed at the danger, immediately cashiered Lambert, Desborow, Berry, Clarke, Barrow, Kelsey, Cobbet. Sir Arthur Hazelrig proposed the impeachment of Lambert for high treason. Fleetwood's commission was vacated, and the command of the army was vested in seven persons, of whom that general was one. The parliament voted, that they would have no more general officers. And they declared it high treason to levy any money without consent of parliament.

But these votes were feeble weapons in opposition to the swords of the soldiery. Lambert drew some troops together, in order to decide the controversy. Okey, who was leading his regiment to the assistance of the parliament, was deserted by them. Morley and Moss brought their regiments into Palace-yard, resolute to oppose the violence of Lambert. But that artful general knew an easy way of disappointing them. He placed his soldiers in the streets which lead to Westminster-hall. When the speaker came in his coach, he ordered the horses to be turned, and very civilly conducted him home. The other members were in like manner intercepted. And the two regiments in Palace-yard, observing that they were exposed to derision, peaceably retired to their quarters. A little before this bold enterprize, a solemn fast had been kept by the army; and it is remarked, that this ceremony was the usual prelude to every signal violence, which they committed.

13th October.

Parliament expelled.

The officers found themselves again invested with supreme authority, of which they intended for ever to retain the substance, however they might bestow on others the empty shadow or appearance. They elected a committee of twenty-three persons, of whom seven were officers. These they pretended to invest with sovereign authority; and they called them a *committee of safety*. They spoke every where of summoning a parliament, chosen by the people; but they really took some steps towards assembling a military parliament, composed of officers elected from every regiment in the service.*q* Throughout the three kingdoms there prevailed nothing but the melancholy fears, to the nobility and gentry, of a bloody massacre and extermination; to the rest of the people, of perpetual servitude, beneath those sanctified robbers, whose union and whose divisions would be equally destructive, and who, under pretence of superior illuminations, would soon extirpate, if possible, all private morality, as they had already done all public law and justice, from the British dominions.

26th October.

Committee of safety.

During the time that England continued in this distracted condition, the other kingdoms of Europe were hastening towards a composure of those differences, by which they had so long been agitated. The parliament, while it preserved authority, instead of following the imprudent politics of Cromwel, and lending assistance to the conquering Swede, embraced the maxims of the Dutch

Foreign affairs.

q Ludlow.

CHAPTER LXII

commonwealth, and resolved, in conjunction with that state, to mediate by force an accommodation between the northern crowns. Montague was sent with a squadron to the Baltic, and carried with him as ambassador Algernon Sidney, the celebrated republican. Sidney found the Swedish monarch employed in the siege of Copenhagen, the capital of his enemy; and was highly pleased, that, with a Roman arrogance, he could check the progress of royal victories, and display in so signal a manner the superiority of freedom above tyranny. With the highest indignation, the ambitious prince was obliged to submit to the imperious mediation of the two commonwealths. "It is cruel," said he, "that laws should be prescribed me by parricides and pedlars." But his whole army was enclosed in an island, and might be starved by the combined squadrons of England and Holland. He was obliged, therefore, to quit his prey, when he had so nearly gotten possession of it; and having agreed to a pacification with Denmark, he retired into his own country, where he soon after died.

The wars between France and Spain were also concluded by the treaty of the Pyrenees. These animosities had long been carried on between the rival states, even while governed by a sister and brother, who cordially loved and esteemed each other. But politics, which had so long prevailed over these friendly affections, now at last yielded to their influence; and never was the triumph more full and complete. The Spanish Low Countries, if not every part of that monarchy, lay almost entirely at the mercy of its enemy. Broken armies, disordered finances, slow and irresolute counsels; by these resources alone were the dispersed provinces of Spain defended against the vigorous power of France. But the queen regent, anxious for the fate of her brother, employed her authority with the cardinal to stop the progress of the French conquests, and put an end to a quarrel, which, being commenced by ambition, and attended with victory, was at last concluded with moderation. The young monarch of France, though aspiring and warlike in his character, was at this time entirely occupied in the pleasures of love and gallantry, and had passively resigned the reins of empire into the hands of his politic minister. And he remained an unconcerned spectator; while an opportunity for conquest was parted with, which he never was able, during the whole course of his active reign, fully to retrieve.

The ministers of the two crowns, Mazarine and don Louis de

Haro, met at the foot of the Pyrenees, in the isle of Pheasants, a place which was supposed to belong to neither kingdom. The negotiation being brought to an issue by frequent conferences between the ministers, the monarchs themselves agreed to a congress; and these two splendid courts appeared in their full lustre amidst those savage mountains. Philip brought his daughter, Mary Therese, along with him; and giving her in marriage to his nephew, Louis, endeavoured to cement by this new tye the incompatible interests of the two monarchies. The French king made a solemn renunciation of every succession, which might accrue to him in right of his consort; a vain formality, too weak to restrain the ungoverned ambition of princes.

The affairs of England were in so great disorder, that it was not possible to comprehend that kingdom in the treaty, or adjust measures with a power, which was in such incessant fluctuation. The king, reduced to despair by the failure of all enterprizes for his restoration, was resolved to try the weak resource of foreign succours; and he went to the Pyrenees at the time when the two ministers were in the midst of their negotiations. Don Louis received him with that generous civility, peculiar to his nation; and expressed great inclination, had the low condition of Spain allowed him, to give assistance to the distressed monarch. The cautious Mazarine, pleading the alliance of France with the English commonwealth, refused even to see him; and though the king offered to marry the cardinal's niece,[r] he could, for the present, obtain nothing but empty professions of respect and protestations of services. The condition of that monarch, to all the world, seemed totally desperate. His friends had been baffled in every attempt for his service: The scaffold had often streamed with the blood of the more active royalists: The spirits of many were broken with tedious imprisonments: The estates of all were burthened by the fines and confiscations, which had been levied upon them: No-one durst openly avow himself of that party: And so small did their number seem to a superficial view, that, even should the nation recover its liberty, which was deemed no wise probable, it was judged uncertain what form of government it would embrace. But amidst all these gloomy prospects, fortune, by a surprizing

[r] K. James's Memoirs.

CHAPTER LXII

revolution, was now paving the way for the king to mount, in peace and triumph, the throne of his ancestors. It was by the prudence and loyalty of general Monk, that this happy change was at last accomplished.

George Monk, to whom the fate was reserved of re-establishing monarchy, and finishing the bloody dissensions of three kingdoms, was the second son of a family in Devonshire, ancient and honourable, but lately, from too great hospitality and expence, somewhat fallen to decay. He betook himself, in early youth, to the profession of arms; and was engaged in the unfortunate expeditions to Cadiz and the isle of Rhé. After England had concluded peace with all her neighbours, he sought military experience in the Low Countries, the great school of war to all the European nations; and he rose to the command of a company under lord Goring. This company consisted of 200 men, of whom a hundred were volunteers, often men of family and fortune, sometimes noblemen, who lived upon their own income in a splendid manner. Such a military turn at that time prevailed among the English!

General Monk.

When the sound of war was first heard in this island, Monk returned to England, partly desirous of promotion in his native country, partly disgusted with some ill usage from the States, of which he found reason to complain. Upon the Scottish pacification, he was employed by the earl of Leicester against the Irish rebels; and having obtained a regiment, was soon taken notice of, for his military skill, and for his calm and deliberate valour. Without ostentation, expence, or caresses, merely by his humane and equal temper, he gained the good-will of the soldiery; who, with a mixture of familiarity and affection, usually called him *honest George Monk;* an honourable appellation, which they still continued to him, even during his greatest elevation. He was remarkable for his moderation in party; and while all around him were inflamed into rage against the opposite faction, he fell under suspicion from the candour and tranquillity of his behaviour. When the Irish army was called over into England, surmises of this kind had been so far credited, that he had even been suspended from his command, and ordered to Oxford, that he might answer the charge laid against him. His established character for truth and sincerity here stood him in great stead; and upon his earnest protestations and declarations, he was soon restored to his regiment, which he joined at the siege of Nantwich. The day after his arrival, Fairfax attacked and defeated the royalists, commanded by Biron; and took colonel Monk prisoner. He was sent to the Tower, where he endured, above two years, all the rigors of poverty and confinement. The king, however, was so mindful as to send him, notwithstanding his own difficulties, a present of 100 guineas; but it was not till after the royalists were totally subdued, that he recovered his liberty. Monk, however distressed, had always refused the most inviting offers from the parliament: But Cromwel, sensible of his merit, having solicited him to engage in the wars against the Irish, who were considered as rebels both by king and parliament; he was not unwilling to repair his broken fortunes by accepting a command, which, he flattered himself, was reconcilable to the strictest principles of honour. Having once engaged with the parliament, he was obliged to obey orders; and found himself necessitated to fight, both against the marquess of Ormond in Ireland, and against the king himself in Scotland. Upon the reduction of the latter kingdom, Monk was left with the supreme command; and by the equality and justice of his administration he was able to give contentment to that restless people, now reduced to subjection by a nation whom they hated. No less acceptable was his authority to the officers and soldiers; and foreseeing, that the good will of the army under his command might some time be of great service to him, he had, with much care and success, cultivated their friendship.

The connexions, which he had formed with Cromwel, his benefactor, preserved him faithful to Richard, who had been enjoined by his father to follow in every thing the directions of general Monk. When the long parliament was restored, Monk, who was not prepared for opposition, acknowledged their authority, and was continued in his command, from which it would not have been safe to attempt dislodging him. After the army had expelled the parliament, he protested against the violence, and resolved, as he pretended, to vindicate their invaded privileges. Deeper designs, either in the king's favour or his own, were, from the beginning, suspected to be the motive of his actions.

Monk declares for the parliament.

A rivalship had long subsisted between him and Lambert; and every body saw the reason why he opposed the elevation of that ambitious general, by whose success his own authority, he knew,

CHAPTER LXII

would soon be subverted. But little friendship had ever subsisted between him and the parliamentary leaders; and it seemed no wise probable, that he intended to employ his industry, and spend his blood, for the advancement of one enemy above another. How early he entertained designs for the king's restoration, we know not with certainty: It is likely, that, as soon as Richard was deposed, he foresaw, that, without such an expedient, it would be impossible ever to bring the nation to a regular settlement. His elder and younger brothers were devoted to the royal cause: The Granvilles, his near relations, and all the rest of his kindred, were in the same interests: He himself was intoxicated with no fumes of enthusiasm, and had maintained no connexions with any of the fanatical tribe. His early engagements had been with the king, and he had left that service without receiving any disgust from the royal family. Since he had inlisted himself with the opposite party, he had been guilty of no violence or rigor, which might render him obnoxious. His return, therefore, to loyalty was easy and open; and nothing could be supposed to counterbalance his natural propensity to that measure, except the views of his own elevation, and the prospect of usurping the same grandeur and authority, which had been assumed by Cromwel. But from such exorbitant, if not impossible projects, the natural tranquillity and moderation of his temper, the calmness and solidity of his genius, not to mention his age, now upon the decline, seem to have set him at a distance. Cromwel himself, he always asserted,[s] could not long have maintained his usurpation; and any other person, even equal to him in genius, it was obvious, would now find it more difficult to practise arts, of which, every one, from experience, was sufficiently aware. It is more agreeable, therefore, to reason as well as candor to suppose, that Monk, as soon as he put himself in motion, had entertained views of effecting the king's restoration; nor ought any objections, derived from his profound silence even to Charles himself, be regarded as considerable. His temper was naturally reserved; his circumstances required dissimulation; the king, he knew, was surrounded with spies and traitors; and upon the whole, it seems hard to interpret that conduct, which ought to exalt our idea of his prudence, as a disparagement of his probity.

[s] Gumble's life of Monk, p. 93.

Sir John Granville, hoping that the general would engage in the king's service, sent into Scotland his younger brother, a clergyman, Dr. Monk, who carried him a letter and invitation from the king. When the doctor arrived, he found, that his brother was then holding a council of officers, and was not to be seen for some hours. In the mean time, he was received and entertained by Price, the general's chaplain, a man of probity, as well as a partizan of the king's. The doctor having an entire confidence in the chaplain, talked very freely to him about the object of his journey, and engaged him, if there should be occasion, to second his applications. At last, the general arrives; the brothers embrace; and after some preliminary conversation, the doctor opens his business. Monk interrupted him to know, whether he had ever before to any body mentioned the subject. "To no body," replied his brother, "but to Price, whom I know to be entirely in your confidence." The general, altering his countenance, turned the discourse; and would enter into no farther confidence with him, but sent him away with the first opportunity. He would not trust his own brother the moment he knew that he had disclosed the secret; though to a man whom he himself could have trusted.[1]

His conduct in all other particulars was full of the same reserve and prudence; and no less was requisite for effecting the difficult work, which he had undertaken. All the officers in his army, of whom he entertained any suspicion, he immediately cashiered: Cobbet, who had been sent by the committee of safety, under pretence of communicating their resolutions to Monk, but really with a view of debauching his army, he committed to custody: He drew together the several scattered regiments: He summoned an assembly, somewhat resembling a convention of states; and having communicated to them his resolution of marching into England, he received a seasonable, though no great supply of money.

Hearing that Lambert was advancing northward with his army, Monk sent Cloberry and two other commissioners to London, with large professions of his inclination to peace, and with offers of terms for an accommodation. His chief aim was to gain time, and relax the preparations of his enemies. The committee of safety fell into the snare. A treaty was signed by Monk's commissioners;

[1] Lord Lansdowne's defence of general Monk.

CHAPTER LXII

but he refused to ratify it, and complained that they had exceeded their powers. He desired, however, to enter into a new negotiation at Newcastle. The committee willingly accepted this fallacious offer.

Meanwhile these military sovereigns found themselves sur- *November.* rounded on all hands with inextricable difficulties. The nation had fallen into total anarchy; and by refusing the payment of all taxes, reduced the army to the greatest necessities. While Lambert's forces were assembling at Newcastle, Hazelrig and Morley took possession of Portsmouth, and declared for the parliament. A party, sent to suppress them, was persuaded by their commander to join in the same declaration. The city apprentices rose in a tumult, and demanded a free parliament. Though they were suppressed by colonel Hewson, a man who from the profession of a cobler had risen to a high rank in the army, the city still discovered symptoms of the most dangerous discontent. It even established a kind of separate government, and assumed the supreme authority within itself. Admiral Lawson with his squadron came into the river, and declared for the parliament. Hazelrig and Morley, hearing of this important event, left Portsmouth, and advanced towards London. The regiments near that city, being solicited by their old officers, who had been cashiered by the committee of safety, revolted again to the parliament. Desborow's regiment, being sent by Lambert to support his friends, no sooner arrived at St. Albans, than it declared for the same assembly.

Fleetwood's hand was found too weak and unstable to support this ill-founded fabric, which, every where around him, was falling into ruins. When he received intelligence of any murmurs among the soldiers, he would prostrate himself in prayer, and could hardly be prevailed with to join the troops. Even when among them, he would, in the midst of any discourse, invite them all to prayer, and put himself on his knees before them. If any of his friends exhorted him to more vigour, they could get no other answer, than that God had spitten in his face, and would not hear him. Men now ceased to wonder, why Lambert had promoted him to the office of general, and had contented himself with the second command in the army.

Lenthal, the speaker, being invited by the officers, again as- *26th of* sumed authority, and summoned together the parliament, which *December.*

twice before had been expelled with so much reproach and ignominy. As soon as assembled, they repealed their act against the
payment of excise and customs; they appointed commissioners for
assigning quarters to the army; and, without taking any notice of
Lambert, they sent orders to the forces under his command immediately to repair to those quarters, which were appointed them.

Lambert was now in a very disconsol te condition. Monk, he
saw, had passed the Tweed at Coldstream, and was advancing
upon him. His own soldiers deserted him in great multitudes, and
joined the enemy. Lord Fairfax too, he heard, had raised forces
behind him, and had possessed himself of York, without declaring
his purpose. The last orders of the parliament so entirely stripped
him of his army, that there remained not with him above a hundred horse: All the rest went to their quarters with quietness and
resignation; and he himself was, some time after, arrested and
committed to the Tower. The other officers, who had formerly
been cashiered by the parliament, and who had resumed their
commands, that they might subdue that assembly, were again
cashiered and confined to their houses. Sir Harry Vane and some
members, who had concurred with the committee of safety, were
ordered into a like confinement. And the parliament now seemed
to be again possessed of more absolute authority than ever, and to
be without any danger of opposition or controul.

The republican party was at this time guided by two men,
Hazelrig and Vane, who were of opposite characters, and mortally
hated each other. Hazelrig, who possessed greater authority in the
parliament, was haughty, imperious, precipitate, vain-glorious;
without civility, without prudence; qualified only by his noisy,
pertinacious obstinacy to acquire an ascendant in public assemblies. Vane was noted, in all civil transactions, for temper, insinuation, address, and a profound judgment; in all religious speculations, for folly and extravagance. He was a perfect enthusiast;
and fancying that he was certainly favoured with inspiration, he
deemed himself, to speak in the language of the times, to be a *man
above ordinances,* and, by reason of his perfection, to be unlimited
and unrestrained by any rules, which govern inferior mortals.
These whimsies, mingling with pride, had so corrupted his excellent understanding, that sometimes he thought himself the person

CHAPTER LXII

deputed to reign on earth for a thousand years over the whole congregation of the faithful.[u]

Monk, though informed of the restoration of the parliament, from whom he received no orders, still advanced with his army, which was near 6000 men: The scattered forces in England were above five times more numerous. Fairfax, who had resolved to declare for the king, not being able to make the general open his intentions, retired to his own house in Yorkshire. In all counties through which Monk passed, the prime gentry flocked to him with addresses; expressing their earnest desire, that he would be instrumental in restoring the nation to peace and tranquillity, and to the enjoyment of those liberties, which by law were their birthright, but of which, during so many years, they had been fatally bereaved: And that, in order to this salutary purpose, he would prevail, either for the restoring of those members, who had been secluded before the king's death, or for the election of a new parliament, who might legally and by general consent, again govern the nation. Though Monk pretended not to favour these addresses, that ray of hope, which the knowledge of his character and situation afforded, mightily animated all men. The tyranny and the anarchy, which now equally oppressed the kingdom; the experience of past distractions, the dread of future convulsions, the indignation against military usurpation, against sanctified hypocrisy: All these motives had united every party, except the most desperate, into ardent wishes for the king's restoration, the only remedy for all these fatal evils.

Scot and Robinson were sent as deputies by the parliament, under pretence of congratulating the general, but in reality to serve as spies upon him. The city dispatched four of their principal citizens to perform like compliments; and at the same time to confirm the general in his inclination to a free parliament, the object of all men's prayers and endeavours. The authority of Monk could scarcely secure the parliamentary deputies from those insults, which the general hatred and contempt towards their masters drew from men of every rank and denomination.

Monk continued his march with few interruptions till he

[u] Clarendon.

reached St. Albans. He there sent a message to the parliament; desiring them to remove from London those regiments, which, though they now professed to return to their duty, had so lately offered violence to that assembly. This message was unexpected, and exceedingly perplexed the house. Their fate, they found, must still depend on a mercenary army; and they were as distant as ever from their imaginary sovereignty. However they found it necessary to comply. The soldiers made more difficulty. A mutiny arose among them. One regiment, in particular, quartered in Somerset-house, expressly refused to yield their place to the northern army. But those officers, who would gladly, on such an occasion, have inflamed the quarrel, were absent or in confinement; and for want of leaders, the soldiers were at last, with great reluctance, obliged to submit. Monk with his army took quarters in Westminster.

3d February. Monk enters London.

6th February.

The general was introduced to the house; and thanks were given him by Lenthal for the eminent services which he had done his country. Monk was a prudent, not an eloquent speaker. He told the house, that the services, which he had been enabled to perform, were no more than his duty, and merited not such praises as those with which they were pleased to honour him: That among many persons of greater worth, who bore their commission, he had been employed as the instrument of providence for effecting their restoration; but he considered this service as a step only to more important services, which it was *their* part to render to the nation: That while on his march, he observed all ranks of men, in all places, to be in earnest expectation of a settlement, after the violent convulsions, to which they had been exposed; and to have no prospect of that blessing but from the dissolution of the present parliament, and from the summoning of a new one, free and full, who, meeting without oaths or engagements, might finally give contentment to the nation: That applications had been made to him for that purpose; but that he, sensible of his duty, had still told the petitioners, that the parliament itself, which was now free and would soon be full, was the best judge of all these measures, and that the whole community ought to acquiesce in their determination: That though he expressed himself in this manner to the people, he must now freely inform the house, that the fewer engagements were exacted, the more comprehensive would their plan prove, and the more satisfaction would it give to the nation:

CHAPTER LXII

And that it was sufficient for public security, if the fanatical party and the royalists were excluded; since the principles of these factions were destructive either of government or of liberty.

This speech, containing matter, which was both agreeable and disagreeable to the house as well as to the nation, still kept every one in suspence, and upheld that uncertainty, in which it seemed the general's interest to retain the public. But it was impossible for the kingdom to remain long in this doubtful situation: The people, as well as the parliament, pushed matters to a decision. During the late convulsions, the payment of taxes had been interrupted: and though the parliament, upon their assembling, renewed the ordinances for impositions, yet so little reverence did the people pay to those legislators, that they gave very slow and unwilling obedience to their commands. The common council of London flatly refused to submit to an assessment, required of them; and declared, that, till a free and lawful parliament imposed taxes, they never should deem it their duty to make any payment. This resolution, if yielded to, would immediately have put an end to the dominion of the parliament: They were determined, therefore, upon this occasion to make at once a full experiment of their own power and of their general's obedience.

Monk received orders to march into the city; to seize twelve persons, the most obnoxious to the parliament; to remove the posts and chains from all the streets; and to take down and break the portcullises and gates of the city: And very few hours were allowed him to deliberate upon the execution of these violent orders. To the great surprize and consternation of all men, Monk prepared himself for obedience. Neglecting the entreaties of his friends, the remonstrances of his officers, the cries of the people, he entered the city in a military manner; he apprehended as many as he could of the proscribed persons, whom he sent to the Tower; with all the circumstances of contempt he broke the gates and portcullises; and having exposed the city to the scorn and derision of all who hated it, he returned in triumph to his quarters in Westminster. *9th February.*

No sooner had the general leisure to reflect, than he found, that this last measure, instead of being a continuation of that cautious ambiguity, which he had hitherto maintained, was taking party without reserve, and laying himself, as well as the nation, at the mercy of that tyrannical parliament, whose power had long been odious, as their persons contemptible, to all men. He resolved, therefore, before it were too late, to repair the dangerous mistake, into which he had been betrayed, and to show the whole world, still more without reserve, that he meant no longer to be the *11th* minister of violence and usurpation. After complaining of the *February.* odious service, in which he had been employed; he wrote a letter to the house, reproaching them, as well with the new cabals which they had formed with Vane and Lambert, as with the encouragement given to a fanatical petition presented by Praisegod Barebone; and he required them, in the name of the citizens, soldiers, and whole commonwealth, to issue writs, within a week, for the filling of their house, and to fix the time for their own dissolution *Declares* and the assembling of a new parliament. Having dispatched this *for a free* letter, which might be regarded, he thought, as an undoubted *parlia-* pledge of his sincerity, he marched with his army into the city, and *ment.* desired Allen, the Mayor, to summon a common-council at Guildhall. He there made many apologies for the indignity, which, two days before, he had been obliged to put upon them; assured them of his perseverance in the measures which he had adopted; and desired that they might mutually plight their faith for a strict union between city and army, in every enterprize for the happiness and settlement of the commonwealth.

It would be difficult to describe the joy and exultation, which displayed itself throughout the city, as soon as intelligence was conveyed of this happy measure, embraced by the general. The prospect of peace, concord, liberty, justice, broke forth at once, from amidst the deepest darkness, in which the nation had ever been involved. The view of past calamities no longer presented dismal prognostics of the future: It tended only to inhance the general exultation for those scenes of happiness and tranquillity, which all men now confidently promised themselves. The royalists, the presbyterians, forgetting all animosities, mingled in common joy and transport, and vowed never more to gratify the ambition of false and factious tyrants, by their calamitous divisions. The populace, more outrageous in their festivity, made the air resound with acclamations, and illuminated every street with signals of jollity and triumph. Applauses of the general were every where intermingled with detestation against the parliament. The most

CHAPTER LXII

ridiculous inventions were adopted, in order to express this latter passion. At every bonfire rumps were roasted; and where these could no longer be found, pieces of flesh were cut into that shape: And the funeral of the parliament (the populace exclaimed) was celebrated by these symbols of hatred and derision.

The parliament, though in the agonies of despair, made still one effort for the recovery of their dominion. They sent a committee with offers to gain the general. He refused to hear them, except in the presence of some of the secluded members. Though several persons, desperate from guilt and fanaticism, promised to invest him with the dignity of supreme magistrate, and to support his government, he would not hearken to such wild proposals. Having fixed a close correspondence with the city, and established its militia in hands, whose fidelity could be relied on, he returned with his army to Westminster, and pursued every proper measure for the settlement of the nation. While he still pretended to maintain republican principles, he was taking large steps towards the re-establishment of the ancient monarchy.

The secluded members, upon the general's invitation, went to the house, and finding no longer any obstruction, they entered, and immediately appeared to be the majority: Most of the independents left the place. The restored members first repealed all the ordinances, by which they had been excluded: They gave Sir George Boothe and his party their liberty and estates: They renewed the general's commission, and enlarged his powers: They fixed an assessment for the support of the fleet and army: And having passed these votes for the present composure of the kingdom, they dissolved themselves, and issued writs for the immediate assembling of a new parliament. This last measure had been previously concerted with the general, who knew, that all men, however different in affections, expectations, and designs, united in their detestation of the long parliament. *21st February. Secluded members restored.*

16th March. Long parliament dissolved.

A council of state was established, consisting of men of character and moderation; most of whom, during the civil wars, had made a great figure among the presbyterians. The militia of the kingdom was put into such hands as would promote order and settlement. These, conjoined with Monk's army, which lay united at London, were esteemed a sufficient check on the more numerous, though dispersed army, of whose inclinations there was still much reason to be diffident. Monk, however, was every day removing the more obnoxious officers, and bringing the troops to a state of discipline and obedience.

Overton, governor of Hull, had declared his resolution to keep possession of that fortress till the coming of king Jesus: But when Alured produced the authority of parliament for his delivering the place to colonel Fairfax, he thought proper to comply.

Montague, who commanded the fleet in the Baltic, had entered into the conspiracy with Sir George Boothe; and pretending want of provisions, had sailed from the Sound towards the coast of England, with an intention of supporting that insurrection of the royalists. On his arrival he received the news of Boothe's defeat, and the total failure of the enterprize. The great difficulties, to which the parliament was then reduced, allowed them no leisure to examine strictly the reasons, which he gave for quitting his station; and they allowed him to retire peaceably to his country-house. The council of state now conferred on him, in conjunction with Monk, the command of the fleet; and secured the naval, as well as military force, in hands favourable to the public settlement.

Notwithstanding all these steps, which were taking towards the re-establishment of monarchy, Monk still maintained the appearance of zeal for a commonwealth, and hitherto allowed no canal of correspondence between himself and the king to be opened. To call a free parliament, and to restore the royal family, were visibly, in the present disposition of the kingdom, one and the same measure: Yet would not the general declare, otherwise than by his actions, that he had adopted the king's interests; and nothing but necessity extorted at last the confession from him. His silence, in the commencement of his enterprize, ought to be no objection to his sincerity; since he maintained the same reserve, at a time, when, consistent with common sense, he could have entertained no other purpose.[w]

There was one Morrice, a gentleman of Devonshire, of a sedentary, studious disposition, nearly related to Monk, and one who had always maintained the strictest intimacy with him. With this friend alone did Monk deliberate concerning that great enterprize, which he had projected. Sir John Granville, who had a commission

[w] See note [E] at the end of the volume.

CHAPTER LXII

from the king, applied to Morrice for access to the general; but received for answer, that the general desired him to communicate his business to Morrice. Granville, though importunately urged, twice refused to deliver his message to any but Monk himself; and this cautious politician, finding him now a person, whose secrecy could be safely trusted, admitted him to his presence, and opened to him his whole intentions. Still he scrupled to commit any thing to writing:[x] He delivered only a verbal message by Granville; assuring the king of his services, giving advice for his conduct, and exhorting him instantly to leave the Spanish territories, and retire into Holland. He was apprehensive lest Spain might detain him as a pledge for the recovery of Dunkirk and Jamaica. Charles followed these directions, and very narrowly escaped to Breda. Had he protracted his journey a few hours, he had certainly, under pretence of honour and respect, been arrested by the Spaniards.

Lockhart, who was governor of Dunkirk, and no wise averse to the king's service, was applied to on this occasion. The state of England was set before him, the certainty of the restoration represented, and the prospect of great favour displayed, if he would anticipate the vows of the kingdom, and receive the king into his fortress. Lockhart still replied, that his commission was derived from an English parliament, and he would not open his gates but in obedience to the same authority.[y] This scruple, though in the present emergence it approaches towards superstition, it is difficult for us entirely to condemn.

The elections for the new parliament went every where in favour of the king's party. This was one of those popular torrents, where the most indifferent, or even the most averse, are transported with the general passion, and zealously adopt the sentiments of the community, to which they belong. The enthusiasts themselves seemed to be disarmed of their fury; and between despair and astonishment gave way to those measures, which, they found, it would be impossible for them, by their utmost efforts, to withstand. The presbyterians, the royalists, being united, formed the voice of the nation, which, without noise, but with infinite ardour, called for the king's restoration. The kingdom was almost entirely in the hands of the former party; and some zealous leaders

---

[x] Lansdowne, Clarendon.   [y] Burnet.

among them began to renew the demand of those conditions, which had been required of the late king in the treaty of Newport: But the general opinion seemed to condemn all those rigorous and jealous capitulations with their sovereign. Harassed with convulsions and disorders, men ardently longed for repose, and were terrified at the mention of negotiations or delays, which might afford opportunity to the seditious army still to breed new confusion. The passion too for liberty, having been carried to such violent extremes, and having produced such bloody commotions, began, by a natural movement, to give place to a spirit of loyalty and obedience; and the public was less zealous in a cause, which was become odious, on account of the calamities, which had so long attended it. After the legal concessions made by the late king, the constitution seemed to be sufficiently secured; and the additional conditions insisted on, as they had been framed during the greatest ardour of the contest, amounted rather to annihilation than a limitation of monarchy. Above all, the general was averse to the mention of conditions; and resolved, that the crown, which he intended to restore, should be conferred on the king entirely free and unincumbered. Without farther scruple, therefore, or jealousy, the people gave their voice in elections for such as they knew to entertain sentiments favourable to monarchy; and all payed court to a party, which, they foresaw, was soon to govern the nation. Though the parliament had voted, that no one should be elected, who had himself, or whose father had borne arms for the late king; little regard was any where payed to this ordinance. The leaders of the presbyterians, the earl of Manchester, lord Fairfax, lord Robarts, Hollis, Sir Anthony Ashley Cooper, Annesley, Lewis, were determined to atone for past transgressions by their present zeal for the royal interests; and from former merits, successes, and sufferings, they had acquired with their party the highest credit and authority.

The affairs of Ireland were in a condition no less favourable to the king. As soon as Monk declared against the English army, he dispatched emissaries into Ireland, and engaged the officers in that kingdom to concur with him in the same measures. Lord Broghill, president of Munster, and Sir Charles Coote, president of Connaught, went so far as to enter into a correspondence with the king, and to promise their assistance for his restoration. In

CHAPTER LXII

conjunction with Sir Theophilus Jones, and other officers, they took possession of the government, and excluded Ludlow, who was zealous for the rump-parliament, but whom they pretended to be in a confederacy with the Committee of Safety. They kept themselves in readiness to serve the king; but made no declarations, till they should see the turn, which affairs took in England.

But all these promising views had almost been blasted by an untoward accident. Upon the admission of the secluded members, the republican party, particularly the late king's judges, were seized with the justest despair, and endeavoured to infuse the same sentiments into the army. By themselves or their emissaries, they represented to the soldiers, that all those brave actions, which had been performed during the war, and which were so meritorious in the eyes of the parliament, would no doubt be regarded as the deepest crimes by the royalists, and would expose the army to the severest vengeance. That in vain did that party make professions of moderation and lenity: The king's death, the execution of so many of the nobility and gentry, the sequestration and imprisonment of the rest, were in their eyes crimes so deep, and offences so personal, as must be prosecuted with the most implacable resentment. That the loss of all arrears, and the cashiering of every officer and soldier, were the lightest punishment, which must be expected: After the dispersion of the army, no farther protection remained to them, either for life or property, but the clemency of enraged victors. And that, even if the most perfect security could be obtained, it were inglorious to be reduced, by treachery and deceit, to subjection under a foe, who, in the open field, had so often yielded to their superior valour.

After these suggestions had been infused into the army, Lambert suddenly made his escape from the Tower, and threw Monk and the council of state into great consternation. They knew Lambert's vigour and activity; they were acquainted with his popularity in the army; they were sensible, that, though the soldiers had lately deserted him, they sufficiently expressed their remorse and their detestation of those, who, by false professions, they found, had so egregiously deceived them. It seemed necessary, therefore, to employ the greatest celerity in suppressing so dangerous a foe: Colonel Ingoldsby, who had been one of the late king's judges, but who was now entirely engaged in the royal cause, was dispatched

22d
April.
after him. He overtook him at Daventry, while he had yet assembled but four troops of horse. One of them deserted him. Another quickly followed the example. He himself, endeavouring to make his escape, was seized by Ingoldsby, to whom he made submissions not suitable to his former character of spirit and valour. Okey, Axtel, Cobbet, Crede, and other officers of that party were taken prisoners with him. All the roads were full of soldiers hastening to join them. In a few days, they had been formidable. And it was thought, that it might prove dangerous for Monk himself to have assembled any considerable body of his republican army for their suppression: So that nothing could be more happy than the sudden extinction of this rising flame.

25th
April.
When the parliament met, they chose Sir Harbottle Grimstone speaker, a man, who, though he had for some time concurred with the late parliament, had long been esteemed affectionate to the king's service. The great dangers, incurred during former usurpations, joined to the extreme caution of the general, kept every one in awe; and none dared for some days, to make any mention of the king. The members exerted their spirit chiefly in bitter invectives against the memory of Cromwel, and in execrations against the 1st May. inhuman murther of their late sovereign. At last, the general, having sufficiently sounded their inclinations, gave directions to Annesley, president of the council, to inform them, that one Sir John Granville, a servant of the king's, had been sent over by his majesty, and was now at the door with a letter to the commons. The The restoration. loudest acclamations were excited by this intelligence. Granville was called in: The letter accompanied with a declaration, greedily read: Without one moment's delay, and without a contradictory vote, a committee was appointed to prepare an answer: And in order to spread the same satisfaction throughout the kingdom, it was voted that the letter and declaration should immediately be published.

The people, freed from the state of suspence, in which they had so long been held, now changed their anxious hope for the unmixt effusions of joy; and displayed a social triumph and exultation, which no private prosperity, even the greatest, is ever able fully to inspire. Traditions remain of men, particularly of Oughtred, the mathematician, who died of pleasure, when informed of this happy and surprising event. The king's declaration was well calcu-

CHAPTER LXII

lated to uphold the satisfaction, inspired by the prospect of public settlement. It offered a general amnesty to all persons whatsoever; and that without any exceptions but such as should afterwards be made by parliament: It promised liberty of conscience; and a concurrence in any act of parliament, which, upon mature deliberation, should be offered, for insuring that indulgence: It submitted to the arbitration of the same assembly, the enquiry into all grants, purchases, and alienations: And it assured the soldiers of all their arrears, and promised them, for the future, the same pay, which they then enjoyed.

The lords, perceiving the spirit, by which the kingdom as well as the commons was animated, hastened to re-instate themselves in their ancient authority, and to take their share in the settlement of the nation. They found the doors of their house open; and all were admitted, even such as had formerly been excluded on account of their pretended delinquency.

The two houses attended; while the king was proclaimed with great solemnity, in Palace-Yard, at White-hall, and at Temple-Bar. *8th May.* The commons voted 500 pounds to buy a jewel for Granville, who had brought them the king's gracious messages: A present of 50,000 pounds was conferred on the king, 10,000 pounds on the duke of York, 5000 pounds on the duke of Gloucester. A committee of lords and commons was dispatched to invite his majesty to return and take possession of the government. The rapidity, with which all these events were conducted, was marvellous, and discovered the passionate zeal and entire unanimity of the nation. Such an impatience appeared, and such an emulation, in lords, and commons, and city, who should make the most lively expressions of their joy and duty; that, as the noble historian expresses it, a man could not but wonder where those people dwelt, who had done all the mischief, and kept the king so many years from enjoying the comfort and support of such excellent subjects. The king himself said, that it must surely have been his own fault, that he had not sooner taken possession of the throne; since he found every body so zealous in promoting his happy restoration.

The respect of foreign powers soon followed the submission of the king's subjects. Spain invited him to return to the Low Countries, and embark in some of her maritime towns. France made protestations of affection and regard, and offered Calais for the same purpose. The states-general sent deputies with a like friendly invitation. The king resolved to accept of this last offer. The people of the republic bore him a cordial affection; and politics no longer restrained their magistrates from promoting and expressing that sentiment. As he passed from Breda to the Hague, he was attended by numerous crowds, and was received with the loudest acclamations; as if themselves, not their rivals in power and commerce, were now restored to peace and security. The states-general in a body, and afterwards the states of Holland apart, performed their compliments with the greatest solemnity: Every person of distinction was ambitious of being introduced to his majesty; all ambassadors and public ministers of kings, princes, or states, repaired to him, and professed the joy of their masters in his behalf: So that one would have thought, that from the united efforts of Christendom, had been derived this revolution, which diffused every where such universal satisfaction.

The English fleet came in sight of Scheveling. Montague had not waited for orders from the parliament; but had persuaded the officers, of themselves, to tender their duty to his majesty. The duke of York immediately went on board, and took the command of the fleet as high admiral.

When the king disembarked at Dover, he was met by the general, whom he cordially embraced. Never subject in fact, probably in his intentions, had deserved better of his king and country. In the space of a few months, without effusion of blood, by his cautious and disinterested conduct alone, he had bestowed settlement on three kingdoms, which had long been torne with the most violent convulsions: And having obstinately refused the most inviting conditions, offered him by the king as well as by every party in the kingdom, he freely restored his injured master to the vacant *29th May.* throne. The king entered London on the 29th of May, which was also his birth-day. The fond imaginations of men interpreted as a happy omen the concurrence of two such joyful periods.

At this aera, it may be proper to stop a moment, and take a general survey of the age, so far as regards manners, finances, arms, commerce, arts and sciences. The chief use of history is, that it affords materials for disquisitions of this nature; and it seems the duty of an historian to point out the proper inferences and conclusions.

CHAPTER LXII

No people could undergo a change more sudden and entire in *Manners* their manners than did the English nation during this period. *and arts.* From tranquillity, concord, submission, sobriety, they passed in an instant to a state of faction, fanaticism, rebellion, and almost frenzy. The violence of the English parties exceeded any thing, which we can now imagine: Had they continued but a little longer, there was just reason to dread all the horrors of the ancient massacres and proscriptions. The military usurpers, whose authority was founded on palpable injustice, and was supported by no national party, would have been impelled by rage and despair into such sanguinary measures; and if these furious expedients had been employed on one side, revenge would naturally have pushed the other party, after a return of power, to retaliate upon their enemies. No social intercourse was maintained between the parties; no marriages or alliances contracted. The royalists, though oppressed, harassed, persecuted, disdained all affinity with their masters. The more they were reduced to subjection, the greater superiority did they affect above those usurpers, who by violence and injustice had acquired an ascendant over them.

The manners of the two factions were as opposite as those of the most distant nations. "Your friends, the Cavaliers," said a parliamentarian to a royalist, "are very dissolute and debauched." "True," replied the royalists, "they have the infirmities of men: But your friends, the Roundheads, have the vices of devils, tyranny, rebellion, and spiritual pride."[z] Riot and disorder, it is certain, notwithstanding the good example set them by Charles I. prevailed very much among his partizans. Being commonly men of birth and fortune, to whom excesses are less pernicious than to the vulgar, they were too apt to indulge themselves in all pleasures, particularly those of the table. Opposition to the rigid preciseness of their antagonists encreased their inclination to good-fellowship; and the character of a man of pleasure was affected among them, as a sure pledge of attachment to the church and monarchy. Even when ruined by confiscations and sequestrations, they endeavoured to maintain the appearance of a careless and social jollity. "As much as hope is superior to fear," said a poor and merry cavalier, "so much is our situation preferable to that of our enemies. We laugh while they tremble."

[z] Sir Philip Warwic.

The gloomy enthusiasm, which prevailed among the parliamentary party, is surely the most curious spectacle presented by any history; and the most instructive, as well as entertaining, to a philosophical mind. All recreations were in a manner suspended by the rigid severity of the presbyterians and independents. Horse-races and cock-matches were prohibited as the greatest enormities.[a] Even bear-baiting was esteemed heathenish and unchristian: The sport of it, not the inhumanity, gave offence. Colonel Hewson, from his pious zeal, marched with his regiment into London, and destroyed all the bears, which were there kept for the diversion of the citizens. This adventure seems to have given birth to the fiction of Hudibras. Though the English nation be naturally candid and sincere, hypocrisy prevailed among them beyond any example in ancient or modern times. The religious hypocrisy, it may be remarked, is of a peculiar nature; and being generally unknown to the person himself, though more dangerous, it implies less falsehood than any other species of insincerity. The Old Testament, preferably to the New, was the favourite of all the sectaries. The eastern poetical style of that composition made it more easily susceptible of a turn, which was agreeable to them.

We have had occasion, in the course of this work, to speak of many of the sects, which prevailed in England: To enumerate them all would be impossible. The quakers, however, are so considerable, at least so singular, as to merit some attention; and as they renounced by principle the use of arms, they never made such a figure in public transactions as to enter into any part of our narrative.

The religion of the quakers, like most others, began with the lowest vulgar, and, in its progress, came at last to comprehend people of better quality and fashion. George Fox, born at Drayton in Lancashire in 1624, was the founder of this sect. He was the son of a weaver, and was himself bound apprentice to a shoe-maker. Feeling a stronger impulse towards spiritual contemplations than towards that mechanical profession, he left his master, and went about the country, cloathed in a leathern doublet, a dress which he long affected, as well for its singularity as its cheapness. That he might wean himself from sublunary objects, he broke off all con-

[a] Killing no Murder.

CHAPTER LXII

nexions with his friends and family, and never dwelled a moment in one place; lest habit should beget new connexions, and depress the sublimity of his aerial meditations. He frequently wandered into the woods, and passed whole days in hollow trees, without company, or any other amusement than his Bible. Having reached that pitch of perfection as to need no other book, he soon advanced to another state of spiritual progress, and began to pay less regard even to that divine composition itself. His own breast, he imagined, was full of the same inspiration, which had guided the prophets and apostles themselves; and by this inward light must every spiritual obscurity be cleared, by this living spirit must the dead letter be animated.

When he had been sufficiently consecrated in his own imagination, he felt that the fumes of self-applause soon dissipate, if not continually supplied by the admiration of others; and he began to seek proselytes. Proselytes were easily gained, at a time when all men's affections were turned towards religion, and when the most extravagant modes of it were sure to be most popular. All the forms of ceremony, invented by pride and ostentation, Fox and his disciples, from a superior pride and ostentation, carefully rejected: Even the ordinary rites of civility were shunned, as the nourishment of carnal vanity and self-conceit. They would bestow no titles of distinction: The name of *friend* was the only salutation, with which they indiscriminately accosted every one. To no person would they make a bow, or move their hat, or give any signs of reverence. Instead of that affected adulation, introduced into modern tongues, of speaking to individuals as if they were a multitude, they returned to the simplicity of ancient languages; and *thou* and *thee* were the only expressions, which, on any consideration, they could be brought to employ.

Dress too, a material circumstance, distinguished the members of this sect. Every superfluity and ornament was carefully retrenched: No plaits to their coat, no buttons to their sleeves: No lace, no ruffles, no embroidery. Even a button to the hat, though sometimes useful, yet not being always so, was universally rejected by them with horror and detestation.

The violent enthusiasm of this sect, like all high passions, being too strong for the weak nerves to sustain, threw the preachers into convulsions, and shakings, and distortions in their limbs; and they thence received the appellation of *quakers*. Amidst the great toleration, which was then granted to all sects, and even encouragement given to all innovations, this sect alone suffered persecution. From the fervour of their zeal, the quakers broke into churches, disturbed public worship, and harassed the minister and audience with railing and reproaches. When carried before a magistrate, they refused him all reverence, and treated him with the same familiarity as if he had been their equal. Sometimes they were thrown into mad-houses, sometimes into prisons: Sometimes whipped, sometimes pilloryed. The patience and fortitude, with which they suffered, begat compassion, admiration, esteem.[b] A supernatural spirit was believed to support them under those sufferings, which the ordinary state of humanity, freed from the illusions of passion, is unable to sustain.

The quakers creeped into the army: But as they preached universal peace, they seduced the military zealots from their profession, and would soon, had they been suffered, have put an end, without any defeat or calamity, to the dominion of the saints. These attempts became a fresh ground of persecution, and a new reason for their progress among the people.

Morals with this sect were carried, or affected to be carried, to the same degree of extravagance as religion. Give a quaker a blow on one cheek, he held up the other: Ask his cloke, he gave you his coat also: The greatest interest could not engage him, in any court of judicature, to swear even to the truth: He never asked more for his wares than the precise sum, which he was determined to accept. This last maxim is laudable, and continues still to be religiously observed by that sect.

No fanatics ever carried farther the hatred to ceremonies, forms, orders, rites, and positive institutions. Even baptism and the Lord's supper, by all other sects believed to be interwoven with

---

[b] The following story is told by Whitlocke, p. 599. Some quakers at Hasington in Northumberland coming to the minister on the Sabbath-day, and speaking to him, the people fell upon the quakers, and almost killed one or two of them, who going out fell on their knees, and prayed God to pardon the people, who knew not what they did; and afterwards speaking to the people, so convinced them of the evil they had done in beating them, that the country people fell a quarrelling, and beat one another more than they had before beaten the quakers.

CHAPTER LXII

the very vitals of christianity, were disdainfully rejected by them. The very sabbath they profaned. The holiness of churches they derided; and they would give to these sacred edifices no other appellation than that of *shops* or *steeple-houses*. No priests were admitted in their sect: Every one had received from immediate illumination a character much superior to the sacerdotal. When they met for divine worship, each rose up in his place, and delivered the extemporary inspirations of the Holy Ghost: Women also were admitted to teach the brethren, and were considered as proper vehicles to convey the dictates of the spirit. Sometimes a great many preachers were moved to speak at once: Sometimes a total silence prevailed in their congregations.

Some quakers attempted to fast forty days in imitation of Christ; and one of them bravely perished in the experiment.[c] A female quaker came naked into the church where the protector sate; being moved by the spirit, as she said, to appear *as a sign* to the people. A number of them fancied, that the renovation of all things had commenced, and that cloaths were to be rejected together with other superfluities. The sufferings, which followed the practice of this doctrine, were a species of persecution not well calculated for promoting it.

James Naylor was a quaker, noted for blasphemy, or rather madness, in the time of the protectorship. He fancied, that he himself was transformed into Christ, and was become the real saviour of the world; and in consequence of this frenzy, he endeavoured to imitate many actions of the Messiah related in the evangelists. As he bore a resemblance to the common pictures of Christ; he allowed his beard to grow in a like form: He raised a person from the dead:[d] He was ministered unto by women:[e] He entered Bristol, mounted on a horse: I suppose, from the difficulty in that place of finding an ass: His disciples spread their garments before him, and cried, "Hosanna to the highest; holy, holy is the Lord God of Sabbaoth." When carried before the magistrate, he would give no other answer to all questions than "thou hast said it." What is remarkable, the parliament thought that the matter de-

---

[c] Whitlocke, p. 624.   [d] Harleyan Miscellany, vol. vi. p. 399. One Dorcas Earberry made oath before a magistrate, that she had been dead two days, and that Naylor had brought her to life.   [e] Id. ibid.

served their attention. Near ten days they spent in enquiries and debates about him.[f] They condemned him to be pilloryed, whipped, burned in the face, and to have his tongue bored through with a red hot iron. All these severities he bore with the usual patience. So far his delusion supported him. But the sequel spoiled all. He was sent to Bridewell, confined to hard labour, fed on bread and water, and debarred from all his disciples, male and female. His illusion dissipated; and after some time, he was contented to come out an ordinary man, and return to his usual occupations.

The chief taxes in England, during the time of the commonwealth, were the monthly assessments, the excise, and the customs. The assessments were levied on personal estates as well as on land;[g] and commissioners were appointed in each county for rating the individuals. The highest assessment amounted to 120,000 pounds a month in England; the lowest was 35,000. The assessments in Scotland were sometimes 10,000 pounds a month;[h] commonly 6000. Those on Ireland 9000. At a medium, this tax might have afforded about a million a year. The excise, during the civil wars, was levied on bread, flesh-meat, as well as beer, ale, strongwaters, and many other commodities. After the king was subdued, bread and flesh-meat were exempted from excise. The customs on exportation were lowered in 1656.[i] In 1650, commissioners were appointed to levy both customs and excises. Cromwel in 1657 returned to the old practice of farming. Eleven hundred thousand pounds were then offered, both for customs and excise, a greater sum than had ever been levied by the commissioners:[k] The whole of the taxes during that period might at a medium amount to above two millions a year; a sum, which, though moderate, much exceeded the revenue of any former king.[l] Sequestrations, compositions, sale of crown and church lands, and of the lands of delinquents, yielded also considerable sums, but very difficult to be estimated. Church lands are said to have been sold for a million.[m] None of these were ever valued at above ten or eleven years pur-

[f] Thurloe, vol. v. p. 708. [g] Scobel, p. 419. [h] Thurloe, vol. ii. p. 476. [i] Scobel, p. 376. [k] Thurloe, vol. vi. p. 425. [l] It appears that the late king's revenue from 1637, to the meeting of the long parliament, was only 900,000 pounds, of which 200,000 may be esteemed illegal. [m] Dr. Walker, p. 14.

chase.[n] The estates of delinquents amounted to above 200,000 pounds a year.[o] Cromwel died more than two millions in debt;[p] though the parliament had left him in the treasury above 500,000 pounds; and in stores, the value of 700,000 pounds.[q]

The committee of danger in April 1648 voted to raise the army to 40,000 men.[r] The same year, the pay of the army was estimated at 80,000 pounds a month.[s] The establishment of the army in 1652, was in Scotland 15,000 foot, 2580 horse, 560 dragoons; in England, 4700 foot, 2520 horse, garrisons 6154. In all, 31,519, besides officers.[t] The army in Scotland was afterwards considerably reduced. The army in Ireland was not much short of 20,000 men; so that upon the whole, the commonwealth maintained in 1652 a standing army of more than 50,000 men. Its pay amounted to a yearly sum of 1,047,715 pounds.[u] Afterwards the protector reduced the establishment to 30,000 men; as appears by the Instrument of Government and Humble Petition and Advice. His frequent enterprizes obliged him from time to time to augment them. Richard had on foot in England an army of 13,258 men, in Scotland 9506, in Ireland about 10,000 men.[w] The foot soldiers had commonly a shilling a day.[x] The horse had two shillings and six-pence; so that many gentlemen and younger brothers of good family inlisted in the protector's cavalry.[y] No wonder, that such men were averse from the re-establishment of civil government, by which, they well knew, they must be deprived of so gainful a profession.

At the time of the battle of Worcester, the parliament had on foot about 80,000 men, partly militia, partly regular forces. The vigour of the commonwealth, and the great capacity of those members, who had assumed the government, never at any time appeared so conspicuous.[z]

The whole revenue of the public during the protectorship of Richard was estimated at 1,868,717 pounds: His annual expences at 2,201,540 pounds. An additional revenue was demanded from parliament.[a]

[n] Thurloe, vol. i. p. 753.   [o] Ibid. vol. ii. p. 414.   [p] Ibid. vol. vii. p. 667.
[q] World's Mistake in Oliver Cromwel.   [r] Whitlocke, p. 298.   [s] Ibid.
p. 378.   [t] Journal, 2d December, 1652.   [u] Id. ibid.   [w] Journal, 6th of
April, 1659.   [x] Thurloe, vol. i. p. 395, vol. ii. p. 414.   [y] Gumble's Life of
Monk.   [z] Whitlocke, p. 477.   [a] Journal, 7th April, 1659.

The commerce and industry of England encreased extremely during the peaceable period of Charles's reign: The trade to the East-Indies and to Guinea became considerable. The English possessed almost the sole trade with Spain. Twenty thousand cloths were annually sent to Turkey.[b] Commerce met with interruption, no doubt, from the civil wars and convulsions, which afterwards prevailed; though it soon recovered after the establishment of the commonwealth. The war with the Dutch, by distressing the commerce of so formidable a rival, served to encourage trade in England: The Spanish war was to an equal degree pernicious. All the effects of the English merchants, to an immense value, were confiscated in Spain. The prevalence of democratical principles engaged the country gentlemen to bind their sons apprentices to merchants;[c] and commerce has ever since been more honourable in England than in any other European kingdom. The exclusive companies, which formerly confined trade, were never expressly abolished by any ordinance of parliament during the commonwealth; but as men payed no regard to the prerogative, whence the charters of these companies were derived, the monopoly was gradually invaded, and commerce encreased by the encrease of liberty. Interest in 1650 was reduced to six per cent.

The customs in England, before the civil wars, are said to have amounted to 500,000 pounds a year:[d] A sum ten times greater than during the best period in queen Elizabeth's reign: But there is probably some exaggeration in this matter.

The Post-house, in 1653, was farmed at 10,000 pounds a year, which was deemed a considerable sum for the three kingdoms. Letters paid only about half the present postage.

From 1619 to 1638, there had been coined 6,900,042 pounds. From 1638 to 1657, the coinage amounted to 7,733,521 pounds.[e] Dr. Davenant has told us, from the registers of the mint, that, between 1558 and 1659, there had been coined 19,832,476 pounds in gold and silver.

The first mention of tea, coffee, and chocolate, is about 1660.[f] Asparagus, artichoaks, colliflower, and a variety of sallads, were about the same time introduced into England.[g]

The colony of New England encreased by means of the puri-

[b] Strafford's Letters, vol. i. p. 421, 423, 430, 467. [c] Clarendon. [d] Lewis Roberts's Treasure of Traffick. [e] Happy future state of England. [f] Anderson, vol. ii. p. 111. [g] Id. ibid.

tans, who fled thither, in order to free themselves from the constraint, which Laud and the church party had imposed upon them; and before the commencement of the civil wars, it is supposed to have contained 25,000 souls.[h] For a like reason, the catholics, afterwards, who found themselves exposed to many hardships, and dreaded still worse treatment, went over to America in great numbers, and settled the colony of Maryland.

Before the civil wars, learning and the fine arts were favoured at court, and a good taste began to prevail in the nation. The king loved pictures, sometimes handled the pencil himself, and was a good judge of the art. The pieces of foreign masters were bought up at a vast price; and the value of pictures doubled in Europe by the emulation between Charles and Philip IV. of Spain, who were touched with the same elegant passion. Vandyke was caressed and enriched at court. Inigo Jones was master of the king's buildings; though afterwards persecuted by the parliament, on account of the part which he had in rebuilding St. Paul's, and for obeying some orders of council, by which he was directed to pull down houses, in order to make room for that edifice. Laws, who had not been surpassed by any musician before him, was much beloved by the king, who called him the father of music. Charles was a good judge of writing, and was thought by some more anxious with regard to purity of style than became a monarch.[i] Notwithstanding his narrow revenue, and his freedom from all vanity, he lived in such magnificence, that he possessed four and twenty palaces, all of them elegantly and compleatly furnished; insomuch, that, when he removed from one to another, he was not obliged to transport any thing along with him.

Cromwel, though himself a barbarian, was not insensible to literary merit. Usher, notwithstanding his being a bishop, received a pension from him. Marvel and Milton were in his service. Waller, who was his relation, was caressed by him. That poet always said, that the Protector himself was not so wholly illiterate as was commonly imagined. He gave a hundred pounds a year to the divinity professor at Oxford; and an historian mentions this bounty as an instance of his love of literature.[k] He intended to have erected a college at Durham for the benefit of the northern counties.

[h] British Empire in America, vol. i. p. 372.   [i] Burnet.   [k] Neale's History of the Puritans, vol. iv. p. 123.

Civil wars, especially when founded on principles of liberty, are not commonly unfavourable to the arts of eloquence and composition; or rather, by presenting nobler and more interesting objects, they amply compensate that tranquillity, of which they bereave the muses. The speeches of the parliamentary orators during this period are of a strain much superior to what any former age had produced in England; and the force and compass of our tongue were then first put to trial. It must, however, be confessed, that the wretched fanaticism, which so much infected the parliamentary party, was no less destructive of taste and science, than of all law and order. Gaiety and wit were proscribed: Human learning despised: Freedom of enquiry detested: Cant and hypocrisy alone encouraged. It was an article positively insisted on in the preliminaries to the treaty of Uxbridge, that all play-houses should for ever be abolished. Sir John Davenant, says Whitlocke,[l] speaking of the year 1658, published an opera, notwithstanding the nicety of the times. All the king's furniture was put to sale: His pictures, disposed of at very low prices, enriched all the collections in Europe: The cartoons, when complete, were only appraised at 300 pounds, though the whole collection of the king's curiosities was sold at above 50,000.[m] Even the royal palaces were pulled in pieces, and the materials of them sold. The very library and medals at St. James's, were intended by the generals to be brought to auction, in order to pay the arrears of some regiments of cavalry, quartered near London: But Selden, apprehensive of the loss, engaged his friend Whitlocke, then lord-keeper for the commonwealth, to apply for the office of librarian. This expedient saved that valuable collection.

It is however remarkable, that the greatest genius by far, that shone out in England during this period, was deeply engaged with these fanatics, and even prostituted his pen in theological controversy, in factious disputes, and in justifying the most violent measures of the party. This was John Milton, whose poems are admirable, though liable to some objections; his prose writings disagreeable, though not altogether defective in genius. Nor are all his poems equal: His Paradise Lost, his Comus, and a few others shine out amidst some flat and insipid compositions: Even in the

[l] P. 639.   [m] Parl. Hist. vol. xix. p. 83.

CHAPTER LXII

Paradise Lost, his capital performance, there are very long passages, amounting to near a third of the work, almost wholly destitute of harmony and elegance, nay, of all vigour of imagination. This natural inequality in Milton's genius was much encreased by the inequalities in his subject; of which some parts are of themselves the most lofty that can enter into human conception; others would have required the most laboured elegance of composition to support them. It is certain, that this author, when in a happy mood, and employed on a noble subject, is the most wonderfully sublime of any poet in any language; Homer and Lucretius and Tasso not excepted. More concise than Homer, more simple than Tasso, more nervous than Lucretius; had he lived in a later age, and learned to polish some rudeness in his verses; had he enjoyed better fortune, and possessed leisure to watch the returns of genius in himself; he had attained the pinnacle of perfection, and borne away the palm of epic poetry.

It is well known, that Milton never enjoyed in his lifetime the reputation which he deserved. His Paradise Lost was long neglected: Prejudices against an apologist for the regicides, and against a work not wholly purged from the cant of former times, kept the ignorant world from perceiving the prodigious merit of that performance. Lord Somers, by encouraging a good edition of it, about twenty years after the author's death, first brought it into request; and Tonson, in his dedication of a smaller edition, speaks of it as a work just beginning to be known. Even during the prevalence of Milton's party, he seems never to have been much regarded; and Whitlocke[n] talks of one Milton, as he calls him, a blind man, who was employed in translating a treaty with Sweden into Latin. These forms of expression are amusing to posterity, who consider how obscure Whitlocke himself, though lord-keeper, and ambassador, and indeed a man of great abilities and merit, has become in comparison of Milton.

It is not strange, that Milton received no encouragement after the restoration: It is more to be admired, that he escaped with his life. Many of the cavaliers blamed extremely that lenity towards him, which was so honourable in the king, and so advantageous to posterity. It is said, that he had saved Davenant's life during the

[n] P. 633.

protectorship; and Davenant in return afforded him like protection after the restoration; being sensible, that men of letters ought always to regard their sympathy of taste as a more powerful band of union, than any difference of party or opinion as a source of animosity. It was during a state of poverty, blindness, disgrace, danger, and old age, that Milton composed his wonderful poem, which not only surpassed all the performances of his cotemporaries, but all the compositions, which had flowed from his pen, during the vigor of his age, and the height of his prosperity. This circumstance is not the least remarkable of all those which attend that great genius. He died in 1674, aged 66.

Waller was the first refiner of English poetry, at least of English rhyme; but his performances still abound with many faults, and what is more material, they contain but feeble and superficial beauties. Gaiety, wit, and ingenuity are their ruling character: They aspire not to the sublime; still less to the pathetic. They treat of love, without making us feel any tenderness; and abound in panegyric, without exciting admiration. The panegyric, however, on Cromwel contains more force than we should expect from the other compositions of this poet.

Waller was born to an ample fortune, was early introduced to the court, and lived in the best company. He possessed talents for eloquence as well as poetry; and till his death, which happened in a good old age, he was the delight of the house of commons. The errors of his life proceeded more from want of courage than of honour or integrity. He died in 1687, aged 82.

Cowley is an author extremely corrupted by the bad taste of his age; but had he lived even in the purest times of Greece or Rome, he must always have been a very indifferent poet. He had no ear for harmony; and his verses are only known to be such by the rhyme, which terminates them. In his rugged untuneable numbers are conveyed sentiments the most strained and distorted; long spun allegories, distant allusions, and forced conceits. Great ingenuity, however, and vigour of thought sometimes break out amidst those unnatural conceptions: A few anacreontics surprise us by their ease and gaiety: His prose writings please, by the honesty and goodness which they express, and even by their spleen and melancholy. This author was much more praised and admired during his life time, and celebrated after his death, than the great Milton. He died in 1667, aged 49.

CHAPTER LXII

Sir John Denham in his Cooper's Hill (for none of his other poems merit attention) has a loftiness and vigour, which had not before him been attained by any English poet, who wrote in rhyme. The mechanical difficulties of that measure retarded its improvement. Shakespeare, whose tragic scenes are sometimes so wonderfully forcible and expressive, is a very indifferent poet, when he attempts to rhyme. Precision and neatness are chiefly wanting in Denham. He died in 1688, aged 73.

No English author in that age was more celebrated both abroad and at home than Hobbes: In our time, he is much neglected: A lively instance how precarious all reputations, founded on reasoning and philosophy! A pleasant comedy, which paints the manners of the age, and exposes a faithful picture of nature, is a durable work, and is transmitted to the latest posterity. But a system, whether physical or metaphysical, commonly owes its success to its novelty; and is no sooner canvassed with impartiality than its weakness is discovered. Hobbes's politics are fitted only to promote tyranny, and his ethics to encourage licentiousness. Though an enemy to religion, he partakes nothing of the spirit of scepticism; but is as positive and dogmatical as if human reason, and his reason in particular, could attain a thorough conviction in these subjects. Clearness and propriety of style are the chief excellencies of Hobbes's writings. In his own person he is represented to have been a man of virtue; a character no wise surprising, notwithstanding his libertine system of ethics. Timidity is the principal fault, with which he is reproached: He lived to an extreme old age, yet could never reconcile himself to the thoughts of death. The boldness of his opinions and sentiments form a remarkable contrast to this part of his character. He died in 1679, aged 91.

Harrington's Oceana was well adapted to that age, when the plans of imaginary republics were the daily subjects of debate and conversation; and even in our time it is justly admired as a work of genius and invention. The idea, however, of a perfect and immortal commonwealth will always be found as chimerical as that of a perfect and immortal man. The style of this author wants ease and fluency; but the good matter, which his work contains, makes compensation. He died in 1677, aged 66.

Harvey is entitled to the glory of having made, by reasoning alone, without any mixture of accident, a capital discovery in one of the most important branches of science. He had also the happiness of establishing at once his theory on the most solid and convincing proofs; and posterity has added little to the arguments suggested by his industry and ingenuity. His treatise of the circulation of the blood is farther embellished by that warmth and spirit, which so naturally accompany the genius of invention. This great man was much favoured by Charles I. who gave him the liberty of using all the deer in the royal forests for perfecting his discoveries on the generation of animals. It was remarked, that no physician in Europe, who had reached forty years of age, ever, to the end of his life, adopted Harvey's doctrine of the circulation of the blood, and that his practice in London diminished extremely, from the reproach drawn upon him, by that great and signal discovery. So slow is the progress of truth in every science, even when not opposed by factious or superstitious prejudices! He died in 1657, aged 79.

This age affords great materials for history; but did not produce any accomplished historian. Clarendon, however, will always be esteemed an entertaining writer, even independant of our curiosity to know the facts, which he relates. His style is prolix and redundant, and suffocates us by the length of its periods: But it discovers imagination and sentiment, and pleases us at the same time that we disapprove of it. He is more partial in appearance than in reality: For he seems perpetually anxious to apologize for the king; but his apologies are often well grounded. He is less partial in his relation of facts, than in his account of characters: He was too honest a man to falsify the former; his affections were easily capable, unknown to himself, of disguising the latter. An air of probity and goodness runs through the whole work; as these qualities did in reality embellish the whole life of the author. He died in 1674, aged 66.

These are the chief performances, which engage the attention of posterity. Those numberless productions, with which the press then abounded; the cant of the pulpit, the declamations of party, the subtilties of theology, all these have long ago sunk in silence and oblivion. Even a writer, such as Selden, whose learning was his chief excellency; or Chillingworth, an acute disputant against the papists will scarcely be ranked among the classics of our language or country.

LXIII

CHARLES II

New ministry – Act of indemnity –
Settlement of the revenue – Trial and execution
of the regicides – Dissolution of the convention –
Parliament – Prelacy restored – Insurrection of the
Millenarians – Affairs of Scotland – Conference
at the Savoy – Arguments for and against a
comprehension – A new parliament – Bishops' seats
restored – Corporation act – Act of uniformity –
King's marriage – Trial of Vane – And
execution – Presbyterian clergy ejected –
Dunkirk sold to the French –
Declaration of indulgence –
Decline of Clarendon's credit

CHARLES II. when he ascended the throne of his ancestors, was   *1660.*
thirty years of age. He possessed a vigorous constitution, a
fine shape, a manly figure, a graceful air; and though his features
were harsh, yet was his countenance in the main lively and engaging. He was in that period of life, when there remains enough of
youth to render the person amiable, without preventing that authority and regard, which attend the years of experience and maturity. Tenderness was excited by the memory of his recent adver-
sities. His present prosperity was the object rather of admiration

than of envy. And as the sudden and surprising revolution, which restored him to his regal rights, had also restored the nation to peace, law, order, and liberty; no prince ever obtained a crown in more favourable circumstances, or was more blest with the cordial affection and attachment of his subjects.

This popularity, the king, by his whole demeanor and behaviour, was well qualified to support and to encrease. To a lively wit and quick comprehension, he united a just understanding and a general observation both of men and things. The easiest manners, the most unaffected politeness, the most engaging gaiety accompanied his conversation and address. Accustomed during his exile to live among his courtiers rather like a companion than a monarch, he retained, even while on the throne, that open affability, which was capable of reconciling the most determined republicans to his royal dignity. Totally devoid of resentment, as well from the natural lenity as carelessness of his temper, he insured pardon to the most guilty of his enemies, and left hopes of favour to his most violent opponents. From the whole tenor of his actions and discourse, he seemed desirous of losing the memory of past animosities, and of uniting every party in an affection for their prince and their native country.

New ministry. Into his council were admitted the most eminent men of the nation, without regard to former distinctions: The presbyterians, equally with the royalists, shared this honour. Annesley was also created earl of Anglesey; Ashley Cooper lord Ashley; Denzil Hollis lord Hollis. The earl of Manchester was appointed lord chamberlain, and lord Say, privy seal. Calamy and Baxter, presbyterian clergymen, were even made chaplains to the king.

Admiral Montague, created earl of Sandwich, was entitled from his recent services to great favour; and he obtained it. Monk, created duke of Albemarle, had performed such signal services, that, according to a vulgar and malignant observation, he ought rather to have expected hatred and ingratitude: Yet was he ever treated by the king with great marks of distinction. Charles's disposition, free from jealousy; and the prudent behaviour of the general, who never over-rated his merits; prevented all those disgusts, which naturally arise in so delicate a situation. The capacity too of Albemarle was not extensive, and his parts were more solid than shining. Though he had distinguished himself in inferior stations,

CHAPTER LXIII

he was imagined, upon familiar acquaintance, not to be wholly equal to those great atchievements, which fortune, united to prudence, had enabled him to perform; and he appeared unfit for the court, a scene of life to which he had never been accustomed. Morrice, his friend, was created secretary of state, and was supported more by his patron's credit than by his own abilities or experience.

But the choice, which the king at first made of his principal ministers and favourites, was the circumstance, which chiefly gave contentment to the nation, and prognosticated future happiness and tranquillity. Sir Edward Hyde, created earl of Clarendon, was chancellor and prime minister: The marquess, created duke of Ormond, was steward of the household: The earl of Southampton, high treasurer: Sir Edward Nicholas, secretary of state. These men, united together in friendship, and combining in the same laudable inclinations, supported each others credit, and pursued the interests of the public.

Agreeable to the present prosperity of public affairs was the universal joy and festivity diffused throughout the nation. The melancholy austerity of the fanatics fell into discredit together with their principles. The royalists, who had ever affected a contrary disposition, found in their recent success new motives for mirth and gaiety; and it now belonged to them to give repute and fashion to their manners. From past experience it had sufficiently appeared, that gravity was very distinct from wisdom, formality from virtue, and hypocrisy from religion. The king himself, who bore a strong propensity to pleasure, served, by his powerful and engaging example, to banish those sour and malignant humours, which had hitherto engendered such confusion. And though the just bounds were undoubtedly passed, when men returned from their former extreme; yet was the public happy in exchanging vices, pernicious to society, for disorders, hurtful chiefly to the individuals themselves, who were guilty of them.

It required some time before the several parts of the state, disfigured by war and faction, could recover their former arrangement: But the parliament immediately fell into good correspondence with the king; and they treated him with the same dutiful regard, which had usually been payed to his predecessors. Being summoned without the king's consent, they received, at first, only the title of a convention; and it was not till he passed an act for that purpose, that they were called by the appellation of parliament. All judicial proceedings, transacted in the name of the commonwealth or protector, were ratified by a new law. And both houses, acknowledging the guilt of the former rebellion, gratefully received, in their own name and in that of all the subjects, his majesty's gracious pardon and indemnity.

Act of
indemnity.
The king, before his restoration, being afraid of reducing any of his enemies to despair, and at the same time unwilling that such enormous crimes as had been committed, should receive a total impunity, had expressed himself very cautiously in his declaration of Breda, and had promised an indemnity to all criminals, but such as should be excepted by parliament. He now issued a proclamation, declaring that such of the late king's judges as did not yield themselves prisoners within fourteen days should receive no pardon. Nineteen surrendered themselves: Some were taken in their flight: Others escaped beyond sea.

The commons seem to have been more inclined to lenity than the lords. The upper house, inflamed by the ill usage, which they had received, were resolved, besides the late king's judges, to except every one, who had sitten in any high court of justice. Nay, the earl of Bristol moved, that no pardon might be granted to those who had any wise contributed to the king's death. So wide an exception, in which every one, who had served the parliament, might be comprehended, gave a general alarm; and men began to apprehend, that this motion was the effect of some court artifice or intrigue. But the king soon dissipated these fears. He came to the house of peers; and in the most earnest terms, passed the act of general indemnity. He urged both the necessity of the thing, and the obligation of his former promise: A promise, he said, which he would ever regard as sacred; since to it he probably owed the satisfaction, which at present he enjoyed, of meeting his people in parliament. This measure of the king's was received with great applause and satisfaction.

After repeated solicitations, the act of indemnity passed both houses, and soon received the royal assent. Those who had an immediate hand in the late king's death, were there excepted: Even Cromwel, Ireton, Bradshaw, and others now dead were attainted, and their estates forfeited. Vane and Lambert, though

CHAPTER LXIII

none of the regicides, were also excepted. St. John and seventeen persons more were deprived of all benefit from this act, if they ever accepted any public employment. All who had sitten in any illegal high court of justice were disabled from bearing offices. These were all the severities, which followed such furious civil wars and convulsions.

The next business was the settlement of the king's revenue. In this work, the parliament had regard to public freedom as well as to the support of the crown. The tenures of wards and liveries had long been regarded as a grievous burthen by the nobility and gentry: Several attempts had been made during the reign of James to purchase this prerogative, together with that of purveyance; and 200,000 pounds a year had been offered that prince in lieu of them: Wardships and purveyance had been utterly abolished by the republican parliament: And even in the present parliament, before the king arrived in England, a bill had been introduced, offering him a compensation for the emoluments of these prerogatives. A hundred thousand pounds a year was the sum agreed to; and half of the excise was settled in perpetuity upon the crown as the fund whence this revenue should be levied. Though that impost yielded more profit, the bargain might be esteemed hard; and it was chiefly the necessity of the king's situation, which induced him to consent to it. No request of the parliament, during the present joy, could be refused them. *Settlement of the revenue.*

Tonnage and poundage and the other half of the excise were granted to the king during life. The parliament even proceeded so far as to vote that the settled revenue of the crown for all charges should be 1,200,000 pounds a year; a sum greater than any English monarch had ever before enjoyed. But as all the princes of Europe were perpetually augmenting their military force, and consequently their expence, it became requisite that England, from motives both of honour and security, should bear some proportion to them, and adapt its revenue to the new system of politics, which prevailed. According to the chancellor's computation, a charge of 800,000 pounds a year, was at present requisite for the fleet and other articles, which formerly cost the crown but eighty thousand.

Had the parliament, before restoring the king, insisted on any farther limitations than those which the constitution already imposed; besides the danger of reviving former quarrels among parties; it would seem, that their precaution had been entirely superfluous. By reason of its slender and precarious revenue, the crown in effect was still totally dependant. Not a fourth part of this sum, which seemed requisite for public expences, could be levied without consent of parliament; and any concessions, had they been thought necessary, might, even after the restoration, be extorted by the commons from their necessitous prince. This parliament showed no intention of employing at present that engine to any such purposes; but they seemed still determined not to part with it entirely, or to render the revenues of the crown fixed and independent. Tho' they voted in general, that 1,200,000 pounds a year should be settled on the king, they scarcely assigned any funds, which could yield two thirds of that sum. And they left the care of fulfilling their engagements to the future consideration of parliament.

In all the temporary supplies, which they voted, they discovered the same cautious frugality. To disband the army, so formidable in itself, and so much accustomed to rebellion and changes of government, was necessary for the security both of king and parliament; yet the commons showed great jealousy in granting the sums, requisite for that end. An assessment of 70,000 pounds a month was imposed; but it was at first voted, to continue only three months: And all the other sums, which they levied for that purpose, by a poll-bill and new assessments, were still granted by parcels; as if they were not, as yet, well assured of the fidelity of the hand, to which the money was entrusted. Having proceeded so far *13th Sept.* in the settlement of the nation, the parliament adjourned itself for some time.

Trial and execution of the regicides. During the recess of parliament, the object, which chiefly interested the public, was the trial and condemnation of the regicides. The general indignation, attending the enormous crime, of which these men had been guilty, made their sufferings the subject of joy to the people: But in the peculiar circumstances of that action, in the prejudices of the times, as well as in the behaviour of the criminals, a mind, seasoned with humanity, will find a plentiful source of compassion and indulgence. Can any one, without concern for human blindness and ignorance, consider the demeanor of general Harrison, who was first brought to his trial? With great courage and elevation of sentiment, he told the court, that the pretended crime, of which he stood accused, was not a deed, performed in a corner: The sound of it had gone forth to most nations; and in the singular and marvellous conduct of it had chiefly appeared the sovereign power of heaven. That he himself, agitated by doubts, had often, with passionate tears, offered up his addresses to the divine Majesty, and earnestly sought for light and conviction: He had still received assurance of a heavenly sanction, and returned from these devout supplications with more serene tranquillity and satisfaction. That all the nations of the earth were, in the eyes of their Creator, less than a drop of water in the bucket; nor were their erroneous judgments aught but darkness compared with divine illuminations. That these frequent illapses of the divine spirit he could not suspect to be interested illusions; since he was conscious, that, for no temporal advantage, would he offer injury to the poorest man or woman that trod upon the earth. That all the allurements of ambition, all the terrors of imprisonment, had not been able, during the usurpation of Cromwel, to shake his steddy resolution, or bend him to a compliance with that deceitful tyrant. And that when invited by him to sit on the right hand of the throne, when offered riches and splendor and dominion, he had disdainfully rejected all temptations; and neglecting the tears of his friends and family, had still, through every danger, held fast his principles and his integrity.

Scot, who was more a republican than a fanatic, had said in the house of commons, a little before the restoration, that he desired no other epitaph to be inscribed on his tomb-stone than this; *Here lies Thomas Scot, who adjudged the king to death.* He supported the same spirit upon his trial.

Carew, a Millenarian, submitted to his trial, *saving to our Lord Jesus Christ his right to the government of these kingdoms.* Some scrupled to say, according to form, that they would be tried by God and their country; because God was not visibly present to judge them. Others said, that they would be tried by the word of God.

No more than six of the late king's judges, Harrison, Scot, Carew, Clement, Jones, and Scrope, were executed: Scrope alone, of all those who came in upon the king's proclamation. He was a gentleman of good family and of a decent character: But it was proved, that he had a little before, in conversation, expressed himself as if he were no wise convinced of any guilt in condemning the king. Axtel, who had guarded the high court of justice, Hacker, who commanded on the day of the king's execution, Coke, the solicitor for the people of England, and Hugh Peters, the fanatical preacher, who inflamed the army and impelled them to regicide: All these were tried, and condemned, and suffered with the king's judges. No saint or confessor ever went to martyrdom with more assured confidence of heaven than was expressed by those criminals, even when the terrors of immediate death, joined to many indignities, were set before them. The rest of the king's judges, by an unexampled lenity, were reprieved; and they were dispersed into several prisons.

This punishment of declared enemies interrupted not the rejoicings of the court: But the death of the duke of Glocester, a young prince of promising hopes, threw a great cloud upon them. The king, by no incident in his life, was ever so deeply affected. Glocester was observed to possess united the good qualities of both his brothers: The clear judgment and penetration of the king; the industry and application of the duke of York. He was also believed to be affectionate to the religion and constitution of his country. He was but twenty years of age, when the small-pox put an end to his life.

The princess of Orange, having come to England, in order to partake of the joy, attending the restoration of her family, with whom she lived in great friendship, soon after sickened and died. The queen-mother payed a visit to her son; and obtained his consent to the marriage of the princess Henrietta, with the duke of Orleans, brother to the French king.

6th Nov. After a recess of near two months, the parliament met, and proceeded in the great work of the national settlement. They established the post-office, wine-licences, and some articles of the revenue. They granted more assessments, and some arrears for paying and disbanding the army. Business, being carred on with great unanimity, was soon dispatched: And after they had sitten near two months, the king, in a speech full of the most gracious expressions, thought proper to dissolve them.

*Dissolu-
tion of the
conven-
tion par-
liament.
29th Dec.*

This house of commons had been chosen during the reign of the old parliamentary party; and though many royalists had creeped in amongst them, yet did it chiefly consist of presbyterians, who had not yet entirely laid aside their old jealousies and principles. Lenthal, a member, having said, that those who first took arms against the king, were as guilty as those who afterwards brought him to the scaffold, was severely reprimanded by order of the house; and the most violent efforts of the long parliament, to secure the constitution, and bring delinquents to justice, were in effect vindicated and applauded.[o] The claim of the two houses to the militia, the first ground of the quarrel, however exorbitant an usurpation, was never expressly resigned by this parliament. They made all grants of money with a very sparing hand. Great arrears being due by the protectors, to the fleet, the army, the navy-office, and every branch of service; this whole debt they threw upon the crown, without establishing funds sufficient for its payment. Yet notwithstanding this jealous care, expressed by the parliament, there prevails a story, that Popham, having sounded the disposition of the members, undertook to the earl of Southampton to procure, during the king's life, a grant of two millions a year, land tax; a sum, which, added to the customs and excise, would for ever have rendered this prince independant of his people. Southampton, it is said, merely from his affection to the king, had unwarily embraced the offer; and it was not till he communicated the matter to the chancellor, that he was made sensible of its pernicious tendency. It is not improbable, that such an offer might have been made, and been hearkened to; but it is no wise probable, that all the interest of the court would ever, with this house of commons, have been able to make it effectual. Clarendon showed his prudence, no less than his integrity, in entirely rejecting it.

The chancellor, from the same principles of conduct, hastened to disband the army. When the king reviewed these veteran troops, he was struck with their beauty, order, discipline, and martial appearance; and being sensible, that regular forces are most necessary implements of royalty, he expressed a desire of finding expedients still to retain them. But his wise minister set before him the dangerous spirit by which these troops were actuated, their enthusiastic genius, their habits of rebellion and mutiny; and he convinced the king, that, till they were disbanded, he never could esteem himself securely established on his throne. No more troops

[o] Journals, vol. viii. p. 24.

were retained than a few guards and garrisons, about 1000 horse, and 4000 foot. This was the first appearance, under the monarchy, of a regular standing army in this island. Lord Mordaunt said, that the king, being possessed of that force, might now look upon himself as the most considerable gentleman in England.[p] The fortifications of Glocester, Taunton, and other towns, which had made resistance to the king during the civil wars, were demolished.

Clarendon not only behaved with wisdom and justice in the office of chancellor: All the counsels, which he gave the king, tended equally to promote the interest of prince and people. Charles, accustomed in his exile to pay entire deference to the judgment of this faithful servant, continued still to submit to his direction; and for some time no minister was ever possessed of more absolute authority. He moderated the forward zeal of the royalists, and tempered their appetite for revenge. With the opposite party, he endeavoured to preserve inviolate all the king's engagements: He kept an exact register of the promises which had been made for any service, and he employed all his industry to fulfil them. This good minister was now nearly allied to the royal family. His daughter, Ann Hyde, a woman of spirit and fine accomplishments, had hearkened, while abroad, to the addresses of the duke of York, and under promise of marriage, had secretly admitted him to her bed. Her pregnancy appeared soon after the restoration; and though many endeavoured to dissuade the king from consenting to so unequal an alliance, Charles, in pity to his friend and minister, who had been ignorant of these engagements, permitted his brother to marry her.[q] Clarendon expressed great uneasiness, at the honour, which he had obtained; and said, that, by being elevated so much above his rank, he thence dreaded a more sudden downfal.

Prelacy restored. Most circumstances of Clarendon's administration have met with applause: His maxims alone in the conduct of ecclesiastical politics have by many been deemed the effect of prejudices, narrow and bigotted. Had the jealousy of royal power prevailed so far with the convention parliament as to make them restore the king

[p] King James's Memoirs. This prince says, that Venner's insurrection furnished a reason or pretence for keeping up the guards, which were intended at first to have been disbanded with the rest of the army.   [q] King James's Memoirs.

with strict limitations, there is no question but the establishment of presbyterian discipline had been one of the conditions most rigidly insisted on. Not only that form of ecclesiastical government is more favourable to liberty than to royal power: It was likewise, on its own account, agreeable to the majority of the house of commons, and suited their religious principles. But as the impatience of the people, the danger of delay, the general disgust towards faction, and the authority of Monk had prevailed over that jealous project of limitations, the full settlement of the hierarchy, together with the monarchy, was a necessary and infallible consequence. All the royalists were zealous for that mode of religion; the merits of the episcopal clergy towards the king, as well as their sufferings on that account, had been great; the laws, which established bishops and the liturgy, were as yet unrepealed by legal authority; and any attempt of the parliament, by new acts, to give the superiority to presbyterianism, had been sufficient to involve the nation again in blood and confusion. Moved by these views, the commons had wisely postponed the examination of all religious controversy, and had left the settlement of the church to the king and to the ancient laws.

The king at first used great moderation in the execution of the laws. Nine bishops still remained alive; and these were immediately restored to their sees: All the ejected clergy recovered their livings: The liturgy, a form of worship decent, and not without beauty, was again admitted into the churches: But at the same time, a declaration was issued, in order to give contentment to the presbyterians, and preserve an air of moderation and neutrality.[r] In this declaration, the king promised, that he would provide suffragan bishops for the larger dioceses; that the prelates should, all of them, be regular and constant preachers; that they should not confer ordination, or exercise any jurisdiction, without the advice and assistance of presbyters, chosen by the diocese; that such alterations should be made in the liturgy, as would render it totally unexceptionable; that in the mean time, the use of that mode of worship should not be imposed on such as were unwilling to receive it; and that the surplice, the cross in baptism, and bowing at the name of Jesus should not be rigidly insisted on. This declara-

[r] Parl. Hist. vol. xxiii. p. 173.

tion was issued by the king as head of the church; and he plainly assumed, in many parts of it, a legislative authority in ecclesiastical matters. But the English government, though more exactly defined by late contests, was not, as yet, reduced, in every particular, to the strict limits of law. And if ever prerogative was justifiably employed, it seemed to be on the present occasion; when all parts of the state were torne with past convulsions, and required the moderating hand of the chief magistrate, to reduce them to their ancient order.

But though these appearances of neutrality were maintained, and a mitigated episcopacy only seemed to be insisted on, it was far from the intention of the ministry always to preserve like regard to the presbyterians. The madness of the fifth-monarchy-men afforded them a pretence for departing from it. Venner, a desperate enthusiast, who had often conspired against Cromwel, having, by his zealous lectures, inflamed his own imagination and that of his followers, issued forth at their head into the streets of London. They were to the number of sixty, compleatly armed, believed themselves invulnerable and invincible, and firmly expected the same success, which had attended Gideon and other heroes of the Old Testament. Every one at first fled before them. One unhappy man, who, being questioned, said, "He was for God and king Charles," was instantly murdered by them. They went triumphantly from street to street, every where proclaiming king Jesus, who, they said, was their invisible leader. At length, the magistrates, having assembled some train-bands, made an attack upon them. They defended themselves with order as well as valour; and after killing many of the assailants, they made a regular retreat into Cane-Wood near Hampstead. Next morning, they were chased thence by a detachment of the guards; but they ventured again to invade the city, which was not prepared to receive them. After committing great disorder, and traversing almost every street of that immense capital, they retired into a house, which they were resolute to defend to the last extremity. Being surrounded, and the house untiled, they were fired upon from every side; and they still refused quarter. The people rushed in upon them, and seized the few who were alive. These were tried, condemned, and executed; and to the last they persisted in affirming, that, if they were deceived, it was the Lord that had deceived them.

Insurrection of the Millenarians.

CHAPTER LXIII

Clarendon and the ministry took occasion from this insurrection to infer the dangerous spirit of the presbyterians and of all
the sectaries: But the madness of the attempt sufficiently proved,
that it had been undertaken by no concert, and never could have
proved dangerous. The well-known hatred too, which prevailed
between the presbyterians and the other sects, should have removed the former from all suspicion of any concurrence in the
enterprize. But as a pretence was wanted, besides their old demer-
its, for justifying the intended rigours against all of them, this
reason, however slight, was greedily laid hold of.

Affairs in Scotland hastened with still quicker steps than those
in England towards a settlement and a compliance with the king.
It was deliberated in the English council, whether that nation
should be restored to its liberty, or whether the forts, erected by
Cromwel, should not still be upheld, in order to curb the mutinous
spirit, by which the Scots in all ages had been so much governed.
Lauderdale, who, from the battle of Worcester to the restoration,
had been detained prisoner in the Tower, had considerable influence with the king; and he strenuously opposed this violent measure. He represented, that it was the loyalty of the Scottish nation,
which had engaged them in an opposition to the English rebels;
and to take advantage of the calamities, into which, on that account, they had fallen, would be regarded as the highest injustice
and ingratitude: That the spirit of that people was now fully subdued by the servitude, under which the usurpers had so long held
them, and would of itself yield to any reasonable compliance with
their legal sovereign, if, by this means, they recovered their liberty
and independence: That the attachment of the Scots towards their
king, whom they regarded as their native prince, was naturally
much stronger than that of the English; and would afford him a
sure resource, in case of any rebellion among the latter: That
republican principles had long been, and still were, very prevalent
with his southern subjects, and might again menace the throne
with new tumults and resistance. That the time would probably
come, when the king, instead of desiring to see English garrisons
in Scotland, would be better pleased to have Scottish garrisons in
England, who, supported by English pay, would be fond to curb
the seditious genius of that opulent nation: And that a people,
such as the Scots, governed by a few nobility, would more easily be

Affairs of
Scotland.

reduced to submission under monarchy, than one, like the English, who breathed nothing but the spirit of democratical equality.

These views induced the king to disband all the forces in Scotland, and to raze all the forts, which had been erected. General Middleton, created earl of that name, was sent commissioner to the parliament, which was summoned. A very compliant spirit was there discovered in all orders of men. The commissioner had even sufficient influence to obtain an act, annulling, at once, all laws, which had passed since the year 1633; on pretext of the violence, which, during that time, had been employed against the king and his father, in order to procure their assent to these statutes. This was a very large, if not an unexampled concession; and, together with many dangerous limitations, overthrew some useful barriers, which had been erected to the constitution. But the tide was now running strongly towards monarchy; and the Scottish nation plainly discovered, that their past resistance had proceeded more from the turbulence of their aristocracy and the bigotry of their ecclesiastics than from any fixed passion towards civil liberty. The lords of articles were restored, with some other branches of prerogative; and royal authority, fortified with more plausible claims and pretences, was, in its full extent, re-established in that kingdom.

The prelacy likewise, by the abrogating of every statute, enacted in favour of presbytery, was thereby tacitly restored; and the king deliberated what use he should make of this concession. Lauderdale, who at bottom was a passionate zealot against episcopacy, endeavoured to persuade him, that the Scots, if gratified in this favourite point of ecclesiastical government, would, in every other demand, be entirely compliant with the king. Charles, though he had no such attachment to prelacy as had influenced his father and grandfather, had suffered such indignities from the Scottish presbyterians, that he ever after bore them a hearty aversion. He said to Lauderdale, that presbyterianism, he thought, was not a religion for a gentleman; and he could not consent to its farther continuance in Scotland. Middleton too and his other ministers persuaded him, that the nation in general was so disgusted with the violence and tyranny of the ecclesiastics, that any alteration of church government would be universally grateful. And Clarendon, as well as Ormond, dreading that the presbyterian sect, if

CHAPTER LXIII

legally established in Scotland, would acquire authority in England and Ireland, seconded the application of these ministers. The resolution was therefore taken to restore prelacy; a measure afterwards attended with many and great inconveniencies: But whether in this resolution Charles chose not the lesser evil, it is very difficult to determine. Sharp who had been commissioned by the presbyterians in Scotland to manage their interests with the king, was persuaded to abandon that party; and as a reward for his compliance, was created archbishop of St. Andrews. The conduct of ecclesiastical affairs was chiefly entrusted to him; and as he was esteemed a traitor and a renegade by his old friends, he became on that account, as well as from the violence of his conduct, extremely obnoxious to them.

Charles had not promised to Scotland any such indemnity as he had ensured to England by the declaration of Breda: And it was deemed more political for him to hold over men's heads, for some time, the terror of punishment; till they should have made the requisite compliances with the new government. Though neither the king's temper nor plan of administration led him to severity; some examples, after such a bloody and triumphant rebellion, seemed necessary; and the marquess of Argyle and one Guthry, were pitched on as the victims. Two acts of indemnity, one passed by the late king in 1641, another by the present in 1651, formed, it was thought, invincible obstacles to the punishment of Argyle; and barred all enquiry into that part of his conduct, which might justly be regarded as the most exceptionable. Nothing remained but to try him for his compliance with the usurpation; a crime common to him with the whole nation, and such a one as the most loyal and affectionate subject might frequently by violence be obliged to commit. To make this compliance appear the more voluntary and hearty, there were produced in court letters, which he had written to Albemarle, while that general commanded in Scotland, and which contained expressions of the most cordial attachment to the established government. But besides the general indignation, excited by Albemarle's discovery of this private correspondence; men thought, that even the highest demonstrations of affection might, during jealous times, be exacted as a necessary mark of compliance from a person of such distinction as Argyle, and could not, by any equitable construction, imply the crime of treason. The parliament, however, scrupled not to pass sentence upon him; and he died with great constancy and courage. As he was universally known to have been the chief instrument of the past disorders and civil wars, the irregularity of his sentence, and several iniquitous circumstances in the method of conducting his trial, seemed on that account to admit of some apology. Lord Lorne, son of Argyle, having ever preserved his loyalty, obtained a gift of the forfeiture. Guthry was a seditious preacher, and had personally affronted the king: His punishment gave surprize to no body. Sir Archibald Johnstone of Warriston was attainted and fled; but was seized in France about two years after, brought over, and executed. He had been very active, during all the late disorders; and was even suspected of a secret correspondence with the English regicides.

Besides these instances of compliance in the Scottish parliament, they voted an additional revenue to the king of 40,000 pounds a year, to be levied by way of excise. A small force was purposed to be maintained by this revenue, in order to prevent like confusions with those to which the kingdom had been hitherto exposed. An act was also passed, declaring the covenant unlawful, and its obligation void and null.

In England, the civil distinctions seemed to be abolished by the lenity and equality of Charles's administration. Cavalier and Round-head were heard of no more: All men seemed to concur in submitting to the king's lawful prerogatives, and in cherishing the just privileges of the people and of parliament. Theological controversy alone still subsisted, and kept alive some sparks of that flame, which had thrown the nation into combustion. While catholics, independents, and other sectaries were content with entertaining some prospect of toleration; prelacy and presbytery struggled for the superiority, and the hopes and fears of both parties kept them in agitation. A conference was held in the Savoy between twelve bishops and twelve leaders among the presbyterian ministers, with an intention, at least on pretence, of bringing about an accommodation between the parties. The surplice, the cross in baptism, the kneeling at the sacrament, the bowing at the name of Jesus, were anew canvassed; and the ignorant multitude were in hopes, that so many men of gravity and learning could not fail, after deliberate argumentation, to agree in all points of contro-

Conference at the Savoy. 25th March.

versy: They were surprized to see them separate more inflamed than ever, and more confirmed in their several prejudices. To enter into particulars would be superfluous. Disputes concerning religious forms are, in themselves, the most frivolous of any; and merit attention only so far as they have influence on the peace and order of civil society.

The king's declaration had promised, that some endeavours should be used to effect a comprehension of both parties; and Charles's own indifference with regard to all such questions seemed a favourable circumstance for the execution of that project. The partizans of a comprehension said, that the presbyterians, as well as the prelatists, having felt by experience the fatal effects of obstinacy and violence, were now well disposed towards an amicable agreement: That the bishops, by relinquishing some part of their authority, and dispensing with the most exceptionable ceremonies, would so gratify their adversaries as to obtain their cordial and affectionate compliance, and unite the whole nation in one faith and one worship: That by obstinately insisting on forms, in themselves insignificant, an air of importance was bestowed on them, and men were taught to continue equally obstinate in rejecting them: That the presbyterian clergy would go every reasonable length, rather than, by parting with their livings, expose themselves to a state of beggary, at best of dependence: And that if their pride were flattered by some seeming alterations, and a pretence given them for affirming, that they had not abandoned their former principles, nothing farther was wanting to produce a thorough union between those two parties, which comprehended the bulk of the nation.

Arguments for and against a comprehension.

It was alledged on the other hand, that the difference between religious sects was founded, not on principle, but on passion; and till the irregular affections of men could be corrected, it was in vain to expect, by compliances, to obtain a perfect unanimity and comprehension: That the more insignificant the objects of dispute appeared, with the more certainty might it be inferred, that the real ground of dissention was different from that which was universally pretended: That the love of novelty, the pride of argumentation, the pleasure of making proselytes, and the obstinacy of contradiction, would for ever give rise to sects and disputes, nor was it possible that such a source of dissention could ever, by any concessions, be entirely exhausted: That the church, by departing from ancient practices and principles, would tacitly acknowledge herself guilty of error, and lose that reverence, so requisite for preserving the attachment of the multitude: And that if the present concessions (which was more than probable) should prove ineffectual, greater must still be made; and in the issue, discipline would be despoiled of all its authority, and worship of all its decency, without obtaining that end, which had been so fondly sought for by these dangerous indulgences.

The ministry were inclined to give the preference to the latter arguments; and were the more confirmed in that intention by the disposition, which appeared in the parliament lately assembled. The royalists and zealous churchmen were at present the popular party in the nation, and, seconded by the efforts of the court, had prevailed in most elections. Not more than fifty-six members of the presbyterian party had obtained seats in the lower house;[s] and these were not able either to oppose or retard the measures of the majority. Monarchy, therefore, and episcopacy, were now exalted to as great power and splendor as they had lately suffered misery and depression. Sir Edward Turner was chosen speaker.

A new parliament. 8th May.

An act was passed for the security of the king's person and government. To intend or devise the king's imprisonment, or bodily harm, or deposition, or levying war against him, was declared, during the life-time of his present majesty, to be high treason. To affirm him to be a papist or heretic, or to endeavour by speech or writing to alienate his subjects' affections from him; these offences were made sufficient to incapacitate the person guilty from holding any employment in church or state. To maintain that the long parliament is not dissolved, or that either or both houses, without the king, are possessed of legislative authority, or that the covenant is binding; was made punishable by the penalty of premunire.

The covenant itself, together with the act for erecting the high court of justice, that for subscribing the engagement, and that for declaring England a commonwealth, were ordered to be burnt by the hands of the hangman. The people assisted with great alacrity on this occasion.

[s] Carte's Answer to the Bystander, p. 79.

CHAPTER LXIII

The abuses of petitioning in the preceding reign had been attended with the worst consequences; and to prevent such irregular practices for the future, it was enacted, that no more than twenty hands should be fixed to any petition, unless with the sanction of three justices, or the major part of the grand jury; and that no petition should be presented to the king or either house by above ten persons. The penalty annexed to a transgression of this law was a fine of a hundred pounds and three months imprisonment.

The bishops, though restored to their spiritual authority, were still excluded from parliament by the law, which the late king had passed, immediately before the commencement of the civil disorders. Great violence, both against the king and the house of peers, had been employed in passing this law; and on that account alone, the partizans of the church were provided with a plausible pretence for repealing it. Charles expressed much satisfaction, when he gave his assent to the act for that purpose. It is certain, that the authority of the crown, as well as that of the church, was interested in restoring the prelates to their former dignity. But those, who deemed every acquisition of the prince a detriment to the people, were apt to complain of this instance of complaisance in the parliament. *Bishops' seats restored.*

After an adjournment of some months, the parliament was again assembled, and proceeded in the same spirit as before. They discovered no design of restoring, in its full extent, the ancient prerogative of the crown: They were only anxious to repair all those breaches, which had been made, not by the love of liberty, but by the fury of faction and civil war. The power of the sword had, in all ages, been allowed to be vested in the crown; and though no law conferred this prerogative, every parliament, till the last of the preceding reign, had willingly submitted to an authority more ancient, and therefore more sacred, than that of any positive statute. It was now thought proper solemnly to relinquish the violent pretensions of that parliament, and to acknowledge, that neither one house, nor both houses, independent of the king, were possessed of any military authority. The preamble to this statute went so far as to renounce all right even of *defensive* arms against the king; and much observation has been made with regard to a concession, esteemed so singular. Were these terms taken in their full *20th Nov.*

literal sense, they imply a total renunciation of limitations to monarchy, and of all privileges in the subject, independent of the will of the sovereign. For as no rights can subsist without some remedy, still less rights exposed to so much invasion from tyranny, or even from ambition; if subjects must never resist, it follows, that every prince, without any effort, policy or violence, is at once rendered absolute and uncontroulable: The sovereign needs only issue an edict, abolishing every authority but his own; and all liberty, from that moment, is in effect annihilated. But this meaning it were absurd to impute to the present parliament, who, though zealous royalists, showed in their measures, that they had not cast off all regard to national privileges. They were probably sensible, that to suppose in the sovereign any such invasion of public liberty is entirely unconstitutional; and that therefore expressly to reserve, upon that event, any right of resistance in the subject, must be liable to the same objection. They had seen that the long parliament, under colour of defence, had begun a violent attack upon kingly power; and after involving the kingdom in blood, had finally lost that liberty, for which they had so imprudently contended. They thought, perhaps erroneously, that it was no longer possible, after such public and such exorbitant pretensions to persevere in that prudent silence, hitherto maintained by the laws; and that it was necessary, by some positive declaration, to bar the return of like inconveniencies. When they excluded, therefore, the right of defence, they supposed, that the constitution remaining firm upon its basis, there never really could be an attack made by the sovereign. If such an attack was at any time made, the necessity was then extreme: And the case of extreme and violent necessity, no laws, they thought, could comprehend; because to such a necessity no laws could beforehand point out a proper remedy.

The other measures of this parliament still discovered a more anxious care to guard against rebellion in the subject than encroachments in the crown: The recent evils of civil war and usurpation had naturally encreased the spirit of submission to the monarch, and had thrown the nation into that dangerous extreme. During the violent and jealous government of the parliament and of the protectors, all magistrates, liable to suspicion, had been expelled the corporations; and none had been admitted, who gave not proofs of affection to the ruling powers, or who refused to

Corpo-
ration
act.

subscribe the covenant. To leave all authority in such hands seemed dangerous; and the parliament, therefore, empowered the king to appoint commissioners for regulating the corporations, and expelling such magistrates as either intruded themselves by violence, or professed principles, dangerous to the constitution, civil and ecclesiastical. It was also enacted, that all magistrates should disclaim the obligation of the covenant, and should declare, both their belief, that it was not lawful, upon any pretence whatsoever, to resist the king, and their abhorrence of the traiterous position of taking arms by the king's authority against his person, or against those who were commissioned by him.

The care of the church was no less attended to by this parliament, than that of monarchy; and the bill of uniformity was a pledge of their sincere attachment to the episcopal hierarchy, and of their antipathy to presbyterianism. Different parties, however, concurred in promoting this bill, which contained many severe clauses. The independents and other sectaries, enraged to find all their schemes subverted by the presbyterians, who had once been their associates, exerted themselves to disappoint that party of the favour and indulgence, to which, from their recent merits in promoting the restoration, they thought themselves justly entitled. By the presbyterians, said they, the war was raised: By them was the populace first incited to tumults: By their zeal, interest, and riches were the armies supported: By their force was the king subdued: And if, in the sequel, they protested against those extreme violences, committed on his person by the military leaders, their opposition came too late, after having supplied these usurpers with the power and the pretences, by which they maintained their sanguinary measures. They had indeed concurred with the royalists in recalling the king: But ought they to be esteemed, on that account, more affectionate to the royal cause? Rage and animosity, from disappointed ambition, were plainly their sole motives; and if the king should now be so imprudent as to distinguish them by any particular indulgences, he would soon experience from them the same hatred and opposition, which had proved so fatal to his father.

The catholics, though they had little interest in the nation, were a considerable party at court; and from their services and sufferings, during the civil wars, it seemed but just to bear them some

1662.
Act of
uniformity.

favour and regard. These religionists dreaded an entire union among the protestants. Were they the sole nonconformists in the nation, the severe execution of penal laws upon their sect seemed an infallible consequence; and they used, therefore, all their interest to push matters to extremity against the presbyterians, who had formerly been their most severe oppressors, and whom they now expected for their companions in affliction. The earl of Bristol, who, from conviction, or interest, or levity, or complaisance for the company with whom he lived, had changed his religion during the king's exile, was regarded as the head of this party.

The church party had, during so many years, suffered such injuries and indignities from the sectaries of every denomination, that no moderation, much less deference, was on this occasion to be expected in the ecclesiastics. Even the laity of that communion seemed now disposed to retaliate upon their enemies, according to the usual measures of party justice. This sect or faction (for it partook of both) encouraged the rumours of plots and conspiracies against the government; crimes, which, without any apparent reason, they imputed to their adversaries. And instead of enlarging the terms of communion, in order to comprehend the presbyterians, they gladly laid hold of the prejudices, which prevailed among that sect, in order to eject them from their livings. By the bill of uniformity it was required, that every clergyman should be re-ordained, if he had not before received episcopal ordination; should declare his assent to every thing contained in the Book of Common Prayer; should take the oath of canonical obedience; should abjure the solemn league and covenant; and should renounce the principle of taking arms, on any pretence whatsoever, against the king.

This bill re-instated the church in the same condition, in which it stood before the commencement of the civil wars; and as the old persecuting laws of Elizabeth still subsisted in their full rigor, and new clauses of a like nature were now enacted, all the king's promises of toleration and of indulgence to tender consciences were thereby eluded and broken. It is true, Charles, in his declaration from Breda, had expressed his intention of regulating that indulgence by the advice and authority of parliament: But this limitation could never reasonably be extended to a total infringement and violation of his engagements. However, it is agreed, that the king did not voluntarily concur with this violent measure, and that the zeal of Clarendon and of the church party among the commons, seconded by the intrigues of the catholics, was the chief cause, which extorted his consent.

The royalists, who now predominated, were very ready to signalize their victory, by establishing those high principles of monarchy, which their antagonists had controverted: But when any real power or revenue was demanded for the crown, they were neither so forward nor so liberal in their concessions as the king would gladly have wished. Though the parliament passed laws for regulating the navy, they took no notice of the army; and declined giving their sanction to this dangerous innovation. The king's debts were become intolerable; and the commons were at last constrained to vote him an extraordinary supply of 1,200,000 pounds, to be levied by eighteen monthly assessments. But besides that this supply was much inferior to the occasion, the king was obliged earnestly to solicit the commons, before he could obtain it; and, in order to convince the house of its absolute necessity, he desired them to examine strictly into all his receipts and disbursements. Finding likewise upon enquiry, that the several branches of revenue fell much short of the sums expected, they at last, after much delay, voted a new imposition of two shillings on each hearth; and this tax they settled on the king during life. The whole established revenue, however, did not, for many years, exceed a million,[f] a sum confessedly too narrow for the public expences. A very rigid frugality at least, which the king seems to have wanted, would have been requisite to make it suffice for the dignity and security of government. After all business was dispatched, the parliament was prorogued. *19th May.*

Before the parliament rose, the court was employed in making preparations for the reception of the new queen, Catherine of Portugal, to whom the king was betrothed, and who had just landed at Portsmouth. During the time, that the protector carried on the war with Spain, he was naturally led to support the Portuguese in their revolt; and he engaged himself by treaty to supply them with 10,000 men for their defence against the Spaniards. On the king's restoration, advances were made by Portugal for the *King's marriage.*

[f] D'Estrades, 25th of July, 1661. Mr. Ralph's History, vol. i. p. 176.

renewal of the alliance; and in order to bind the friendship closer, an offer was made of the Portuguese princess, and a portion of 500,000 pounds, together with two fortresses, Tangiers in Africa and Bombay in the East Indies. Spain, who, after the peace of the Pyrenees, bent all her force to recover Portugal, now in appearance abandoned by France, took the alarm, and endeavoured to fix Charles in an opposite interest. The catholic king offered to adopt any other princess as a daughter of Spain, either the princess of Parma, or, what he thought more popular, some protestant princess, the daughter of Denmark, Saxony, or Orange: And on any of these, he promised to confer a dowry equal to that which was offered by Portugal. But many reasons inclined Charles rather to accept of the Portuguese proposals. The great disorders in the government and finances of Spain made the execution of her promises be much doubted; and the king's urgent necessities demanded some immediate supply of money. The interest of the English commerce likewise seemed to require, that the independancy of Portugal should be supported, lest the union of that crown with Spain should put the whole treasures of America into the hands of one potentate. The claims too of Spain upon Dunkirk and Jamaica, rendered it impossible, without farther concessions, to obtain the cordial friendship of that power: And on the other hand, the offer, made by Portugal, of two such considerable fortresses, promised a great accession to the naval force of England. Above all, the proposal of a protestant princess was no allurement to Charles, whose inclinations led him strongly to give the preference to a catholic alliance. According to the most probable accounts,[u] the resolution of marrying the daughter of Portugal was taken by the king, unknown to all his ministers; and no remonstrances could prevail with him to alter his intentions. When the matter was laid before the council, all voices concurred in ap-

[u] Carte's Ormond, vol. ii. p. 254. This account seems better supported, than that in Ablancourt's Memoirs, that the chancellor chiefly pushed the Portuguese alliance. The secret transactions of the court of England could not be supposed to be much known to a French resident at Lisbon: And whatever opposition the chancellor might make, he would certainly endeavour to conceal it from the queen and all her family; and even in the parliament and council would support the resolution already taken. *Clarendon himself says in his Memoirs, that he never either opposed or promoted the Portuguese match.*

proving the resolution; and the parliament expressed the same complaisance. And thus was concluded, seemingly with universal consent, the inauspicious marriage with Catherine, a princess of virtue, but who was never able either by the graces of her person or humour, to make herself agreeable to the king. The report, however, of her natural incapacity to have children, seems to have been groundless; since she was twice declared to be pregnant.[w]

21st May.

The festivity of these espousals was clouded by the trial and execution of criminals. Berkstead, Cobbet, and Okey, three regicides, had escaped beyond sea; and after wandering some time concealed in Germany, came privately to Delft, having appointed their families to meet them in that place. They were discovered by Downing, the king's resident in Holland, who had formerly served the protector and commonwealth in the same station, and who once had even been chaplain to Okey's regiment. He applied for a warrant to arrest them. It had been usual for the States to grant these warrants; though at the same time, they had ever been careful secretly to advertise the persons, that they might be enabled to make their escape. This precaution was eluded by the vigilance and dispatch of Downing. He quickly seized the criminals, hurried them on board a frigate which lay off the coast, and sent them to England. These three men behaved with more moderation and submission than any of the other regicides, who had suffered. Okey in particular, at the place of execution, prayed for the king, and expressed his intention, had he lived, of submitting peaceably to the established government. He had risen during the wars from being a chandler in London to a high rank in the army; and in all his conduct appeared to be a man of humanity and honour. In consideration of his good character and of his dutiful behaviour, his body was given to his friends to be buried.

The attention of the public was much engaged by the trial of two distinguished criminals, Lambert and Vane. These men, though none of the late king's judges, had been excepted from the general indemnity, and committed to prison. The convention-parliament, however, was so favourable to them, as to petition the king, if they should be found guilty, to suspend their execution: But this new parliament, more zealous for monarchy, applied for

[w] Lord Landsdown's Defence of general Monk. Temple, vol. ii. p. 154.

their trial and condemnation. Not to revive disputes, which were better buried in oblivion, the indictment of Vane did not comprehend any of his actions during the war between the king and parliament: It extended only to his behaviour after the late king's death, as member of the council of state, and secretary of the navy, where fidelity to the trust, reposed in him, required his opposition to monarchy.

Vane wanted neither courage nor capacity to avail himself of this advantage. He urged, that, if a compliance with the government, at that time established in England, and the acknowledging of its authority were to be regarded as criminal, the whole nation had incurred equal guilt, and none would remain, whose innocence could entitle them to try or condemn him for his pretended treasons: That, according to these maxims, wherever an illegal authority was established by force, a total and universal destruction must ensue; while the usurpers proscribed one part of the nation for disobedience, the lawful prince punished the other for compliance: That the legislature of England, foreseeing this violent situation, had provided for public security by the famous statute of Henry VII.; in which it was enacted, that no man, in case of any revolution, should ever be questioned for his obedience to the king in being: That whether the established government were a monarchy or a commonwealth, the reason of the thing was still the same; nor ought the expelled prince to think himself entitled to allegiance, so long as he could not afford protection: That it belonged not to private persons, possessed of no power, to discuss the title of their governors; and every usurpation, even the most flagrant, would equally require obedience with the most legal establishment: That the controversy between the late king and his parliament was of the most delicate nature; and men of the greatest probity had been divided in their choice of the party which they should embrace: That the parliament, being rendered indissoluble but by its own consent, was become a kind of co-ordinate power with the king; and as the case was thus entirely new and unknown to the constitution, it ought not to be tried rigidly by the letter of the ancient laws: That for his part, all the violences, which had been put upon the parliament, and upon the person of the sovereign, he had ever condemned; nor had he once appeared in the house for some time before and after the execution of the king:

CHAPTER LXIII

That, finding the whole government thrown into disorder, he was still resolved, in every revolution, to adhere to the commons, the root, the foundation of all lawful authority: That in prosecution of this principle, he had chearfully undergone all the violence of Cromwel's tyranny; and would now, with equal alacrity, expose himself to the rigours of perverted law and justice: That though it was in his power, on the king's restoration, to have escaped from his enemies, he was determined, in imitation of the most illustrious names of antiquity, to perish in defence of liberty, and to give testimony with his blood for that honourable cause, in which he had been inlisted: And, that, besides the ties, by which God and nature had bound him to his native country, he was voluntarily engaged by the most sacred covenant, whose obligation no earthly power should ever be able to make him relinquish.

All the defence, which Vane could make, was fruitless. The court, considering more the general opinion of his active guilt in the beginning and prosecution of the civil wars, than the articles of treason charged against him, took advantage of the letter of the law, and brought him in guilty. His courage deserted him not upon his condemnation. Though timid by nature, the persuasion of a just cause supported him against the terrors of death; while his enthusiasm, excited by the prospect of glory, embellished the conclusion of a life, which, through the whole course of it, had been so much disfigured by the prevalence of that principle. Lest pity for a courageous sufferer should make impression on the populace, drummers were placed under the scaffold, whose noise, as he began to launch out in reflections on the government, drowned his voice, and admonished him to temper the ardour of his zeal. He was not astonished at this unexpected incident. In all his behaviour, there appeared a firm and animated intrepidity; and he considered death but as a passage to that eternal felicity, which he believed to be prepared for him.

This man, so celebrated for his parliamentary talents, and for his capacity in business, has left some writings behind him: They treat, all of them, of religious subjects, and are absolutely unintelligible: No traces of eloquence, or even of common sense appear in them. A strange paradox! did we not know, that men of the greatest genius, where they relinquish by principle the use of their reason, are only enabled, by their vigour of mind, to work them-

11th June.

*and ex-
ecution.
14th June.*

selves the deeper into error and absurdity. It was remarkable, that, as Vane, by being the chief instrument of Strafford's death, had first opened the way for that destruction, which overwhelmed the nation; so by his death he closed the scene of blood. He was the last that suffered on account of the civil wars. Lambert, though condemned, was reprieved at the bar; and the judges declared, that, if Vane's behaviour had been equally dutiful and submissive, he would have experienced like lenity in the king. Lambert survived his condemnation near thirty years. He was confined to the isle of Guernesey; where he lived contented, forgetting all his past schemes of greatness, and entirely forgotten by the nation: He died a Roman catholic.

Presbyterian clergy ejected. 24th Aug.

However odious Vane and Lambert were to the presbyterians, that party had no leisure to rejoice at their condemnation. The fatal St. Bartholomew approached; the day, when the clergy were obliged by the late law, either to relinquish their livings, or to sign the articles required of them. A combination had been entered into by the more zealous of the presbyterian ecclesiastics to refuse the subscription; in hopes, that the bishops would not venture at once to expel so great a number of the most popular preachers. The catholic party at court, who desired a great rent among the protestants, encouraged them in this obstinacy, and gave them hopes, that the king would protect them in their refusal. The king himself, by his irresolute conduct, contributed, either from design or accident, to encrease this opinion. Above all, the terms of subscription had been made strict and rigid, on purpose to disgust all the zealous and scrupulous among the presbyterians, and deprive them of their livings. About 2000 of the clergy, in one day, relinquished their cures; and to the astonishment of the court, sacrificed their interest to their religious tenets. Fortified by society in their sufferings, they were resolved to undergo any hardships, rather than openly renounce those principles, which, on other occasions, they were so apt, from interest, to warp or elude. The church enjoyed the pleasure of retaliation; and even pushed, as usual, the vengeance farther than the offence. During the dominion of the parliamentary party, a fifth of each living had been left to the ejected clergyman; but this indulgence, though at first insisted on by the house of peers, was now refused to the presbyterians. However difficult to conciliate peace among theologians, it was hoped by many, that some relaxation in the terms of communion might have kept the presbyterians united to the church, and have cured those ecclesiastical factions, which had been so fatal, and were still so dangerous. Bishoprics were offered to Calamy, Baxter, and Reynolds, leaders among the presbyterians; the last only could be prevailed on to accept. Deaneries and other preferments were refused by many.

The next measure of the king has not had the good fortune to be justified by any party; but is often considered, on what grounds I shall not determine, as one of the greatest mistakes, if not blemishes, of his reign. It is the sale of Dunkirk to the French. The parsimonious maxims of the parliament, and the liberal, or rather careless disposition of Charles, were ill suited to each other; and notwithstanding the supplies voted him, his treasury was still very empty and very much indebted. He had secretly received the sum of 200,000 crowns from France for the support of Portugal; but the forces sent over to that country, and the fleets, maintained in order to defend it, had already cost the king that sum, and together with it, near double the money, which had been payed as the queen's portion.[x] The time fixed for payment of his sister's portion to the duke of Orleans was approaching. Tangiers, a fortress from which great benefit was expected, was become an additional burthen to the crown; and Rutherford, who now commanded in Dunkirk, had encreased the charge of that garrison to a hundred and twenty thousand pounds a year. These considerations had such influence, not only on the king, but even on Clarendon, that this uncorrupt minister was the most forward to advise accepting a sum of money in lieu of a place which, he thought, the king, from the narrow state of his revenue, was no longer able to retain. By the treaty with Portugal, it was stipulated, that Dunkirk should never be yielded to the Spaniards: France was therefore the only purchaser that remained. D'Estrades was invited over by a letter from the chancellor himself, in order to conclude the bargain. Nine hundred thousand pounds were demanded: One hundred thousand were offered. The English by degrees lowered their demand; the French raised their offer: And the bargain was concluded at

Dunkirk sold to the French.

[x] D'Estrades, 17th of August, 1662. There was above half of 500,000 pounds really paid as the queen's portion.

400,000 pounds. The artillery an stores were valued at a fifth of the sum.[y] The importance of this sale was not, at that time, sufficiently known, either abroad or at home.[z] The French monarch himself, so fond of acquisitions, and so good a judge of his own interests, thought, that he had made a hard bargain,[a] and this sum, in appearance so small, was the utmost, which he would allow his ambassador to offer.

Declaration of indulgence. 26th Dec.

A new incident discovered such a glimpse of the king's character and principles as, at first, the nation was somewhat at a loss how to interpret, but such as subsequent events, by degrees, rendered sufficiently plain and manifest. He issued a declaration on pretence of mitigating the rigours, contained in the act of uniformity. After expressing his firm resolution to observe the general indemnity, and to trust entirely to the affections of his subjects, not to any military power, for the support of his throne; he mentioned the promises of liberty of conscience, contained in his declaration of Breda. And he subjoined, that, "as in the first place he had been zealous to settle the uniformity of the church of England, in discipline, ceremony and government, and shall ever constantly maintain it: So as for what concerns the penalties upon those who, living peaceably, do not conform themselves thereunto, through scruple and tenderness of misguided conscience, but modestly and without scandal perform their devotions in their own way, he should make it his special care, so far as in him lay, without invading the freedom of parliament, to incline their wisdom next approaching sessions to concur with him in making some such act for that

[y] D'Estrades, 21st of August, 12th of September, 1662.   [z] It appears, however, from many of D'Estrades's letters, particularly that of the 21st of August, 1661, that the king might have transferred Dunkirk to the parliament, who would not have refused to bear the charges of it, but were unwilling to give money to the king for that purpose. The king on the other hand was jealous, lest the parliament should acquire any separate dominion or authority in a branch of administration, which seemed so little to belong to them: A proof that the government was not yet settled into that composure, and mutual confidence, which is absolutely requisite for conducting it.   [a] Id. 3d of October, 1662. The chief importance indeed of Dunkirk to the English was, that it was able to distress their trade, when in the hands of the French: But it was Lewis the XIVth who first made it a good sea-port. If ever England have occasion to transport armies to the continent, it must be in support of some ally whose towns serve to the same purpose as Dunkirk would, if in the hands of the English.

CHAPTER LXIII

purpose, as may enable him to exercise, with a more universal satisfaction, that power of dispensing, which he conceived to be inherent in him."[b] Here a most important prerogative was exercised by the king; but under such artful reserves and limitations as might prevent the full discussion of the claim, and obviate a breach between him and his parliament. The foundation of this measure lay much deeper, and was of the utmost consequence.

The king, during his exile, had imbibed strong prejudices in favour of the catholic religion; and according to the most probable accounts, had already been secretly reconciled in form to the church of Rome. The great zeal, expressed by the parliamentary party against all papists, had always, from a spirit of opposition, inclined the court and all the royalists to adopt more favourable sentiments towards that sect, which, through the whole course of the civil wars, had strenuously supported the rights of the sovereign. The rigour too, which the king, during his abode in Scotland, had experienced from the presbyterians, disposed him to run into the other extreme, and to bear a kindness to the party, most opposite in its genius to the severity of those religionists. The solicitations and importunities of the queen-mother, the contagion of the company which he frequented, the view of a more splendid and courtly mode of worship, the hopes of indulgence in pleasure; all these causes operated powerfully on a young prince, whose careless and dissolute temper made him incapable of adhering closely to the principles of his early education. But if the thoughtless humour of Charles rendered him an easy convert to popery, the same disposition ever prevented the theological tenets of that sect from taking any fast hold of him. During his vigorous state of health, while his blood was warm and his spirits high; a contempt and disregard to all religion held possession of his mind; and he might more properly be denominated a deist than a catholic. But in those revolutions of temper, when the love of raillery gave place to reflection, and his penetrating, but negligent understanding was clouded with fears and apprehensions, he had starts of more sincere conviction; and a sect, which always possessed his inclination, was then master of his judgment and opinion.[c]

[b] Kennet's Register, p. 850. [c] The author confesses, that the king's zeal for popery was apt, at intervals, to go farther than is here supposed, as appears from many passages in James the Second's Memoirs.

But though the king thus fluctuated, during his whole reign, between irreligion, which he more openly professed, and popery, to which he retained a secret propensity, his brother, the duke of York, had zealously adopted all the principles of that theological party. His eager temper and narrow understanding made him a thorough convert, without any reserve from interest, or doubts from reasoning and enquiry. By his application to business, he had acquired a great ascendant over the king, who, though possessed of more discernment, was glad to throw the burthen of affairs on the duke, of whom he entertained little jealousy. On pretence of easing the protestant dissenters, they agreed upon a plan for introducing a general toleration, and giving the catholics the free exercise of their religion; at least, the exercise of it in private houses. The two brothers saw with pleasure so numerous and popular a body of the clergy refuse conformity; and it was hoped, that, under shelter of their name, the small and hated sect of the catholics might meet with favour and protection.

1663.
18th Feb.
But while the king pleaded his early promises of toleration, and insisted on many other plausible topics, the parliament, who sat a little after the declaration was issued, could by no means be satisfied with this measure. The declared intention of easing the dissenters, and the secret purpose of favouring the catholics, were equally disagreeable to them; and in these prepossessions they were encouraged by the king's ministers themselves, particularly the chancellor. The house of commons represented to the king, that his declaration of Breda contained no promise to the presbyterians and other dissenters, but only an expression of his intentions, upon supposition of the concurrence of parliament: That even if the nonconformists had been entitled to plead a promise, they had entrusted this claim, as all their other rights and privileges, to the house of commons, who were their representatives, and who now freed the king from that obligation: That it was not to be supposed, that his majesty and the houses were so bound by that declaration as to be incapacitated from making any laws, which might be contrary to it: That even at the king's restoration, there were laws of uniformity in force, which could not be dispensed with but by act of parliament: And that the indulgence intended would prove most pernicious both to church and state, would open the door to schism, encourage faction, disturb the

CHAPTER LXIII

public peace, and discredit the wisdom of the legislature. The king did not think proper, after this remonstrance, to insist any farther at present on the project of indulgence.

In order to deprive the catholics of all hopes, the two houses concurred in a remonstrance against them. The king gave a gracious answer; though he scrupled not to profess his gratitude towards many of that persuasion, on account of their faithful services in his father's cause and in his own. A proclamation, for form's sake, was soon after issued against Jesuits and Romish priests: But care was taken, by the very terms of it, to render it ineffectual. The parliament had allowed, that all foreign priests, belonging to the two queens, should be excepted, and that a permission for them to remain in England should still be granted. In the proclamation, the word, *foreign,* was purposely omitted; and the queens were thereby authorized to give protection to as many English priests as they should think proper.

That the king might reap some advantage from his compliances, however fallacious, he engaged the commons anew into an examination of his revenue, which, chiefly by the negligence in levying it, had proved, he said, much inferior to the public charges. Notwithstanding the price of Dunkirk, his debts, he complained, amounted to a considerable sum; and to satisfy the commons, that the money formerly granted him, had not been prodigally expended, he offered to lay before them the whole account of his disbursements. It is however agreed on all hands, that the king, though, during his banishment, he had managed his small and precarious income with great order and economy, had now much abated of these virtues, and was unable to make his royal revenues suffice for his expences. The commons, without entering into too nice a disquisition, voted him four subsidies; and this was the last time, that taxes were levied in that manner.

Several laws were made this session with regard to trade. The militia also came under consideration, and some rules were established for ordering and arming it. It was enacted, that the king should have no power of keeping the militia under arms above fourteen days in the year. The situation of this island, together with its great naval power, has always occasioned other means of security, however requisite, to be much neglected amongst us: And the parliament showed here a very superfluous jealousy of the king's strictness in disciplining the militia. The principles of liberty rather require a contrary jealousy.

The earl of Bristol's friendship with Clarendon, which had subsisted, with great intimacy, during their exile and the distresses of the royal party, had been considerably impaired since the restoration, by the chancellor's refusing his assent to some grants, which Bristol had applied for to a court lady: And a little after, the latter nobleman, agreeably to the impetuosity and indiscretion of his temper, broke out against the minister in the most outrageous manner. He even entered a charge of treason against him before the house of peers; but had concerted his measures so imprudently, that the judges, when consulted, declared, that, neither for its matter nor its form, could the charge be legally received. The articles indeed resemble more the incoherent altercations of a passionate enemy, than a serious accusation, fit to be discussed by a court of judicature; and Bristol himself was so ashamed of his conduct and defeat, that he absconded during some time. Notwithstanding his fine talents, his eloquence, his spirit, and his courage, he could never regain the character, which he lost by this hasty and precipitate measure.

Decline of Clarendon's credit. But though Clarendon was able to elude this rash assault, his credit at court was sensibly declining; and in proportion as the king found himself established on the throne, he began to alienate himself from a minister, whose character was so little suited to his own. Charles's favour for the catholics was always opposed by Clarendon, public liberty was secured against all attempts of the over-zealous royalists, prodigal grants of the king were checked or refused, and the dignity of his own character was so much consulted by the chancellor, that he made it an inviolable rule, as did also his friend, Southampton, never to enter into any connexion with the royal mistresses. The king's favourite was Mrs. Palmer, afterwards created dutchess of Cleveland; a woman prodigal, rapacious, dissolute, violent, revengeful. She failed not in her turn to undermine Clarendon's credit with his master; and her success was at this time made apparent to the whole world. Secretary Nicholas, the chancellor's great friend, was removed from his place; and Sir Harry Bennet, his avowed enemy, was advanced to that office. Bennet was soon after created lord Arlington.

Though the king's conduct had hitherto, since his restoration,

CHAPTER LXIII

been, in the main, laudable, men of penetration began to observe, that those virtues, by which he had, at first, so much dazzled and enchanted the nation, had great show, but not equal solidity. His good understanding lost much of its influence by his want of application; his bounty was more the result of a facility of disposition than any generosity of character; his social humour led him frequently to neglect his dignity; his love of pleasure was not attended with proper sentiment, and decency; and while he seemed to bear a good will to every one that approached him, he had a heart not very capable of friendship, and he had secretly entertained a very bad opinion and distrust of mankind. But above all, what sullied his character in the eyes of good judges was his negligent ingratitude towards the unfortunate cavaliers, whose zeal and sufferings in the royal cause had known no bounds. This conduct however in the king may, from the circumstances of his situation and temper, admit of some excuse; at least, of some alleviation. As he had been restored more by the efforts of his reconciled enemies than of his ancient friends, the former pretended a title to share his favour; and being, from practice, acquainted with public business, they were better qualified to execute any trust committed to them. The king's revenues were far from being large, or even equal to his necessary expences; and his mistresses, and the companions of his mirth and pleasures, gained by solicitation every request from his easy temper. The very poverty, to which the more zealous royalists had reduced themselves, by rendering them insignificant, made them unfit to support the king's measures, and caused him to deem them a useless incumbrance. And as many false and ridiculous claims of merit were offered, his natural indolence, averse to a strict discussion or enquiry, led him to treat them all with equal indifference. The parliament took some notice of the poor cavaliers. Sixty thousand pounds were at one time distributed among them: Mrs. Lane also and the Penderells had handsome presents and pensions from the king. But the greater part of the royalists still remained in poverty and distress; aggravated by the cruel disappointment in their sanguine hopes, and by seeing favour and preferment bestowed upon their most inveterate foes. With regard to the act of indemnity and oblivion, they universally said, that it was an act of indemnity to the king's enemies, and of oblivion to his friends.

LXIV

A new session – Rupture with Holland –
A new session – Victory of the English – Rupture
with France – Rupture with Denmark –
New session – Five-mile act – Sea-fight of
four days – Victory of the English – Fire of
London – Advances towards peace – Disgrace at
Chatham – Peace of Breda – Clarendon's fall –
and banishment – State of France – Character
of Lewis XIV. – French invasion of
the Low Countries – Negotiations –
Triple league – Treaty of
Aix-la-chapelle – Affairs of
Scotland – and of Ireland

1664.
16th
March.
A new
session.

THE NEXT SESSION of parliament discovered a continuance of the same principles, which had prevailed in all the foregoing. Monarchy and the church were still the objects of regard and affection. During no period of the present reign, did this spirit more evidently pass the bounds of reason and moderation.

The king in his speech to the parliament had ventured openly to demand a repeal of the triennial act; and he even went so far as to declare, that, notwithstanding the law, he never would allow any parliament to be assembled by the methods prescribed in that

CHAPTER LXIV

statute. The parliament, without taking offence at this declaration, repealed the law; and in lieu of all the securities, formerly provided, satisfied themselves with a general clause, "that parliaments should not be interrupted above three years at the most." As the English parliament had now raised itself to be a regular check and controul upon royal power; it is evident, that they ought still to have preserved a regular security for their meeting, and not have trusted entirely to the good-will of the king, who, if ambitious or enterprising, had so little reason to be pleased with these assemblies. Before the end of Charles's reign, the nation had occasion to feel very sensibly the effects of this repeal.

By the act of uniformity, every clergyman, who should officiate without being properly qualified, was punishable by fine and imprisonment: But this security was not thought sufficient for the church. It was now enacted, that, wherever five persons above those of the same household, should assemble in a religious congregation, every one of them was liable, for the first offence, to be imprisoned three months, or pay five pounds; for the second, to be imprisoned six months, or pay ten pounds; and for the third to be transported seven years, or pay a hundred pounds. The parliament had only in their eye the malignity of the sectaries: They should have carried their attention farther, to the chief cause of that malignity, the restraint under which they laboured.

The commons likewise passed a vote, that the wrongs, dishonours, and indignities, offered to the English by the subjects of the United Provinces, were the greatest obstructions to all foreign trade: And they promised to assist the king with their lives and fortunes in asserting the rights of his crown against all opposition whatsoever. This was the first open step towards a Dutch war. We must explain the causes and motives of this measure.

That close union and confederacy, which, during a course of *Rupture* near seventy-years, has subsisted, almost without interruption or *with* jealousy, between England and Holland, is not so much founded *Holland.* on the natural unalterable interests of these states, as on their terror of the growing power of the French monarch, who, without their combination, it is apprehended, would soon extend his dominion over Europe. In the first years of Charles's reign, when the ambitious genius of Lewis had not, as yet, displayed itself; and when the great force of his people was, in some measure, unknown even to themselves, the rivalship of commerce, not checked by any other jealousy or apprehension, had in England begotten a violent enmity against the neighbouring republic.

Trade was beginning, among the English, to be a matter of general concern; but notwithstanding all their efforts and advantages, their commerce seemed hitherto to stand upon a footing, which was somewhat precarious. The Dutch, who, by industry and frugality, were enabled to undersell them in every market, retained possession of the most lucrative branches of commerce; and the English merchants had the mortification to find, that all attempts to extend their trade were still turned, by the vigilance of their rivals, to their loss and dishonour. Their indignation encreased, when they considered the superior naval power of England; the bravery of her officers and seamen; her favourable situation, which enabled her to intercept the whole Dutch commerce. By the prospect of these advantages, they were strongly prompted, from motives less just than political, to make war upon the States; and at once to ravish from them by force, what they could not obtain, or could obtain but slowly, by superior skill and industry.

The careless, unambitious temper of Charles rendered him little capable of forming so vast a project as that of engrossing the commerce and naval power of Europe; yet could he not remain altogether insensible to such obvious and such tempting prospects. His genius, happily turned towards mechanics, had inclined him to study naval affairs, which, of all branches of business, he both loved the most, and understood the best. Though the Dutch, during his exile, had expressed towards him more civility and friendship, than he had received from any other foreign power; the Louvestein or aristocratic faction, which, at this time, ruled the commonwealth, had fallen into close union with France; and could that party be subdued, he might hope, that his nephew, the young prince of Orange, would be re-instated in the authority, possessed by his ancestors, and would bring the States to a dependence under England. His narrow revenues made it still requisite for him to study the humours of his people, which now ran violently towards war; and it has been suspected, though the suspicion was not justified by the event, that the hopes of diverting some of the supplies to his private use were not overlooked by this necessitous monarch.

CHAPTER LXIV

The duke of York, more active and enterprizing, pushed more eagerly the war with Holland. He desired an opportunity of distinguishing himself: He loved to cultivate commerce: He was at the head of a new African company, whose trade was extremely checked by the settlements of the Dutch: And perhaps, the religious prejudices, by which that prince was always so much governed, began, even so early, to instil into him an antipathy against a protestant commonwealth, the bulwark of the reformation. Clarendon and Southampton, observing that the nation was not supported by any foreign alliance, were averse to hostilities; but their credit was now on the decline.

By these concurring motives, the court and parliament were *17th May.* both of them inclined to a Dutch war. The parliament was prorogued without voting supplies: But as they had been induced, without any open application from the crown, to pass that vote above-mentioned against the Dutch encroachments, it was reasonably considered as sufficient sanction for the vigorous measures, which were resolved on.

Downing, the English minister at the Hague, a man of an insolent, impetuous temper, presented a memorial to the States, containing a list of those depredations, of which the English complained. It is remarkable, that all the pretended depredations preceded the year 1662, when a treaty of league and alliance had been renewed with the Dutch; and these complaints were then thought either so ill grounded or so frivolous, that they had not been mentioned in the treaty. Two ships alone, the Bonaventure and the Good-hope, had been claimed by the English; and it was agreed, that the claim should be prosecuted by the ordinary course of justice. The States had consigned a sum of money, in case the cause should be decided against them; but the matter was still in dependance. Cary, who was entrusted by the proprietors with the management of the law-suit for the Bonaventure, had resolved to accept of thirty thousand pounds, which were offered him; but was hindered by Downing, who told him, that the claim was a matter of state between the two nations, not a concern of private persons.[d] These circumstances give us no favourable idea of the justice of the English pretensions.

[d] Temple, vol. ii. p. 42.

Charles confined not himself to memorials and remonstrances. Sir Robert Holmes was secretly dispatched with a squadron of twenty-two ships to the coast of Africa. He not only expelled the Dutch from cape Corse, to which the English had some pretensions: He likewise seized the Dutch settlements of cape Verde and the isle of Goree, together with several ships trading on that coast. And having sailed to America, he possessed himself of Nova Belgia, since called New York; a territory, which James the first had given by patent to the earl of Stirling, but which had never been planted but by the Hollanders. When the States complained of these hostile measures, the king, unwilling to avow what he could not well justify, pretended to be totally ignorant of Holmes's enterprize. He likewise confined that admiral to the Tower; but some time after released him.

The Dutch, finding that their applications for redress were likely to be eluded, and that a ground of quarrel was industriously sought for by the English, began to arm with diligence. They even exerted, with some precipitation, an act of vigour, which hastened on the rupture. Sir John Lawson and de Ruyter had been sent with combined squadrons into the Mediterranean, in order to chastise the pyratical states on the coast of Barbary; and the time of their separation and return was now approaching. The States secretly dispatched orders to de Ruyter, that he should take in provisions at Cadiz; and sailing towards the coast of Guinea, should retaliate on the English, and put the Dutch in possession of those settlements whence Holmes had expelled them. De Ruyter, having a considerable force on board, met with no opposition in Guinea. All the new acquisitions of the English, except cape Corse, were recovered from them. They were even dispossessed of some old settlements. Such of their ships as fell into his hands were seized by de Ruyter. That admiral sailed next to America. He attacked Barbadoes, but was repulsed. He afterwards committed hostilities on Long Island.

Meanwhile, the English preparations for war were advancing with vigor and industry. The king had received no supplies from parliament; but by his own funds and credit he was enabled to equip a fleet: The city of London lent him 100,000 pounds: The spirit of the nation seconded his armaments: He himself went from port to port, inspecting with great diligence, and encour-

CHAPTER LXIV

aging the work: And in a little time the English navy was put in a formidable condition. Eight hundred thousand pounds are said to have been expended on this armament. When Lawson arrived, and communicated his suspicion of de Ruyter's enterprize, orders were issued for seizing all Dutch ships; and 135 fell into the hands of the English. These were not declared prizes, till afterwards, when war was proclaimed.

The parliament, when it met, granted a supply, the largest by far that had ever been given to a king of England, yet scarcely sufficient for the present undertaking. Near two millions and a half were voted, to be levied by quarterly payments in three years. The avidity of the merchants, together with the great prospect of success, had animated the whole nation against the Dutch.

24th Nov. A new session.

A great alteration was made this session in the method of taxing the clergy. In almost all the other monarchies of Europe, the assemblies, whose consent was formerly requisite to the enacting of laws, were composed of three estates, the clergy, the nobility, and the commonalty, which formed so many members of the political body, of which the king was considered as the head. In England too, the parliament was always represented as consisting of three estates; but their separation was never so distinct as in other kingdoms. A convocation, however, had usually sitten at the same time with the parliament; though they possessed not a negative voice in the passing of laws, and assumed no other temporal power than that of imposing taxes on the clergy. By reason of ecclesiastical preferments, which he could bestow, the king's influence over the church was more considerable than over the laity; so that the subsidies, granted by the convocation, were commonly greater than those which were voted by parliament. The church, therefore, was not displeased to depart tacitly from the right of taxing herself, and allow the commons to lay impositions on ecclesiastical revenues, as on the rest of the kingdom. In recompence, two subsidies, which the convocation had formerly granted, were remitted, and the parochial clergy were allowed to vote at elections. Thus the church of England made a barter of power for profit. Their convocations, having become insignificant to the crown, have been much disused of late years.

The Dutch saw, with the utmost regret, a war approaching, whence they might dread the most fatal consequences, but which

afforded no prospect of advantage. They tried every art of negotiation, before they would come to extremities. Their measures
were at that time directed by John de Wit, a minister equally
eminent for greatness of mind, for capacity, and for integrity.
Though moderate in his private deportment, he knew how to
adopt in his public counsels that magnanimity, which suits the
minister of a great state. It was ever his maxim, that no independent government should yield to another any evident point of
reason or equity; and that all such concessions, so far from preventing war, served to no other purpose than to provoke fresh
claims and insults. By his management a spirit of union was preserved in all the provinces; great sums were levied; and a navy was
equipped, composed of larger ships than the Dutch had ever built
before, and able to cope with the fleet of England.

1665.
22d Feb.

As soon as certain intelligence arrived of de Ruyter's enterprizes, Charles declared war against the States. His fleet, consisting
of 114 sail, besides fire-ships and ketches, was commanded by the
duke of York, and under him by prince Rupert and the earl of

3d June.
Victory
of the
English.

Sandwich. It had about 22,000 men on board. Obdam, who was
admiral of the Dutch navy, of nearly equal force, declined not the
combat. In the heat of action, when engaged in close fight with the
duke of York, Obdam's ship blew up. This accident much discouraged the Dutch, who fled towards their own coast. Tromp alone,
son of the famous admiral, killed during the former war, bravely
sustained with his squadron the efforts of the English, and protected the rear of his countrymen. The vanquished had nineteen
ships sunk and taken. The victors lost only one. Sir John Lawson
died soon after of his wounds.

It is affirmed, and with an appearance of reason, that this
victory might have been rendered more complete, had not orders
been issued to slacken sail by Brounker, one of the duke's bed-
chamber, who pretended authority from his master. The duke
disclaimed the orders; but Brounker never was sufficiently punished for his temerity.[e] It is allowed, however, that the duke be-

---

[e] King James in his Memoirs gives an account of this affair different from
what we meet with in any historian. He says, that, while he was asleep,
Brounker brought orders to Sir John Harman, captain of the ship, to
slacken sail. Sir John remonstrated, but obeyed. After some time, finding
that his falling back was likely to produce confusion in the fleet, he hoisted

CHAPTER LXIV

haved with great bravery during the action. He was long in the thickest of the fire. The earl of Falmouth, lord Muskerry, and Mr. Boyle, were killed by one shot at his side, and covered him all over with their brains and gore. And it is not likely, that, in a pursuit, where even persons of inferior station, and of the most cowardly disposition, acquire courage, a commander should feel his spirits to flag, and should turn from the back of an enemy, whose face he had not been afraid to encounter.

This disaster threw the Dutch into consternation, and determined de Wit, who was the soul of their councils, to exert his military capacity, in order to support the declining courage of his countrymen. He went on board the fleet, which he took under his command; and he soon remedied all those disorders, which had been occasioned by the late misfortune. The genius of this man was of the most extensive nature. He quickly became as much master of naval affairs, as if he had from his infancy been educated in them; and he even made improvements in some parts of pilotage and sailing, beyond what men expert in those arts had ever been able to attain.

The misfortunes of the Dutch determined their allies to act for their assistance and support. The king of France was engaged in a defensive alliance with the States; but as his naval force was yet in its infancy, he was extremely averse, at that time, from entering into a war with so formidable a power as England. He long tried to mediate a peace between the states, and for that purpose sent an embassy to London, which returned without effecting any thing. Lord Hollis, the English ambassador at Paris, endeavoured to draw over Lewis to the side of England; and, in his master's name, made him the most tempting offers. Charles was content to abandon all the Spanish Low Countries to the French, without pretending to

Rupture with France.

---

the sail as before: So that the prince coming soon after on the quarter deck, and finding all things as he left them, knew nothing of what had passed during his repose. No body gave him the least intimation of it. It was long after, that he heard of it, by a kind of accident; and he intended to have punished Brounker by martial law; but just about that time, the house of commons took up the question and impeached him, which made it impossible for the duke to punish him otherwise than by dismissing him his service. Brounker, before the house, never pretended, that he had received any orders from the duke.

a foot of ground for himself; provided Lewis would allow him to pursue his advantages against the Dutch.*f* But the French monarch, though the conquest of that valuable territory was the chief object of his ambition, rejected the offer as contrary to his interests: He thought, that if the English had once established an uncontroulable dominion over the sea and over commerce, they would soon be able to render his acquisitions a dear purchase to him. When de Lionne, the French secretary, assured Van Beuninghen, ambassador of the States, that this offer had been pressed on his master during six months, "I can readily believe it," replied the Dutchman; "I am sensible that it is the interest of England."*g*

Such were the established maxims at that time with regard to the interests of princes. It must however be allowed, that the politics of Charles, in making this offer, were not a little hazardous. The extreme weakness of Spain would have rendered the French conquests easy and infallible; but the vigour of the Dutch, it might be foreseen, would make the success of the English much more precarious. And even were the naval force of Holland totally annihilated, the acquisition of the Dutch commerce to England could not be relied on as a certain consequence; nor is trade a constant attendant of power, but depends on many other, and some of them very delicate, circumstances.

Though the king of France was resolved to support the Hollanders in that unequal contest, in which they were engaged; he yet protracted his declaration, and employed the time in naval preparations, both in the ocean and the Mediterranean. The king of Denmark mean while was resolved not to remain an idle spectator of the contest between the maritime powers. The part which he acted was the most extraordinary: He made a secret agreement with Charles to seize all the Dutch ships in his harbours, and to share the spoils with the English, provided they would assist him in executing this measure. In order to encrease his prey, he perfidiously invited the Dutch to take shelter in his ports; and accordingly the East India fleet, very richly laden, had put into Bergen. Sandwich, who now commanded the English navy (the duke having gone ashore) dispatched Sir Thomas Tiddiman with a squad-

---

f D'Estrades, 19th of December, 1664.   *g* D'Estrades, 14th August, 1665.

ron to attack them; but whether from the king of Denmark's delay in sending orders to the governor, or, what is more probable, from his avidity in endeavouring to engross the whole booty, the English admiral, though he behaved with great bravery, failed of his purpose. The Danish governor fired upon him; and the Dutch, having had leisure to fortify themselves, made a gallant resistance.

3d August.

The king of Denmark, seemingly ashamed of his conduct, concluded with Sir Gilbert Talbot, the English envoy, an offensive alliance against the States; and at the very same time, his resident at the Hague, by his orders, concluded an offensive alliance against England. To this latter alliance he adhered, probably from jealousy of the encreasing naval power of England; and he seized and confiscated all the English ships in his harbours. This was a sensible check to the advantages, which Charles had obtained over the Dutch. Not only a blow was given to the English commerce; the king of Denmark's naval force was also considerable, and threatened every moment a conjunction with the Hollanders. That prince stipulated to assist his ally with a fleet of thirty sail; and he received in return a yearly subsidy of 1,500,000 crowns, of which 300,000 were paid by France.

Rupture with Denmark.

The king endeavoured to counterbalance these confederacies by acquiring new friends and allies. He had dispatched Sir Richard Fanshaw into Spain, who met with a very cold reception. That monarchy was sunk into a state of weakness, and was menaced with an invasion from France; yet could not any motive prevail with Philip to enter into cordial friendship with England. Charles's alliance with Portugal, the detention of Jamaica and Tangiers, the sale of Dunkirk to the French; all these offences sunk so deep in the mind of the Spanish monarch, that no motive of interest was sufficient to outweigh them.

The bishop of Munster was the only ally that Charles could acquire. This prelate, a man of restless enterprize and ambition, had entertained a violent animosity against the States; and he was easily engaged, by the promise of subsidies from England, to make an incursion on that republic. With a tumultuary army of near 20,000 men, he invaded her territories, and met with weak resistance. The land forces of the States were as feeble and ill-governed, as their fleets were gallant and formidable. But after his committing great ravages in several of the provinces, a stop was put to the progress of this warlike prelate. He had not military skill sufficient to improve the advantages which fortune had put into his hands: The king of France sent a body of 6000 men to oppose him: Subsidies were not regularly remitted him from England; and many of his troops deserted for want of pay: The elector of Brandenburgh threatened him with an invasion in his own state: And on the whole, he was glad to conclude a peace under the mediation of France. On the first surmise of his intentions, Sir William Temple was sent from London with money to fix him in his former alliance; but found, that he arrived too late.

The Dutch, encouraged by all these favourable circumstances, continued resolute to exert themselves to the utmost in their own defence. De Ruyter, their great admiral, was arrived from his expedition to Guinea: Their Indian fleet was come home in safety: Their harbours were crowded with merchant ships: Faction at home was appeased: The young prince of Orange had put himself under the tuition of the States of Holland, and of de Wit, their pensionary, who executed his trust with honour and fidelity: And the animosity, which the Hollanders entertained against the attack of the English, so unprovoked, as they thought it, made them thirst for revenge, and hope for better success in their next enterprize. Such vigour was exerted in the common cause, that, in order to man the fleet, all merchant ships were prohibited to sail, and even the fisheries were suspended.[h]

The English likewise continued in the same disposition, though another more grievous calamity had joined itself to that of war. *10th Octob.* The plague had broken out in London; and that with such violence as to cut off, in a year, near 90,000 inhabitants. The king was obliged to summon the parliament at Oxford.

New session. A good agreement still subsisted between the king and parliament. They, on their part, unanimously voted him the supply demanded, twelve hundred and fifty thousand pounds, to be levied in two years by monthly assessments. And he, to gratify them; *Five-mile-act.* passed the five-mile-act, which has given occasion to grievous and not unjust complaints. The church, under pretence of guarding monarchy against its inveterate enemies, persevered in the project of wreaking her own enmity against the nonconformists. It was

[h] Tromp's life. D'Estrades, 5th of February 1665.

CHAPTER LXIV

enacted, that no dissenting teacher, who took not the non-resistance oath above mentioned, should, except upon the road, come within five miles of any corporation, or of any place, where he had preached after the act of oblivion. The penalty was a fine of fifty pounds, and six months imprisonment. By ejecting the nonconforming clergy from their churches, and prohibiting all separate congregations, they had been rendered incapable of gaining any livelihood by their spiritual profession. And now, under colour of removing them from places, where their influence might be dangerous, an expedient was fallen upon to deprive them of all means of subsistence. Had not the spirit of the nation undergone a change, these violences were preludes to the most furious persecution.

However prevalent the hierarchy, this law did not pass without opposition. Besides several peers, attached to the old parliamentary party, Southampton himself, though Clarendon's great friend, expressed his disapprobation of these measures. But the church party, not discouraged with this opposition, introduced into the house of commons a bill for imposing the oath of non-resistance on the whole nation. It was rejected only by three voices. The parliament, after a short session, was prorogued.

31st Octob.

After France had declared war, England was evidently over-matched in force. Yet she possessed this advantage by her situation, that she lay between the fleets of her enemies, and might be able, by speedy and well-concerted operations, to prevent their junction. But such was the unhappy conduct of her commanders, or such the want of intelligence in her ministers, that this circumstance turned rather to her prejudice. Lewis had given orders to the duke of Beaufort, his admiral, to sail from Toulon; and the French squadron, under his command, consisting of above forty sail,[i] was now commonly supposed to be entering the channel. The Dutch fleet, to the number of seventy-six sail, was at sea, under the command of de Ruyter and Tromp, in order to join him. The duke of Albemarle and prince Rupert commanded the English fleet, which exceeded not seventy-four sail. Albemarle, who, from his successes under the protector, had too much learned to despise the enemy, proposed to detach prince Rupert with twenty ships, in

1666.

[i] D'Estrades, 21st of May 1666.

order to oppose the duke of Beaufort. Sir George Ayscue, well acquainted with the bravery and conduct of de Ruyter, protested against the temerity of this resolution: But Albemarle's authority prevailed. The remainder of the English set sail to give battle to the Dutch; who, seeing the enemy advance quickly upon them, cut their cables, and prepared for the combat. The battle that ensued, is one of the most memorable, that we read of in story; whether we consider its long duration, or the desperate courage, with which it was fought. Albemarle made here some atonement by his valour for the rashness of the attempt. No youth, animated by glory and ambitious hopes, could exert himself more than did this man, who was now in the decline of life, and who had reached the summit of honours. We shall not enter minutely into particulars. It will be sufficient to mention the chief events of each day's engagement.

Sea fight of four days.

1st June.

In the first day, Sir William Berkeley, vice-admiral, leading the van, fell into the thickest of the enemy, was overpowered, and his ship taken. He himself was found dead in his cabin, all covered with blood. The English had the weather-gage of the enemy; but as the wind blew so hard, that they could not use their lower tire, they derived but small advantage from this circumstance. The Dutch shot, however, fell chiefly on their sails and rigging; and few ships were sunk or much damaged. Chain-shot was at that time a new invention; commonly attributed to de Wit. Sir John Harman exerted himself extremely on this day. The Dutch admiral, Evertz, was killed in engaging him. Darkness parted the combatants.

The second day, the wind was somewhat fallen, and the combat became more steady and more terrible. The English now found, that the greatest valour cannot compensate the superiority of numbers, against an enemy who is well conducted, and who is not defective in courage. De Ruyter and Van Tromp, rivals in glory and enemies from faction, exerted themselves in emulation of each other; and de Ruyter had the advantage of disengaging and saving his antagonist, who had been surrounded by the English, and was in the most imminent danger. Sixteen fresh ships joined the Dutch fleet during the action: And the English were so shattered, that their fighting ships were reduced to twenty-eight, and they found themselves obliged to retreat towards their own coast. The Dutch followed them, and were on the point of renewing the combat; when a calm, which came a little before night, prevented the engagement.

CHAPTER LXIV

Next morning, the English were obliged to continue their retreat; and a proper disposition was made for that purpose. The shattered ships were ordered to stretch ahead; and sixteen of the most entire followed them in good order, and kept the enemy in awe. Albemarle himself closed the rear, and presented an undaunted countenance to his victorious foes. The earl of Ossory, son of Ormond, a gallant youth, who sought honour and experience in every action throughout Europe, was then on board the admiral. Albemarle confessed to him his intention rather to blow up his ship and perish gloriously, than yield to the enemy. Ossory applauded this desperate resolution.

About two o'clock, the Dutch had come up with their enemy, and were ready to renew the fight; when a new fleet was descried from the south, crowding all their sail to reach the scene of action. The Dutch flattered themselves that Beaufort was arrived, to cut off the retreat of the vanquished: The English hoped, that prince Rupert had come, to turn the scale of action. Albemarle, who had received intelligence of the prince's approach, bent his course towards him. Unhappily, Sir George Ayscue, in a ship of a hundred guns, the largest in the fleet, struck on the Galloper sands, and could receive no assistance from his friends, who were hastening to join the reinforcement. He could not even reap the consolation of perishing with honour, and revenging his death on his enemies. They were preparing fireships to attack him, and he was obliged to strike. The English sailors, seeing the necessity, with the utmost indignation surrendered themselves prisoners.

Albemarle and prince Rupert were now determined to face the enemy; and next morning the battle began afresh, with more equal force than ever, and with equal valour. After long cannonading, the fleets came to a close combat; which was continued with great violence, till parted by a mist. The English retired first into their harbours.

Though the English, by their obstinate courage, reaped the chief honour in this engagement, it is somewhat uncertain, who obtained the victory. The Hollanders took a few ships; and having some appearances of advantage, expressed their satisfaction by all the signs of triumph and rejoicing. But as the English fleet was repaired in a little time, and put to sea more formidable than ever, together with many of those ships, which the Dutch had boasted to have burned or destroyed; all Europe saw, that those two brave nations were engaged in a contest, which was not likely, on either side, to prove decisive.

It was the conjunction alone of the French, that could give a decisive superiority to the Dutch. In order to facilitate this conjunction, de Ruyter, having repaired his fleet, posted himself at the mouth of the Thames. The English, under prince Rupert and Albemarle, were not long in coming to the attack. The numbers of each fleet amounted to about eighty sail; and the valour and experience of the commanders, as well as of the seamen, rendered the engagement fierce and obstinate. Sir Thomas Allen, who commanded the white squadron of the English, attacked the Dutch van, which he entirely routed; and he killed the three admirals who commanded it. Van Tromp engaged Sir Jeremy Smith; and during the heat of action, he was separated from de Ruyter and the main body, whether by accident or design was never certainly known. De Ruyter, with conduct and valour, maintained the combat against the main body of the English; and though overpowered by numbers, kept his station, till night ended the engagement. Next day, finding the Dutch fleet scattered and discouraged, his high spirit submitted to a retreat, which yet he conducted with such skill, as to render it equally honourable to himself as the greatest victory. Full of indignation however at yielding the superiority to the enemy, he frequently exclaimed, "My God! what a wretch am I? among so many thousand bullets, is there not one to put an end to my miserable life?" One de Witte, his son-in-law, who stood near, exhorted him, since he sought death, to turn upon the English, and render his life a dear purchase to the victors. But de Ruyter esteemed it more worthy a brave man to persevere to the uttermost, and, as long as possible, to render service to his country. All that night and next day, the English pressed upon the rear of the Dutch; and it was chiefly by the redoubled efforts of de Ruyter, that the latter saved themselves in their harbours.

The loss, sustained by the Hollanders in this action, was not very considerable; but as violent animosities had broken out between the two admirals, who engaged all the officers on one side or other, the consternation, which took place, was great among the provinces. Tromp's commission was at last taken from him; but though several captains had misbehaved, they were so effectually protected by their friends in the magistracy of the towns, that most

25th July. Victory of the English.

CHAPTER LXIV

of them escaped punishment, many were still continued in their commands.

The English now rode incontestible masters of the sea, and insulted the Dutch in their harbours. A detachment under Holmes was sent into the road of Vlie, and burned a hundred and forty merchantmen, two men of war, together with Brandaris, a large and rich village on the coast. The Dutch merchants, who lost by this enterprize, uniting themselves to the Orange faction, exclaimed against an administration, which, they pretended, had brought such disgrace and ruin on their country. None but the firm and intrepid mind of de Wit could have supported itself under such a complication of calamities.

The king of France, apprehensive that the Dutch would sink under their misfortunes; at least, that de Wit, his friend, might be dispossessed of the administration, hastened the advance of the duke of Beaufort. The Dutch fleet likewise was again equipped; and under the command of de Ruyter, cruised near the straits of Dover. Prince Rupert with the English navy, now stronger than ever, came full sail upon them. The Dutch admiral thought proper to decline the combat, and retired into St. John's road near Bulloigne. Here he sheltered himself, both from the English, and from a furious storm, which arose. Prince Rupert too was obliged to retire into St. Helens; where he stayed some time, in order to repair the damages, which he had sustained. Mean while the duke of Beaufort proceeded up the channel, and passed the English fleet unperceived; but he did not find the Dutch, as he expected. De Ruyter had been seized with a fever: Many of the chief officers had fallen into sickness: A contagious distemper was spread through the fleet: And the States thought it necessary to recall them into their harbours, before the enemy should be refitted. The French king, anxious for his navy, which, with so much care and industry, he had lately built, dispatched orders to Beaufort, to make the best of his way to Brest. That admiral had again the good fortune to pass the English. One ship alone, the Ruby, fell into the hands of the enemy.

While the war continued without any decisive success on either side, a calamity happened in London, which threw the people into great consternation. Fire, breaking out in a baker's house near the bridge, spread itself on all sides with such rapidity, that no efforts

3d Sept.
Fire of London.

could extinguish it, till it laid in ashes a considerable part of the city. The inhabitants, without being able to provide effectually for their relief, were reduced to be spectators of their own ruin; and were pursued from street to street by the flames, which unexpectedly gathered round them. Three days and nights did the fire advance; and it was only by the blowing up of houses, that it was at last extinguished. The king and duke used their utmost endeavours to stop the progress of the flames; but all their industry was unsuccessful. About four hundred streets, and thirteen thousand houses were reduced to ashes.

The causes of this calamity were evident. The narrow streets of London, the houses built entirely of wood, the dry season, and a violent east wind which blew; these were so many concurring circumstances, which rendered it easy to assign the reason of the destruction that ensued. But the people were not satisfied with this obvious account. Prompted by blind rage, some ascribed the guilt to the republicans, others to the catholics; though it is not easy to conceive how the burning of London could serve the purposes of either party. As the papists were the chief objects of public detestation, the rumour, which threw the guilt on them, was more favourably received by the people. No proof however, or even presumption, after the strictest enquiry by a committee of parliament, ever appeared to authorize such a calumny; yet in order to give countenance to the popular prejudice, the inscription, engraved by authority on the monument, ascribed this calamity to that hated sect. This clause was erazed by order of king James, when he came to the throne; but after the revolution it was replaced. So credulous, as well as obstinate, are the people, in believing every thing, which flatters their prevailing passion!

The fire of London, though at that time a great calamity, has proved in the issue beneficial both to the city and the kingdom. The city was rebuilt in a very little time; and care was taken to make the streets wider and more regular than before. A discretionary power was assumed by the king to regulate the distribution of the buildings, and to forbid the use of lath and timber, the materials, of which the houses were formerly composed. The necessity was so urgent, and the occasion so extraordinary, that no exceptions were taken at an exercise of authority, which otherwise might have been deemed illegal. Had the king been enabled to carry his power still

CHAPTER LXIV

farther, and made the houses be rebuilt with perfect regularity, and entirely upon one plan; he had much contributed to the convenience, as well as embellishment of the city. Great advantages, however, have resulted from the alterations; though not carried to the full length. London became much more healthy after the fire. The plague, which used to break out with great fury twice or thrice every century, and indeed was always lurking in some corner or other of the city, has scarcely ever appeared since that calamity.

The parliament met soon after, and gave the sanction of law to those regulations made by royal authority; as well as appointed commissioners for deciding all such questions of property, as might arise from the fire. They likewise voted a supply of 1,800,000 pounds to be levied, partly by a poll-bill, partly by assessments. Though their enquiry brought out no proofs, which could fix on the papists the burning of London, the general aversion against that sect still prevailed; and complaints were made, probably without much foundation, of its dangerous encrease. Charles, at the desire of the commons, issued a proclamation for the banishment of all priests and jesuits; but the bad execution of this, as well as of former edicts, destroyed all confidence in his sincerity, whenever he pretended an aversion towards the catholic religion. Whether suspicions of this nature had diminished the king's popularity, is uncertain; but it appears, that the supply was voted much later than Charles expected, or even than the public necessities seemed to require. The intrigues of the duke of Buckingham, a man who wanted only steadiness to render him extremely dangerous, had somewhat embarrassed the measures of the court: And this was the first time that the king found any considerable reason to complain of a failure of confidence in this house of commons. The rising symptoms of ill humour tended, no doubt, to quicken the steps, which were already making towards a peace with foreign enemies.

Charles began to be sensible, that all the ends, for which the war had been undertaken, were likely to prove entirely abortive. The Dutch, even when single, had defended themselves with vigor, and were every day improving in their military skill and preparations. Though their trade had suffered extremely, their extensive credit enabled them to levy great sums; and while the seamen of England loudly complained of want of pay, the Dutch navy was regularly

Advances towards peace.

1667.

supplied with money and every thing requisite for its subsistence. As two powerful kings now supported them, every place, from the extremity of Norway to the coasts of Bayonne, was become hostile to the English. And Charles, neither fond of action, nor stimulated by any violent ambition, earnestly fought for means of restoring tranquillity to his people, disgusted with a war, which, being joined with the plague and fire, had proved so fruitless and destructive.

The first advances towards an accommodation were made by England. When the king sent for the body of Sir William Berkeley, he insinuated to the States his desire of peace on reasonable terms; and their answer corresponded in the same amicable intentions. Charles, however, to maintain the appearance of superiority, still insisted, that the States should treat at London; and they agreed to make him this compliment so far as concerned themselves: But being engaged in alliance with two crowned heads, they could not, they said, prevail with these to depart in that respect from their dignity. On a sudden, the king went so far on the other side as to offer the sending of ambassadors to the Hague; but this proposal, which seemed honourable to the Dutch, was meant only to divide and distract them, by affording the English an opportunity to carry on cabals with the disaffected party. The offer was therefore rejected; and conferences were secretly held in the queen-mother's apartments at Paris, where the pretensions of both parties were discussed. The Dutch made equitable proposals, either that all things should be restored to the same condition in which they stood before the war; or that both parties should continue in possession of their present acquisitions. Charles accepted of the latter proposal; and almost every thing was adjusted, except the disputes with regard to the isle of Polerone. This island lies in the East Indies, and was formerly valuable for its produce of spices. The English had been masters of it; but were dispossessed at the time when the violences were committed against them at Amboyna. Cromwel had stipulated to have it restored; and the Hollanders, having first entirely destroyed all the spice trees, maintained, that they had executed the treaty, but that the English had been anew expelled during the course of the war. Charles renewed his pretensions to this island; and as the reasons on both sides began to multiply, and seemed to require a long discussion, it was agreed to transfer the treaty to some other place; and Charles made choice of Breda.

CHAPTER LXIV

Lord Hollis and Henry Coventry were the English ambassadors. They immediately desired, that a suspension of arms should be agreed to, till the several claims could be adjusted: But this proposal, seemingly so natural, was rejected by the credit of de Wit. That penetrating and active minister, thoroughly acquainted with the characters of princes and the situation of affairs, had discovered an opportunity of striking a blow, which might at once restore to the Dutch the honour lost during the war, and severely revenge those injuries, which he ascribed to the wanton ambition and injustice of the English.

Whatever projects might have been formed by Charles for secreting the money granted him by parliament, he had hitherto failed in his intention. The expences of such vast armaments had exhausted all the supplies;[k] and even a great debt was contracted to the seamen. The king therefore was resolved to save, as far as possible, the last supply of 1,800,000 pounds; and to employ it for payment of his debts, as well those which had been occasioned by the war, as those which he had formerly contracted. He observed, that the Dutch had been with great reluctance forced into the war, and that the events of it were not such as to inspire them with great desire of its continuance. The French, he knew, had been engaged into hostilities by no other motive than that of supporting their ally; and were now more desirous than ever of putting an end to the quarrel. The differences between the parties were so inconsiderable, that the conclusion of peace appeared infallible; and nothing but forms, at least some vain points of honour, seemed to remain for the ambassadors at Breda to discuss. In this situation, Charles, moved by an ill-timed frugality, remitted his preparations, and exposed England to one of the greatest affronts, which it has ever received. Two small squadrons alone were equipped; and during a war with such potent and martial enemies, every thing was left almost in the same situation as in times of the most profound tranquillity.

De Wit protracted the negotiations at Breda, and hastened the

[k] The Dutch had spent on the war near 40 millions of livres a year, above three millions sterling: A much greater sum than had been granted by the English parliament. D'Estrades, 24th of December, 1665; 1st of January, 1666. Temple, vol. i. p. 71. It was probably the want of money which engaged the king to pay the seamen with tickets; a contrivance which proved so much to their loss.

naval preparations. The Dutch fleet appeared in the Thames under the command of de Ruyter, and threw the English into the utmost consternation. A chain had been drawn across the river Medway; some fortifications had been added to Sheerness and Upnore castle: But all these preparations were unequal to the present necessity. Sheerness was soon taken; nor could it be saved by the valour of Sir Edward Sprague, who defended it. Having the advantage of a spring tide, and an easterly wind, the Dutch pressed *10th June.* on, and broke the chain, though fortified by some ships, which had *Disgrace* been there sunk by orders of the duke of Albemarle. They burned *at* the three ships, which lay to guard the chain, the Matthias, the *Chatham.* Unity, and the Charles the Fifth. After damaging several vessels, and possessing themselves of the hull of the Royal Charles, which the English had burned, they advanced with six men of war, and five fire-ships, as far as Upnore castle, where they burned the Royal Oak, the Loyal London, and the Great James. Captain Douglas, who commanded on board the Royal Oak, perished in the flames, though he had an easy opportunity of escaping. "Never was it known," he said, "that a Douglas had left his post without orders."[l] The Hollanders fell down the Medway without receiving any considerable damage; and it was apprehended, that they might next tide sail up the Thames, and extend their hostilities even to the bridge of London. Nine ships were sunk at Woolwich, four at Blackwall: Platforms were raised in many places, furnished with artillery: The train bands were called out; and every place was in a violent agitation. The Dutch sailed next to Portsmouth, where they made a fruitless attempt: They met with no better success at Plymouth: They insulted Harwich: They sailed again up the Thames as far as Tilbury, where they were repulsed. The whole coast was in alarm; and had the French thought proper at this time to join the Dutch fleet, and to invade England, consequences the most fatal might justly have been apprehended. But Lewis had no intention to push the victory to such extremities. His interest required, that a balance should be kept between the two maritime powers; not that an uncontrouled superiority should be given to either.

Great indignation prevailed amongst the English, to see an

---

[l] Temple, vol. ii. p. 41.

enemy, whom they regarded as inferior, whom they had expected totally to subdue, and over whom they had gained many honourable advantages, now of a sudden ride undisputed masters of the ocean, burn their ships in their very harbours, fill every place with confusion, and strike a terror into the capital itself. But though the cause of all these disasters could be ascribed neither to bad fortune, to the misconduct of admirals, nor to the ill-behaviour of seamen, but solely to the avarice, at least to the improvidence, of the government; no dangerous symptoms of discontent appeared, and no attempt for an insurrection was made by any of those numerous sectaries, who had been so openly branded for their rebellious principles, and who upon that supposition had been treated with such severity.[m]

In the present distress, two expedients were embraced: An army of 12,000 men was suddenly levied; and the parliament, though it lay under prorogation, was summoned to meet. The houses were very thin; and the only vote, which the commons passed, was an address for breaking the army; which was complied with. This expression of jealousy shewed the court what they might expect from that assembly; and it was thought more prudent to prorogue them till next winter.

But the signing of the treaty at Breda extricated the king from his present difficulties. The English ambassadors received orders to recede from those demands, which, however frivolous in themselves, could not now be relinquished, without acknowledging a superiority in the enemy. Polerone remained with the Dutch; satisfaction for the ships, Bonaventure and Goodhope, the pretended grounds of the quarrel, was no longer insisted on; Acadie was yielded to the French. The acquisition of New-York, a settlement so important by its situation, was the chief advantage which the English reaped from a war, in which the national character of bravery had shone out with lustre, but where the misconduct of the government, especially in the conclusion, had been no less apparent. *10th July. Peace of Breda.*

To appease the people by some sacrifice seemed requisite be-

[m] Some nonconformists however, both in Scotland and England, had kept a correspondence with the States, and had entertained projects for insurrections, but they were too weak even to attempt the execution of them. D'Estrades, 13th October, 1665.

*Clar-
endon's
fall.*

fore the meeting of parliament; and the prejudices of the nation pointed out the victim. The chancellor was at this time much exposed to the hatred of the public, and of every party, which divided the nation. All the numerous sectaries regarded him as their determined enemy; and ascribed to his advice and influence, those persecuting laws, to which they had lately been exposed. The catholics knew, that while he retained any authority, all their credit with the king and the duke would be entirely useless to them, nor must they ever expect any favour or indulgence. Even the royalists, disappointed in their sanguine hopes of preferment, threw a great load of envy on Clarendon, into whose hands the king seemed at first to have resigned the whole power of government. The sale of Dunkirk, the bad payment of the seamen, the disgrace at Chatham, the unsuccessful conclusion of the war; all these misfortunes were charged on the chancellor, who, though he had ever opposed the rupture with Holland, thought it still his duty to justify what he could not prevent. A building, likewise, of more expence and magnificence than his slender fortune could afford, being unwarily undertaken by him, much exposed him to public reproach, as if he had acquired great riches by corruption. The populace gave it commonly the appellation of Dunkirk House.

The king himself, who had always more revered than loved the chancellor, was now totally estranged from him. Amidst the dissolute manners of the court, that minister still maintained an inflexible dignity, and would not submit to any condescensions, which he deemed unworthy of his age and character. Buckingham, a man of profligate morals, happy in his talent for ridicule, but exposed in his own conduct to all the ridicule, which he threw on others, still made him the object of his raillery, and gradually lessened in the king that regard, which he bore to his minister. When any difficulties arose, either for want of power or money, the blame was still thrown on him, who, it was believed, had carefully at the restoration checked all lavish concessions to the king. And what perhaps touched Charles more nearly, he found in Clarendon, it is said, obstacles to his pleasures as well as to his ambition.

The king, disgusted with the homely person of his consort, and desirous of having children, had hearkened to proposals of obtaining a divorce, on pretence either of her being pre-engaged to

CHAPTER LXIV

another, or of having made a vow of chastity before her marriage. He was farther stimulated by his passion for Mrs. Stuart, daughter of a Scotch gentleman; a lady of great beauty, and whose virtue he had hitherto found impregnable: But Clarendon, apprehensive of the consequences attending a disputed title, and perhaps anxious for the succession of his own grandchildren, engaged the duke of Richmond to marry Mrs. Stuart, and thereby put an end to the king's hopes. It is pretended, that Charles never forgave this disappointment.

When politics, therefore, and inclination both concurred to make the king sacrifice Clarendon to popular prejudices, the memory of his past services was not able any longer to delay his fall. The great seal was taken from him, and given to Sir Orlando Bridgeman, by the title of Lord Keeper. Southampton the treasurer was now dead, who had persevered to the utmost in his attachments to the chancellor. The last time he appeared at the council table, he exerted his friendship with a vigour, which neither age nor infirmities could abate. "This man," said he, speaking of Clarendon, "is a true protestant, and an honest Englishman; and while he enjoys power, we are secure of our laws, liberties, and religion. I dread the consequences of his removal."

But the fall of the chancellor was not sufficient to gratify the malice of his enemies: His total ruin was resolved on. The duke of York in vain exerted his interest in behalf of his father-in-law. Both prince and people united in promoting that violent measure; and no means were thought so proper for ingratiating the court with a parliament, which had so long been governed by that very minister, who was now to be the victim of their prejudices.

Some popular acts paved the way for the session; and the parliament, in their first address, gave the king thanks for these instances of his goodness, and among the rest, they took care to mention his dismission of Clarendon. The king, in reply, assured the houses, that he would never again employ that nobleman in any public office whatsoever. Immediately, the charge against him was opened in the house of commons by Mr. Seymour, afterwards Sir Edward, and consisted of seventeen articles. The house, without examining particulars, farther than hearing general affirmations, that all would be proved, immediately voted his impeachment. Many of the articles[n] we know to be either false or frivolous; and such of them, as we are less acquainted with, we may fairly presume to be no better grounded. His advising the sale of Dunkirk, seems the heaviest and truest part of the charge; but a mistake in judgment, allowing it to be such, where there appears no symptoms of corruption or bad intentions, it would be very hard to impute as a crime to any minister. The king's necessities, which occasioned that measure, cannot with any appearance of reason be charged on Clarendon; and chiefly proceeded from the over-frugal maxims of the parliament itself, in not granting the proper supplies to the crown.

When the impeachment was carried up to the peers, as it contained an accusation of treason in general, without specifying any particulars, it seemed not a sufficient ground for committing Clarendon to custody. The precedents of Strafford and Laud were not, by reason of the violence of the times, deemed a proper authority; but as the commons still insisted upon his commitment, it was necessary to appoint a free conference between the houses. The lords persevered in their resolution; and the commons voted this conduct to be an obstruction to public justice, and a precedent of evil and dangerous tendency. They also chose a committee to draw up a vindication of their own proceedings.

Clarendon, finding that the popular torrent, united to the violence of power, ran with impetuosity against him, and that a defence, offered to such prejudiced ears, would be entirely ineffectual, thought proper to withdraw. At Calais, he wrote a paper addressed to the house of lords. He there said, that his fortune, which was but moderate, had been gained entirely by the lawful, avowed profits of his office, and by the voluntary bounty of the king; that during the first years after the restoration he had always concurred in opinion with the other counsellors, men of such reputation that no one could entertain suspicions of their wisdom or integrity; that his credit soon declined, and however he might disapprove of some measures, he found it vain to oppose them; that his repugnance to the Dutch war, the source of all the public grievances, was always generally known, as well as his disapprobation of many unhappy steps taken in conducting it; and that

[n] See note [F] at the end of the volume.

CHAPTER LXIV

whatever pretence might be made of public offences, his real crime, that which had exasperated his powerful enemies, was his frequent opposition to exorbitant grants, which the importunity of suitors had extorted from his majesty.

The lords transmitted this paper to the commons under the appellation of a libel; and by a vote of both houses, it was condemned to be burned by the hands of the hangman. The parliament next proceeded to exert their legislative power against Clarendon, and passed a bill of banishment and incapacity, which received the royal assent. He retired into France, where he lived in a private manner. He survived his banishment six years; and he employed his leisure chiefly in reducing into order the History of the Civil Wars, for which he had before collected materials. The performance does honour to his memory; and except Whitlocke's Memorials, is the most candid account of those times, composed by any contemporary author. *Clarendon's banishment.*

Clarendon was always a friend to the liberty and constitution of his country. At the commencement of the civil wars, he had entered into the late king's service, and was honoured with a great share in the esteem and friendship of that monarch: He was pursued with unrelenting animosity by the Long Parliament: He had shared all the fortunes and directed all the counsels of the present king during his exile: He had been advanced to the highest trust and offices after the restoration: Yet all these circumstances, which might naturally operate with such force, either on resentment, gratitude, or ambition, had no influence on his uncorrupted mind. It is said, that when he first engaged in the study of the law, his father exhorted him with great earnestness to shun the practice too common in that profession, of straining every point in favour of prerogative, and perverting so useful a science to the oppression of liberty: And in the midst of these rational and virtuous counsels, which he re-iterated, he was suddenly seized with an apoplexy, and expired in his son's presence. This circumstance gave additional weight to the principles, which he inculcated.

The combination of king and subject to oppress so good a minister affords, to men of opposite dispositions, an equal occasion of inveighing against the ingratitude of princes, or ignorance of the people. Charles seems never to have mitigated his resentment against Clarendon; and the national prejudices pursued him to his retreat in France. A company of English soldiers, being quartered near him, assaulted his house, broke open the doors, gave him a dangerous wound on the head, and would have proceeded to the last extremities, had not their officers, hearing of the violence, happily interposed.

1668.

The next expedient, which the king embraced, in order to acquire popularity, is more deserving of praise; and, had it been steadily pursued, would probably have rendered his reign happy, certainly his memory respected. It is the Triple Alliance of which I speak; a measure, which gave entire satisfaction to the public.

State of France.

The glory of France, which had long been eclipsed, either by domestic factions, or by the superior force of the Spanish monarchy, began now to break out with great lustre, and to engage the attention of the neighbouring nations. The independent power and mutinous spirit of the nobility were subdued: The popular pretensions of the parliament restrained: The Hugonot party reduced to subjection: That extensive and fertile country, enjoying every advantage both of climate and situation, was fully peopled with ingenious and industrious inhabitants: And while the spirit of the nation discovered all the vigour and bravery requisite for great enterprizes, it was tamed to an entire submission under the will of the sovereign.

Character of Lewis XIV.

The sovereign, who now filled the throne, was well adapted, by his personal character, both to encrease and to avail himself of these advantages. Lewis XIV. endowed with every quality, which could enchant the people, possessed many which merit the approbation of the wise. The masculine beauty of his person was embellished with a noble air: The dignity of his behaviour was tempered with affability and politeness: Elegant without effeminacy, addicted to pleasure without neglecting business, decent in his very vices, and beloved in the midst of arbitrary power; he surpassed all contemporary monarchs, as in grandeur, so likewise in fame and glory.

His ambition, regulated by prudence, not by justice, had carefully provided every means of conquest; and before he put himself in motion, he seemed to have absolutely ensured success. His finances were brought into order: A naval power created: His armies encreased and disciplined: Magazines and military stores provided: And though the magnificence of his court was supported

CHAPTER LXIV

beyond all former example, so regular was the economy observed, and so willingly did the people, now enriched by arts and commerce, submit to multiplied taxes, that his military force much exceeded what in any preceding age had ever been employed by any European monarch.

The sudden decline and almost total fall of the Spanish monarchy, opened an inviting field to so enterprising a prince, and seemed to promise him easy and extensive conquests. The other nations of Europe, feeble or ill-governed, were astonished at the greatness of his rising empire; and all of them cast their eyes towards England, as the only power, which could save them from that subjection, with which they seemed to be so nearly threatened.

The animosity, which had anciently subsisted between the English and French nations, and which had been suspended for above a century by the jealousy of Spanish greatness, began to revive and to exert itself. The glory of preserving the balance of Europe, a glory so much founded on justice and humanity, flattered the ambition of England; and the people were eager to provide for their own future security, by opposing the progress of so hated a rival. The prospect of embracing such measures had contributed, among other reasons, to render the peace of Breda so universally acceptable to the nation. By the death of Philip IV. king of Spain, an inviting opportunity, and some very slender pretences, had been afforded to call forth the ambition of Lewis.

At the treaty of the Pyrenees, when Lewis espoused the Spanish princess, he had renounced every title of succession to every part of the Spanish monarchy; and this renunciation had been couched in the most accurate and most precise terms, that language could afford. But on the death of his father-in-law, he retracted his renunciation, and pretended, that natural rights, depending on blood and succession, could not be annihilated by any extorted deed or contract. Philip had left a son, Charles II. of Spain; but as the queen of France was of a former marriage, she laid claim to a considerable province of the Spanish monarchy, even to the exclusion of her brother. By the customs of some parts of Brabant, a female of a first marriage was preferred to a male of a second, in the succession to private inheritances; and Lewis thence inferred, that his queen had acquired a right to the dominion of that important dutchy.

*French in-
vasion of
the Low
Countries.*

A claim of this nature was more properly supported by military force than by argument and reasoning. Lewis appeared on the frontiers of the Netherlands with an army of 40,000 men, commanded by the best generals of the age, and provided with every thing necessary for action. The Spaniards, though they might have foreseen this measure, were totally unprepared. Their towns, without magazines, fortifications, or garrisons, fell into the hands of the French king, as soon as he presented himself before them. Athe, Lisle, Tournay, Oudenarde, Courtray, Charleroi, Binche were immediately taken: And it was visible, that no force in the Low Countries was able to stop or retard the progress of the French arms.

This measure, executed with such celerity and success, gave great alarm to almost every court in Europe. It had been observed with what dignity, or even haughtiness, Lewis, from the time he began to govern, had ever supported all his rights and pretensions. D'Estrades, the French ambassador, and Watteville, the Spanish, having quarrelled in London, on account of their claims for precedency, the French monarch was not satisfied, till Spain sent to Paris a solemn embassy, and promised never more to revive such contests. Crequi, his ambassador at Rome, had met with an affront from the pope's guards: The pope, Alexander VII. had been constrained to break his guards, to send his nephew to ask pardon, and to allow a pillar to be erected in Rome itself, as a monument of his own humiliation. The king of England too had experienced the high spirit and unsubmitting temper of Lewis. A pretension to superiority in the English flag having been advanced, the French monarch remonstrated with such vigour, and prepared himself to resist with such courage, that Charles found it more prudent to desist from his vain and antiquated claims. The king of England, said Lewis to his ambassador D'Estrades, may know my force, but he knows not the sentiments of my heart: Every thing appears to me contemptible in comparison of glory.[o] These measures of conduct had given strong indications of his character: But the invasion of Flanders discovered an ambition, which, being supported by such overgrown power, menaced the general liberties of Europe.

As no state lay nearer the danger, none was seized with more

[o] 25th of January, 1662.

CHAPTER LXIV

terror than the United Provinces. They were still engaged, together with France, in a war against England; and Lewis had promised them, that he would take no step against Spain without previously informing them: But, contrary to this assurance, he kept a total silence, till on the very point of entering upon action. If the renunciation, made at the treaty of the Pyrenees, was not valid, it was foreseen, that upon the death of the king of Spain, a sickly infant, the whole monarchy would be claimed by Lewis; after which it would be vainly expected to set bounds to his pretensions. Charles, acquainted with these well-grounded apprehensions of the Dutch, had been the more obstinate in insisting on his own conditions at Breda; and by delaying to sign the treaty, had imprudently exposed himself to the signal disgrace, which he received at Chatham. De Wit, sensible that a few weeks delay would be of no consequence in the Low Countries, took this opportunity of striking an important blow, and of finishing the war with honour to himself and to his country.

Negotiations meanwhile commenced for the saving of Flanders; but no resistance was made to the French arms. The Spanish ministers exclaimed every where against the flagrant injustice of Lewis's pretensions, and represented it to be the interest of every power in Europe, even more than of Spain itself, to prevent his conquest of the Low Countries. The emperor and the German princes discovered evident symptoms of discontent; but their motions were slow and backward. The States, tho' terrified at the prospect of having their frontier exposed to so formidable a foe, saw no resource, no means of safety. England indeed seemed disposed to make opposition to the French; but the variable and impolitic conduct of Charles kept that republic from making him any open advances, by which she might lose the friendship of France, without acquiring any new ally. And though Lewis, dreading a combination of all Europe, had offered terms of accommodation, the Dutch apprehended, lest these, either from the obstinacy of the Spaniards, or the ambition of the French, should never be carried into execution.

Negotiations.

Charles resolved with great prudence to take the first step towards a confederacy. Sir William Temple, his resident at Brussels, received orders to go secretly to the Hague, and to concert with the States the means of saving the Netherlands. This man, whom philosophy had taught to despise the world, without rendering him unfit for it, was frank, open, sincere, superior to the little tricks of vulgar politicians: And meeting in de Wit with a man of the same generous and enlarged sentiments, he immediately opened his master's intentions, and pressed a speedy conclusion. A treaty was from the first negotiated between these two statesmen with the same cordiality, as if it were a private transaction between intimate companions. Deeming the interests of their country the same, they gave full scope to that sympathy of character, which disposed them to an entire reliance on each other's professions and engagements. And though jealousy against the house of Orange might inspire de Wit with an aversion to a strict union with England, he generously resolved to sacrifice all private considerations to the public service.

Temple insisted on an offensive league between England and Holland, in order to oblige France to relinquish all her conquests: But de Wit told him, that this measure was too bold and precipitate to be agreed to by the States. He said, that the French were the old and constant allies of the republic; and till matters came to extremities, she never would deem it prudent to abandon a friendship so well established, and rely entirely on a treaty with England, which had lately waged so cruel a war against her: That ever since the reign of Elizabeth, there had been such a fluctuation in the English councils, that it was not possible, for two years together, to take any sure or certain measures with that kingdom: That though the present ministry, having entered into views so conformable to national interest, promised greater firmness and constancy, it might still be unsafe, in a business of such consequence, to put entire confidence in them: That the French monarch was young, haughty, and powerful; and if treated in so imperious a manner, would expose himself to the greatest extremities rather than submit: That it was sufficient, if he could be constrained to adhere to the offers, which he himself had already made; and if the remaining provinces of the Low Countries could be thereby saved from the danger, with which they were at present threatened: And that the other powers, in Germany and the north, whose assistance they might expect, would be satisfied with putting a stop to the French conquests, without pretending to recover the places already lost.

The English minister was content to accept of the terms, pro-

CHAPTER LXIV

posed by the pensionary. Lewis had offered to relinquish all the queen's rights on condition either of keeping the conquests, which he had made last campaign, or of receiving, in lieu of them, Franchecomté, together with Cambray, Aire, and St. Omers. De Wit and Temple founded their treaty upon this proposal. They agreed to offer their mediation to the contending powers, and oblige France to adhere to this alternative, and Spain to accept of it. If Spain refused, they agreed, that France should not prosecute her claim by arms, but leave it entirely to England and Holland to employ force for making the terms effectual. And the remainder of the Low Countries they thenceforth guaranteed to Spain. A defensive alliance was likewise concluded between Holland and England.

The articles of this confederacy were soon adjusted by such candid and able negotiators: But the greatest difficulty still remained. By the constitution of the republic, all the towns in all the provinces must give their consent to every alliance; and besides that this formality could not be dispatched in less than two months, it was justly to be dreaded, that the influence of France would obstruct the passing of the treaty in some of the smaller cities. D'Estrades, the French ambassador, a man of abilities, hearing of the league, which was on the carpet, treated it lightly; "Six weeks hence," said he, "we shall speak to it." To obviate this difficulty, de Wit had the courage, for the public good, to break through the laws in so fundamental an article; and by his authority, he prevailed with the States General at once to sign and ratify the league: Though they acknowledged, that, if that measure should displease *13th Jan.* their constituents, they risqued their heads by this irregularity. After sealing, all parties embraced with great cordiality. Temple cried out, *At Breda, as friends: Here, as brothers.* And de Wit added, that now the matter was finished, it looked like a miracle.

Room had been left in the treaty for the accession of Sweden, *Triple* which was soon after obtained; and thus was concluded in five days *league.* the triple league; an event received with equal surprise and approbation by the world. Notwithstanding the unfortunate conclusion of the last war, England now appeared in her proper station, and, by this wise conduct, had recovered all her influence and credit in Europe. Temple likewise received great applause; but to all the compliments made him on the occasion, he modestly replied, that to remove things from their center, or proper element, required force and labour; but that of themselves they easily returned to it.

The French monarch was extremely displeased with this measure. Not only bounds were at present set to his ambition: Such a barrier was also raised as seemed for ever impregnable. And though his own offer was made the foundation of the treaty, he had prescribed so short a time for the acceptance of it, that he still expected, from the delays and reluctance of Spain, to find some opportunity of eluding it. The court of Madrid showed equal displeasure. To relinquish any part of the Spanish provinces, in lieu of claims, so apparently unjust, and these urged with such violence and haughtiness, inspired the highest disgust. Often did the Spaniards threaten to abandon entirely the Low Countries rather than submit to so cruel a mortification; and they endeavoured, by this menace, to terrify the mediating powers into more vigorous measures for their support. But Temple and de Wit were better acquainted with the views and interests of Spain. They knew, that she must still retain the Low Countries, as a bond of connexion with the other European powers, who alone, if her young monarch should happen to die without issue, could ensure her independency against the pretensions of France. They still urged, there-

Treaty of Aix-la-Chapelle. fore, the terms of the triple league, and threatened Spain with war in case of refusal. The plenipotentiaries of all the powers met at Aix-la-Chapelle. Temple was minister for England; Van Beuninghen for Holland; D'Ohna for Sweden.

Spain at last, pressed on all hands, accepted of the alternative offered; but in her very compliance, she gave strong symptoms of ill-humour and discontent. It had been apparent, that the Hollanders, entirely neglecting the honour of the Spanish monarchy, had been anxious only for their own security; and, provided they could remove Lewis to a distance from their frontier, were more indifferent what progress he made in other places. Sensible of these views, the queen-regent of Spain resolved still to keep them in an anxiety, which might for the future be the foundation of an union more intimate than they were willing at present to enter into. Franchecomté, by a vigorous and well concerted plan of the French king, had been conquered, in fifteen days, during a rigorous season, and in the midst of winter. She chose therefore to

CHAPTER LXIV

recover this province, and to abandon all the towns conquered in Flanders during the last campaign. By this means, Lewis extended his garrisons into the heart of the Low-countries; and a very feeble barrier remained to the Spanish provinces.

But notwithstanding the advantages of his situation, the French monarch could entertain small hopes of ever extending his conquests on that quarter, which lay the most exposed to his ambition, and where his acquisitions were of most importance. The triple league guaranteed the remaining provinces to Spain; and the emperor and other powers of Germany, whose interest seemed to be intimately concerned, were invited to enter into the same confederacy. Spain herself, having, about this time, under the mediation of Charles, made peace on equal terms with Portugal, might be expected to exert more vigour and opposition to her haughty and triumphant rival. The great satisfaction, expressed in England, on account of the counsels now embraced by the court, promised the hearty concurrence of parliament in every measure, which could be proposed for opposition to the grandeur of France. And thus all Europe seemed to repose herself with security under the wings of that powerful confederacy, which had been so happily formed for her protection. It is now time to give some account of the state of affairs in Scotland and in Ireland.

The Scottish nation, though they had never been subject to the arbitrary power of their prince, had but very imperfect notions of law and liberty; and scarcely in any age had they ever enjoyed an administration, which had confined itself within the proper boundaries. By their final union alone with England, their once hated adversary, they have happily attained the experience of a government perfectly regular, and exempt from all violence and injustice. Charles, from his aversion to business, had entrusted the affairs of that country to his ministers, particularly Middleton; and these could not forbear making very extraordinary stretches of authority. *Affairs of Scotland.*

There had been intercepted a letter, written by lord Lorne to lord Duffus, in which, a little too plainly, but very truly, he complained, that his enemies had endeavoured by falshood to prepossess the king against him. But he said, that he had now discovered them, had defeated them, and had gained the person, meaning the earl of Clarendon, upon whom the chief of them depended. This letter was produced before the parliament; and Lorne was tried upon an old, tyrannical, absurd law against *Leasing-making;* by which it was rendered criminal to belie the subjects to the king, or create in him an ill opinion of them. He was condemned to die: But Charles was much displeased with the sentence, and granted him a pardon.[p]

It was carried in parliament, that twelve persons, without crime, witness, trial, or accuser, should be declared incapable of all trust or office; and to render this injustice more egregious, it was agreed, that these persons should be named by ballot: A method of voting, which several republics had adopted at elections, in order to prevent faction and intrigue; but which could serve only as a cover to malice and iniquity, in the inflicting of punishments. Lauderdale, Crawford, and sir Robert Murray, among others, were incapacitated: But the king, who disapproved of this injustice, refused his assent.[q]

An act was passed against all persons, who should move the king for restoring the children of those who were attainted by parliament; an unheard-of restraint on applications for grace and mercy. No penalty was affixed; but the act was but the more violent and tyrannical on that account. The court-lawyers had established it as a maxim, that the assigning of a punishment was a limitation of the crown: Whereas a law, forbidding anything, though without a penalty, made the offenders criminal. And in that case, they determined, that the punishment was arbitrary; only that it could not extend to life. Middleton as commissioner passed this act; though he had no instructions for that purpose.

An act of indemnity passed; but at the same time it was voted, that all those who had offended during the late disorders, should be subjected to fines; and a committee of parliament was appointed for imposing them. These proceeded without any regard to some equitable rules, which the king had prescribed to them.[r] The most obnoxious compounded secretly. No consideration was had, either of men's riches, or of the degrees of their guilt: No proofs were produced: Enquiries were not so much as made: But as fast as information was given in against any man, he was marked down for a particular fine: And all was transacted in a secret

[p] Burnet, p. 149.   [q] Burnet, p. 152.   [r] Id. p. 147.

CHAPTER LXIV

committee. When the list was read in parliament, exceptions were made to several: Some had been under age during the civil wars; some had been abroad. But it was still replied, that a proper time would come, when every man should be heard in his own defence. The only intention, it was said, of setting the fines was, that such persons should have no benefit by the act of indemnity, unless they paid the sum demanded: Every one that chose to stand upon his innocence, and renounce the benefit of the indemnity, might do it at his peril. It was well known, that no one would dare so far to set at defiance so arbitrary an administration. The king wrote to the council, ordering them to supersede the levying of those fines: But Middleton found means, during some time, to elude these orders.[s] And at last, the king obliged his ministers to compound for half the sums, which had been imposed. In all these transactions, and in most others, which passed during the present reign, we still find the moderating hand of the king, interposed to protect the Scots from the oppressions, which their own countrymen, employed in the ministry, were desirous of exercising over them.

But the chief circumstance, whence were derived all the subsequent tyranny and disorders in Scotland, was the execution of the laws for the establishment of episcopacy; a mode of government, to which a great part of the nation had entertained an unsurmountable aversion. The rights of patrons had for some years been abolished; and the power of electing ministers had been vested in the kirk-session, and lay-elders. It was now enacted, that all incumbents, who had been admitted upon this title, should receive a presentation from the patron, and should be instituted anew by the bishop, under the penalty of deprivation. The more rigid presbyterians concerted measures among themselves, and refused obedience: They imagined, that their number would protect them. Three hundred and fifty parishes, above a third of the kingdom, were at once declared vacant. The western counties chiefly were obstinate in this particular. New ministers were sought for all over the kingdom; and no one was so ignorant or vicious as to be rejected. The people, who loved extremely and respected their former teachers; men remarkable for the severity of their manners, and their fervor in preaching; were inflamed

[s] Burnet, p. 201.

against these intruders, who had obtained their livings under such invidious circumstances, and who took no care, by the regularity of their manners, to soften the prejudices entertained against them. Even most of those, who retained their livings by compliance, fell under the imputation of hypocrisy, either by their shewing a disgust to the new model of ecclesiastical government, which they had acknowledged; or on the other hand, by declaring, that their former adherence to presbytery and the covenant had been the result of violence and necessity. And as Middleton and the new ministry indulged themselves in great riot and disorder, to which the nation had been little accustomed, an opinion universally prevailed, that any form of religion, offered by such hands, must be profane and impious.

The people, notwithstanding their discontents, were resolved to give no handle against them, by the least symptom of mutiny or sedition: But this submissive disposition, instead of procuring a mitigation of the rigours, was made use of as an argument for continuing the same measures, which by their vigour, it was pretended, had produced so prompt an obedience. The king, however, was disgusted with the violence of Middleton,[t] and he made Rothes commissioner in his place. This nobleman was already president of the council; and soon after was made lord keeper and treasurer. Lauderdale still continued secretary of state, and commonly resided at London.

Affairs remained in a peaceable state, till the severe law was made in England against conventicles.[u] The Scottish parliament imitated that violence, by passing a like act. A kind of high commission court was appointed by the privy-council, for executing this rigorous law, and for the direction of ecclesiastical affairs. But even this court, illegal as it might be deemed, was much preferable to the method next adopted. Military force was let loose by the council. Wherever the people had generally forsaken their churches, the guards were quartered throughout the country. Sir James Turner commanded them, a man whose natural ferocity of temper was often inflamed by the use of strong liquors. He went about, and received from the clergy lists of those who absented themselves from church, or were supposed to frequent con-

[t] Burnet, p. 202.   [u] 1664.

CHAPTER LXIV

venticles. Without any proof or legal conviction, he demanded a
fine from them, and quartered soldiers on the supposed delinquents, till he received payment. As an insurrection was dreaded
during the Dutch war, new forces were levied, and intrusted to the
command of Dalziel and Drummond; two officers, who had served
the king during the civil wars, and had afterwards engaged in the
service of Russia, where they had encreased the native cruelty of
their disposition. A full career was given to their tyranny by the
Scottish ministry. Representations were made to the king against
these enormities. He seemed touched with the state of the country;
and besides giving orders, that the ecclesiastical commission
should be discontinued, he signified his opinion, that another way
of proceeding was necessary for his service.[w]

This lenity of the king's came too late to remedy the disorders.
The people, inflamed with bigotry, and irritated by ill usage, rose
in arms. They were instigated by Guthry, Semple, and other
preachers. They surprised Turner in Dumfries, and resolved to
have put him to death; but finding, that his orders, which fell into
their hands, were more violent than his execution of them, they
spared his life. At Laneric, after many prayers, they renewed the
covenant, and published their manifesto; in which they professed
all submission to the king: They desired only the re-establishment
of presbytery and of their former ministers. As many gentlemen of
their party had been confined on suspicion; Wallace and Lear-
mont, two officers, who had served, but in no high rank, were
entrusted by the populace with the command. Their force never
exceeded two thousand men; and though the country in general
bore them favour, men's spirits were so subdued, that the rebels
could expect no farther accession of numbers. Dalziel took the
field to oppose their progress. Their number was now diminished
to 800; and these, having advanced near Edinburgh, attempted to
find their way back into the west by Pentland Hills. They were
attacked by the king's forces.[x] Finding that they could not escape,
they stopped their march. Their clergy endeavoured to infuse
courage into them. After singing some psalms, the rebels turned
on the enemy; and being assisted by the advantage of the ground,
they received the first charge very resolutely. But that was all the

[w] Burnet, p. 213.   [x] 28th November, 1666.

action: Immediately, they fell into disorder, and fled for their lives. About forty were killed on the spot, and a hundred and thirty taken prisoners. The rest, favoured by the night, and by the weariness, and even by the pity of the king's troops, made their escape.

The oppressions which these people had suffered, the delusions under which they laboured, and their inoffensive behaviour during the insurrection, made them the objects of compassion: Yet were the king's ministers, particularly Sharpe, resolved to take severe vengeance. Ten were hanged on one gibbet at Edinburgh: Thirty-five before their own doors in different places. These criminals might all have saved their lives, if they would have renounced the covenant. The executions were going on, when the king put a stop to them. He said, that blood enough had already been shed; and he wrote a letter to the privy-council, in which he ordered, that such of the prisoners as should simply promise to obey the laws for the future, should be set at liberty, and that the incorrigible should be sent to the plantations.[y] This letter was brought by Burnet, archbishop of Glasgow; but not being immediately delivered to the council by Sharpe, the president,[z] one Maccail had in the interval been put to the torture, under which he expired. He seemed to die in an exstacy of joy. "Farewel sun, moon, and stars; farewel world and time; farewel weak and frail body: Welcome eternity, welcome angels and saints, welcome Saviour of the world, and welcome God, the judge of all!" Such were his last words: And these animated speeches he uttered with an accent and manner, which struck all the bystanders with astonishment.

Affairs of Ireland.   The settlement of Ireland after the restoration was a work of greater difficulty than that of England, or even of Scotland. Not only the power, during the former usurpations, had there been vested in the king's enemies: The whole property, in a manner, of the kingdom had also been changed; and it became necessary to redress but with as little violence as possible, many grievous hardships and iniquities, which were there complained of.

The Irish catholics had in 1648 concluded a treaty with Ormond, the king's lieutenant, in which they had stipulated pardon for their past rebellion, and had engaged under certain conditions

[y] Burnet, p. 237.   [z] Wodrow's History, vol. i. p. 255.

to assist the royal cause: And though the violence of the priests and the bigotry of the people had prevented, in a great measure, the execution of this treaty; yet were there many, who having strictly, at the hazard of their lives, adhered to it, seemed on that account well entitled to reap the fruits of their loyalty. Cromwel, having without distinction expelled all the native Irish from the three provinces of Munster, Leinster, and Ulster, had confined them to Connaught and the county of Clare; and among those who had thus been forfeited, were many whose innocence was altogether unquestionable. Several protestants likewise, and Ormond among the rest, had all along opposed the Irish rebellion; yet having afterwards embraced the king's cause against the parliament, they were all of them attainted by Cromwel. And there were many officers, who had, from the commencement of the insurrection, served in Ireland, and who, because they would not desert the king, had been refused all their arrears by the English Commonwealth.

To all these unhappy sufferers some justice seemed to be due: But the difficulty was to find the means of redressing such great and extensive iniquities. Almost all the valuable parts of Ireland had been measured out and divided, either to the adventurers, who had lent money to the parliament for the suppression of the Irish rebellion, or to the soldiers, who had received land in lieu of their arrears. These could not be dispossessed, because they were the most powerful and only armed part of Ireland; because it was requisite to favour them, in order to support the protestant and English interest in that kingdom; and because they had generally, with a seeming zeal and alacrity, concurred in the king's restoration. The king, therefore, issued a proclamation; in which he promised to maintain their settlement, and at the same time engaged to give redress to the innocent sufferers. There was a quantity of land as yet undivided in Ireland; and from this and some other funds, it was thought possible for the king to fulfil both these engagements.

A court of claims was erected, consisting altogether of English commissioners, who had no connexion with any of the parties, into which Ireland was divided. Before these were laid four thousand claims of persons craving restitution on account of their innocence; and the commissioners had found leisure to examine only six hundred. It already appeared, that, if all these were to be restored, the funds, whence the adventurers and soldiers must get reprisals, would fall short of giving them any tolerable satisfaction. A great alarm and anxiety seized all ranks of men: The hopes and fears of every party were excited: These eagerly grasped at recovering their paternal inheritance: Those were resolute to maintain their new acquisitions.

The duke of Ormond was created lord-lieutenant; being the only person, whose prudence and equity could compose such jarring interests. A parliament was assembled at Dublin; and as the lower house was almost entirely chosen by the soldiers and adventurers, who still kept possession, it was extremely favourable to that interest. The house of peers showed greater impartiality.

An insurrection was projected, together with a surprizal of the castle of Dublin, by some of the disbanded soldiers; but this design was happily defeated by the vigilance of Ormond. Some of the criminals were punished. Blood, the most desperate of them, escaped into England.

But affairs could not long remain in the confusion and uncertainty, into which they had fallen. All parties seemed willing to abate somewhat of their pretensions, in order to attain some stability; and Ormond interposed his authority for that purpose. The soldiers and adventurers agreed to relinquish a third of their possessions; and as they had purchased their lands at very low prices, they had reason to think themselves favoured by this composition. All those, who had been attainted on account of their adhering to the king, were restored; and some of the innocent Irish. It was a hard situation, that a man was obliged to prove himself innocent, in order to recover possession of the estate, which he and his ancestors had ever enjoyed: But the hardship was augmented, by the difficult conditions annexed to this proof. If the person had ever lived in the quarters of the rebels, he was not admitted to plead his innocence; and he was, for that reason alone, supposed to have been a rebel. The heinous guilt of the Irish nation made men the more readily overlook any iniquity, which might fall on individuals; and it was considered, that, though it be always the interest of all good government to prevent injustice, it is not always possible to remedy it, after it has had a long course, and has been attended with great successes.

CHAPTER LXIV

Ireland began to attain a state of some composure when it was disturbed by a violent act, passed by the English parliament, which prohibited the importation of Irish cattle into England.[a] Ormond remonstrated strongly against this law. He said, that the present trade, carried on between England and Ireland, was extremely to the advantage of the former kingdom, which received only provisions, or rude materials, in return for every species of manufacture: That if the cattle of Ireland were prohibited, the inhabitants of that island had no other commodity, by which they could pay England for their importations, and must have recourse to other nations for a supply: That the industrious inhabitants of England, if deprived of Irish provisions, which made living cheap, would be obliged to augment the price of labour, and thereby render their manufactures too dear to be exported to foreign markets: That the indolent inhabitants of Ireland, finding provisions fall almost to nothing, would never be induced to labour, but would perpetuate to all generations their native sloth and barbarism: That by cutting off almost entirely the trade between the kingdoms, all the natural bands of union were dissolved, and nothing remained to keep the Irish in their duty but force and violence: And that by reducing that kingdom to extreme poverty, it would be even rendered incapable of maintaining that military power, by which, during its well grounded discontents, it must necessarily be retained in subjection.

The king was so much convinced of the justness of these reasons, that he used all his interest to oppose the bill; and he openly declared, that he could not give his assent to it with a safe conscience. But the commons were resolute in their purpose. Some of the rents of England had fallen of late years, which had been ascribed entirely to the importation of Irish cattle: Several intrigues had contributed to inflame that prejudice, particularly those of Buckingham and Ashley, who were desirous of giving Ormond disturbance in his government: And the spirit of tyranny, of which nations are as susceptible as individuals, had extremely animated the English to exert their superiority over their dependant state. No affair could be conducted with greater violence than this was by the commons. They even went so far in the pream-

[a] In 1666.

ble of the bill as to declare the importation of Irish cattle to be a *nuisance*. By this expression, they gave scope to their passion, and at the same time barred the king's prerogative, by which he might think himself entitled to dispense with a law, so full of injustice and bad policy. The lords expunged the word; but as the king was sensible, that no supply would be given by the commons, unless they were gratified in their prejudices, he was obliged both to employ his interest with the peers for making the bill pass, and to give the royal assent to it. He could not, however, forbear expressing his displeasure at the jealousy entertained against him, and at the intention, which the commons discovered of retrenching his prerogative.

This law brought great distress for some time upon the Irish; but it has occasioned their applying with greater industry to manufactures, and has proved in the issue beneficial to that kingdom.

LXV

SINCE THE RESTORATION, England had attained a situation,   *1668.* which had never been experienced in any former period of her government, and which seemed the only one, that could fully ensure, at once, her tranquillity and her liberty: The king was in continual want of supply from the parliament; and he seemed willing to accommodate himself to that dependent situation. Instead of reviving those claims of prerogative, so strenuously insisted on by his predecessors, Charles had strictly confined himself within the limits of law, and had courted, by every art of popularity, the affections of his subjects. Even the severities, however blameable, which he had exercised against nonconformists, are to be considered as expedients, by which he strove to ingratiate himself with that party, which predominated in parliament. But notwithstanding these promising appearances, there were many circumstances, which kept the government from resting steddily on that bottom, on which it was placed. The crown having lost almost all its ancient demesnes, relied entirely on voluntary grants of the people; and the commons not fully accustomed to this new situation, were not yet disposed to supply with sufficient liberality the necessities of the crown. They imitated too strictly the example of their predecessors in a rigid frugality of public money; and neither sufficiently considered the indigent condition of their prince, nor the general state of Europe; where every nation, by its increase both of magnificence and force, had made great additions to all public expences. Some considerable sums, indeed, were bestowed on Charles; and the patriots of that age, tenacious of ancient maxims, loudly upbraided the commons with prodigality: But if we may judge by the example of a later period, when the government has become more regular, and the harmony of its parts has been more happily adjusted, the parliaments of this reign seem rather to have merited a contrary reproach.

The natural consequence of the poverty of the crown was, besides feeble irregular transactions in foreign affairs, a continual uncertainty in its domestic administration. No one could answer with any tolerable assurance for the measures of the house of commons. Few of the members were attached to the court by any other band than that of inclination. Royalists indeed in their principles, but unexperienced in business, they lay exposed to every rumour or insinuation; and were driven by momentary gusts or currents, no less than the populace themselves. Even the attempts made to gain an ascendant over them, by offices, and, as it is believed, by bribes and pensions, were apt to operate in a manner contrary to what was intended by the ministers. The novelty of the practice conveyed a general, and indeed a just, alarm; while at the same time, the poverty of the crown rendered this influence very limited and precarious.

CHAPTER LXV

The character of Charles was ill fitted to remedy those defects in the constitution. He acted in the administration of public affairs, as if government were a pastime, rather than a serious occupation; and by the uncertainty of his conduct, he lost that authority, which could alone bestow constancy on the fluctuating resolutions of the parliament. His expences too, which sometimes perhaps exceeded the proper bounds, were directed more by inclination than by policy; and while they encreased his dependance on the parliament, they were not calculated fully to satisfy either the interested or disinterested part of that assembly.

The parliament met after a long adjournment; and the king promised himself every thing from the attachment of the commons. All his late measures had been calculated to acquire the good will of his people; and above all, the triple league, it was hoped, would be able to efface all the disagreeable impressions left by the unhappy conclusion of the Dutch war. But a new attempt made by the court, and a laudable one too, lost him, for a time, the effect of all these endeavours. Buckingham, who was in great favour with the king, and carried on many intrigues among the commons, had also endeavoured to support connexions with the nonconformists; and he now formed a scheme, in concert with the lord keeper, Sir Orlando Bridgeman, and the chief justice, Sir Matthew Hale, two worthy patriots, to put an end to those severities, under which these religionists had so long laboured. It was proposed to reconcile the presbyterians by a comprehension, and to grant a toleration to the independants and other sectaries. Favour seems not, by this scheme, as by others embraced during the present reign, to have been intended the catholics: Yet were the zealous commons so disgusted, that they could not be prevailed on even to give the king thanks for the triple league, however laudable that measure was then, and has ever since been esteemed. They immediately voted an address for a proclamation against conventicles. Their request was complied with; but as the king still dropped some hints of his desire to reconcile his protestant subjects, the commons passed a very unusual vote, that no man should bring into the house any bill of that nature. The king in vain reiterated his solicitations for supply; represented the necessity of equipping a fleet; and even offered, that the money, which they should grant, should be collected and issued for that purpose by

8th of February.
A parliament.

commissioners appointed by the house. Instead of complying, the commons voted an enquiry into all the miscarriages during the late war; the slackening of sail after the duke's victory from false orders delivered by Brounker, the miscarriage at Berghen, the division of the fleet under prince Rupert and Albemarle, the disgrace at Chatham. Brounker was expelled the house, and ordered to be impeached. Commissioner Pet, who had neglected orders issued for the security of Chatham, met with the same fate. These impeachments were never prosecuted. The house at length, having been indulged in all their prejudices, were prevailed with to vote the king three hundred and ten thousand pounds, by an imposition on wine and other liquors; after which they were adjourned.

11th of May.   Public business, besides being retarded by the disgust of the commons against the tolerating maxims of the court, met with obstructions this session from a quarrel between the two houses. Skinner, a rich merchant in London, having suffered some injuries from the East India company, laid the matter by petition before the house of lords, by whom he was relieved in costs and damages to the amount of five thousand pounds. The commons voted, that the lords, in taking cognizance of this affair, originally, without any appeal from inferior courts, had acted in a manner not agreeable to the laws of the land, and tending to deprive the subject of the right, ease, and benefit, due to him by these laws; and that Skinner, in prosecuting the suit after this manner, had infringed the privileges of the commons: For which offence, they ordered him to be taken into custody. Some conferences ensued between the houses; where the lords were tenacious of their right of judicature, and maintained, that the method, in which they had exercised it, was quite regular. The commons rose into a great ferment; and went so far as to vote, that "whoever should be aiding or assisting in putting in execution the order or sentence of the house of lords, in the case of Skinner against the East-India company, should be deemed a betrayer of the rights and liberties of the commons of England, and an infringer of the privileges of the house of commons." They rightly judged, that it would not be easy, after this vote, to find any one, who would venture to incur their indignation. The proceedings indeed of the lords seem in this case to have been unusual and without precedent.

CHAPTER LXV

The king's necessities obliged him again to assemble the parliament, who showed some disposition to relieve him. The price, however, which he must pay for this indulgence, was his yielding to new laws against conventicles. His complaisance in this particular contributed more to gain the commons, than all the pompous pretences of supporting the triple alliance, that popular measure, by which he expected to make such advantage. The quarrel between the two houses was revived; and as the commons had voted only four hundred thousand pounds, with which the king was not satisfied, he thought proper before they had carried their vote into a law, to prorogue them. The only business finished this short session was the receiving of the report of the committee appointed for examining the public accounts. On the first inspection of this report, there appears a great sum, no less than a million and a half, unaccounted for; and the natural inference is, that the king had much abused the trust reposed in him by parliament. But a more accurate inspection of particulars serves, in a great measure, to remove this imputation. The king indeed went so far as to tell the parliament from the throne, "That he had fully informed himself of that matter, and did affirm, that no part of those monies, which they had given him, had been diverted to other uses, but on the contrary, besides all those supplies, a very great sum had been raised out of his standing revenue and credit, and a very great debt contracted; and all for the war." Though artificial pretences have often been employed by kings in their speeches to parliament, and by none more than Charles, it is somewhat difficult to suspect him of a direct lie and falshood. He must have had some reasons, and perhaps not unplausible ones, for this affirmation, of which all his hearers, as they had the accounts lying before them, were at that time competent judges.[b]

The method, which all parliaments had hitherto followed, was to vote a particular sum for the supply, without any distinction or any appropriation to particular services. So long as the demands of the crown were small and casual, no great inconveniencies arose from this practice. But as all the measures of government were now changed, it must be confessed, that, if the king made a just

1669.
9th of October.

11th of December.

[b] See note [G] at the end of the volume.

application of public money, this inaccurate method of proceeding, by exposing him to suspicion, was prejudicial to him. If he were inclined to act otherwise, it was equally hurtful to the people. For these reasons, a contrary practice, during all the late reigns, has constantly been followed by the commons.

1670.
14th
February.

When the parliament met after the prorogation, they entered anew upon the business of supply, and granted the king an additional duty, during eight years, of twelve pounds on each tun of Spanish wine imported, eight on each tun of French. A law also passed empowering him to sell the fee farm rents; the last remains of the demesnes, by which the ancient kings of England had been supported. By this expedient he obtained some supply for his present necessities, but left the crown, if possible, still more dependent than before. How much money might be raised by these sales is uncertain; but it could not be near one million eight hundred thousand pounds, the sum assigned by some writers.[c]

The act against conventicles passed, and received the royal assent. It bears the appearance of mitigating the former persecuting laws; but if we may judge by the spirit, which had broken out almost every session during this parliament, it was not intended as any favour to the nonconformists. Experience probably had taught, that laws over rigid and severe could not be executed. By this act the hearer in a conventicle (that is, in a dissenting assembly, where more than five were present, besides the family) was fined five shillings for the first offence, ten for the second; the preacher twenty pounds for the first offence, forty for the second. The person, in whose house the conventicle met, was amerced a like sum with the preacher. One clause is remarkable; that, if any dispute should arise with regard to the interpretation of any part of the act, the judges should always explain the doubt in the sense least favourable to conventicles, it being the intention of parliament entirely to suppress them. Such was the zeal of the commons, that they violated the plainest and most established maxims of civil policy, which require, that, in all criminal prosecutions, favour should always be given to the prisoner.

The affair of Skinner still remained a ground of quarrel be-

[c] Mr. Carte, in his vindication of the Answer to the Bystander, p. 99, says, that the sale of the fee farm rents would not yield above one hundred thousand pounds; and his reasons appear well founded.

CHAPTER LXV

tween the two houses; but the king prevailed with the peers to accept of the expedient proposed by the commons, that a general razure should be made of all the transactions with regard to that disputed question.

Some attempts were made by the king to effect a union between England and Scotland: Though they were too feeble to remove all the difficulties, which obstructed that useful and important undertaking. Commissioners were appointed to meet, in order to regulate the conditions: But the design, chiefly by the intrigues of Lauderdale, soon after came to nothing.

The king, about this time, began frequently to attend the debates of the house of peers. He said, that they amused him, and that he found them no less entertaining than a play. But deeper designs were suspected. As he seemed to interest himself extremely in the cause of lord Roos, who had obtained a divorce from his wife on the accusation of adultery, and applied to parliament for leave to marry again; people imagined, that Charles intended to make a precedent of the case, and that some other pretence would be found for getting rid of the queen. Many proposals to this purpose, it is said, were made him by Buckingham: But the king, how little scrupulous soever in some respects, was incapable of any action harsh or barbarous; and he always rejected every scheme of this nature. A suspicion however of such intentions, it was observed, had, at this time, begotten a coldness between the two royal brothers.

We now come to a period, when the king's counsels, which had hitherto, in the main, been good, though negligent and fluctuating, became, during some time, remarkably bad, or even criminal; and breeding incurable jealousies in all men, were followed by such consequences as had almost terminated in the ruin both of prince and people. Happily, the same negligence still attended him; and, as it had lessened the influence of the good, it also diminished the effect of the bad measures, which he embraced.

It was remarked, that the committee of council, established for foreign affairs, was entirely changed; and that prince Rupert, the duke of Ormond, secretary Trevor, and lord keeper Bridgeman, men in whose honour the nation had great confidence, were never called to any deliberations. The whole secret was entrusted to five persons, Clifford, Ashley, Buckingham, Arlington, and Lauder-

The Cabal.

dale. These men were known by the appellation of the Cabal, a word which the initial letters of their names happened to compose. Never was there a more dangerous ministry in England, nor one more noted for pernicious counsels.

Their characters.

Lord Ashley, soon after known by the name of earl of Shaftesbury, was one of the most remarkable characters of the age, and the chief spring of all the succeeding movements. During his early youth, he had engaged in the late king's party; but being disgusted with some measures of prince Maurice, he soon deserted to the parliament. He insinuated himself into the confidence of Cromwel; and as he had great influence with the presbyterians, he was serviceable in supporting, with his party, the authority of that usurper. He employed the same credit in promoting the restoration; and on that account both deserved and acquired favour with the king. In all his changes, he still maintained the character of never betraying those friends whom he deserted; and which-ever party he joined, his great capacity and singular talents soon gained him their confidence, and enabled him to take the lead among them. No station could satisfy his ambition, no fatigues were insuperable to his industry. Well acquainted with the blind attachment of faction, he surmounted all sense of shame: And relying on the subtilty of his contrivances, he was not startled with enterprizes, the most hazardous and most criminal. His talents, both of public speaking and private insinuation, shone out in an eminent degree; and amidst all his furious passions, he possessed a sound judgment of business, and still more of men. Though fitted by nature for beginning and pushing the greatest undertakings, he was never able to conduct any to a happy period; and his eminent abilities, by reason of his insatiable desires, were equally dangerous to himself, to the prince, and to the people.

The duke of Buckingham possessed all the advantages, which a graceful person, a high rank, a splendid fortune, and a lively wit could bestow; but by his wild conduct, unrestrained either by prudence or principle, he found means to render himself in the end odious and even insignificant. The least interest could make him abandon his honour; the smallest pleasure could seduce him from his interest; the most frivolous caprice was sufficient to counterbalance his pleasure. By his want of secrecy and constancy, he destroyed his character in public life; by his contempt of order and

CHAPTER LXV

economy, he dissipated his private fortune; by riot and debauchery, he ruined his health; and he remained at last as incapable of doing hurt, as he had ever been little desirous of doing good, to mankind.

The earl, soon after created duke of Lauderdale, was not defective in natural, and still less in acquired, talents; but neither was his address graceful, nor his understanding just. His principles, or, more properly speaking, his prejudices, were obstinate, but unable to restrain his ambition: His ambition was still less dangerous than the tyranny and violence of his temper. An implacable enemy, but a lukewarm friend; insolent to his inferiors, but abject to his superiors; though in his whole character and deportment, he was almost diametrically opposite to the king, he had the fortune, beyond any other minister, to maintain, during the greater part of his reign, an ascendant over him.

The talents of parliamentary eloquence and intrigue had raised Sir Thomas Clifford; and his daring impetuous spirit gave him weight in the king's councils. Of the whole cabal, Arlington was the least dangerous either by his vices or his talents. His judgment was sound, though his capacity was but moderate; and his intentions were good, though he wanted courage and integrity to persevere in them. Together with Temple and Bridgeman, he had been a great promoter of the triple league; but he threw himself with equal alacrity into opposite measures, when he found them agreeable to his master. Clifford and he were secretly catholics: Shaftesbury, though addicted to astrology, was reckoned a deist: Buckingham had too little reflection to embrace any steady principles: Lauderdale had long been a bigotted and furious presbyterian; and the opinions of that sect still kept possession of his mind, how little soever they appeared in his conduct.

The dark counsels of the cabal, though from the first they gave anxiety to all men of reflection, were not thoroughly known but by the event. Such seem to have been the views, which they, in concurrence with some catholic courtiers, who had the ear of their sovereign, suggested to the king and the duke, and which these princes too greedily embraced. They said, that the parliament, though the spirit of party, for the present, attached them to the crown, were still more attached to those powers and privileges, which their predecessors had usurped from the sovereign: That

Their counsels.

after the first flow of kindness was spent, they had discovered evident symptoms of discontent; and would be sure to turn against the king all the authority which they yet retained, and still more those pretensions which it was easy for them in a moment to revive: That they not only kept the king in dependence by means of his precarious revenue, but had never discovered a suitable generosity, even in those temporary supplies, which they granted him: That it was high time for the prince to rouze himself from his lethargy, and to recover that authority, which his predecessors, during so many ages, had peaceably enjoyed: That the great error or misfortune of his father was the not having formed any close connexion with foreign princes, who, on the breaking out of the rebellion, might have found their interest in supporting him: That the present alliances, being entered into with so many weaker potentates, who themselves stood in need of the king's protection, could never serve to maintain, much less augment, the royal authority: That the French monarch alone, so generous a prince, and by blood so nearly allied to the king, would be found both able and willing, if gratified in his ambition, to defend the common cause of kings against usurping subjects: That a war, undertaken against Holland by the united force of two such mighty potentates, would prove an easy enterprize, and would serve all the purposes which were aimed at: That under pretence of that war, it would not be difficult to levy a military force, without which, during the prevalence of republican principles among his subjects, the king would vainly expect to defend his prerogative: That his naval power might be maintained, partly by the supplies, which, on other pretences, would previously be obtained from parliament; partly by subsidies from France; partly by captures, which might easily be made on that opulent republic: That in such a situation, attempts to recover the lost authority of the crown would be attended with success; nor would any malcontents dare to resist a prince, fortified by so powerful an alliance; or if they did, they would only draw more certain ruin on themselves and on their cause: And that by subduing the States, a great step would be made towards a reformation of the government; since it was apparent, that that republic, by its fame and grandeur, fortified, in his factious subjects, their attachment to what they vainly termed their civil and religious liberties.

CHAPTER LXV

These suggestions happened fatally to concur with all the inclinations and prejudices of the king; his desire of more extensive
authority, his propensity to the catholic religion, his avidity for
money. He seems likewise, from the very beginning of his reign, to
have entertained great jealousy of his own subjects, and, on that
account, a desire of fortifying himself by an intimate alliance with
France. So early as 1664, he had offered the French monarch to
allow him without opposition to conquer Flanders, provided that
prince would engage to furnish him with ten thousand infantry,
and a suitable number of cavalry, in case of any rebellion in England.[d] As no dangerous symptom at that time appeared, we are left
to conjecture, from this incident, what opinion Charles had conceived of the factious disposition of his people.

Even during the time, when the triple alliance was the most
zealously cultivated, the king never seems to have been entirely
cordial in those salutary measures, but still to have cast a longing
eye towards the French alliance. Clifford, who had much of his
confidence, said imprudently, "Notwithstanding all this joy, we
must have a second war with Holland." The accession of the Emperor to that alliance had been refused by England on frivolous
pretences. And many unfriendly cavils were raised against the
States with regard to Surinam and the conduct of the East India
company.[e] But about April 1669, the strongest symptoms appeared of those fatal measures, which were afterwards more
openly pursued.

De Wit, at that time, came to Temple; and told him, that he
payed him a visit as a friend, not as a minister. The occasion was
to acquaint him with a conversation which he had lately had with
Puffendorf, the Swedish agent, who had passed by the Hague in
the way from Paris to his own country. The French ministers,
Puffendorf said, had taken much pains to persuade him, that the
Swedes would very ill find their account in those measures, which
they had lately embraced: That Spain would fail them in all her
promises of subsidies; nor would Holland alone be able to support
them: That England would certainly fail them, and had already
adopted counsels directly opposite to those which by the triple
league she had bound herself to pursue: And that the resolution

[d] D'Estrades, 21st July, 1667.   [e] See note [H] at the end of the volume.

was not the less fixed and certain, because the secret was as yet communicated to very few either in the French or English court. When Puffendorf seemed incredulous, Turenne showed him a letter from Colbert de Crossy, the French minister at London; in which, after mentioning the success of his negotiations, and the favourable disposition of the chief ministers there, he added, "And I have at last made them sensible of the full extent of his majesty's bounty."*f* From this incident it appears, that the infamous practice of selling themselves to foreign princes, a practice, which, notwithstanding the malignity of the vulgar, is certainly rare among men in high office, had not been scrupled by Charles's ministers, who even obtained their master's consent to this dishonourable corruption.

But while all men of penetration, both abroad and at home, were alarmed with these incidents, the visit, which the king received from his sister, the duchess of Orleans, was the foundation of still stronger suspicions. Lewis, knowing the address and insinuation of that amiable princess, and the great influence, which she had gained over her brother, had engaged her to employ all her good offices, in order to detach Charles from the triple league, which, he knew, had fixed such unsurmountable barriers to his ambition; and he now sent her to put the last hand to the plan of their conjunct operations. That he might the better cover this negotiation, he pretended to visit his frontiers, particularly the great works which he had undertaken at Dunkirk; and he carried *16th May.* the queen and the whole court along with him. While he remained on the opposite shore, the duchess of Orleans went over to England; and Charles met her at Dover, where they passed ten days together in great mirth and festivity. By her artifices and caresses, *Alliance with France.* she prevailed on Charles to relinquish the most settled maxims of honour and policy, and to finish his engagements with Lewis for the destruction of Holland; as well as for the subsequent change of religion in England.

But Lewis well knew Charles's character, and the usual fluctuation of his counsels. In order to fix him in the French interests, he resolved to bind him by the tyes of pleasure, the only ones which with him were irresistible; and he made him a present of a French

f Temple, vol. ii. p. 179.

CHAPTER LXV

mistress, by whose means he hoped, for the future, to govern him. The dutchess of Orleans brought with her a young lady of the name of Queroüaille, whom the king carried to London, and soon after created dutchess of Portsmouth. He was extremely attached to her during the whole course of his life; and she proved a great means of supporting his connexions with her native country.

The satisfaction, which Charles reaped from his new alliance, received a great check by the death of his sister, and still more by those melancholy circumstances which attended it. Her death was sudden, after a few days illness; and she was seized with the malady upon drinking a glass of succory-water. Strong suspicions of poison arose in the court of France, and were spread all over Europe; and as her husband had discovered many symptoms of jealousy and discontent on account of her conduct, he was universally believed to be the author of the crime. Charles himself, during some time, was entirely convinced of his guilt; but upon receiving the attestation of physicians, who, on opening her body, found no foundation for the general rumour, he was, or pretended to be satisfied. The duke of Orleans indeed did never, in any other circumstance of his life, betray such dispositions as might lead him to so criminal an action; and a lady, it is said, drank the remains of the same glass, without feeling any inconvenience. The sudden death of princes is commonly accompanied with these dismal surmises; and therefore less weight is in this case to be laid on the suspicions of the public.

Charles, instead of breaking with France upon this incident, took advantage of it to send over Buckingham, under pretence of condoling with the duke of Orleans, but in reality to concert farther measures for the projected war. Never ambassador received greater caresses. The more destructive the present measures were to the interests of England, the more natural was it for Lewis to load with civilities, and even with favours, those whom he could engage to promote them.

The journey of Buckingham augmented the suspicions in Holland, which every circumstance tended still farther to confirm. Lewis made a sudden irruption into Lorraine; and though he missed seizing the duke himself, who had no surmise of the danger, and who narrowly escaped, he was soon able, without resistance, to make himself master of the whole country. The French

monarch was so far unhappy, that, though the most tempting
opportunities offered themselves, he had not commonly so much
as the pretence of equity and justice to cover his ambitious measures. This acquisition of Lorraine ought to have excited the jealousy of the contracting powers in the triple league, as much as an
invasion of Flanders itself; yet did Charles turn a deaf ear to all
remonstrances, made him upon that subject.

But what tended chiefly to open the eyes of de Wit and the
States, with regard to the measures of England, was the sudden
recal of Sir William Temple. This minister had so firmly established his character of honour and integrity, that he was believed
incapable even of obeying his master's commands, in promoting
measures which he esteemed pernicious to his country; and so
long as he remained in employment, de Wit thought himself assured of the fidelity of England. Charles was so sensible of this
prepossession, that he ordered Temple to leave his family at the
Hague, and pretended, that that minister would immediately return, after having conferred with the king about some business,
where his negotiation had met with obstructions. De Wit made the
Dutch resident inform the English court, that he should consider
the recal of Temple as an express declaration of a change of measures in England; and should even know what interpretation to
put upon any delay of his return.

24th Oct.
A parlia-
ment.

While these measures were secretly in agitation, the parliament
met, according to adjournment. The king made a short speech,
and left the business to be enlarged upon by the keeper. That
minister much insisted on the king's great want of supply; the
mighty encrease of the naval power of France, now triple to what
it was before the last war with Holland; the decay of the English
navy; the necessity of fitting out next year a fleet of fifty sail; the
obligations which the king lay under by several treaties to exert
himself for the common good of christendom. Among other treaties, he mentioned the triple alliance, and the defensive league
with the States.

The artifice succeeded. The house of commons, entirely satisfied with the king's measures, voted him considerable supplies. A
land tax for a year was imposed of a shilling a pound; two shillings
a pound on two thirds of the salaries of offices; fifteen shillings on
every hundred pounds of bankers' money and stock; an additional

CHAPTER LXV

excise upon beer for six years, and certain impositions upon law proceedings for nine years. The parliament had never before been in a more liberal humour; and never surely was it less merited by the counsels of the king and of his ministers.[g]

The commons passed another bill, for laying a duty on tobacco, Scotch salt, glasses, and some other commodities. Against this bill the merchants of London appeared by petition before the house of lords. The lords entered into their reasons, and began to make amendments on the bill sent up by the commons. This attempt was highly resented by the lower house, as an encroachment on the right, which they pretended to possess alone, of granting money to the crown. Many remonstrances passed between the two houses; and by their altercations the king was obliged to prorogue the parliament; and he thereby lost the money which was intended him. This is the last time that the peers have revived any pre-

1671.

22d April.

[g] This year, on the 3d of January, died George Monk, duke of Albemarle, at Newhall in Essex, after a languishing illness, and in the sixty-third year of his age. He left a great estate of 5,000 l. a year in land, and 60,000 l. in money, acquired by the bounty of the king, and encreased by his own frugality in his later years. Bishop Burnet, who, agreeably to his own factious spirit, treats this illustrious personage with great malignity, reproaches him with avarice: But as he appears not to have been in the least tainted with rapacity, his frugal conduct may more candidly be imputed to the habits, acquired in early life, while he was possessed of a very narrow fortune. It is indeed a singular proof of the strange power of faction, that any malignity should pursue the memory of a nobleman, the tenor of whose life was so unexceptionable, and who, by restoring the antient and legal and free government to three kingdoms, plunged in the most destructive anarchy, may safely be said to be the subject, in these islands, who, since the beginning of time, rendered the most durable and most essential services to his native country. The means also, by which he atchieved his great undertakings, were almost entirely unexceptionable. His temporary dissimulation, being absolutely necessary, could scarcely be blameable. He had received no trust from that mungrel, pretended, usurping parliament whom he dethroned; therefore could betray none: He even refused to carry his dissimulation so far as to take the oath of abjuration against the king. I confess, however, that the Rev. Dr. Douglas has shown me, from the Clarendon papers, an original letter of his to Sir Arthur Hazzlerig, containing very earnest, and certainly false protestations of his zeal for a commonwealth. It is to be lamented, that so worthy a man, and of such plain manners, should ever have found it necessary to carry his dissimulation to such a height. His family ended with his son.

tensions of that nature. Ever since, the privilege of the commons, in all other places, except in the house of peers, has passed for uncontroverted.

There was a private affair, which during this session disgusted the house of commons, and required some pains to accommodate it. The usual method of those who opposed the court in the money bills, was, if they failed in the main vote, as to the extent of the supply, to levy the money upon such funds as they expected would be unacceptable, or would prove deficient. It was proposed to lay an imposition upon playhouses: The courtiers objected, that the players were the king's servants, and a part of his pleasure. Sir John Coventry, a gentleman of the country party, asked, "whether the king's pleasure lay among the male or the female players?" This stroke of satire was aimed at Charles, who, besides his mistresses of higher quality, entertained at that time two actresses, Davis and Nell Gwin. The king received not the raillery with the good humour, which might have been expected. It was said, that this being the first time, that respect to majesty had been publicly violated, it was necessary, by some severe chastisement, to make Coventry an example to all who might incline to tread in his footsteps. Sands, Obrian, and some other officers of the guards were ordered to way-lay him, and to set a mark upon him. He defended himself with bravery, and after wounding several of the assailants, was disarmed with some difficulty. They cut his nose to the bone, in order, as they said, to teach him what respect he owed to the king. The commons were inflamed by this indignity offered to one of their members, on account of words spoken in the house. They *Coventry* passed a law, which made it capital to maim any person; and they *act.* enacted, that those criminals, who had assaulted Coventry, should be incapable of receiving a pardon from the crown.

There was another private affair transacted about this time, by which the king was as much exposed to the imputation of a capricious lenity, as he was here blamed for unnecessary severity. *Blood's* Blood, a disbanded officer of the protector's, had been engaged in *crimes.* the conspiracy for raising an insurrection in Ireland; and on account of this crime he himself had been attainted, and some of his accomplices capitally punished. The daring villain meditated revenge upon Ormond, the lord lieutenant. Having by artifice drawn off the duke's footmen, he attacked his coach in the night

CHAPTER LXV

time, as it drove along St. James's street in London; and he made himself master of his person. He might here have finished the crime, had he not meditated refinements in his vengeance: He was resolved to hang the duke at Tyburn; and for that purpose bound him, and mounted him on horseback behind one of his companions. They were advanced a good way into the fields; when the duke, making efforts for his liberty, threw himself to the ground, and brought down with him the assassin to whom he was fastened. They were struggling together in the mire; when Ormond's servants, whom the alarm had reached, came and saved him. Blood and his companions, firing their pistols in a hurry at the duke, rode off, and saved themselves by means of the darkness.

Buckingham was at first, with some appearances of reason, suspected to be the author of this attempt. His profligate character, and his enmity against Ormond, exposed him to that imputation. Ossory soon after came to court; and seeing Buckingham stand by the king, his colour rose, and he could not forbear expressing himself to this purpose. "My lord, I know well, that you are at the bottom of this late attempt upon my father: But I give you warning; if by any means he come to a violent end, I shall not be at a loss to know the author: I shall consider you as the assassin: I shall treat you as such; and wherever I meet you, I shall pistol you, though you stood behind the king's chair; and I tell it you in his majesty's presence, that you may be sure I shall not fail of performance."[h] If there was here any indecorum, it was easily excused in a generous youth, when his father's life was exposed to danger.

A little after, Blood formed a design of carrying off the crown and regalia from the Tower; a design, to which he was prompted, as well by the surprising boldness of the enterprize, as by the views of profit. He was near succeeding. He had bound and wounded Edwards, the keeper of the jewel-office, and had gotten out of the Tower with his prey; but was overtaken and seized, with some of his associates. One of them was known to have been concerned in the attempt upon Ormond; and Blood was immediately concluded to be the ringleader. When questioned, he frankly avowed the enterprize; but refused to tell his accomplices. "The fear of death,"

[h] Carte's Ormond, vol. ii. p. 225.

he said, "should never engage him, either to deny a guilt, or betray a friend." All these extraordinary circumstances made him the general subject of conversation; and the king was moved by an idle curiosity to see and speak with a person, so noted for his courage and his crimes. Blood might now esteem himself secure of pardon; and he wanted not address to improve the opportunity. He told Charles, that he had been engaged, with others, in a design to kill him with a carabine above Battersea, where his majesty often went to bathe: That the cause of this resolution was the severity exercised over the consciences of the godly, in restraining the liberty of their religious assemblies: That when he had taken his stand among the reeds, full of these bloody resolutions, he found his heart checked with an awe of majesty; and he not only relented himself, but diverted his associates from their purpose: That he had long ago brought himself to an entire indifference about life, which he now gave for lost; yet could he not forbear warning the king of the danger which might attend his execution: That his associates had bound themselves by the strictest oaths to revenge the death of any of the confederacy: And that no precaution or power could secure any one from the effects of their desperate resolutions.

Whether these considerations excited fear or admiration in the king, they confirmed his resolution of granting a pardon to Blood; but he thought it a point of decency first to obtain the duke of Ormond's consent. Arlington came to Ormond in the king's name, and desired that he would not prosecute Blood, for reasons which he was commanded to give him. The duke replied, that his majesty's commands were the only reason, that could be given; and being sufficient, he might therefore spare the rest. Charles carried his kindness to Blood still farther: He granted him an estate of five hundred pounds a year in Ireland; he encouraged his attendance about his person; he shewed him great countenance, and many applied to him for promoting their pretensions at court. And while old Edwards, who had bravely ventured his life, and had been wounded, in defending the crown and regalia, was forgotten and neglected, this man, who deserved only to be stared at, and detested as a monster, became a kind of favourite.

Errors of this nature in private life have often as bad an influence as miscarriages, in which the public is more immediately

CHAPTER LXV

concerned. Another incident happened this year, which infused a general displeasure, and still greater apprehensions, into all men. The dutchess of York died; and in her last sickness, she made open profession of the Romish religion, and finished her life in that communion. This put an end to that thin disguise, which the duke had hitherto worn; and he now openly declared his conversion to the church of Rome. Unaccountable terrors of popery, ever since the accession of the house of Stuart, had prevailed throughout the nation; but these had formerly been found so groundless, and had been employed to so many bad purposes, that surmises of this nature were likely to meet with the less credit among all men of sense; and nothing but the duke's imprudent bigotry could have convinced the whole nation of this change of religion. Popery, which had hitherto been only a hideous spectre, was now become a real ground of terror; being openly and zealously embraced by the heir to the crown, a prince of industry and enterprize; while the king himself was not entirely free from like suspicions.

Duke declares himself catholic.

It is probable, that the new alliance with France inspired the duke with the courage to make open profession of his religion, and rendered him more careless of the affections and esteem of the English. This alliance became every day more apparent. Temple was declared to be no longer ambassador to the States; and Downing, whom the Dutch regarded as the inveterate enemy of their republic, was sent over in his stead. A ground of quarrel was sought by means of a yacht, dispatched for lady Temple. The captain sailed through the Dutch fleet, which lay on their own coasts; and he had orders to make them strike, to fire on them, and to persevere till they should return his fire. The Dutch admiral, Van Ghent, surprised at this bravado, came on board the yacht, and expressed his willingness to pay respect to the British flag, according to former practice: But that a fleet, on their own coasts, should strike to a single vessel, and that not a ship of war, was, he said, such an innovation, that he durst not, without express orders, agree to it. The captain, thinking it dangerous, as well as absurd, to renew firing in the midst of the Dutch fleet, continued his course; and for that neglect of orders was committed to the Tower.

This incident, however, furnished Downing with a new article to encrease those vain pretences on which it was purposed to ground the intended rupture. The English court delayed several months before they complained; lest, if they had demanded satisfaction more early, the Dutch might have had time to grant it. Even when Downing delivered his memorial, he was bound by his instructions not to accept of any satisfaction after a certain number of days; a very imperious manner of negotiating, and impracticable in Holland, where the forms of the republic render delays absolutely unavoidable. An answer, however, though refused by Downing, was sent over to London; with an ambassador extraordinary, who had orders to use every expedient, that might give satisfaction to the court of England. That court replied, that the answer of the Hollanders was ambiguous and obscure; but they would not specify the articles or expressions, which were liable to that objection. The Dutch ambassador desired the English minister to draw the answer in what terms they pleased; and he engaged to sign it: The English ministry replied, that it was not their business to draw papers for the Dutch. The ambassador brought them the draught of an article, and asked them whether it were satisfactory: The English answered, that, when he had signed and delivered it, they would tell him their mind concerning it. The Dutchman resolved to sign it at a venture; and on his demanding a new audience, an hour was appointed for that purpose: But when he attended, the English refused to enter upon business, and told him, that the season for negotiating was now past.[i]

1672.   Long and frequent prorogations were made of the parliament; lest the houses should declare themselves with vigour against counsels, so opposite to the inclination as well as interests of the public. Could we suppose, that Charles, in his alliance against Holland, really meant the good of his people, that measure must pass for an extraordinary, nay, a romantic, strain of patriotism, which could lead him, in spite of all difficulties, and even in spite of themselves, to seek the welfare of the nation. But every step, which he took in this affair, became a proof to all men of penetration, that the present war was intended against the religion and

---

[i] England's Appeal, p. 22. This year, on the 12th of November, died, in his retreat, and in the 60th year of his age, Thomas lord Fairfax, who performed many great actions, without being a memorable personage, and allowed himself to be carried into many criminal enterprizes, with the best and most upright intentions. His daughter and heir was married to George Villiers, duke of Buckingham.

CHAPTER LXV

liberties of his own subjects, even more than against the Dutch themselves. He now acted in every thing, as if he were already an absolute monarch, and was never more to lie under the controul of national assemblies.

The long prorogations of parliament, if they freed the king from the importunate remonstrances of that assembly, were however attended with this inconvenience, that no money could be procured to carry on the military preparations against Holland. Under pretence of maintaining the triple league, which, at that very time, he had firmly resolved to break, Charles had obtained a large supply from the commons; but this money was soon exhausted by debts and expences. France had stipulated to pay two hundred thousand pounds a year during the war; but that supply was inconsiderable, compared to the immense charge of the English navy. It seemed as yet premature to venture on levying money, without consent of parliament; since the power of taxing themselves was the privilege, of which the English were, with reason, particularly jealous. Some other resource must be fallen on. The king had declared, that the staff of treasurer was ready for any one, that could find an expedient for supplying the present necessities. Shaftesbury dropped a hint to Clifford, which the latter immediately seized, and carried to the king, who granted him the promised reward, together with a peerage. This expedient was the shutting up of the Exchequer, and the retaining of all the payments, which should be made into it.

3d January. Exchequer shut.

It had been usual for the bankers to carry their money to the Exchequer, and to advance it upon security of the funds, by which they were afterwards re-imbursed, when the money was levied on the public. The bankers, by this traffic, got eight, sometimes ten, per cent. for sums, which either had been consigned to them without interest, or which they had borrowed at six per cent.: Profits, which they dearly paid for by this egregious breach of public faith. The measure was so suddenly taken, that none had warning of the danger. A general confusion prevailed in the city, followed by the ruin of many. The bankers stopped payment; the merchants could answer no bills; distrust took place every where, with a stagnation of commerce, by which the public was universally affected. And men, full of dismal apprehensions, asked each other, what must be the scope of those mysterious counsels, whence the parliament and all men of honour were excluded, and which commenced by the forfeiture of public credit, and an open violation of the most solemn engagements, both foreign and domestic.

Declaration of indulgence.

Another measure of the court contains something laudable, when considered in itself; but if we reflect on the motive whence it proceeded, as well as the time when it was embraced, it will furnish a strong proof of the arbitrary and dangerous counsels, pursued at present by the king and his ministry. Charles resolved to make use of his supreme power in ecclesiastical matters; a power, he said, which was not only inherent in him, but which had been recognized by several acts of parliament. By virtue of this authority, he issued a proclamation; suspending the penal laws, enacted against all nonconformists or recusants whatsoever; and granting to the protestant dissenters the public exercise of their religion, to the catholics the exercise of it in private houses. A fruitless experiment of this kind, opposed by the parliament, and retracted by the king, had already been made a few years after the restoration; but Charles expected, that the parliament, whenever it should meet, would now be tamed to greater submission, and would no longer dare to controul his measures. Meanwhile, the dissenters, the most inveterate enemies of the court, were mollified by these indulgent maxims: And the catholics, under their shelter, enjoyed more liberty than the laws had hitherto allowed them.

15th March.

At the same time, the act of navigation was suspended by royal will and pleasure: A measure, which, though a stretch of prerogative, seemed useful to commerce, while all the seamen were employed on board the royal navy. A like suspension had been granted, during the first Dutch war, and was not much remarked; because men had, at that time, entertained less jealousy of the crown. A proclamation was also issued, containing rigorous clauses in favour of pressing: Another full of menaces against those who presumed to speak undutifully of his majesty's measures, and even against those who heard such discourse, unless they informed in due time against the offenders: Another against importing or vending any sort of painted earthen ware, "except those of China, upon pain of being grievously fined, and suffering the utmost punishment, which might be lawfully inflicted upon contemners of his majesty's royal authority." An army had been levied; and it was found, that discipline could not be enforced without the exer-

CHAPTER LXV

cise of martial law, which was therefore established by order of council, though contrary to the petition of right. All these acts of power, how little important soever in themselves, savoured strongly of arbitrary government, and were nowise suitable to that legal administration, which the parliament, after such violent convulsions and civil wars, had hoped to have established in the kingdom.

It may be worth remarking, that the lord-keeper refused to affix the great seal to the declaration for suspending the penal laws; and was for that reason, though under other pretences, removed from his office. Shaftesbury was made chancellor in his place; and thus another member of the Cabal received the reward of his counsels.

Foreign transactions kept pace with these domestic occurrences. An attempt, before the declaration of war, was made on the Dutch Smyrna fleet by Sir Robert Holmes. This fleet consisted of seventy sail, valued at a million and a half; and the hopes of seizing so rich a prey had been a great motive for engaging Charles in the present war, and he had considered that capture as a principal resource for supporting his military enterprizes. Holmes, with nine frigates and three yachts, had orders to go on this command; and he passed Sprague in the channel, who was returning with a squadron from a cruize in the Mediterranean. Sprague informed him of the near approach of the Hollanders; and had not Holmes, from a desire of engrossing the honour and profit of the enterprize, kept the secret of his orders, the conjunction of these squadrons had rendered the success infallible. When Holmes approached the Dutch, he put on an amicable appearance, and invited the admiral, Van Ness, who commanded the convoy, to come on board of him; One of his captains gave a like insidious invitation to the rear-admiral. But these officers were on their guard. They had received an intimation of the hostile intentions of the English, and had already put all the ships of war and merchantmen in an excellent posture of defence. Three times were they valiantly assailed by the English; and as often did they valiantly defend themselves. In the third attack one of the Dutch ships of war was taken: and three or four of their most inconsiderable merchantmen fell into the enemies' hands. The rest, fighting with skill and courage, continued their course; and favoured by a mist,

Attack of the Smyrna fleet.

13th March.

got safe into their own harbours. This attempt is denominated perfidious and pyratical by the Dutch writers, and even by many of the English. It merits at least the appellation of irregular; and as it had been attended with bad success, it brought double shame upon the contrivers. The English ministry endeavoured to apologize for the action, by pretending that it was a casual rencounter, arising from the obstinacy of the Dutch, in refusing the honours of the flag: But the contrary was so well known, that even Holmes himself had not the assurance to persist in this asseveration.

Till this incident the States, notwithstanding all the menaces and preparations of the English, never believed them thoroughly in earnest; and had always expected, that the affair would terminate, either in some demands of money, or in some proposals for the advancement of the prince of Orange. The French themselves had never much reckoned on assistance from England; and scarcely could believe, that their ambitious projects would, contrary to every maxim of honour and policy, be forwarded by that power, which was most interested, and most able to oppose them. But Charles was too far advanced to retreat. He immediately issued a declaration of war against the Dutch; and surely reasons more false and frivolous never were employed to justify a flagrant violation of treaty. Some complaints are there made of injuries done to the East India company, which yet that company disavowed: The detention of some English in Surinam is mentioned; though it appears, that these persons had voluntarily remained there: The refusal of a Dutch fleet on their own coasts to strike to an English yacht, is much aggravated: And to piece up all these pretensions, some abusive pictures are mentioned, and represented as a ground of quarrel. The Dutch were long at a loss what to make of this article; till it was discovered, that a portrait of Cornelius de Wit, brother to the pensionary, painted by order of certain magistrates of Dort, and hung up in a chamber of the town-house, had given occasion to the complaint. In the perspective of this portrait, the painter had drawn some ships on fire in a harbour. This was construed to be Chatham, where de Wit had really distinguished himself, and had acquired honour; but little did he imagine, that, while the insult itself, committed in open war, had so long been forgiven, the picture of it should draw such severe vengeance upon his country. The conclusion of this man-

17th March. War declared with Holland.

CHAPTER LXV

ifesto, where the king still professed his resolution of adhering to the triple alliance, was of a piece with the rest of it.

Lewis's declaration of war contained more dignity, if undisguised violence and injustice could merit that appellation. He pretended only, that the behaviour of the Hollanders had been such, that it did not consist with his glory any longer to bear it. That monarch's preparations were in great forwardness; and his ambition was flattered with the most promising views of success. Sweden was detached from the triple league: The bishop of Munster was engaged by the payment of subsidies to take part with France: The elector of Cologne had entered into the same alliance; and having consigned Bonne and other towns into the hands of Lewis, magazines were there erected; and it was from that quarter that France purposed to invade the United Provinces. The standing force of that kingdom amounted to a hundred and eighty thousand men; and with more than half of this great army was the French king now approaching to the Dutch frontiers. The order, economy, and industry of Colbert, equally subservient to the ambition of the prince and happiness of the people, furnished unexhausted treasures: These, employed by the unrelenting vigilance of Louvois, supplied every military preparation, and facilitated all the enterprizes of the army: Condé, Turenne, seconded by Luxembourg, Crequi, and the most renowned generals of the age, conducted this army, and by their conduct and reputation inspired courage into every one. The monarch himself, surrounded with a brave nobility, animated his troops by the prospect of reward, or, what was more valued, by the hopes of his approbation. The fatigues of war gave no interruption to gaiety: Its dangers furnished matter for glory: And in no enterprize did the genius of that gallant and polite people ever break out with more distinguished lustre.

Though de Wit's intelligence in foreign courts was not equal to the vigilance of his domestic administration, he had, long before, received many surmises of this fatal confederacy; but he prepared not for defence, so early or with such industry, as the danger required. A union of England with France was evidently, he saw, destructive to the interests of the former kingdom; and therefore, overlooking or ignorant of the humours and secret views of Charles, he concluded it impossible, that such pernicious projects

could ever really be carried into execution. Secure in this fallacious reasoning, he allowed the republic to remain too long in
that defenceless situation, into which many concurring accidents
had conspired to throw her.

Weakness of the States. By a continued and successful application to commerce, the
people were become unwarlike, and confided entirely for their
defence in that mercenary army, which they maintained. After the
treaty of Westphalia, the States, trusting to their peace with Spain,
and their alliance with France, had broken a great part of this
army, and did not support with sufficient vigilance the discipline
of the troops which remained. When the aristocratic party prevailed, it was thought prudent to dismiss many of the old experienced officers, who were devoted to the house of Orange; and
their place was supplied by raw youths, the sons or kinsmen of
burgomasters, by whose interest the party was supported. These
new officers, relying on the credit of their friends and family,
neglected their military duty; and some of them, it is said, were
even allowed to serve by deputies, to whom they assigned a small
part of their pay. During the war with England, all the forces of
that nation had been disbanded: Lewis's invasion of Flanders, followed by the triple league, occasioned the dismission of the French
regiments: And the place of these troops, which had ever had a
chief share in the honour and fortune of all the wars in the Low
Countries, had not been supplied by any new levies.

De Wit, sensible of this dangerous situation, and alarmed by the
reports which came from all quarters, exerted himself to supply
those defects, to which it was not easy of a sudden to provide a
suitable remedy. But every proposal, which he could make, met
with opposition from the Orange party, now become extremely
formidable. The long and uncontrouled administration of this
statesman had begotten envy: The present incidents roused up his
enemies and opponents, who ascribed to his misconduct alone the
bad situation of the republic: And, above all, the popular affection
to the young prince, which had so long been held in violent constraint, and had thence acquired new accession of force, began to
display itself, and to threaten the commonwealth with some great
convulsion. William III, prince of Orange, was in the twenty-
second year of his age, and gave strong indications of those great
qualities, by which his life was afterwards so much distinguished.

CHAPTER LXV

De Wit himself, by giving him an excellent education, and instructing him in all the principles of government and sound policy, had generously contributed to make his rival formidable. Dreading the precarious situation of his own party, he was always resolved, he said, by conveying to the prince the knowledge of affairs, to render him capable of serving his country, if any future emergence should ever throw the administration into his hands. The conduct of William had hitherto been extremely laudable. Notwithstanding his powerful alliances with England and Brandenburgh, he had expressed his resolution of depending entirely on the States for his advancement; and the whole tenor of his behaviour suited extremely the genius of that people. Silent and thoughtful; given to hear and to enquire; of a sound and steady understanding; firm in what he once resolved, or once denied; strongly intent on business, little on pleasure: By these virtues he engaged the attention of all men. And the people, sensible that they owed their liberty, and very existence, to his family, and remembering, that his great uncle, Maurice, had been able, even in more early youth, to defend them against the exorbitant power of Spain, were desirous of raising this prince to all the authority of his ancestors, and hoped, from his valour and conduct alone, to receive protection against those imminent dangers, with which they were at present threatened.

While these two powerful factions struggled for superiority, every scheme for defence was opposed, every project retarded. What was determined with difficulty, was executed without vigour. Levies indeed were made, and the army compleated to seventy thousand men; [k] The prince was appointed both general and admiral of the commonwealth, and the whole military power was put into his hands. But new troops could not of a sudden acquire discipline and experience: And the partizans of the prince were still unsatisfied, as long as the *perpetual edict,* so it was called, remained in force; by which he was excluded from the stadtholdership, and from all share in the civil administration.

It had always been the maxim of de Wit's party to cultivate naval affairs with extreme care, and to give the fleet a preference above the army, which they represented as the object of an unrea-

[k] Temple, vol. i. p. 75.

sonable partiality in the princes of Orange. The two violent wars, which had of late been waged with England, had exercised the valour, and improved the skill of the sailors. And, above all, de Ruyter, the greatest sea commander of the age, was closely connected with the Lovestein party; and every one was disposed, with confidence and alacrity, to obey him. The equipment of the fleet was therefore hastened by de Wit; in hopes, that, by striking at first a successful blow, he might inspire courage into the dismayed States, and support his own declining authority. He seems to have been, in a peculiar manner, incensed against the English; and he resolved to take revenge on them for their conduct, of which, he thought, he himself and his country had such reason to complain. By the offer of a close alliance for mutual defence, they had seduced the republic to quit the alliance of France; but no sooner had she embraced these measures, than they formed leagues for her destruction, with that very power, which they had treacherously engaged her to offend. In the midst of full peace, nay, during an intimate union, they attacked her commerce, her only means of subsistence; and, moved by shameful rapacity, had invaded that property, which, from a reliance on their faith, they had hoped to find unprotected and defenceless. Contrary to their own manifest interest, as well as to their honour, they still retained a malignant resentment for her successful conclusion of the former war; a war, which had, at first, sprung from their own wanton insolence and ambition. To repress so dangerous an enemy, would, de Wit imagined, give peculiar pleasure, and contribute to the future security of his country, whose prosperity was so much the object of general envy.

Actuated by like motives and views, de Ruyter put to sea with a formidable fleet, consisting of ninety-one ships of war and forty-four fire-ships. Cornelius de Wit was on board, as deputy from the States. They sailed in quest of the English, who were under the command of the duke of York, and who had already joined the French under Mareschal d'Etrées. The combined fleets lay at Sole-bay in a very negligent posture; and Sandwich, being an experienced officer, had given the duke warning of the danger; but received, it is said, such an answer as intimated, that there was more of caution than of courage in his apprehensions. Upon the appearance of the enemy, every one ran to his post with precip-

Battle of Solebay. 28th May.

itation, and many ships were obliged to cut their cables, in order to be in readiness. Sandwich commanded the van; and though determined to conquer or to perish, he so tempered his courage with prudence, that the whole fleet was visibly indebted to him for its safety. He hastened out of the bay, where it had been easy for de Ruyter with his fire-ships to have destroyed the combined fleets, which were crowded together; and by this wise measure he gave time to the duke of York, who commanded the main body, and to mareschal d'Etrées, admiral of the rear, to disengage themselves. He himself meanwhile rushed into battle with the Hollanders; and by presenting himself to every danger, had drawn upon him all the bravest of the enemy. He killed Van Ghent, a Dutch admiral, and beat off his ship: He sunk another ship, which ventured to lay him aboard: He sunk three fire-ships, which endeavoured to grapple with him: And though his vessel was torn in pieces with shot, and of a thousand men she contained, near six hundred were laid dead upon the deck, he continued still to thunder with all his artillery in the midst of the enemy. But another fire-ship, more fortunate than the preceding, having laid hold of his vessel, her destruction was now inevitable. Warned by Sir Edward Haddock, his captain, he refused to make his escape, and bravely embraced death as a shelter from that ignominy, which a rash expression of the duke's, he thought, had thrown upon him.

Sandwich killed.

During this fierce engagement with Sandwich, de Ruyter remained not inactive. He attacked the duke of York, and sought him with such fury for above two hours, that of two and thirty actions, in which that admiral had been engaged, he declared this combat to be the most obstinately disputed. The duke's ship was so shattered, that he was obliged to leave her, and remove his flag to another. His squadron was overpowered with numbers; till Sir Joseph Jordan, who had succeeded to Sandwich's command, came to his assistance; and the fight, being more equally balanced, was continued till night, when the Dutch retired, and were not followed by the English. The loss sustained by the fleets of the two maritime powers was nearly equal, if it did not rather fall more heavy on the English. The French suffered very little, because they had scarcely been engaged in the action; and as this backwardness is not their national character, it was concluded, that they had received secret orders to spare their ships, while the Dutch and

English should weaken each other by their mutual animosity. Almost all the other actions during the present war tended to confirm this suspicion.

It might be deemed honourable for the Dutch to have fought with some advantage the combined fleets of two such powerful nations; but nothing less than a complete victory could serve the purpose of de Wit, or save his country from those calamities, which from every quarter threatened to overwhelm her. He had expected, that the French would make their attack on the side of Maestricht, which was well fortified, and provided with a good garrison; but Lewis, taking advantage of his alliance with Cologne, resolved to invade the enemy on that frontier, which he knew to be more feeble and defenceless. The armies of that elector, and those of Munster appeared on the other side of the Rhine, and divided the force and attention of the States. The Dutch troops, too weak to defend so extensive a frontier, were scattered into so many towns, that no considerable body remained in the field; and a strong garrison was scarcely to be found in any fortress. Lewis passed the Meuse at Viset; and laying siege to Orsoi, a town of the elector of Brandenburgh's, but garrisoned by the Dutch, he carried it in three days. He divided his army, and invested at once Burik, Wesel, Emerik, and Rhimberg, four places regularly fortified, and not unprovided with troops: In a few days all these places were surrendered. A general astonishment had seized the Hollanders, from the combination of such powerful princes against the republic; and no where was resistance made, suitable to the ancient glory or present greatness of the state. Governors without experience commanded troops without discipline; and despair had universally extinguished that sense of honour, by which alone, men, in such dangerous extremities, can be animated to a valorous defence.

14th May.

Progress of the French.

Lewis advanced to the banks of the Rhine, which he prepared to pass. To all the other calamities of the Dutch was added the extreme drought of the season, by which the greatest rivers were much diminished, and in some places rendered fordable. The French cavalry, animated by the presence of their prince, full of impetuous courage, but ranged in exact order, flung themselves into the river: The infantry passed in boats: A few regiments of Dutch appeared on the other side, who were unable to make resis-

2d June.

CHAPTER LXV

tance. And thus was executed without danger, but not without glory, the passage of the Rhine; so much celebrated, at that time, by the flattery of the French courtiers, and transmitted to posterity by the more durable flattery of their poets.

Each success added courage to the conquerors, and struck the vanquished with dismay. The prince of Orange, though prudent beyond his age, was but newly advanced to the command, unacquainted with the army, unknown to them; and all men, by reason of the violent factions which prevailed, were uncertain of the authority on which they must depend. It was expected, that the fort of Skink, famous for the sieges which it had formerly sustained, would make some resistance; but it yielded to Turenne in a few days. The same general made himself master of Arnheim, Knotzembourg, and Nimeguen, as soon as he appeared before them. Doesbourg at the same time opened its gates to Lewis: Soon after, Harderwic, Amersfort, Campen, Rhenen, Viane, Elberg, Zwol, Cuilemberg, Wageninguen, Lochem, Woerden, fell into the enemies' hands. Groll and Deventer surrendered to the mareschal Luxembourg, who commanded the troops of Munster. And every hour brought to the States news of the rapid progess of the French, and of the cowardly defence of their own garrisons.

The prince of Orange, with his small and discouraged army, retired into the province of Holland; where he expected, from the natural strength of the country, since all human art and courage failed, to be able to make some resistance. The town and province of Utrecht sent deputies, and surrendered themselves to Lewis. Naerden, a place within three leagues of Amsterdam, was seized by the marquis of Rochfort, and had he pushed on to Muyden, he had easily gotten possession of it. Fourteen stragglers of his army having appeared before the gates of that town, the magistrates sent them the keys; but a servant maid, who was alone in the castle, having raised the drawbridge, kept them from taking possession of that fortress. The magistrates afterwards, finding the party so weak, made them drunk, and took the keys from them. Muyden is so near to Amsterdam, that its cannon may infest the ships which enter that city.

Lewis with a splendid court made a solemn entry into Utrecht, *25th June.* full of glory, because every where attended with success; though more owing to the cowardice and misconduct of his enemies, than to his own valour or prudence. The three provinces were already in his hands, Guelderland, Overyssel, and Utrecht; Groninghen was threatened; Friezeland was exposed: The only difficulty lay in Holland and Zealand; and the monarch deliberated concerning the proper measures for reducing them. Condé and Turenne exhorted him to dismantle all the towns, which he had taken, except a few; and fortifying his main army by the garrisons, put himself in a condition of pushing his conquests. Louvois, hoping that the other provinces, weak and dismayed, would prove an easy prey, advised him to keep possession of places, which might afterwards serve to retain the people in subjection. His council was followed; though it was found, soon after, to have been the most impolitic.

Consterna-tion of the Dutch. Meanwhile the people, throughout the republic, instead of collecting a noble indignation against the haughty conqueror, discharged their rage upon their own unhappy minister, on whose prudence and integrity every one formerly bestowed the merited applause. The bad condition of the armies was laid to his charge: The ill choice of governors was ascribed to his partiality: As instances of cowardice multiplied, treachery was suspected; and his former connections with France being remembered, the populace believed, that he and his partizans had now combined to betray them to their most mortal enemy. The prince of Orange, notwithstanding his youth and inexperience, was looked on as the only saviour of the state; and men were violently driven by their fears into his party, to which they had always been led by favour and inclination.

Amsterdam alone seemed to retain some courage; and by forming a regular plan of defence, endeavoured to infuse spirit into the other cities. The magistrates obliged the burgesses to keep a strict watch: The populace, whom want of employment might engage to mutiny, were maintained by regular pay, and armed for the defence of the public. Some ships, which lay useless in the harbour, were refitted, and stationed to guard the city: And the sluices being opened, the neighbouring country, without regard to the damage sustained, was laid under water. All the province followed the example, and scrupled not, in this extremity, to restore to the sea those fertile fields, which with great art and expence had been won from it.

The states were assembled, to consider, whether any means

CHAPTER LXV

were left to save the remains of their lately flourishing, and now distressed Commonwealth. Though they were surrounded with waters, which barred all access to the enemy, their deliberations were not conducted with that tranquillity, which could alone suggest measure, proper to extricate them from their present difficulties. The nobles gave their vote, that, provided their religion, liberty, and sovereignty could be saved, every thing else should without scruple be sacrificed to the conqueror. Eleven towns concurred in the same sentiments. Amsterdam singly declared against all treaty with insolent and triumphant enemies: But notwithstanding that opposition, ambassadors were dispatched to implore the pity of the two combined monarchs. It was resolved to sacrifice to Lewis, Maestricht and all the frontier towns, which lay without the bounds of the seven provinces; and to pay him a large sum for the charges of the war.

Lewis deliberated with his ministers Louvois and Pomponne, concerning the measures which he should embrace in the present emergence; and fortunately for Europe, he still preferred the violent counsels of the former. He offered to evacuate his conquests on condition, that all duties lately imposed on the commodities of France, should be taken off: That the public exercise of the Romish religion should be permitted in the United Provinces; the churches shared with the catholics; and their priests maintained by appointments from the States: That all the frontier towns of the republic should be yielded to him, together with Nimeguen, Skink, Knotzembourg, and that part of Guelderland which lay on the other side of the Rhine; as likewise the isle of Bommel, that of Voorn, the fortress of St. Andrew, those of Louvestein and Crevecoeur: That the States should pay him the sum of twenty millions of livres for the charges of the war: That they should every year send him a solemn embassy, and present him with a golden medal, as an acknowledgment, that they owed to him the preservation of that liberty, which, by the assistance of his predecessors, they had formerly acquired: And that they should give entire satisfaction to the king of England: And he allowed them but ten days for the acceptance of these demands.

The ambassadors, sent to London, met with still worse reception: No minister was allowed to treat with them; and they were retained in a kind of confinement. But notwithstanding this rigorous conduct of the court, the presence of the Dutch ambassadors excited the sentiments of tender compassion, and even indignation, among the people in general, especially among those who could foresee the aim and result of those dangerous counsels. The two most powerful monarchs, they said, in Europe, the one by land, the other by sea, have, contrary to the faith of solemn treaties, combined to exterminate an illustrious republic: What a dismal prospect does their success afford to the neighbours of the one, and to the subjects of the other? Charles had formed the triple league, in order to restrain the power of France: A sure proof, that he does not now err from ignorance. He had courted and obtained the applauses of his people by that wise measure: As he now adopts contrary counsels, he must surely expect by their means to render himself independent of his people, whose sentiments are become so indifferent to him. During the entire submission of the nation, and dutiful behaviour of the parliament, dangerous projects, without provocation, are formed to reduce them to subjection; and all the foreign interests of the people are sacrificed, in order the more surely to bereave them of their domestic liberties. Lest any instance of freedom should remain within their view, the United Provinces, the real barrier of England, must be abandoned to the most dangerous enemy of England; and by an universal combination of tyranny against laws and liberty, all mankind, who have retained, in any degree, their precious, though hitherto precarious, birthrights, are for ever to submit to slavery and injustice.

Though the fear of giving umbrage to his confederate had engaged Charles to treat the Dutch ambassadors with such rigour, he was not altogether without uneasiness, on account of the rapid and unexpected progress of the French arms. Were Holland entirely conquered, its whole commerce and naval force, he perceived, must become an accession to France; the Spanish Low Countries must soon follow; and Lewis, now independent of his ally, would no longer think it his interest to support him against his discontented subjects. Charles, though he never carried his attention to very distant consequences, could not but foresee these obvious events; and though incapable of envy or jealousy, he was touched with anxiety, when he found every thing yield to the French arms, while such vigorous resistance was made to his own. He soon dismissed the Dutch ambassadors, lest they should cabal

CHAPTER LXV

among his subjects, who bore them great favour: But he sent over Buckingham and Arlington, and soon after lord Halifax, to negotiate anew with the French king, in the present prosperous situation of that monarch's affairs.

These ministers passed through Holland; and as they were supposed to bring peace to the distressed republic, they were every where received with the loudest acclamations. "God bless the king of England! God bless the prince of Orange! Confusion to the States!" This was every where the cry of the populace. The ambassadors had several conferences with the States and the prince of Orange; but made no reasonable advances towards an accommodation. They went to Utrecht, where they renewed the league with Lewis, and agreed, that neither of the kings should make peace with Holland but by common consent. They next gave in their pretensions, of which the following are the principal articles: That the Dutch should give up the honour of the flag, without the least reserve or limitation; nor should whole fleets, even on the coast of Holland, refuse to strike or lower their topsails to the smallest ship, carrying the British flag: That all persons, guilty of treason against the king, or of writing seditious libels, should, on complaint, be banished for ever the dominions of the States: That the Dutch should pay the king a million sterling towards the charges of the war, together with ten thousand pounds a-year, for permission to fish on the British seas: That they should share the Indian trade with the English: That the prince of Orange and his descendants should enjoy the sovereignty of the United Provinces: at least, that they should be invested with the dignities of Stadtholder, Admiral and General, in as ample a manner as had ever been enjoyed by any of his ancestors: And that the isle of Walcheren, the city and castle of Sluis, together with the isles of Cadsant, Gorée, and Vorne, should be put into the king's hands, as a security for the performance of articles.

The terms proposed by Lewis bereaved the republic of all security against any invasion by land from France: Those demanded by Charles exposed them equally to an invasion by sea from England: And when both were united, they appeared absolutely intolerable, and reduced the Hollanders, who saw no means of defence, to the utmost despair. What extremely augmented their distress, were the violent factions, with which they continued to be every where agitated. De Wit, too pertinacious in defence of his own system of liberty, while the very being of the Commonwealth was threatened, still persevered in opposing the repeal of the perpetual edict, now become the object of horror to the Dutch populace. Their rage at last broke all bounds, and bore every thing before it. They rose in an insurrection at Dort, and by force constrained their burgo-masters to sign the repeal, so much demanded. This proved a signal of a general revolt throughout all the provinces.

30th June.

At Amsterdam, the Hague, Middlebourg, Rotterdam, the people flew to arms, and trampling under foot the authority of their magistrates, obliged them to submit to the prince of Orange. They expelled from their office such as displeased them: They required the prince to appoint others in their place: And agreeably to the proceedings of the populace in all ages, provided they might wreak their vengeance on their superiors, they expressed great indifference for the protection of their civil liberties.

Prince of Orange Stadt-holder.

The superior talents and virtues of de Wit made him, on this occasion, the chief object of envy, and exposed him to the utmost rage of popular prejudice. Four assassins, actuated by no other motive than mistaken zeal, had assaulted him in the streets; and after giving him many wounds, had left him for dead. One of them was punished: The others were never questioned for the crime. His brother, Cornelius, who had behaved with prudence and courage on board the fleet, was obliged by sickness to come ashore; and he was now confined to his house at Dort. Some assassins broke in upon him; and it was with the utmost difficulty that his family and servants could repel their violence. At Amsterdam, the house of the brave de Ruyter, the sole resource of the distressed commonwealth, was surrounded by the enraged populace; and his wife and children were for some time exposed to the most imminent danger.

One Tichelaer, a barber, a man noted for infamy, accused Cornelius de Wit of endeavouring by bribes to engage him in the design of poisoning the prince of Orange. The accusation, though attended with the most improbable and even absurd circumstances, was greedily received by the credulous multitude, and Cornelius was cited before a court of judicature. The judges, either blinded by the same prejudices, or not daring to oppose the popu-

CHAPTER LXV

lar torrent, condemned him to suffer the question. This man, who
had bravely served his country in war, and who had been invested
with the highest dignities, was delivered into the hands of the
executioner, and torn in pieces by the most inhuman torments.
Amidst the severe agonies which he endured, he still made
protestations of his innocence, and frequently repeated an ode
of Horace, which contained sentiments suited to his deplorable
condition:

Justum et tenacem propositi virum, &c.[1]

The judges, however, condemned him to lose his offices, and to
be banished the commonwealth. The pensionary, who had not
been terrified from performing the part of a kind brother, and
faithful friend during this prosecution, resolved not to desert him
on account of the unmerited infamy, which was endeavoured to be
thrown upon him. He came to his brother's prison, determined to
accompany him to the place of his exile. The signal was given to
the populace. They rose in arms: They broke open the doors of the
prison; they pulled out the two brothers; and a thousand hands

*Massacre
of the
de Wits.*

[1] Which may be thus translated.

> The man, whose mind on virtue bent,
> Pursues some greatly good intent,
>   With undiverted aim,
> Serene beholds the angry crowd;
> Nor can their clamours, fierce and loud,
>   His stubborn honour tame.
>
> Not the proud tyrant's fiercest threat,
> Nor storms, that from their dark retreat
>   The lawless surges wake,
> Not Jove's dread bolt that shakes the pole,
> The firmer purpose of his soul
>   With all its power can shake.
>
> Shou'd Nature's frame in ruins fall,
> And chaos o'er the sinking ball
>   Resume primeval sway,
> His courage chance and fate defies,
> Nor feels the wreck of earth and skies
>   Obstruct its destin'd way.
>   BLACKLOCKE.

vied who should first be imbrued in their blood. Even their death did not satiate the brutal rage of the multitude. They exercised on the dead bodies of those virtuous citizens, indignities too shocking to be recited; and till tired with their own fury, they permitted not the friends of the deceased to approach, or to bestow on them the honours of a funeral, silent and unattended.

The massacre of the de Wits put an end for the time to the remains of their party; and all men, from fear, inclination, or prudence, concurred in expressing the most implicit obedience to the prince of Orange. The republic, though half subdued by foreign force, and as yet dismayed by its misfortunes, was now firmly united under one leader, and began to collect the remains of its *Good* pristine vigour. William, worthy of that heroic family from which *conduct* he sprang, adopted sentiments becoming the head of a brave and *of the* free people. He bent all his efforts against the public enemy: He *prince.* sought not against his country any advantages, which might be dangerous to civil liberty. Those intolerable conditions, demanded by their insolent enemies, he exhorted the States to reject with scorn; and by his advice they put an end to negotiations, which served only to break the courage of their fellow-citizens, and delay the assistance of their allies. He showed them, that the numbers and riches of the people, aided by the advantages of situation, would still be sufficient, if they abandoned not themselves to despair, to resist, at least retard, the progress of their enemies, and preserve the remaining provinces, till the other nations of Europe, sensible of the common danger, could come to their relief. He represented, that, as envy at their opulence and liberty had produced this mighty combination against them, they would in vain expect by concessions to satisfy foes, whose pretensions were as little bounded by moderation as by justice. He exhorted them to remember the generous valour of their ancestors, who, yet in the infancy of the state, preferred liberty to every human consideration; and rouzing their spirits to an obstinate defence, repelled all the power, riches, and military discipline of Spain. And he professed himself willing to tread in the steps of his illustrious predecessors, and hoped, that, as they had honoured him with the same affection, which their ancestors paid to the former princes of Orange, they would second his efforts with the same constancy and manly fortitude.

CHAPTER LXV

The spirit of the young prince infused itself into his hearers. Those who lately entertained thoughts of yielding their necks to subjection were now bravely determined to resist the haughty victor, and to defend those last remains of their native soil, of which neither the irruptions of Lewis nor the inundation of waters had as yet bereaved them. Should even the ground fail them on which they might combat, they were still resolved not to yield the generous strife; but flying to their settlements in the Indies, erect a new empire in those remote regions, and preserve alive, even in the climates of slavery, that liberty, of which Europe was become unworthy. Already they concerted measures for executing this extraordinary resolution; and found, that the vessels, contained in their harbours, could transport above two hundred thousand inhabitants to the East-Indies.

The combined princes, finding at last some appearance of opposition, bent all their efforts to seduce the prince of Orange, on whose valour and conduct the fate of the commonwealth entirely depended. The sovereignty of the province of Holland was offered him, and the protection of England and France, to insure him, as well against the invasion of foreign enemies, as the insurrection of his subjects. All proposals were generously rejected; and the prince declared his resolution to retire into Germany, and to pass his life in hunting on his lands there, rather than abandon the liberty of his country, or betray the trust reposed in him. When Buckingham urged the inevitable destruction which hung over the United Provinces, and asked him, whether he did not see, that the commonwealth was ruined; *There is one certain means,* replied the prince, *by which I can be sure never to see my country's ruin; I will die in the last ditch.*

The people in Holland had been much incited to espouse the prince's party, by the hopes, that the king of England, pleased with his nephew's elevation, would abandon those dangerous engagements, into which he had entered, and would afford his protection to the distressed republic. But all these hopes were soon found to be fallacious. Charles still persisted in his alliance with France; and the combined fleets approached the coast of Holland, with an English army on board, commanded by count Schomberg. It is pretended, that an unusual tide carried them off the coast; and that Providence thus interposed, in an extraordinary manner, to save the republic from the imminent danger, to which it was exposed. Very tempestuous weather, it is certain, prevailed all the rest of the season; and the combined fleets either were blown to a distance, or durst not approach a coast, which might prove fatal to them. Lewis, finding that his enemies gathered courage behind their inundations, and that no farther success was likely for the present to attend his arms, had retired to Versailles.

The other nations of Europe regarded the subjection of Holland as the forerunner of their own slavery, and retained no hopes of defending themselves, should such a mighty accession be made to the already exorbitant power of France. The emperor, though he lay at a distance, and was naturally slow in his undertakings, began to put himself in motion; Brandenburgh shewed a disposition to support the States; Spain had sent some forces to their assistance; and by the present efforts of the prince of Orange, and the prospect of relief from their allies, a different face of affairs began already to appear. Groninghen was the first place that stopped the progress of the enemy: The bishop of Munster was repulsed from before that town, and obliged to raise the siege with loss and dishonour. Naerden was attempted by the prince of Orange; but mareschal Luxembourg, breaking in upon his entrenchments with a sudden irruption, obliged him to abandon the enterprize.

1673.
4th of
Feb.
A parlia-
ment.

There was no ally, on whom the Dutch more relied for assistance, than the parliament of England, which the king's necessities at last obliged him to assemble. The eyes of all men, both abroad and at home, were fixed on this session, which met after prorogations continued for near two years. It was evident how much the king dreaded the assembling of his parliament; and the discontents, universally excited by the bold measures entered into, both in foreign and domestic administration, had given but too just foundation for his apprehensions.

The king, however, in his speech, addressed them with all the appearance of cordiality and confidence. He said, that he would have assembled them sooner, had he not been desirous to allow them leisure for attending their private affairs, as well as to give his people respite from taxes and impositions: That since their last meeting, he had been forced into a war, not only just but necessary; necessary both for the honour and interest of the nation:

CHAPTER LXV

That in order to have peace at home, while he had war abroad, he had issued his declaration of indulgence to dissenters, and had found many good effects to result from that measure: That he heard of some exceptions, which had been taken to this exercise of power; but he would tell them plainly, that he was resolved to stick to his declaration; and would be much offended at any contradiction: And that though a rumour had been spread, as if the new levied army had been intended to controul law and property, he regarded that jealousy as so frivolous, that he was resolved to augment his forces next spring, and did not doubt but they would consider the necessity of them in their supplies. The rest of the business he left to the chancellor.

The chancellor enlarged on the same topics, and added many extraordinary positions of his own. He told them, that the Hollanders were the common enemies of all monarchies, especially that of England, their only competitor for commerce and naval power, and the sole obstacle to their views of attaining an universal empire, as extensive as that of ancient Rome: That, even during their present distress and danger, they were so intoxicated with these ambitious projects, as to slight all treaty, nay, to refuse all cessation of hostilities: That the king, in entering on this war, did no more than prosecute those maxims, which had engaged the parliament to advise and approve of the last; and he might therefore safely say, that *it was their war:* That the States being the eternal enemies of England, both by interest and inclination, the parliament had wisely judged it necessary to extirpate them, and had laid it down as an eternal maxim, that *delenda est Carthago,* this hostile government by all means is to be subverted: And that though the Dutch pretended to have assurances, that the parliament would furnish no supplies to the king, he was confident, that this hope, in which they extremely trusted, would soon fail them.

Before the commons entered upon business, there lay before them an affair, which discovered, beyond a possibility of doubt, the arbitrary projects of the king; and the measures, taken upon it, proved, that the house was not at present in a disposition to submit to them. It had been the constant undisputed practice, ever since the parliament in 1604, for the house, in case of any vacancy, to issue out writs for new elections; and the chancellor, who, before that time, had had some precedents in his favour, had ever afterwards abstained from all exercise of that authority. This indeed was one of the first steps, which the commons had taken in establishing and guarding their privileges; and nothing could be more requisite than this precaution, in order to prevent the clandestine issuing of writs, and to ensure a fair and free election. No one but so desperate a minister as Shaftesbury, who had entered into a regular plan for reducing the people to subjection, could have entertained thoughts of breaking in upon a practice so reasonable and so well established, or could have hoped to succeed in so bold an enterprize. Several members had taken their seats upon irregular writs issued by the chancellor; but the house was no sooner assembled, and the speaker placed in the chair, than a motion was made against them; and the members themselves had the modesty to withdraw. Their election was declared null; and new writs, in the usual form, were issued by the speaker.

The next step taken by the commons had the appearance of some more complaisance; but in reality proceeded from the same spirit of liberty and independence. They entered a resolution, that, in order to supply his majesty's extraordinary occasions, for that was the expression employed, they would grant eighteen months assessment, at the rate of 70,000 pounds a month, amounting in the whole to 1,260,000 pounds. Though unwilling to come to a violent breach with the king, they would not express the least approbation of the war; and they gave him the prospect of this supply, only that they might have permission to proceed peaceably in the redress of the other grievances, of which they had such reason to complain.

No grievance was more alarming, both on account of the secret views from which it proceeded, and the consequences which might attend it, than the declaration of indulgence. A remonstrance was immediately framed against that exercise of prerogative. The king defended his measure. The commons persisted in their opposition to it; and they represented, that such a practice, if admitted, might tend to interrupt the free course of the laws, and alter the legislative power, which had always been acknowledged to reside in the king and the two houses. All men were in expectation, with regard to the issue of this extraordinary affair. The king seemed engaged in honour to support his measure; and in order to prevent all opposition, he had positively declared that he would support it.

CHAPTER LXV

The commons were obliged to persevere, not only because it was dishonourable to be foiled, where they could plead such strong reasons, but also because, if the king prevailed in his pretensions, an end seemed to be put to all the legal limitations of the constitution.

It is evident, that Charles was now come to that delicate crisis, which he ought at first to have foreseen, when he embraced those desperate counsels; and his resolutions, in such an event, ought long ago to have been entirely fixed and determined. Besides his usual guards, he had an army encamped at Blackheath under the command of mareschal Schomberg, a foreigner; and many of the officers were of the catholic religion. His ally, the French king, he might expect, would second him, if force became requisite for restraining his discontented subjects, and supporting the measures, which by common consent they had agreed to pursue. But the king was startled, when he approached so dangerous a precipice, as that which lay before him. Were violence once offered, there could be no return, he saw, to mutual confidence and trust with his people; the perils attending foreign succours, especially from so mighty a prince, were sufficiently apparent; and the success, which his own arms had met with in the war, was not so great, as to encrease his authority, or terrify the malcontents from opposition. The desire of power, likewise, which had engaged Charles in these precipitate measures, had less proceeded, we may observe, from ambition than from love of ease. Strict limitations of the constitution rendered the conduct of business complicated and troublesome; and it was impossible for him, without much contrivance and intrigue, to procure the money necessary for his pleasures, or even for the regular support of government. When the prospect, therefore, of such dangerous opposition presented itself, the same love of ease inclined him to retract what it seemed so difficult to maintain; and his turn of mind, naturally pliant and careless, made him find little objection to a measure, which a more haughty prince would have embraced with the utmost reluctance. That he might yield with the better grace, he asked the opinion of the house of peers, who advised him to comply with the commons. Accordingly the king sent for the declaration, and with his own hands broke the seals. The commons expressed the utmost satisfaction with this measure, and the most entire duty to his majesty.

Declaration of indulgence recalled.

Charles assured them, that he would willingly pass any law, offered him, which might tend to give them satisfaction in all their just grievances.

Shaftesbury, when he found the king recede at once from so capital a point, which he had publicly declared his resolution to maintain, concluded, that all schemes for enlarging royal authority were vanished, and that Charles was utterly incapable of pursuing such difficult and such hazardous measures. The parliament, he foresaw, might push their enquiries into those counsels, which were so generally odious; and the king, from the same facility of disposition, might abandon his ministers to their vengeance. He resolved, therefore, to make his peace in time with that party, which was likely to predominate, and to atone for all his violences in favour of monarchy, by like violences in opposition to it. Never turn was more sudden, or less calculated to save appearances. Immediately, he entered into all the cabals of the country party; and discovered to them, perhaps magnified, the arbitrary designs of the court, in which he himself had borne so deep a share. He was received with open arms by that party, who stood in need of so able a leader; and no questions were asked with regard to his late apostacy. The various factions, into which the nation had been divided, and the many sudden revolutions, to which the public had been exposed, had tended much to debauch the minds of men, and to destroy the sense of honour and decorum in their public conduct.

But the parliament, though satisfied with the king's compliance, had not lost all those apprehensions, to which the measures of the court had given so much foundation. A law passed for imposing a test on all who should enjoy any public office. Besides taking the oaths of allegiance and supremacy, and receiving the sacrament in the established church; they were obliged to abjure all belief in the doctrine of transubstantiation. As the dissenters had seconded the efforts of the commons against the king's declaration of indulgence, and seemed resolute to accept of no toleration in an illegal manner, they had acquired great favour with the parliament; and a project was adopted to unite the whole protestant interest against the common enemy, who now began to appear formidable. A bill passed the commons for the ease and relief of the protestant nonconformists; but met with some difficulties, at least delays, in the house of peers.

CHAPTER LXV

The resolution for supply was carried into a law; as a recompence to the king for his concessions. An act, likewise, of general pardon and indemnity was passed, which screened the ministers from all farther enquiry. The parliament probably thought, that the best method of reclaiming the criminals was to shew them, that their case was not desperate. Even the remonstrance, which the commons voted of their grievances, may be regarded as a proof, that their anger was, for the time, somewhat appeased. None of the capital points are there touched on; the breach of the triple league, the French alliance, or the shutting up of the exchequer. The sole grievances mentioned are an arbitrary imposition on coals for providing convoys, the exercise of martial law, the quartering and pressing of soldiers; and they prayed, that, after the conclusion of the war, the whole army should be disbanded. The king gave them a gracious, though an evasive answer. When business was finished, the two houses adjourned themselves.

29th of March.

Though the king had receded from his declaration of indulgence, and thereby had tacitly relinquished the dispensing power, he was still resolved, notwithstanding his bad success both at home and abroad, to persevere in his alliance with France, and in the Dutch war, and consequently in all those secret views, whatever they were, which depended on those fatal measures. The money, granted by parliament, sufficed to equip a fleet, of which prince Rupert was declared admiral: For the duke was set aside by the test. Sir Edward Sprague and the earl of Ossory commanded under the prince. A French squadron joined them, commanded by d'Etrées. The combined fleets set sail towards the coast of Holland, and found the enemy, lying at anchor, within the sands at Schonvelt. There is a natural confusion attending sea-fights, even beyond other military transactions; derived from the precarious operations of winds and tides, as well as from the smoke and darkness, in which every thing is there involved. No wonder, therefore, that accounts of those battles are apt to contain uncertainties and contradictions; especially when delivered by writers of the hostile nations, who take pleasure in exalting the advantages of their own countrymen, and depressing those of the enemy. All we can say with certainty of this battle, is, that both sides boasted of the victory; and we may thence infer, that the event was not decisive. The Dutch, being near home, retired into their harbours. In a

28th of May. Sea-fight.

4th June.
Another
sea-fight.

week, they were refitted, and presented themselves again to the combined fleets. A new action ensued, not more decisive than the foregoing. It was not fought with great obstinacy on either side; but whether the Dutch or the allies first retired, seems to be a matter of uncertainty. The loss in the former of these actions fell chiefly on the French, whom the English, diffident of their intentions, took care to place under their own squadrons; and they thereby exposed them to all the fire of the enemy. There seems not to have been a ship lost on either side in the second engagement.

It was sufficient glory to de Ruyter, that, with a fleet much inferior to the combined squadrons of France and England, he could fight them without any notable disadvantage; and it was sufficient victory, that he could defeat the project of a descent in Zealand, which, had it taken place, had endangered, in the present circumstances, the total overthrow of the Dutch commonwealth. Prince Rupert was also suspected not to favour the king's projects for subduing Holland, or enlarging his authority at home; and from these motives he was thought not to have pressed so hard on the enemy, as his well-known valour gave reason to expect. It is indeed remarkable, that, during this war, though the English with their allies much over-matched the Hollanders, they were not able to gain any advantage over them; while in the former war, though often overborne by numbers, they still exerted themselves with the greatest courage, and always acquired great renown, sometimes even signal victories. But they were disgusted at the present measures, which they deemed pernicious to their country; they were not satisfied in the justice of the quarrel; and they entertained a perpetual jealousy of their confederates, whom, had they been permitted, they would, with much more pleasure, have destroyed than even the enemy themselves.

If prince Rupert was not favourable to the designs of the court, he enjoyed as little favour from the court, at least from the duke, who, though he could no longer command the fleet, still possessed the chief authority in the admiralty. The prince complained of a total want of every thing, powder, shot, provisions, beer, and even water; and he went into harbour, that he might refit his ships, and supply their numerous necessities. After some weeks he was refitted, and he again put to sea. The hostile fleets met at the mouth of the Texel, and fought the last battle, which, during the course

11th of
August.
Another
sea-fight.

of so many years, these neighbouring maritime powers have disputed with each other. De Ruyter, and under him Tromp, commanded the Dutch in this action, as in the two former: For the prince of Orange had reconciled these gallant rivals; and they retained nothing of their former animosity, except that emulation, which made them exert themselves with more distinguished bravery against the enemies of their country. Brankert was opposed to d'Etrées, de Ruyter to prince Rupert, Tromp to Sprague. It is to be remarked, that in all actions these brave admirals last mentioned had still selected each other, as the only antagonists worthy each others valour; and no decisive advantage had as yet been gained by either of them. They fought in this battle, as if there were no mean between death and victory.

D'Etrees and all the French squadron, except rear admiral Martel, kept at a distance; and Brankert, instead of attacking them, bore down to the assistance of de Ruyter, who was engaged in furious combat with prince Rupert. On no occasion did the prince acquire more deserved honour: His conduct, as well as valour, shone out with signal lustre. Having disengaged his squadron from the numerous enemies, with whom he was every where surrounded, and having joined Sir John Chichely, his rear admiral, who had been separated from him, he made haste to the relief of Sprague, who was hard pressed by Tromp's squadron. The Royal Prince, in which Sprague first engaged, was so disabled, that he was obliged to hoist his flag on board the St. George; while Tromp was for a like reason obliged to quit his ship, the Golden Lion, and go on board the Comet. The fight was renewed with the utmost fury by these valorous rivals, and by the rear admirals, their seconds. Ossory, rear admiral to Sprague, was preparing to board Tromp, when he saw the St. George terribly torn, and in a manner disabled. Sprague was leaving her in order to hoist his flag on board a third ship, and return to the charge; when a shot, which had passed through the St. George, took his boat, and sunk her. The admiral was drowned, to the great regret of Tromp himself, who bestowed on his valour the deserved praises.

Prince Rupert found affairs in this dangerous situation, and saw most of the ships in Sprague's squadron disabled from fight. The engagement however was renewed, and became very close and bloody. The prince threw the enemy into disorder. To encrease it, he sent among them two fire-ships; and at the same time made a signal to the French to bear down; which if they had done, a decisive victory must have ensued. But the prince, when he saw that they neglected his signal, and observed that most of his ships were in no condition to keep the sea long, wisely provided for their safety by making easy sail towards the English coast. The victory in this battle was as doubtful, as in all the actions fought during the present war.

The turn, which the affairs of the Hollanders took by land, was more favourable. The prince of Orange besieged and took Naerden; and from this success gave his country reason to hope for still more prosperous enterprizes. Montecuculi, who commanded the Imperialists on the Upper Rhine, deceived, by the most artful conduct, the vigilance and penetration of Turenne, and making a sudden march, sat down before Bonne. The prince of Orange's conduct was no less masterly; while he eluded all the French generals, and leaving them behind him, joined his army to that of the Imperialists. Bonne was taken in a few days: Several other places in the electorate of Cologne fell into the hands of the allies: And the communication being thus cut off between France and the United Provinces, Lewis was obliged to recal his forces, and to abandon all his conquests, with greater rapidity than he had at first made them. The taking of Maestricht was the only advantage, which he gained this campaign.

Congress of Cologne.
A congress was opened at Cologne under the mediation of Sweden; but with small hopes of success. The demands of the two kings were such as must have reduced the Hollanders to perpetual servitude. In proportion as the affairs of the States rose, the kings sunk in their demands; but the States still sunk lower in their offers; and it was found impossible for the parties ever to agree on any conditions. After the French evacuated Holland, the congress broke up; and the seizure of prince William of Furstenburg by the Imperialists afforded the French and English a good pretence for leaving Cologne. The Dutch ambassadors in their memorials expressed all the haughtiness and disdain, so natural to a free state, which had met with such unmerited ill usage.

20th Oct.
A parliament.
The parliament of England was now assembled, and discovered much greater symptoms of ill humour, than had appeared in the last session. They had seen for some time a negociation of mar-

CHAPTER LXV

riage carried on between the duke of York and the archduchess of Inspruc, a catholic of the Austrian family; and they had made no opposition. But when that negociation failed, and the duke applied to a princess of the house of Modena, then in close alliance with France; this circumstance, joined to so many other grounds of discontent, raised the commons into a flame; and they remonstrated with the greatest zeal against the intended marriage. The king told them, that their remonstrance came too late; and that the marriage was already agreed on, and even celebrated by proxy. The commons still insisted; and proceeding to the examination of the other parts of government, they voted the standing army a grievance, and declared, that they would grant no more supply, unless it appeared, that the Dutch were so obstinate as to refuse all reasonable conditions of peace. To cut short these disagreeable attacks, the king resolved to prorogue the parliament; and with *4th Nov.* that intention he came unexpectedly to the house of peers, and sent the usher to summon the commons. It happened, that the speaker and the usher nearly met at the door of the house; but the speaker being within, some of the members suddenly shut the door, and cried, *To the chair, to the chair;* while others cried, *The black rod is at the door.* The speaker was hurried to the chair; and the following motions were instantly made: That the alliance with France is a grievance; that the evil counsellors about the king are a grievance; that the duke of Lauderdale is a grievance, and not fit to be trusted or employed. There was a general cry, *To the question, to the question:* But the usher knocking violently at the door, the speaker leaped from the chair, and the house rose in great confusion.

During the interval, Shaftesbury, whose intrigues with the malcontent party were now become notorious, was dismissed from the office of chancellor; and the great seal was given to sir Heneage Finch, by the title of lord keeper. The test had incapacitated Clifford; and the white staff was conferred on sir Thomas Osborne, soon after created earl of Danby, a minister of abilities, who had risen by his parliamentary talents. Clifford retired into the country, and soon after died.

The parliament had been prorogued, in order to give the duke *1674.* leisure to finish his marriage; but the king's necessities soon *7th Feb.* obliged him again to assemble them; and by some popular acts he paved the way for the session. But all his efforts were in vain. The disgust of the commons was fixed in foundations too deep to be easily removed. They began with applications for a general fast; by which they intimated, that the nation was in a very calamitous condition: They addressed against the king's guards, which they represented as dangerous to liberty, and even as illegal, since they never had yet received the sanction of parliament: They took some steps towards establishing a new and more rigorous test against popery: And what chiefly alarmed the court, they made an attack on the members of the cabal, to whose pernicious counsels they imputed all their present grievances. Clifford was dead: Shaftesbury had made his peace with the country party, and was become their leader: Buckingham was endeavouring to imitate Shaftesbury; but his intentions were as yet known to very few. A motion was therefore made in the house of commons for his impeachment: He desired to be heard at the bar; but expressed himself in so confused and ambiguous a manner, as gave little satisfaction. He was required to answer precisely to certain queries, which they proposed to him. These regarded all the articles of misconduct abovementioned; and among the rest, the following query seems remarkable. "By whose advice was the army brought up to overawe the debates and resolutions of the house of commons?" This shews to what length the suspicions of the house were at that time carried. Buckingham, in all his answers, endeavoured to exculpate himself, and to load Arlington. He succeeded not in the former intention: The commons voted an address for his removal. But Arlington, who was on many accounts obnoxious to the house, was attacked. Articles were drawn up against him; though the impeachment was never prosecuted.

The king plainly saw, that he could expect no supply from the commons for carrying on a war, so odious to them. He resolved therefore to make a separate peace with the Dutch, on the terms which they had proposed through the channel of the Spanish ambassador. With a cordiality, which, in the present disposition on both sides, was probably but affected, but which was obliging, he asked advice of the parliament. The parliament unanimously concurred, both in thanks for this gracious condescension, and in their advice for peace. Peace was accordingly concluded. The honour of the flag was yielded by the Dutch in the most extensive terms: A

Peace with Holland.

CHAPTER LXV

regulation of trade was agreed to: All possessions were restored to the same condition as before the war: The English planters in Surinam were allowed to remove at pleasure: And the States agreed to pay to the king the sum of eight hundred thousand patacoons, near three hundred thousand pounds. Four days after *28th Feb.* the parliament was prorogued, the peace was proclaimed in London, to the great joy of the people. Spain had declared, that she could no longer remain neuter, if hostilities were continued against Holland; and a sensible decay of trade was foreseen, in case a rupture should ensue with that kingdom. The prospect of this loss contributed very much to encrease the national aversion to the present war, and to enliven the joy for its conclusion.

There was in the French service a great body of English, to the number of ten thousand men, who had acquired honour in every action, and had greatly contributed to the successes of Lewis. These troops, Charles said, he was bound by treaty not to recall; but he obliged himself to the States by a secret article not to allow them to be recruited. His partiality to France prevented a strict execution of this engagement.

LXVI

Schemes of the Cabal –
Remonstrances of Sir William Temple –
Campaign of 1674 – A Parliament – Passive
obedience – A Parliament – Campaign of 1675 –
Congress of Nimeguen – Campaign of 1676 –
Uncertain conduct of the King – A Parliament –
Campaign of 1677 – Parliament's distrust
of the King – Marriage of the Prince
of Orange with the Lady Mary – Plan of peace –
Negociations – Campaign of 1678 –
Negociations – Peace of Nimeguen –
State of affairs in Scotland

1674.
Schemes
of the
Cabal.

IF WE CONSIDER the projects of the famous Cabal, it will appear hard to determine, whether the end, which those ministers pursued, were more blameable and pernicious, or the means, by which they were to effect it, more impolitic and imprudent. Though they might talk only of recovering or fixing the king's authority; their intention could be no other than that of making him absolute: Since it was not possible to regain or maintain, in opposition to the people, any of those powers of the crown, abolished by late law or custom, without subduing the people, and rendering the royal prerogative entirely uncontroulable. Against such a scheme, they might foresee, that every part of the nation would declare themselves, not only the old parliamentary faction, which, though they kept not in a body, were still numerous; but even the greatest royalists, who were indeed attached to monarchy, but desired to see it limited and restrained by law. It had appeared, that the present parliament, though elected during the greatest prevalence of the royal party, was yet tenacious of popular privileges, and retained a considerable jealousy of the crown, even before they had received any just ground of suspicion. The guards, therefore, together with a small army, new levied, and undisciplined, and composed too of Englishmen, were almost the only domestic resources, which the king could depend on in the prosecution of these dangerous counsels.

The assistance of the French king was, no doubt, deemed by the Cabal a considerable support in the schemes which they were forming; but it is not easily conceived, that they could imagine themselves capable of directing and employing an associate of so domineering a character. They ought justly to have suspected, that it would be the sole intention of Lewis, as it evidently was his interest, to raise incurable jealousies between the king and his people; and that he saw how much a steddy uniform government in this island, whether free or absolute, would form invincible barriers to his ambition. Should his assistance be demanded; if he sent a small supply, it would serve only to enrage the people, and render the breach altogether irreparable; if he furnished a great force, sufficient to subdue the nation, there was little reason to trust his generosity, with regard to the use, which he would make of this advantage.

In all its other parts, the plan of the Cabal, it must be confessed, appears equally absurd and incongruous. If the war with Holland were attended with great success, and involved the subjection of the republic; such an accession of force must fall to Lewis, not to Charles: And what hopes afterwards of resisting by the greatest unanimity so mighty a monarch? How dangerous, or rather how ruinous to depend upon his assistance against domestic discontents? If the Dutch, by their own vigour, and the assistance of allies, were able to defend themselves, and could bring the war to an equality, the French arms would be so employed abroad, that no considerable reinforcement could thence be expected to second the king's enterprizes in England. And might not the project of over-awing or subduing the people be esteemed, of itself, sufficiently odious, without the aggravation of sacrificing that State, which they regarded as their best ally, and with which, on many accounts, they were desirous of maintaining the greatest concord and strictest confederacy?

Whatever views likewise might be entertained of promoting by these measures the catholic religion; they could only tend to render all the other schemes abortive, and make them fall with inevitable ruin upon the projectors. The catholic religion, indeed, where it is established, is better fitted than the protestant for supporting an absolute monarchy; but would any man have thought of it as the means of acquiring arbitrary authority in England, where it was more detested than even slavery itself?

It must be allowed, that the difficulties, and even inconsistencies, attending the schemes of the Cabal, are so numerous and obvious, that one feels at first an inclination to deny the reality of those schemes, and to suppose them entirely the chimeras of calumny and faction. But the utter impossibility of accounting, by any other hypothesis, for those strange measures embraced by the court, as well as for the numerous circumstances, which accompanied them, obliges us to acknowledge (though there remains no direct evidence of it)[m] that a formal plan was laid for changing the

[m] Since the publication of this History, the Author has had occasion to see the most direct and positive evidence of this conspiracy. From the humanity and candour of the principal of the Scotch College at Paris, he was admitted to peruse James the Second's Memoirs, kept there. They amount to several volumes of small folio, all writ with that prince's own hand, and comprehending the remarkable incidents of his life from his early youth till near the time of his death. His account of the French alliance is as follows: The intention of the king and duke was chiefly to change the religion of England, which they deemed an easy undertaking, because of the great propensity, as they imagined, of the cavaliers and church party to popery: The treaty with Lewis was concluded at Versailles in the end of 1669, or beginning of 1670, by Lord Arundel of Wardour, whom no historian mentions as having had any hand in these transactions. The purport of it was, that Lewis was to give Charles 200,000 pounds a year in quarterly payments, in order to enable him to settle the catholic religion in England; and he was also to supply him with an army of 6000 men in case of any insurrection. When that work was finished, England was to join with France in making war upon Holland. In case of success, Lewis was to have the inland prov-

religion, and subverting the constitution, of England, and that the king and the ministry were in reality conspirators against the people. What is most probable in human affairs is not always true; and a very minute circumstance, overlooked in our speculations, serves often to explain events, which may seem the most surprizing and unaccountable. Though the king possessed penetration and a

---

inces, the prince of Orange Holland in sovereignty, and Charles, Sluice, the Brille, Walkeren, with the rest of the sea ports as far as Mazeland Sluice. The king's project was first to effect the change of religion in England; but the dutchess of Orleans, in the interview at Dover, persuaded him to begin with the Dutch war, contrary to the remonstrances of the duke of York, who insisted that Lewis, after serving his own purposes, would no longer trouble himself about England. The duke makes no mention of any design to render the king absolute; but that was, no doubt, implied in the other project, which was to be effected entirely by royal authority. The king was so zealous a papist, that he wept for joy when he saw the prospect of re-uniting his kingdom to the catholic church.

Sir John Dalrymple has since published some other curious particulars with regard to this treaty. We find, that it was concerted and signed with the privity alone of four popish counsellors of the king's, Arlington, Arundel, Clifford and Sir Richard Bealing. The secret was kept from Buckingham, Ashley, and Lauderdale. In order to engage them to take part in it, a very refined and a very mean artifice was fallen upon by the king. After the secret conclusion and signature of the treaty, the king pretended to these three ministers that he wished to have a treaty and alliance with France for mutual support, and for a Dutch war; and when various pretended obstacles and difficulties were surmounted, a sham-treaty was concluded with their consent and approbation, containing every article of the former real treaty, except that of the king's change of religion. However, there was virtually involved even in this treaty, the assuming of absolute government in England: For the support of French troops, and a war with Holland, so contrary to the interests and inclinations of his people, could mean nothing else. One cannot sufficiently admire the absolute want of common sense which appears throughout the whole of this criminal transaction. For if popery was so much the object of national horror, that even the king's three ministers, Buckingham, Ashley, and Lauderdale, and such profligate ones too, either would not, or durst not receive it, what hopes could he entertain of forcing the nation into that communion? Considering the state of the kingdom, full of veteran and zealous soldiers, bred during the civil wars, it is probable that he had not kept the crown two months after a declaration so wild and extravagant. This was probably the reason why the king of France and the French ministers always dissuaded him from taking off the mask, till the successes of the Dutch war should render that measure prudent and practicable.

sound judgment, his capacity was chiefly fitted for smaller matters,[n] and the ordinary occurrences of life; nor had he application enough to carry his view to distant consequences, or to digest and adjust any plan of political operations. As he scarcely ever thought twice on any one subject, every appearance of advantage was apt to seduce him; and when he found his way obstructed by unlooked-for difficulties, he readily turned aside into the first path, where he expected more to gratify the natural indolence of his disposition. To this versatility or pliancy of genius, he himself was inclined to trust; and he thought, that, after trying an experiment for enlarging his authority, and altering the national religion, he could easily, if it failed, return into the ordinary channel of government. But the suspicions of the people, though they burst not forth at once, were by this attempt rendered altogether incurable; and the more they reflected on the circumstances, attending it, the more resentment and jealousy were they apt to entertain. They observed, that the king never had any favourite; that he was never governed by his ministers, scarcely even by his mistresses; and that he himself was the chief spring of all public counsels. Whatever appearance, therefore, of a change might be assumed, they still suspected, that the same project was secretly in agitation; and they deemed no precaution too great to secure them against the pernicious consequences of such measures.

The king, sensible of this jealousy, was inclined thenceforth not to trust his people, of whom he had even before entertained a great diffidence; and though obliged to make a separate peace, he still kept up connexions with the French monarch. He apologized for deserting his ally, by representing to him all the real undissembled difficulties, under which he laboured; and Lewis, with the greatest complaisance and good humour, admitted the validity of his excuses. The duke likewise, conscious that his principles and conduct had rendered him still more obnoxious to the people, maintained on his own account a separate correspondence with the French court, and entered into particular connexions with Lewis, which these princes dignified with the name of friendship. The duke had only in view to secure his succession, and favour the catholics; and it must be acknowledged to his praise, that, though his schemes

[n] Duke of Buckingham's character of K. Charles II.

CHAPTER LXVI

were, in some particulars, dangerous to the people, they gave the king no just ground of jealousy. A dutiful subject, and an affectionate brother, he knew no other rule of conduct than obedience; and the same unlimited submission, which afterwards, when king, he exacted of his people, he was ever willing, before he ascended the throne, to pay to his sovereign.

As the king was at peace with all the world, and almost the only prince in Europe placed in that agreeable situation, he thought proper to offer his mediation to the contending powers, in order to compose their differences. France, willing to negociate under so favourable a mediator, readily accepted of Charles's offer; but, it was apprehended, that, for a like reason, the allies would be inclined to refuse it. In order to give a sanction to his new measures, the king invited Temple from his retreat, and appointed him ambassador to the States. That wise minister, reflecting on the unhappy issue of his former undertakings, and the fatal turn of counsels, which had occasioned it, resolved, before he embarked anew, to acquaint himself, as far as possible, with the real intentions of the king, in those popular measures, which he seemed again to have adopted. After blaming the dangerous schemes of the Cabal, which Charles was desirous to excuse, he told his majesty very plainly, that he would find it extremely difficult, if not absolutely impossible, to introduce into England the same system of government and religion, which was established in France: That the universal bent of the nation was against both; and it required ages to change the genius and sentiments of a people: That many, who were at bottom indifferent in matters of religion, would yet oppose all alterations on that head; because they considered, that nothing but force of arms could subdue the reluctance of the people against popery; after which, they knew, there could be no security for civil liberty: That in France every circumstance had long been adjusted to that system of government, and tended to its establishment and support: That the commonalty, being poor and dispirited, were of no account; the nobility, engaged by the prospect or possession of numerous offices, civil and military, were entirely attached to the court; the ecclesiastics, retained by like motives, added the sanction of religion to the principles of civil policy: That in England a great part of the landed property belonged either to the yeomanry or middling gentry; the king had

Remonstrances of Sir W. Temple.

few offices to bestow; and could not himself even subsist, much less maintain an army, except by the voluntary supplies of his parliament: That if he had an army on foot, yet, if composed of Englishmen, they would never be prevailed on to promote ends, which the people so much feared and hated: That the Roman catholics in England were not the hundredth part of the nation, and in Scotland not the two hundredth; and it seemed against all common sense to hope, by one part, to govern ninety-nine, who were of contrary sentiments and dispositions: And that foreign troops, if few, would tend only to inflame hatred and discontent; and how to raise and bring over at once, or to maintain many, it was very difficult to imagine. To these reasonings Temple added the authority of Gourville, a Frenchman, for whom, he knew, the king had entertained a great esteem. "A king of England," said Gourville, "who will be *the man of his people,* is the greatest king in the world: But if he will be any thing more, he is nothing at all." The king heard, at first, this discourse with some impatience; but being a dextrous dissembler, he seemed moved at last, and laying his hand on Temple's, said, with an appearing cordiality, "And I will be the man of my people."

Temple, when he went abroad, soon found, that the scheme of mediating a peace was likely to prove abortive. The allies, besides their jealousy of the king's mediation, expressed a great ardour for the continuance of war. Holland had stipulated with Spain never to come to an accommodation, till all things in Flanders were restored to the condition, in which they had been left by the Pyrenean treaty. The emperor had high pretensions in Alsace; and as the greater part of the empire joined in the alliance, it was hoped, that France, so much over-matched in force, would soon be obliged to submit to the terms demanded of her. The Dutch, indeed, oppressed by heavy taxes, as well as checked in their commerce, were desirous of peace; and had few or no claims of their own to retard it: But they could not in gratitude, or even in good policy, abandon allies, to whose protection they had so lately been indebted for their safety. The prince of Orange likewise, who had great influence in their councils, was all on fire for military fame, and was well pleased to be at the head of armies, from which such mighty successes were expected. Under various pretences, he eluded, during the whole campaign, the meeting with Temple;

CHAPTER LXVI

and after the troops were sent into winter-quarters, he told that minister, in his first audience, that, till greater impression were made on France, reasonable terms could not be hoped for; and it were therefore vain to negotiate.

The success of the campaign had not answered expectation. *Campaign* The prince of Orange, with a superior army, was opposed in *of 1674.* Flanders to the prince of Condé, and had hoped to penetrate into France by that quarter, where the frontier was then very feeble. After long endeavouring, though in vain, to bring Condé to a battle, he rashly exposed, at Seneffe, a wing of his army; and that active prince failed not at once to see and to seize the advantage. But this imprudence of the prince of Orange was amply compensated by his behaviour in that obstinate and bloody action which ensued. He rallied his dismayed troops; he led them to the charge; he pushed the veteran and martial troops of France; and he obliged the prince of Condé, notwithstanding his age and character, to exert greater efforts, and to risque his person more, than in any action, where, even during the heat of youth, he had ever commanded. After sun-set, the action was continued by the light of the moon; and it was darkness at last, not the weariness of the combatants, which put an end to the contest, and left the victory undecided. "The prince of Orange," said Condé, with candour and generosity, "has acted in every thing like an old captain, except venturing his life too like a young soldier." Oudenarde was afterwards invested by the prince of Orange; but he was obliged by the Imperial and Spanish generals to raise the siege on the approach of the enemy. He afterwards besieged and took Grave; and at the beginning of winter, the allied armies broke up, with great discontents and complaints on all sides.

The allies were not more successful in other places. Lewis in a few weeks reconquered Franchecomté. In Alsace, Turenne displayed, against a much superior enemy, all that military skill, which had long rendered him the most renowned captain of his age and nation. By a sudden and forced march, he attacked and beat at Sintzheim the duke of Lorrain and Caprara, general of the Imperialists. Seventy thousand Germans poured into Alsace, and took up their quarters in that province. Turenne, who had retired into Lorrain, returned unexpectedly upon them. He attacked and defeated a body of the enemy at Mulhausen. He chaced from

Colmar the elector of Brandenburgh, who commanded the German troops. He gained a new advantage at Turkheim. And having dislodged all the allies, he obliged them to repass the Rhine, full of shame for their multiplied defeats, and still more, of anger and complaints against each other.

In England, all these events were considered by the people with great anxiety and concern; though the king and his ministers affected great indifference with regard to them. Considerable alterations were about this time made in the English ministry. Buckingham was dismissed, who had long, by his wit and entertaining humour, possessed the king's favour. Arlington, now chamberlain, and Danby the treasurer, possessed chiefly the king's confidence. Great hatred and jealousy took place between these ministers; and public affairs were somewhat disturbed by their quarrels. But Danby daily gained ground with his master. And Arlington declined in the same proportion. Danby was a frugal minister; and by his application and industry, he brought the revenue into tolerable order. He endeavoured so to conduct himself as to give offence to no party; and the consequence was, that he was able entirely to please none. He was a declared enemy to the French alliance; but never possessed authority enough to overcome the prepossessions, which the king and the duke retained towards it. It must be ascribed to the prevalence of that interest, aided by money, remitted from Paris, that the parliament was assembled so late this year; lest they should attempt to engage the king in measures against France, during the ensuing campaign. They met not till the approach of summer.[o]

1675.
13th
April.

A par-
liament.

Every step, taken by the commons, discovered that ill humour and jealousy, to which the late open measures of the king, and his present secret attachments gave but too just foundation. They drew up a new bill against popery, and resolved to insert in it many severe clauses for the detection and prosecution of priests: They presented addresses a second time against Lauderdale; and when the king's answer was not satisfactory, they seemed still determined to persevere in their applications: An accusation was moved

[o] This year, on the 25th of March, died Henry Cromwel, second son of the protector, in the 47th year of his age. He had lived unmolested in a private station, ever since the king's restoration, which he rather favoured than opposed.

CHAPTER LXVI

against Danby; but upon examining the several articles, it was not found to contain any just reasons of a prosecution; and was therefore dropped: They applied to the king for recalling his troops from the French service; and as he only promised, that they should not be recruited, they appeared to be much dissatisfied with the answer: A bill was brought in, making it treason to levy money without authority of parliament: Another vacating the seats of such members as accepted of offices: Another to secure the personal liberty of the subject, and to prevent sending any person prisoner beyond sea.

That the court party might not be idle, during these attacks, a bill for a new test was introduced into the house of peers by the earl of Lindesey. All members of either house, and all who possessed any office, were by this bill required to swear, that it was not lawful, upon any pretence whatsoever, to take arms against the king; that they abhorred the traiterous position of taking arms by his authority against his person, or against those who were commissioned by him; and that they will not at any time endeavour the alteration of the protestant religion, or of the established government either in church or state.

Passive obedience.

Great opposition was made to this bill; as might be expected from the present disposition of the nation. During seventeen days, the debates were carried on with much zeal; and all the reason and learning of both parties were displayed on the occasion. The question, indeed, with regard to resistance, was a point, which entered into the controversies of the old parties, cavalier and roundhead; as it made an essential part of the present disputes between court and country. Few neuters were found in the nation: But among such as could maintain a calm indifference, there prevailed sentiments wide of those which were adopted by either party. Such persons thought, that all general, speculative declarations of the legislature, either for or against resistance, were equally impolitic, and could serve to no other purpose, than to signalize in their turn the triumph of one faction over another: That the simplicity retained in the ancient laws of England, as well as in the laws of every other country, ought still to be preserved, and was best calculated to prevent the extremes on either side: That the absolute exclusion of resistance, in all possible cases, was founded on *false* principles; its express admission might be attended with *dangerous* consequences; and there was no necessity for exposing the public to either inconvenience: That if a choice must necessarily be made in the case, the preference of utility to truth in public institutions was apparent; nor could the supposition of resistance, beforehand and in general terms, be safely admitted in any government: That even in mixt monarchies, where that supposition seemed most requisite, it was yet entirely superfluous; since no man, on the approach of extraordinary necessity, could be at a loss, though not directed by legal declarations, to find the proper remedy: That even those who might, at a distance, and by scholastic reasoning, exclude all resistance, would yet hearken to the voice of nature; when evident ruin, both to themselves and to the public, must attend a strict adherence to their pretended principles: That the question, as it ought thus to be entirely excluded from all determinations of the legislature, was, even among private reasoners, somewhat frivolous, and little better than a dispute of words: That the one party could not pretend, that resistance ought ever to become a familiar practice; the other would surely have recourse to it in great extremities: And thus the difference could only turn on the degrees of danger or oppression, which would warrant this irregular remedy; a difference, which, in a general question, it was impossible, by any language, precisely to fix or determine.

There were many other absurdities in this test, particularly that of binding men by oath not to alter the government either in church or state; since all human institutions are liable to abuse, and require continual amendments, which are, in reality, so many alterations. It is not indeed possible to make a law, which does not innovate, more or less, in the government. These difficulties produced such obstructions to the bill, that it was carried only by two voices in the house of peers. All the popish lords, headed by the earl of Bristol, voted against it. It was sent down to the house of commons, where it was likely to undergo a scrutiny still more severe.

But a quarrel, which ensued between the two houses, prevented the passing of every bill, projected during the present session. One Dr. Shirley, being cast in a lawsuit before chancery against Sir John Fag, a member of the house of commons, preferred a petition of appeal to the house of peers. The Lords received it, and summoned Fag to appear before them. He com-

CHAPTER LXVI

plained to the lower house, who espoused his cause. They not only maintained, that no member of their house could be summoned before the peers: They also asserted, that the upper house could receive no appeals from any court of equity; a pretension, which extremely retrenched the jurisdiction of the peers, and which was contrary to the practice that had prevailed during this whole century. The commons send Shirley to prison; the lords assert their powers. Conferences are tried; but no accommodation ensues. Four lawyers are sent to the Tower by the commons, for transgressing the orders of the house, and pleading in this cause before the peers. The peers denominate this arbitrary commitment a breach of the great charter, and order the lieutenant of the Tower to release the prisoners: He declines obedience: They apply to the king, and desire him to punish the lieutenant for his contempt. The king summons both houses; exhorts them to unanimity; and informs them, that the present quarrel had arisen from the contrivance of his and their enemies, who expected by that means to force a dissolution of the parliament. His advice has no effect: The commons continue as violent as ever; and the king, finding that no business could be finished, at last prorogued the parliament.

8th June.

When the parliament was again assembled, there appeared not in any respect a change in the dispositions of either house. The king desired supplies, as well for the building of ships as for taking off anticipations, which lay upon his revenue. He even confessed, that he had not been altogether so frugal as he might have been, and as he resolved to be for the future; though he asserted, that, to his great satisfaction, he had found his expences by no means so exorbitant as some had represented them. The commons took into consideration the subject of supply. They voted 300,000 pounds for the building of ships; but they appropriated the sum by very strict clauses. They passed a resolution not to grant any supply for taking off the anticipations of the revenue.*p* This vote was carried in a full house, by a majority of four only: So nearly were the parties balanced. The quarrel was revived, to which Dr. Shirley's

13th Oct. A parliament.

---

p Several historians have affirmed, that the commons found, this session, upon enquiry, that the king's revenue was 1,600,000 pounds a year, and that the necessary expence was but 700,000 pounds; and have appealed to the Journals for a proof. But there is not the least appearance of this in the Journals; and the fact is impossible.

cause had given occasion. The proceedings of the commons discovered the same violence as during the last session. A motion was made in the house of peers, but rejected, for addressing the king to dissolve the present parliament. The king contented himself *22d Nov.* with proroguing them to a very long term. Whether these quarrels between the houses arose from contrivance or accident was not certainly known. Each party might, according to their different views, esteem themselves either gainers or losers by them. The court might desire to obstruct all attacks from the commons, by giving them other employment. The country party might desire the dissolution of a parliament, which, notwithstanding all disgusts, still contained too many royalists, ever to serve all the purposes of the malcontents.

Soon after the prorogation, there passed an incident, which in itself is trivial, but tends strongly to mark the genius of the English government, and of Charles's administration, during this period. The liberty of the constitution, and the variety as well as violence of the parties, had begotten a propensity for political conversation; and as the coffee-houses in particular were the scenes, where the conduct of the king and the ministry was canvassed with great freedom, a proclamation was issued to suppress these places of rendezvous. Such an act of power, during former reigns, would have been grounded entirely on the prerogative; and before the accession of the house of Stuart, no scruple would have been entertained with regard to that exercise of authority. But Charles, finding doubts to arise upon his proclamation, had recourse to the judges, who supplied him with a chicane, and that too a frivolous one, by which he might justify his proceedings. The law, which settled the excise, enacted, that licences for retailing liquors might be refused to such as could not find security for payment of the duties. But coffee was not a liquor subjected to excise; and even this power of refusing licences was very limited, and could not reasonably be extended beyond the intention of the act. The king, therefore, observing the people to be much dissatisfied, yielded to a petition of the coffee-men, who promised for the future to restrain all seditious discourse in their houses; and the proclamation was recalled.

Campaign of 1675. This campaign proved more fortunate to the confederates than any other during the whole war. The French took the field in

CHAPTER LXVI

Flanders with a numerous army; and Lewis himself served as a volunteer under the prince of Condé. But notwithstanding his great preparations, he could gain no advantages but the taking of Huy and Limbourg, places of small consequence. The prince of Orange with a considerable army opposed him in all his motions; and neither side was willing, without a visible advantage, to hazard a general action, which might be attended either with the entire loss of Flanders on the one hand, or the invasion of France on the other. Lewis, tired of so unactive a campaign, returned to Versailles; and the whole summer passed in the Low-Countries without any memorable event.

Turenne commanded on the Upper Rhine, in opposition to his great rival, Montecuculi, general of the Imperialists. The object of the latter was to pass the Rhine, to penetrate into Alsace, Lorraine, or Burgundy, and to fix his quarters in these provinces: The aim of the former was to guard the French frontiers, and to disappoint all the schemes of his enemy. The most consummate skill was displayed on both sides; and if any superiority appeared in Turenne's conduct, it was chiefly ascribed to his greater vigour of body, by which he was enabled to inspect all the posts in person, and could on the spot take the justest measures for the execution of his designs. By posting himself on the German side of the Rhine, he not only kept Montecuculi from passing that river: He had also laid his plan in so masterly a manner, that, in a few days he must have obliged the Germans to decamp, and have gained a considerable advantage over them; when a period was put to his life, by a random shot, which struck him on the breast as he was taking a view of the enemy. The consternation of his army was inexpressible. The French troops, who, a moment before, were assured of victory, now considered themselves as entirely vanquished; and the Germans, who would have been glad to compound for a safe retreat, expected no less than the total destruction of their enemy. But de Lorges, nephew to Turenne, succeeded him in the command, and possessed a great share of the genius and capacity of his predecessor. By his skilful operations, the French were enabled to repass the Rhine, without considerable loss; and this retreat was deemed equally glorious with the greatest victory. The valour of the English troops, who were placed in the rear, greatly contributed to save the French army. They had been seized with the same passion as the native troops of France, for their brave general, and fought with ardour to revenge his death on the Germans. The duke of Marlborough, then captain Churchill, here learned the rudiments of that art, which he afterwards practised with such fatal success against France.

The prince of Condé left the army in Flanders under the command of Luxembourg; and carrying with him a considerable reinforcement, succeeded to Turenne's command. He defended Alsace from the Germans, who had passed the Rhine, and invaded that province. He obliged them first to raise the siege of Hagenau, then that of Saberne. He eluded all their attempts to bring him to a battle. And having dexterously prevented them from establishing themselves in Alsace, he forced them, notwithstanding their superiority of numbers, to repass the Rhine, and to take up winter quarters in their own country.

After the death of Turenne, a detachment of the German army was sent to the siege of Treves: An enterprize, in which the Imperialists, the Spaniards, the Palatine, the duke of Lorraine, and many other princes passionately concurred. The project was well concerted, and executed with vigor. Mareschal Crequi, on the other hand, collected an army, and advanced with a view of forcing the Germans to raise the siege. They left a detachment to guard their lines, and under the command of the dukes of Zell and Osnaburgh, marched in quest of the enemy. At Consarbric, they fell unexpectedly, and with superior numbers, on Crequi, and put him to rout. He escaped with four attendants only; and throwing himself into Treves, resolved, by a vigorous defence, to make atonement for his former error or misfortune. The garrison was brave, but not abandoned to that total despair, by which their governor was actuated. They mutinied against his obstinacy; capitulated for themselves; and because he refused to sign the capitulation, they delivered him a prisoner into the hands of the enemy.

It is remarkable, that this defeat, given to Crequi, is almost the only one, which the French received at land, from Rocroi to Blenheim, during the course of above sixty years; and these too, full of bloody wars against potent and martial enemies: Their victories almost equal the number of years during that period. Such was the vigour and good conduct of that monarchy! And such too were the

CHAPTER LXVI

resources and refined policy of the other European nations, by which they were enabled to repair their losses, and still to confine that mighty power nearly within its ancient limits! A fifth part of these victories would have sufficed, in another period, to have given to France the empire of Europe.

The Swedes had been engaged, by the payment of large subsidies, to take part with Lewis, and invade the territories of the elector of Brandenburgh in Pomerania. That elector, joined by some Imperialists from Silesia, fell upon them with bravery and success. He soon obliged them to evacuate his part of that country, and he pursued them into their own. He had an interview with the king of Denmark, who had now joined the confederates, and resolved to declare war against Sweden. These princes concerted measures for pushing the victory.

To all these misfortunes against foreign enemies were added some domestic insurrections of the common people in Guienne and Brittany. Though soon suppressed, they divided the force and attention of Lewis. The only advantage, gained by the French, was at sea. Messina in Sicily had revolted; and a fleet under the duke de Vivonne was dispatched to support the rebels. The Dutch had sent a squadron to assist the Spaniards. A battle ensued, where de Ruyter was killed. This event alone was thought equivalent to a victory.

The French, who, twelve years before, had scarcely a ship of war in any of their harbours, had raised themselves, by means of perseverance and policy, to be, in their present force, though not in their resources, the first maritime power in Europe. The Dutch, while in alliance with them against England, had supplied them with several vessels, and had taught them the rudiments of the difficult art of ship building. The English next, when in alliance with them against Holland, instructed them in the method of fighting their ships, and of preserving order in naval engagements. Lewis availed himself of every opportunity to aggrandize his people, while Charles, sunk in indolence and pleasure, neglected all the noble arts of government; or if at any time he roused himself from his lethargy, that industry, by reason of the unhappy projects which he embraced, was often more pernicious to the public than his inactivity itself. He was as anxious to promote the naval power of France, as if the safety of his crown had depended on it; and many of the plans executed in that kingdom, were first, it is said,[q] digested and corrected by him.

1676.

Con-gress of Nimeguen.

The successes of the allies had been considerable the last campaign; but the Spaniards and Imperialists well knew, that France was not yet sufficiently broken, nor willing to submit to the terms which they resolved to impose upon her. Though they could not refuse the king's mediation, and Nimeguen, after many difficulties, was at last fixed on as the place of congress; yet under one pretence or other, they still delayed sending their ambassadors, and no progress was made in the negociation. Lord Berkeley, Sir William Temple, and Sir Lionel Jenkins, were the English ministers at Nimeguen. The Dutch, who were impatient for peace, soon appeared: Lewis, who hoped to divide the allies, and who knew, that he himself could neither be seduced nor forced into a disadvantageous peace, sent ambassadors: The Swedes, who hoped to recover by treaty what they had lost by arms, were also forward to negociate. But as these powers could not proceed of themselves to settle terms, the congress, hitherto, served merely as an amusement to the public.

Campaign of 1676.

It was by the events of the campaign, not the conferences among the negotiators, that the articles of peace were to be determined. The Spanish towns, ill fortified and worse defended, made but a feeble resistance to Lewis; who, by laying up magazines during the winter, was able to take the field early in the spring, before the forage could be found in the open country. In the month of April he laid siege to Condé, and took it by storm in four days. Having sent the duke of Orleans to besiege Bouchaine, a small but important fortress, he posted himself so advantageously with his main army, as to hinder the confederates from relieving it, or fighting without disadvantage. The prince of Orange, in spite of the difficulties of the season, and the want of provisions, came in sight of the French army; but his industry served to no other purpose than to render him spectator of the surrender of Bouchaine. Both armies stood in awe of each other, and were unwilling to hazard an action, which might be attended with the most important consequences. Lewis, though he wanted not personal

[q] Welwood, Burnet, Coke.

CHAPTER LXVI

courage, was little enterprizing in the field; and being resolved this campaign to rest contented with the advantages which he had so early obtained, he thought proper to entrust his army to mareschal Schomberg, and retired himself to Versailles. After his departure, the prince of Orange laid siege to Maestricht; but meeting with an obstinate resistance, he was obliged, on the approach of Schomberg, who in the mean time had taken Aire, to raise the siege. He was incapable of yielding to adversity, or bending under misfortunes: But he began to foresee, that, by the negligence and errors of his allies, the war in Flanders must necessarily have a very unfortunate issue.

On the Upper Rhine, Philipsbourg was taken by the Imperialists. In Pomerania, the Swedes were so unsuccessful against the Danes and Brandenburghers, that they seemed to be losing apace all those possessions, which, with so much valour and good fortune, they had acquired in Germany.

About the beginning of winter, the congress of Nimeguen was pretty full, and the plenipotentiaries of the emperor and Spain, two powers strictly conjoined by blood and alliance, at last appeared. The Dutch had threatened, if they absented themselves any longer, to proceed to a separate treaty with France. In the conferences and negociations, the dispositions of the parties became every day more apparent.

The Hollanders, loaded with debts, and harassed with taxes, *1677.* were desirous of putting an end to a war; in which, besides the disadvantages attending all leagues, the weakness of the Spaniards, the divisions and delays of the Germans, prognosticated nothing but disgrace and misfortune. Their commerce languished; and what gave them still greater anxiety, the commerce of England, by reason of her neutrality, flourished extremely; and they were apprehensive, lest advantages, once lost, would never thoroughly be regained. They had themselves no farther motive for continuing the war, than to secure a good frontier to Flanders; but gratitude to their allies still engaged them to try, whether another campaign might procure a peace, which would give general satisfaction. The prince of Orange, urged by motives of honour, of ambition, and of animosity against France, endeavoured to keep them steady to this resolution.

The Spaniards, not to mention the other incurable weaknesses, into which their monarchy was fallen, were distracted with domestic dissentions between the parties of the queen regent and Don John, natural brother to their young sovereign. Though unable of themselves to defend Flanders, they were resolute not to conclude a peace, which would leave it exposed to every assault or inroad; and while they made the most magnificent promises to the States, their real trust was in the protection of England. They saw, that, if that small but important territory were once subdued by France, the Hollanders, exposed to so terrible a power, would fall into dependance, and would endeavour, by submissions, to ward off that destruction, to which a war in the heart of their state must necessarily expose them. They believed, that Lewis, sensible how much greater advantages he might reap from the alliance than from the subjection of the republic, which must scatter its people, and depress its commerce, would be satisfied with very moderate conditions, and would turn his enterprizes against his other neighbours. They thought it impossible but the people and parliament of England, foreseeing these obvious consequences, must at last force the king to take part in the affairs of the continent, in which their interests were so deeply concerned. And they trusted, that even the king himself, on the approach of so great a danger, must open his eyes, and sacrifice his prejudices, in favour of France, to the safety of his own dominions.

Uncertain conduct of the king. But Charles here found himself entangled in such opposite motives and engagements, as he had not resolution enough to break, or patience to unravel. On the one hand, he always regarded his alliance with France as a sure resource in case of any commotions among his own subjects; and whatever schemes he might still retain for enlarging his authority, or altering the established religion, it was from that quarter alone he could expect assistance. He had actually in secret sold his neutrality to France, and he received remittances of a million of livres a-year, which was afterwards encreased to two millions; a considerable supply in the present embarrassed state of his revenue. And he dreaded, lest the parliament should treat him as they had formerly done his father; and after they had engaged him in a war on the continent, should take advantage of his necessities, and make him purchase supplies by sacrificing his prerogative, and abandoning his ministers.

CHAPTER LXVI

On the other hand, the cries of his people and parliament, seconded by Danby, Arlington, and most of his ministers, incited him to take part with the allies, and to correct the unequal balance of power in Europe. He might apprehend danger from opposing such earnest desires: He might hope for large supplies if he concurred with them: And however inglorious and indolent his disposition, the renown of acting as arbiter of Europe, would probably at intervals rouze him from his lethargy, and move him to support the high character, with which he stood invested.

It is worthy of observation, that, during this period, the king was, by every one, abroad and at home, by France and by the allies, allowed to be the undisputed arbiter of Europe; and no terms of peace, which he would have prescribed, could have been refused by either party. Though France afterwards found means to resist the same alliance, joined with England; yet was she then obliged to make such violent efforts as quite exhausted her; and it was the utmost necessity, which pushed her to find resources, far surpassing her own expectations. Charles was sensible, that, so long as the war continued abroad, he should never enjoy ease at home, from the impatience and importunity of his subjects; yet could he not resolve to impose a peace by openly joining himself with either party. Terms advantageous to the allies must lose him the friendship of France: The contrary would enrage his parliament. Between these views, he perpetually fluctuated; and from his conduct, it is observable, that a careless, remiss disposition, agitated by opposite motives, is capable of as great inconsistencies as are incident even to the greatest imbecillity and folly.

The parliament was assembled; and the king made them a plausible speech, in which he warned them against all differences among themselves; expressed a resolution to do his part for bringing their consultations to a happy issue; and offered his consent to any laws for the farther security of their religion, liberty, and property. He then told them of the decayed condition of the navy; and asked money for repairing it: He informed them, that part of his revenue, the additional excise, was soon to expire: And he added these words, "You may at any time see the yearly established expence of the government, by which it will appear, that, the constant and unavoidable charge being paid, there will remain no

15th Feb.
A parliament.

overplus towards answering those contingencies, which may happen in all kingdoms, and which have been a considerable burthen on me this last year."

Before the parliament entered upon business, they were stopped by a doubt, concerning the legality of their meeting. It had been enacted by an old law of Edward III. "That parliaments should be held once every year, or oftener, if need be." The last prorogation had been longer than a year; and being supposed on that account illegal, it was pretended to be equivalent to a dissolution. The consequence seems by no means just; and besides, a later act, that which repealed the triennial law, had determined, that it was necessary to hold parliaments only once in three years. Such weight, however, was put on this cavil, that Buckingham, Shaftesbury, Salisbury, and Wharton, insisted strenuously in the house of peers on the invalidity of the parliament, and the nullity of all its future acts. For such dangerous positions, they were sent to the Tower, there to remain during the pleasure of his majesty and the house. Buckingham, Salisbury, and Wharton made submissions, and were soon after released. But Shaftesbury, more obstinate in his temper, and desirous of distinguishing himself by his adherence to liberty, sought the remedy of law; and being rejected by the judges, he was at last, after a twelve-month's imprisonment, obliged to make the same submissions; upon which he was also released.

The commons at first seemed to proceed with temper. They granted the sum of 586,000 pounds, for building thirty ships; though they strictly appropriated the money to that service. Estimates were given in of the expence; but it was afterwards found that they fell short near 100,000 pounds. They also voted, agreeably to the king's request, the continuance of the additional excise for three years. This excise had been granted for nine years in 1668. Every thing seemed to promise a peaceable and an easy session.

Campaign of 1677. But the parliament was roused from this tranquillity by the news received from abroad. The French king had taken the field in the middle of February, and laid siege to Valenciennes, which he carried in a few days by storm. He next invested both Cambray and St. Omers. The prince of Orange, alarmed with his progress, hastily assembled an army, and marched to the relief of St. Omers. He

CHAPTER LXVI

was encountered by the French, under the duke of Orleans and mareschal Luxembourg. The prince possessed great talents for war; courage, activity, vigilance, patience; but still he was inferior in genius to those consummate generals, opposed to him by Lewis; and though he always found means to repair his losses, and to make head in a little time against the victors, he was, during his whole life, unsuccessful. By a masterly movement of Luxembourg, he was here defeated, and obliged to retreat to Ypres. Cambray and St. Omers were soon after surrendered to Lewis.

This success, derived from such great power and such wise conduct, infused a just terror into the English parliament. They addressed the king, representing the danger to which the kingdom was exposed from the greatness of France; and praying, that his majesty, by such alliances as he should think fit, would both secure his own dominions and the Spanish Netherlands, and thereby quiet the fears of his people. The king, desirous of eluding this application, which he considered as a kind of attack on his measures, replied in general terms, that he would use all means for the preservation of Flanders, consistent with the peace and safety of his kingdoms. This answer was an evasion, or rather a denial. The commons, therefore, thought proper to be more explicit. They entreated him not to defer the entering into such alliances as might attain that great end: And in case war with the French king should be the result of his measures, they promised to grant him all the aids and supplies, which would enable him to support the honour and interest of the nation. The king was also more explicit in his reply. He told them, that the only way to prevent danger, was to put him in a condition to make preparations for their security. This message was understood to be a demand of money. The parliament accordingly empowered the king to borrow on the additional excise 200,000 pounds at seven per cent.: A very small sum indeed; but which they deemed sufficient, with the ordinary revenue, to equip a good squadron, and thereby put the nation in security, till farther resolutions should be taken.

But this concession fell far short of the king's expectations. He therefore informed them, that, unless they granted him the sum of 600,000 pounds upon new funds, it would not be possible for him, without exposing the nation to manifest danger, *to speak or act those things,* which would answer the end of their several addresses. The house took this message into consideration: But before they came to any resolution, the king sent for them to Whitehall, where he told them, upon the word of a king, that they should not repent any trust, which they would repose in him for the safety of his kingdom; that he would not for any consideration break credit with them, or employ their money to other uses, than those for which they intended it; but that he would not hazard, either his own safety or theirs, by taking any vigorous measures, or forming new alliances, till he were in a better condition both to defend his subjects, and offend his enemies. This speech brought affairs to a short issue. The king required them to trust him with a large sum: He pawned his royal word for their security: They must either run the risque of losing their money, or fail of those alliances which they had projected, and at the same time declare to all the world the highest distrust of their sovereign.

Parlia-ment's distrust of the king. But there were many reasons which determined the house of commons to put no trust in the king. They considered, that the pretence of danger was obviously groundless; while the French were opposed by such powerful alliances on the continent, while the king was master of a good fleet at sea, and while all his subjects were so heartily united in opposition to foreign enemies. That the only justifiable reason, therefore, of Charles's backwardness, was not the apprehension of danger from abroad, but a diffidence, which he might perhaps have entertained of his parliament; lest, after engaging him in foreign alliances for carrying on war, they should take advantage of his necessities, and extort from him concessions dangerous to his royal dignity. That this parliament, by their past conduct, had given no foundation for such suspicions, and were so far from pursuing any sinister ends, that they had granted supplies for the first Dutch war; for maintaining the triple league, though concluded without their advice; even for carrying on the second Dutch war, which was entered into contrary to their opinion, and contrary to the manifest interests of the nation. That on the other hand, the king had, by former measures, excited very reasonable jealousies in his people, and did with a bad grace require at present their trust and confidence. That he had not scrupled to demand supplies for maintaining the triple league, at the very moment he was concerting measures for breaking it, and had accordingly employed to that purpose the supplies, which he had

CHAPTER LXVI

obtained by those delusive pretences. That his union with France, during the war against Holland, must have been founded on projects the most dangerous to his people; and as the same union was still secretly maintained, it might justly be feared, that the same projects were not yet entirely abandoned. That he could not seriously intend to prosecute vigorous measures against France; since he had so long remained entirely unconcerned during such obvious dangers; and, till prompted by his parliament, whose proper business it was not to take the lead in those parts of administration, had suspended all his activity. That if he really meant to enter into a cordial union with his people, he would have taken the first step, and have endeavoured, by putting trust in them, to restore that confidence, which he himself, by his rash conduct, had first violated. That it was in vain to ask so small a sum as 600,000 pounds, in order to secure him against the future attempts of the parliament; since that sum must soon be exhausted by a war with France, and he must again fall into that dependance, which was become, in some degree, essential to the constitution. That if he would form the necessary alliances, that sum, or a greater, would instantly be voted; nor could there be any reason to dread, that the parliament would immediately desert measures, in which they were engaged by their honour, their inclination, and the public interest. That the real ground, therefore, of the king's refusal was neither apprehension of danger from foreign enemies, nor jealousy of parliamentary encroachments; but a desire of obtaining the money, which he intended, notwithstanding his royal word, to employ to other purposes. And that by using such dishonourable means to so ignoble an end, he rendered himself still more unworthy the confidence of his people.

The house of commons was now regularly divided into two parties, the court and the country. Some were inlisted in the court-party by offices, nay, a few by bribes secretly given them; a practice first begun by Clifford, a dangerous minister: But great numbers were attached merely by inclination; so far as they esteemed the measures of the court agreeable to the interests of the nation. Private views and faction had likewise drawn several into the country party: But there were also many of that party, who had no other object than the public good. These disinterested members on both sides fluctuated between the factions; and gave the superiority sometimes to the court, sometimes to the opposition.[r] In the present emergence, a general distrust of the king prevailed; and the parliament resolved not to hazard their money, in expectation of alliances, which, they believed, were never intended to be formed. Instead of granting the supply, they voted an address, wherein they "besought his majesty to enter into a league, offensive and defensive, with the States General of the United Provinces, against the growth and power of the French king, and for the preservation of the Spanish Netherlands; and to make such other alliances with the confederates as should appear fit and useful to that end." They supported their advice with reasons; and promised speedy and effectual supplies, for preserving his majesty's honour and ensuring the safety of the public. The king pretended the highest anger at this address, which he represented as a dangerous encroachment upon his prerogative. He reproved the commons in severe terms; and ordered them immediately to be adjourned.

8th May.

It is certain, that this was the critical moment, when the king both might with ease have preserved the balance of power in Europe, which it has since cost this island a great expence of blood and treasure to restore, and might by perseverance have at last regained, in some tolerable measure, after all past errors, the confidence of his people. This opportunity being neglected, the wound became incurable; and notwithstanding *his* momentary appearances of vigour against France and popery, and *their* momentary inclinations to rely on his faith: *he* was still believed to be at bottom engaged in the same interests, and *they* soon relapsed into distrust and jealousy. The secret memoirs of this reign, which have since been published,[s] prove beyond a doubt, that the king had at

[r] Temple's Memoirs, vol. i. p. 458.   [s] Such as the letters, which passed betwixt Danby and Montague, the king's ambassador at Paris; Temple's Memoirs, and his Letters. In these last, we see that the king never made any proposals of terms but what were advantageous to France, and the prince of Orange believed them to have always been concerted with the French ambassador. Vol. i. p. 439.

In Sir John Dalrymple's Appendix, p. 103, it appears, that the king had signed himself, without the participation of his ministers, a secret treaty with France, and had obtained a pension on the promise of his neutrality: A fact, which renders his *royal word,* solemnly given to his subjects, one of the most dishonourable and most scandalous acts, that ever proceeded from a throne.

CHAPTER LXVI

this time concerted measures with France, and had no intention to enter into a war in favour of the allies. He had entertained no view, therefore, even when he pawned his ROYAL WORD to his people, than to procure a grant of money; and he trusted, that, while he eluded their expectations, he could not afterwards want pretences for palliating his conduct.

Negotiations meanwhile were carried on between France and Holland, and an eventual treaty was concluded; that is, all their differences were adjusted, provided they could afterwards satisfy their allies on both sides. This work, though in appearance difficult, seemed to be extremely forwarded, by farther bad successes on the part of the confederates, and by the great impatience of the Hollanders; when a new event happened, which promised a more prosperous issue to the quarrel with France, and revived the hopes of all the English, who understood the interests of their country.

The king saw, with regret, the violent discontents, which prevailed in the nation, and which seemed every day to augment upon him. Desirous by his natural temper to be easy himself, and to make every body else easy, he sought expedients to appease those murmurs, which, as they were very disagreeable for the present, might in their consequences prove extremely dangerous. He knew, that, during the late war with Holland, the malcontents at home had made applications to the prince of Orange; and if he continued still to neglect the prince's interests, and to thwart the inclinations of his own people, he apprehended lest their common complaints should cement a lasting union between them. He saw, that the religion of the duke inspired the nation with dismal apprehensions; and though he had obliged his brother to allow the young princesses to be educated in the protestant faith, something farther, he thought, was necessary, in order to satisfy the nation. He entertained, therefore, proposals for marrying the prince of Orange to the lady Mary, the elder princess, and heir apparent to the crown (for the duke had no male issue), and he hoped, by so tempting an offer, to engage him intirely in his interests. A peace he purposed to make; such as would satisfy France, and still preserve his connections with that crown: And he intended to sanctify it by the approbation of the prince, whom he found to be extremely revered in England, and respected throughout Europe. All the reasons for this alliance were seconded by the solicitations of Danby, and also of Temple, who was at that time in England:

And Charles at last granted permission to the prince, when the campaign should be over, to pay him a visit.

1oth Oct.   The king very graciously received his nephew at Newmarket. He would have entered immediately upon business; but the prince desired first to be acquainted with the lady Mary: And he declared, that, contrary to the usual sentiments of persons of his rank, he placed a great part of happiness in domestic satisfaction, and would not, upon any consideration of interest or politics, match himself with a person disagreeable to him. He was introduced to the princess, whom he found in the bloom of youth, and extremely amiable both in her person and her behaviour. The king now thought, that he had a double tye upon him, and might safely expect his compliance with every proposal: He was surprized to find the prince decline all discourse of business, and refuse to concert any terms for the general peace, till his marriage should be finished. He foresaw, he said, from the situation of affairs, that his allies were likely to have hard terms; and he never would expose himself to the reproach of having sacrificed their interests to promote his own purposes. Charles still believed, notwithstanding the cold, severe manner of the prince, that he would abate of this rigid punctilio of honour; and he protracted the time, hoping, by his own insinuation and address, as well as by the allurements of love and ambition, to win him to compliance. One day, Temple found the prince in very bad humour, repenting that he had ever come to England, and resolute in a few days to leave it: But before he went, the king, he said, must chuse the terms, on which they should hereafter live together: He was sure it must be like the greatest friends or the greatest enemies: And he desired Temple to inform his master next morning of these intentions. Charles was struck with this menace, and foresaw how the prince's departure would be interpreted by the people. He resolved, therefore, imme-

23rd Octob. Marriage of the prince of Orange with the lady Mary.   diately to yield with a good grace; and having paid a compliment to his nephew's honesty, he told Temple, that the marriage was concluded, and desired him to inform the duke of it, as of an affair already resolved on. The duke seemed surprized; but yielded a prompt obedience: Which, he said, was his constant maxim to whatever he found to be the king's pleasure. No measure during this reign gave such general satisfaction. All parties strove who should most applaud it. And even Arlington, who had been kept

CHAPTER LXVI

out of the secret, told the prince, "That some things good in themselves, were spoiled by the manner of doing them, as some things bad were mended by it; but he would confess, that this was a thing so good in itself, that the manner of doing it could not spoil it."

This marriage was a great surprize to Lewis, who, accustomed to govern every thing in the English court, now found so important a step taken, not only without his consent, but without his knowledge or participation. A conjunction of England with the allies, and a vigorous war in opposition to French ambition, were the consequences immediately expected, both abroad and at home: But to check these sanguine hopes, the king, a few days after the marriage, prolonged the adjournment of the parliament from the third of December to the fourth of April. This term was too late for granting supplies, or making preparations for war; and could be chosen by the king for no other reason, than as an atonement to France for his consent to the marriage. It appears also that Charles secretly received from Lewis the sum of two millions of livres on account of this important service.[t]

The king, however, entered into consultations with the prince, together with Danby and Temple, concerning the terms which it would be proper to require of France. After some debate, it was agreed, that France should restore Lorrain to the duke; with Tournay, Valenciennes, Condé, Aeth, Charleroi, Courtray, Oudenarde, and Binche to Spain, in order to form a good frontier for the Low Countries. The prince insisted that Franchecomté should likewise be restored; and Charles thought, that, because he had patrimonial estates of great value in that province, and deemed his property more secure in the hands of Spain, he was engaged by such views to be obstinate in that point: But the prince declared, that to procure but one good town to the Spaniards in Flanders, he would willingly relinquish all those possessions. As the king still insisted on the impossibility of wresting Franchecomté from Lewis, the prince was obliged to acquiesce.

Notwithstanding this concession to France, the projected peace was favourable to the allies; and it was a sufficient indication of vigour in the king, that he had given his assent to it. He farther agreed to send over a minister instantly to Paris, in order to pro-

Plan of peace.

[t] Sir John Dalrymple's Appendix, p. 112.

pose these terms. This minister was to enter into no treaty: He was to allow but two days for the acceptance or refusal of the terms: Upon the expiration of these, he was presently to return: And in case of refusal, the king promised to enter immediately into the confederacy. To carry so imperious a message, and so little expected from the English court, Temple was the person pitched on, whose declared aversion to the French interest was not likely to make him fail of vigour and promptitude in the execution of his commission.

But Charles next day felt a relenting in this assumed vigour. Instead of Temple he dispatched the earl of Feversham, a creature of the duke's, and a Frenchman by birth: And he said, that the message being harsh in itself, it was needless to aggravate it by a disagreeable messenger. The prince left London; and the king, at his departure, assured him, that he never would abate in the least point of the scheme concerted, and would enter into war with Lewis, if he rejected it.

Negocia-
tions.

Lewis received the message with seeming gentleness and complacency. He told Feversham, that the king of England well knew, that he might always be master of the peace; but some of the towns in Flanders, it seemed very hard to demand, especially Tournay, upon whose fortifications such immense sums had been expended: He would therefore take some short time to consider of an answer. Feversham said, that he was limited to two days stay: But when that time was elapsed, he was prevailed on to remain some few days longer; and he came away at last without any positive answer. Lewis said, that he hoped his brother would not break with him for one or two towns: And with regard to them too, he would send orders to his ambassador at London to treat with the king himself. Charles was softened by the softness of France; and the blow was thus artfully eluded. The French ambassador, Barillon, owned at last, that he had orders to yield all except Tournay, and even to treat about some equivalent for that fortress, if the king absolutely insisted upon it. The prince was gone, who had given spirit to the English court; and the negociation began to draw out into messages and returns from Paris.

By intervals, however, the king could rouze himself, and show still some firmness and resolution. Finding that affairs were not likely to come to any conclusion with France, he summoned, notwithstanding the long adjournment, the parliament on the fifteenth of January; an unusual measure, and capable of giving alarm to the French court. Temple was sent for to the council, and the king told him, that he intended he should go to Holland, in order to form a treaty of alliance with the States; and that the purpose of it should be, like the triple league, to force both France and Spain to accept of the terms proposed. Temple was sorry to find this act of vigour qualified by such a regard to France, and by such an appearance of indifference and neutrality between the parties. He told the king, that the resolution agreed on, was to begin the war in conjunction with all the confederates, in case of no direct and immediate answer from France: That this measure would satisfy the prince, the allies, and the people of England; advantages which could not be expected from such an alliance with Holland alone: That France would be disobliged, and Spain likewise; nor would the Dutch be satisfied with such a faint imitation of the triple league, a measure concerted when they were equally at peace with both parties. For these reasons, Temple declined the employment; and Lawrence Hyde, second son of chancellor Clarendon, was sent in his place.

The Prince of Orange could not regard without contempt such *1678.* symptoms of weakness and vigour conjoined in the English counsels. He was resolved, however, to make the best of a measure, which he did not approve; and as Spain secretly consented, that her ally should form a league, which was seemingly directed against her as well as France, but which was to fall only on the latter, the States concluded the treaty in the terms proposed by *6th Jan.* the king.

Meanwhile, the English parliament met, after some new adjournments; and the king was astonished, that, notwithstanding *28th Jan.* the resolute measures, which, he thought, he had taken, great distrust and jealousy and discontent were apt, at intervals, still to prevail among the members. Though in his speech he had allowed, that a good peace could no longer be expected from negociation, and assured them, that he was resolved to enter into a war for that purpose; the commons did not forbear to insert in their reply several harsh and even unreasonable clauses. Upon his reproving them, they seemed penitent, and voted, that they would assist his majesty in the prosecution of the war. A fleet of ninety sail, an army of thirty thousand men, and a million of money were also voted. Great difficulties were made by the commons with regard to the army, which the house, judging by past measures, believed to be intended more against the liberties of England than against the progress of the French Monarch. To this perilous situation had the king reduced both himself and the nation. In all debates, severe speeches were made, and were received with seeming approbation: The duke and the treasurer began to be apprehensive of impeachments: Many motions against the king's ministers were lost by a small majority: The commons appointed a day to consider the state of the kingdom with regard to popery: And they even went so far as to vote, that, how urgent soever the occasion, they would lay no farther charge on the people, till secured against the prevalence of the catholic party. In short, the parliament was impatient for war whenever the king seemed averse to it; but grew suspicious of some sinister design as soon as he complied with their requests, and seemed to enter into their measures.

The king was enraged at this last vote: He reproached Temple with his popular notions, as he termed them; and asked him how he thought the house of commons could be trusted for carrying on the war, should it be entered on, when in the very commencement they made such declarations. The uncertainties indeed of Charles's conduct were so multiplied, and the jealousies on both sides so incurable, that even those, who approached nearest the scene of action, could not determine, whether the king ever seriously meant to enter into a war, or whether, if he did, the house of commons would not have taken advantage of his necessities, and made him purchase supplies by a great sacrifice of his authority.[u]

The king of France knew how to avail himself of all the advantages, which these distractions afforded him. By his emissaries, he represented to the Dutch, the imprudence of their depending on England; where an indolent king, averse to all war, especially with France, and irresolute in his measures, was actuated only by the uncertain breath of a factious parliament. To the aristocratical party, he remarked the danger of the prince's alliance with the royal family of England, and revived their apprehensions; lest, in imitation of his father, who had been honoured with the same alliance, he should violently attempt to enlarge his authority, and

[u] Temple, vol. i. p. 461.

*Campaign
of 1678.*

enslave his native country. In order to enforce these motives with
farther terrors, he himself took the field very early in the spring;
and after threatening Luxembourg, Mons, and Namur, he suddenly sat down before Ghent and Ypres, and in a few weeks made
himself master of both places. This success gave great alarm to the
Hollanders, who were no wise satisfied with the conduct of England, or with the ambiguous treaty lately concluded; and it quick-
ened all their advances towards an accommodation.

Immediately after the parliament had voted the supply, the
king began to inlist forces; and such was the ardour of the English
for a war with France, that an army of above 20,000 men, to the
astonishment of Europe, was completed in a few weeks. Three
thousand men under the duke of Monmouth, were sent over to
secure Ostend: Some regiments were recalled from the French
service: A fleet was fitted out with great diligence: And a quadru-
ple alliance was projected between England, Holland, Spain, and
the Emperor.

But these vigorous measures received a sudden damp from a
passionate address of the lower house; in which they justified all
their past proceedings, that had given disgust to the king; desired
to be acquainted with the measures taken by him; prayed him to
dismiss evil counsellors; and named in particular the duke of Lauderdale, on whose removal they strenuously insisted. The king told
them, that their address was so extravagant, that he was not willing
speedily to give it the answer, which it deserved. And he began
again to lend an ear to the proposals of Lewis, who offered him
great sums of money, if he would consent to France's making an
advantageous peace with the allies.

*Negoti-
ations.*

Temple, though pressed by the king, refused to have any concern in so dishonourable a negotiation: But he informs us, that the
king said, there was one article proposed, which so incensed him,
that, as long as he lived, he should never forget it. Sir William goes
no farther; but the editor of his works, the famous Dr. Swift, says,
that the French, before they would agree to any payment, required
as a preliminary, that the king should engage never to keep above
8000 regular troops in Great Britain.[w] Charles broke into a passion. "God's-fish," said he, his usual oath, "does my brother of

[w] To wit, 3000 men for Scotland, and the usual guards and garrisons in
England, amounting to near 5000 men. Sir J. Dalrymple's App. p. 161.

France think to serve me thus? Are all his promises to make me absolute master of my people come to this? Or does he think *that* a thing to be done with eight thousand men?"

Van Beverning was the Dutch ambassador at Nimeguen, a man of great authority with the States. He was eager for peace, and was persuaded, that the reluctance of the king and the jealousies of the parliament would for ever disappoint the allies in their hopes of succour from England. Orders were sent him by the States to go to the French king at Ghent, and to concert the terms of a general treaty, as well as procure a present truce for six weeks. The terms agreed on were much worse for the Spaniards, than those which had been planned by the king and the prince of Orange. Six towns, some of them of no great importance, were to be restored to them: But Ypres, Condé, Valenciennes, and Tournay, in which consisted the chief strength of their frontier, were to remain with France.

Great murmurs arose in England when it was known, that Flanders was to be left in so defenceless a condition. The chief complaints were levelled against the king, who, by his concurrence at first, by his favour afterwards, and by his delays at last, had raised the power of France to such an enormous height, that it threatened the general liberties of Europe. Charles, uneasy under these imputations, dreading the consequence of losing the affections of his subjects, and perhaps disgusted with the secret article proposed by France, began to wish heartily for war, which, he hoped, would have restored him to his ancient popularity.

An opportunity unexpectedly offered itself for his displaying these new dispositions. While the ministers at Nimeguen were concerting the terms of a general treaty, the marquis de Balbaces, the Spanish ambassador, asked the ambassadors of France, at what time France intended to restore the six towns in Flanders. They made no difficulty in declaring, that the king, their master, being obliged to see an entire restitution made to the Swedes of all they had lost in the war, could not evacuate these towns till that crown had received satisfaction; and that this detention of places was the only means to induce the powers of the north to accept of the peace.

The States immediately gave the king intelligence of a pretension, which might be attended with such dangerous consequences. The king was both surprised and angry. He immediately dispatched Temple to concert with the States vigorous measures for opposing France. Temple in six days concluded a treaty, by which Lewis was obliged to declare within sixteen days after the date, that he would presently evacuate the towns: And in case of his refusal, Holland was bound to continue the war, and England to declare immediately against France, in conjunction with the whole confederacy.

16th July.

All these warlike measures were so ill seconded by the parliament, where even the French ministers were suspected, with reason,[x] of carrying on some intrigues, that the commons renewed their former jealousies against the king, and voted the army imme-

---

[x] Sir John Dalrymple, in his Appendix, has given us, from Barillon's dispatches in the Secretary's office at Paris, a more particular detail of these intrigues. They were carried on with lord Russel, lord Hollis, lord Berkshire, the duke of Buckingham, Algernon Sydney, Montague, Bulstrode, col. Titus, sir Edward Harley, sir John Baber, sir Roger Hill, Boscawen, Littleton, Powle, Harbord, Hambden, sir Thomas Armstrong, Hotham, Herbert, and some others of less note. Of these, lord Russel and lord Hollis alone refused to touch any French money: All the others received presents or bribes from Barillon. But we are to remark, that the party views of these men, and their well-founded jealousies of the king and duke, engaged them, independently of the money, into the same measures that were suggested to them by the French ambassador. The intrigues of France, therefore, with the parliament were a mighty small engine in the political machine. Those with the king, which have always been known, were of infinitely greater consequence. The sums distributed to all these men, excepting Montague, did not exceed 16,000 pounds in three years; and therefore could have little weight in the two houses, especially when opposed to the influence of the crown. Accordingly we find, in all Barillon's dispatches, a great anxiety that the parliament should never be assembled. The conduct of these English patriots was more mean than criminal; and monsieur Courten says, that two hundred thousand livres employed by the Spaniards and Germans, would have more influence than two millions distributed by France. See Sir J. Dalrymple's App. p. 111. It is amusing to observe the general, and I may say national, rage excited by the late discovery of this secret negotiation; chiefly on account of Algernon Sydney, whom the blind prejudices of party had exalted into a hero. His ingratitude and breach of faith, in applying for the king's pardon, and immediately on his return entering into cabals for rebellion, form a conduct much more criminal than the taking of French gold: Yet the former circumstance was always known, and always disregarded. But every thing connected with France is supposed, in England, to be polluted beyond all possibility of expiation. Even lord Russel, whose conduct in this negotiation was only factious, and that in an ordinary degree, is imagined to be dishonoured by the same discovery.

diately to be disbanded. The king by a message represented the danger of disarming before peace were finally concluded; and he recommended to their consideration, whether he could honourably recal his forces from those towns in Flanders, which were put under his protection, and which had at present no other means of defence. The commons agreed to prolong the term with regard to these forces. Every thing indeed in Europe bore the appearance of war. France had positively declared, that she would not evacuate the six towns before the requisite cession was made to Sweden; and her honour seemed now engaged to support that declaration. Spain and the Empire, disgusted with the terms of peace imposed by Holland, saw with pleasure the prospect of a powerful support from the new resolutions of Charles. Holland itself, encouraged by the prince of Orange and his party, was not displeased to find, that the war would be renewed on more equal terms. The allied army under that prince was approaching towards Mons, then blockaded by France. A considerable body of English under the duke of Monmouth, was ready to join him.

Charles usually passed a great part of his time in the women's apartments, particularly those of the duchess of Portsmouth; where, among other gay company, he often met with Barillon, the French ambassador, a man of polite conversation, who was admitted into all the amusements of that inglorious, but agreeable monarch. It was the charms of this sauntering, easy life, which, during his later years, attached Charles to his mistresses. By the insinuations of Barillon and the duchess of Portsmouth, an order was, in an unguarded hour, procured, which instantly changed the face of affairs in Europe. One du Cros, a French fugitive monk, was sent to Temple, directing him to apply to the Swedish ambassador, and persuade him not to insist on the conditions required by France, but to sacrifice to general peace those interests of Sweden. Du Cros, who had secretly received instructions from Barillon, published every where in Holland the commission with which he was intrusted; and all men took the alarm. It was concluded, that Charles's sudden alacrity for war was as suddenly extinguished, and that no steady measures could ever be taken with England. The king afterwards, when he saw Temple, treated this important matter in raillery; and said laughing, that the rogue du Cros had outwitted them all.

CHAPTER LXVI

The negotiations however at Nimeguen still continued; and the French ambassadors spun out the time, till the morning of the critical day, which, by the late treaty between England and Holland, was to determine, whether a sudden peace or a long war were to have place in Christendom. The French ambassadors came then to Van Beverning, and told him, that they had received orders to consent to the evacuation of the towns, and immediately to conclude and sign the peace. Van Beverning might have refused compliance, because it was now impossible to procure the consent and concurrence of Spain; but he had entertained so just an idea of the fluctuations in the English counsels, and was so much alarmed by the late commission given to du Cros, that he deemed it fortunate for the republic to finish on any terms a dangerous war, where they were likely to be very ill supported. The papers were instantly drawn, and signed by the ministers of France and Holland between eleven and twelve o'clock at night. By this treaty, France secured the possession of Franchecomté, together with Cambray, Aire, St. Omers, Valenciennes, Tournay, Ypres, Bouchaine, Cassel, &c. and restored to Spain only Charleroi, Courtrai, Oudenard, Aeth, Ghent, and Limbourg.

1st August.

Next day Temple received an express from England, which brought the ratifications of the treaty lately concluded with the States, together with orders immediately to proceed to the exchange of them. Charles was now returned to his former inclinations for war with France.

Van Beverning was loudly exclaimed against by the ambassadors of the allies at Nimeguen, especially those of Brandenburg and Denmark, whose masters were obliged by the treaty to restore all their acquisitions. The ministers of Spain and the emperor were sullen and disgusted; and all men hoped, that the States, importuned and encouraged by continual solicitations from England, would disavow their ambassador, and renew the war. The prince of Orange even took an extraordinary step, in order to engage them to that measure; or perhaps to give vent to his own spleen and resentment. The day after signing the peace at Nimeguen, he attacked the French army at St. Dennis near Mons; and gained some advantage over Luxembourg, who rested secure on the faith of the treaty, and concluded the war to be finished. The prince knew, at least had reason to believe, that the peace was signed, though it had not been formally notified to him; and he here sacrificed wantonly, without a proper motive, the lives of many brave men on both sides, who fell in this sharp and well contested action.

Hyde was sent over with a view of persuading the States to disavow Van Beverning; and the king promised, that England, if she might depend on Holland, would immediately declare war, and would pursue it, till France were reduced to reasonable conditions. Charles at present went farther than words. He hurried on the embarkation of his army for Flanders; and all his preparations wore a hostile appearance. But the States had been too often deceived to trust him any longer. They ratified the treaty signed at Nimeguen; and all the other powers of Europe were at last, after much clamour and many disgusts, obliged to accept of the terms prescribed to them.

Peace of Nimeguen. Lewis had now reached the height of that glory, which ambition can afford. His ministers and negotiators appeared as much superior to those of all Europe in the cabinet, as his generals and armies had been experienced in the field. A successful war had been carried on against an alliance, composed of the greatest potentates in Europe. Considerable conquests had been made, and his territories enlarged on every side. An advantageous peace was at last concluded, where he had given the law. The allies were so enraged against each other, that they were not likely to cement soon in any new confederacy. And thus he had, during some years, a real prospect of attaining the monarchy of Europe, and of exceeding the empire of Charlemagne, perhaps equalling that of ancient Rome. Had England continued much longer in the same condition, and under the same government, it is not easy to conceive, that he could have failed of his purpose.

In proportion as these circumstances exalted the French, they excited indignation among the English, whose animosity, rouzed by terror, mounted to a great height against that rival nation. Instead of taking the lead in the affairs of Europe, Charles, they thought, had, contrary to his own honour and interest, acted a part entirely subservient to the common enemy; and in all his measures had either no project at all, or such as was highly criminal and dangerous. While Spain, Holland, the emperor, the princes of Germany called aloud on England to lead them to victory and to

CHAPTER LXVI

liberty, and conspired to raise her to a station more glorious than she had ever before attained; her king, from mean pecuniary motives, had secretly sold his alliance to Lewis, and was bribed into an interest contrary to that of his people. His active schemes in conjunction with France were highly pernicious; his neutrality was equally ignominious; and the jealous, refractory behaviour of the parliament, though in itself dangerous, was the only remedy for so many greater ills, with which the public, from the misguided counsels of the king, was so nearly threatened. Such were the dispositions of men's minds at the conclusion of the peace of Nimeguen: And these dispositions naturally prepared the way for the events which followed.

We must now return to the affairs of Scotland, which we left in some disorder, after the suppression of the insurrection in 1666. The king, who at that time endeavoured to render himself popular in England, adopted like measures in Scotland; and he entrusted the government into the hands chiefly of Tweddale, and Sir Robert Murray, men of prudence and moderation. These ministers made it their principal object to compose the religious differences, which ran high, and for which scarcely any modern nation but the Dutch, had as yet found the proper remedy. As rigour and restraint had failed of success in Scotland, a scheme of *comprehension* was tried; by which it was intended to diminish greatly the authority of bishops, to abolish their negative voice in the ecclesiastical courts, and to leave them little more than the right of precedency among the presbyters. But the presbyterian zealots entertained great jealousy against this scheme. They remembered, that, by such gradual steps, king James had endeavoured to introduce episcopacy. Should the ears and eyes of men be once reconciled to the name and habit of bishops, the whole power of the function, they dreaded, would soon follow: The least communication with unlawful and antichristian institutions they esteemed dangerous and criminal: *Touch not, taste not, handle not;* this cry went out amongst them: And the king's ministers at last perceived, that they should prostitute the dignity of government, by making advances, to which the malcontents were determined not to correspond.

The next project adopted was that of *indulgence.* In prosecution of this scheme, the most popular of the expelled preachers, with-

State of affairs in Scotland.

out requiring any terms of submission to the established religion, were settled in vacant churches; and small salaries of about twenty pounds a-year were offered to the rest, till they should otherwise be provided for. These last refused the king's bounty, which they considered as the wages of a criminal silence. Even the former soon repented their compliance. The people, who had been accustomed to hear them rail against their superiors, and preach to the times, as they termed it, deemed their sermons languid and spiritless, when deprived of these ornaments. Their usual gifts, they thought, had left them, on account of their submission, which was stigmatized as erastianism. They gave them the appellation, not of ministers of Christ, but of *the king's curates;* as the clergy of the established church were commonly denominated the *bishop's curates.* The preachers themselves returned in a little time to their former practices, by which they hoped to regain their former dominion over the minds of men. The conventicles multiplied daily in the west: The clergy of the established church were insulted: The laws were neglected: The covenanters even met daily in arms at their places of worship: And though they usually dispersed themselves after divine service, yet the government took a just alarm at seeing men, who were so entirely governed by their seditious teachers, dare to set authority at defiance, and during a time of full peace, to put themselves in a military posture.

There was here, it is apparent, in the political body, a disease dangerous and inveterate; and the government had tried every remedy, but the true one, to allay and correct it. An unlimited *toleration,* after sects have diffused themselves and are strongly rooted, is the only expedient, which can allay their fervour, and make the civil union acquire a superiority above religious distinctions. But as the operations of this regimen are commonly gradual, and at first imperceptible, vulgar politicians are apt, for that reason, to have recourse to more hasty and more dangerous remedies. It is observable too, that these non-conformists in Scotland neither offered nor demanded toleration; but laid claim to an entire superiority, and to the exercise of extreme rigour against their adversaries. The covenant, which they idolized, was a persecuting, as well as a seditious band of confederacy; and the government, instead of treating them like madmen, who should be soothed, and flattered, and deceived into tranquillity, thought themselves intitled to a rigid obedience, and were too apt, from a mistaken policy, to retaliate upon the dissenters, who had erred from the spirit of enthusiasm.

Amidst these disturbances, a new parliament was assembled at Edinburgh;[y] and Lauderdale was sent down commissioner. The zealous presbyterians, who were the chief patrons of liberty, were too obnoxious to resist, with any success, the measures of government; and in parliament the tide still ran strongly in favour of monarchy. The commissioner had such influence as to get two acts passed, which were of great consequence to the ecclesiastical and civil liberties of the kingdom. By the one, it was declared, that the settling of all things with regard to the external government of the church was a right of the crown: That whatever related to ecclesiastical meetings, matters, and persons, was to be ordered, according to such directions as the king should send to his privy council: And that these, being published by them, should have the force of laws. The other act regarded the militia, which the king by his own authority had two years before established, instead of the army which was disbanded. By this act, the militia was settled, to the number of 22,000 men, who were to be constantly armed, and regularly disciplined. And it was farther enacted, that these troops should be held in readiness to march into England, Ireland, or any part of the king's dominions, for any cause in which his majesty's authority, power, or greatness was concerned; on receiving orders, not from the king himself, but from the privy council of Scotland.

Lauderdale boasted extremely of his services in procuring these two laws. The king by the former was rendered absolute master of the church, and might legally, by his edict, re-establish, if he thought proper, the catholic religion in Scotland. By the latter he saw a powerful force ready at his call: He had even the advantage of being able to disguise his orders under the name of the privy council; and in case of failure in his enterprizes, could, by such a pretence, apologize for his conduct to the parliament of England. But in proportion as these laws were agreeable to the king, they gave alarm to the English commons, and were the chief cause of the redoubled attacks, which they made upon Lauderdale. These attacks, however, served only to fortify him in his interest

[y] 19th of October, 1669.

with the king; and though it is probable, that the militia of Scotland, during the divided state of that kingdom, would, if matters had come to extremities, have been of little service against England; yet did Charles regard the credit of it as a considerable support to his authority: And Lauderdale, by degrees, became the prime or rather sole minister for Scotland. The natural indolence of the king disposed him to place entire confidence in a man, who had so far extended the royal prerogative, and who was still disposed to render it absolutely uncontroulable.

In a subsequent session of the same parliament,[z] a severe law was enacted against conventicles. Ruinous fines were imposed both on the preachers and hearers, even if the meetings had been in houses; but field conventicles were subjected to the penalty of death and confiscation of goods: Four hundred marks Scotch were offered as a reward to those who should seize the criminals; and they were indemnified for any slaughter, which they might commit in the execution of such an undertaking. And as it was found difficult to get evidence against these conventicles, however numerous, it was enacted by another law, that, whoever, being required by the council, refused to give information upon oath, should be punished by arbitrary fines, by imprisonment, or by banishment to the plantations. Thus all persecution naturally, or rather necessarily, adopts the iniquities, as well as rigours, of the inquisition. What a considerable part of the society consider as their duty and honour, and even many of the opposite party are apt to regard with compassion and indulgence, can by no other expedient be subjected to such severe penalties as the natural sentiments of mankind appropriate only to the greatest crimes.

Though Lauderdale found this ready compliance in the parliament, a party was formed against him, of which duke Hamilton was the head. This nobleman, with Tweddale, and others, went to London, and applied to the king, who, during the present depression and insignificance of parliament, was alone able to correct the abuses of Lauderdale's administration. But even their complaints to him might be dangerous; and all approaches of truth to the throne were barred by the ridiculous law against leasing-making; a law, which seems to have been extorted by the ancient nobles, in

[z] 28th of July, 1670.

order to protect their own tyranny, oppression, and injustice. Great precautions, therefore, were used by the Scottish malcontents in their representations to the king; but no redress was obtained. Charles loaded them with caresses, and continued Lauderdale in his authority.

A very bad, at least a severe use was made of this authority. The privy council dispossessed twelve gentlemen or noblemen of their houses,[a] which were converted into so many garrisons, established for the suppression of conventicles. The nation, it was pretended, was really, on account of these religious assemblies, in a state of war; and by the ancient law, the king, in such an emergence, was empowered to place a garrison in any house, where he should judge it expedient.

It were endless to recount every act of violence and arbitrary authority exercised during Lauderdale's administration. All the lawyers were put from the bar, nay, banished by the king's order twelve miles from the capital, and by that means the whole justice of the kingdom was suspended for a year; till these lawyers were brought to declare it as their opinion, that all appeals to parliament were illegal. A letter was procured from the king, for expelling twelve of the chief magistrates of Edinburgh, and declaring them incapable of all public office; though their only crime had been their want of compliance with Lauderdale. The burroughs of Scotland have a privilege of meeting once a-year by their deputies in order to consider the state of trade, and make bye laws for its regulation: In this convention a petition was voted, complaining of some late acts, which obstructed commerce, and praying the king, that he would impower his commissioner, in the next session of parliament, to give his assent for repealing them. For this presumption, as it was called, several of the members were fined and imprisoned. One More, a member of parliament, having moved in the house, that, in imitation of the English parliament, no bill should pass except after three readings, he was, for this pretended offence, immediately sent to prison by the commissioner.

The private deportment of Lauderdale was as insolent and provoking as his public administration was violent and tyrannical. Justice likewise was universally perverted by faction and interest:

[a] In 1675.

And from the great rapacity of that duke, and still more of his dutchess, all offices and favours were openly put to sale. No-one was allowed to approach the throne who was not dependant on him; and no remedy could be hoped for or obtained against his manifold oppressions. The case of Mitchel shows, that this minister was as much destitute of truth and honour as of lenity and justice.

Mitchel was a desperate fanatic, and had entertained a resolution of assassinating Sharpe, archbishop of St. Andrews, who, by his former apostasy and subsequent rigour, had rendered himself extremely odious to the covenanters. In the year 1668, Mitchel fired a pistol at the primate, as he was sitting in his coach; but the bishop of Orkney, stepping into the coach, happened to stretch out his arm, which intercepted the ball, and was much shattered by it. This happened in the principal street of the city; but so generally was the archbishop hated, that the assassin was allowed peaceably to walk off; and having turned a street or two, and thrown off a wig, which disguised him, he immediately appeared in public, and remained altogether unsuspected. Some years after, Sharpe remarked one, who seemed to eye him very eagerly; and being still anxious, lest an attempt of assassination should be renewed, he ordered the man to be seized and examined. Two loaded pistols were found upon him; and as he was now concluded to be the author of the former attempt, Sharpe promised, that, if he would confess his guilt, he should be dismissed without any punishment. Mitchel (for the conjecture was just), was so credulous as to believe him; but was immediately produced before the council by the faithless primate. The council, having no proof against him, but hoping to involve the whole body of covenanters in this odious crime, solemnly renewed the promise of pardon, if he would make a full discovery; and it was a great disappointment to them, when they found, upon his confession, that only one person, who was now dead, had been acquainted with his bloody purpose. Mitchel was then carried before a court of judicature, and required to renew his confession; but being apprehensive, lest, tho' a pardon for life had been promised him, other corporal punishment might still be inflicted, he refused compliance; and was sent back to prison. He was next examined before the council, under pretence of his being concerned in the insurrection at Pentland; and though

CHAPTER LXVI

no proof appeared against him, he was put to the question, and, contrary to the most obvious principles of equity, was urged to accuse himself. He endured the torture with singular resolution, and continued obstinate in the denial of a crime, of which, it is believed, he really was not guilty. Instead of obtaining his liberty, he was sent to the Bass, a very high rock, surrounded by the sea; at this time converted into a state prison, and full of the unhappy covenanters. He there remained in great misery, loaded with irons; till the year 1677, when it was resolved by some new examples to strike a fresh terror into the persecuted, but still obstinate enthusiasts. Mitchel was then brought before a court of judicature, and put upon his trial, for an attempt to assassinate an archbishop and a privy counsellor. His former confession was pleaded against him, and was proved by the testimony of the duke of Lauderdale, lord commissioner, lord Hatton his brother, the earl of Rothes, and the primate himself. Mitchel, besides maintaining that the privy counsel was no court of judicature, and that a confession before them was not judicial, asserted, that he had been engaged to make that confession by a solemn promise of pardon. The four privy counsellors denied upon oath, that any such promise had ever been given. The prisoner then desired, that the council books might be produced in court; and even offered a copy of that day's proceedings to be read; but the privy counsellors maintained, that, after they had made oath, no farther proof could be admitted, and that the books of council contained the king's secrets, which were on no account to be divulged. They were not probably aware, when they swore, that the clerk having engrossed the promise of pardon in the narrative of Mitchel's confession, the whole minute had been signed by the chancellor, and that the proofs of their perjury were by that means committed to record. Though the prisoner was condemned, Lauderdale was still inclined to pardon him; but the unrelenting primate rigorously insisted upon his execution, and said, that, if assassins remained unpunished, his life must be exposed to perpetual danger. Mitchel was accordingly executed at Edinburgh in January 1678. Such a complication of cruelty and treachery shews the character of those ministers, to whom the king had, at this time, entrusted the government of Scotland.

Lauderdale's administration, besides the iniquities arising from the violence of his temper, and the still greater iniquities inseparable from all projects of persecution, was attended with other circumstances, which engaged him in severe and arbitrary measures. An absolute government was to be introduced, which on its commencement is often most rigorous; and tyranny was still obliged, for want of military power, to cover itself under an appearance of law; a situation which rendered it extremely aukward in its motions, and by provoking opposition, extended the violence of its oppressions.

The rigours exercised against conventicles, instead of breaking the spirit of the fanatics, had tended only, as is usual, to render them more obstinate, to encrease the fervour of their zeal, to link them more closely together, and to inflame them against the established hierarchy. The commonalty, almost every where in the south, particularly in the western counties, frequented conventicles without reserve; and the gentry, though they themselves commonly abstained from these illegal places of worship, connived at this irregularity in their inferiors. In order to interest the former on the side of the persecutors, a bond or contract was by order of the privy council tendered to the landlords in the west, by which they were to engage for the good behaviour of their tenants; and in case any tenant frequented a conventicle, the landlord was to subject himself to the same fine as could by law be exacted from the delinquent. It was ridiculous to give sanction to laws by voluntary contracts: It was iniquitous to make one man answerable for the conduct of another: It was illegal to impose such hard conditions upon men, who had no wise offended. For these reasons, the greater part of the gentry refused to sign these bonds; and Lauderdale, enraged at this opposition, endeavoured to break their spirit by expedients, which were still more unusual and more arbitrary.

The law enacted against conventicles, had called them seminaries of rebellion. This expression, which was nothing but a flourish of rhetoric, Lauderdale and the privy council were willing to understand in a literal sense; and because the western counties abounded in conventicles, though otherwise in profound peace, they pretended that these counties were in a state of actual war and rebellion. They made therefore an agreement with some highland chieftains to call out their clans, to the number of 8000 men: To these they joined the guards, and the militia of Angus: And they

CHAPTER LXVI

sent the whole to live at free quarters upon the lands of such as had refused the bonds illegally required of them. The obnoxious counties were the most populous and most industrious in Scotland. The highlanders were the people the most disorderly and the least civilized. It is easy to imagine the havoc and destruction which ensued. A multitude, not accustomed to discipline, averse to the restraint of laws, trained up in rapine and violence, were let loose amidst those whom they were taught to regard as enemies to their prince and to their religion. Nothing escaped their ravenous hands: By menaces, by violence, and sometimes by tortures, men were obliged to discover their concealed wealth. Neither age, nor sex, nor innocence afforded protection: And the gentry, finding that even those who had been most compliant, and who had subscribed the bonds, were equally exposed to the rapacity of those barbarians, confirmed themselves still more in the resolution of refusing them. The voice of the nation was raised against this enormous outrage; and after two months free quarter, the highlanders were sent back to their hills, loaded with the spoils and execrations of the west.

Those who had been engaged to subscribe the bonds, could find no security but by turning out such tenants as they suspected of an inclination to conventicles, and thereby depopulating their estates. To encrease the misery of these unhappy farmers, the council enacted, that none should be received any where, or allowed a habitation, who brought not a certificate of his conformity from the parish-minister. That the obstinate and refractory might not escape farther persecution, a new device was fallen upon. By the law of Scotland, any man, who should go before a magistrate, and swear that he thought himself in danger from another, might obtain a writ of *law-burrows,* as it is called; by which the latter was bound, under the penalty of imprisonment and outlawry, to find security for his good behaviour. Lauderdale entertained the absurd notion of making the king sue out writs of law-burrows against his subjects. On this pretence, the refusers of the bonds were summoned to appear before the council, and were required to bind themselves, under the penalty of two years' rent, neither to frequent conventicles themselves, nor allow their family and tenants to be present at those unlawful assemblies. Thus chicanery was joined to tyranny; and the majesty of the king, instead of being exalted, was in reality prostituted; as if he were obliged to seek the same security, which one neighbour might require of another.

It was an old law, but seldom executed, that a man, who was accused of any crime, and did not appear, in order to stand his trial, might be *intercommuned*, that is, he might be publicly outlawed; and whoever afterwards, either on account of business, relation, nay charity, had the least intercourse with him, was subjected to the same penalties as could by law be inflicted on the criminal himself. Several writs of intercommuning were now issued against the hearers and preachers in conventicles; and by this severe and even absurd law, crimes and guilt went on multiplying in a geometrical proportion. Where laws themselves are so violent, it is no wonder that an administration should be tyrannical.

Lest the cry of an oppressed people should reach the throne, the council forbad, under severe penalties, all noblemen or gentlemen of landed property to leave the kingdom: A severe edict, especially where the sovereign himself resided in a foreign country. Notwithstanding this act of council, Cassils first, afterwards Hamilton and Tweddale, went to London, and laid their complaints before the king. These violent proceedings of Lauderdale were opposite to the natural temper of Charles; and he immediately issued orders for discontinuing the bonds and the writs of law-burrows. But as he was commonly little touched with what lay at a distance, he entertained not the proper indignation against those who had abused his authority: Even while he retracted these oppressive measures, he was prevailed with to avow and praise them in a letter, which he wrote to the privy council. This proof of confidence might fortify the hands of the ministry; but the king ran a manifest risque of losing the affections of his subjects, by not permitting, even those who were desirous of it, to distinguish between him and their oppressors.

It is reported,[b] that Charles, after a full hearing of the debates concerning Scottish affairs, said, "I perceive, that Lauderdale has been guilty of many bad things against the people of Scotland; but I cannot find, that he has acted any thing contrary to my interest." A sentiment unworthy of a sovereign!

During the absence of Hamilton and the other discontented

[b] Burnet.

CHAPTER LXVI

lords, the king allowed Lauderdale to summon a convention of estates at Edinburgh. This assembly, besides granting some money, bestowed applause on all Lauderdale's administration, and in their addresses to the king, expressed the highest contentment and satisfaction. But these instances of complaisance had the contrary effect in England from what was expected by the contrivers of them. All men there concluded, that in Scotland the very voice of liberty was totally suppressed; and that, by the prevalence of tyranny, grievances were so rivetted, that it was become dangerous even to mention them, or complain to the prince, who alone was able to redress them. From the slavery of the neighbouring kingdom, they inferred the arbitrary disposition of the king; and from the violence with which sovereign power was there exercised, they apprehended the miseries, which might ensue to themselves upon their loss of liberty. If persecution, it was asked, by a protestant church could be carried to such extremes, what might be dreaded from the prevalence of popery, which had ever, in all ages, made open profession of exterminating by fire and sword every opposite sect or communion? And if the first approaches towards unlimited authority were so tyrannical, how dismal its final establishment; when all dread of opposition shall at last be removed by mercenary armies, and all sense of shame by long and inveterate habit?

LXVII

The Popish plot – Oates's narrative –
And character – Coleman's letters – Godfrey's
murder – General consternation – The parliament –
Zeal of the parliament – Bedloe's narrative –
Accusation of Danby – His impeachment –
Dissolution of the long parliament –
Its character – Trial of Coleman – Of Ireland –
New elections – Duke of Monmouth – Duke of York
retires to Brussels – New parliament –
Danby's impeachment – Popish plot –
New council – Limitations on a popish successor –
Bill of exclusion – Habeas corpus bill – Prorogation
and dissolution of the parliament – Trial and
execution of the five jesuits – And of
Langhorne – Wakeman acquitted –
State of affairs in Scotland –
Battle of Bothwel bridge

1678.   THE ENGLISH NATION, ever since the fatal league with France,
had entertained violent jealousies against the court; and the
subsequent measures, adopted by the king, had tended more to
encrease than cure the general prejudices. Some mysterious de-

332

sign was still suspected in every enterprize and profession: Arbitrary power and popery were apprehended as the scope of all projects: Each breath or rumour made the people start with anxiety: Their enemies, they thought, were in their very bosom, and had gotten possession of their sovereign's confidence. While in this timorous, jealous disposition, the cry of a *plot* all on a sudden struck their ears: They were wakened from their slumber; and like men affrighted and in the dark, took every figure for a spectre. The terror of each man became the source of terror to another. And an universal panic being diffused, reason and argument and common sense and common humanity lost all influence over them. From this disposition of men's minds we are to account for the progress of the POPISH PLOT, and the credit given to it; an event, which would otherwise appear prodigious and altogether inexplicable.

The Popish plot.

On the 12th of August, one Kirby, a chemist, accosted the king, as he was walking in the park: "Sir," said he, "keep within the company: Your enemies have a design upon your life; and you may be shot in this very walk." Being asked the reason of these strange speeches, he said, that two men, called Grove and Pickering, had engaged to shoot the king, and Sir George Wakeman, the queen's physician, to poison him. This intelligence, he added, had been communicated to him by doctor Tongue; whom, if permitted, he would introduce to his majesty. Tongue was a divine of the church of England; a man active, restless, full of projects, void of understanding. He brought papers to the king, which contained information of a plot, and were digested into forty-three articles. The king, not having leisure to peruse them, sent them to the treasurer, Danby, and ordered the two informers to lay the business before that minister. Tongue confessed to Danby, that he himself had not drawn the papers, that they had been secretly thrust under his door, and that, though he suspected, he did not certainly know, who was the author. After a few days, he returned, and told the treasurer, that his suspicions, he found, were just; and that the author of the intelligence, whom he had met twice or thrice in the street, had acknowledged the whole matter, and had given him a more particular account of the conspiracy, but desired, that his name might be concealed, being apprehensive lest the papists should murder him.

The information was renewed with regard to Grove's and Pickering's intentions of shooting the king; and Tongue even pretended, that, at a particular time, they were to set out for Windsor with that intention. Orders were given for arresting them, as soon as they should appear in that place: But though this alarm was more than once renewed, some frivolous reasons were still found by Tongue for their having delayed the journey. And the king concluded, both from these evasions, and from the mysterious, artificial manner of communicating the intelligence, that the whole was an imposture.

Tongue came next to the treasurer, and told him, that a pacquet of letters, written by jesuits concerned in the plot, was that night to be put into the post-house for Windsor, directed to Bennifield, a jesuit, confessor to the duke. When this intelligence was conveyed to the king, he replied, that the pacquet mentioned had a few hours before been brought to the duke by Bennifield; who said, that he suspected some bad design upon him, that the letters seemed to contain matters of a dangerous import, and that he knew them not to be the hand-writing of the persons whose names were subscribed to them. This incident still farther confirmed the king in his incredulity.

The matter had probably slept for ever, had it not been for the anxiety of the duke; who, hearing that priests and jesuits and even his own confessor had been accused, was desirous, that a thorough enquiry should be made by the council into the pretended conspiracy. Kirby and Tongue were enquired after, and were now found to be living in close connection with Titus Oates, the person who was said to have conveyed the first intelligence to Tongue. Oates affirmed, that he had fallen under suspicion with the jesuits; that he had received three blows with a stick, and a box on the ear from the provincial of that order, for revealing their conspiracy; And that, over-hearing them speak of their intentions to punish him more severely he had withdrawn, and concealed himself. This man, in whose breast was lodged a secret, involving the fate of kings and kingdoms, was allowed to remain in such necessity, that Kirby was obliged to supply him with daily bread; and it was a joyful surprize to him, when he heard, that the council was at last disposed to take some notice of his intelligence. But as he expected more encouragement from the public, than from the king or his ministers, he thought proper, before he was presented to the council, to go with his two companions to Sir Edmondsbury Godfrey, a noted and active justice of peace, and to give evidence before him of all the articles of the conspiracy.

The wonderful intelligence, which Oates conveyed both to Godfrey and the council, and afterwards to the parliament, was to this purpose.ᶜ The pope, he said, on examining the matter in the congregation *de propaganda,* had found himself entitled to the possession of England and Ireland on account of the heresy of prince and people, and had accordingly assumed the sovereignty of these kingdoms. This supreme power he had thought proper to delegate to the society of Jesuits; and de Oliva, general of that order, in consequence of the papal grant, had exerted every act of regal authority, and particularly had supplied, by commissions under the seal of the society, all the chief offices, both civil and military. Lord Arundel was created chancellor, lord Powis treasurer, Sir William Godolphin privy seal, Coleman secretary of state, Langhorne attorney general, lord Bellasis general of the papal army, lord Peters lieutenant general, lord Stafford pay-master; and inferior commissions, signed by the provincial of the Jesuits, were distributed all over England. All the dignities too of the church were filled, and many of them with Spaniards and other foreigners. The provincial had held a consult of the Jesuits under his authority; where the king, whom they opprobriously called the Black Bastard, was solemnly tried and condemned as a heretic; and a resolution taken to put him to death. Father Le Shee (for so this great plotter and informer called father la Chaise, the noted confessor of the French king) had consigned in London ten thousand pounds to be paid to any man, who should merit it by this assassination. A Spanish provincial had expressed like liberality: The prior of the Benedictines was willing to go the length of six thousand: The Dominicans approved of the action; but pleaded poverty. Ten thousand pounds had been offered to Sir George Wakeman, the queen's physician, who demanded fifteen thousand, as a reward for so great a service: His demand was complied with; and five thousand had been paid him by advance. Lest this means should fail, four Irish ruffians had been hired by the Jesuits, at the rate of twenty guineas a-piece, to stab the king at Windsor; and

Oates's narrative.

___
ᶜ Oates's narrative.

Coleman, secretary to the late duchess of York, had given the messenger, who carried them orders, a guinea to quicken his diligence. Grove and Pickering were also employed to shoot the king with silver bullets: The former was to receive the sum of fifteen hundred pounds; the latter, being a pious man, was to be rewarded with thirty thousand masses, which, estimating masses at a shilling a-piece, amounted to a like value. Pickering would have executed his purpose, had not the flint at one time dropped out of his pistol, at another time the priming. Coniers, the Jesuit, had bought a knife at the price of ten shillings, which, he thought, was not dear, considering the purpose for which he intended it, to wit, stabbing the king. Letters of subscription were circulated among the catholics all over England to raise a sum for the same purpose. No less than fifty Jesuits had met in May last, at the White-horse tavern, where it was unanimously agreed to put the king to death. This synod did afterwards, for more convenience, divide themselves into many lesser cabals or companies; and Oates was employed to carry notes and letters from one to another, all tending to the same end, of murthering the king. He even carried, from one company to another, a paper, in which they formally expressed their resolution of executing that deed; and it was regularly subscribed by all of them. A wager of a hundred pounds was laid, and stakes made, that the king should eat no more Christmas pyes. In short, it was determined, to use the expression of a Jesuit, that if he would not become R. C. (Roman Catholic) he should no longer be C.R. (Charles Rex). The great fire of London had been the work of the Jesuits, who had employed eighty or eighty-six persons for that purpose, and had expended seven hundred fire-balls; but they had a good return for their money; for they had been able to pilfer goods from the fire to the amount of fourteen thousand pounds: The Jesuits had also raised another fire on St. Margaret's Hill, whence they had stolen goods to the value of two thousand pounds; Another at Southwark: And it was determined in like manner to burn all the chief cities in England. A paper model was already framed for the firing of London; the stations were regularly marked out, where the several fires were to commence; and the whole plan of operations was so concerted, that precautions were taken by the Jesuits to vary their measures, according to the variation of the wind. Fire-balls were familiarly called among them Teuxbury mustard pills; and were said to contain a notable biting sauce. In the great fire, it had been determined to murther the king; but he had displayed such diligence and humanity in extinguishing the flames, that even the Jesuits relented, and spared his life. Besides these assassinations and fires; insurrections, rebellions, and massacres were projected by that religious order in all the three kingdoms. There were twenty thousand catholics in London, who would rise in four-and-twenty hours or less; and Jennison, a Jesuit, said, that they mighty easily cut the throats of a hundred thousand protestants. Eight thousand catholics had agreed to take arms in Scotland. Ormond was to be murthered by four Jesuits; a general massacre of the Irish protestants was concerted; and forty thousand black bills were already provided for that purpose. Coleman had remitted two hundred thousand pounds to promote the rebellion in Ireland; and the French king was to land a great army in that island. Poole, who wrote the Synopsis, was particularly marked out for assassination; as was also Dr. Stillingfleet, a controversial writer against the papists. Burnet tells us, that Oates paid him the same compliment. After all this havoc, the crown was to be offered to the duke, but on the following conditions; that he receive it as gift from the pope; that he confirm all the papal commissions for offices and employments; that he ratify all past transactions, by pardoning the incendiaries, and the murderers of his brother and of the people; and that he consent to the utter extirpation of the protestant religion. If he refuse these conditions, he himself was immediately to be poisoned or assassinated. *To pot James must go*; according to the expression ascribed by Oates to the Jesuits.

Oates, the informer of this dreadful plot, was himself the most infamous of mankind. He was the son of an anabaptist preacher, *And character.* chaplain to colonel Pride; but having taken orders in the church, he had been settled in a small living by the duke of Norfolk. He had been indicted for perjury; and by some means had escaped. He was afterwards a chaplain on board the fleet; whence he had been dismissed on complaint of some unnatural practices, not fit to be named. He then became a convert to the catholics; but he afterwards boasted, that his conversion was a mere pretence, in order to get into their secrets and to betray them.[d] He was sent over to the Jesuits' college at St. Omers, and though above thirty years of age,

[d] Burnet, Echard, North, L'Estrange, &c.

he there lived some time among the students. He was dispatched on an errand to Spain; and thence returned to St. Omers; where the Jesuits, heartily tired of their convert, at last dismissed him from their seminary. It is likely, that, from resentment of this usage, as well as from want and indigence, he was induced, in combination with Tongue, to contrive that plot, of which he accused the catholics.

This abandoned man, when examined before the council, betrayed his impostures in such a manner, as would have utterly discredited the most consistent story, and the most reputable evidence. While in Spain, he had been carried, he said, to Don John, who promised great assistance to the execution of the catholic designs. The king asked him, what sort of a man Don John was: He answered, a tall lean man; directly contrary to truth, as the king well knew.[e] He totally mistook the situation of the Jesuits' college at Paris.[f] Though he pretended great intimacies with Coleman, he knew him not, when placed very near him; and had no other excuse than that his sight was bad in candle-light. [g] He fell into like mistakes with regard to Wakeman.

Notwithstanding these objections, great attention was paid to Oates's evidence, and the plot became very soon the subject of conversation, and even the object of terror to the people. The violent animosity, which had been excited against the catholics in general, made the public swallow the grossest absurdities when they accompanied an accusation of those religionists: And the more diabolical any contrivance appeared, the better it suited the tremendous idea entertained of a Jesuit. Danby likewise, who stood in opposition to the French and catholic interest at court, was willing to encourage every story, which might serve to discredit that party. By his suggestion, when a warrant was signed for arresting Coleman, there was inserted a clause for seizing his papers; a circumstance attended with the most important consequences.

Coleman's letters. Coleman, partly on his own account, partly by orders from the duke, had been engaged in a correspondence with father la Chaise, with the pope's nuncio at Brussels, and with other catholics abroad; and being himself a fiery zealot, busy and sanguine, the expressions in his letters often betrayed great violence and indis-

[e] Burnet, North.   [f] North.   [g] Burnet, North, Trials.

cretion. His correspondence, during the years 1674, 1675, and part of 1676, was seized, and contained many extraordinary passages. In particular he said to la Chaise, "We have here a mighty work upon our hands, no less than the conversion of three kingdoms, and by that perhaps the utter subduing of a pestilent heresy, which has a long time domineered over a great part of this northern world. There were never such hopes of success, since the days of queen Mary, as now in our days. God has given us a prince," meaning the duke, "who is become (may I say a miracle) zealous of being the author and instrument of so glorious a work; but the opposition we are sure to meet with is also like to be great: So that it imports us to get all the aid and assistance we can." In another letter he said, "I can scarce believe myself awake, or the thing real, when I think of a prince in such an age as we live in, converted to such a degree of zeal and piety, as not to regard any thing in the world in comparison of God Almighty's glory, the salvation of his own soul, and the conversion of our poor kingdom." In other passages the interests of the crown of England, those of the French king, and those of the catholic religion are spoken of as inseparable. The duke is also said to have connected his interests unalterably with those of Lewis. The king himself, he affirms, is always inclined to favour the catholics, when he may do it without hazard. "Money," Coleman adds, "cannot fail of persuading the king to any thing. There is nothing it cannot make him do, were it ever so much to his prejudice. It has such an absolute power over him, that he cannot resist it. Logic, built upon money, has in our court more powerful charms than any other sort of argument." For these reasons, he proposed to father la Chaise, that the French king should remit the sum of 300,000 pounds, on condition that the parliament be dissolved; a measure, to which, he affirmed, the king was, of himself, sufficiently inclined, were it not for his hopes of obtaining money from that assembly. The parliament, he said, had already constrained the king to make peace with Holland, contrary to the interests of the catholic religion, and of his most christian majesty: And if they should meet again, they would surely engage him farther, even to the making of war against France. It appears also from the same letters, that the assembling of the parliament so late as April in the year 1675, had been procured by the intrigues of the catholic and French party, who thereby intended to show the Dutch and their confederates, that they could expect no assistance from England.

When the contents of these letters were publicly known, they diffused the panic, with which the nation began already to be seized on account of the popish plot. Men reasoned more from their fears and their passions than from the evidence before them. It is certain, that the restless and enterprizing spirit of the catholic church, particularly of the Jesuits, merits attention, and is, in some degree, dangerous to every other communion. Such zeal of proselytism actuates that sect, that its missionaries have penetrated into every nation of the globe; and, in one sense, there is a *popish plot* perpetually carrying on against all states, protestant, pagan, and mahometan. It is likewise very probable, that the conversion of the duke, and the favour of the king had inspired the catholic priests with new hopes of recovering in these islands their lost dominion, and gave fresh vigour to that intemperate zeal, by which they are commonly actuated. Their first aim was to obtain a toleration; and such was the evidence, they believed, of their theological tenets, that, could they but procure entire liberty, they must infallibly in time open the eyes of the people. After they had converted considerable numbers, they might be enabled, they hoped, to reinstate themselves in full authority, and entirely to suppress that heresy, with which the kingdom had so long been infected. Though these dangers to the protestant religion were distant, it was justly the object of great concern to find, that the heir of the crown was so blinded with bigotry, and so deeply engaged in foreign interests; and that the king himself had been prevailed on, from low interests, to hearken to his dangerous insinuations. Very bad consequences might ensue from such perverse habits and attachments; nor could the nation and parliament guard against them with too anxious a precaution. But that the Roman pontiff could hope to assume the sovereignty of these kingdoms; a project, which, even during the darkness of the eleventh and twelfth centuries, would have appeared chimerical: That he should delegate this authority to the Jesuits; that order in the Romish church, which was the most hated: That a massacre could be attempted of the protestants, who surpassed the catholics a hundred fold, and were invested with the whole authority of the state: That the king himself was to be assassinated, and even the duke, the only support of their party: These were such absurdities as no human testimony was sufficient to prove; much less the evidence of one man, who was noted for infamy, and who could not keep himself, every moment, from falling into the grossest inconsistencies. Did such intelligence deserve even so much attention as to be refuted, it would appear, that Coleman's letters were sufficient alone to destroy all its credit. For how could so long a train of correspondence be carried on, by a man so much trusted by the party; and yet no traces of insurrections, if really intended, of fires, massacres, assassinations, invasions, be ever discovered in any single passage of these letters? But all such reflections, and many more, equally obvious, were vainly employed against that general prepossession, with which the nation was seized. Oates's plot and Coleman's were universally confounded together: And the evidence of the latter being unquestionable, the belief of the former, aided by the passions of hatred and of terror, took possession of the whole people.

There was danger, however, lest time might open the eyes of the public; when the murther of Godfrey completed the general delusion, and rendered the prejudices of the nation absolutely incurable. This magistrate had been missing some days; and after much search, and many surmises, his body was found lying in a ditch at Primrose-hill: The marks of strangling were thought to appear about his neck, and some contusions on his breast: His own sword was sticking in the body; but as no considerable quantity of blood ensued on drawing it, it was concluded, that it had been thrust in after his death, and that he had not killed himself: He had rings on his fingers and money in his pocket: It was therefore inferred, that he had not fallen into the hands of robbers. Without farther reasoning, the cry rose, that he had been assassinated by the papists, on account of his taking Oates's evidence. This clamour was quickly propagated, and met with universal belief. The panic spread itself on every side with infinite rapidity; and all men, astonished with fear, and animated with rage, saw in Godfrey's fate all the horrible designs ascribed to the Catholics; and no farther doubt remained of Oates's veracity. The voice of the nation united against that hated sect; and notwithstanding that the bloody conspiracy was supposed to be now detected, men could scarcely be persuaded, that their lives were yet in safety. Each hour teemed with new rumours and surmizes. Invasions from abroad, insur-

17th Octob. Godfrey's murther.

General consternation.

rections at home, even private murthers and poisonings were apprehended. To deny the reality of the plot was to be an accomplice: To hesitate was criminal: Royalist, Republican; Churchman, Sectary; Courtier, Patriot; all parties concurred in the illusion. The city prepared for its defence, as if the enemy were at its gates: The chains and posts were put up: And it was a noted saying at that time of Sir Thomas Player, the chamberlain, that, were it not for these precautions, all the citizens might rise next morning with their throats cut.[h]

In order to propagate the popular frenzy, several artifices were employed. The dead body of Godfrey was carried into the city, attended by vast multitudes. It was publicly exposed in the streets, and viewed by all ranks of men; and every one, who saw it, went away inflamed, as well by the mutual contagion of sentiments, as by the dismal spectacle itself. The funeral pomp was celebrated with great parade. The corpse was conducted through the chief streets of the city: Seventy-two clergymen marched before: Above a thousand persons of distinction followed after: And at the funeral-sermon, two able-bodied divines mounted the pulpit, and stood on each side of the preacher, lest, in paying the last duties to this unhappy magistrate, he should, before the whole people, be murthered by the Papists.[i]

In this disposition of the nation, reason could no more be heard than a whisper in the midst of the most violent hurricane. Even at present, Godfrey's murther can scarcely, upon any system, be rationally accounted for. That he was assassinated by the Catholics, seems utterly improbable. These religionists could not be engaged to commit that crime from *policy*, in order to deter other magistrates from acting against them. Godfrey's fate was no wise capable of producing that effect, unless it were publicly known, that the Catholics were his murtherers; an opinion, which, it was easy to foresee, must prove the ruin of their party. Besides, how many magistrates, during more than a century, had acted in the most violent manner against the Catholics, without its being ever suspected, that any one had been cut off by assassination? Such jealous times as the present were surely ill fitted for beginning these dangerous experiments. Shall we therefore say, that the Catholics

[h] North, p. 206.   [i] North, p. 205.

were pushed on, not by policy, but by blind *revenge* against Godfrey? But Godfrey had given them little or no occasion of offence in taking Oates's evidence. His part was merely an act of form, belonging to his office; nor could he, or any man in his station, possibly refuse it. In the rest of his conduct, he lived on good terms with the Catholics, and was far from distinguishing himself by his severity against that sect. It is even certain, that he had contracted an intimacy with Coleman, and took care to inform his friend of the danger, to which, by reason of Oates's evidence, he was at present exposed.

There are some writers, who, finding it impossible to account for Godfrey's murther by the machinations of the Catholics, have recourse to the opposite supposition. They lay hold of that obvious presumption, that those commit the crime who reap advantage by it; and they affirm that it was Shaftesbury and the heads of the popular party, who perpetrated that deed, in order to throw the odium of it on the Papists. If this supposition be received, it must also be admitted, that the whole plot was the contrivance of those politicians; and that Oates acted altogether under their direction. But it appears, that Oates, dreading probably the opposition of powerful enemies, had very anxiously acquitted the duke, Danby, Ormond, and all the ministry; persons who were certainly the most obnoxious to the popular leaders. Besides, the whole texture of the plot contains such low absurdity, that it is impossible to have been the invention of any man of sense or education. It is true, the more monstrous and horrible the conspiracy, the better was it fitted to terrify, and thence to convince, the populace: But this effect, we may safely say, no one could before-hand have expected; and a fool was in this case more likely to succeed than a wise man. Had Shaftesbury laid the plan of a popish conspiracy, he had probably rendered it moderate, consistent, credible; and on that very account had never met with the prodigious success, with which Oates's tremendous fictions were attended.

We must, therefore be contented to remain for ever ignorant of the actors in Godfrey's murther; and only pronounce in general, that that event, in all likelihood, had no connexion, one way or other, with the popish plot. Any man, especially so active a magistrate as Godfrey, might, in such a city as London, have many enemies, of whom his friends and family had no suspicion. He was a melancholy man; and there is some reason, notwithstanding the pretended appearances to the contrary, to suspect that he fell by his own hands. The affair was never examined with tranquillity, or even with common sense, during the time; and it is impossible for us, at this distance, certainly to account for it.

No one doubted but the papists had assassinated Godfrey; but still the particular actors were unknown. A proclamation was issued by the king, offering a pardon and a reward of five hundred pounds to any one who should discover them. As it was afterwards surmized, that the terror of a like assassination would prevent discovery, a new proclamation was issued, promising absolute protection to any one who should reveal the secret. Thus were indemnity, money, and security offered to the fairest bidder: And no one needed to fear, during the present fury of the people, that his evidence would undergo too severe a scrutiny.

21st Octob. The parliament. While the nation was in this ferment, the parliament was assembled. In his speech the king told them, that, though they had given money for disbanding the army,[k] he had found Flanders so exposed, that he had thought it necessary still to keep them on foot, and doubted not but this measure would meet with their approbation. He informed them, that his revenue lay under great anticipations, and at best was never equal to the constant and necessary expence of government; as would appear from the state of it, which he intended to lay before them. He also mentioned the plot, formed against his life by Jesuits; but said, that he would forbear delivering any opinion of the matter, lest he should seem to say too much or too little; and that he would leave the scrutiny of it entirely to the law.

The king was anxious to keep the question of the popish plot from the parliament; where, he suspected, many designing people would very much abuse the present credulity of the nation: But Danby, who hated the catholics, and courted popularity, and perhaps hoped, that the king, if his life were believed in danger from the Jesuits, would be more cordially loved by the nation, had entertained opposite designs; and the very first day of the session, he opened the matter in the house of peers. The king was extremely

---

[k] They had granted him 600,000 pounds for disbanding the army, for reimbursing the charges of his naval armament, and for paying the princess of Orange's portion.

displeased with this temerity, and told his minister, "Though you do not believe it, you will find, that you have given the parliament a handle to ruin yourself, as well as to disturb all my affairs; and you will surely live to repent it." Danby had afterwards sufficient reason to applaud the sagacity of his master.

The cry of the plot was immediately echoed from one house to the other. The authority of parliament gave sanction to that fury, with which the people were already agitated. An address was voted for a solemn fast: A form of prayer was contrived for that solemnity; and because the popish plot had been omitted in the first draught, it was carefully ordered to be inserted; lest omniscience should want intelligence, to use the words of an historian.[1]

Zeal of the parliament.

In order to continue and propagate the alarm, addresses were voted for laying before the house such papers as might discover the horrible conspiracy; for the removal of popish recusants from London; for administering every where the oaths of allegiance and supremacy; for denying access at court to all unknown or suspicious persons; and for appointing the trainbands of London and Westminster to be in readiness. The lords Powis, Stafford, Arundel, Peters, and Bellasis were committed to the Tower, and were soon after impeached for high treason. And both houses, after hearing Oates's evidence, voted, "That the lords and commons are of opinion, that there hath been, and still is, a damnable and hellish plot, contrived and carried on by the popish recusants, for assassinating the king, for subverting the government, and for rooting out and destroying the protestant religion."

So vehement were the houses, that they sat every day, forenoon and afternoon, on the subject of the plot: For no other business could be attended to. A committee of lords were appointed to examine prisoners and witnesses: Blank warrants were put into their hands, for the commitment of such as should be accused or suspected. Oates, who, though his evidence were true, must, by his own account, be regarded as an infamous villain, was by every one applauded, caressed, and called the saviour of the nation. He was recommended by the parliament to the King. He was lodged in Whitehall, protected by guards, and encouraged by a pension of 1200 pounds a-year.

[1] North, p. 207.

Bedloe's
nar-
rative.
It was not long before such bountiful encouragement brought forth new witnesses. William Bedloe, a man, if possible, more infamous than Oates, appeared next upon the stage. He was of very low birth, had been noted for several cheats and even thefts, had travelled over many parts of Europe under borrowed names, and frequently passed himself for a man of quality, and had endeavoured, by a variety of lyes and contrivances, to prey upon the ignorant and unwary. When he appeared before the council, he gave intelligence of Godfrey's murther only, which, he said, had been perpetrated in Somerset-house, where the queen lived, by papists, some of them servants in her family. He was questioned about the plot; but utterly denied all knowledge of it, and also asserted, that he had no acquaintance with Oates. Next day, when examined before the committee of lords, he bethought himself better, and was ready to give an ample account of the plot, which he found so anxiously enquired into. This narrative he made to tally, as well as he could, with that of Oates, which had been published: But that he might make himself acceptable by new matter, he added some other circumstances, and these, still more tremendous and extraordinary. He said, that ten thousand men were to be landed from Flanders in Burlington Bay, and immediately to seize Hull: That Jersey and Guernsey were to be surprized by forces from Brest; and that a French Fleet was, all last summer, hovering in the Channel for that purpose: That the lords Powis and Peters were to form an army in Radnorshire, to be joined by another army, consisting of twenty or thirty thousand religious men and pilgrims, who were to land at Milford Haven from St. Iago in Spain: That there were forty thousand men ready in London; besides those, who would, on the alarm, be posted at every alehouse door, in order to kill the soldiers, as they came out of their quarters: That lord Stafford, Coleman, and father Ireland had money sufficient to defray the expences of all these armaments: That he himself was to receive four thousand pounds, as one that could murder a man; as also a commission from lord Bellasis, and a benediction from the pope: That the king was to be assassinated; all the protestants massacred, who would not seriously be converted; the government offered to ONE, if he would consent to hold it of the church; but if he should refuse that condition, as was suspected, the supreme authority would be given to certain lords

under the nomination of the pope. In a subsequent examination before the commons, Bedloe added (for these men always brought out their intelligence successively and by piece-meal), that lord Carrington was also in the conspiracy for raising men and money against the government; as was likewise lord Brudenel. These noblemen, with all the other persons mentioned by Bedloe, were immediately committed to custody by the parliament.

It is remarkable, that the only resource of Spain, in her present decayed condition, lay in the assistance of England; and, so far from being in a situation to transport ten thousand men for the invasion of that kingdom, she had solicited and obtained English forces to be sent into the garrisons of Flanders, which were not otherwise able to defend themselves against the French. The French too, we may observe, were, at that very time, in open war with Spain, and yet are supposed to be engaged in the same design against England; as if religious motives were become the sole actuating principle among sovereigns. But none of these circumstances, however obvious, were able, when set in opposition to multiplied horrors, antipathies, and prejudices, to engage the least attention of the populace: For such the whole nation were at this time become. The popish plot passed for incontestible: And had not men soon expected with certainty the legal punishment of these criminals, the catholics had been exposed to the hazard of an universal massacre. The torrent indeed of national prejudices ran so high, that no one, without the most imminent danger, durst venture openly to oppose it; nay, scarcely any one, without great force of judgment, could even secretly entertain an opinion contrary to the prevailing sentiments. The loud and unanimous voice of a great nation has mighty authority over weak minds; and even later historians are so swayed by the concurring judgment of such multitudes, that some of them have esteemed themselves sufficiently moderate, when they affirmed, that many circumstances of the plot were true, though some were added, and others much magnified. But it is an obvious principle, that a witness, who perjures himself in one circumstance, is credible in none: And the authority of the plot, even to the end of the prosecutions, stood entirely upon witnesses. Though the catholics had been suddenly and unexpectedly detected, at the very moment, when their conspiracy, it is said, was ripe for execution; no arms, no ammunition, no money, no commissions, no papers, no letters, after the most rigorous search, ever were discovered, to confirm the evidence of Oates and Bedloe. Yet still the nation, though often frustrated, went on in the eager pursuit and confident belief of the conspiracy: And even the manifold inconsistencies and absurdities, contained in the narratives, instead of discouraging them, served only as farther incentives to discover the bottom of the plot, and were considered as slight objections, which a more complete information would fully remove. In all history, it will be difficult to find such another instance of popular frenzy and bigoted delusion.

In order to support the panic among the people, especially among the citizens of London, a pamphlet was published with this title, "A narrative and impartial discovery of the horrid popish plot, carried on for burning and destroying the cities of London and Westminster with their suburbs: setting forth the several consults, orders, and resolutions of the jesuits, concerning the same: By captain William Bedloe, lately engaged in that horrid design, and one of the popish committee for carrying on such fires." Every fire, which had happened for several years past, is there ascribed to the machinations of the jesuits, who purposed, as Bedloe said, by such attempts, to find an opportunity for the general massacre of the protestants; and in the mean time, were well pleased to enrich themselves by pilfering goods from the fire.

The king, though he scrupled not, wherever he could speak freely, to throw the highest ridicule on the plot, and on all who believed it; yet found it necessary to adopt the popular opinion before the parliament. The torrent, he saw, ran too strong to be controuled; and he could only hope, by a seeming compliance, to be able, after some time, to guide and direct and elude its fury. He made therefore a speech to both houses; in which he told them, that he would take the utmost care of his person during these times of danger; that he was as ready as their hearts could wish, to join with them in all means for establishing the protestant religion, not only during his own time, but for all future ages; and that, provided the right of succession were preserved, he would consent to any laws for restraining a popish successor: And in conclusion, he exhorted them to think of effectual means for the conviction of popish recusants; and he highly praised the duty and loyalty of all

CHAPTER LXVII

his subjects, who had discovered such anxious concern for his safety.

These gracious expressions abated nothing of the vehemence of parliamentary proceedings. A bill was introduced for a new test, in which popery was denominated idolatry; and all members, who refused this test, were excluded from both houses. The bill passed the commons without much opposition; but in the upper house the duke moved, that an exception might be admitted in his favour. With great earnestness, and even with tears in his eyes, he told them, that he was now to cast himself on their kindness, in the greatest concern, which he could have in the world; and he protested, that, whatever his religion might be, it should only be a private *thing* between God and his own soul, and never should appear in his public conduct. Notwithstanding this strong effort, in so important a point, he prevailed only by two voices; a sufficient indication of the general disposition of the people. "I would not have," said a noble peer, in the debate on this bill, "so much as a popish man or a popish woman to remain here; not so much as a popish dog or a popish bitch; not so much as a popish cat to pur or mew about the king." What is more extraordinary; this speech met with praise and approbation.

Encouraged by this general fury, the witnesses went still a step farther in their accusations; and though both Oates and Bedloe had often declared, that there was no other person of distinction, whom they knew to be concerned in the plot, they were now so audacious as to accuse the queen herself of entering into the design against the life of her husband. The commons, in an address to the king, gave countenance to this scandalous accusation; but the lords would not be prevailed with to join in the address. It is here, if any where, that we may suspect the suggestions of the popular leaders to have had place. The king, it was well known, bore no great affection to his consort; and now, more than ever, when his brother and heir was so much hated, had reason to be desirous of issue, which might quiet the jealous fears of his people. This very hatred, which prevailed against the duke, would much facilitate, he knew, any expedient that could be devised for the exclusion of that prince: and nothing farther seemed requisite for the king, than to give way in this particular to the rage and fury of the nation. But Charles, notwithstanding all allurements of pleasure, or interest, or safety, had the generosity to protect his injured consort. "They think," said he, "I have a mind to a new wife; but for all that, I will not see an innocent woman abused." [m] He immediately ordered Oates to be strictly confined, seized his papers, and dismissed his servants; and this daring informer was obliged to make applications to parliament, in order to recover his liberty.

During this agitation of men's minds, the parliament gave new attention to the militia; a circumstance, which, even during times of greatest tranquillity, can never prudently be neglected. They passed a bill, by which it was enacted, that a regular militia should be kept in arms, during six weeks of the year, and a third part of them do duty every fortnight of that time. The popular leaders probably intended to make use of the general prejudices, and even to turn the arms of the people against the prince.[n] But Charles refused his assent to the bill, and told the parliament, that he would not, were it for half an hour, part so far with the power of the sword: But if they would contrive any other bill for ordering the militia, and still leave it in his power to assemble or dismiss them as he thought proper, he would willingly give it the royal assent. The commons, dissatisfied with this negative, though the king had never before employed that prerogative, immediately voted that all the new-levied forces should be disbanded. They passed a bill, granting money for that purpose; but to shew their extreme jealousy of the crown, besides appropriating the money by the strictest clauses, they ordered it to be paid, not into the exchequer, but into the chamber of London. The lords demurred with regard to so extraordinary a clause, which threw a violent reflection on the king's ministers, and even on himself; and by that means the act remained in suspence.

Accusation of Danby. It was no wonder, that the present ferment and credulity of the nation engaged men of infamous character and indigent circumstances to become informers; when persons of rank and condition could be tempted to give into that scandalous practice. Montague, the king's ambassador at Paris, had procured a seat in the lower house; and without obtaining or asking the king's leave, he suddenly came over to England. Charles, suspecting his intention,

---

[m] North's Examen. p. 186.   [n] Burnet, vol. i. p. 437.

ordered his papers to be seized; but Montague, who foresaw this measure, had taken care to secrete one paper, which he immediately laid before the house of commons. It was a letter from the treasurer Danby, written in the beginning of the year, during the negociations at Nimeguen for the general peace. Montague was there directed to make a demand of money from France; or in other words, the king was willing secretly to sell his good offices to Lewis, contrary to the general interests of the confederates, and even to those of his own kingdoms. The letter, among other particulars, contains these words: "In case the conditions of peace shall be accepted, the king expects to have six millions of livres a year for three years, from the time that this agreement shall be signed between his majesty and the king of France; because it will probably be two or three years before the parliament will be in humour to give him any supplies after the making of any peace with France; and the ambassador here has always agreed to that sum; but not for so long a time." Danby was so unwilling to engage in this negociation, that the king, to satisfy him, subjoined with his own hand these words: "This letter is writ by my order, C. R." Montague, who revealed this secret correspondence, had even the baseness to sell his base treachery at a high price to the French monarch.[o]

The commons were inflamed with this intelligence against Danby; and carrying their suspicions farther than the truth, they concluded, that the king had all along acted in concert with the French court; and that every step, which he had taken in conjunction with the allies, had been illusory and deceitful. Desirous of getting to the bottom of so important a secret, and being pushed by Danby's numerous enemies, they immediately voted an impeachment of high treason against that minister, and sent up six articles to the house of peers. These articles were, That he had traiterously engrossed to himself regal power, by giving instructions to his majesty's ambassadors, without the participation of the secretaries of state, or the privy-council: That he had traiterously endeavoured to subvert the government, and introduce arbitrary power; and to that end, had levied and continued an army, contrary to act of parliament: That he had traiterously en- *His impeachment.*

[o] Appendix to Sir John Dalrymple's Memoirs.

deavoured to alienate the affections of his majesty's subjects, by negociating a disadvantageous peace with France, and procuring money for that purpose: That he was popishly affected, and had traiterously concealed, after he had notice, the late horrid and bloody plot, contrived by the papists against his majesty's person and government: That he had wasted the king's treasure: And that he had, by indirect means, obtained several exorbitant grants from the crown.

It is certain, that the treasurer, in giving instructions to an ambassador, had exceeded the bounds of his office; and as the genius of a monarchy, strictly limited, requires, that the proper minister should be answerable for every abuse of power, the commons, though they here advanced a new pretension, might justify themselves by the utility, and even necessity of it. But in other respects their charge against Danby was very ill grounded. That minister made it appear to the house of lords, not only that Montague, the informer against him, had all along promoted the money-negociations with France, but that he himself was ever extremely averse to the interests of that crown, which he esteemed pernicious to his master, and to his country. The French nation, he said, had always entertained, as he was certainly informed, the highest contempt, both of the king's person and government. His diligence, he added, in tracing and discovering the popish plot, was generally known; and if he had common sense, not to say common honesty, he would surely be anxious to preserve the life of a master, by whom he was so much favoured. He had wasted no treasure, because there was no treasure to waste. And though he had reason to be grateful for the king's bounty, he had made more moderate acquisitions than were generally imagined, and than others in his office had often done, even during a shorter administration.

The house of peers plainly saw, that, allowing all the charge of the commons to be true, Danby's crime fell not under the statute of Edward III.; and though the words, *treason* and *traiterously*, had been carefully inserted in several articles, this appellation could not change the nature of things, or subject him to the penalties annexed to that crime. They refused, therefore, to commit Danby upon this irregular charge: The commons insisted on their demand; and a great contest was likely to arise, when the king, who had already seen sufficient instances of the ill-humour of the parliament, thought proper to prorogue them. This prorogation was soon after followed by a dissolution; a desperate remedy in the present disposition of the nation. But the disease, it must be owned, the king had reason to esteem desperate. The utmost rage had been discovered by the commons, on account of the popish plot; and their fury began already to point against the royal family, if not against the throne itself. The duke had been struck at in several motions: The treasurer had been impeached: All supply had been refused, except on the most disagreeable conditions: Fears, jealousies, and antipathies were every day multiplying in parliament: And though the people were strongly infected with the same prejudices, the king hoped, that, by dissolving the present cabals, a set of men might be chosen, more moderate in their persuits, and less tainted with the virulence of faction. *30th Dec. Dissolution of the long parliament.*

Thus came to a period a parliament, which had sitten during the whole course of this reign one year excepted. Its conclusion was very different from its commencement. Being elected during the joy and festivity of the restoration, it consisted almost entirely of royalists; who were disposed to support the crown by all the liberality, which the habits of that age would permit. Alarmed by the alliance with France, they gradually withdrew their confidence from the king; and finding him still to persevere in a foreign interest, they proceeded to discover symptoms of the most refractory and most jealous disposition. The popish plot pushed them beyond all bounds of moderation; and before their dissolution, they seemed to be treading fast in the footsteps of the last long parliament, on whose conduct they threw at first such violent blame. In all their variations, they had still followed the opinions and prejudices of the nation; and ever seemed to be more governed by humour and party-views than by public interest, and more by public interest than by any corrupt or private influence. *Its character.*

During the sitting of the parliament, and after its prorogation and dissolution, the trials of the pretended criminals were carried on; and the courts of judicature, places, which, if possible, ought to be kept more pure from injustice than even national assemblies themselves, were strongly infected with the same party rage and bigoted prejudices. Coleman, the most obnoxious of the conspirators, was first brought to his trial. His letters were produced *Trial of Coleman.*

against him. They contained, as he himself confessed, much indiscretion: But unless so far as it is illegal to be a zealous catholic, they seemed to prove nothing criminal, much less treasonable against him. Oates and Bedloe deposed, that he had received a commission, signed by the superior of the jesuits, to be papal secretary of state, and had consented to the poisoning, shooting, and stabbing of the king: He had even, according to Oates's deposition, advanced a guinea to promote those bloody purposes. These wild stories were confounded with the projects contained in his letters; and Coleman received sentence of death. The sentence was soon after executed upon him.[p] He suffered with calmness and constancy, and to the last persisted in the strongest protestations of his innocence.

Of Ireland. Coleman's execution was succeeded by the trial of father Ireland, who, it is pretended, had signed, together with fifty jesuits, the great resolution of murdering the king. Grove and Pickering, who had undertaken to shoot him, were tried at the same time. The only witnesses against the prisoners were still Oates and Bedloe. Ireland affirmed, that he was in Staffordshire all the month of August last, a time when Oates's evidence made him in London. He proved his assertion by good evidence, and would have proved it by undoubted; had he not, most iniquitously, been debarred, while in prison, from all use of pen, ink, and paper, and denied the liberty of sending for witnesses. All these men, before their arraignment, were condemned in the opinion of the judges, jury, and spectators; and to be a jesuit, or even a catholic, was of itself a sufficient proof of guilt. The chief justice,[q] in particular, gave sanction to all the narrow prejudices and bigoted fury of the populace. Instead of being counsel for the prisoners, as his office required, he pleaded the cause against them, brow-beat their witnesses, and on every occasion represented their guilt as certain and uncontroverted. He even went so far as publicly to affirm, that the papists had not the same principles which protestants have, and therefore were not entitled to that common *credence*, which the principles and practices of the latter call for. And when the jury brought in their verdict against the prisoners, he said, "You have done, gentlemen, like very good subjects, and very good Chris-

[p] 3d of December.   [q] Sir William Scroggs.

CHAPTER LXVII

tians, that is to say, like very good Protestants: And now much good may their 30,000 masses do them." Alluding to the masses, by which Pickering was to be rewarded for murdering the king. All these unhappy men went to execution, protesting their innocence: a circumstance, which made no impression on the spectators. The opinion, that the jesuits allowed of lies and mental reservations for promoting a good cause, was at this time so universally received, that no credit was given to testimony delivered either by that order, or by any of their disciples. It was forgotten, that all the conspirators, engaged in the gun-powder treason, and Garnet, the jesuit, among the rest, had freely on the scaffold made confession of their guilt.

1679.
14th Jan.

Though Bedloe had given information of Godfrey's murder, he still remained a single evidence against the persons accused; and all the allurements of profit and honour had not hitherto tempted any one to confirm the testimony of that informer. At last, means were found to compleat the legal evidence. One Prance, a silversmith, and a catholic, had been accused by Bedloe of being an accomplice in the murder; and upon his denial had been thrown into prison, loaded with heavy irons, and confined to the condemned hole, a place cold, dark, and full of nastiness. Such rigours were supposed to be exercised by orders from the secret committee of lords, particularly Shaftesbury and Buckingham; who, in examining the prisoners, usually employed (as is said, and indeed sufficiently proved) threatenings and promises, rigour and indulgence, and every art, under pretence of extorting the truth from them. Prance had not courage to resist, but confessed himself an accomplice in Godfrey's murder. Being asked concerning the plot, he also thought proper to be acquainted with it, and conveyed some intelligence to the council. Among other absurd circumstances, he said that one Le Fevre bought a second-hand sword of him; because he knew not, as he said, what times were at hand: And Prance expressing some concern for poor tradesmen, if such times came; Le Fevre replied, that it would be better for tradesmen, if the catholic religion were restored: And particularly, that there would be more church work for silversmiths. All this information, with regard to the plot as well as the murder of Godfrey, Prance solemnly retracted, both before the king and the secret committee: But being again thrown into prison, he was induced, by new terrors and new sufferings, to confirm his first information, and was now produced as a sufficient evidence.

Hill, Green, and Berry were tried for Godfrey's murder; all of them men of low stations. Hill was servant to a physician: The other two belonged to the popish chapel at Somerset-house. It is needless to run over all the particulars of a long trial: It will be sufficient to say, that Bedloe's evidence and Prance's were in many circumstances totally irreconcileable; that both of them laboured under unsurmountable difficulties, not to say gross absurdities; and that they were invalidated by contrary evidence, which is altogether convincing. But all was in vain: The prisoners were condemned and executed. They all denied their guilt at their execution; and as Berry died a protestant, this circumstance was regarded as very considerable: But, instead of its giving some check to the general credulity of the people, men were only surprised, that a protestant could be induced at his death to persist in so manifest a falshood.

Feb. 21st and 28th.

As the army could neither be kept up, nor disbanded without money, the king, how little hopes soever he could entertain of more compliance, found himself obliged to summon a new parliament. The blood, already shed on account of the popish plot, instead of satiating the people, served only as an incentive to their fury; and each conviction of a criminal was hitherto regarded as a new proof of those horrible designs, imputed to the papists. This election is perhaps the first in England, which, since the commencement of the monarchy, had been carried on by a violent contest between the parties, and where the court interested itself, to a high degree, in the choice of the national representatives. But all its efforts were fruitless, in opposition to the torrent of prejudices, which prevailed. Religion, liberty, property, even the lives of men were now supposed to be at stake; and no security, it was thought, except in a vigilant parliament, could be found against the impious and bloody conspirators. Were there any part of the nation, to which the ferment, occasioned by the popish plot, had not as yet propagated itself; the new elections, by interesting the whole people in public concerns, tended to diffuse it into the remotest corner; and the consternation, universally excited, proved an excellent engine for influencing the electors. All the zealots of the former parliament were re-chosen: New ones were

New elections.

CHAPTER LXVII

added: The presbyterians in particular, being transported with the most inveterate antipathy against popery, were very active and very successful in the elections. That party, it is said, first began at this time the abuse of splitting their freeholds, in order to multiply votes and electors. By accounts, which came from every part of England, it was concluded, that the new representatives would, if possible, exceed the old in their refractory opposition to the court, and furious persecution of the catholics.

The king was alarmed, when he saw so dreadful a tempest arise from such small and unaccountable beginnings. His life, if Oates and Bedloe's information were true, had been aimed at by the catholics: Even the duke's was in danger: The higher, therefore, the rage mounted against popery, the more should the nation have been reconciled to these princes, in whom, it appeared, the church of Rome reposed no confidence. But there is a sophistry, which attends all the passions; especially those into which the populace enter. Men gave credit to the informers, so far as concerned the guilt of the catholics: But they still retained their old suspicions, that these religionists were secretly favoured by the king, and had obtained the most entire ascendant over his brother. Charles had too much penetration not to see the danger, to which the succession, and even his own crown and dignity, now stood exposed. A numerous party, he found, was formed against him; on the one hand, composed of a populace, so credulous from prejudice, so blinded with religious antipathy, as implicitly to believe the most palpable absurdities; and conducted, on the other hand, by leaders so little scrupulous, as to endeavour, by encouraging perjury, subornation, lyes, impostures, and even by shedding innocent blood, to gratify their own furious ambition, and subvert all legal authority. Rouzed from his lethargy by so eminent a peril, he began to exert that vigour of mind, of which, on great occasions, he was not destitute; and without quitting in appearance his usual facility of temper, he collected an industry, firmness, and vigilance, of which he was believed altogether incapable. These qualities, joined to dexterity and prudence, conducted him happily through the many shoals, which surrounded him; and he was at last able to make the storm fall on the heads of those who had blindly raised, or artfully conducted it.

One chief step, which the king took, towards gratifying and

appeasing his people and parliament, was, desiring the duke to withdraw beyond sea, that no farther suspicion might remain of the influence of popish counsels. The duke readily complied; but first required an order for that purpose, signed by the king; lest his absenting himself should be interpreted as a proof of fear or of guilt. He also desired, that his brother should satisfy him, as well as the public, by a declaration of the illegitimacy of the duke of Monmouth.

Duke of Mon- mouth.

James duke of Monmouth was the king's natural son by Lucy Walters, and born about ten years before the restoration. He possessed all the qualities, which could engage the affections of the populace; a distinguished valour, an affable address, a thoughtless generosity, a graceful person. He rose still higher in the public favour, by reason of the universal hatred, to which the duke, on account of his religion, was exposed. Monmouth's capacity was mean; his temper pliant: So that, notwithstanding his great popularity, he had never been dangerous, had he not implicitly resigned himself to the guidance of Shaftesbury, a man of such a restless temper, such subtle wit, and such abandoned principles. That daring politician had flattered Monmouth with the hopes of succeeding to the crown. The story of a contract of marriage, passed between the king and Monmouth's mother, and secretly kept in a certain *black box,* had been industriously spread abroad, and was greedily received by the multitude. As the horrors of popery still pressed harder on them, they might be induced, either to adopt that fiction, as they had already done many others more incredible, or to commit open violation on the right of succession. And it would not be difficult, it was hoped, to persuade the king, who was extremely fond of his son, to give him the preference above a brother, who, by his imprudent bigotry, had involved him in such inextricable difficulties. But Charles, in order to cut off all such expectations, as well as to remove the duke's apprehensions, took care, in full council, to make a declaration of Monmouth's illegitimacy, and to deny all promise of marriage with his mother. The duke, being gratified in so reasonable a request, willingly complied with the king's desire, and retired to Brussels.

Duke of York retires to Brussels.

6th March. New par- liament.

But the king soon found, that, notwithstanding this precaution, notwithstanding his concurrence in the prosecution of the popish plot, notwithstanding the zeal which he expressed, and even at this time exercised against the catholics; he had no wise obtained the confidence of his parliament. The refractory humour of the lower house appeared in the first step, which they took upon their assembling. It had ever been usual for the commons, in the election of their speaker, to consult the inclinations of the Sovereign; and even the long parliament in 1641 had not thought proper to depart from so established a custom. The king now desired, that the choice should fall on Sir Thomas Meres: But Seymour, speaker to the last parliament, was instantly called to the chair, by a vote which seemed unanimous. The king, when Seymour was presented to him for his approbation, rejected him, and ordered the commons to proceed to a new choice. A great flame was excited. The commons maintained, that the king's approbation was merely a matter of form, and that he could not, without giving a reason, reject the speaker chosen: The king, that, since he had the power of rejecting, he might, if he pleased, keep the reason in his own breast. As the question had never before been started, it might seem difficult to find principles, upon which it could be decided.[r] By way of compromise, it was agreed to set aside both candidates. Gregory, a lawyer, was chosen; and the election was ratified by the king. It has ever since been understood, that the choice of the speaker lies in the house; but that the king retains the power of rejecting any person disagreeable to him.

Seymour was deemed a great enemy to Danby; and it was the influence of that nobleman, as commonly supposed, which had engaged the king to enter into this ill-timed controversy with the commons. The impeachment, therefore, of Danby was on that account the sooner revived; and it was maintained by the commons, that notwithstanding the intervening dissolution, every part of that proceeding stood in the same condition in which it had been left by the last parliament: A pretension, which, though unusual, seems tacitly to have been yielded them. The king had before hand had the precaution to grant a pardon to Danby; and, in order to

Danby's impeachment.

---

[r] In 1566, the speaker said to Q. Elizabeth, that without her allowance the election of the house was of no significance. D'Ewes's Journal, p. 97. In the parliament 1592, 1593, the speaker, who was Sir Edward Coke, advances a like position. D'Ewes, p. 459. Townshend, p. 35. So that this pretension of the commons seems to have been somewhat new; like many of their other powers and privileges.

screen the chancellor from all attacks by the commons, he had taken the great seal into his own hands, and had himself affixed it to the parchment. He told the parliament, that, as Danby had acted in every thing by his orders, he was in no respect criminal; that his pardon, however, he would insist upon; and if it should be found any wise defective in form, he would renew it again and again, till it should be rendered entirely compleat: But that he was resolved to deprive him of all employments, and to remove him from court.

The commons were no wise satisfied with this concession. They pretended, that no pardon of the crown could be pleaded in bar of an impeachment by the commons. The prerogative of mercy had hitherto been understood to be altogether unlimited in the king; and this pretension of the commons, it must be confessed, was entirely new. It was however not unsuitable to the genius of a monarchy, strictly limited; where the king's ministers are supposed to be for ever accountable to national assemblies, even for such abuses of power as they may commit by orders from their master. The present emergence, while the nation was so highly inflamed, was the proper time for pushing such popular claims; and the commons failed not to avail themselves of this advantage. They still insisted on the impeachment of Danby. The peers, in compliance with them, departed from their former scruples, and ordered Danby to be taken into custody. Danby absconded. The commons passed a bill, appointing him to surrender himself before a certain day or, in default of it, attainting him. A bill had passed the upper house, mitigating the penalty to banishment; but after some conferences, the peers thought proper to yield to the violence of the commons; and the bill of attainder was carried. Rather than undergo such severe penalties, Danby appeared, and was immediately committed to the Tower.

While a protestant nobleman met with such violent prosecution, it was not likely that the catholics would be over-looked by the zealous commons. The credit of the popish plot still stood upon the oaths of a few infamous witnesses. Though such immense preparations were supposed to have been made in the very bowels of the kingdom, no traces of them, after the most rigorous enquiry, had as yet appeared. Though so many thousands, both abroad and at home, had been engaged in the dreadful secret; neither hope, nor fear, nor remorse, nor levity, nor suspicions, nor

*Popish
plot.*

CHAPTER LXVII

private resentment had engaged any one to confirm the evidence. Though the catholics, particularly the Jesuits, were represented as guilty of the utmost indiscretion, insomuch that they talked of the king's murder as common news, and wrote of it in plain terms by the common post; yet, among the great number of letters seized, no one contained any part of so complicated a conspiracy. Though the informers pretended, that, even after they had resolved to betray the secret, many treasonable commissions and papers had passed through their hands; they had not had the precaution to keep any one of them, in order to fortify their evidence. But all these difficulties, and a thousand more, were not found too hard of digestion by the nation and parliament. The prosecution and farther discovery of the plot were still the object of general concern. The commons voted, that, if the king should come to an untimely end, they would revenge his death upon the papists; not reflecting that this sect were not his only enemies. They promised rewards to new discoverers; not considering the danger, which they incurred, of granting bribes to perjury. They made Bedloe a present of 500 pounds; and particularly recommended the care of his safety to the duke of Monmouth. Colonel Sackville, a member, having, in a private company, spoken opprobriously of those who affirmed that there was any plot, was expelled the house. The peers gave power to their committees to send for and examine such as would maintain the innocence of those who had been condemned for the plot. A pamphlet having been published to discredit the informers, and to vindicate the catholic lords in the Tower, these lords were required to discover the author, and thereby to expose their own advocate to prosecution. And both houses concurred in renewing the former vote, that the papists had undoubtedly entered into a *horrid* and *treasonable* conspiracy against the king, the state, and the protestant religion.

It must be owned, that this extreme violence, in prosecution of so absurd an imposture, disgraces the noble cause of liberty, in which the parliament was engaged. We may even conclude from such impatience of contradiction, that the prosecutors themselves retained a secret suspicion, that the general belief was but ill grounded. The politicians among them were afraid to let in light, lest it might put an end to so useful a delusion: The weaker and less dishonest party took care, by turning their eyes aside, not to see a truth, so opposite to those furious passions, by which they were actuated, and in which they were determined obstinately to persevere.

Sir William Temple had lately been recalled from his foreign employments; and the king, who, after the removal of Danby, had no one with whom he could so much as discourse with freedom of public affairs, was resolved, upon Coventry's dismission, to make him one of his secretaries of state. But that philosophical patriot, too little interested for the intrigues of a court, too full of spleen and delicacy for the noisy turbulence of popular assemblies, was alarmed at the universal discontents and jealousies, which prevailed, and was determined to make his retreat, as soon as possible, from a scene which threatened such confusion. Meanwhile, he could not refuse the confidence, with which his master honoured him; and he resolved to employ it to the public service. He represented to the king, that, as the jealousies of the nation were extreme, it was necessary to cure them by some new remedy, and to restore that mutual confidence, so requisite for the safety both of king and people: That to refuse every thing to the parliament in their present disposition, or to yield every thing, was equally dangerous to the constitution as well as to public tranquillity: That if the king would introduce into his councils such men as enjoyed the confidence of his people, fewer concessions would probably be required; or if unreasonable demands were made, the king, under the sanction of such counsellors, might be enabled, with the greater safety, to refuse them: And that the heads of the popular party, being gratified with the king's favour, would probably abate of that violence by which they endeavoured at present to pay court to the multitude.

New council. The king assented to these reasons; and, in concert with Temple, he laid the plan of a new privy-council, without whose advice he declared himself determined for the future to take no measure of importance. This council was to consist of thirty persons, and was never to exceed that number. Fifteen of the chief officers of the crown were to be continued, who, it was supposed, would adhere to the king, and, in case of any extremity, oppose the exorbitancies of faction. The other half of the council was to be composed, either of men of character, detached from the court, or of those who possessed chief credit in both houses. And the king, in filling up the names of his new council, was well pleased to find, that the members, in land and offices, possessed to the amount of 300,000 pounds a-year; a sum nearly equal to the whole property of the house of commons, against whose violence the new council was intended as a barrier to the throne.[s]

This experiment was tried, and seemed at first to give some satisfaction to the public. The earl of Essex, a nobleman of the popular party, son of that lord Capel who had been beheaded a little after the late king, was created treasurer in the room of Danby: The earl of Sunderland, a man of intrigue and capacity, was made secretary of state: Viscount Halifax, a fine genius, possessed of learning, eloquence, industry, but subject to inquietude, and fond of refinements, was admitted into the council. These three, together with Temple, who often joined them, though he kept himself more detached from public business, formed a kind of cabinet council, from which all affairs received their first digestion. Shaftesbury was made president of the council; contrary to the advice of Temple, who foretold the consequence of admitting a man of so dangerous a character into any part of the public administration.

As Temple foresaw, it happened. Shaftesbury finding, that he possessed no more than the appearance of court-favour, was resolved still to adhere to the popular party, by whose attachment he enjoyed an undisputed superiority in the lower house, and possessed great influence in the other. The very appearance of court-favour, empty as it was, tended to render him more dangerous. His partizans, observing the progress which he had already made, hoped, that he would soon acquire the entire ascendant; and he constantly flattered them, that if they persisted in their purpose, the king, from indolence, and necessity, and fondness for Mon-

---

[s] Their names were: Prince Rupert, the archbishop of Canterbury, lord Finch, chancellor, earl of Shaftesbury, president, earl of Anglesea, privy seal, duke of Albemarle, duke of Monmouth, duke of Newcastle, duke of Lauderdale, duke of Ormond, marquess of Winchester, marquess of Worcester, earl of Arlington, earl of Salisbury, earl of Bridgwater, earl of Sunderland, earl of Essex, earl of Bath, viscount Fauconberg, viscount Halifax, bishop of London, lord Robarts, lord Hollis, lord Russel, lord Cavendish, secretary Coventry, Sir Francis North, chief justice, Sir Henry Capel, Sir John Ernley, Sir Thomas Chicheley, Sir William Temple, Edward Seymour, Henry Powle.

mouth, would at last be induced, even at the expence of his brother's right, to make them every concession.

Besides, the antipathy to popery, as well as jealousy of the king and duke, had taken too fast possession of men's minds, to be removed by so feeble a remedy, as this new council, projected by Temple. The commons, soon after the establishment of that council, proceeded so far as to vote unanimously, "That the duke of York's being a papist, and the hopes of his coming to the crown, had given the highest countenance to the present conspiracies and designs of the papists against the king and the protestant religion." It was expected, that a bill for excluding him the throne would soon be brought in. To prevent this bold measure, the king concerted some limitations, which he proposed to the parliament. He introduced his plan by the following gracious expressions: "And to shew you, that, while you are doing your parts, my thoughts have not been misemployed, but that it is my constant care to do every thing, that may preserve your religion, and secure it for the future in all events, I have commanded my lord chancellor to mention several particulars; which, I hope, will be an evidence, that, in all things, which concern the public security, I shall not follow your zeal, but lead it."

Limitations on a popish successor. The limitations projected were of the utmost importance, and deprived the successor of the chief branches of royalty. A method was there chalked out, by which the nation, on every new reign, could be ensured of having a parliament, which the king should not, for a certain time, have it in his power to dissolve. In case of a popish successor, the prince was to forfeit the right of conferring any ecclesiastical preferments: No member of the privy council, no judge of the common law or in chancery, was to be put in or displaced but by consent of parliament: And the same precaution was extended to the military part of the government; to the lord lieutenants and deputy lieutenants of the counties, and to all officers of the navy. The chancellor of himself added, "It is hard to invent another restraint; considering how much the revenue will depend upon the consent of parliament, and how impossible it is to raise money without such consent. But yet, if anything else can occur to the wisdom of parliament, which may farther secure religion and liberty against a popish successor, without defeating the right of succession itself, his majesty will readily consent to it."

CHAPTER LXVII

It is remarkable, that, when these limitations were first laid before the council, Shaftesbury and Temple were the only members, who argued against them. The reasons, which they employed, were diametrically opposite. Shaftesbury's opinion was, that the restraints were insufficient; and that nothing but the total exclusion of the duke could give a proper security to the kingdom. Temple on the other hand thought, that the restraints were so rigorous as even to subvert the constitution; and that shackles, put upon a popish successor, would not afterwards be easily cast off by a protestant. It is certain, that the duke was extremely alarmed when he heard of this step taken by the king, and that he was better pleased even with the bill of exclusion itself, which, he thought, by reason of its violence and injustice, could never possibly be carried into execution. There is also reason to believe, that the king would not have gone so far, had he not expected, from the extreme fury of the commons, that his concessions would be rejected, and that the blame of not forming a reasonable accommodation would by that means lie entirely at their door.

It soon appeared, that Charles had entertained a just opinion of the dispositions of the house. So much were the commons actuated by the cabals of Shaftesbury and other malcontents; such violent antipathy prevailed against popery, that the king's concessions, though much more important than could reasonably have been expected, were not embraced. A bill was brought in for the total exclusion of the duke from the crown of England and Ireland. It was there declared that the sovereignty of these kingdoms, upon the king's death or resignation should devolve to the person next in succession after the duke; that all acts of royalty, which that prince should afterwards perform, should not only be void, but be deemed treason; that if he so much as entered any of these dominions, he should be deemed guilty of the same offence; and that all who supported his title, should be punished as rebels and traitors. This important bill, which implied banishment as well as exclusion, passed the lower house by a majority of seventy-nine.

Bill of exclusion.

The commons were not so wholly employed about the exclusion-bill as to overlook all other securities to liberty. The country party, during all the last parliament, had much exclaimed against the bribery and corruption of the members; and the same reproach had been renewed against the present parliament. An enquiry was made into a complaint, which was so dangerous to the honour of that assembly; but very little foundation was found for it. Sir Stephen Fox, who was the pay-master, confessed to the house, that nine members received pensions to the amount of three thousand four hundred pounds: And after a rigorous enquiry by a secret committee, eight more pensioners were discovered. A sum also, about twelve thousand pounds, had been occasionally given or lent to others. The writers of that age pretend, that Clifford and Danby had adopted opposite maxims with regard to pecuniary influence. The former endeavoured to gain the leaders and orators of the house, and deemed the others of no consequence. The latter thought it sufficient to gain a majority, however composed. It is likely, that the means, rather than the intention, were wanting to both these ministers.

Pensions and bribes, though it be difficult entirely to exclude them, are dangerous expedients for government; and cannot be too carefully guarded against, nor too vehemently decried by every one who has a regard to the virtue and liberty of a nation. The influence, however, which the crown acquires from the disposal of places, honours, and preferments, is to be esteemed of a different nature. This engine of power may become too forcible, but it cannot altogether be abolished, without the total destruction of monarchy, and even of all regular authority. But the commons at this time were so jealous of the crown, that they brought in a bill, which was twice read, excluding from the lower house all who possessed any lucrative office.

The standing army and the king's guards were by the commons voted to be illegal: A new pretension, it must be confessed; but necessary for the full security of liberty and a limited constitution.

Habeas corpus bill.

Arbitrary imprisonment is a grievance, which, in some degree, has place almost in every government, except in that of Great Britain; and our absolute security from it we owe chiefly to the present parliament; a merit, which makes some atonement for the faction and violence, into which their prejudices had, in other particulars, betrayed them. The great charter had laid the foundation of this valuable part of liberty; the petition of right had renewed and extended it; but some provisions were still wanting, to render it complete, and prevent all evasion or delay from ministers and judges. The act of *habeas corpus,* which passed this session, served these purposes. By this act, it was prohibited to send any one to a prison beyond sea. No judge, under severe penalties, must refuse to any prisoner a writ of *habeas corpus,* by which the gaoler was directed to produce in court the body of the prisoner (whence the writ has its name), and to certify the cause of his detainer and imprisonment. If the gaol lie within twenty miles of the judge, the writ must be obeyed in three days; and so proportionably for greater distances: Every prisoner must be indicted the first term after his commitment, and brought to trial in the subsequent term. And no man, after being enlarged by order of court, can be re-committed for the same offence. This law seems necessary for the protection of liberty in a mixed monarchy; and as it has not place in any other form of government, this consideration alone may induce us to prefer our present constitution to all others. It must, however, be confessed, that there is some difficulty to reconcile with such extreme liberty the full security and the regular police of a state, especially the police of great cities. It may also be doubted, whether the low state of the public revenue in this period, and of the military power, did not still render some discretionary author-ity in the crown necessary to the support of government.

During these zealous efforts for the protection of liberty, no complaisance for the crown was discovered by this parliament. The king's revenue lay under great debts and anticipations: Those branches, granted in the years 1669 and 1670, were ready to ex-pire. And the fleet was represented by the king as in great decay and disorder. But the commons, instead of being affected by these distresses of the crown, trusted chiefly to them for passing the exclusion-bill, and for punishing and displacing all the ministers who were obnoxious to them. They were therefore in no haste to relieve the king; and grew only the more assuming on account of his complaints and uneasiness. Jealous however of the army, they granted the same sum of 206,000 pounds, which had been voted for disbanding it by the last parliament; though the vote, by reason of the subsequent prorogation and dissolution, joined to some scruples of the lords, had not been carried into an act. This money was appropriated by very strict clauses; but the commons insisted not as formerly upon its being paid into the chamber of London.

The impeachment of the five popish lords in the Tower, with that of the earl of Danby, was carried on with vigour. The power of this minister, and his credit with the king, rendered him extremely obnoxious to the popular leaders; and the commons hoped, that, if he were pushed to extremity, he would be obliged, in order to justify his own conduct, to lay open the whole intrigue of the French alliance, which they suspected to contain a secret of the most dangerous nature. The king, on his part, apprehensive of the same consequences, and desirous to protect his minister, who was become criminal merely by obeying orders, employed his whole interest to support the validity of that pardon, which had been granted him. The lords appointed a day for the examination of the question, and agreed to hear counsel on both sides: But the commons would not submit their pretensions to the discussion of argument and enquiry. They voted, that whoever should presume, without their leave, to maintain before the house of peers the validity of Danby's pardon, should be accounted a betrayer of the liberties of the English commons. And they made a demand, that the bishops, whom they knew to be devoted to the court, should be removed, not only when the trial of the earl should commence, but also when the validity of his pardon should be discussed.

The bishops before the reformation had always enjoyed a seat in parliament: But so far were they antiently from regarding that dignity as a privilege, that they affected rather to form a separate order in the state, independent of the civil magistrate, and accountable only to the pope and to their own order. By the constitutions, however, of Clarendon, enacted during the reign of Henry II. they were obliged to give their presence in parliament; but as the canon law prohibited them from assisting in capital trials, they were allowed in such cases the privilege of absenting themselves. A practice, which was at first voluntary, became afterwards a rule; and on the earl of Strafford's trial, the bishops, who would gladly have attended, and who were no longer bound by the canon law, were yet obliged to withdraw. It had been usual for them to enter a protest, asserting their right to sit; and this protest, being considered as a mere form, was always admitted and disregarded. But here was started a new question of no small importance. The commons, who were now enabled, by the violence of the people, and the necessities of the crown, to make new acquisitions of powers and privileges, insisted, that the bishops had no more title to vote in the question of the earl's pardon than in the impeachment itself. The bishops asserted, that the pardon was merely a preliminary; and that, neither by the canon law nor the practice of parliament, were they ever obliged, in capital cases, to withdraw till the very commencement of the trial itself. If their absence were considered as a privilege, which was its real origin, it depended on their own choice, how far they would insist upon it. If regarded as a diminution of their right of peerage, such unfavourable customs ought never to be extended beyond the very circumstance established by them; and all arguments, from a pretended parity of reason, were in that case of little or no authority.

The house of lords was so much influenced by these reasons, that they admitted the bishops' right to vote, when the validity of the pardon should be examined. The commons insisted still on their withdrawing; and thus a quarrel being commenced between the two houses, the king, who expected nothing but fresh instances of violence from this parliament, began to entertain thoughts of laying hold of so favourable a pretence, and of finishing the session by a prorogation. While in this disposition, he was alarmed with sudden intelligence, that the house of commons was preparing a remonstrance, in order to inflame the nation still farther upon the favourite topics of the plot and of popery. He hastened, *27th May.* therefore, to execute his intention, even without consulting his new council, by whose advice he had promised to regulate his whole conduct. And thus were disappointed all the projects of the malcontents, who were extremely enraged at this vigorous measure of the king's. Shaftesbury publicly threatened, that he would have the head of whoever had advised it. The parliament was soon *Proroga-* after dissolved without advice of council; and writs were issued for *tion and* a new parliament. The king was willing to try every means, which *dissolu-* gave a prospect of more compliance in his subjects; and, in case of *tion of* failure, the blame, he hoped, would lie on those whose obstinacy *the par-* forced him to extremities. *liament.*

10th July.

But even during the recess of parliament, there was no interruption to the prosecution of the catholics accused of the plot: The king found himself obliged to give way to this popular fury. White- *Trial* bread, provincial of the jesuits, Fenwic, Gavan, Turner, and Har- *and exe-* court, all of them of the same order, were first brought to their *cution of* trial. Besides Oates and Bedloe, Dugdale, a new witness, appeared *the five* against the prisoners. This man had been steward to lord Aston, *jesuits.*

and, though poor, possessed a character somewhat more reputable than the other two: But his account of the intended massacres and assassinations was equally monstrous and incredible. He even asserted, that 200,000 papists in England were ready to take arms. The prisoners proved by sixteen witnesses from St. Omers, students and most of them young men of family, that Oates was in that seminary, at the time when he swore that he was in London: But as they were catholics and disciples of the jesuits, their testimony, both with the judges and jury, was totally disregarded. Even the reception, which they met with in court, was full of outrage and mockery. One of them saying, that Oates always continued at St. Omers, if he could believe his senses: "You papists," said the chief justice, "are taught not to believe your senses." It must be confessed, that Oates, in opposition to the students of St. Omers, found means to bring evidence of his having been at that time in London: But this evidence, though it had, at that time, the appearance of some solidity, was afterwards discovered, when Oates himself was tried for perjury, to be altogether deceitful. In order farther to discredit that witness, the jesuits proved by undoubted testimony, that he had perjured himself in father Ireland's trial, whom they shewed to have been in Staffordshire at the very time when Oates swore that he was committing treason in London. But all these pleas availed them nothing against the general prejudices. They received sentence of death; and were executed, persisting to their last breath in the most solemn, earnest, and deliberate, though disregarded, protestations of their innocence.

And of Langhorne. The next trial was that of Langhorne, an eminent lawyer, by whom all the concerns of the jesuits were managed. Oates and Bedloe swore, that all the papal commissions by which the chief offices in England were filled with catholics, passed through his hands. When verdict was given against the prisoner, the spectators expressed their savage joy by loud acclamations. So high indeed had the popular rage mounted, that the witnesses for this unhappy man, on approaching the court, were almost torn in pieces by the rabble: One in particular was bruised to such a degree, as to put his life in danger. And another, a woman, declared, that, unless the court could afford her protection, she durst not give evidence: But as the judges could go no farther than promise to punish such as should do her any injury, the prisoner himself had the humanity to wave her testimony.

CHAPTER LXVII

So far the informers had proceeded with success: Their accusation was hitherto equivalent to a sentence of death. The first check which they received, was on the trial of Sir George Wakeman, the queen's physician, whom they accused of an intention to poison the king. It was a strong circumstance in favour of Wakeman, that Oates, in his first information before the council, had accused him only upon hearsay; and when asked by the chancellor, whether he had any thing farther to charge him with, he added, "God forbid I should say any thing against Sir George: For I know nothing more against him." On the trial he gave positive evidence of the prisoner's guilt. There were many other circumstances which favoured Wakeman: But what chiefly contributed to his acquittal, was the connexion of his cause with that of the queen, whom no one, even during the highest prejudices of the times, could sincerely believe guilty. The great importance of the trial made men recollect themselves, and recal that good sense and humanity, which seemed, during some time, to have abandoned the nation. The chief justice himself, who had hitherto favoured the witnesses, exaggerated the plot, and railed against the prisoners, was observed to be considerably mollified, and to give a favourable charge to the jury. Oates and Bedloe had the assurance to attack him to his face, and even to accuse him of partiality before the council. The whole party, who had formerly much extolled his conduct, now made him the object of their resentment. Wakeman's acquittal was indeed a sensible mortification to the furious prosecutors of the plot, and fixed an indelible stain upon the witnesses. But Wakeman, after he recovered his liberty, finding himself exposed to such inveterate enmity, and being threatened with farther prosecutions, thought it prudent to retire beyond sea: And his flight was interpreted as a proof of guilt, by those who were still resolved to persist in the belief of the conspiracy.

Wakeman acquitted. 18th July.

The great discontents in England, and the refractory disposition of the parliament, drew the attention of the Scottish covenanters, and gave them a prospect of some time putting an end to those oppressions, under which they had so long laboured. It was suspected to have been the policy of Lauderdale and his associates to push these unhappy men to extremities, and force them into rebellion, with a view of reaping profit from the forfeitures and attainders, which would ensue upon it. But the covenanters, aware of this policy, had hitherto forborne all acts of hostility; and

State of affairs in Scotland.

that tyrannical minister had failed of his purpose. An incident at last happened, which brought on an insurrection in that country.

The covenanters were much enraged against Sharpe, the primate, whom they considered as an apostate from their principles, and whom they experienced to be an unrelenting persecutor of all those who dissented from the established worship. He had an officer under him, one Carmichael, no less zealous than himself against conventicles, and who by his violent prosecutions had rendered himself extremely obnoxious to the fanatics. A company of these had way-laid him on the road near St. Andrews, with an intention, if not of killing him, at least of chastizing him so severely as would afterwards render him more cautious in persecuting the nonconformists.[t] While looking out for their prey, they were surprized at seeing the archbishop's coach pass by; and they immediately interpreted this incident as a declaration of the secret purpose of providence against him. But when they observed, that almost all his servants, by some accident, were absent, they no longer doubted, but heaven had here delivered their capital enemy into their hands. Without farther deliberation, they fell upon him; dragged him from his coach; tore him from the arms of his daughter, who interposed with cries and tears; and piercing him with redoubled wounds, left him dead on the spot, and immediately dispersed themselves.

3d May.

This atrocious action served the ministry as a pretence for a more violent persecution against the fanatics, on whom, without distinction, they threw the guilt of those furious assassins. It is indeed certain, that the murder of Sharpe had excited an universal joy among the covenanters, and that their blind zeal had often led them, in their books and sermons, to praise and recommend the assassination of their enemies, whom they considered as the enemies of all true piety and godliness. The stories of Jael and Sisera, of Ehud and Eglon, resounded from every pulpit. The officers, quartered in the west, received more strict orders to find out and disperse all conventicles; and for that reason the covenanters, instead of meeting in small bodies, were obliged to celebrate their worship in numerous assemblies, and to bring arms for their security. At Rutherglen, a small borough near Glasgow, they openly set

---

[t] Wodrow's History of the sufferings of the church of Scotland, vol. ii. p. 28.

forth a declaration against prelacy; and in the market-place burned several acts of parliament and acts of council, which had established that mode of ecclesiastical government, and had prohibited conventicles. For this insult on the supreme authority, they purposely chose the 29th of May, the anniversary of the restoration; and previously extinguished the bonfires, which had been kindled for that solemnity.

Captain Graham, afterwards viscount Dundee, an active and enterprizing officer, attacked a great conventicle upon Loudonhill, and was repulsed with the loss of thirty men. The covenanters, finding that they were unwarily involved in such deep guilt, were engaged to persevere, and to seek, from their valour and fortune alone, for that indemnity, which the severity of the government left them no hopes of ever being able otherwise to obtain. They pushed on to Glasgow; and though at first repulsed, they afterwards made themselves masters of that city; dispossessed the established clergy; and issued proclamations, in which they declared, that they fought against the king's supremacy, against popery and prelacy, and against a popish successor.

How accidental soever this insurrection might appear, there is reason to suspect, that some great men, in combination with the popular leaders in England, had secretly instigated the covenanters to proceed to such extremities,[u] and hoped for the same effects that had forty years before ensued from the disorders in Scotland. The king also, apprehensive of like consequences, immediately dispatched thither Monmouth with a small body of English cavalry. That nobleman joined to these troops the Scottish guards, and some regiments of militia, levied from the well affected counties; and with great celerity marched in quest of the rebels. They had taken post near Bothwel castle, between Hamilton and Glasgow; where there was no access to them but over a bridge, which a small body was able to defend against the king's forces. They shewed judgment in the choice of their post, but discovered neither judgment nor valour in any other step of their conduct. No nobility and few gentry had joined them: The clergy were in reality the generals; and the whole army never exceeded 8000 men. Monmouth attacked the bridge; and the body of rebels, who defended

Battle of Bothwelbridge.

22d June.

---

[u] Algernon Sidney's letters, p. 90.

it, maintained their post, as long as their ammunition lasted. When they sent for more, they received orders to quit their ground, and to retire backwards. This imprudent measure occasioned an immediate defeat to the covenanters. Monmouth passed the bridge without opposition, and drew up his forces, opposite to the enemy. His cannon alone put them to rout. About 700 fell in the pursuit: For properly speaking there was no action. Twelve hundred were taken prisoners; and were treated by Monmouth with a humanity, which they had never experienced in their own countrymen. Such of them as would promise to live peaceably were dismissed. About three hundred, who were so obstinate as to refuse this easy condition, were shipped for Barbadoes; but unfortunately perished in the voyage. Two of their clergy were hanged. Monmouth was of a generous disposition; and besides, aimed at popularity in Scotland. The king intended to intrust the government of that kingdom in his hands. He had married a Scottish lady, heir of a great family, and allied to all the chief nobility. And Lauderdale, as he was now declining in his parts, and was much decayed in his memory, began to lose with the king that influence, which he had maintained during so many years; notwithstanding the efforts of his numerous enemies both in Scotland and England, and notwithstanding the many violent and tyrannical actions, of which he had been guilty. Even at present he retained so much influence as to poison all the good intentions, which the king, either of himself or by Monmouth's suggestion, had formed with regard to Scotland. An act of indemnity was granted; but Lauderdale took care, that it should be so worded as rather to afford protection to himself and his associates, than to the unhappy covenanters. And though orders were given to connive thenceforwards at all conventicles, he found means, under a variety of pretences, to elude the execution of them. It must be owned however to his praise, that he was the chief person, who, by his counsel, occasioned the expeditious march of the forces and the prompt orders given to Monmouth; and thereby disappointed all the expectations of the English malcontents, who, reflecting on the disposition of men's minds in both kingdoms, had entertained great hopes from the progress of the Scottish insurrection.

LXVIII

State of parties – State of the ministry –
Meal-tub plot – Whig and Tory – A new parliament –
Violence of the commons – Exclusion bill –
Arguments for and against the exclusion –
Exclusion-bill rejected – Trial of Stafford –
His execution – Violence of the commons –
Dissolution of the parliament – New
parliament at Oxford – Fitzharris's
case – Parliament dissolved –
Victory of the royalists

THE KING, observing that the whole nation concurred at first in the belief and prosecution of the popish plot, had found it necessary for his own safety to pretend, in all public speeches and transactions, an entire belief and acquiescence in that famous absurdity, and by this artifice he had eluded the violent and irresistible torrent of the people. When a little time and recollection, as well as the execution of the pretended conspirators, had somewhat moderated the general fury, he was now enabled to form a considerable party, devoted to the interests of the crown, and determined to oppose the pretensions of the malcontents.

In every mixed government, such as that of England, the bulk of the nation will always incline to preserve the entire frame of the constitution; but according to the various prejudices, interests, and

1679.

State of parties.

dispositions of men, some will ever attach themselves with more passion to the regal, others to the popular part of the government. Though the king, after his restoration, had endeavoured to abolish the distinction of parties, and had chosen his ministers from among all denominations; no sooner had he lost his popularity, and exposed himself to general jealousy, than he found it necessary to court the old cavalier party, and to promise them full compensation for that neglect, of which they had hitherto complained. The present emergence made it still more necessary for him to apply for their support; and there were many circumstances, which determined them, at this time, to fly to the assistance of the crown, and to the protection of the royal family.

A party, strongly attached to monarchy, will naturally be jealous of the right of succession, by which alone, they believe, stability to be preserved in the government, and a barrier fixed against the encroachments of popular assemblies. The project, openly embraced, of excluding the duke, appeared to that party a dangerous innovation: And the design, secretly projected, of advancing Monmouth, made them apprehensive, lest the inconveniencies of a disputed succession should be propagated to all posterity. While the jealous lovers of liberty maintained, that a king, whose title depended on the parliament, would naturally be more attentive to the interests, at least to the humours of the people; the passionate admirers of monarchy considered all dependance as a degradation of kingly government, and a great step towards the establishment of a commonwealth in England.

But though his union with the political royalists brought great accession of force to the king, he derived no less support from the confederacy, which he had, at this time, the address to form with the church of England. He represented to the ecclesiastics the great number of presbyterians and other sectaries, who had entered into the popular party; the encouragement and favour which they met with; the loudness of their cries with regard to popery and arbitrary power. And he made the established clergy and their adherents apprehend, that the old scheme for the abolition of prelacy as well as monarchy was revived, and that the same miseries and oppressions awaited them, to which, during the civil wars and usurpations, they had so long been exposed.

The memory also of those dismal times united many indifferent and impartial persons to the crown, and begat a dread lest the zeal for liberty should engraft itself on fanaticism, and should once more kindle a civil war in the kingdom. Had not the king still retained the prerogative of dissolving the parliament, there was indeed reason to apprehend the renewal of all the pretensions and violences, which had ushered in the last commotions. The one period appeared an exact counter-part to the other: But still discerning judges could perceive, both in the spirit of the parties and in the genius of the prince, a material difference; by means of which Charles was enabled at last, though with the imminent peril of liberty, to preserve the peace of the nation.

The cry against popery was loud; but it proceeded less from religious than from party zeal, in those who propagated, and even in those who adopted it. The spirit of enthusiasm had occasioned so much mischief, and had been so successfully exploded, that it was not possible, by any artifice, again to revive and support it. Cant had been ridiculed; hypocrisy detected; the pretensions to a more thorough reformation, and to greater purity, had become suspicious; and instead of denominating themselves the *godly* party, the appellation affected at the beginning of the civil wars, the present patriots were content with calling themselves the *good* and the *honest* party: [w] A sure prognostic, that their measures were not to be so furious, nor their pretensions so exorbitant.

The king too, though not endowed with the integrity and strict principles of his father, was happy in a more amiable manner, and more popular address. Far from being distant, stately, or reserved, he had not a grain of pride or vanity in his whole composition,[x] but was the most affable, best bred man alive. He treated his subjects like noblemen, like gentlemen, like freemen; not like vassals or boors. His professions were plausible, his whole behaviour engaging; so that he won upon the hearts, even while he lost the good opinion of his subjects, and often balanced their judgment of things by their personal inclination.[y] In his public conduct likewise, though he had sometimes embraced measures dangerous to the liberty and religion of his people, he had never been found to persevere obstinately in them, but had always returned into that

[w] Temple, vol. i. p. 335.   [x] Temple, vol. i. p. 449.   [y] Dissertation on parties, letter vii.

path, which their united opinion seemed to point out to him. And upon the whole, it appeared to many cruel and even iniquitous, to remark too rigorously the failings of a prince, who discovered so much facility in correcting his errors, and so much lenity in pardoning the offences committed against himself.

The general affection, borne the king, appeared signally about this time. He fell sick at Windsor; and had two or three fits of a fever, so violent as made his life be thought in danger. A general consternation seized all ranks of men, encreased by the apprehensions entertained of his successor. In the present disposition of men's minds, the king's death, to use an expression of sir William Temple,[z] was regarded as the end of the world. The malcontents, it was feared, would proceed to extremities, and immediately kindle a civil war in the kingdom. Either their entire success, or entire failure, or even the balance and contest of parties, seemed all of them events equally fatal. The king's chief counsellors, therefore, *State of the ministry.* Essex, Halifax, and Sunderland, who stood on bad terms with Shaftesbury and the popular party, advised him to send secretly for the duke, that, in case of any sinister accident, that prince might be ready to assert his right against the opposition, which he *2d Sept.* was likely to meet with. When the duke arrived, he found his brother out of danger; and it was agreed to conceal the invitation, which he had received. His journey, however, was attended with important consequences. He prevailed on the king to disgrace Monmouth, whose projects were now known and avowed; to deprive him of his command in the army; and to send him beyond sea. He himself returned to Brussels; but made a short stay in that place. He obtained leave to retire to Scotland, under pretence still of quieting the apprehensions of the English nation; but in reality with a view of securing that kingdom in his interests.

Though Essex and Halifax had concurred in the resolution of inviting over the duke, they soon found, that they had not obtained his confidence, and that even the king, while he made use of their service, had no sincere regard for their persons. Essex in disgust resigned the treasury: Halifax retired to his country-seat: Temple, despairing of any accommodation among such enraged parties, withdrew almost entirely to his books and his gardens. The

---

[z] Vol. i. p. 342.

CHAPTER LXVIII

king, who changed ministers as well as measures with great indifference, bestowed at this time his chief confidence on Hyde, Sunderland, and Godolphin. Hyde succeeded Essex in the treasury.

All the king's ministers, as well as himself, were extremely
averse to the meeting of the new parliament, which they expected
to find as refractory as any of the preceding. The elections had
gone mostly in favour of the country party. The terrors of the plot
had still a mighty influence over the populace; and the apprehensions of the duke's bigoted principles and arbitrary character
weighed with men of sense and reflection. The king therefore
resolved to prorogue the parliament, that he might try, whether
time would allay those humours, which, by every other expedient,
he had in vain attempted to mollify. In this measure he did not
expect the concurrence of his council. He knew, that those popular
leaders, whom he had admitted, would zealously oppose a resolution, which disconcerted all their schemes; and that the royalists
would not dare, by supporting it, to expose themselves to the
vengeance of the parliament, when it should be assembled. These
reasons obliged him to take this step entirely of himself; and he
only declared his resolution in council. It is remarkable, that,
though the king had made profession never to embrace any measure without the advice of these counsellors, he had often broken
that resolution, and had been necessitated, in affairs of the greatest
consequence, to controul their opinion. Many of them in disgust
threw up about this time; particularly lord Russel, the most popular man in the nation, as well from the mildness and integrity of his
character, as from his zealous attachment to the religion and liberties of his country. Though carried into some excesses, his intentions were ever esteemed upright; and being heir to the greatest fortune in the kingdom, as well as void of ambition, men
believed, that nothing but the last necessity could ever engage him
to embrace any desperate measures. Shaftesbury, who was, in most
particulars, of an opposite character, was removed by the king
from the office of president of the council; and the earl of Radnor,
a man who possessed whimsical talents and splenetic virtues, was
substituted in his place.

It was the favour and countenance of the parliament, which
had chiefly encouraged the rumour of plots; but the nation had
gotten so much into that vein of credulity, and every necessitous

villain was so much incited by the success of Oates and Bedloe, that, even during the prorogation, the people were not allowed to remain in tranquillity. There was one Dangerfield, a fellow who had been burned in the hand for crimes, transported, whipped, pilloried four times, fined for cheats, outlawed for felony, convicted of coining, and exposed to all the public infamy, which the laws could inflict on the basest and most shameful enormities. The credulity of the people, and the humour of the times enabled even this man to become a person of consequence. He was the author *Meal-tub-* of a new incident, called the meal-tub-plot, from the place where *plot.* some papers, relating to it, were found. The bottom of this affair it is difficult, and not very material, to discover. It only appears, that Dangerfield, under pretence of betraying the conspiracies of the presbyterians, had been countenanced by some catholics of condition, and had even been admitted to the duke's presence and the king's. And that under pretence of revealing new popish plots, he had obtained access to Shaftesbury and some of the popular leaders. Which side he intended to cheat, is uncertain; or whether he did not rather mean to cheat both: But he soon found, that the belief of the nation was more open to a popish than a presbyterian plot; and he resolved to strike in with the prevailing humour. Though no weight could be laid on his testimony, great clamour was raised; as if the court, by way of retaliation, had intended to load the presbyterians with the guilt of a false conspiracy. It must be confessed, that the present period, by the prevalence and suspicion of such mean and ignoble arts on all sides, throws a great stain on the British annals.

17th   One of the most innocent artifices, practised by party men at
Nov.   this time, was the additional ceremony, pomp, and expence, with which a pope-burning was celebrated in London: The spectacle served to entertain, and amuse, and inflame the populace. The duke of Monmouth likewise came over without leave, and made a triumphant procession through many parts of the kingdom, extremely caressed and admired by the people. All these arts seemed requisite to support the general prejudices, during the long interval of parliament. Great endeavours were also used to obtain the *1680.*   king's consent for the meeting of that assembly. Seventeen peers presented a petition to this purpose. Many of the corporations imitated the example. Notwithstanding several marks of dis-

pleasure, and even a menacing proclamation from the king, petitions came from all parts, earnestly insisting on a session of parliament. The danger of popery, and the terrors of the plot were never forgotten in any of these addresses.

Tumultuous petitioning was one of the chief artifices by which the malcontents in the last reign had attacked the crown: And though the manner of subscribing and delivering petitions was now somewhat regulated by act of parliament, the thing itself still remained; and was an admirable expedient for infesting the court, for spreading discontent, and for uniting the nation in any popular clamour. As the king found no law, by which he could punish those importunate, and, as he deemed them, undutiful solicitations, he was obliged to encounter them by popular applications of a contrary tendency. Wherever the church and court party prevailed, addresses were framed, containing expressions of the highest regard to his majesty, the most entire acquiescence in his wisdom, the most dutiful submission to his prerogative, and the deepest *abhorrence* of those, who endeavoured to encroach upon it, by prescribing to him any time for assembling the parliament. Thus the nation came to be distinguished into *petitioners* and *abhorrers*. Factions indeed were at this time extremely animated against each other. The very names, by which each party denominated its antagonist, discover the virulence and rancour, which prevailed. For besides petitioner and abhorrer, appellations which were soon forgotten, this year is remarkable for being the epoch of the well-known epithets of W H I G and T O R Y, by which, and sometimes without any material difference, this island has been so long divided. The court party reproached their antagonists with their affinity to the fanatical conventiclers in Scotland, who were known by the name of whigs: The country party found a resemblance between the courtiers and the popish banditti in Ireland, to whom the appellation of tory was affixed. And after this manner, these foolish terms of reproach came into public and general use; and even at present seem not nearer their end than when they were first invented.

Whig and tory.

The king used every art to encourage his partizans, and to reconcile the people to his government. He persevered in the great zeal which he affected against popery. He even allowed several priests to be put to death, for no other crime than their having received orders in the Romish church. It is singular, that one of them, called Evans, was playing at tennis, when the warrant for his immediate execution was notified to him: He swore, that he would play out his set first. Charles, with the same view of acquiring popularity, formed an alliance with Spain, and also offered an alliance to Holland: But the Dutch, terrified with the great power of France, and seeing little resource in a country so distracted as England, declined acceptance. He had sent for the duke from Scotland, but desired him to return, when the time of assembling the parliament began to approach.

It was of great consequence to the popular party, while the meeting of parliament depended on the king's will, to keep the law, whose operations are perpetual, entirely on their side. The sheriffs of London by their office return the juries: It had been usual for the mayor to nominate one sheriff by drinking to him; and the common hall had ever without dispute confirmed the mayor's choice. Sir Robert Clayton, the mayor, appointed one who was not acceptable to the popular party: The common-hall rejected him; and Bethel and Cornish, two independants, and republicans, and of consequence deeply engaged with the malcontents, were chosen by a majority of voices. In spite of all remonstrances and opposition, the citizens persisted in their choice; and the court party was obliged for the present to acquiesce.

Juries however were not so partial in the city; but that reason and justice, even when the popish plot was in question, could sometimes prevail. The earl of Castlemaine, husband to the dutchess of Cleveland, was acquitted about this time, though accused by Oates and Dangerfield of an intention to assassinate the king. Sir Thomas Gascoigne, a very aged gentleman in the north, being accused by two servants, whom he had dismissed for dishonesty, received a like verdict. These trials were great blows to the plot, which now began to stagger, in the judgment of most men, except those who were entirely devoted to the country party. But in order still to keep alive the zeal against popery, the earl of Shaftesbury appeared in Westminster-hall, attended by the earl of Huntingdon, the lords Russel, Cavendish, Grey, Brandon, Sir Henry Caverly, Sir Gilbert Gerrard, Sir William Cooper, and other persons of distinction, and presented to the grand jury of Middlesex reasons for indicting the duke of York as a popish recusant. While

23d
June.

CHAPTER LXVIII

the jury were deliberating on this extraordinary presentment, the chief justice sent for them, and suddenly, even somewhat irregularly, dismissed them. Shaftesbury however obtained the end for which he had undertaken this bold measure: He showed to all his followers the desperate resolution, which he had embraced, never to admit of any accommodation or composition with the duke. By such daring conduct he gave them assurance, that he was fully determined not to desert their cause; and he engaged them to a like devoted perseverance in all the measures, which he should suggest to them.

As the kingdom was regularly and openly divided into two zealous parties, it was not difficult for the king to know, that the majority of the new house of commons was engaged in interests opposite to the court: But that he might leave no expedient untried, which could compose the unhappy differences among his subjects, he resolved, at last, after a long interval, to assemble the parliament. In his speech, he told them, that the several prorogations, which he had made, had been very advantageous to his neighbours, and very useful to himself: That he had employed that interval in perfecting with the crown of Spain an alliance, which had often been desired by former parliaments, and which, he doubted not, would be extremely agreeable to them: That, in order to give weight to this measure, and render it beneficial to Christendom, it was necessary to avoid all domestic dissensions, and to unite themselves firmly in the same views and purposes: That he was determined, that nothing on his part should be wanting to such a salutary end; and provided the succession were preserved in its due and legal course, he would concur in any expedient for the security of the protestant religion: That the farther examination of the popish plot and the punishment of the criminals were requisite for the safety both of king and kingdom. And after recommending to them the necessity of providing, by some supplies, for the safety of Tangiers, he proceeded in these words: "But that which I value above all the treasure in the world, and which I am sure will give us greater strength and reputation both at home and abroad than any treasure can do, is a perfect union among ourselves. Nothing but this can restore the kingdom to that strength and vigour which it seems to have lost, and raise us again to that consideration, which England hath usually possessed. All

21st.
Octob.
A new
parlia-
ment.

Europe have their eyes upon this assembly, and think their own happiness and misery, as well as ours, will depend upon it. If we should be so unhappy as to fall into misunderstandings among ourselves to that degree as would render our friendship unsafe to trust to, it will not be wondered at, if our neighbours should begin to take new resolutions, and perhaps such as may be fatal to us. Let us therefore take care, that we do not gratify our enemies, and discourage our friends, by any unseasonable disputes. If any such do happen, the world will see, that it is no fault of mine: For I have done all that it was possible for me to do, to keep you in peace, while I live, and to leave you so, when I die. But from so great prudence and so good affection as yours, I can fear nothing of this kind; but do rely upon you all, that you will do your best endeavours to bring this parliament to a good and happy conclusion."

Violence of the commons.

All these mollifying expressions had no influence with the commons. Every step, which they took, betrayed the zeal, with which they were animated. They voted, that it was the undoubted right of the subject to petition the king for the calling and sitting of parliament. Not content with this decision, which seems justifiable in a mixed monarchy, they fell with the utmost violence on all those *abhorrers,* who, in their addresses to the crown, had expressed their disapprobation of those petitions. They did not reflect, that it was as lawful for one party of men, as for another, to express their sense of public affairs; and that the best established right may, in particular circumstances, be abused, and even the exercise of it become an object of abhorrence. For this offence, they expelled Sir Thomas Withens. They appointed a committee for farther enquiry into such members as had been guilty of a like crime; and complaints were lodged against lord Paston, Sir Robert Malverer, Sir Bryan Stapleton, Taylor, and Turner. They addressed the king against Sir George Jefferies, recorder of London, for his activity in the same cause; and they frightened him into a resignation of his office, in which he was succeeded by Sir George Treby, a great leader of the popular party. They voted an impeachment against North, chief justice of the common pleas, for drawing the proclamation against tumultuous petitions: But upon examination found the proclamation so cautiously worded, that it afforded them no handle against him. A petition had been

CHAPTER LXVIII

presented to the king from Taunton. "How dare you deliver me such a paper?" said the king to the person who presented it. "Sir," replied he, "my name is DARE." For this saucy reply, but under other pretences, he had been tried, fined, and committed to prison. The commons now addressed the king for his liberty and for remitting his fine. Some printers also and authors of seditious libels they took under their protection.

Great numbers of the abhorrers, from all parts of England, were seized by order of the commons, and committed to custody. The liberty of the subject, which had been so carefully guarded by the great charter, and by the late law of habeas corpus, was every day violated by their arbitrary and capricious commitments. The chief jealousy, it is true, of the English constitution is naturally and justly directed against the crown; nor indeed have the commons any other means of securing their privileges than by commitments, which, as they cannot beforehand be exactly determined by law, must always appear in some degree arbitrary. Sensible of these reasons, the people had hitherto, without murmuring, seen this discretionary power exercised by the house: But as it was now carried to excess, and was abused to serve the purposes of faction, great complaints against it were heard from all quarters. At last, the vigour and courage of one Stowel of Exeter, an abhorrer, put an end to the practice. He refused to obey the serjeant at arms, stood upon his defence, and said that he knew of no law, by which they pretended to commit him. The house, finding it equally dangerous to proceed or to recede, got off by an evasion: They inserted in their votes, that Stowel was indisposed, and that a month's time was allowed him for the recovery of his health.

But the chief violence of the house of commons appeared in all their transactions with regard to the plot, which they prosecuted with the same zeal and the same credulity as their predecessors. They renewed the former vote, which affirmed the reality of the horrid popish plot; and, in order the more to terrify the people, they even asserted, that, notwithstanding the discovery, the plot still subsisted. They expelled Sir Robert Can, and Sir Robert Yeomans, who had been complained of, for saying, that there was no popish, but there was a presbyterian plot. And they greatly lamented the death of Bedloe, whom they called a material witness, and on whose testimony they much depended. He had been seized with a fever at Bristol; had sent for chief justice North; confirmed all his former evidence, except that with regard to the duke and the queen; and desired North to apply to the king for some money to relieve him in his necessities. A few days after, he expired; and the whole party triumphed extremely in these circumstances of his death: As if such a testimony could be deemed the affirmation of a dying man, as if his confession of perjury in some instances could assure his veracity in the rest, and as if the perseverance of one profligate could outweigh the last words of so many men, guilty of no crime but that of popery.

The commons even endeavoured, by their countenance and protection, to remove the extreme infamy, with which Dangerfield was loaded, and to restore him to the capacity of being an evidence. The whole tribe of informers they applauded and rewarded: Jennison, Turberville, Dugdale, Smith, la Faria, appeared before them; and their testimony, however frivolous or absurd, met with a favourable reception: The king was applied to in their behalf for pensions and pardons: Their narratives were printed with that sanction, which arose from the approbation of the house: Dr. Tongue was recommended for the first considerable church preferment, which should become vacant. Considering men's determined resolution to believe, instead of admiring that a palpable falshood should be maintained by witnesses, it may justly appear wonderful, that no better evidence was ever produced against the catholics.

The principal reasons, which still supported the clamour of the popish plot, were the apprehensions entertained by the people, of the duke of York, and the resolution, embraced by their leaders, of *Exclusion-* excluding him from the throne. Shaftesbury and many consid-*bill.* erable men of the party, had rendered themselves irreconcileable with him, and could find their safety no way but in his ruin. Monmouth's friends hoped, that the exclusion of that prince would make way for their patron. The resentment against the duke's apostacy, the love of liberty, the zeal for religion, the attachment to faction; all these motives incited the country party. And above all, what supported the resolution of adhering to the exclusion, and rejecting all other expedients offered, was the hope artfully encouraged, that the king would at last be obliged to yield to their demand. His revenues were extremely burdened; and even if free, could scarcely suffice for the necessary charges of government, much less for that pleasure and expence, to which he was inclined. Though he had withdrawn his countenance from Monmouth, he was known secretly to retain a great affection for him. On no occasion had he ever been found to persist obstinately against difficulties and importunity. And as his beloved mistress, the dutchess of Portsmouth, had been engaged, either from lucrative views, or the hopes of making the succession fall on her own children, to unite herself with the popular party; this incident was regarded as a favourable prognostic of their success. Sunderland, secretary of state, who had linked his interest with that of the dutchess, had concurred in the same measure.

But besides friendship for his brother and a regard to the right of succession, there were many strong reasons, which had determined Charles to persevere in opposing the exclusion. All the royalists and the devotees to the church; that party by which alone monarchy was supported; regarded the right of succession as inviolable; and if abandoned by the king in so capital an article, it was to be feared, that they would, in their turn, desert his cause, and deliver him over to the pretensions and usurpations of the country party. The country party, or the whigs, as they were called, if they did not still retain some propensity towards a republic, were at least affected with a violent jealousy of regal power; and it was equally to be dreaded, that, being enraged with past opposition and animated by present success, they would, if they prevailed in this pretension, be willing as well as able, to reduce the prerogative within very narrow limits. All menaces therefore, all promises were in vain employed against the king's resolution: He never would be prevailed on to desert his friends, and put himself into the hands of his enemies. And having voluntarily made such important concessions, and tendered, over and over again, such strong limitations, he was well pleased to find them rejected by the obstinacy of the commons; and hoped, that, after the spirit of opposition had spent itself in fruitless violence, the time would come, when he might safely appeal against his parliament to his people.

So much were the popular leaders determined to carry matters to extremities, that in less than a week after the commencement of the session, a motion was made for bringing in an exclusion-bill, and a committee was appointed for that purpose. This bill differed in nothing from the former, but in two articles, which showed still an encrease of zeal in the commons: The bill was to be read to the people twice a-year in all the churches of the kingdom, and every one, who should support the duke's title was rendered incapable of receiving a pardon but by act of parliament.

The debates were carried on with great violence on both sides. The bill was defended by Sir William Jones, who had now resigned his office of attorney-general, by lord Russel, by Sir Francis Winnington, Sir Harry Capel, Sir William Pulteney, by colonel Titus, *10th Nov.* Treby, Hambden, Montague. It was opposed by Sir Leoline Jenkins, secretary of state, Sir John Ernley, chancellor of the exchequer, by Hyde, Seymour, Temple. The arguments, transmitted to us, may be reduced to the following topics.

Arguments for and against the exclusion. In every government, said the exclusionists, there is somewhere an authority absolute and supreme; nor can any determination, how unusual soever, which receives the sanction of the legislature, admit afterwards of dispute or controul. The liberty of a constitution, so far from diminishing this absolute power, seems rather to add force to it, and to give it greater influence over the people. The more members of the state concur in any legislative decision, and the more free their voice; the less likelihood is there, that any opposition will be made to those measures, which receive the final sanction of their authority. In England, the legislative power is lodged in king, lords, and commons, which comprehend every order of the community: And there is no pretext for exempting any circumstance of government, not even the succession of the crown, from so full and decisive a jurisdiction. Even express declarations have, in this particular, been made of parliamentary authority: Instances have occurred, where it has been exerted: And though prudential reasons may justly be alledged, why such innovations should not be attempted but on extraordinary occasions, the power and right are for ever vested in the community. But if any occasion can be deemed extraordinary, if any emergence can require unusual expedients, it is the present; when the heir to the crown has renounced the religion of the state, and has zealously embraced a faith, totally hostile and incompatible. A prince of that communion can never put trust in a people, so prejudiced against him: The people must be equally diffident of such a prince: Foreign and destructive alliances will seem to one

CHAPTER LXVIII

the only protection of his throne: Perpetual jealousy, opposition, faction, even insurrections will be employed by the other as the sole securities for their liberty and religion. Though theological principles, when set in opposition to passions, have often small influence on mankind in general, still less on princes; yet when they become symbols of faction, and marks of party distinctions, they concur with one of the strongest passions in the human frame, and are then capable of carrying men to the greatest extremities. Notwithstanding the better judgment and milder disposition of the king; how much has the influence of the duke already disturbed the tenor of government? How often engaged the nation into measures totally destructive of their foreign interests and honour, of their domestic repose and tranquillity? The more the absurdity and incredibility of the popish plot are insisted on, the stronger reason it affords for the exclusion of the duke; since the universal belief of it discovers the extreme antipathy of the nation to his religion, and the utter impossibility of ever bringing them to acquiesce peaceably under the dominion of such a sovereign. The prince, finding himself in so perilous a situation, must seek for security by desperate remedies, and by totally subduing the privileges of a nation, which had betrayed such hostile dispositions towards himself, and towards every thing which he deems the most sacred. It is in vain to propose limitations and expedients. Whatever share of authority is left in the duke's hands, will be employed to the destruction of the nation; and even the additional restraints, by discovering the public diffidence and aversion, will serve him as incitements to put himself in a condition entirely superior and independant. And as the laws of England still make resistance treason, and neither do nor can admit of any positive exceptions; what folly to leave the kingdom in so perilous and absurd a situation; where the greatest virtue will be exposed to the most severe proscription, and where the laws can only be saved by expedients, which these same laws have declared the highest crime and enormity?

The court party reasoned in an opposite manner. An authority, they said, wholly absolute and uncontroulable is a mere chimera, and is no where to be found in any human institutions. All government is founded on opinion and a sense of duty; and wherever the supreme magistrate, by any law or positive prescription, shocks an

opinion regarded as fundamental, and established with a firmness
equal to that of his own authority, he subverts the principle, by
which he himself is established, and can no longer hope for obedience. In European monarchies, the right of succession is justly
esteemed a fundamental; and even though the whole legislature
be vested in a single person, it would never be permitted him by an
edict, to disinherit his lawful heir, and call a stranger or more
distant relation to the throne. Abuses in other parts of government
are capable of redress, from more dispassionate enquiry or better
information of the sovereign, and till then ought patiently to be
endured: But violations of the right of succession draw such terrible consequences after them as are not to be paralleled by any
other grievance or inconvenience. Vainly is it pleaded, that England is a mixed monarchy; and that a law, assented to by king,
lords, and commons, is enacted by the concurrence of every part
of the state: It is plain, that there remains a very powerful party,
who may indeed be out-voted, but who never will deem a law,
subversive of hereditary right, any wise valid or obligatory. Limitations, such as are proposed by the king, give no shock to the
constitution, which, in many particulars, is already limited; and
they may be so calculated as to serve every purpose, sought for by
an exclusion. If the ancient barriers against regal authority have
been able, during so many ages, to remain impregnable; how
much more, those additional ones, which, by depriving the monarch of power, tend so far to their own security? The same jealousy
too of religion, which has engaged the people to lay these restraints upon the successor, will extremely lessen the number of his
partizans, and make it utterly impracticable for him, either by
force or artifice, to break the fetters, imposed upon him. The
king's age and vigorous state of health promise him a long life:
And can it be prudent to tear in pieces the whole state, in order to
provide against a contingency, which, it is very likely, may never
happen? No human schemes can secure the public in all possible,
imaginable, events; and the bill of exclusion itself, however accurately framed, leaves room for obvious and natural suppositions,
to which it pretends not to provide any remedy. Should the duke
have a son, after the king's death must that son, without any default of his own, forfeit his title? or must the princess of Orange
descend from the throne, in order to give place to the lawful

CHAPTER LXVIII

successor? But were all these reasonings false, it still remains to be considered, that, in public deliberations, we seek not the expedient, which is best in itself, but the best of such as are practicable. The king willingly consents to limitations, and has already offered some which are of the utmost importance: But he is determined to endure any extremity rather than allow the right of succession to be invaded. Let us beware of that factious violence, which leads to demand more than will be granted; lest we lose the advantage of those beneficial concessions, and leave the nation, on the king's demise, at the mercy of a zealous prince, irritated with the ill usage, which, he imagines, he has already met with.

In the house of commons, the reasoning of the exclusionists appeared the more convincing; and the bill passed by a great majority. It was in the house of peers that the king expected to oppose it with success. The court party was there so prevalent, that it was carried only by a majority of two to pay so much regard to the bill as even to commit it. When it came to be debated, the contest was violent. Shaftesbury, Sunderland, and Essex argued *15th Nov.* for it: Halifax chiefly conducted the debate against it, and displayed an extent of capacity and a force of eloquence, which had never been surpassed in that assembly. He was animated, as well by the greatness of the occasion, as by a rivalship with his uncle Shaftesbury; whom, during that day's debate, he seemed, in the judgment of all, to have totally eclipsed. The king was present during the whole debate, which was prolonged till eleven at night. The bill was thrown out by a considerable majority. All the bishops, *Exclusion* except three, voted against it. Besides the influence of the court *bill* over them; the church of England, they imagined or pretended, *rejected.* was in greater danger from the prevalence of presbyterianism than of popery, which, though favoured by the duke, and even by the king, was extremely repugnant to the genius of the nation.

The commons discovered much ill humour upon this disappointment. They immediately voted an address for the removal of Halifax from the king's councils and presence for ever. Though the pretended cause was his advising the late frequent prorogations of parliament, the real reason was apparently his vigorous opposition to the exclusion-bill. When the king applied for money to enable him to maintain Tangiers, which he declared his present revenues totally unable to defend; instead of complying, they voted such an address as was in reality a remonstrance, and one little less violent than that famous remonstrance, which ushered in the civil wars. All the abuses of government, from the beginning almost of the reign, are there insisted on; the Dutch war, the alliance with France, the prorogations and dissolutions of parliament; and as all these measures, as well as the *damnable* and *hellish* plot, are there ascribed to the machinations of papists, it was plainly insinuated, that the king had, all along, lain under the influence of that party, and was in reality the chief conspirator against the religion and liberties of his people.

The commons, though they conducted the great business of the exclusion with extreme violence and even imprudence, had yet much reason for the jealousy, which gave rise to it: But their vehement prosecution of the popish plot even after so long an interval, discovers such a spirit, either of credulity or injustice, as admits of no apology. The impeachment of the catholic lords in the Tower was revived; and as viscount Stafford, from his age, infirmities, and narrow capacity, was deemed the least capable of defending himself, it was determined to make him the first victim, that his condemnation might pave the way for a sentence against the rest. The chancellor, now created earl of Nottingham, was appointed high steward for conducting the trial.

30th Nov.

Three witnesses were produced against the prisoner; Oates, Dugdale, and Turberville. Oates swore, that he saw Fenwic, the jesuit, deliver to Stafford a commission signed by de Oliva, general of the jesuits, appointing him pay-master to the papal army, which was to be levied for the subduing of England: For this ridiculous imposture still maintained its credit with the commons. Dugdale gave testimony, that the prisoner, at Tixal, a seat of lord Aston's, had endeavoured to engage him in the design of murdering the king; and had promised him, besides the honour of being sainted by the church, a reward of 500 pounds for that service. Turberville deposed, that the prisoner, in his own house at Paris, had made him a like proposal. To offer money for murdering a king, without laying down any scheme, by which the assassin may insure some probability or possibility of escape, is so incredible in itself, and may so easily be maintained by any prostitute evidence, that an accusation of that nature, not accompanied with circumstances, ought very little to be attended to by any court of judicature. But

Trial of Stafford,

CHAPTER LXVIII

notwithstanding the small hold, which the witnesses afforded, the prisoner was able in many material particulars, to discredit their testimony. It was sworn by Dugdale, that Stafford had assisted in a great consult of the catholics held at Tixal; but Stafford proved by undoubted testimony, that at the time assigned he was in Bath, and in that neighbourhood. Turberville had served a noviciate among the Dominicans; but having deserted the convent, he had enlisted as a trooper in the French army; and being dismissed that service, he now lived in London, abandoned by all his relations, and exposed to great poverty. Stafford proved, by the evidence of his gentleman and his page, that Turberville had never, either at Paris or at London, been seen in his company; and it might justly appear strange, that a person, who had so important a secret in his keeping, was so long entirely neglected by him.

The clamour and outrage of the populace, during the trial, were extreme: Great abilities and eloquence were displayed by the managers, Sir William Jones, Sir Francis Winnington, and serjeant Maynard: Yet did the prisoner, under all these disadvantages, make a better defence than was expected, either by his friends or his enemies: The unequal contest, in which he was engaged, was a plentiful source of compassion to every mind, seasoned with humanity. He represented, that, during a course of forty years, from the very commencement of the civil wars, he had, through many dangers, difficulties and losses, still maintained his loyalty: And was it credible, that now, in his old age, easy in his circumstances, but dispirited by infirmities, he would belye the whole course of his life, and engage against his royal master, from whom he had ever received kind treatment, in the most desperate and most bloody of all conspiracies? He remarked the infamy of the witnesses; the contradictions and absurdities of their testimony; the extreme indigence in which they had lived, though engaged, as they pretended, in a conspiracy with kings, princes, and nobles; the credit and opulence to which they were at present raised. With a simplicity and tenderness more persuasive than the greatest oratory, he still made protestations of his innocence, and could not forbear, every moment, expressing the most lively surprize and indignation at the audacious impudence of the witnesses.

It will appear astonishing to us, as it did to Stafford himself, that the peers, after a solemn trial of six days, should, by a majority of twenty-four voices, give sentence against him. He received however with resignation the fatal verdict. *God's holy name be praised,* was the only exclamation which he uttered. When the high-steward told him, that the peers would intercede with the king for remitting the more cruel and ignominious parts of the sentence, hanging and quartering; he burst into tears: But he told the lords, that he was moved to this weakness, by his sense of their goodness, not by any terror of that fate, which he was doomed to suffer.

It is remarkable, that, after Charles, as is usual in such cases, had remitted to Stafford the hanging and quartering, the two sheriffs, Bethel and Cornish, indulging their own republican humour, and complying with the prevalent spirit of their party, ever jealous of monarchy, started a doubt with regard to the king's power of exercising even this small degree of lenity. "Since he cannot pardon the whole," said they, "how can he have power to remit any part of the sentence?" They proposed the doubt to both houses: The peers pronounced it superfluous; and even the commons, apprehensive lest a question of this nature might make way for Stafford's escape, gave this singular answer. "This house is *content,* that the sheriffs do execute William late viscount Stafford by severing his head from his body *only.*" Nothing can be a stronger proof of the fury of the times, than that lord Russel, notwithstanding the virtue and humanity of his character, seconded in the house this barbarous scruple of the sheriffs.

In the interval between the sentence and execution, many efforts were made to shake the resolution of the infirm and aged prisoner, and to bring him to some confession of the treason, for which he was condemned. It was even rumoured, that he had confessed; and the zealous partymen, who, no doubt, had secretly, notwithstanding their credulity, entertained some doubts with regard to the reality of the popish conspiracy, expressed great triumph on the occasion. But Stafford, when again called before the house of peers, discovered many schemes, which had been laid by himself and others for procuring a toleration to the catholics, at least a mitigation of the penal laws, enacted against them: And he protested, that this was the sole treason, of which he had ever been guilty.

Stafford now prepared himself for death with the intrepidity, which became his birth and station, and which was the natural

CHAPTER LXVIII

result of the innocence and integrity, which, during the course of a long life, he had ever maintained: His mind seemed even to collect new force from the violence and oppression, under which he laboured. When going to execution, he called for a cloak to defend him against the rigour of the season. "Perhaps," said he, "I may shake with cold; but, I trust in God, not for fear." On the scaffold, he continued, with reiterated and earnest asseverations, to make protestations of his innocence: All his fervour was exercised on that point: When he mentioned the witnesses, whose perjuries had bereaved him of life, his expressions were full of mildness and of charity. He solemnly disavowed all those immoral principles, which over-zealous protestants had ascribed without distinction to the church of Rome: And he hoped, he said, that the time was now approaching, when the present delusion would be dissipated; and when the force of truth, though late, would engage the whole world to make reparation to his injured honour.

29th Dec.

and execution.

The populace, who had exulted at Stafford's trial and condemnation, were now melted into tears, at the sight of that tender fortitude, which shone forth in each feature, and motion, and accent of this aged noble. Their profound silence was only interrupted by sighs and groans. With difficulty they found speech to assent to those protestations of innocence, which he frequently repeated: "We believe you, my lord! God bless you, my lord!" These expressions with a faultering accent flowed from them. The executioner himself was touched with sympathy. Twice he lifted up the ax, with an intent to strike the fatal blow; and as often felt his resolution to fail him. A deep sigh was heard to accompany his last effort, which laid Stafford for ever at rest. All the spectators seemed to feel the blow. And when the head was held up to them with the usual cry, *This is the head of a traitor,* no clamour of assent was uttered. Pity, remorse, and astonishment had taken possession of every heart, and displayed itself in every countenance.

This is the last blood which was shed on account of the popish plot: An incident, which, for the credit of the nation, it were better to bury in eternal oblivion; but which it is necessary to perpetuate, as well to maintain the truth of history, as to warn, if possible, their posterity and all mankind never again to fall into so shameful, so barbarous a delusion.

The execution of Stafford gratified the prejudices of the country party; but it contributed nothing to their power and security: On the contrary, by exciting commiseration, it tended still farther to encrease that disbelief of the whole plot, which began now to prevail. The commons, therefore, not to lose the present opportunity, resolved to make both friends and enemies sensible of their power. They passed a bill for easing the protestant dissenters, and for repealing the persecuting statute of the thirty-fifth of Elizabeth: This laudable bill was likewise carried through the house of peers. The chief justice was very obnoxious for dismissing the grand jury in an irregular manner, and thereby disappointing that bold measure of Shaftesbury and his friends, who had presented the duke as a recusant. For this crime the commons sent up an impeachment against him; as also against Jones and Weston, two of the judges, who, in some speeches from the bench, had gone so far as to give to many of the first reformers the appellation of fanatics.

The king, in rejecting the exclusion bill, had sheltered himself securely behind the authority of the house of peers; and the commons had been deprived of the usual pretence, to attack the sovereign himself, under colour of attacking his ministers and counsellors. In prosecution however of the scheme, which he had formed, of throwing the blame on the commons in case of any rupture, he made them a new speech. After warning them, that a neglect of this opportunity would never be retrieved, he added these words: "I did promise you the fullest satisfaction, which your hearts could wish, for the security of the protestant religion, and to concur with you in any remedies, which might consist with preserving the succession of the crown in its due and legal course of descent. I do again, with the same reservations, renew the same promises to you: And being thus ready on my part to do all that can reasonably be expected from me, I should be glad to know from you, as soon as may be, how far I shall be assisted by you, and what it is you desire from me."

The most reasonable objection against the limitations, proposed by the king, is, that they introduced too considerable an innovation in the government, and almost totally annihilated the power of the future monarch. But considering the present disposition of the commons and their leaders, we may fairly presume, that this objection would have small weight with them, and that their disgust against the court would rather incline them to diminish than support regal authority. They still hoped, from the king's urgent necessities and his usual facility, that he would throw himself wholly into their hands; and that thus, without waiting for the accession of the duke, they might immediately render themselves absolute masters of the government. The commons, therefore, besides insisting still on the exclusion, proceeded to bring in bills of an important, and some of them of an alarming nature: One to renew the triennial act, which had been so inadvertently repealed in the beginning of the reign: A second to make the office of judge during good behaviour: A third to declare the levying of money without consent of parliament to be high treason: A fourth to order an association for the safety of his majesty's person, for defence of the protestant religion, for the preservation of the protestant subjects against all invasions and opposition whatsoever, and for preventing the duke of York or any papist from succeeding to the crown. The memory of the covenant was too recent for men to overlook the consequences of such an association: And the king, who was particularly conversant in Davila, could not fail of recollecting a memorable foreign instance, to fortify this domestic experience.

Violence of the commons.

The commons also passed many votes, which, though they had not the authority of laws, served however to discover the temper and disposition of the house. They voted, that whoever had advised his majesty to refuse the exclusion bill, were promoters of popery and enemies to the king and kingdom. In another vote, they named the marquess of Worcester, the earls of Clarendon, Feversham, and Halifax, Laurence Hyde, and Edward Seymour, as those dangerous enemies; and they requested his majesty to remove them from his person and councils for ever: They voted, that, till the exclusion bill were passed, they could not, consistent with the trust reposed in them, grant the king any manner of supply. And lest he should be enabled, by any other expedient, to support the government, and preserve himself independant, they passed another vote, in which they declared, that whoever should hereafter lend, by way of advance, any money upon those branches of the king's revenue, arising from customs, excise, or hearth money, should be judged a hinderer of the sitting of parliament, and be responsible for the same in parliament.

The king might presume, that the peers, who had rejected the exclusion bill, would still continue to defend the throne, and that none of the dangerous bills, introduced into the other house, would ever be presented for the royal assent and approbation. But as there remained no hopes of bringing the commons to any better temper, and as their farther sitting served only to keep faction alive, and to perpetuate the general ferment of the nation, he came secretly to a resolution of proroguing them. They got intelligence about a quarter of an hour before the black rod came to their door. Not to lose such precious time, they passed in a tumultuous manner some extraordinary resolutions. They voted, *that* whosoever advised his majesty to prorogue this parliament to any other purpose than in order to pass the bill of exclusion, was a betrayer of the king, of the protestant religion, and of the kingdom of England; a promoter of the French interest, and a pensioner of France: *That* thanks be given to the city of London for their manifest loyalty, and for their care and vigilance in the preservation of the king and of the protestant religion: *That* it is the opinion of this house, that that city was burned in the year 1666 by the papists, designing thereby to introduce arbitrary power and popery into the kingdom: *That* humble application be made to his majesty for restoring the duke of Monmouth to all his offices and commands, from which, it appears to the house, he had been removed by the influence of the duke of York. And *that* it is the opinion of the house that the prosecution of the protestant dissenters upon the penal laws is at this time grievous to the subject, a weakening of the protestant interest, an encouragement of popery, and dangerous to the peace of the kingdom.

1681.
10th Jan.
Dissolution of the parliament.

The king passed some laws of no great importance: But the bill for repealing the thirty-fifth of Elizabeth, he privately ordered the clerk of the crown not to present to him. By this artifice, which was equally disobliging to the country party as if the bill had been rejected, and at the same time implied some timidity in the king, that salutary act was for the present eluded. The king had often of himself attempted, and sometimes by irregular means, to give indulgence to nonconformists: But besides that he had usually expected to comprehend the catholics in this liberty, the present refractory disposition of the sectaries had much incensed him against them; and he was resolved, if possible, to keep them still at mercy.

CHAPTER LXVIII

The last votes of the commons seemed to be an attempt of forming indirectly an association against the crown, after they found, that their association bill could not pass: The dissenting interest, the city, and the duke of Monmouth, they endeavoured to connect with the country party. A civil war indeed never appeared so likely as at present; and it was high time for the king to dissolve a parliament, which seemed to have entertained such dangerous projects. Soon after, he summoned another. Though he observed, that the country party had established their interest so strongly in all the electing burroughs, that he could not hope for any disposition more favourable in the new parliament, this expedient was still a prosecution of his former project, of trying every method, by which he might form an accommodation with the commons: And if all failed, he hoped, that he could the better justify to his people, at least to his party, a final breach with them.

It had always been much regretted by the royalists, during the civil wars, that the long parliament had been assembled at Westminster, and had thereby received force and encouragement from the vicinity of a potent and factious city, which had zealously embraced their party. Though the king was now possessed of guards, which in some measure overawed the populace, he was determined still farther to obviate all inconveniencies; and he summoned the new parliament to meet at Oxford. The city of London showed how just a judgment he had formed of their dispositions. Besides re-electing the same members, they voted thanks to them for their former behaviour, in endeavouring to discover the depth of the *horrid* and *hellish* popish plot, and to exclude the duke of York, the principal cause of the ruin and misery, impending over the nation. Monmouth with fifteen peers presented a petition against assembling the parliament at Oxford, "where the two houses," they said, "could not be in safety; but would be easily exposed to the swords of the papists and their adherents, of whom too many had creeped into his majesty's guards." These insinuations, which pointed so evidently at the king himself, were not calculated to persuade him, but to inflame the people.

The exclusionists might have concluded, both from the king's dissolution of the last parliament, and from his summoning of the present to meet at Oxford, that he was determined to maintain his declared resolution of rejecting their favourite bill: But they still flattered themselves, that his urgent necessities would influence his easy temper, and finally gain them the ascendant. The leaders came to parliament, attended not only by their servants, but by numerous bands of their partizans. The four city members in particular were followed by great multitudes, wearing ribbons, in which were woven these words, *No popery! No slavery!* The king had his guards regularly mustered: His party likewise endeavoured to make a show of their strength: And on the whole, the assembly at Oxford rather bore the appearance of a tumultuous Polish diet, than of a regular English parliament.

21st. March.

The king, who had hitherto employed the most gracious expressions to all his parliaments, particularly the two last, thought proper to address himself to the present in a more authoritative manner. He complained of the unwarrantable proceedings of the former house of commons; and said, that, as he would never use arbitrary government himself, neither would he ever suffer it in others. By calling, however, this parliament so soon, he had sufficiently shown, that no past irregularities could inspire him with a prejudice against those assemblies. He now afforded them, he added, yet another opportunity of providing for the public safety; and to all the world had given one evidence more, that on his part he had not neglected the duty incumbent on him.

New parliament at Oxford.

The commons were not over-awed by the magisterial air of the king's speech. They consisted almost entirely of the same members; they chose the same speaker; and they instantly fell into the same measures, the impeachment of Danby, the repeal of the persecuting statute of Elizabeth, the enquiry into the popish plot, and the bill of exclusion. So violent were they on this last article, that no other expedient, however plausible, could so much as be hearkened to. Ernley, one of the king's ministers, proposed, that the duke should be banished, during life, five hundred miles from England, and that on the king's demise the next heir should be constituted regent with regal power: Yet even this expedient, which left the duke only the bare title of king, could not, though seconded by Sir Thomas Lyttleton and Sir Thomas Mompesson, obtain the attention of the house. The past disappointments of the country party, and the opposition made by the court, had only rendered them more united, more haughty, and more determined. No method but their own, of excluding the duke, could give them any satisfaction.

CHAPTER LXVIII

There was one Fitz-harris, an Irish catholic, who had insin- *Fitz-*
uated himself into the dutchess of Portsmouth's acquaintance, and *harris's*
had been very busy in conveying to her intelligence of any libel *case.*
written by the country party, or of any designs entertained against
her or against the court. For services of this kind, and perhaps too,
from a regard to his father, Sir Edward Fitz-harris, who had been
an eminent royalist, he had received from the king a present of 250
pounds. This man met with one Everard, a Scotchman, a spy of the
exclusionists, and an informer concerning the popish plot; and he
engaged him to write a libel against the king, the duke, and the
whole administration. What Fitz-harris's intentions were, cannot
well be ascertained: It is probable, as he afterwards asserted, that
he meant to carry this libel to his patron, the dutchess, and to make
a merit of the discovery. Everard, who suspected some other design, and who was well pleased on his side to have the merit of a
discovery with his patrons, resolved to betray his friend: He posted
Sir William Waller, a noted justice of peace, and two persons more
behind the hangings, and gave them an opportunity of seeing and
hearing the whole transaction. The libel, sketched out by Fitz-
harris, and executed partly by him, partly by Everard, was the most
furious, indecent, and outrageous performance imaginable; and
such as was fitter to hurt than serve any party, which should be so
imprudent as to adopt it. Waller carried the intelligence to the
king, and obtained a warrant for committing Fitz-harris, who happened, at that very time, to have a copy of the libel in his pocket.
Finding himself now delivered over to the law, he resolved to pay
court to the popular party, who were alone able to protect him, and
by whom he observed almost all trials to be governed and directed.
He affirmed, that he had been employed by the court to write the
libel, in order to throw the odium of it on the exclusionists: But this
account, which was within the bounds of credibility, he disgraced
by circumstances, which are altogether absurd and improbable.
The intention of the ministers, he said, was to send about copies to
all the heads of the country party; and the moment they received
them, they were to be arrested, and a conspiracy to be imputed to
them. That he might merit favour by still more important intelligence, he commenced a discoverer of the great popish plot; and
he failed not to confirm all the tremendous circumstances, insisted
on by his predecessors. He said, that the second Dutch war was

entered into with a view of extirpating the protestant religion, both abroad and at home; that father Parry, a jesuit, on the disappointment by the peace, told him, that the catholics resolved to murder the king, and had even engaged the queen in that design: that the envoy of Modena offered him 10,000 pounds to kill the king, and upon his refusal the envoy said, that the duchess of Mazarine, who was as expert at poisoning as her sister, the countess of Soissons, would, with a little phial, execute that design; that upon the king's death the army in Flanders was to come over, and massacre the protestants; that money was raised in Italy for recruits and supplies, and there should be no more parliaments; and that the duke was privy to this whole plan, and had even entered into the design of Godfrey's murder, which was executed in the manner related by Prance.

The popular leaders had, all along, been very desirous of having an accusation against the duke; and though Oates and Bedloe, in their first evidence, had not dared to go so far, both Dugdale and Dangerfield had afterwards been encouraged to supply so material a defect, by comprehending him in the conspiracy. The commons, therefore, finding that Fitz-harris was also willing to serve this purpose, were not ashamed to adopt his evidence, and resolved for that end to save him from the destruction, with which he was at present threatened. The king had removed him from the city-prison, where he was exposed to be tampered with by the exclusionists; had sent him to the Tower; and had ordered him to be prosecuted by an indictment at common law. In order to prevent his trial and execution, an impeachment was voted by the commons against him, and sent up to the lords. That they might shew the greater contempt of the court, they ordered, by way of derision, that the impeachment should be carried up by secretary Jenkins; who was so provoked by the intended affront, that he at first refused obedience; though afterwards, being threatened with commitment, he was induced to comply. The lords voted to remit the affair to the ordinary courts of justice, before whom, as the attorney-general informed them, it was already determined to try Fitz-harris. The commons maintained, that the peers were obliged to receive every impeachment from the commons; and this indeed seems to have been the first instance of their refusal: They therefore voted, that the lords, in rejecting their impeachment, had

CHAPTER LXVIII

denied justice, and had violated the constitution of parliament. They also declared, that whatever inferior court should proceed against Fitz-harris, or any one that lay under impeachment, would be guilty of a high breach of privilege. Great heats were likely to ensue; and as the king saw no appearance of any better temper in the commons, he gladly laid hold of the opportunity, afforded by a quarrel between the two houses; and he proceeded to a dissolution of the parliament. The secret was so well kept, that the commons had no intimation of it, till the black rod came to their door, and summoned them to attend the king at the house of peers.

Parliament dissolved.

This vigorous measure, though it might have been foreseen, excited such astonishment in the country party, as deprived them of all spirit, and reduced them to absolute despair. They were sensible, though too late, that the king had finally taken his resolution, and was determined to endure any extremity rather than submit to those terms, which they had resolved to impose upon him. They found, that he had patiently waited till affairs should come to full maturity; and having now engaged a national party on his side, had boldly set his enemies at defiance. No parliament, they knew, would be summoned for some years; and during that long interval, the court, though perhaps at the head of an inferior party, yet being possessed of all authority, would have every advantage over a body, dispersed and disunited. These reflections crowded upon every one; and all the exclusionists were terrified, lest Charles should follow the blow by some action more violent, and immediately take vengeance on them for their long and obstinate opposition to his measures. The king on his part was no less apprehensive, lest despair might prompt them to have recourse to force, and make some sudden attempt upon his person. Both parties therefore hurried from Oxford; and in an instant, that city, so crowded and busy, was left in its usual emptiness and tranquillity.

The court party gathered force from the dispersion and astonishment of their antagonists, and adhered more firmly to the king, whose resolutions, they now saw, could be entirely depended on. The violences of the exclusionists were every where exclaimed against and aggravated; and even the reality of the plot, that great engine of their authority, was openly called in question. The clergy

Victory of the royalists.

especially were busy in this great revolution; and being moved, partly by their own fears, partly by the insinuations of the court, they represented all their antagonists as sectaries and republicans, and rejoiced in escaping those perils, which they believed to have been hanging over them. Principles the most opposite to civil liberty, were every where inforced from the pulpit, and adopted in numerous addresses; where the king was flattered in his present measures, and congratulated on his escape from parliaments. Could words have been depended on, the nation appeared to be running fast into voluntary servitude, and seemed even ambitious of resigning into the king's hands all the privileges, transmitted to them, through so many ages, by their gallant ancestors.

But Charles had sagacity enough to distinguish between men's real internal sentiments, and the language, which zeal and opposition to a contrary faction may sometimes extort from them. Notwithstanding all these professions of duty and obedience, he was resolved not to trust, for a long time, the people with a new election, but to depend entirely on his own economy for alleviating those necessities, under which he laboured. Great retrenchments were made in the houshold: Even his favourite navy was neglected: Tangiers, though it had cost great sums of money, was a few years after abandoned and demolished. The mole was entirely destroyed; and the garrison, being brought over to England, served to augment that small army, which the king relied on, as the solid basis of his authority. It had been happy for the nation, had Charles used his victory with justice and moderation equal to the prudence and dexterity, with which he obtained it.

The first step, taken by the court, was the trial of Fitz-harris. Doubts were raised by the jury with regard to their power of trying him, after the concluding vote of the commons: But the judges took upon them to decide the question in the affirmative; and the jury were obliged to proceed. The writing of the libel was clearly proved upon Fitz-harris: The only question was with regard to his intentions. He asserted, that he was a spy of the court, and had accordingly carried the libel to the duchess of Portsmouth; and he was desirous, that the jury should, in this transaction, consider him as a cheat, not as a traitor. He failed however somewhat in the proof; and was brought in guilty of treason by the jury.

Finding himself entirely in the hands of the king, he now retracted all his former impostures with regard to the popish plot, and even endeavoured to atone for them by new impostures against the country party. He affirmed, that these fictions had been extorted from him by the suggestions and artifices of Treby the recorder, and of Bethel and Cornish, the two sheriffs: This account he persisted in even at his execution; and though men knew, that nothing could be depended on, which came from one so corrupt, and so lost to all sense of honour; yet were they inclined, from his perseverance, to rely somewhat more on his veracity in these last asseverations. But it appears, that his wife had some connexions with Mrs. Wall, the favourite maid of the duchess of Portsmouth; and Fitz-harris hoped, if he persisted in a story agreeable to the court, that some favour might, on that account, be shown to his family.

It is amusing to reflect on the several lights, in which this story has been represented by the opposite factions. The country party affirmed, that Fitz-harris had been employed by the court, in order to throw the odium of the libel on the exclusionists, and thereby give rise to a protestant plot: The court party maintained, that the exclusionists had found out Fitz-harris, a spy of the ministers, and had set him upon this undertaking, from an intention of loading the court with the imputation of such a design upon the exclusionists. Rather than acquit their antagonists, both sides were willing to adopt an account the most intricate and incredible. It was a strange situation, in which the people, at this time, were placed; to be every day tortured with these perplexed stories, and inflamed with such dark suspicions against their fellow-citizens. This was no less than the fifteenth false plot, or sham plot, as they were then called, with which the court, it was imagined, had endeavoured to load their adversaries.[a]

The country party had intended to make use of Fitz-harris's evidence against the duke and the catholics; and his execution was therefore a great mortification to them. But the king and his ministers were resolved not to be contented with so slender an advantage. They were determined to pursue the victory, and to employ against the exclusionists those very offensive arms, however unfair, which that party had laid up in store against their antagonists.

[a] College's trial.

The whole gang of spies, witnesses, informers, suborners, who had so long been supported and encouraged by the leading patriots, finding now that the king was entirely master, turned short upon their old patrons, and offered their service to the ministers. To the disgrace of the court and of the age, they were received with hearty welcome; and their testimony or rather perjury made use of, in order to commit legal murder upon the opposite party. With an air of triumph and derision it was asked, "Are not these men good witnesses, who have established the popish plot, upon whose testimony Stafford and so many catholics have been executed, and whom you yourselves have so long celebrated as men of credit and veracity? You have admitted them into your bosom: They are best acquainted with your treasons: They are determined in another shape to serve their king and country: And you cannot complain, that the same measure, which you meted to others, should now, by a righteous doom or vengeance, be measured out to you."

It is certain, that the principle of retaliation may serve in some cases as a full apology, in others as an alleviation, for a conduct which would otherwise be exposed to great blame. But these infamous arts, which poison justice in its very source, and break all the bands of human society, are so detestable and dangerous, that no pretence of retaliation can be pleaded as an apology or even an alleviation of the crime incurred by them. On the contrary, the greater indignation the king and his ministers felt, when formerly exposed to the perjuries of abandoned men, the more reluctance should they now have discovered against employing the same instruments of vengeance upon their antagonists.

The first person, on whom the ministers fell, was one College, a London joiner, who had become extremely noted for his zeal against popery, and was much connected with Shaftesbury and the leaders of the country party: For as they relied much upon the populace, men of College's rank and station were useful to them. College had been in Oxford armed with sword and pistol during the sitting of the parliament; and this was made the foundation of his crime. It was pretended that a conspiracy had been entered into to seize the king's person, and detain him in confinement, till he should make the concessions demanded of him. The sheriffs of London were in strong opposition to the court; and it was not strange, that the grand jury named by them rejected the bill

CHAPTER LXVIII

against College. The prisoner was therefore sent to Oxford, where the treason was said to have been committed. Lord Norris, a courtier, was sheriff of the county; and the inhabitants were in general devoted to the court party. A jury was named, consisting entirely of royalists; and though they were men of credit and character, yet such was the factious rage, which prevailed, that little justice could be expected by the prisoner. Some papers, containing hints and directions for his defence, were taken from him, as he was conducted to his trial: An iniquity, which some pretended to justify by alledging, that a like violence had been practised against a prisoner during the fury of the popish plot. Such wild notions of retaliation were at that time propagated by the court party.

The witnesses produced against College were Dugdale, Turberville, Haynes, Smith; men who had before given evidence against the catholics, and whom the jury, for that very reason, regarded as the most perjured villains. College, though beset with so many toils, and oppressed with so many iniquities, defended himself with spirit, courage, capacity, presence of mind; and he invalidated the evidence of the crown, by convincing arguments and undoubted testimony: Yet did the jury, after half an hour's deliberation, bring in a verdict against him. The inhuman spectators received the verdict with a shout of applause: But the prisoner was no wise dismayed. At his execution, he maintained the same manly fortitude, and still denied the crime imputed to him. His whole conduct and demeanour prove him to have been a man led astray only by the fury of the times, and to have been governed by an honest, but indiscreet zeal for his country and his religion.

Thus the two parties, actuated by mutual rage, but cooped up within the narrow limits of the law, levelled with poisoned daggers the most deadly blows against each other's breast, and buried in their factious divisions all regard to truth, honour, and humanity.

LXIX

State of affairs in Ireland –
Shaftesbury acquitted – Argyle's trial –
State of affairs in Scotland – State of the ministry
in England – New nomination of sheriffs – Quo
warrantos – Great power of the crown –
A conspiracy – Shaftesbury retires
and dies – Rye-house plot – Conspiracy
discovered – Execution of the conspirators –
Trial of lord Russel – His execution – Trial of
Algernon Sidney – His execution – State
of the nation – State of foreign affairs –
King's sickness and death –
and character

1681.
*State of
affairs
in Ire-
land.*

WHEN THE CABAL entered into the mysterious alliance with France, they took care to remove the duke of Ormond from the committee of foreign affairs; and nothing tended farther to increase the national jealousy, entertained against the new measures, than to see a man of so much loyalty, as well as probity and honour, excluded from public councils. They had even so great interest with the king as to get Ormond recalled from the government of Ireland; and lord Robarts, afterwards earl of Radnor, succeeded him in that important employment. Lord Berkeley succeeded Robarts; and the earl of Essex, Berkeley. At last in the year 1677, Charles cast his eye again upon Ormond, whom he had so long neglected; and sent him over lieutenant to Ireland. "I have done every thing," said the king, "to disoblige that man; but it is not in my power to make him my enemy." Ormond, during his disgrace, had never joined the malcontents, nor encouraged those clamours, which, with too much reason, but often for bad purposes, were raised against the king's measures. He even thought it his duty, regularly, though with dignity, to pay his court at Whitehall; and to prove that his attachments were founded on gratitude, inclination, and principle, not on any temporary advantages. All the expressions, which dropped from him, while neglected by the court, showed more of good humour, than any prevalence of spleen and indignation. "I can do you no service," said he to his friends, "I have only the power left by my applications to do you some hurt." When colonel Cary Dillon solicited him to second his pretensions for an office, and urged that he had no friends but God and his grace: "Alas! poor Cary," replied the duke, "I pity thee: Thou couldest not have two friends, that possess less interest at court." "I am thrown bye," said he, on another occasion, "like an old rusty clock; yet even that neglected machine, twice in twenty-four hours, points right."

On such occasions, when Ormond, from decency, paid his attendance at court, the king, equally ashamed to show him civility and to neglect him, was abashed and confounded. "Sir," said the profligate Buckingham, "I wish to know whether it be the duke of Ormond, that is out of favour with your majesty, or your majesty with the duke of Ormond; for, of the two, you seem the most out of countenance."

When Charles found it his interest to show favour to the old royalists and to the church of England, Ormond, who was much revered by that whole party, could not fail of recovering, together with the government of Ireland, his former credit and authority. His administration, when lord lieutenant, corresponded to the general tenor of his life; and tended equally to promote the interests of prince and people, of protestant and catholic. Ever firmly attached to the established religion, he was able, even during those jealous times, to escape suspicion, though he gratified not vulgar prejudices by any persecution of the popish party. He encreased the revenue of Ireland to three hundred thousand pounds a year: He maintained a regular army of ten thousand men: He supported a well disciplined militia of twenty thousand: And though the act of settlement had so far been infringed, that catholics were permitted to live in corporate towns, they were guarded with so careful an eye, that the most timorous protestant never apprehended any danger from them.

The chief object of Essex's ambition was to return to the station of lord lieutenant, where he had behaved with honour and integrity: Shaftesbury and Buckingham bore an extreme hatred to Ormond, both from personal and party considerations: The great aim of the anti-courtiers was to throw reflections on every part of the king's government. It could be no surprize, therefore, to the lord lieutenant to learn, that his administration was attacked in parliament, particularly by Shaftesbury; but he had the satisfaction, at the same time, to hear of the keen, though polite defence, made by his son, the generous Ossory. After justifying several particulars of Ormond's administration against that intriguing patriot, Ossory proceeded in the following words: "Having spoken of what the lord lieutenant has done, I presume with the same truth to tell your lordships what he has not done. He never advised the breaking of the triple league; he never advised the shutting up of the exchequer; he never advised the declaration for a toleration; he never advised the falling out with the Dutch and the joining with France: He was not the author of that most excellent position *Delenda est Carthago,* that Holland, a protestant country, should, contrary to the true interests of England, be totally destroyed. I beg that your lordships will be so just as to judge of my father and all men, according to their actions and their counsels." These few sentences, pronounced by a plain gallant soldier, noted for probity, had a surprising effect upon the audience, and confounded all the rhetoric of his eloquent and factious adversary. The prince of Orange, who esteemed the former character as much as he despised the latter, could not forbear congratulating by letter the earl of Ossory on this new species of victory, which he had obtained.

Ossory, though he ever kept at a distance from faction, was the most popular man in the kingdom; though he never made any compliance with the corrupt views of the court, was beloved and respected by the king. An universal grief appeared on his death, which happened about this time, and which the populace, as is usual wherever they are much affected, foolishly ascribed to poison. Ormond bore the loss with patience and dignity; though he ever retained a pleasing, however melancholy, sense of the signal merit of Ossory. "I would not exchange my dead son," said he, "for any living son in Christendom."

These particularities may appear a digression; but it is with pleasure, I own, that I relax myself for a moment in the contemplation of these humane and virtuous characters, amidst that scene of fury and faction, fraud and violence, in which at present our narration has unfortunately engaged us.

Besides the general interest of the country party to decry the conduct of all the king's ministers, the prudent and peaceable administration of Ormond was in a particular manner displeasing to them. In England, where the catholics were scarcely one to a hundred, means had been found to excite an universal panic, on account of insurrections and even massacres, projected by that sect; and it could not but seem strange that in Ireland, where they exceeded the protestants six to one, there should no symptoms appear of any combination or conspiracy. Such an incident, when duly considered, might even in England shake the credit of the plot, and diminish the authority of those leaders, who had so long, with such industry, inculcated the belief of it on the nation. Rewards, therefore, were published in Ireland to any that would bring intelligence or become witnesses; and some profligates were sent over to that kingdom, with a commission to seek out evidence against the catholics. Under pretence of searching for arms or papers, they broke into houses, and plundered them: They threw innocent men into prison, and took bribes for their release: And after all their diligence, it was with difficulty, that that country, commonly fertile enough in witnesses, could furnish them with any fit for their purpose.

At last, one Fitzgerald appeared, followed by Ivey, Sanson, Dennis, Bourke, two Macnamaras, and some others. These men were immediately sent over to England; and though they possessed neither character sufficient to gain belief even for truth, nor sense to invent a credible falshood, they were caressed, rewarded, supported and recommended by the earl of Shaftesbury. Oliver

Plunket, the titular primate of Ireland, a man of peaceable dispositions, was condemned and executed upon such testimony. And the Oxford parliament entered so far into the matter as to vote, that they were entirely satisfied in the reality of the *horrid* and *damnable* Irish plot. But such decisions, though at first regarded as infallible, had now lost much of their authority; and the public still remained somewhat indifferent and incredulous.

After the dissolution of the parliament, and the subsequent victory of the royalists, Shaftesbury's evidences, with Turberville, Smith, and others, addressed themselves to the ministers, and gave information of high treason against their former patron. It is sufficiently scandalous, that intelligence, conveyed by such men, should have been attended to; but there is some reason to think, that the court agents, nay the ministers, nay the king himself,[b] went farther, and were active in endeavouring, though in vain, to find more reputable persons to support the blasted credit of the Irish witnesses. Shaftesbury was committed to prison, and his indictment was presented to the grand jury. The new sheriffs of London, Shute and Pilkington, were engaged as deeply as their predecessors in the country party; and they took care to name a jury devoted to the same cause: A precaution quite necessary, when it was scarcely possible to find men indifferent or attached to neither party. As far as swearing could go, the treason was clearly proved against Shaftesbury; or rather so clearly as to merit no kind of credit or attention. That veteran leader of a party, enured from his early youth to faction and intrigue, to cabals and conspiracies, was represented as opening without reserve his treasonable intentions to these obscure banditti, and throwing out such violent and outrageous reproaches upon the king, as none but men of low education, like themselves, could be supposed to employ. The draught of an association, it is true, against popery and the duke, was found in Shaftesbury's cabinet; and dangerous inferences might be drawn from many clauses of that paper. But it did not appear, that it had been framed by Shaftesbury, or so much as approved by him. And as projects of an association had been proposed in parliament, it was very natural for this nobleman, or his correspondents, to be thinking of some plan, which it might be proper to lay before

Shaftesbury acquitted.

[b] See captain Wilkinson's narrative.

CHAPTER LXIX

that assembly. The grand jury, therefore, after weighing all these circumstances, rejected the indictment; and the people, who attended the hall, testified their joy by the loudest acclamations, which were echoed throughout the whole city.

About this time a scheme of oppression was laid in Scotland, after a manner still more flagrant, against a nobleman much less obnoxious than Shaftesbury; and as that country was reduced to a state of almost total subjection, the project had the good fortune to succeed.

The earl of Argyle, from his youth, had distinguished himself *Argyle's* by his loyalty, and his attachment to the royal family. Though his *trial.* father was head of the covenanters, he himself refused to concur in any of their measures; and when a commission of colonel was given him by the convention of states, he forbore to act upon it, till it should be ratified by the king. By his respectful behaviour, as well as by his services, he made himself acceptable to Charles, when that prince was in Scotland: And even after the battle of Worcester, all the misfortunes, which attended the royal cause, could not engage him to desert it. Under Middleton he obstinately persevered to harass and infest the victorious English; and it was not till he received orders from that general, that he would submit to accept of a capitulation. Such jealousy of his loyal attachments was entertained by the commonwealth and protector, that a pretence was soon after fallen upon to commit him to prison; and his confinement was rigorously continued till the restoration. The king, sensible of his services, had remitted to him his father's forfeiture, and created him earl of Argyle; and when a most unjust sentence was passed upon him by the Scottish parliament, Charles had anew remitted it. In the subsequent part of this reign, Argyle behaved himself dutifully; and though he seemed not disposed to go all lengths with the court, he always appeared, even in his opposition, to be a man of mild dispositions and peaceable deportment.

A parliament was summoned at Edinburgh this summer, and the duke was appointed commissioner. Besides granting money to the king and voting the indefeasible right of succession, this parliament enacted a test, which all persons, possessed of offices, civil, military, or ecclesiastical, were bound to take. In this test, the king's supremacy was asserted, the covenant renounced, passive obedience assented to, and all obligations disclaimed of endeavouring any alteration in civil or ecclesiastical establishments. This was the state of the test, as proposed by the courtiers; but the country party proposed also to insert a clause, which could not with decency be refused, expressing the person's adherence to the protestant religion. The whole was of an enormous length, considered as an oath; and what was worse, a confession of faith was there ratified, which had been imposed a little after the reformation, and which contained many articles altogether forgotten by the parliament and nation. Among others, the doctrine of resistance was inculcated; so that the test, being voted in a hurry, was found on examination to be a medley of contradiction and absurdity. Several persons, the most attached to the crown, scrupled to take it: The bishops and many of the clergy remonstrated: The earl of Queensberry refused to swear, except he might be allowed to add an explanation: And even the privy council thought it necessary to publish for general satisfaction a solution of some difficulties, attending the test.

Though the courtiers could not reject the clause of adhering to the protestant religion, they proposed, as a necessary mark of respect, that all princes of the blood should be exempted from taking the oath. This exception was zealously opposed by Argyle; who observed, that the sole danger to be dreaded for the protestant religion must proceed from the perversion of the royal family. By insisting on such topics, he drew on himself the secret indignation of the duke, of which he soon felt the fatal consequences.

When Argyle took the test as a privy counsellor, he subjoined, in the duke's presence, an explanation, which he had beforehand communicated to that prince, and which he believed to have been approved by him. It was in these words: "I have considered the test, and am very desirous of giving obedience as far as I can. I am confident, that the parliament never intended to impose contradictory oaths: Therefore I think no man can explain it but for himself. Accordingly, I take it as far as it is consistent with itself, and the protestant religion. And I do declare, that I mean not to bind myself, in my station, and in a lawful way, from wishing, and endeavouring any alteration, which I think to the advantage of church or state, and not repugnant to the protestant religion and my loyalty: And this I understand as a part of my oath." The duke,

CHAPTER LXIX

as was natural, heard these words with great tranquillity: No one took the least offence: Argyle was admitted to sit that day in council: And it was impossible to imagine, that a capital offence had been committed, where occasion seemed not to have been given, so much as for a frown or reprimand.

Argyle was much surprized, a few days after, to find, that a warrant was issued for committing him to prison; that he was indicted for high treason, leasing-making, and perjury; and that from these innocent words an accusation was extracted, by which he was to forfeit honours, life, and fortune. It is needless to enter into particulars, where the iniquity of the whole is so apparent. Though the sword of justice was displayed, even her semblance was not put on; and the forms alone of law were preserved, in order to sanctify, or rather aggravate the oppression. Of five judges, three did not scruple to find the guilt of treason and leasing-making to be incurred by the prisoner: A jury of fifteen noblemen gave verdict against him: And the king, being consulted, ordered the sentence to be pronounced; but the execution of it to be suspended, till farther orders.

It was pretended by the duke and his creatures, that Argyle's life and fortune were not in any danger, and that the sole reason for pushing the trial to such extremities against him was in order to make him renounce some hereditary jurisdictions, which gave his family a dangerous authority in the highlands, and obstructed the course of public justice. But allowing the end to be justifiable, the means were infamous; and such as were incompatible, not only with a free, but a civilized government. Argyle had therefore no reason to trust any longer to the justice or mercy of such enemies: He made his escape from prison; and till he should find a ship for Holland, he concealed himself during some time in London. The king heard of his lurking-place, but would not allow him to be arrested.[c] All the parts however of his sentence, as far as the government in Scotland had power, were rigorously executed; his estate confiscated, his arms reversed and torne.

It would seem, that the genuine passion for liberty was at this time totally extinguished in Scotland: There was only preserved a spirit of mutiny and sedition, encouraged by a mistaken zeal for

State of affairs in Scotland.

[c] Burnet, vol. i. p. 522.

religion. Cameron and Cargil, two furious preachers, went a step beyond all their brethren: They publicly excommunicated the king for his tyranny and his breach of the covenant; and they renounced all allegiance to him. Cameron was killed by the troops in an action at Airs-Moss; Cargil was taken and hanged. Many of their followers were tried and convicted. Their lives were offered them if they would say *God save the king:* But they would only agree to pray for his repentance. This obstinacy was much insisted on as an apology for the rigors of the administration: But if duly considered, it will rather afford reason for a contrary inference. Such unhappy delusion is an object rather of commiseration than of anger: And it is almost impossible, that men could have been carried to such a degree of frenzy, unless provoked by a long train of violence and oppression.

1682.   As the king was master in England, and no longer dreaded the clamours of the country party, he permitted the duke to pay him a visit; and was soon after prevailed on to allow of his return to England, and of his bearing a part in the administration. The duke went to Scotland, in order to bring up his family, and settle the government of that country; and he chose to take his passage by sea. The ship struck on a sand-bank, and was lost: The duke escaped in the barge; and it is pretended, that, while many persons of rank and quality were drowned, and among the rest, Hyde, his brother-in-law, he was very careful to save several of his dogs and priests: For these two species of favourites are coupled together by some writers. It has likewise been asserted, that the barge might safely have held more persons, and that some who swam to it were thrust off, and even their hands cut, in order to disengage them. But every action of every eminent person, during this period, is so liable to be misinterpreted and misrepresented by faction, that we ought to be very cautious in passing judgment on too slight evidence. It is remarkable, that the sailors on board the ship, though they felt themselves sinking, and saw inevitable death before their eyes, yet as soon as they observed the duke to be in safety, gave a loud shout, in testimony of their joy and satisfaction.

The duke, during his abode in Scotland, had behaved with great civility towards the gentry and nobility; and by his courtly demeanor had much won upon their affections: But his treatment of the enthusiasts was still somewhat rigorous; and in many instances he appeared to be a man of a severe, if not an unrelenting temper. It is even asserted, that he sometimes assisted at the torture of criminals, and looked on with tranquillity, as if he were considering some curious experiment.[d] He left the authority in the hands of the earl of Aberdeen, chancellor, and the earl of Queensberry, treasurer: A very arbitrary spirit appeared in their administration. A gentleman of the name of Weir was tried, because he had kept company with one who had been in rebellion; though that person had never been marked out by process or proclamation. The inferences, upon which Weir was condemned (for a prosecution by the government and a condemnation were in Scotland the same thing) hung upon each other, after the following manner. No man, it was supposed, could have been in a rebellion, without being exposed to suspicion in the neighbourhood: If the neighbourhood had suspected him, it was to be presumed, that each individual had likewise heard of the grounds of suspicion: Every man was bound to declare to the government his suspicion against every man, and to avoid the company of traitors: To fail in this duty was to participate in the treason: The conclusion on the whole was, You have conversed with a rebel; therefore you are yourself a rebel. A reprieve was with some difficulty procured for Weir; but it was seriously determined to make use of the precedent. Courts of judicature were erected in the southern and western counties, and a strict inquisition carried on against this new species of crime. The term of three years was appointed for the continuance of these courts; after which an indemnity was promised. Whoever would take the test, was instantly entitled to the benefit of this indemnity. The presbyterians, alarmed with such tyranny, from which no man could deem himself safe, began to think of leaving the country; and some of their agents were sent to England, in order to treat with the proprietors of Carolina for a settlement in that colony. Any condition seemed preferable to the living in their native country, which, by the prevalence of persecution and violence, was become as insecure to them as a den of robbers.

Above two thousand persons were out-lawed on pretence of

[d] Burnet, vol. i. p. 583. Wodrow, vol. ii. p. 169. This last author, who is much the better authority, mentions only one instance, that of Spreul, which seems to have been an extraordinary one.

their conversing or having intercourse with rebels,[e] and they were continually hunted in their retreat by soldiers, spies, informers, and oppressive magistrates. It was usual to put ensnaring questions to people, living peaceably in their own houses; such as, "Will you renounce the covenant? Do you esteem the rising at Bothwel to be rebellion? Was the killing of the archbishop of St. Andrews murder?" And when the poor deluded creatures refused to answer, capital punishments were inflicted on them.[f] Even women were brought to the gibbet for this pretended crime. A number of fugitives, rendered frantic by oppression, had published a seditious declaration; renouncing allegiance to Charles Stuart, whom they called, as they, for their parts, had indeed some reason to esteem him, a tyrant. This incident afforded the privy council a pretence for an unusual kind of oppression. Soldiers were dispersed over the country, and power was given to all commission officers, even the lowest, to oblige every one they met with, to abjure the declaration; and upon refusal, instantly, without farther questions, to shoot the delinquent.[g] It were endless, as well as shocking, to enumerate all the instances of persecution, or, in other words, of absurd tyranny, which at that time prevailed in Scotland. One of them however is so singular, that I cannot forbear relating it.

Three women were seized; [h] and the customary oath was tendered to them, by which they were to abjure the seditious declaration abovementioned. They all refused, and were condemned to a capital punishment by drowning. One of them was an elderly woman: The other two were young; one eighteen years of age, the other only thirteen. Even these violent persecutors were ashamed to put the youngest to death: But the other two were conducted to the place of execution, and were tied to stakes within the sea-mark at low-water: A contrivance, which rendered their death lingering and dreadful. The elderly woman was placed farthest in, and by the rising of the waters was first suffocated. The younger, partly terrified with the view of her companion's death, partly subdued by the entreaty of her friends, was prevailed with to say *God save the King.* Immediately the spectators called out, that she had submit-

[e] Wodrow, vol. ii. Appendix, 94.   [f] Ibid. vol. ii. passim.   [g] Ibid. vol. ii. p. 434.   [h] Wodrow, vol. ii. p. 505.

ted; and she was loosened from the stake. Major Winram, the officer who guarded the execution, again required her to sign the abjuration; and upon her refusal, he ordered her instantly to be plunged in the water, where she was suffocated.

The severity of the administration in Scotland is in part to be ascribed to the duke's temper, to whom the king had consigned over the government of that country, and who gave such attention to affairs as to allow nothing of moment to escape him. Even the government of England, from the same cause, began to be somewhat infected with the same severity. The duke's credit was great at court. Though neither so much beloved nor esteemed as the king, he was more dreaded; and thence an attendance more exact, as well as a submission more obsequious, was paid to him. The saying of Waller was remarked, that Charles, in spite to the parliament, who had determined, that the duke should not succeed him, was resolved, that he should reign even in his lifetime.

The king however, who loved to maintain a balance in his councils, still supported Halifax, whom he created a marquess, and made privy seal; though ever in opposition to the duke. This man, who possessed the finest genius and most extensive capacity, of all employed in public affairs during the present reign, affected a species of neutrality between the parties, and was esteemed the head of that small body, known by the denomination of *Trimmers*. This conduct, which is more natural to men of integrity than of ambition, could not however procure him the former character; and he was always, with reason, regarded as an intriguer rather than a patriot. Sunderland, who had promoted the exclusion-bill, and who had been displaced on that account, was again, with the duke's consent, brought into the administration. The extreme duplicity, at least variableness, of this man's conduct, through the whole course of his life, made it be suspected, that it was by the king's direction he had mixed with the country party. Hyde, created earl of Rochester, was first commissioner of the treasury, and was entirely in the duke's interests.

State of the ministry in England.

The king himself was obliged to act as the head of a party; a disagreeable situation for a prince, and always the source of much injustice and oppression. He knew how obnoxious the dissenters were to the church; and he resolved, contrary to the maxims of toleration, which he had hitherto supported in England, to gratify his friends by the persecution of his enemies. The laws against conventicles were now rigorously executed; an expedient, which, the king knew, would diminish neither the numbers nor influence of the nonconformists; and which is therefore to be deemed more the result of passion than of policy. Scarcely any persecution serves the intended purpose but such as amounts to a total extermination.

Though the king's authority made every day great advances, it still met with considerable obstacles, chiefly from the city, which was entirely in the hands of the malcontents. The juries, in particular, named by the sheriffs, were not likely to be impartial judges between the crown and the people; and after the experiments already made in the case of Shaftesbury and that of College, treason, it was apprehended, might there be committed with impunity. There could not therefore be a more important service to the court than to put affairs upon a different footing. Sir John Moore, the mayor, was gained by secretary Jenkins, and encouraged to insist upon the customary privilege of his office, of naming one of the sheriffs. Accordingly, when the time of election came, he drank to North, a Levant merchant, who accepted of that expensive office. The country party said, that, being lately returned from Turkey, he was, on account of his recent experience, better qualified to serve the purposes of the court. A poll was opened for the election of another sheriff; and here began the contest. The majority of the common-hall, headed by the two sheriffs of the former year, refused to acknowledge the mayor's right of appointing one sheriff, but insisted that both must be elected by the livery. Papillon and Dubois were the persons whom the country party agreed to elect: Box was pointed out by the courtiers. The poll was opened; but as the mayor would not allow the election to proceed for two vacancies, the sheriffs and he separated, and each carried on the poll apart. The country party, who voted with the sheriffs for Papillon and Dubois, were much more numerous than those who voted with the mayor for Box: But as the mayor insisted, that his poll was the only legal one, he declared Box to be duly elected. All difficulties however were not surmounted. Box, apprehensive of the consequences, which might attend so dubious an election, fined off; and the mayor found it necessary to proceed to a new choice. When the matter was proposed to the common-hall,

New nomination of sheriffs.

24th of June.

a loud cry was raised, No election! No election! The two sheriffs already elected, Papillon and Dubois, were insisted on as the only legal magistrates. But as the mayor still maintained, that Box alone had been legally chosen, and that it was now requisite to supply his place, he opened books anew; and during the tumult and confusion of the citizens, a few of the mayor's partizans elected Rich, unknown to and unheeded by the rest of the livery. North and Rich were accordingly sworn in sheriffs for the ensuing year; but it was necessary to send a guard of the train bands to protect them in entering upon their office. A new mayor of the court party was soon after chosen by means, as is pretended, still more violent and irregular.

25th of October.

Thus the country party were dislodged from their strong hold in the city; where, ever since the commencement of factions in the English government, they had, without interruption, almost without molestation, maintained a superiority. It had been happy, had the partialities, hitherto objected to juries, been corrected, without giving place to partialities of an opposite kind: But in the present distracted state of the nation, an equitable neutrality was almost impossible to be attained. The court and church party, who were now named on juries, made justice subservient to their factious views; and the king had a prospect of obtaining full revenge on his enemies. It was not long before the effects of these alterations were seen. When it was first reported, that the duke intended to leave Scotland, Pilkington, at that time sheriff, a very violent man had broken out in these terms, "He has already burned the city; and he is now coming to cut all our throats?" For these scandalous expressions, the duke sued Pilkington; and enormous damages to the amount of 100,000 pounds were decreed him. By the law of England, ratified in the great charter, no fine or damages ought to extend to the total ruin of a criminal. Sir Patience Ward, formerly mayor, who gave evidence for Pilkington, was sued for perjury, and condemned to the pillory: A severe sentence, and sufficient to deter all witnesses from appearing in favour of those, who were prosecuted by the court.

But though the crown had obtained so great a victory in the city, it was not quite decisive; and the contest might be renewed every year at the election of magistrates. An important project, therefore, was formed, not only to make the king master of the

1683.
Quo warrantos.

city, but by that precedent to gain him uncontrouled influence in all the corporations of England, and thereby give the greatest wound to the legal constitution, which the most powerful and most arbitrary monarchs had ever yet been able to inflict. A writ of *quo warranto* was issued against the city; that is, an enquiry into the validity of its charter. It was pretended, that the city had forfeited all its privileges, and ought to be declared no longer a corporation, on account of two offences, which the court of aldermen and common council had committed. After the great fire in 1666, all the markets had been rebuilt, and had been fitted up with many conveniences; and, in order to defray the expence, the magistrates had imposed a small toll on goods brought to market: in the year 1679, they had addressed the king against the prorogation of parliament, and had employed the following terms: "Your petitioners are greatly surprized at the late prorogation, whereby the prosecution of the public justice of the kingdom, and the making of necessary provisions for the preservation of your majesty and your protestant subjects, have received interruption." These words were pretended to contain a scandalous reflection on the king and his measures. The cause of the city was defended against the attorney and solicitor generals, by Treby and Pollexsen.

These last pleaded, that, since the foundation of the monarchy, no corporation had ever yet been exposed to forfeiture, and the thing itself implied an absurdity: That a corporation, as such, was incapable of all crime or offence, and none were answerable for any iniquity but the persons themselves, who committed it: That the members, in choosing magistrates, had entrusted them with legal powers only; and where the magistrates exceeded these powers, their acts were void, but could never involve the body itself in any criminal imputation: That such had ever been the practice of England, except at the Reformation, when the monasteries were abolished; but this was an extraordinary case; and it was even thought necessary to ratify afterwards the whole transaction by act of parliament: That corporate bodies, framed for public good, and calculated for perpetual duration, ought not to be annihilated for the temporary faults of their members, who might themselves, without hurting the community, be questioned for their offences: That even a private estate, if entailed, could not be forfeited to the crown, on account of treason, committed by the tenant for life; but upon his demise went to the next in remainder: That the offences, objected to the city, far from deserving so severe a punishment, were not even worthy of the smallest reprehension. That all corporations were invested with the power of making bye-laws; and the smallest borough in England had ever been allowed to carry the exercise of this power farther than London had done in the instance complained of: That the city, having, at its own expence, repaired the markets, which were built too on its own estate, might as lawfully claim a small recompence from such as brought commodities thither, as a man might require rent for a house, of which he was possessed. That those who disliked the condition, might abstain from the market; and whoever paid, had done it voluntarily: That it was an avowed right of the subjects to petition; nor had the city in their address abused this privilege: That the king himself had often declared, the parliament often voted, the nation to be in danger from the popish plot; which, it is evident, could not be fully prosecuted but in a parliamentary manner: That the impeachment of the popish lords was certainly obstructed by the frequent prorogations; as was also the enacting of necessary laws, and providing for the defence of the nation: That the loyalty of the city, no less than their regard to self-preservation, might prompt them to frame the petition; since it was acknowledged, that the king's life was every moment exposed to the most imminent danger from the popish conspiracy: That the city had not accused the king of obstructing justice, much less of having any such intention; since it was allowed, that evil counsellors were alone answerable for all the pernicious consequences of any measure: And that it was unaccountable, that two public deeds, which had not, during so long a time, subjected to any, even the smallest penalty, the persons guilty of them, should now be punished so severely upon the corporation, which always was, and always must be innocent.

It is evident, that those who would apologize for the measures of the court, must, in this case, found their arguments, not on law, but reasons of state. The judges, therefore, who condemned the city, are inexcusable; since the sole object of their determinations must ever be the pure principles of justice and equity. But the office of judge was at that time held during pleasure; and it was impossible, that any cause, where the court bent its force, could ever be carried against it. After sentence was pronounced, the city

12th June.

applied in a humble manner to the king; and he agreed to restore their charter, but in return they were obliged to submit to the following regulations: That no mayor, sheriff, recorder, common serjeant, town clerk, or coroner, should be admitted to the exercise of his office without his majesty's approbation: That if the king disapprove twice of the mayor or sheriffs elected, he may by commission appoint these magistrates: That the mayor and court of aldermen may, with his majesty's leave, displace any magistrate: And that no alderman, in case of a vacancy, shall be elected without consent of the court of aldermen, who, if they disapprove twice of the choice, may fill the vacancy.

Great power of the crown.

All the corporations in England, having the example of London before their eyes, saw how vain it would prove to contend with the court, and were, most of them, successively induced to surrender their charters into the king's hands. Considerable sums were exacted for restoring the charters; and all offices of power and profit were left at the disposal of the crown. It seems strange, that the independent royalists, who never meant to make the crown absolute, should yet be so elated with the victory obtained over their adversaries, as to approve of a precedent, which left no national privileges in security, but enabled the king under like pretences, and by means of like instruments, to recall anew all those charters, which at present he was pleased to grant. And every friend to liberty must allow, that the nation, whose constitution was thus broken in the shock of faction, had a right, by every prudent expedient, to recover that security, of which it was so unhappily bereaved.

While so great a faction adhered to the crown, it is apparent, that resistance, however justifiable, could never be prudent; and all wise men saw no expedient but peaceably to submit to the present grievances. There was however a party of malcontents, so turbulent in their disposition, that, even before this last iniquity, which laid the whole constitution at the mercy of the king, they had meditated plans of resistance; at a time when it could be as little justifiable as prudent. In the spring 1681,[i] a little before the Ox-

---

[i] Lord Grey's secret history of the Rye-house plot. This is the most full and authentic account of all these transactions; but is in the main confirmed by bishop Sprat, and even Burnet, as well as by the trials and dying confessions of the conspirators: So that nothing can be more unaccountable than

CHAPTER LXIX

ford parliament, the king was seized with a fit of sickness at Windsor, which gave great alarm to the public. The duke of Monmouth, *A con-* lord Russel, lord Grey, instigated by the restless Shaftesbury, had *spiracy.* agreed, in case the king's sickness should prove mortal, to rise in arms and to oppose the succession of the duke. Charles recovered; but these dangerous projects were not laid aside. The same conspirators, together with Essex and Salisbury, were determined to continue the Oxford parliament, after the king, as was daily expected, should dissolve it; and they engaged some leaders among the commons in the same desperate measure. They went so far as to detain several lords in the house, under pretence of signing a protest against rejecting Fitz-harris's impeachment: But hearing that the commons had broken up in great consternation, they were likewise obliged at last to separate. Shaftesbury's imprisonment and trial put an end for some time to these machinations; and it was not till the new sheriffs were imposed on the city that they were revived. The leaders of the country party began then to apprehend themselves in imminent danger; and they were well pleased to find, that the citizens were struck with the same terror, and were thence inclined to undertake the most perilous enterprizes. Besides the city, the gentry and nobility in several counties of England were solicited to rise in arms. Monmouth engaged the earl of Macclesfield, lord Brandon, Sir Gilbert Gerrard, and other gentlemen in Cheshire; lord Russel fixed a correspondence with Sir William Courtney, Sir Francis Rowles, Sir Francis Drake, who promised to raise the west; and Trenchard in particular, who had interest in the disaffected town of Taunton, assured him of considerable assistance from that neighbourhood. Shaftesbury and his emissary, Ferguson, an independent clergyman and a restless plotter, managed the correspondence in the city, upon which the confederates chiefly relied. The whole train was ready to take fire; but was prevented by the caution of lord Russel, who induced Monmouth to delay the enterprize. Shaftesbury in the mean time was so much affected with the sense of his danger, that he had left his house, and secretly lurked in the city; meditating all those desper-

---

that any one should pretend, that this conspiracy was an imposture like the popish plot. Monmouth's declaration published in the next reign, confesses a consult for extraordinary remedies.

ate schemes, which disappointed revenge and ambition could inspire. He exclaimed loudly against delay, and represented to his confederates, that having gone so far, and entrusted the secret into so many hands, there was no safety for them but in a bold and desperate prosecution of their purpose. The projects were therefore renewed: Meetings of the conspirators were appointed in different houses, particularly in Shephard's, an eminent wine-merchant in the city: The plan of an insurrection was laid in London, Cheshire, Devonshire, and Bristol: The several places of rendezvous in the city were concerted; and all the operations fixed. The state of the guards was even viewed by Monmouth and Armstrong, and an attack on them pronounced practicable: A declaration to justify the enterprize to the public was read and agreed to: And every circumstance seemed now to render an insurrection unavoidable; when a new delay was procured by Trenchard, who declared, that the rising in the west could not for some weeks be in sufficient forwardness.

Shaftesbury was enraged at these perpetual cautions and delays in an enterprize, which, he thought, nothing but courage and celerity could render effectual: He threatened to commence the insurrection with his friends in the city alone; and he boasted, that he had ten thousand *brisk boys,* as he called them, who, on a motion of his finger, were ready to fly to arms. Monmouth, Russel, and the other conspirators, were, during some time, in apprehensions, lest despair should push him into some dangerous measure; when they heard, that, after a long combat between fear and rage, he had at last abandoned all hopes of success, and had retired into Holland. He lived in a private manner at Amsterdam; and for greater security desired to be admitted into the magistracy of that city: But his former violent counsels against the Dutch commonwealth were remembered; and all applications from him were rejected. He died soon after; and his end gave neither sorrow to his friends, nor joy to his enemies. His furious temper, notwithstanding his capacity, had done great injury to the cause, in which he was engaged. The violences and iniquities, which he suggested and encouraged, were greater than even faction itself could endure; and men could not forbear sometimes recollecting, that the same person, who had become so zealous a patriot, was once a most prostitute courtier. It is remarkable, that this man, whose principles and conduct were,

Shaftes-
bury
retires
and dies.

in all other respects, so exceptionable, proved an excellent chancellor; and that all his decrees, while he possessed that high office, were equally remarkable for justness and for integrity. So difficult is it to find in history a character either wholly bad or perfectly good; though the prejudices of party make writers run easily into the extremes both of panegyric and of satire!

After Shaftesbury's departure, the conspirators found some difficulty in renewing the correspondence with the city malcontents, who had been accustomed to depend solely on that nobleman. Their common hopes, however, as well as common fears, made them at last have recourse to each other; and a regular project of an insurrection was again formed. A council of six was erected, consisting of Monmouth, Russel, Essex, Howard, Algernon Sidney, and John Hambden, grandson of the great parliamentary leader. These men entered into an agreement with Argyle and the Scottish malcontents; who engaged, that, upon the payment of 10,000 pounds for the purchase of arms in Holland, they would bring the covenanters into the field. Insurrections likewise were anew projected in Cheshire, and the west, as well as in the city; and some meetings of the leaders were held, in order to reduce these projects into form. The conspirators differed extremely in their views. Sidney was passionate for a commonwealth. Essex had embraced the same project. But Monmouth had entertained hopes of acquiring the crown for himself. Russel, as well as Hambden, was much attached to the ancient constitution, and intended only the exclusion of the duke and the redress of grievances. Lord Howard was a man of no principle, and was ready to embrace any party, which his immediate interest should recommend to him. But notwithstanding this difference of characters and of views, their common hatred of the duke and the present administration united them in one party; and the dangerous experiment of an insurrection was fully resolved on.

While these schemes were concerting among the leaders, there was an inferior order of conspirators, who held frequent meetings; and, together with the insurrection, carried on projects quite unknown to Monmouth, and the cabal of six. Among these men were *Rye-house* colonel Rumsey, an old republican officer, who had distinguished *plot.* himself in Portugal, and had been recommended to the king by mareschal Schomberg; lieutenant colonel Walcot, likewise a republican officer; Goodenough, under-sheriff of London, a zealous and noted party-man; West, Tyley, Norton, Ayloffe, lawyers; Ferguson, Rouse, Hone, Keiling, Holloway, Bourne, Lee, Rumbald. Most of these last were merchants or tradesmen; and the only persons of this confederacy, who had access to the leaders of the party, were Rumsey and Ferguson. When these men met together, they indulged themselves in the most desperate and most criminal discourse: They frequently mentioned the assassination of the king and the duke, to which they had given the familiar appellation of *lopping:* They even went so far as to have thought of a scheme for that purpose. Rumbald, who was a maltster, possessed a farm, called the Rye-house, which lay on the road to Newmarket, whither the king commonly went once a-year, for the diversion of the races. A plan of this farm had been laid before some of the conspirators by Rumbald, who showed them how easy it would be, by over-turning a cart, to stop at that place the king's coach; while they might fire upon him from the hedges, and be enabled afterwards, through bye-lanes and cross the fields, to make their escape. But though the plausibility of this scheme gave great pleasure to the conspirators, no concerted design was as yet laid, nor any men, horses, or arms provided: The whole was little more than loose discourse, the overflowings of their zeal and rancour. The house, in which the king lived at Newmarket, took fire accidentally; and he was obliged to leave that place eight days sooner than he intended. To this circumstance his safety was afterwards ascribed, when the conspiracy was detected; and the court party could not sufficiently admire the wise dispensations of providence. It is indeed certain, that as the king had thus unexpectedly left Newmarket, he was worse attended than usual; and Rumbald informed his confederates with regret what a fine opportunity was thus unfortunately lost.

Conspiracy discovered.

Among the conspirators I have mentioned Keiling, a salter in London. This man had been engaged in a bold measure, of arresting the mayor of London, at the suit of Papillon and Dubois, the ousted sheriffs; and being liable to prosecution for that action, he thought it safest to purchase a pardon, by revealing the conspiracy, in which he was deeply concerned. He brought to secretary Jenkins intelligence of the assassination plot; but as he was a single evidence, the secretary, whom many false plots had proba-

12th June.

CHAPTER LXIX

bly rendered incredulous, scrupled to issue warrants for the commitment of so great a number of persons. Keiling therefore, in order to fortify his testimony, engaged his brother in treasonable discourse with Goodenough, one of the conspirators; and Jenkins began now to give more attention to the intelligence. The conspirators had got some hint of the danger, in which they were involved; and all of them concealed themselves. One person alone, of the name of Barber, an instrument-maker, was seized; and as his confession concurred in many particulars with Keiling's information, the affair seemed to be put out of all question; and a more diligent search was every where made after the conspirators.

West, the lawyer, and colonel Rumsey, finding the perils, to which they were exposed in endeavouring to escape, resolved to save their own lives at the expence of their companions; and they surrendered themselves with an intention of becoming evidence. West could do little more than confirm the testimony of Keiling with regard to the assassination plot; but Rumsey, besides giving additional confirmation of the same design, was at last, though with much difficulty, led to reveal the meetings at Shephard's. Shephard was immediately apprehended; and had not courage to maintain fidelity to his confederates. Upon his information, orders were issued for arresting the great men engaged in the conspiracy. Monmouth absconded: Russel was sent to the Tower: Gray was arrested, but escaped from the messenger: Howard was taken, while he concealed himself in a chimney; and being a man of profligate morals, as well as indigent circumstances, he scrupled not, in hopes of a pardon and a reward, to reveal the whole conspiracy. Essex, Sidney, Hambden were immediately apprehended upon his evidence. Every day some of the conspirators were detected in their lurking-places, and thrown into prison.

Lieutenant colonel Walcot was first brought to his trial. This man, who was once noted for bravery, had been so far overcome by the love of life, that he had written to secretary Jenkins, and had offered upon promise of pardon to turn evidence: But no sooner had he taken this mean step, than he felt more generous sentiments arise in him; and he endeavoured, though in vain, to conceal himself. The witnesses against him were Rumsey, West, Shephard, together with Bourne, a brewer. His own letter to the secretary was produced, and rendered the testimony of the wit-

Execution of the conspirators.

nesses unquestionable. Hone and Rouse were also condemned. These two men, as well as Walcot, acknowledged, at their execution, the justice of the sentence; and from their trial and confession it is sufficiently apparent, that the plan of an insurrection had been regularly formed; and that even the assassination had been often talked of, and not without the approbation of many of the conspirators.

Trial of lord Russel, The condemnation of these criminals was probably intended as a preparative to the trial of lord Russel, and served to impress the public with a thorough belief of the conspiracy, as well as a horror against it. The witnesses produced against the noble prisoner were Rumsey, Shephard, and lord Howard. Rumsey swore, that he himself had been introduced to the cabal at Shephard's, where Russel was present; and had delivered them a message from Shaftesbury, urging them to hasten the intended insurrection: But had received for answer, that it was found necessary to delay the design, and that Shaftesbury must therefore, for some time, rest contented. This answer, he said, was delivered by Ferguson; but was assented to by the prisoner. He added, that some discourse had been entered into about taking a survey of the guards; and he thought that Monmouth, Gray, and Armstrong undertook to view them. Shephard deposed, that his house had beforehand been bespoken by Ferguson for the secret meeting of the conspirators, and that he had been careful to keep all his servants from approaching them, and had served them himself. Their discourse, he said, ran chiefly upon the means of surprizing the guards; and it was agreed, that Monmouth and his two friends should take a survey of them. The report, which they brought next meeting, was, that the guards were remiss, and that the design was practicable: But he did not affirm, that any resolution was taken of executing it. The prisoner, he thought, was present at both these meetings; but he was sure, that at least he was present at one of them. A declaration, he added, had been read by Ferguson in Russel's presence: The reasons of the intended insurrection were there set forth, and all the public grievances fully displayed.

Lord Howard had been one of the cabal of six, established after Shaftesbury's flight; and two meetings had been held by the conspirators, one at Hambden's, another at Russel's. Howard deposed, that, at the first meeting, it was agreed to begin the insur-

CHAPTER LXIX

rection in the country before the city; the places were fixed, the proper quantity and kind of arms agreed on, and the whole plan of operations concerted: That at the second meeting, the conversation chiefly turned upon their correspondence with Argyle and the discontented Scots, and that the principal management of that affair was entrusted to Sidney, who had sent one Aaron Smith into Scotland with proper instructions. He added, that in these deliberations no question was put, or votes collected; but there was no contradiction; and, as he took it, all of them, and the prisoner among the rest, gave their consent.

Rumsey and Shephard were very unwilling witnesses against lord Russel; and it appears from Gray's Secret History,[k] that, if they had pleased, they could have given a more explicit testimony against him. This reluctance, together with the difficulty in recollecting circumstances of a conversation, which had passed above eight months before, and which the persons had not at that time any intention to reveal, may beget some slight objection to their evidence. But on the whole, it was undoubtedly proved, that the insurrection had been deliberated on by the prisoner, and fully resolved; the surprisal of the guards deliberated on, but not fully resolved; and that an assassination had never once been mentioned nor imagined by him. So far the matter of fact seems certain: But still, with regard to law, there remained a difficulty, and that of an important nature.

The English laws of treason, both in the manner of defining that crime, and in the proof required, are the mildest and most indulgent, and consequently the most equitable, that are any where to be found. The two chief species of treason, contained in the statute of Edward III., are the compassing and intending of the king's death, and the actually levying of war against him; and by the law of Mary, the crime must be proved by the concurring testimony of two witnesses, to some overt act, tending to these purposes. But the lawyers, partly desirous of paying court to the sovereign, partly convinced of ill consequences, which might attend such narrow limitations, had introduced a greater latitude, both in the proof and definition of the crime. It was not required, that the two witnesses should testify the same precise overt act: It

[k] Page 43.

was sufficient, that they both testified some overt act of the same treason; and though this evasion may seem a subtilty, it had long prevailed in the courts of judicature, and had at last been solemnly fixed by parliament at the trial of lord Stafford. The lawyers had used the same freedom with the law of Edward III. They had observed, that, by that statute, if a man should enter into a conspiracy for a rebellion, should even fix a correspondence with foreign powers for that purpose, should provide arms and money, yet, if he were detected and no rebellion ensued, he could not be tried for treason. To prevent this inconvenience, which it had been better to remedy by a new law, they had commonly laid their indictment for intending the death of the king, and had produced the intention of rebellion as a proof of that other intention. But though this form of indictment and trial was very frequent, and many criminals had received sentence upon it, it was still considered as somewhat irregular, and was plainly confounding, by a sophism, two species of treason, which the statute had accurately distinguished. What made this refinement still more exceptionable, was, that a law had passed soon after the restoration; in which the consulting or the intending of a rebellion, was, during Charles's life-time, declared treason; and it was required, that the prosecution should be commenced within six months after the crime was committed. But notwithstanding this statute, the lawyers had persevered, as they still do persevere, in the old form of indictment; and both Sir Harry Vane and Oliver Plunket, titular primate of Ireland, had been tried by it. Such was the general horror, entertained against the old republicans, and the popish conspirators, that no one had murmured against this interpretation of the statute; and the lawyers thought, that they might follow the precedent, even in the case of the popular and beloved lord Russel. Russel's crime fell plainly within the statute of Charles the IId; but the facts sworn to by Rumsey and Shephard were beyond the six months required by law, and to the other facts Howard was a single witness. To make the indictment, therefore, more extensive, the intention of murdering the king was comprehended in it; and for proof of this intention the conspiracy for raising a rebellion was assigned; and what seemed to bring the matter still nearer, the design of attacking the king's guards.

Russel perceived this irregularity, and desired to have the point

CHAPTER LXIX

argued by counsel: The chief justice told him, that this favour could not be granted, unless he previously confessed the facts charged upon him. The artificial confounding of the two species of treason, though a practice supported by many precedents, is the chief, but not the only hardship, of which Russel had reason to complain on his trial. His defence was feeble; and he contented himself with protesting, that he never had entertained any design against the life of the king: His veracity would not allow him to deny the conspiracy for an insurrection. The jury were men of fair and reputable characters, but zealous royalists: After a short deliberation, they brought in the prisoner guilty.

Applications were made to the king for a pardon: Even money, to the amount of a hundred thousand pounds, was offered to the dutchess of Portsmouth by the old earl of Bedford, father to Russel. The king was inexorable. He had been extremely harassed with the violence of the country party; and he had observed, that the prisoner, besides his secret designs, had always been carried to the highest extremity of opposition in parliament. Russel had even adopted a sentiment, similar to what we meet with in a letter of the younger Brutus. Had his father, he said, advised the king to reject the exclusion-bill, he would be the first to move for a parliamentary impeachment against him. When such determined resolution was observed, his popularity, his humanity, his justice, his very virtues became so many crimes, and were used as arguments against sparing him. Charles therefore would go no farther than remitting the more ignominious part of the sentence, which the law requires to be pronounced against traitors. "Lord Russel," said he, "shall find, that I am possessed of that prerogative, which, in the case of lord Stafford, he thought proper to deny me." As the fury of the country party had rendered it impossible for the king, without the imminent danger of his crown, to pardon so many catholics, whom he firmly believed innocent, and even affectionate and loyal to him; he probably thought, that, since the edge of the law was now ready to fall upon that party themselves, they could not reasonably expect, that he would interpose to save them.

Russel's consort, a woman of virtue, daughter and heir of the good earl of Southampton, threw herself at the king's feet, and pleaded with many tears the merits and loyalty of her father, as an atonement for those errors, into which honest, however mistaken principles had seduced her husband. These supplications were the last instance of female weakness (if they deserve the name) which she betrayed. Finding all applications vain, she collected courage, and not only fortified herself against the fatal blow, but endeavoured by her example to strengthen the resolution of her unfortunate lord. With a tender and decent composure they took leave of each other on the day of his execution. "The bitterness of death is now past," said he, when he turned from her. Lord Cavendish had lived in the closest intimacy with Russel, and deserted not his friend in the present calamity. He offered to manage his escape, by changing cloaths with him, and remaining at all hazards in his place. Russel refused to save his own life, by an expedient which might expose his friend to so many hardships. When the duke of Monmouth by message offered to surrender himself, if Russel thought that this measure would any wise contribute to his safety; "It will be no advantage to me," he said, "to have my friends die with me." Some of his expressions discover, not only composure, but good humour in this melancholy extremity. The day before his execution he was seized with a bleeding at the nose. "I shall not now let blood to divert this distemper," said he to doctor Burnet who attended him, "that will be done to-morrow." A little before the sheriffs conducted him to the scaffold, he wound up his watch. "Now I have done," said he, "with time, and henceforth must think solely of eternity."

21st July.

The scaffold was erected in Lincoln's Inn Fields, a place distant from the Tower; and it was probably intended, by conducting Russel through so many streets, to show the mutinous city their beloved leader, once the object of all their confidence, now exposed to the utmost rigours of the law. As he was the most popular among his own party; so was he ever the least obnoxious to the opposite faction: And his melancholy fate united every heart, sensible of humanity, in a tender compassion for him. Without the least change of countenance, he laid his head on the block; and at two strokes, it was severed from his body.

and execution.

In the speech, which he delivered to the sheriffs, he was very anxious to clear his memory from any imputation of ever intending the king's death, or any alteration in the government: He could not explicitly confess the projected insurrection without hurting his friends, who might still be called in question for it; but

CHAPTER LXIX

he did not purge himself of that design, which, in the present condition of the nation, he regarded as no crime. By many passages in his speech he seems to the last to have lain under the influence of party zeal; a passion, which, being nourished by a social temper, and cloathing itself under the appearance of principle, it is almost impossible for a virtuous man, who has acted in public life, ever thoroughly to eradicate. He professed his entire belief in the popish plot: And he said, that, though he had often heard the seizure of the guards mentioned, he had ever disapproved of that attempt. To which he added, that the massacring of so many innocent men in cool blood was so like a popish practice, that he could not but abhor it. Upon the whole, the integrity and virtuous intentions, rather than the capacity, of this unfortunate nobleman, seem to have been the shining parts of his character.

Algernon Sidney was next brought to his trial. This gallant person, son of the earl of Leicester, had entered deeply into the war against the late king; and though no wise tainted with enthusiasm, he had so far shared in all the counsels of the independant republican party, as to have been named on the high court of justice which tried and condemned that monarch: He thought not proper, however, to take his seat among the judges. He ever opposed Cromwel's usurpation with zeal and courage; and after making all efforts against the restoration, he resolved to take no benefit of the general indemnity, but chose voluntary banishment, rather than submit to a government and family, which he abhorred. As long as the republican party had any existence, he was active in every scheme, however unpromising, which tended to promote their cause: But at length, in 1677, finding it necessary for his private affairs to return to England, he had applied for the king's pardon, and had obtained it. When the factions, arising from the popish plot, began to run high, Sidney, full of those ideas of liberty, which he had imbibed from the great examples of antiquity, joined the popular party; and was even willing to seek a second time, through all the horrors of civil war, for his adored republic.

Trial of Algernon Sidney.

From this imperfect sketch of the character and conduct of this singular personage, it may easily be conceived how obnoxious he was become to the court and ministry: What alone renders them blameable was the illegal method, which they took, for effecting their purpose against him. On Sidney's trial they produced a great

number of witnesses, who proved the reality of a plot in general;
and when the prisoner exclaimed, that all these evidences said
nothing of him, he was answered, that this method of proceeding,
however irregular, had been practised in the prosecutions of the
popish conspirators: A topic more fit to condemn one party than
to justify the other. The only witness, who deposed against Sidney,
was lord Howard; but as the law required two witnesses, a strange
expedient was fallen on to supply this deficiency. In ransacking the
prisoner's closet, some discourses on government were found; in
which he had maintained principles, favourable indeed to liberty,
but such as the best and most dutiful subjects in all ages have been
known to embrace; the original contract, the source of power from
a consent of the people, the lawfulness of resisting tyrants, the
preference of liberty to the government of a single person. These
papers were asserted to be equivalent to a second witness, and even
to many witnesses. The prisoner replied, that there was no other
reason for ascribing these papers to him as the author, besides a
similitude of hand; a proof, which was never admitted in criminal
prosecutions: That allowing him to be the author, he had composed them solely for his private amusement, and had never published them to the world, or even communicated them to any
single person: That, when examined, they appeared, by the colour
of the ink to have been written many years before, and were in vain
produced as evidence of a present conspiracy against the government: And that where the law positively requires two witnesses,
one witness, attended with the most convincing circumstances,
could never suffice; much less, when supported by a circumstance
so weak and precarious. All these arguments, though urged by the
prisoner with great courage and pregnancy of reason, had no
influence. The violent and inhuman Jefferies was now chief justice; and by his direction a partial jury was easily prevailed on to
give verdict against Sidney. His execution followed a few days
after: He complained, and with reason, of the iniquity of the sentence; but he had too much greatness of mind to deny those conspiracies with Monmouth and Russel, in which he had been engaged. He rather gloried, that he now suffered for that *good old
cause,* in which, from his earliest youth, he said, he had inlisted
himself.

The execution of Sidney is regarded as one of the greatest

*17th
Dec.
His ex-
ecution.*

blemishes of the present reign. The evidence against him, it must be confessed, was not legal; and the jury, who condemned him, were, for that reason, very blameable. But that after sentence passed by a court of judicature, the king should interpose and pardon a man, who, though otherwise possessed of merit, was undoubtedly guilty, who had ever been a most inflexible and most inveterate enemy to the royal family, and who lately had even abused the king's clemency, might be an act of heroic generosity, but can never be regarded as a necessary and indispensible duty.

Howard was also the sole evidence against Hambden; and his testimony was not supported by any material circumstance. The crown-lawyers therefore found it in vain to try the prisoner for treason: They laid the indictment only for a misdemeanour, and obtained sentence against him. The fine imposed was exorbitant; no less than forty thousand pounds.

Holloway, a merchant of Bristol, one of the conspirators, had fled to the West-Indies, and was now brought over. He had been out-lawed; but the year, allowed him for surrendering himself, was not expired. A trial was therefore offered him: But as he had at first confessed his being engaged in a conspiracy for an insurrection, and even allowed that he had heard some discourse of an assassination, though he had not approved of it, he thought it more expedient to throw himself on the king's mercy. He was executed, persisting in the same confession.

Sir Thomas Armstrong, who had been seized in Holland, and sent over by Chidley, the king's minister, was precisely in the same situation with Holloway: But the same favour, or rather justice, was refused him. The lawyers pretended, that, unless he had voluntarily surrendered himself before the expiration of the time assigned, he could not claim the privilege of a trial; not considering that the seizure of his person ought in equity to be supposed the accident which prevented him. The king, bore a great enmity against this gentleman, by whom he believed the duke of Monmouth to have been seduced from his duty: He also asserted that Armstrong had once promised Cromwel to assassinate him; though it must be confessed, that the prisoner justified himself from this imputation by very strong arguments. These were the reasons of that injustice, which was now done him. It was apprehended, that sufficient evidence of his guilt could not be produced; and that even the partial juries, which were now returned, and which allowed themselves to be entirely directed by Jefferies and other violent judges, would not give sentence against him.

On the day that Russel was tried, Essex, a man eminent both for virtues and abilities, was found in the Tower with his throat cut. The coroner's inquest brought in their verdict, *self-murther:* Yet because two children ten years old (one of whom too departed from his evidence) had affirmed, that they heard a great noise from his window, and that they saw a hand throw out a bloody razor; these circumstances were laid hold of, and the murder was ascribed to the king and the duke, who happened that morning to pay a visit to the Tower. Essex was subject to fits of deep melancholy, and had been seized with one immediately upon his commitment: He was accustomed to maintain the lawfulness of suicide: And his countess, upon a strict enquiry, which was committed to the care of Dr. Burnet, found no reason to confirm the suspicion: Yet could not all these circumstances, joined to many others, entirely remove the imputation. It is no wonder, that faction is so productive of vices of all kinds: For, besides that it inflames all the passions, it tends much to remove those great restraints, honour and shame; when men find, that no iniquity can lose them the applause of their own party, and no innocence secure them against the calumnies of the opposite.

But though there is no reason to think, that Essex had been murdered by any orders from court, it must be acknowledged that an unjustifiable use in Russel's trial was made of that incident. The king's counsel mentioned it in their pleadings as a strong proof of the conspiracy; and it is said to have had great weight with the jury. It was insisted on in Sidney's trial for the same purpose.

State of the nation. Some memorable causes, tried about this time, though they have no relation to the Rye-house conspiracy, show the temper of the bench and of the juries. Oates was convicted of having called the duke a popish traitor; was condemned in damages to the amount of one hundred thousand pounds; and was adjudged to remain in prison till he should make payment. A like sentence was passed upon Dutton-Colt for a like offence. Sir Samuel Barnardiston was fined ten thousand pounds; because in some private letters which had been intercepted, he had reflected on the government. This gentleman was obnoxious, because he had been

CHAPTER LXIX

foreman of that jury, which rejected the bill against Shaftesbury. A pretence was therefore fallen upon for punishing him; though such a precedent may justly be deemed a very unusual act of severity, and sufficient to destroy all confidence in private friendship and correspondence.

There is another remarkable trial, which shows the disposition of the courts of judicature, and which, though it passed in the ensuing year, it may not be improper to relate in this place. One Rosewel, a presbyterian preacher, was accused by three women of having spoken treasonable words in a sermon. They swore to two or three periods, and agreed so exactly together, that there was not the smallest variation in their depositions. Rosewel on the other hand made a very good defence. He proved, that the witnesses were lewd and infamous persons. He proved, that, even during Cromwel's usurpations, he had always been a royalist; that he prayed constantly for the king in his family: and that in his sermons he often inculcated the obligations of loyalty. And as to the sermon, of which he was accused, several witnesses, who heard it, and some who wrote it in short hand, deposed that he had used no such expressions as those which were imputed to him. He offered his own notes as a farther proof. The women could not show by any circumstance or witness, that they were at his meeting. And the expressions, to which they deposed, were so gross, that no man in his senses could be supposed to employ them before a mixt audience. It was also urged, that it appeared next to impossible for three women to remember so long a period upon one single hearing, and to remember it so exactly, as to agree to a tittle in their depositions with regard to it. The prisoner offered to put the whole upon this issue: He would pronounce, with his usual tone of voice, a period as long as that to which they had sworn; and then let them try to repeat it, if they could. What was more unaccountable, they had forgotten even the text of his sermon; nor did they remember any single passage, but the words, to which they gave evidence. After so strong a defence, the solicitor general thought not proper to make any reply: Even Jefferies went no farther than some general declamations against conventicles and presbyterians: Yet so violent were party-prejudices, that the jury gave a verdict against the prisoner; which however appeared so palpably unjust, that it was not carried into execution.

The duke of Monmouth had absconded on the first discovery of the conspiracy; and the court could get no intelligence of him. At length, Halifax, who began to apprehend the too great prevalence of the royal party, and who thought, that Monmouth's interest would prove the best counterpoize to the duke's, discovered his retreat, and prevailed on him to write two letters to the king, full of the tenderest and most submissive expressions. The king's fondness was revived; and he permitted Monmouth to come to court. He even endeavoured to mediate a reconciliation between his son and his brother; and having promised Monmouth, that his testimony should never be employed against any of his friends, he engaged him to give a full account of the plot. But, in order to put the country party to silence, he called next day an extraordinary council; and informed them, that Monmouth had showed great penitence for the share which he had had in the late conspiracy, and had expressed his resolutions never more to engage in such criminal enterprizes. He went so far as to give orders, that a paragraph to the like purpose should be inserted in the Gazette. Monmouth kept silence till he had obtained his pardon in form: But finding, that, by taking this step, he was entirely disgraced with his party, and that, even though he should not be produced in court as an evidence, his testimony, being so publicly known, might have weight with juries on any future trial, he resolved at all hazards to retrieve his honour. His emissaries, therefore, received orders to deny, that he had ever made any such confession as that which was imputed to him; and the party exclaimed, that the whole was an imposture of the court. The king provoked at this conduct, banished Monmouth his presence, and afterwards ordered him to depart the kingdom.

The court was aware, that the malcontents in England had held a correspondence with those of Scotland; and that Baillie of Jerviswood, a man of merit and learning, with two gentlemen of the name of Campbel, had come to London, under pretence of negociating the settlement of the Scottish presbyterians in Carolina, but really with a view of concerting measures with the English conspirators. Baillie was sent prisoner to Edinburgh; but as no evidence appeared against him, the council required him to swear, that he would answer all questions, which should be propounded to him. He refused to submit to so iniquitous a condition; and a

CHAPTER LXIX

fine of six thousand pounds was imposed upon him. At length, two persons, Spence and Carstares, being put to the torture, gave evidence which involved the earl of Tarras and some others, who, in order to save themselves, were reduced to accuse Baillie. He was brought to trial; and being in so languishing a condition from the treatment which he had met with in prison, that it was feared he would not survive that night, he was ordered to be executed the very afternoon on which he received sentence.

The severities, exercised during this part of the present reign, were much contrary to the usual tenor of the king's conduct; and though those who studied his character more narrowly, have pronounced, that towards great offences he was rigid and inexorable, the nation were more inclined to ascribe every unjust or hard measure to the prevalence of the duke, into whose hands the king had, from indolence, not from any opinion of his brother's superior capacity, resigned the reins of government. The crown indeed gained great advantage from the detection of the conspiracy, and lost none by the rigorous execution of the conspirators: The horror entertained against the assassination-plot, which was generally confounded with the project for an insurrection, rendered the whole party unpopular, and reconciled the nation to the measures of the court. The most loyal addresses came from all parts; and the doctrine of submission to the civil magistrate, and even of an unlimited passive obedience, became the reigning principle of the times. The university of Oxford passed a solemn decree, condemning some doctrines, which they termed republican, but which indeed are, most of them, the only tenets, on which liberty and a limited constitution can be founded. The faction of the exclusionists, lately so numerous, powerful, and zealous, were at the king's feet; and were as much fallen in their spirit as in their credit with the nation. Nothing that had the least appearance of opposition to the court, could be hearkened to by the public.[l]

The king endeavoured to encrease his present popularity by every art; and knowing, that the suspicion of popery was of all

1684.

[l] In the month of November this year died Prince Rupert, in the sixty-third year of his age. He had left his own country so early, that he had become an entire Englishman, and was even suspected, in his latter days, of a biass to the country party. He was for that reason much neglected at court. The duke of Lauderdale died also this year.

others the most dangerous, he judged it proper to marry his niece, the lady Anne, to prince George, brother to the king of Denmark. All the credit, however, and persuasion of Halifax could not engage him to call a parliament, or trust the nation with the election of a new representative. Though his revenues were extremely burthened, he rather chose to struggle with the present difficulties, than try an experiment, which, by raising afresh so many malignant humours, might prove dangerous to his repose. The duke likewise zealously opposed this proposal, and even engaged the king in measures, which could have no tendency, but to render any accommodation with a parliament altogether impracticable. Williams, who had been speaker during the two last parliaments, was prosecuted for warrants, issued by him, in obedience to orders of the house: A breach of privilege, which, it seemed not likely, any future house of commons would leave unquestioned. Danby and the popish lords, who had so long been confined in the Tower, and who saw no prospect of a trial in parliament, applied by petition, and were admitted to bail: A measure just in itself, but deemed a great encroachment on the privileges of that assembly. The duke, contrary to law, was restored to the office of high admiral, without taking the test.

Had the least grain of jealousy or emulation been mixed in the king's character; had he been actuated by that concern for his people's or even for his own honour, which his high station demanded, he would have hazarded many domestic inconveniencies rather than allow France to domineer in so haughty a manner as that which at present she assumed in every negociation. The peace of Nimeguen, imposed by the Dutch on their unwilling allies, had disjointed the whole confederacy; and all the powers, engaged in it, had disbanded their supernumerary troops, which they found it difficult to subsist. Lewis alone still maintained a powerful army, and by his preparations rendered himself every day more formidable. He now acted as if he were the sole sovereign in Europe, and as if all other princes were soon to become his vassals. Courts or chambers were erected in Metz and Brisac, for re-uniting such territories as had ever been members of any part of his new conquests. They made inquiry into titles buried in the most remote antiquity. They cited the neighbouring princes to appear before them, and issued decrees, expelling them the contested territories. The important town of Strasbourg, an ancient and a free state, was

State of foreign affairs.

CHAPTER LXIX

seized by Lewis: Alost was demanded of the Spaniards, on a frivolous, and even ridiculous pretence; and upon their refusal to
yield it, Luxembourg was blockaded, and soon after taken.[m] Genoa
had been bombarded, because the Genoese had stipulated to build
some gallies for the Spaniards; and, in order to avoid more severe
treatment, that republic was obliged to yield to the most mortifying
conditions. The empire was insulted in its head and principal
members; and used no other expedient for redress, than impotent
complaints and remonstrances.

Spain was so enraged at the insolent treatment which she met
with, that, without considering her present weak condition, she
declared war against her haughty enemy: She hoped that the other
powers of Europe, sensible of the common danger, would fly to
her assistance. The prince of Orange, whose ruling passions were
love of war and animosity against France, seconded every where
the applications of the Spaniards. In the year 1681, he made a
journey to England, in order to engage the king into closer measures with the confederates. He also proposed to the States to
make an augmentation of their forces; but several of the provinces,
and even the town of Amsterdam, had been gained by the French,
and the proposal was rejected. The prince's enemies derived the
most plausible reasons of their opposition from the situation of
England, and the known and avowed attachments of the English
monarch.

No sooner had Charles dismissed his parliament, and embraced the resolution of governing by prerogative alone, than he
dropped his new alliance with Spain and returned to his former
dangerous connections with Lewis. This prince had even offered
to make him arbiter of his differences with Spain; and the latter
power, sensible of Charles's partiality, had refused to submit to
such a disadvantageous proposal. Whether any money was now
remitted to England, we do not certainly know: But we may fairly
presume, that the king's necessities were in some degree relieved
by France.[n] And though Charles had reason to apprehend the

[m] It appears from Sir John Dalrymple's Appendix, that the king received
from France a million of livres for his connivance at the seizure of Luxembourg, beside his ordinary pension.   [n] The following passage is an
extract from M. Barillon's letters kept in the *Depot des Affaires etrangeres* at
Versailles. It was lately communicated to the author while in France. Convention verbale arretée le 1 avril 1681. Charles 2 s'engage a ne rien omettre

utmost danger from the great, and still encreasing, naval power of that kingdom, joined to the weak condition of the English fleet, no consideration was able to rouze him from his present lethargy.

It is here we are to fix the point of the highest exaltation, which the power of Lewis or that of any European prince, since the age of Charlemagne, had ever attained. The monarch, most capable of opposing his progress was entirely engaged in his interests; and the Turks, invited by the malcontents of Hungary, were preparing to invade the emperor, and to disable that prince from making head against the progress of the French power. Lewis may even be accused of oversight, in not making sufficient advantage of such favourable opportunities, which he was never afterwards able to recall. But that monarch, though more governed by motives of ambition than by those of justice or moderation, was still more actuated by the suggestions of vanity. He contented himself with insulting and domineering over all the princes and free states of Europe; and he thereby provoked their resentment, without sub-duing their power. While every one, who approached his person, and behaved with submission to his authority, was treated with the highest politeness; all the neighbouring potentates had succes-sively felt the effects of his haughty imperious disposition. And by indulging his poets, orators, and courtiers in their flatteries, and in their prognostications of universal empire, he conveyed faster, than by the prospect of his power alone, the apprehension of general conquest and subjection.

1685. The French greatness never, during his whole reign, inspired Charles with any apprehensions; and Clifford, it is said, one of his

---

pour pouvoir faire connoitre à sa majesté qu'elle avoit raison de prendre confiance en lui; a se degager peu a peu de l'alliance avec l'Espagne, & a se mettre en etat de ne point etre contraint par son parlement de faire quelque chose d'opposé aux nouveaux engagemens qu'il prenoit. En con-sequence le roi promet un subside de deux millions la premiere des trois années de cet engagement & 500,000 écus les deux autres, se contentant de la parole de sa majesté Britannique, d'agir à l'egard de sa majesté con-formement aux obligations qu'il lui avoit. Le Sr. Hyde demanda que le roi s'engagea a ne point attaquer les pays bas & meme Strasbourg, temoignant que le roi son maitre ne pourroit s'empecher de secourir les pais bas, quand même son parlement ne seroit point assemblé. M. Barillon lui repondit en termes generaux par ordre du roi, que sa majesté n' avoit point intention de rompre la paix, & qu'il n'engageroit pas sa majesté Britannique en choses contraires à ses veritables interets.

most favoured ministers, went so far as to affirm, that it were better for the king to be viceroy under a great and generous monarch, than a slave to five hundred of his own insolent subjects. The ambition, therefore, and uncontrouled power of Lewis were no diminution of Charles's happiness; and in other respects his condition seemed at present more eligible than it had ever been since his restoration. A mighty faction, which had shaken his throne, and menaced his family, was totally subdued; and by their precipitate indiscretion had exposed themselves both to the rigour of the laws and to public hatred. He had recovered his former popularity in the nation; and what probably pleased him more than having a compliant parliament, he was enabled to govern altogether without one. But it is certain, that the king, amidst all these promising circumstances, was not happy or satisfied. Whether he found himself exposed to difficulties for want of money, or dreaded a recoil of the popular humour from the present arbitrary measures, is uncertain. Perhaps the violent, imprudent temper of the duke, by pushing Charles upon dangerous attempts, gave him apprehension and uneasiness. He was overheard one day to say, in opposing some of the duke's hasty counsels, "Brother, I am too old to go again to my travels: You may, if you chuse it." Whatever was the cause of the king's dissatisfaction, it seems probable, that he was meditating some change of measures, and had formed a new plan of administration. He was determined, it is thought, to send the duke to Scotland, to recall Monmouth, to summon a parliament, to dismiss all his unpopular ministers, and to throw himself entirely on the good will and affections of his subjects.[v] Amidst these truly wise and virtuous designs, he was seized with a sudden fit, which resembled an apoplexy; and though he was recovered from it by bleeding, he languished only for a few days, and then expired, in the fifty-fifth year of his age, and twenty-fifth of his reign. He was so happy in a good constitution of body, and had ever been so remarkably careful of his health, that his death struck as great a surprize into his subjects, as if he had been in the flower of his youth. And their great concern for him, owing to their affection for his person, as well as their dread of his successor, very naturally, when joined to the critical time of his death, begat the sus-

King's sickness,

and death. 6th Feb.

[v] King James's Memoirs confirm this rumor, as also D'Avaux's Negotiations, 14 Dec. 1684.

picion of poison. All circumstances however considered, this suspicion must be allowed to vanish; like many others, of which all histories are full.

During the few days of the king's illness, clergymen of the church of England attended him; but he discovered a total indifference towards their devotions and exhortations. Catholic priests were brought, and he received the sacrament from them, accompanied with the other rites of the Romish church. Two papers were found in his cabinet, written with his own hand, and containing arguments in favour of that communion. The duke had the imprudence immediately to publish these papers, and thereby both confirmed all the reproaches of those who had been the greatest enemies to his brother's measures, and afforded to the world a specimen of his own bigotry.

and character.
If we survey the character of Charles II. in the different lights, which it will admit of, it will appear various, and give rise to different and even opposite sentiments. When considered as a companion, he appears the most amiable and engaging of men; and indeed, in this view, his deportment must be allowed altogether unexceptionable. His love of raillery was so tempered with good breeding, that it was never offensive: His propensity to satire was so checked with discretion, that his friends never dreaded their becoming the object of it: His wit, to use the expression of one who knew him well, and who was himself a good judge, *p* could not be said so much to be very refined or elevated, qualities apt to beget jealousy and apprehension in company, as to be a plain, gaining, well-bred, recommending kind of wit. And though perhaps he talked more than strict rules of behaviour might permit, men were so pleased with the affable, communicative deportment of the monarch, that they always went away contented both with him and with themselves. This indeed is the most shining part of the king's character; and he seems to have been sensible of it: For he was fond of dropping the formality of state, and of relapsing every moment into the companion.

In the duties of private life his conduct, though not free from exception, was, in the main, laudable. He was an easy generous lover, a civil obliging husband, a friendly brother, an indulgent

p Marquess of Halifax.

CHAPTER LXIX

father, and a good natured master.*q* The voluntary friendships, however, which this prince contracted, nay, even his sense of gratitude, were feeble; and he never attached himself to any of his ministers or courtiers with a sincere affection. He believed them to have no motive in serving him but self-interest; and he was still ready, in his turn, to sacrifice them to present ease or convenience.

With a detail of his private character we must set bounds to our panegyric on Charles. The other parts of his conduct may admit of some apology, but can deserve small applause. He was indeed so much fitted for private life, preferably to public, that he even possessed order, frugality, and economy in the former: Was profuse, thoughtless, and negligent in the latter. When we consider him as a sovereign, his character, though not altogether destitute of virtue, was in the main dangerous to his people, and dishonourable to himself. Negligent of the interests of the nation, careless of its glory, averse to its religion, jealous of its liberty, lavish of its treasure, sparing only of its blood; he exposed it by his measures, though he ever appeared but in sport, to the danger of a furious civil war, and even to the ruin and ignominy of a foreign conquest. Yet may all these enormities, if fairly and candidly examined, be imputed, in a great measure, to the indolence of his temper; a fault, which, however unfortunate in a monarch, it is impossible for us to regard with great severity.

It has been remarked of Charles, that he never said a foolish thing nor ever did a wise one: A censure, which, though too far carried, seems to have some foundation in his character and deportment. When the king was informed of this saying, he observed, that the matter was easily accounted for: For that his discourse was his own, his actions were the ministry's.

If we reflect on the appetite for power inherent in human nature, and add to it the king's education in foreign countries, and among the cavaliers, a party which would naturally exaggerate the late usurpations of popular assemblies upon the rights of monarchy; it is not surprizing, that civil liberty should not find in him a very zealous patron. Harassed with domestic faction, weary of calumnies and complaints, oppressed with debts, straitened in his revenue, he sought, though with feeble efforts, for a form of gov-

q Duke of Buckingham.

ernment, more simple in its structure and more easy in its management. But his attachment to France, after all the pains, which we have taken, by enquiry and conjecture, to fathom it, contains still something, it must be confessed, mysterious and inexplicable. The hopes of rendering himself absolute by Lewis's assistance seem so chimerical, that they could scarcely be retained with such obstinacy by a prince of Charles's penetration: And as to pecuniary subsidies, he surely spent much greater sums in one season, during the second Dutch war, than were remitted him from France during the whole course of his reign. I am apt therefore to imagine, that Charles was in this particular guided chiefly by inclination, and by a prepossession in favour of the French nation. He considered that people as gay, sprightly, polite, elegant, courteous, devoted to their prince, and attached to the catholic faith; and for these reasons he cordially loved them. The opposite character of the Dutch had rendered them the objects of his aversion; and even the uncourtly humours of the English made him very indifferent towards them. Our notions of interest are much warped by our affections; and it is not altogether without example, that a man may be guided by national prejudices, who has ever been little biassed by private and personal friendship.

The character of this prince has been elaborately drawn by two great masters, perfectly well acquainted with him, the duke of Buckingham and the marquess of Halifax; not to mention several elegant strokes given by Sir William Temple. Dr. Welwood likewise and bishop Burnet have employed their pencil on the same subject: But the former is somewhat partial in his favour; as the latter is by far too harsh and malignant. Instead of finding an exact parallel between Charles II. and the emperor Tiberius, as asserted by that prelate, it would be more just to remark a full contrast and opposition. The emperor seems as much to have surpassed the king in abilities, as he falls short of him in virtue. Provident, wise, active, jealous, malignant, dark, sullen, unsociable, reserved, cruel, unrelenting, unforgiving; these are the lights, under which the Roman tyrant has been transmitted to us. And the only circumstance, in which, it can justly be pretended, he was similar to Charles, is his love of women, a passion which is too general to form any striking resemblance, and which that detestable and detested monster shared also with unnatural appetites.

LXX

JAMES II

King's first transactions –
A parliament – Arguments for and against
a revenue for life – Oates convicted of perjury –
Monmouth's invasion – His defeat – and execution –
Cruelties of Kirke – and of Jefferies – State of affairs
in Scotland – Argyle's invasion – defeat – and
execution – A parliament – French persecutions –
The dispensing power – State of Scotland – State
of Ireland – Breach betwixt the king and the
church – Court of ecclesiastical commission –
Sentence against the bishop of London –
Suspension of the penal laws – State of
Ireland – Embassy to Rome – Attempt
on Magdalen College – Imprisonment –
trial, and acquittal of the bishops –
Birth of the prince of Wales

THE FIRST ACT of James's reign was to assemble the privy council; where, after some praises bestowed on the memory of his predecessor, he made professions of his resolution to maintain the established government, both in church and state. Though he had been reported, he said, to have imbibed arbitrary prin-

1685.
King's
first trans-
actions.

449

ciples, he knew that the laws of England were sufficient to make him as great a monarch as he could wish; and he was determined never to depart from them. And as he had heretofore ventured his life in defence of the nation, he would still go as far as any man in maintaining all its just rights and liberties.

This discourse was received with great applause, not only by the council, but by the nation. The king universally passed for a man of great sincerity and great honour; and as the current of favour ran at that time for the court, men believed, that his intentions were conformable to his expressions. "We have now," it was said, "the word of a king; and a word never yet broken." Addresses came from all quarters, full of duty, nay, of the most servile adulation. Every one hastened to pay court to the new monarch.[r] And James had reason to think, that, notwithstanding the violent efforts made by so potent a party for his exclusion, no throne in Europe was better established than that of England.

The king, however, in the first exercise of his authority, shewed, that either he was not sincere in his professions of attachment to the laws, or that he had entertained so lofty an idea of his own legal power, that even his utmost sincerity would tend very little to secure the liberties of the people. All the customs and the greater part of the excise had been settled by parliament on the late king during life, and consequently the grant was now expired; nor had the successor any right to levy these branches of revenue. But James issued a proclamation, ordering the customs and excise to be paid as before; and this exertion of power he would not deign to qualify by the least act or even appearance of condescension. It was proposed to him, that, in order to prevent the ill effects of any intermission in levying these duties, entries should be made, and bonds for the sums be taken from the merchants and brewers: But the payment be suspended till the parliament should give author-

---

[r] The quakers' address was esteemed somewhat singular for its plainness and simplicity. It was conceived in these terms: "We are come to testify our sorrow for the death of our good friend Charles, and our joy for thy being made our governor. We are told thou art not of the persuasion of the church of England, no more than we: Wherefore we hope thou wilt grant us the same liberty, which thou allowest thyself. Which doing, we wish thee all manner of happiness."

CHAPTER LXX

ity to receive it. This precaution was recommended as an expression of deference to that assembly, or rather to the laws: But for that very reason, probably, it was rejected by the king, who thought, that the commons would thence be invited to assume more authority, and would regard the whole revenue, and consequently the whole power, of the crown, as dependent on their good will and pleasure.

The king likewise went openly, and with all the ensigns of his dignity, to mass, an illegal meeting: And by this imprudence he displayed at once his arbitrary disposition, and the bigotry of his principles: These two great characteristics of his reign, and bane of his administration. He even sent Caryl, as his agent, to Rome, in order to make submissions to the pope, and to pave the way for a solemn re-admission of England into the bosom of the catholic church. The pope, Innocent the XIth, prudently advised the king not to be too precipitate in his measures, nor rashly attempt what repeated experience might convince him was impracticable. The Spanish ambassador, Ronquillo, deeming the tranquillity of England necessary for the support of Spain, used the freedom to make like remonstrances. He observed to the king, how busy the priests appeared at court, and advised him not to assent with too great facility to their dangerous counsels. "Is it not the custom in Spain," said James, "for the king to consult with his confessor?" "Yes," replied the ambassador, "and it is for that very reason our affairs succeed so ill."

James gave hopes on his accession, that he would hold the balance of power more steadily than his predecessor; and that France, instead of rendering England subservient to her ambitious projects, would now meet with strong opposition from that kingdom. Besides applying himself to business with industry, he seemed jealous of national honour, and expressed great care, that no more respect should be paid to the French ambassador at London than his own received at Paris. But these appearances were not sufficiently supported, and he found himself immediately under the necessity of falling into a union with that great monarch, who, by his power as well as his zeal, seemed alone able to assist him, in the projects formed for promoting the catholic religion in England.

Notwithstanding the king's prejudices, all the chief offices of the crown continued still in the hands of protestants. Rochester was treasurer; his brother Clarendon chamberlain; Godolphin chamberlain to the queen; Sunderland secretary of state; Halifax president of the council. This nobleman had stood in opposition to James during the last years of his brother's reign; and when he attempted, on the accession, to make some apology for his late measures, the king told him, that he would forget every thing past, except his behaviour during the bill of exclusion. On other occasions, however, James appeared not of so forgiving a temper. When the principal exclusionists came to pay their respects to the new sovereign, they either were not admitted, or were received very coldly, sometimes even with frowns. This conduct might suit the character, which the king so much affected, of sincerity: But by showing, that a king of England could resent the quarrels of a duke of York, he gave his people no high idea either of his lenity or magnanimity.

On all occasions, the king was open in declaring, that men must now look for a more active and more vigilant government, and that he would retain no ministers, who did not practise an unreserved obedience to his commands. We are not indeed to look for the springs of his administration so much in his council and chief officers of state, as in his own temper, and in the character of those persons, with whom he secretly consulted. The queen had great influence over him; a woman of spirit, whose conduct had been popular till she arrived at that high dignity. She was much governed by the priests, especially the jesuits; and as these were also the king's favourites, all public measures were taken originally from the suggestions of these men, and bore evident marks of their ignorance in government, and of the violence of their religious zeal.

The king however had another attachment, seemingly not very consistent with this devoted regard to his queen and to his priests: It was to Mrs. Sedley, whom he soon after created countess of Dorchester, and who expected to govern him with the same authority, which the duchess of Portsmouth had possessed during the former reign. But James, who had entertained the ambition of converting his people, was told, that the regularity of his life ought to correspond to the sanctity of his intentions; and he was pre-

CHAPTER LXX

vailed with to remove Mrs. Sedley from court: A resolution in which he had not the courage to persevere. Good agreement between the mistress and the confessor of princes is not commonly a difficult matter to compass: But in the present case these two potent engines of command were found very incompatible. Mrs. Sedley, who possessed all the wit and ingenuity of her father, Sir Charles, made the priests and their counsels the perpetual object of her raillery; and it is not to be doubted, but they, on their part, redoubled their exhortations with their penitent to break off so criminal an attachment.

How little inclination soever the king, as well as his queen and priests, might bear to an English parliament, it was absolutely necessary, at the beginning of the reign, to summon that assembly. The low condition, to which the whigs or country party had fallen during the last years of Charles's reign, the odium under which they laboured on account of the Rye-house conspiracy; these causes made that party meet with little success in the elections. The general resignation too of the charters had made the corporations extremely dependent; and the recommendations of the court, though little assisted, at that time, by pecuniary influence, were become very prevalent. The new house of commons, therefore, *A parliament.* consisted almost entirely of zealous tories and churchmen; and were of consequence strongly biassed, by their affections, in favour of the measures of the crown.

The discourse, which the king made to the parliament, was *19th of May.* more fitted to work on their fears than their affections. He repeated indeed, and with great solemnity, the promise which he had made before the privy-council, of governing according to the laws, and of preserving the established religion: But at the same time he told them, that he positively expected they would settle his revenue, and during life too, as in the time of his brother. "I might use many arguments," said he, "to inforce this demand; the benefit of trade, the support of the navy, the necessities of the crown, and the well-being of the government itself, which I must not suffer to be precarious: But I am confident, that your own consideration and your sense of what is just and reasonable, will suggest to you whatever on this occasion might be enlarged upon. There is indeed one popular argument," added he, "which may be urged against compliance with my demand: Men may think, that by feeding me from time to time with such supplies as they think convenient, they will better secure frequent meetings of parliament: But as this is the first time I speak to you from the throne, I must plainly tell you, that such an expedient would be very improper to employ with me, and that the best way to engage me to meet you often is always to use me well."

It was easy to interpret this language of the king's. He plainly intimated, that he had resources in his prerogative for supporting the government, independent of their supplies; and that so long as they complied with his demands, he would have recourse to them; but that any ill usage on their part would set him free from those measures of government, which he seemed to regard more as voluntary than as necessary. It must be confessed, that no parliament in England was ever placed in a more critical situation, nor where more forcible arguments could be urged, either for their opposition to the court, or their compliance with it.

Reasons for and against a revenue during life.
It was said on the one hand, that jealousy of royal power was the very basis of the English constitution, and the principle, to which the nation was beholden for all that liberty, which they enjoy above the subjects of other monarchies. That this jealousy, though, at different periods, it may be more or less intense, can never safely be laid asleep, even under the best and wisest princes. That the character of the present sovereign afforded cause for the highest vigilance, by reason of the arbitrary principles, which he had imbibed; and still more, by reason of his religious zeal, which it is impossible for him ever to gratify, without assuming more authority than the constitution allows him. That power is to be watched in its very first encroachments; nor is any thing ever gained by timidity and submission. That every concession adds new force to usurpation; and at the same time, by discovering the dastardly dispositions of the people, inspires it with new courage and enterprize. That as arms were intrusted altogether in the hands of the prince, no check remained upon him but the dependent condition of his revenue; a security therefore which it would be the most egregious folly to abandon. That all the other barriers, which, of late years, had been erected against arbitrary power, would be found, without this capital article, to be rather pernicious and destructive. That new limitations in the constitution stimulated the monarch's inclination to surmount the laws, and required frequent

CHAPTER LXX

meetings of parliament, in order to repair all the breaches, which either time or violence may have made upon that complicated fabric. That recent experience during the reign of the late king, a prince who wanted neither prudence nor moderation, had sufficiently proved the solidity of all these maxims. That his parliament, having rashly fixed his revenue for life, and at the same time repealed the triennial bill, found that they themselves were no longer of importance, and that liberty, not protected by national assemblies, was exposed to every outrage and violation. And that the more openly the king made an unreasonable demand, the more obstinately ought it to be refused; since it is evident, that his purpose in making it cannot possibly be justifiable.

On the other hand it was urged, that the rule of watching the very first encroachments of power could only have place, where the opposition to it could be regular, peaceful, and legal. That though the refusal of the king's present demand might seem of this nature, yet in reality it involved consequences, which led much farther than at first sight might be apprehended. That the king in his speech had intimated, that he had resources in his prerogative, which, in case of opposition from parliament, he thought himself fully entitled to employ. That if the parliament openly discovered an intention of reducing him to dependence, matters must presently be brought to a crisis, at a time the most favourable to his cause, which his most sanguine wishes could ever have promised him. That if we cast our eyes abroad, to the state of affairs on the continent, and to the situation of Scotland and Ireland; or, what is of more importance, if we consider the disposition of men's minds at home, every circumstance would be found adverse to the cause of liberty. That the country party, during the late reign, by their violent, and in many respects unjustifiable measures in parliament, by their desperate attempts out of parliament, had exposed their principles to general hatred, and had excited extreme jealousy in all the royalists and zealous churchmen, who now formed the bulk of the nation. That it would not be acceptable to that party to see this king worse treated than his brother in point of revenue, or any attempts made to keep the crown in dependence. That they thought parliaments as liable to abuse as courts, and desired not to see things in a situation, where the king could not, if he found it necessary, either prorogue or dissolve those assemblies. That if the present parliament, by making great concessions, could gain the king's confidence, and engage him to observe the promises now given them, every thing would by gentle methods succeed to their wishes. That if, on the contrary, after such instances of compliance, he formed any designs on the liberty and religion of the nation, he would, in the eyes of all mankind, render himself altogether inexcusable, and the whole people would join in opposition to him. That resistance could scarcely be attempted twice; and there was therefore the greater necessity for waiting till time and incidents had fully prepared the nation for it. That the king's prejudices in favour of popery, though in the main pernicious, were yet so far fortunate, that they rendered the connexion inseparable between the national religion and national liberty. And that if any illegal attempts were afterwards made, the church, which was at present the chief support of the crown, would surely catch the alarm, and would soon dispose the people to an effectual resistance.

These last reasons, enforced by the prejudices of party, prevailed in parliament; and the commons, besides giving thanks for the king's speech, voted unanimously, that they would settle on his present majesty during life all the revenue enjoyed by the late king at the time of his demise. That they might not detract from this generosity by any symptoms of distrust, they also voted unanimously, that the house entirely relied on his majesty's royal word and repeated declarations to support the religion of the church of England; but they added, that that religion was dearer to them than their lives. The speaker, in presenting the revenue-bill, took care to inform the king of their vote with regard to religion; but could not, by so signal a proof of confidence, extort from him one word, in favour of that religion, on which, he told his majesty, they set so high a value. Notwithstanding the grounds of suspicion, which this silence afforded, the house continued in the same liberal disposition. The king having demanded a farther supply for the navy and other purposes, they revived those duties on wines and vinegar, which had once been enjoyed by the late king; and they added some impositions on tobacco and sugar. This grant amounted on the whole to about six hundred thousand pounds a year.

The house of lords were in a humour no less compliant. They

CHAPTER LXX

even went some lengths towards breaking in pieces all the remains of the popish plot; that once formidable engine of bigotry and faction.

A little before the meeting of parliament, Oates had been tried for perjury on two indictments. One for deposing, that he was present at a consult of jesuits in London the twenty-fourth of April, 1679: Another for deposing, that father Ireland was in London between the eighth and twelfth of August, and in the beginning of September in the same year. Never criminal was convicted on fuller and more undoubted evidence. Two and twenty persons, who had been students at St. Omers, most of them men of credit and family, gave evidence, that Oates had entered into that seminary about Christmas in the year 1678, and had never been absent but one night, till the month of July following. Forty-seven witnesses, persons also of untainted character, deposed that father Ireland, on the third of August, 1679, had gone to Staffordshire, where he resided till the middle of September; and, what some years before would have been regarded as a very material circumstance, nine of these witnesses were protestants, of the church of England. Oates's sentence was, to be fined a thousand marks on each indictment, to be whipped on two different days from Aldgate to Newgate, and from Newgate to Tyburn, to be imprisoned during life, and to be pilloried five times every year. The impudence of the man supported itself under the conviction, and his courage under the punishment. He made solemn appeals to Heaven, and protestations of the veracity of his testimony: Though the whipping was so cruel, that it was evidently the intention of the court to put him to death by that punishment, he was enabled, by the care of his friends, to recover: And he lived to king William's reign; when a pension of four hundred pounds a year was settled on him. A considerable number still adhered to him in his distresses, and regarded him as the martyr of the protestant cause. The populace were affected with the sight of a punishment, more severe than is commonly inflicted in England. And the sentence of perpetual imprisonment was deemed illegal.

Oates convicted of perjury.

The conviction of Oates's perjury was taken notice of by the house of peers. Besides freeing the popish lords, Powis, Arundel, Bellasis, and Tyrone, together with Danby, from the former impeachment by the commons, they went so far as to vote a reversal of Stafford's attainder, on account of the falshood of that evidence, on which he had been condemned. This bill fixed so deep a reproach on the former proceedings of the exclusionists, that it met with great opposition among the lords; and it was at last, after one reading, dropped by the commons. Though the reparation of injustice be the second honour, which a nation can attain; the present emergence seemed very improper for granting so full a justification to the catholics, and throwing so foul a stain on the protestants.

Monmouth's invasion.

The course of parliamentary proceedings was interrupted by the news of Monmouth's arrival in the west with three ships from Holland. No sooner was this intelligence conveyed to the parliament, than they voted, that they would adhere to his majesty with their lives and fortunes. They passed a bill of attainder against Monmouth; and they granted a supply of four hundred thousand pounds for suppressing his rebellion. Having thus strengthened the hands of the king, they adjourned themselves.

Monmouth, when ordered to depart the kingdom, during the late reign, had retired to Holland; and as it was well known, that he still enjoyed the favour of his indulgent father, all marks of honour and distinction were bestowed upon him by the prince of Orange. After the accession of James, the prince thought it necessary to dismiss Monmouth and all his followers; and that illustrious fugitive retired to Brussels. Finding himself still pursued by the king's severity, he was pushed, contrary to his judgment as well as inclination, to make a rash and premature attempt upon England. He saw that James had lately mounted the throne, not only without opposition, but seemingly with the good will and affections of his subjects. A parliament was sitting, which discovered the greatest disposition to comply with the king, and whose adherence, he knew, would give a sanction and authority to all public measures. The grievances of this reign were hitherto of small importance; and the people were not as yet in a disposition to remark them with great severity. All these considerations occurred to Monmouth; but such was the impatience of his followers, and such the precipitate humour of Argyle, who set out for Scotland a little before him, that no reasons could be attended to; and this unhappy man was driven upon his fate.

CHAPTER LXX

The imprudence, however, of this enterprize did not at first *11th* appear. Though on his landing at Lime in Dorsetshire, he had *June.* scarcely a hundred followers; so popular was his name, that in four days he had assembled above two thousand horse and foot. They were indeed, almost all of them, the lowest of the people, and the declaration, which he published, was chiefly calculated to suit the prejudices of the vulgar, or the most bigotted of the whig-party. He called the king, duke of York; and denominated him a traitor, a tyrant, an assassin, and a popish usurper. He imputed to him the fire of London, the murder of Godfrey and of Essex, nay the poisoning of the late king. And he invited all the people to join in opposition to his tyranny.

The duke of Albemarle, son to him who had restored the royal family, assembled the militia of Devonshire to the number of 4000 men, and took post at Axminister, in order to oppose the rebels; but observing, that his troops bore a great affection to Monmouth, he thought proper to retire. Monmouth, though he had formerly given many proofs of personal courage, had not the vigour of mind requisite for an undertaking of this nature. From an ill grounded diffidence of his men, he neglected to attack Albemarle; an easy enterprize, by which he might both have acquired credit and have supplied himself with arms. Lord Gray, who commanded his horse, discovered himself to be a notorious coward; yet such was the softness of Monmouth's nature, that Gray was still continued in his command. Fletcher of Salton, a Scotchman, a man of signal probity and fine genius, had been engaged by his republican principles in this enterprize, and commanded the cavalry together with Gray: But being insulted by one, who had newly joined the army, and whose horse he had in a hurry made use of, he was prompted by passion, to which he was much subject, to discharge a pistol at the man; and he killed him on the spot. This incident obliged him immediately to leave the camp; and the loss of so gallant an officer was a great prejudice to Monmouth's enterprize.

The next station of the rebels was Taunton, a disaffected town, which gladly and even fondly received them, and re-inforced them with considerable numbers. Twenty young maids of some rank presented Monmouth with a pair of colours of their handiwork, together with a copy of the bible. Monmouth was here persuaded to take upon him the title of king, and assert the legitimacy of his birth; a claim, which he advanced in his first declaration, but whose discussion he was determined, he then said, during some time to postpone. His numbers had now increased to six thousand; and he was obliged every day, for want of arms, to dismiss a great many, who crowded to his standard. He entered Bridgewater, Wells, Frome; and was proclaimed in all these places: But forgetting, that such desperate enterprizes can only be rendered successful by the most adventurous courage, he allowed the expectations of the people to languish, without attempting any considerable undertaking.

While Monmouth, by his imprudent and misplaced caution, was thus wasting time in the West, the king employed himself in making preparations to oppose him. Six regiments of British troops were called over from Holland: The army was considerably augmented: And regular forces, to the number of 3000 men, were dispatched under the command of Feversham and Churchill, in order to check the progress of the rebels.

Monmouth, observing that no considerable men joined him, finding that an insurrection, which was projected in the city, had not taken place, and hearing that Argyle, his confederate, was already defeated and taken; sunk into such despondency, that he had once resolved to withdraw himself, and leave his unhappy followers to their fate. His followers expressed more courage than their leader, and seemed determined to adhere to him in every fortune. The negligent disposition, made by Feversham, invited Monmouth to attack the king's army at Sedgemoor near Bridgewater; and his men in this action showed what a native courage and a principle of duty, even when unassisted by discipline, is able to perform. They threw the veteran forces into disorder; drove them from their ground; continued the fight till their ammunition failed them; and would at last have obtained a victory, had not the misconduct of Monmouth and the cowardice of Gray prevented it. After a combat of three hours the rebels gave way; and were followed with great slaughter. About 1500 fell in the battle and pursuit. And thus was concluded in a few weeks this enterprize, rashly undertaken, and feebly conducted.

Monmouth fled from the field of battle above twenty miles till his horse sunk under him. He then changed cloaths with a peasant

5th July. Monmouth defeated,

CHAPTER LXX

in order to conceal himself. The peasant was discovered by the pursuers, who now redoubled the diligence of their search. At last, the unhappy Monmouth was found, lying in the bottom of a ditch, and covered with fern: His body depressed with fatigue and hunger; his mind by the memory of past misfortunes, by the prospect of future disasters. Human nature is unequal to such calamitous situations; much more, the temper of a man, softened by early prosperity, and accustomed to value himself solely on military bravery. He burst into tears when seized by his enemies; and he seemed still to indulge the fond hope and desire of life. Though he might have known, from the greatness of his own offences, and the severity of James's temper, that no mercy could be expected, he wrote him the most submissive letters, and conjured him to spare the issue of a brother, who had ever been so strongly attached to his interest. James, finding such symptoms of depression and despondency in the unhappy prisoner, admitted him to his presence, in hopes of extorting a discovery of his accomplices: But Monmouth would not purchase life, however loved, at the price of so much infamy. Finding all efforts vain, he assumed courage from despair, and prepared himself for death, with a spirit, better suited to his rank and character. This favourite of the people was attended to the scaffold with a plentiful effusion of tears. He warned the executioner not to fall into the error, which he had committed in beheading Russel, where it had been necessary to repeat the blow. This precaution severed only to dismay the executioner. He struck a feeble blow on Monmouth, who raised his head from the block, and looked him in the face, as if reproaching him for his failure. He gently laid down his head a second time; and the executioner struck him again and again to no purpose. He then threw aside the ax, and cried out that he was incapable of finishing the bloody office. The sheriff olbiged him to renew the attempt; and at two blows more the head was severed from the body. *and executed. 15th July.*

Thus perished in the thirty-sixth year of his age a nobleman, who, in less turbulent times, was well qualified to be an ornament of the court, even to be serviceable to his country. The favour of his prince, the caresses of faction, and the allurements of popularity, seduced him into enterprizes, which exceeded his capacity. The good-will of the people still followed him in every fortune. Even after his execution, their fond credulity flattered them with hopes of seeing him once more at their head. They believed, that the person executed was not Monmouth, but one, who, having the fortune to resemble him nearly, was willing to give this proof of his extreme attachment, and to suffer death in his stead.

This victory, obtained by the king in the commencement of his reign, would naturally, had it been managed with prudence, have tended much to encrease his power and authority. But by reason of the cruelty, with which it was prosecuted, and of the temerity, with which it afterwards inspired him, it was a principal cause of his sudden ruin and downfall.

Such arbitrary principles had the court instilled into all its servants, that Feversham, immediately after the victory, hanged above twenty prisoners; and was proceeding in his executions, when the bishop of Bath and Wells warned him, that these unhappy men were now by law entitled to a trial, and that their execution would be deemed a real murther. This remonstrance however did not stop the savage nature of colonel Kirke, a soldier of fortune, who had long served at Tangiers, and had contracted, from his intercourse with the Moors, an inhumanity less known in European and in free countries. At his first entry into Bridgewater, he hanged nineteen prisoners without the least enquiry into the merits of their cause. As if to make sport with death, he ordered a certain number to be executed, while he and his company should drink the king's health, or the queen's, or that of chief-justice Jefferies. Observing their feet to quiver in the agonies of death, he cried that he would give them music to their dancing; and he immediately commanded the drums to beat and the trumpets to sound. By way of experiment, he ordered one man to be hung up three times, questioning him at each interval, whether he repented of his crime: But the man obstinately asserting, that, notwithstanding the past, he still would willingly engage in the same cause, Kirke ordered him to be hung in chains. One story, commonly told of him, is memorable for the treachery, as well as barbarity, which attended it. A young maid pleaded for the life of her brother, and flung herself at Kirke's feet, armed with all the charms, which beauty and innocence, bathed in tears, could bestow upon her. The tyrant was inflamed with desire, not softened into love or clemency. He promised to grant her request, provided that she, in

Cruelty of colonel Kirke.

CHAPTER LXX

her turn, would be equally compliant to him. The maid yielded to the conditions: But after she had passed the night with him, the wanton savage, next morning, showed her from the window her brother, the darling object for whom she had sacrificed her virtue, hanging on a gibbet, which he had secretly ordered to be there erected for the execution. Rage and despair and indignation took possession of her mind, and deprived her for ever of her senses. All the inhabitants of that country, innocent as well as guilty, were exposed to the ravages of this barbarian. The soldiery were let loose to live at free quarters; and his own regiment, instructed by his example, and encouraged by his exhortations, distinguished themselves in a particular manner by their outrages. By way of pleasantry he used to call them *his lambs;* an appellation, which was long remembered with horror in the west of England.

The violent Jefferies succeeded after some interval; and showed the people, that the rigours of law might equal, if not exceed, the ravages of military tyranny. This man, who wantoned in cruelty, had already given a specimen of his character in many trials, where he presided; and he now set out with a savage joy, as to a full harvest of death and destruction. He began at Dorchester; and thirty rebels being arraigned, he exhorted them, but in vain, to save him, by their free confession, the trouble of trying them: And when twenty-nine were found guilty, he ordered them, as an additional punishment of their disobedience, to be led to immediate execution. Most of the other prisoners, terrified with this example, pleaded guilty; and no less than two hundred and ninety-two received sentence at Dorchester. Of these, eighty were executed. Exeter was the next stage of his cruelty: Two hundred and forty-three were there tried, of whom a great number were condemned and executed. He also opened his commission at Taunton and Wells; and every where carried consternation along with him. The juries were so struck with his menaces, that they gave their verdict with precipitation; and many innocent persons, it is said, were involved with the guilty. And on the whole, besides those who were butchered by the military commanders, two hundred and fifty-one are computed to have fallen by the hand of justice. The whole country was strowed with the heads and limbs of traitors. Every village almost beheld the dead carcass of a wretched inhabitant. And all the rigours of justice, unabated by any appearance of clemency, were fully displayed to the people by the inhuman Jefferies.

Of all the executions, during this dismal period, the most remarkable were those of Mrs. Gaunt and lady Lisle, who had been accused of harbouring traitors. Mrs. Gaunt was an anabaptist, noted for her beneficence, which she extended to persons of all professions and persuasions. One of the rebels, knowing her humane disposition, had recourse to her in his distress, and was concealed by her. Hearing of the proclamation, which offered an indemnity and rewards to such as discovered criminals, he betrayed his benefactress, and bore evidence against her. He received a pardon as a recompence for his treachery; she was burned alive for her charity.

Lady Lisle was widow of one of the regicides, who had enjoyed great favour and authority under Cromwel, and who having fled, after the restoration, to Lauzanne in Swisserland, was there assassinated by three Irish ruffians, who hoped to make their fortune by this piece of service. His widow was now prosecuted for harbouring two rebels the day after the battle of Sedgemoor; and Jefferies pushed on the trial with an unrelenting violence. In vain did the aged prisoner plead, that these criminals had been put into no proclamation; had been convicted by no verdict; nor could any man be denominated a traitor, till the sentence of some legal court was passed upon him: That it appeared not by any proof, that she was so much as acquainted with the guilt of the persons, or had heard of their joining the rebellion of Monmouth; That though she might be obnoxious on account of her family, it was well known, that her heart was ever loyal, and that no person in England had shed more tears for that tragical event, in which her husband had unfortunately borne too great a share: And that the same principles, which she herself had ever embraced, she had carefully instilled into her son, and had, at that very time, sent him to fight against those rebels, whom she was now accused of harbouring. Though these arguments did not move Jefferies, they had influence on the jury. Twice they seemed inclined to bring in a favourable verdict: They were as often sent back with menaces and reproaches; and at last were constrained to give sentence against the prisoner. Notwithstanding all applications for pardon,

CHAPTER LXX

the cruel sentence was executed. The king said, that he had given Jefferies a promise not to pardon her: An excuse, which could serve only to aggravate the blame against himself.

It might have been hoped, that, by all these bloody executions, a rebellion, so precipitate, so ill supported, and of such short duration, would have been sufficiently expiated: But nothing could satiate the spirit of rigour, which possessed the administration. Even those multitudes, who received pardon, were obliged to atone for their guilt by fines, which reduced them to beggary; or where their former poverty made them incapable of paying, they were condemned to cruel whippings or severe imprisonments. Nor could the innocent escape the hands, no less rapacious than cruel, of the chief justice. Prideaux, a gentleman of Devonshire, being thrown into prison, and dreading the severe and arbitrary spirit, which at that time met with no controul, was obliged to buy his liberty of Jefferies at the price of fifteen thousand pounds; though he could never so much as learn the crime of which he was accused.

Goodenough, the seditious under-sheriff of London, who had been engaged in the most bloody and desperate part of the Rye-house conspiracy, was taken prisoner after the battle of Sedgemoor, and resolved to save his own life, by an accusation of Cornish, the sheriff, whom he knew to be extremely obnoxious to the court. Colonel Rumsey joined him in the accusation; and the prosecution was so hastened, that the prisoner was tried, condemned, and executed in the space of a week. The perjury of the witnesses appeared immediately after; and the king seemed to regret the execution of Cornish. He granted his estate to his family, and condemned the witnesses to perpetual imprisonment.

The injustice of this sentence against Cornish, was not wanted to disgust the nation with the court: The continued rigour of the other executions had already impressed an universal hatred against the ministers of justice, attended with compassion for the unhappy sufferers, who, as they had been seduced into this crime by mistaken principles, bore their punishment with the spirit and zeal of martyrs. The people might have been willing on this occasion to distinguish between the king and his ministers: But care was taken to prove, that the latter had done nothing but what was agreeable to their master. Jefferies, on his return, was immediately, for those eminent services, created a peer; and was soon after vested with the dignity of chancellor. It is pretended, however, with some appearance of authority, that the king was displeased with these cruelties, and put a stop to them by orders, as soon as proper information of them was conveyed to him.[s]

State of affairs in Scotland.
We must now take a view of the state of affairs in Scotland; where the fate of Argyle had been decided before that of Monmouth. Immediately after the king's accession, a parliament had been summoned at Edinburgh; and all affairs were there conducted by the duke of Queensberry the commissioner, and the earl of Perth chancellor. The former had resolved to make an entire surrender of the liberties of his country; but was determined still to adhere to its religion: The latter entertained no scruple of paying court even by the sacrifice of both. But no courtier, even the most prostitute, could go farther than the parliament itself towards a resignation of their liberties. In a vote, which they called an offer of duty, after adopting the fabulous history of a hundred and eleven Scottish monarchs, they acknowledged, that all these princes, by the primary and fundamental law of the state, had been vested with a *solid* and *absolute* authority. They declared their abhorrence of all principles and positions, derogatory to the king's sacred, supreme, sovereign, absolute power, of which none, they said, whether single persons or collective bodies, can participate, but in dependance on him and by commission from him. They promised, that the whole nation, between sixteen and sixty, shall be in readiness for his majesty's service, where and as oft as it shall be his royal pleasure to require them. And they annexed the whole excise, both of inland and foreign commodities, for ever to the crown.

All the other acts of this assembly savoured of the same spirit. They declared it treason for any person to refuse the test, if tendered by the council. To defend the obligation of the covenant, subjected a person to the same penalty. To be present at any conventicle, was made punishable with death and confiscation of moveables. Even such as refused to give testimony, either in cases of treason or nonconformity, were declared equally punishable as if guilty of those very crimes: An excellent prelude to all the rigours of an inquisition. It must be confessed, that nothing could

[s] Life of lord keeper North, p. 260. K. James's Memoirs, p. 144.

equal the abject servility of the Scottish nation during this period but the arbitrary severity of the administration.

It was in vain, that Argyle summoned a people, so lost to all sense of liberty, so degraded by repeated indignities, to rise in vindication of their violated laws and privileges. Even those who declared for him, were, for the greater part, his own vassals; men, who, if possible, were still more sunk in slavery than the rest of the nation. He arrived, after a prosperous voyage, in Argyleshire, attended by some fugitives from Holland; among the rest, by Sir Patric Hume, a man of mild dispositions, who had been driven to this extremity by a continued train of oppression. The privy council was beforehand apprized of Argyle's intentions. The whole militia of the kingdom, to the number of twenty-two thousand men, were already in arms; and a third part of them, with the regular forces, were on their march to oppose him. All the considerable gentry of his clan were thrown into prison. And two ships of war were on the coast to watch his motions. Under all these discouragements he yet made a shift, partly from terror, partly from affection, to collect and arm a body of about two thousand five hundred men; but soon found himself surrounded on all sides with insuperable difficulties. His arms and ammunition were seized: His provisions cut off: The marquess of Athole pressed him on one side; lord Charles Murray on another; the duke of Gordon hung upon his rear; the earl of Dunbarton met him in front. His followers daily fell off from him; but Argyle, resolute to persevere, broke at last with the shattered remains of his troops into the disaffected part of the Low Countries, which he had endeavoured to allure to him by declarations for the covenant. No one showed either courage or inclination to join him; and his small and still decreasing army, after wandering about for a little time, was at last defeated and dissipated without an enemy. Argyle himself was seized and carried to Edinburgh; where, after enduring many indignities with a gallant spirit, he was publicly executed. He suffered on the former unjust sentence, which had been passed upon him. The rest of his followers either escaped or were punished by transportation: Rumbold and Ayloffe, two Englishmen, who had attended Argyle on this expedition, were executed.

The king was so elated with this continued tide of prosperity that he began to undervalue even an English parliament, at all times formidable to his family; and from his speech to that assem-

Argyle's invasion,

defeat,

and execution.

9th Nov.
A parliament.

bly, which he had assembled early in the winter, he seems to have thought himself exempted from all rules of prudence or necessity of dissimulation. He plainly told the two houses, that the militia, which had formerly been so much magnified, was now found, by experience in the last rebellion, to be altogether useless; and he required a new supply, in order to maintain those additional forces, which he had levied. He also took notice, that he had employed a great many catholic officers, and that he had, in their favour, dispensed with the law, requiring the test to be taken by every one that possessed any public office. And to cut short all opposition, he declared, that, having reaped the benefit of their service during such times of danger, he was determined, neither to expose them afterwards to disgrace, nor himself, in case of another rebellion, to the want of their assistance.

Such violent aversion did this parliament bear to opposition; so great dread had been instilled of the consequences attending any breach with the king; that it is probable, had he used his dispensing power without declaring it, no enquiries would have been made, and time might have reconciled the nation to this dangerous exercise of prerogative. But to invade at once their constitution, to threaten their religion, to establish a standing army, and even to require them, by their concurrence, to contribute towards all these measures, exceeded the bounds of their patience; and they began, for the first time, to display some small remains of English spirit and generosity. When the king's speech was taken into consideration by the commons, many severe reflections were thrown out against the present measures; and the house was with seeming difficulty engaged to promise in a general vote, that they would grant some supply. But instead of finishing that business, which could alone render them acceptable to the king, they proceeded to examine the dispensing power; and they voted an address to the king against it. Before this address was presented, they resumed the consideration of the supply, and as one million two hundred thousand pounds were demanded by the court, and two hundred thousand proposed by the country-party, a middle course was chosen, and seven hundred thousand, after some dispute, were at last voted. The address against the dispensing power was expressed in the most respectful and submissive terms; yet was it very ill received by the king, and his answer contained a flat denial,

CHAPTER LXX

uttered with great warmth and vehemence. The commons were so daunted with this reply, that they kept silence a long time; and when Coke, member for Derby, rose up and said, "I hope we are all Englishmen, and not to be frightened with a few hard words;" so little spirit appeared in that assembly, often so refractory and mutinous, that they sent him to the Tower for bluntly expressing a free and generous sentiment. They adjourned, without fixing a day for the consideration of his majesty's answer; and on their next meeting, they submissively proceeded to the consideration of the supply, and even went so far as to establish funds for paying the sum voted, in nine years and a half. The king, therefore, had in effect, almost without contest or violence, obtained a complete victory over the commons; and that assembly, instead of guarding their liberties, now exposed to manifest peril, conferred an additional revenue on the crown; and by rendering the king in some degree independent, contributed to increase those dangers, with which they had so much reason to be alarmed.

The next opposition came from the house of peers, which has not commonly taken the lead on these occasions; and even from the bench of bishops, where the court usually expects the greatest complaisance and submission. The upper house had been brought, in the first days of the session, to give general thanks for the king's speech; by which compliment they were understood, according to the practice of that time, to have acquiesced in every part of it: Yet notwithstanding that step, Compton, bishop of London, in his own name and that of his brethren, moved that a day should be appointed for taking the speech into consideration: He was seconded by Halifax, Nottingham, and Mordaunt. Jefferies, the chancellor, opposed the motion; and seemed inclined to use in that house the same arrogance, to which on the bench he had so long been accustomed: But he was soon taught to know his place; and he proved, by his behaviour, that insolence, when checked, naturally sinks into meanness and cowardice. The bishop of London's motion prevailed.

The king might reasonably have presumed, that, even if the peers should so far resume courage as to make an application against his dispensing power, the same steddy answer, which he had given to the commons, would make them relapse into the same timidity; and he might by that means have obtained a considerable supply, without making any concessions in return. But so imperious was his temper, so lofty the idea which he had entertained of his own authority, and so violent the schemes suggested by his own bigotry and that of his priests; that, without any delay, without waiting for any farther provocation, he immediately proceeded to a prorogation. He continued the parliament during a year and a half by four more prorogations; but having in vain tried by separate applications, to break the obstinacy of the leading members, he at last dissolved that assembly. And as it was plainly impossible for him to find among his protestant subjects a set of men more devoted to royal authority, it was universally concluded, that he intended thenceforth to govern entirely without parliaments.

Never king mounted the throne of England with greater advantages than James; nay, possessed greater facility, if that were any advantage, of rendering himself and his posterity absolute: But all these fortunate circumstances tended only, by his own misconduct, to bring more sudden ruin upon him. The nation seemed disposed of themselves to resign their liberties, had he not, at the same time, made an attempt upon their religion: And he might even have succeeded in surmounting at once their liberties and religion, had he conducted his schemes with common prudence and discretion. Openly to declare to the parliament, so early in his reign, his intention to dispense with the tests, struck an universal alarm throughout the nation; infused terror into the church, which had hitherto been the chief support of monarchy; and even disgusted the army, by whose means alone he could now purpose to govern. The former horror against popery was revived by polemical books and sermons; and in every dispute the victory seemed to be gained by the protestant divines, who were heard with more favourable ears, and who managed the controversy with more learning and eloquence. But another incident happened at this time, which tended mightily to excite the animosity of the nation against the catholic communion.

Lewis XIV. having long harassed and molested the protestants, at last revoked entirely the edict of Nantz; which had been enacted by Harry IV. for securing them the free exercise of their religion; which had been declared irrevocable; and which during the experience of near a century, had been attended with no sensible inconvenience. All the iniquities, inseparable from persecution, were exercised against those unhappy religionists; who became obstinate in proportion to the oppressions which they suffered, and either covered under a feigned conversion a more violent abhorrence of the catholic communion, or sought among foreign nations for that liberty, of which they were bereaved in their native country. Above half a million of the most useful and industrious subjects deserted France; and exported, together with immense sums of money, those arts and manufactures, which had chiefly tended to enrich that kingdom. They propagated every where the most tragical accounts of the tyranny, exercised against them, and revived among the protestants all that resentment against the bloody and persecuting spirit of popery, to which so many incidents in all ages had given too much foundation. Near fifty thousand refugees passed over into England; and all men were disposed, from their representations, to entertain the utmost horror against the projects, which they apprehended to be formed by the king for the abolition of the protestant religion. When a prince of so much humanity and of such signal prudence as Lewis could be engaged, by the bigotry of his religion alone, without any provocation, to embrace such sanguinary and impolitic measures; what might be dreaded, they asked, from James, who was so much inferior in these virtues, and who had already been irritated by such obstinate and violent opposition? In vain did the king affect to throw the highest blame on the persecutions in France: In vain did he afford the most real protection and assistance to the distressed Hugonots. All these symptoms of toleration were regarded as insidious; opposite to the avowed principles of his sect, and belied by the severe administration, which he himself had exercised against the nonconformists in Scotland.

The smallest approach towards the introduction of popery, *1686.* must, in the present disposition of the people, have afforded reason of jealousy; much more so wide a step as that of dispensing with the tests, the sole security, which the nation, being disappointed of the exclusion-bill, found provided against those dreaded innovations. Yet was the king resolute to persevere in his purpose; and having failed in bringing over the parliament, he made an attempt, with more success, for establishing his dispensing power, by a verdict of the judges. Sir Edward Hales, a new proselyte, had accepted a commission of colonel; and directions

Dispensing power.

were given his coachman to prosecute him for the penalty of five hundred pounds, which the law, establishing the tests, had granted to informers. By this feigned action, the king hoped, both from the authority of the decision, and the reason of the thing, to put an end to all questions with regard to his dispensing power.

It could not be expected, that the lawyers, appointed to plead against Hales, would exert great force on that occasion: But the cause was regarded with such anxiety by the public, that it has been thoroughly canvassed in several elaborate discourses;[t] and could men divest themselves of prejudice, there want not sufficient materials, on which to form a true judgment. The claim and exercise of the dispensing power is allowed to be very ancient in England; and though it seems at first to have been copied from papal usurpations, it may plainly be traced up as high as the reign of Henry III. In the feudal governments, men were more anxious to secure their private property than to share in the public administration; and provided no innovations were attempted on their rights and possessions, the care of executing the laws, and ensuring general safety was without jealousy entrusted to the sovereign. Penal statutes were commonly intended to arm the prince with more authority for that purpose; and being in the main calculated for promoting his influence as first magistrate, there seemed no danger in allowing him to dispense with their execution, in such particular cases as might require an exception or indulgence. That practice had so much prevailed, that the parliament itself had more than once acknowledged this prerogative of the crown; particularly during the reign of Henry V. when they enacted the law against aliens,[u] and also when they passed the statute of provisors.[w] But though the general tenor of the penal statutes was such as gave the king a superior interest in their execution beyond any of his subjects; it could not but sometimes happen in a mixed government, that the parliament would desire to enact laws, by which the regal

[t] Particularly Sir Edward Herbert's defence in the state trials, and Sir Robert Atkins's enquiry concerning the dispensing power. [u] Rot. parl. 1 Hen. V. n. xv. [w] Ibid. 1 Hen V. n. xxii. It is remarkable, however, that in the reign of Richard the Second, the parliament granted the king only a temporary power of dispensing with the statute of provisors. Rot. parl. 15 Rich. II. n. i. A plain implication that he had not, of himself, such prerogative. So uncertain were many of these points at that time.

CHAPTER LXX

power, in some particulars, even where private property was not immediately concerned, might be regulated and restrained. In the twenty-third of Henry VI. a law of this kind was enacted, prohibiting any man from serving in a county as sheriff above a year, and a clause was inserted, by which the king was disabled from granting a dispensation. Plain reason might have taught, that this law, at least, should be exempted from the king's prerogative: But as the dispensing power still prevailed in other cases, it was soon able, aided by the servility of the courts of judicature, even to overpower this statute, which the legislature had evidently intended to secure against violation. In the reign of Henry VII. the case was brought to a trial before all the judges in the exchequer-chamber; and it was decreed, that, notwithstanding the strict clause abovementioned, the king might dispense with the statute: He could first, it was alleged, dispense with the prohibitory clause, and then with the statute itself. This opinion of the judges, though seemingly absurd, had ever since passed for undoubted law: The practice of continuing the sheriffs had prevailed: And most of the property in England had been fixed by decisions, which juries, returned by such sheriffs, had given in the courts of judicature. Many other dispensations of a like nature may be produced; not only such as took place by intervals, but such as were uniformly continued. Thus the law was dispensed with, which prohibited any man from going a judge of assize into his own county; that which rendered all Welchmen incapable of bearing offices in Wales; and that which required every one, who received a pardon for felony, to find sureties for his good behaviour. In the second of James I. a new consultation of all the judges had been held upon a like question: This prerogative of the crown was again unanimously affirmed: [x] And it became an established principle in English jurisprudence, that, though the king could not allow of what was morally unlawful, he could permit what was only prohibited by positive statute. Even the jealous house of commons, who extorted the petition of right from Charles I. made no scruple, by the mouth of Glanville, their manager, to allow of the dispensing power in its full extent; [y] and in the famous trial of ship-money, Holborne, the

---

[x] Sir Edward Coke's reports, seventh report.   [y] State Trials, vol. vii. first edit. p. 205. Parl. hist. vol. viii. p. 132.

popular lawyer, had, freely, and in the most explicit terms, made the same concession.[z] Sir Edward Coke, the great oracle of English law, had not only concurred with all other lawyers in favour of this prerogative; but seems even to believe it so inherent in the crown, that an act of parliament itself could not abolish it.[a] And he particularly observes, that no law can impose such a disability of enjoying offices as the king may not dispense with; because the king, from the law of nature, has a right to the service of all his subjects. This particular reason, as well as all the general principles, is applicable to the question of the tests; nor can the dangerous consequence of granting dispensations in that case be ever allowed to be pleaded before a court of judicature. Every prerogative of the crown, it may be said, admits of abuse: Should the king pardon all criminals, law must be totally dissolved: Should he declare and continue perpetual war against all nations, inevitable ruin must ensue: Yet these powers are entrusted to the sovereign; and we must be content, as our ancestors were, to depend upon his prudence and discretion in the exercise of them.

Though this reasoning seems founded on such principles as are usually admitted by lawyers, the people had entertained such violent prepossessions against the use, which James here made of his prerogative, that he was obliged, before he brought on Hales's cause, to displace four of the judges, Jones, Montague, Charleton and Nevil; and even Sir Edward Herbert, the chief justice, though a man of acknowledged virtue, yet, because he here supported the pretensions of the crown, was exposed to great and general reproach. Men deemed a dispensing, to be in effect the same with a repealing power; and they could not conceive, that less authority was necessary to repeal than to enact any statute. If one penal law was dispensed with, any other might undergo the same fate: And by what principle could even the laws, which define property, be afterwards secured from violation? The test act had ever been conceived the great barrier of the established religion under a popish successor: As such it had been insisted on by the parliament; as such granted by the king; as such, during the debates with

---

[z] State trials, vol. v. first edit. p. 171.   [a] Sir Edward Coke's reports, twelfth report, p. 18.

CHAPTER LXX

regard to the exclusion, recommended by the chancellor. By what magic, what chicane of law, is it now annihilated, and rendered of no validity? These questions were every where asked; and men, straitened by precedents and decisions of great authority, were reduced either to question the antiquity of this prerogative itself, or to assert, that even the practice of near five centuries could not bestow on it sufficient authority.[b] It was not considered, that the present difficulty or seeming absurdity had proceeded from late innovations introduced into the government. Ever since the beginning of this century, the parliament had, with a laudable zeal, been acquiring powers and establishing principles, favourable to law and liberty: The authority of the crown had been limited in many important particulars: And penal statutes were often calculated to secure the constitution against the attempts of ministers, as well as to preserve general peace, and repress crimes and immoralities. A prerogative however, derived from very ancient, and almost uniform practice, the dispensing power, still remained, or was supposed to remain with the crown; sufficient in an instant to overturn this whole fabric, and to throw down all fences of the constitution. If this prerogative, which carries on the face of it, such strong symptoms of an absolute authority in the prince, had yet, in ancient times, subsisted with some degree of liberty in the subject; this fact only proves, that scarcely any human government, much less one erected in rude and barbarous times, is entirely consistent and uniform in all its parts. But to expect, that the dispensing power could, in any degree, be rendered compatible with those accurate and regular limitations, which had of late been established, and which the people were determined to maintain, was a vain hope; and though men knew not upon what principles they could deny that prerogative, they saw, that, if they would preserve their laws and constitution, there was an absolute necessity for denying, at least for abolishing it. The revolution alone, which soon succeeded, happily put an end to all these disputes: By means of it, a more uniform edifice was at last erected: The monstrous inconsistence, so visible between the ancient Gothic parts of the fabric and the recent plans of liberty, was fully corrected: And

[b] Sir Robert Atkins, p. 21.

to their mutual felicity, king and people were finally taught to know their proper boundaries.[c]

Whatever topics lawyers might find to defend James's dispensing power, the nation thought it dangerous, if not fatal, to liberty; and his resolution of exercising it may on that account be esteemed no less alarming, than if the power had been founded on the most recent and most flagrant usurpation. It was not likely, that an authority, which had been assumed, through so many obstacles, would in his hands lie long idle and unemployed. Four catholic lords were brought into the privy council, Powis, Arundel, Bellasis, and Dover. Halifax, finding, that, notwithstanding his past merits, he possessed no real credit or authority, became refractory in his opposition; and his office of privy seal was given to Arundel. The king was open, as well as zealous, in the desire of making converts; and men plainly saw, that the only way to acquire his affection and confidence was by a sacrifice of their religion. Sunderland, some time after, scrupled not to gain favour at this price. Rochester, the treasurer, though the king's brother-in-law, yet, because he refused to give this instance of complaisance, was turned out of his office: The treasury was put in commission, and Bellasis was placed at the head of it. All the courtiers were disgusted, even such as had little regard to religion. The dishonour, as well as distrust, attending renegades, made most men resolve, at all hazards, to adhere to their ancient faith.

[c] It is remarkable, that the convention, summoned by the prince of Orange, did not, even when they had the making of their own terms in *the declaration of rights,* venture to condemn the dispensing power in general, which had been uniformly exercised by the former kings of England. They only condemned it so far, *as it had been assumed and exercised of late,* without being able to tell wherein the difference lay. But in the *bill of rights,* which passed about a twelvemonth after, the parliament took care to secure themselves more effectually against a branch of prerogative, incompatible with all legal liberty and limitations; and they excluded, in positive terms, all dispensing power in the crown. Yet even then the house of lords rejected that clause of the bill, which condemned the exercise of this power in former kings, and obliged the commons to rest content with abolishing it for the future. There needs no other proof of the irregular nature of the old English government, than the existence of such a prerogative, always exercised and never questioned, till the acquisition of real liberty discovered, at last, the danger of it. See the Journals.

CHAPTER LXX

In Scotland, James's zeal for proselytism was more successful. *State of* The earls of Murray, Perth, and Melfort were brought over to the *Scotland.* court religion; and the two latter noblemen made use of a very courtly reason for their conversion: They pretended, that the papers, found in the late king's cabinet, had opened their eyes, and had convinced them of the preference due to the catholic religion. Queensberry, who showed not the same complaisance, fell into total disgrace, notwithstanding his former services, and the important sacrifices, which he had made to the measures of the court. These merits could not even ensure him of safety against the vengeance, to which he stood exposed. His rival, Perth, who had been ready to sink under his superior interest, now acquired the ascendant; and all the complaints, exhibited against him, were totally obliterated. His faith, according to a saying of Halifax, had made him whole.

But it was in Ireland chiefly, that the mask was wholly taken off, *State of* and that the king thought himself at liberty to proceed, to the full *Ireland.* extent of his zeal and his violence. The duke of Ormond was recalled, and though the primate and lord Granard, two protestants, still possessed the authority of justices, the whole power was lodged in the hands of Talbot, the general, soon after created earl of Tyrconnel; a man, who, from the blindness of his prejudices and fury of his temper, was transported with the most immeasurable ardour for the catholic cause. After the suppression of Monmouth's rebellion, orders were given by Tyrconnel to disarm all the protestants, on pretence of securing the public peace, and keeping their arms in a few magazines for the use of the militia. Next, the army was new-modelled; and a great number of officers were dismissed, because it was pretended, that they or their fathers had served under Cromwel and the republic. The injustice was not confined to them. Near three hundred officers more were afterwards broken, though many of them had purchased their commissions: About four or five thousand private soldiers, because they were protestants, were dismissed; and being stripped even of their regimentals, were turned out to starve in the streets. While these violences were carrying on, Clarendon, who had been named lord lieutenant, came over; but he soon found, that, as he had refused to give the king the desired pledge of fidelity, by changing his religion, he possessed no credit or authority. He was even a kind of prisoner in the hands of Tyrconnel; and as he gave all opposition in his power to the precipitate measures of the catholics, he was soon after recalled, and Tyrconnel substituted in his place. The unhappy protestants now saw all the civil authority, as well as the military force, transferred into the hands of their inveterate enemies; inflamed with hereditary hatred, and stimulated by every motive, which the passion either for power, property, or religion could inspire. Even the barbarous banditti were let loose to prey on them in their present defenceless condition. A renewal of the ancient massacres was apprehended; and great multitudes, struck with the best grounded terror, deserted the kingdom, and infused into the English nation a dread of those violences, to which, after some time, they might justly, from the prevalence of the catholics, think themselves exposed.

All judicious persons of the catholic communion were disgusted with these violent measures, and could easily foresee the consequences. But James was entirely governed by the rash counsels of the queen and of his confessor, father Peters, a jesuit, whom he soon after created a privy counsellor. He thought too, that, as he was now in the decline of life, it was necessary for him, by hasty steps, to carry his designs into execution; lest the succession of the princess of Orange should overturn all his projects. In vain did Arundel, Powis, ard Bellasis remonstrate, and suggest more moderate and cautious measures. These men had seen and felt, during the prosecution of the popish plot, the extreme antipathy, which the nation bore to their religion; and though some subsequent incidents had seemingly allayed that spirit, they knew, that the settled habits of the people were still the same, and that the smallest incident was sufficient to renew the former animosty. A very moderate indulgence, therefore, to the catholic religion would have satisfied them; and all attempts to acquire power, much more to produce a change of the national faith, they deemed dangerous and destructive.[d]

Breach betwixt the king and the church.

On the first broaching of the popish plot, the clergy of the church of England had concurred in the prosecution of it, with the same violence and credulity as the rest of the nation: But dreading afterwards the prevalence of republican and presbyterian prin-

[d] D'Avaux, 10 January, 1687.

CHAPTER LXX

ciples, they had been engaged to support the measures of the court; and to their assistance chiefly, James had owed his succession to the crown. Finding that all these services were forgotten, and that the catholic religion was the king's sole favourite, the church had commenced an opposition to court measures; and popery was now acknowledged the more immediate danger. In order to prevent inflammatory sermons on this popular subject, James revived some directions to preachers, which had been promulgated by the late king, in the beginning of his reign, when no design against the national religion was yet formed, or at least apprehended. But in the present delicate and interesting situation of the church, there was little reason to expect that orders, founded on no legal authority, would be rigidly obeyed by preachers, who saw no security to themselves but in preserving the confidence and regard of the people. Instead of avoiding controversy, according to the king's injunctions, the preachers every where declaimed against popery; and among the rest, Dr. Sharpe, a clergyman of London, particularly distinguished himself, and affected to throw great contempt on those who had been induced to change their religion by such pitiful arguments as the Romish missionaries could suggest. This topic, being supposed to reflect on the king, gave great offence at court; and positive orders were issued to the bishop of London, his diocesan, immediately to suspend Sharpe, till his majesty's pleasure should be farther known. The prelate replied, that he could not possibly obey these commands, and that he was not empowered, in such a summary manner, to inflict any punishment even upon the greatest delinquent. But neither this obvious reason, nor the most dutiful submissions, both of the prelate and of Sharpe himself, could appease the court. The king was determined to proceed with violence in the prosecution of this affair. The bishop himself he resolved to punish for disobedience to his commands; and the expedient, which he employed for that purpose, was of a nature at once the most illegal and most alarming.

Among all the engines of authority formerly employed by the crown, none had been more dangerous or even destructive to liberty, than the court of high commission, which, together with the star-chamber, had been abolished in the reign of Charles I. by act of parliament; in which a clause was also inserted, prohibiting

Court
of eccle-
siastical
commis-
sion.

the erection, in all future times, of that court, or any of a like nature. But this law was deemed by James no obstacle; and an ecclesiastical commission was anew issued, by which seven[e] commissioners were vested with full and unlimited authority over the church of England. On them were bestowed the same inquisitorial powers, possessed by the former court of high commission: They might proceed upon bare suspicion; and the better to set the law at defiance, it was expressly inserted in their patent itself, that they were to exercise their jurisdiction, notwithstanding any law or statute to the contrary. The king's design to subdue the church was now sufficiently known; and had he been able to establish the authority of this new-erected court, his success was infallible. A more sensible blow could not be given both to national liberty and religion; and happily the contest could not be tried in a cause more iniquitous and unpopular than that against Sharpe and the bishop of London.

The prelate was cited before the commissioners. After denying the legality of the court, and claiming the privilege of all Christian bishops to be tried by the metropolitan and his suffragans; he pleaded in his own defence, that, as he was obliged, if he had suspended Sharpe, to act in the capacity of a judge, he could not, consistent either with law or equity, pronounce sentence without a previous citation and trial: That he had by petition represented this difficulty to his majesty; and not receiving any answer, he had reason to think, that his petition had given entire satisfaction: That in order to shew farther his deference, he had advised Sharpe to abstain from preaching, till he had justified his conduct to the king; an advice, which, coming from a superior, was equivalent to a command, and had accordingly met with the proper obedience: That he had thus in his apprehension conformed himself to his majesty's pleasure; but if he should still be found wanting to his duty in any particular, he was now willing to crave pardon, and to make reparation. All this submission, both in Sharpe and the prelate, had no effect: It was determined to have an example: Orders were accordingly sent to the commissioners to proceed:

[e] The persons named were the archbishop of Canterbury, Sancroft; the bishop of Durham, Crew; of Rochester, Sprat; the earl of Rochester, Sunderland, chancellor Jefferies, and lord chief justice Herbert. The archbishop refused to act, and the bishop of Chester was substituted in his place.

CHAPTER LXX

And by a majority of votes the bishop, as well as the doctor, was suspended.

Sentence against the bishop of London.

Almost the whole of this short reign consists of attempts always imprudent, often illegal, sometimes both, against whatever was most loved and revered by the nation: Even such schemes of the king's as might be laudable in themselves, were so disgraced by his intentions, that they serve only to aggravate the charge against him. James was become a great patron of toleration, and an enemy to all those persecuting laws, which, from the influence of the church, had been enacted both against the dissenters and catholics. Not content with granting dispensations to particular persons, he assumed a power of issuing a declaration of general indulgence, and of suspending at once all the penal statutes, by which a conformity was required to the established religion. This was a strain of authority, it must be confessed, quite inconsistent with law and a limited constitution; yet was it supported by many strong precedents in the history of England. Even after the principles of liberty were become more prevalent, and began to be well understood, the late king had, oftener than once, and without giving much umbrage, exerted this dangerous power: He had in 1662 suspended the execution of a law, which regulated carriages: During the two Dutch wars, he had twice suspended the act of navigation: And the commons in 1666, being resolved, contrary to the king's judgment, to enact that iniquitous law against the importation of Irish cattle, found it necessary, in order to obviate the exercise of this prerogative, which they desired not at that time entirely to deny or abrogate, to call that importation a nuisance.

Penal laws suspended.

Though the former authority of the sovereign was great in civil affairs, it was still greater in ecclesiastical; and the whole despotic power of the popes was often believed, in virtue of the supremacy, to have devolved to the crown. The last parliament of Charles I. by abolishing the power of the king and convocation to frame canons without consent of parliament, had somewhat diminished the supposed extent of the supremacy; but still very considerable remains of it, at least very important claims, were preserved, and were occasionally made use of by the sovereign. In 1662, Charles, pleading both the rights of his supremacy and his suspending power, had granted a general indulgence or toleration; and in 1672 he renewed the same edict: Though the remonstrances of his parliament obliged him, on both occasions, to retract; and in the last instance, the triumph of law over prerogative was deemed very great and memorable. In general, we may remark, that, where the exercise of the suspending power was agreeable and useful, the power itself was little questioned: Where the exercise was thought liable to exceptions, men not only opposed it, but proceeded to deny altogether the legality of the prerogative, on which it was founded.

1687. James, more imprudent and arbitrary than his predecessor, issued his proclamation, suspending all the penal laws in ecclesiastical affairs, and granting a general liberty of conscience to all his subjects. He was not deterred by the reflection, both that this scheme of indulgence was already blasted by two fruitless attempts; and that in such a government as that of England, it was not sufficient that a prerogative be approved of by some lawyers and antiquaries: If it was condemned by the general voice of the nation, and yet was still exerted, the victory over national liberty was no less signal than if obtained by the most flagrant injustice and usurpation. These two considerations indeed would rather serve to recommend this project to James; who deemed himself superior in vigour and activity to his brother, and who probably thought, that his people enjoyed no liberties, but by his royal concession and indulgence.

In order to procure a better reception for his edict of toleration, the king, finding himself opposed by the church, began to pay court to the dissenters; and he imagined, that, by playing one party against another, he should easily obtain the victory over both; a refined policy which it much exceeded his capacity to conduct. His intentions were so obvious, that it was impossible for him ever to gain the sincere confidence and regard of the nonconformists. They knew, that the genius of their religion was diametrically opposite to that of the catholics, the sole object of the king's affection. They were sensible, that both the violence of his temper, and the maxims of his religion, were repugnant to the principles of toleration. They had seen, that, on his accession, as well as during his brother's reign, he had courted the church at their expence; and it was not till his dangerous schemes were rejected by the prelates, that he had recourse to the nonconformists. All his favours, therefore, must, to every man of judgment among the sectaries, have appeared insidious: Yet such was the pleasure reaped from present ease, such the animosity of the dissenters against the church, who had so long subjected them to the rigours of persecution, that they every where expressed the most entire duty to the king, and compliance with his measures, and could not forbear rejoicing extremely in the present depression of their adversaries.

But had the dissenters been ever so much inclined to shut their eyes with regard to the king's intentions, the manner of conducting his scheme in Scotland was sufficient to discover the secret. The king first applied to the Scottish parliament, and desired an indulgence for the catholics alone, without comprehending the presbyterians: But that assembly, though more disposed than even the parliament of England, to sacrifice their civil liberties, resolved likewise to adhere pertinaciously to their religion; and they rejected for the first time the king's application. James therefore found himself obliged to exert his prerogative; and he now thought it prudent to interest a party among his subjects, besides the catholics, in supporting this act of authority. To the surprize of the harassed and persecuted presbyterians, they heard the principles of toleration every where extolled, and found that full permission was granted to attend conventicles; an offence, which, even during this reign, had been declared no less than a capital enormity. The king's declaration, however, of indulgence contained clauses, sufficient to depress their joy. As if popery were already predominant, he declared, "that he never would use force or *invincible necessity* against any man on account of his persuasion or the protestant religion:" A promise surely of toleration given to the protestants with great precaution, and admitting a considerable latitude for persecution and violence. It is likewise remarkable, that the king declared in express terms, "that he had thought fit, by his sovereign authority, prerogative royal, and *absolute* power, which all his subjects were to obey *without reserve,* to grant this royal toleration." The dangerous designs of other princes are to be collected by a comparison of their several actions, or by a discovery of their more secret counsels: But so blinded was James with zeal, so transported by his imperious temper, that even his proclamations and public edicts contain expressions, which, without farther enquiry, may suffice to his condemnation.

The English well knew, that the king, by the constitution of their government, thought himself intitled, as indeed he was, to as ample authority in his southern, as in his northern kingdom; and therefore, though the declaration of indulgence published for England was more cautiously expressed, they could not but be alarmed by the arbitrary treatment, to which their neighbours were exposed. It is even remarkable, that the English declaration contained clauses of a strange import. The king there promised, that he would maintain his loving subjects in all their properties and possessions, as well of church and abbey lands as of any other. Men thought, that, if the full establishment of popery were not at hand, this promise was quite superfluous; and they concluded, that the king was so replete with joy on the prospect of that glorious event, that he could not, even for a moment, refrain from expressing it.

State of Ireland. But what afforded the most alarming prospect, was the continuance and even encrease of the violent and precipitate conduct of affairs in Ireland. Tyrconnel was now vested with full authority; and carried over with him as chancellor one Fitton, a man who was taken from a jail, and who had been convicted of forgery and other crimes, but who compensated for all his enormities by a headlong zeal for the catholic religion. He was even heard to say from the bench, that the protestants were all rogues, and that there was not one among forty thousand that was not a traitor, a rebel, and a villain. The whole strain of the administration was suitable to such sentiments. The catholics were put in possession of the council table, of the courts of judicature, and of the bench of justices. In order to make them masters of the parliament, the same violence was exercised that had been practised in England. The charters of Dublin and of all the corporations were annulled; and new charters were granted, subjecting the corporations to the will of the sovereign. The protestant freemen were expelled, catholics introduced; and the latter sect, as they always were the majority in number, were now invested with the whole power of the kingdom. The act of settlement was the only obstacle to their enjoying the whole property; and Tyrconnel had formed a scheme for calling a parliament, in order to reverse that act, and empower the king to bestow all the lands of Ireland on his catholic subjects. But in this scheme he met with opposition from the moderate catholics in the

CHAPTER LXX

king's council. Lord Bellasis went even so far as to affirm with an oath, "that that fellow in Ireland was fool and madman enough to ruin ten kingdoms." The decay of trade, from the desertion of the protestants, was represented; the sinking of the revenue; the alarm communicated to England: And by these considerations the king's resolutions were for some time suspended; though it was easy to foresee, from the usual tenor of his conduct, which side would at last preponderate.

But the king was not content with discovering in his own king-doms the imprudence of his conduct: He was resolved, that all Europe should be witness of it. He publickly sent the earl of Castel-maine ambassador extra-ordinary to Rome, in order to express his obeisance to the Pope, and to make advances for reconciling his kingdoms, in form, to the catholic communion. Never man, who came on so important an errand, met with so many neglects and even affronts, as Castelmaine. The pontiff, instead of being pleased with this forward step, concluded, that a scheme, con-ducted with so much indiscretion, could never possibly be success-ful. And as he was engaged in a violent quarrel with the French monarch, a quarrel which interested him more nearly than the conversion of England, he bore little regard to James, whom he believed too closely connected with his capital enemy. *Embassy to Rome.*

The only proof of complaisance, which James received from the Pontiff was his sending a nuncio to England, in return for the embassy. By act of parliament any communication with the Pope was made treason: Yet so little regard did the king pay to the laws, that he gave the nuncio a public and solemn reception at Windsor. The duke of Somerset, one of the bed-chamber, because he refused to assist at this ceremony, was dismissed from his employ-ment. The nuncio resided openly in London during the rest of this reign. Four catholic bishops were publicly consecrated in the king's chapel, and sent out under the title of vicars apostolical, to exercise the episcopal function in their respective dioceses. Their pastoral letters, directed to the lay catholics of England were printed and dispersed by the express allowance and permission of the king. The regular clergy of that communion appeared at court in the habits of their order; and some of them were so indiscreet as to boast, that, in a little time, they hoped to walk in procession through the capital.

While the king shocked in the most open manner all the principles and prejudices of his protestant subjects, he could not sometimes but be sensible, that he stood in need of their assistance for the execution of his designs. He had himself, by virtue of his prerogative, suspended the penal laws, and dispensed with the test; but he would gladly have obtained the sanction of parliament to these acts of power; and he knew, that, without this authority, his edicts alone would never afford a durable security to the catholics. He had employed, therefore, with the members of parliament many private conferences, which were then called *closetings;* and he used every expedient of reasons, menaces and promises to break their obstinacy in this particular. Finding all his efforts fruitless, he had dissolved the parliament, and was determined to call a new one, from which he expected more complaisance and submission. By the practice of annulling the charters, the king was become master of all the corporations, and could at pleasure change every where the whole magistracy. The church party, therefore, by whom the crown had been hitherto so remarkably supported, and to whom the king visibly owed his safety from all the efforts of his enemies, was deprived of authority; and the dissenters, those very enemies, were, first in London, and afterwards in every other corporation, substituted in their place. Not content with this violent and dangerous innovation, the king appointed certain regulators to examine the qualifications of electors; and directions were given them to exclude all such as adhered to the test and penal statutes.*f* Queries to this purpose were openly proposed in all places, in order to try the sentiments of men, and enable the king to judge of the proceedings of the future parliament. The power of the crown was at this time so great; and the revenue, managed by James's frugality, so considerable and independant; that, if he had embraced any national party, he had been ensured of success; and might have carried his authority to what length he pleased. But the catholics, to whom he had entirely

---

f The elections in some places, particularly in York, were transferred from the people to the magistrates, who, by the new charter, were all named by the crown. Sir John Reresby's memoirs, p. 272. This was in reality nothing different from the king's naming the members. The same act of authority had been employed in all the burroughs of Scotland.

devoted himself, were scarcely the hundredth part of the people. Even the protestant nonconformists, whom he so much courted, were little more than the twentieth; and what was worse, reposed no confidence in the unnatural alliance contracted with the catholics, and in the principles of toleration, which, contrary to their usual practice in all ages, seemed at present to be adopted by that sect. The king therefore, finding little hopes of success, delayed the summoning of a parliament, and proceeded still in the exercise of his illegal and arbitrary authority.

The whole power in Ireland had been committed to catholics. In Scotland, all the ministers, whom the king chiefly trusted, were converts to that religion. Every great office in England, civil and military, was gradually transferred from the protestants. Rochester and Clarendon, the king's brothers-in-law, though they had ever been faithful to his interests, could not, by all their services, atone for their adherence to the national religion; and had been dismissed from their employments. The violent Jefferies himself, though he had sacrificed justice and humanity to the court; yet, because he refused also to give up his religion, was declining in favour and interest. Nothing now remained but to open the door in the church and universities to the intrusion of the catholics. It was not long before the king made this rash effort; and by constraining the prelacy and established church to seek protection in the principles of liberty, he at last left himself entirely without friends and adherents.

Father Francis, a Benedictine, was recommended by the king's mandate to the university of Cambridge for the degree of master of arts; and as it was usual for the university to confer that degree on persons eminent for learning, without regard to their religion; and as they had even admitted lately the secretary to the ambassador of Morocco; the king on that account thought himself the better intitled to compliance. But the university considered, that there was a great difference between a compliment bestowed on foreigners, and degrees which gave a title to vote in all the elections and statutes of the university, and which, if conferred on the catholics, would infallibly in time render that sect entirely superior. They therefore refused to obey the king's mandate, and were cited to appear before the court of ecclesiastical commission. The vice chancellor was suspended by that court; but as the university chose a man of spirit to succeed him, the king thought proper for the present to drop his pretensions.

Attempt upon Magdalen college.

The attempt upon the university of Oxford was prosecuted with more inflexible obstinacy, and was attended with more important consequences. This university had lately, in their famous decree, made a solemn profession of passive obedience; and the court probably expected, that they would show their sincerity, when their turn came to practise that doctrine; which, though, if carried to the utmost extent, it be contrary both to reason and to nature, is apt to meet with the more effectual opposition from the latter principle. The president of Magdalen college, one of the richest foundations in Europe, dying about this time, a mandate was sent in favour of Farmer, a new convert, but one, who, besides his being a catholic, had not in other respects the qualifications required by the statutes for enjoying that office. The fellows of the college made submissive applications to the king for recalling his mandate; but before they received an answer, the day came, on which, by their statutes, they were obliged to proceed to an election. They chose Dr. Hough, a man of virtue, as well as of the firmness and vigour requisite for maintaining his own rights and those of the university. In order to punish the college for this contumacy, as it was called, an inferior ecclesiastical commission was sent down, and the new president and the fellows were cited before it. So little regard had been paid to any consideration besides religion, that Farmer, on enquiry, was found guilty of the lowest and most scandalous vices; insomuch that even the ecclesiastical commissioners were ashamed to insist on his election. A new mandate, therefore, was issued in favour of Parker, lately created bishop of Oxford, a man of a prostitute character, but who, like Farmer, atoned for all his vices by his avowed willingness to embrace the catholic religion. The college represented, that all presidents had ever been appointed by election, and there were few instances of the king's interposing by his recommendation in favour of any candidate; that having already made a regular election of a president, they could not deprive him of his office, and, during his life-time, substitute any other in his place; that, even if there were a vacancy, Parker, by the statutes, of their founder, could not be chosen; that they had all of them bound themselves

CHAPTER LXX

by oath to observe these statutes, and never on any account to accept of a dispensation; and that the college had at all times so much distinguished itself by its loyalty, that nothing but the most invincible necessity could now oblige them to oppose his majesty's inclinations. All these reasons availed them nothing. The president and all the fellows, except two who complied, were expelled the college; and Parker was put in possession of the office. This act of violence, of all those which were committed during the reign of James, is perhaps the most illegal and arbitrary. When the dispensing power was the most strenuously insisted on by court lawyers, it had still been allowed, that the statutes, which regard private property, could not legally be infringed by that prerogative: Yet in this instance it appeared, that even these were not now secure from invasion. The privileges of a college are attacked: Men are illegally dispossessed of their property, for adhering to their duty, to their oaths, and to their religion: The fountains of the church are attempted to be poisoned; nor would it be long, it was concluded, ere all ecclesiastical, as well as civil preferments, would be bestowed on such as, negligent of honour, virtue, and sincerity, basely sacrificed their faith to the reigning superstition. Such were the general sentiments; and as the universities have an intimate connexion with the ecclesiastical establishments, and mightily interest all those who have there received their education, this arbitrary proceeding begat an universal discontent against the king's administration.

The next measure of the court was an insult still more open on the ecclesiastics, and rendered the breach between the king and that powerful body fatal, as well as incurable. It is strange that James, when he felt, from the sentiments of his own heart, what a mighty influence religious zeal had over him, should yet be so infatuated as never once to suspect, that it might possibly have a proportionable authority over his subjects. Could he have profited by repeated experience, he had seen instances enow of their strong aversion to that communion, which, from a violent, imperious temper, he was determined, by every possible expedient, to introduce into his kingdoms.

The king published a second declaration of indulgence, almost in the same terms with the former; and he subjoined an order, that, immediately after divine service, it should be read by the   *1688.*

clergy in all the churches. As they were known universally to disapprove of the use made of the suspending power, this clause, they thought, could be meant only as an insult upon them; and they were sensible, that, by their compliance, they should expose themselves, both to public contempt, on account of their tame behaviour, and to public hatred, by their indirectly patronizing so obnoxious a prerogative.[g] They were determined, therefore, almost universally to preserve the regard of the people; their only protection, while the laws were become of so little validity, and while the court was so deeply engaged in opposite interests. In order to encourage them in this resolution, six prelates, namely, Lloyde bishop of St. Asaph, Ken of Bath and Wells, Turner of Ely, Lake of Chichester, White of Peterborough, and Trelawney of Bristol, met privately with the primate, and concerted the form of a petition to the king. They there represent in few words, that, though possessed of the highest sense of loyalty, a virtue of which the church of England had given such eminent testimonies; and though desirous of affording ease in a legal way to all protestant dissenters; yet, because the declaration of indulgence was founded on a prerogative, formerly declared illegal by parliament, they could not, in prudence, honour, or conscience, so far make themselves parties as the distribution of it all over the kingdom would be interpreted to amount to. They therefore besought the king, that he would not insist upon their reading that declaration.[h]

[g] When Charles dissolved his last parliament, he set forth a declaration giving his reasons for that measure, and this declaration the clergy had been ordered to read to the people after divine service. These orders were agreeable to their party prejudices, and they willingly submitted to them. The contrary was now the case.   [h] The words of the petition were: That the great averseness found in themselves to their distributing and publishing in all their churches your majesty's late declaration for liberty of conscience, proceeds neither from any want of duty and obedience to your majesty (our holy mother, the church of England, being both in her principles and her constant practice unquestionably loyal, and having to her great honour been more than once publicly acknowledged to be so by your gracious majesty) nor yet from any want of tenderness to dissenters, in relation to whom we are willing to come to such a temper as shall be thought fit, when the matter shall be considered and settled in parliament and convocation. But among many other considerations, from this especially, because that declaration is founded upon such a dispensing power as hath been often declared illegal in parliament, and particularly in the

CHAPTER LXX

The king was incapable, not only of yielding to the greatest opposition, but of allowing the slightest and most respectful contradiction to pass uncensured. He immediately embraced a resolution (and his resolutions, when once embraced, were inflexible) of punishing the bishops, for a petition so popular in its matter, and so prudent and cautious in the expression. As the petition was delivered him in private, he summoned them before the council; and questioned them whether they would acknowledge it. The bishops saw his intention, and seemed long desirous to decline answering: But being pushed by the chancellor, they at last avowed the petition. On their refusal to give bail, an order was immediately drawn for their commitment to the Tower; and the crown lawyers received directions to prosecute them for the seditious libel, which, it was pretended, they had composed and uttered.

The people were already aware of the danger, to which the prelates were exposed; and were raised to the highest pitch of anxiety and attention with regard to the issue of this extraordinary affair. But when they beheld these fathers of the church brought from court under the custody of a guard, when they saw them embarked in vessels on the river, and conveyed towards the Tower, all their affection for liberty, all their zeal for religion, blazed up at once; and they flew to behold this affecting spectacle. The whole shore was covered with crowds of prostrate spectators, who at once implored the blessing of those holy pastors, and addressed their petitions towards Heaven for protection during this extreme danger, to which their country and their religion stood exposed. Even the soldiers, seized with the contagion of the same spirit, flung themselves on their knees before the distressed prelates, and craved the benediction of those criminals, whom they were appointed to guard. Some persons ran into the water, that they might participate more nearly in those blessings, which the prelates were distributing on all around them. The bishops themselves, during

Imprison-ment,

year 1662 and 1672, and in the beginning of your majesty's reign, and is a matter of so great moment and consequence to the whole nation both in church and state, that your petitioners cannot in prudence, honour, or conscience so far make themselves parties to it as a distribution of it all over the nation and the solemn publication of it once and again, even in God's house, and in the time of divine service, must amount to in common and reasonable construction.

this triumphant suffering, augmented the general favour, by the most lowly submissive deportment; and they still exhorted the people to fear God, honour the king, and maintain their loyalty; expressions more animating than the most inflammatory speeches. And no sooner had they entered the precincts of the Tower than they hurried to chapel, in order to return thanks for those afflictions, which Heaven, in defence of its holy cause, had thought them worthy to endure.

Trial,   Their passage, when conducted to their trial, was, if possible, attended by greater crowds of anxious spectators. All men saw the dangerous crisis, to which affairs were reduced, and were sensible, that the king could not have put the issue on a cause more unfavourable for himself than that in which he had so imprudently engaged. Twenty-nine temporal peers (for the other prelates kept aloof) attended the prisoners to Westminster-hall; and such crowds of gentry followed the procession, that scarcely was any room left for the populace to enter. The lawyers for the bishops were Sir Robert Sawyer, Sir Francis Pemberton, Pollexsen, Treby, and Sommers. No cause, even during the prosecution of the popish plot, was ever heard with so much zeal and attention. The popular torrent, which, of itself, ran fierce and strong, was now farther irritated by the opposition of government.

The council for the bishops pleaded, that the law allowed subjects, if they thought themselves aggrieved in any particular, to apply by petition to the king, provided they kept within certain bounds, which the same law prescribed to them, and which in the present petition the prelates had strictly observed: That an active obedience in cases, which were contrary to conscience, was never pretended to be due to government; and law was allowed to be the great measure of the compliance and submission of subjects: That when any person found commands to be imposed upon him, which he could not obey, it was more respectful in him to offer his reasons for refusal, than to remain in a sullen and refractory silence: That it was no breach of duty in subjects, even though not called upon, to discover their sense of public measures, in which every one had so intimate a concern: That the bishops in the present case were called upon, and must either express their approbation by compliance, or their disapprobation by petition:

CHAPTER LXX

That it could be no sedition to deny the prerogative of suspending the laws; because there really was no such prerogative, nor ever could be, in a legal and limited government: That even if this prerogative were real, it had yet been frequently controverted before the whole nation, both in Westminster-hall, and in both houses of parliament: and no one had ever dreamed of punishing the denial of it as criminal: That the prelates, instead of making an appeal to the people, had applied in private to his majesty, and had even delivered their petition so secretly, that, except by the confession extorted from them before the council, it was found impossible to prove them the authors: And that though the petition was afterwards printed and dispersed, it was not so much as attempted to be proved, that they had the least knowledge of the publication.

These arguments were convincing in themselves, and were heard with a favourable disposition by the audience. Even some of the judges, though their seats were held during pleasure, declared themselves in favour of the prisoners. The jury however, from what cause is unknown, took several hours to deliberate, and kept, during so long a time, the people in the most anxious expectation. But when the wished for verdict, *not guilty,* was at last pronounced, the intelligence was echoed through the hall, was conveyed to the crowds without, was carried into the city, and was propagated with infinite joy throughout the kingdom.

17th June. and acquittal of the bishops.

Ever since Monmouth's rebellion, the king had, every summer, encamped his army on Hounslow heath, that he might both improve their discipline, and by so unusual a spectacle over-awe the mutinous people. A popish chapel was openly erected in the midst of the camp, and great pains were taken, though in vain, to bring over the soldiers to that communion. The few converts whom the priests had made, were treated with such contempt and ignominy, as deterred every one from following the example. Even the Irish officers, whom the king introduced into the army, served rather, from the aversion borne them, to weaken his interest among them. It happened, that the very day, on which the trial of the bishops was finished, James had reviewed the troops, and had retired into the tent of lord Feversham, the general; when he was surprized to hear a great uproar in the camp, attended with the most extravagant symptoms of tumultuary joy. He suddenly enquired the cause, and was told by Feversham, "It was nothing but the rejoicing of the soldiers for the acquittal of the bishops." "Do you call that nothing?" replied he, "but so much the worse for them."

The king was still determined to rush forward in the same course, in which he was already, by his precipitate career, so fatally advanced. Though he knew, that every order of men, except a handful of catholics, were enraged at his past measures, and still more terrified with the future prospect; though he saw that the same discontents had reached the army, his sole resource during the general disaffection: Yet was he incapable of changing his measures, or even of remitting his violence in the prosecution of them. He struck out two of the judges, Powel and Holloway, who had appeared to favour the bishops: He issued orders to prosecute all those clergymen who had not read his declaration; that is, the whole church of England, two hundred excepted: He sent a mandate to the new fellows, whom he had obtruded on Magdalen-college, to elect for president, in the room of Parker, lately deceased, one Gifford, a doctor of the Sorbonne, and titular bishop of Madura: And he is even said to have nominated the same person to the see of Oxford. So great an infatuation is perhaps an object of compassion rather than of anger: And is really surprizing in a man, who, in other respects, was not wholly deficient in sense and accomplishments.

A few days before the acquittal of the bishops, an event happened, which, in the king's sentiments, much overbalanced all the mortifications, received on that occasion. The queen was delivered of a son, who was baptized by the name of James. This blessing was impatiently longed for, not only by the king and queen, but by all the zealous catholics both abroad and at home. They saw, that the king was past middle age; and that on his death the succession must devolve to the prince and princess of Orange, two zealous protestants, who would soon replace every thing on ancient foundations. Vows therefore were offered at every shrine for a male successor: Pilgrimages were undertaken, particularly one to Loretto, by the dutchess of Modena; and success was chiefly attributed to that pious journey. But in proportion as this event was agreeable to the catholics, it encreased the disgust of the protestants, by depriving them of that pleasing, though somewhat distant prospect, in which at present they flattered themselves.

10th June. Birth of the prince of Wales.

CHAPTER LXX

Calumny even went so far as to ascribe to the king the design of imposing on the world a supposititious child, who might be educated in his principles, and after his death support the catholic religion in his dominions. The nation almost universally believed him capable, from bigotry, of committing any crime; as they had seen, that, from like motives, he was guilty of every imprudence: And the affections of nature, they thought, would be easily sacrificed to the superior motive of propagating a catholic and orthodox faith. The present occasion was not the first, when that calumny had been invented. In the year 1682, the queen, then dutchess of York, had been pregnant; and rumours were spread that an imposture would at that time be obtruded upon the nation: But happily, the infant proved a female, and thereby spared the party all the trouble of supporting their improbable fiction.[i]

[i] This story is taken notice of in a weekly paper, the Observator, published at that very time, 23d of August, 1682: Party zeal is capable of swallowing the most incredible story; but it is surely singular, that the same calumny, when once baffled, should yet be renewed with such success.

LXXI

1688.   WHILE EVERY MOTIVE, civil and religious, concurred to alienate from the king every rank and denomination of men, it
might be expected, that his throne would, without delay, fall to

pieces by its own weight: But such is the influence of established government; so averse are men from beginning hazardous enterprizes; that, had not an attack been made from abroad, affairs might long have remained in their present delicate situation, and James might at last have prevailed in his rash, and ill concerted projects.

The prince of Orange, ever since his marriage with the lady Mary, had maintained a very prudent conduct; agreeably to the sound understanding, with which he was so eminently endowed. He made it a maxim to concern himself little in English affairs, and never by any measure to disgust any of the factions, or give umbrage to the prince, who filled the throne. His natural inclination, as well as his interest, led him to employ himself with assiduous industry in the transactions on the continent, and to oppose the grandeur of the French monarch, against whom he had long, both from personal and political considerations, conceived a violent animosity. By this conduct, he gratified the prejudices of the whole English nation: But as he crossed the inclinations of Charles, who sought peace by compliance with France, he had much declined in the favour and affections of that monarch. *Conduct of the prince of Orange.*

James on his accession found it so much his interest to live on good terms with the heir apparent, that he showed the prince some demonstrations of friendship; and the prince, on his part, was not wanting in every instance of duty and regard towards the king. On Monmouth's invasion, he immediately dispatched over six regiments of British troops, which were in the Dutch service; and he offered to take the command of the king's forces against the rebels. How little soever he might approve of James's administration, he always kept a total silence on the subject, and gave no countenance to those discontents, which were propagated with such industry throughout the nation.

It was from the application of James himself, that the prince first openly took any part in English affairs. Notwithstanding the lofty ideas, which the king had entertained of his prerogative, he found, that the edicts, emitted from it, still wanted much of the authority of laws, and that the continuance of them might in the issue become dangerous, both to himself and to the catholics, whom he desired to favour. An act of parliament alone could insure the indulgence or toleration, which he had laboured to establish; and he hoped, that, if the prince would declare in favour of that scheme, the members, who had hitherto resisted all his own applications, would at last be prevailed with to adopt it. The consent, therefore, of the prince to the repeal of the penal statutes and of the test was strongly solicited by the king; and in order to engage him to agree to that measure, hopes were given,[k] that England would second him in all those enterprizes, which his active and extensive genius had with such success planned on the continent. He was at this time the center of all the negociations of Christendom.

He forms a league against France.

The emperor and the king of Spain, as the prince well knew, were enraged by the repeated injuries, which they had suffered from the ambition of Lewis, and still more by the frequent insults, which his pride had made them undergo. He was apprized of the influence of these monarchs over the catholic princes of the empire: He had himself acquired great authority with the protestant: And he formed a project of uniting Europe in one general league against the encroachments of France, which seemed so nearly to threaten the independance of all its neighbours.

No characters are more incompatible than those of a conqueror and a persecutor; and Lewis soon found, that besides his weakening France by the banishment of so many useful subjects, the refugees had enflamed all the protestant nations against him, and had raised him enemies, who, in defence of their religion as well as liberty, were obstinately resolved to oppose his progress. The city of Amsterdam and other towns in Holland, which had before fallen into a dependance on France, being terrified with the accounts, which they every moment received, of the furious persecutions against the Hugonots, had now dropped all domestic faction, and had entered into an entire confidence with the prince of Orange.[l] The protestant princes of the empire formed a separate league at Magdebourg for the defence of their religion. The English were anew enraged at the blind bigotry of their sovereign, and were disposed to embrace the most desperate resolutions against him. From a view of the state of Europe during this period, it appears, that Lewis, besides sullying an illustrious reign, had

[k] Burnet, vol. i. p. 712. D'Avaux, 15th of April, 1688.   [l] D'Avaux, 24th of July, 1681; 10th of June, 15th of October, 11th of November, 1688; vol. iv. p. 30.

CHAPTER LXXI

wantonly by this persecution raised invincible barriers to his arms, which otherwise it had been difficult, if not impossible, to resist.

The prince of Orange knew how to avail himself of all these advantages. By his intrigues and influence there was formed at Augsbourg a league, in which the whole empire united for its defence against the French monarch. Spain and Holland became parties in the alliance. The accession of Savoy was afterwards obtained. Sweden and Denmark seemed to favour the same cause. But though these numerous states composed the greater part of Europe, the league was still deemed imperfect and unequal to its end; so long as England maintained that neutrality, in which she had hitherto persevered.

James, though more prone to bigotry, was more sensible to his own and to national honour than his brother; and had he not been restrained by the former motive, he would have maintained with more spirit the interests and independance of his kingdoms. When a prospect, therefore, appeared of effecting his religious schemes by opposing the progress of France, he was not averse to that measure; and he gave his son-in-law room to hope, that, by concurring with his views in England, he might prevail with him to second those projects, which the prince was so ambitious of promoting.

A more tempting offer could not be made to a person of his enterprizing character: But the objections to that measure, upon deliberation, appeared to him unsurmountable. The king, he observed, had incurred the hatred of his own subjects: Great apprehensions were entertained of his designs: The only resource, which the nation saw, was in the future succession of the prince and princess: Should *he* concur in those dreaded measures, he should draw on himself all the odium, under which the king laboured: The nation might even refuse to bear the expence of alliances, which would in that case become so suspicious: And he might himself incur danger of losing a succession, which was awaiting him, and which the egregious indiscretion of the king seemed even to give him hopes of reaping, before it should devolve to him by the course of nature. The prince, therefore, would go no farther than to promise his consent to the repeal of the penal statutes, by which the nonconformists as well as catholics were exposed to punishment: The test he deemed a security absolutely necessary for the established religion.

Refuses to concur with the king.

The king did not remain satisfied with a single trial. There was one Stuart, a Scotch lawyer, who had been banished for pretended treasonable practices; but who had afterwards obtained a pardon, and had been recalled. By the king's directions, Stuart wrote several letters to pensionary Fagel, with whom he had contracted an acquaintance in Holland; and besides urging all the motives for an unlimited toleration, he desired, that his reasons should, in the king's name, be communicated to the prince and princess of Orange. Fagel during a long time made no reply; but finding, that his silence was construed into an assent, he at last expressed his own sentiments and those of their Highnesses. He said, that it was their fixed opinion, that no man, merely because he differed from the established faith, should ever, while he remained a peaceable subject, be exposed to any punishment or even vexation. That the prince and princess gave heartily their consent for repealing legally all the penal statutes, as well those which had been enacted against the catholics as against the protestant nonconformists; and would concur with the king in any measure for that purpose. That the test was not to be considered as a penalty inflicted on the professors of any religion, but as a security provided for the established worship. That it was no punishment on men to be excluded from public offices, and to live peaceably on their own revenues or industry. That even in the United Provinces, which were so often cited as models of toleration, though all sects were admitted, yet civil offices were enjoyed by the professors of the established religion alone. That military commands, indeed, were sometimes bestowed on catholics; but as they were conferred with great precaution, and still lay under the controul of the magistrate, they could give no just reason for umbrage. And that their Highnesses, however desirous of gratifying the king, and of endeavouring, by every means, to render his reign peaceable and happy, could not agree to any measure, which would expose their religion to such imminent danger.

When this letter was published, as it soon was, it inspired great courage into the protestants of all denominations, and served to keep them united in their opposition to the encroachments of the catholics. On the other hand, the king, who was not content with a simple toleration for his own religion, but was resolved, that it should enjoy great credit, if not an absolute superiority, was extremely disgusted, and took every occasion to express his displeasure, as well against the prince of Orange as the United Provinces. He gave the Algerine pyrates, who preyed on the Dutch, a reception in his harbours, and liberty to dispose of their prizes. He revived some complaints of the East India company with regard to the affair of Bantam.[m] He required the six British regiments in the Dutch service to be sent over. He began to put his navy in a formidable condition. And from all his movements, the Hollanders entertained apprehensions, that he sought only an occasion and pretence for making war upon them.

The prince in his turn resolved to push affairs with more vigour, and to preserve all the English protestants in his interests, as well as maintain them firm in their present union against the catholics. He knew, that men of education in England were, many of them, retained in their religion more by honour than by principle;[n] and that, though every one was ashamed to be the first proselyte, yet if the example were once set by some eminent persons, interest would every day make considerable conversions to a communion, which was so zealously encouraged by the sovereign. Dykvelt therefore was sent over as envoy to England; and the prince gave him instructions, besides publicly remonstrating on the conduct of affairs both at home and abroad, to apply in his name, after a proper manner, to every sect and denomination. To the church party he sent assurances of favour and regard, and protested, that his education in Holland had no wise prejudiced him against episcopal government. The nonconformists were exhorted not to be deceived by the fallacious caresses of a popish court, but to wait patiently, till, in the fullness of time, laws, enacted by protestants, should give them that toleration, which, with so much reason, they had long demanded. Dykvelt executed his commission with such dexterity, that all orders of men cast their eyes toward Holland, and expected thence a deliverance from those dangers, with which their religion and liberty were so nearly threatened.

Many of the most considerable persons, both in church and state, made secret applications to Dykvelt, and through him to the prince of Orange. Admiral Herbert too, though a man of great

Resolves to oppose the king.

Is applied to by the English.

---

[m] D'Avaux, 21st of January, 1687.   [n] Burnet.

expence, and seemingly of little religion, had thrown up his employments, and had retired to the Hague, where he assured the prince of the disaffection of the seamen, by whom that admiral was extremely beloved. Admiral Russel, cousin german to the unfortunate lord of that name, passed frequently between England and Holland, and kept the communication open with all the great men of the protestant party. Henry Sidney, brother to Algernon, and uncle to the earl of Sunderland, came over under pretence of drinking the waters at Spaw, and conveyed still stronger assurances of an universal combination against the measures of the king. Lord Dumblaine, son of the earl of Danby, being master of a frigate, made several voyages to Holland, and carried from many of the nobility tenders of duty, and even considerable sums of money,[o] to the prince of Orange.

There remained, however, some reasons, which retained all parties in awe, and kept them from breaking out into immediate hostility. The prince, on the one hand, was afraid of hazarding, by violent measures, an inheritance, which the laws ensured to the princess; and the English protestants, on the other, from the prospect of her succession, still entertained hopes of obtaining at last a peaceable and a safe redress of all their grievances. But when a son was born to the king, both the prince and the English nation were reduced to despair, and saw no resource but in a confederacy for their mutual interests. And thus the event, which James had so long made the object of his most ardent prayers, and from which he expected the firm establishment of his throne, proved the immediate cause of his ruin and downfall.

Zuylestein, who had been sent over to congratulate the king on the birth of his son, brought back to the prince invitations from most of the great men in England, to assist them, by his arms, in the recovery of their laws and liberties. The bishop of London, the earls of Danby, Nottingham, Devonshire, Dorset, the duke of Norfolk, the lords Lovelace, Delamere, Paulet, Eland, Mr. Hambden, Powle, Lester, besides many eminent citizens of London; all these persons, though of opposite parties, concurred in their applications to the prince. The whigs, suitably to their ancient principles of liberty, which had led them to attempt the exclusion bill, easily

Coalition of parties.

---

[o] D'Avaux, 14th and 24th of September, 8th and 15th of October, 1688.

agreed to oppose a king, whose conduct had justified whatever his worst enemies had prognosticated concerning his succession. The tories and the church party, finding their past services forgotten, their rights invaded, their religion threatened, agreed to drop for the present all over-strained doctrines of submission, and attend to the great and powerful dictates of nature. The nonconformists, dreading the caresses of known and inveterate enemies, deemed the offers of toleration more secure from a prince, educated in those principles, and accustomed to that practice. And thus all faction was for a time laid asleep in England; and rival parties, forgetting their animosity, had secretly concurred in a design of resisting their unhappy and misguided sovereign. The earl of Shrewsbury, who had acquired great popularity by deserting, at this time, the catholic religion, in which he had been educated, left his regiment, mortgaged his estate for forty thousand pounds, and made a tender of his sword and purse to the prince of Orange. Lord Wharton, notwithstanding his age and infirmities, had taken a journey for the same purpose. Lord Mordaunt was at the Hague, and pushed on the enterprize with that ardent and courageous spirit, for which he was so eminent. Even Sunderland, the king's favourite minister, is believed to have entered into a correspondence with the prince; and at the expence of his own honour and his master's interests, to have secretly favoured a cause, which, he foresaw, was likely soon to predominate.[p]

The prince was easily engaged to yield to the applications of the English, and to embrace the defence of a nation, which, during its present fears and distresses, regarded him as its sole protector. The great object of his ambition was to be placed at the head of a confederate army, and by his valour to avenge the injuries, which he himself, his country, and his allies, had sustained from the haughty Lewis. But while England remained under the present government, he despaired of ever forming a league which would be able, with any probability of success, to make opposition against that powerful monarch. The tyes of affinity could not be supposed to have great influence over a person of the prince's rank and temper; much more, as he knew, that they were at first unwillingly

[p] D'Avaux was always of that opinion. See his negotiations 6th and 20th May, 18th, 27th of September, 22d of November, 1688. On the whole, that opinion is the most probable.

contracted by the king, and had never since been cultivated by any essential favours or good offices. Or should any reproach remain upon him for violating the duties of private life; the glory of delivering oppressed nations would, he hoped, be able, in the eyes of reasonable men, to make ample compensation. He could not well expect, on the commencement of his enterprize, that it would lead him to mount the throne of England: But he undoubtedly foresaw, that its success would establish his authority in that kingdom. And so egregious was James's temerity, that there was no advantage, so great or obvious, which that prince's indiscretion might not afford his enemies.

The prince of Orange, throughout his whole life, was peculiarly happy in the situations, in which he was placed. He saved his own country from ruin, he restored the liberties of these kingdoms, he supported the general independency of Europe. And thus, though his virtue, it is confessed, be not the purest, which we meet with in history, it will be difficult to find any person, whose actions and conduct have contributed more eminently to the general interests of society and of mankind.

Prince's prepa-rations.
The time, when the prince entered on his enterprize, was well chosen; as the people were then in the highest ferment, on account of the insult, which the imprisonment and trial of the bishops had put upon the church, and indeed upon all the protestants of the nation. His method of conducting his preparations was no less wise and politic. Under other pretences he had beforehand made considerable augmentations to the Dutch navy; and the ships were at that time lying in harbour. Some additional troops were also levied; and sums of money, raised for other purposes, were diverted by the prince to the use of this expedition. The States had given him their entire confidence; and partly from terror of the power of France, partly from disgust at some restraints laid on their commerce in that kingdom, were sensible how necessary success in this enterprize was become to their domestic happiness and security. Many of the neighbouring princes regarded him as their guardian and protector, and were guided by him in all their counsels. He held conferences with Castanaga, governor of the Spanish Netherlands, with the electors of Brandenburgh and Saxony, with the Landgrave of Hesse-Cassel, and with the whole house of

CHAPTER LXXI

Lunenbourg. It was agreed, that these princes should replace the troops employed against England, and should protect the United Provinces during the absence of the prince of Orange. Their forces were already on their march for that purpose: A considerable encampment of the Dutch army was formed at Nimeguen: Every place was in movement; and though the roots of this conspiracy reached from one end of Europe to the other, so secret were the prince's counsels, and so fortunate was the situation of affairs, that he could still cover his preparations under other pretences; and little suspicion was entertained of his real intentions.

The king of France, menaced by the league of Augsbourg, had resolved to strike the first blow against the allies; and having sought a quarrel with the emperor and the elector Palatine, he had invaded Germany with a great army, and had laid siege to Philipsbourg. The elector of Cologne, who was also bishop of Liege and Munster, and whose territories almost entirely surrounded the United Provinces, had died about this time; and the candidates for that rich succession were prince Clement of Bavaria, supported by the house of Austria, and the cardinal of Furstemberg, a prelate dependant on France. The pope, who favoured the allies, was able to throw the balance between the parties, and prince Clement was chosen; a circumstance which contributed extremely to the security of the States. But as the cardinal kept possession of many of the fortresses, and had applied to France for succour, the neighbouring territories were full of troops; and by this means the preparations of the Dutch and their allies seemed intended merely for their own defence against the different enterprizes of Lewis.

All the artifices, however, of the prince could not entirely conceal his real intentions from the sagacity of the French court. D'Avaux, Lewis's envoy at the Hague, had been able, by a comparison of circumstances, to trace the purposes of the preparations in Holland; and he instantly informed his master of the discovery. Lewis conveyed the intelligence to James; and accompanied the information with an important offer. He was willing to join a squadron of French ships to the English fleet; and to send over any number of troops, which James should judge requisite for his security. When this proposal was rejected, he again offered to raise

Offers of France to the king.

the siege of Philipsbourg, to march his army into the Netherlands, and by the terror of his arms to detain the Dutch forces in their own country. This proposal met with no better reception.

Rejected. James was not, as yet, entirely convinced, that his son-in-law intended an invasion upon England. Fully persuaded, himself, of the sacredness of his own authority, he fancied, that a like belief had made deep impression on his subjects; and notwithstanding the strong symptoms of discontent which broke out every where, such an universal combination in rebellion appeared to him no wise credible. His army, in which he trusted, and which he had considerably augmented, would easily be able, he thought, to repel foreign force, and to suppress any sedition among the populace. A small number of French troops, joined to these, might tend only to breed discontent; and afford them a pretence for mutinying against foreigners, so much feared and hated by the nation. A great body of auxiliaries might indeed secure him both against an invasion from Holland, and against the rebellion of his own subjects; but would be able afterwards to reduce him to dependance, and render his authority entirely precarious. Even the French invasion of the Low Countries might be attended with dangerous consequences; and would suffice, in these jealous times, to revive the old suspicion of a combination against Holland, and against the protestant religion; a suspicion, which had already produced such discontents in England. These were the views suggested by Sunderland; and it must be confessed, that the reasons, on which they were founded, were sufficiently plausible; as indeed the situation, to which the king had reduced himself, was, to the last degree, delicate and perplexing.

Still Lewis was unwilling to abandon a friend and ally, whose interests he regarded as closely connected with his own. By the suggestion of Skelton, the king's minister at Paris, orders were sent to D'Avaux to remonstrate with the States in Lewis's name against those preparations, which they were making to invade England. The strict amity, said the French minister, which subsists between the two monarchs will make Lewis regard every attempt against his ally as an act of hostility against himself. This remonstrance had a bad effect, and put the States in a flame. What is this alliance, they asked, between France and England, which has been so carefully

CHAPTER LXXI

concealed from us? Is it of the same nature with the former; meant for our destruction and for the extirpation of the protestant religion? If so, it is high time for us to provide for our own defence, and to anticipate those projects, which are forming against us.

Even James was displeased with this officious step taken by Lewis for his service. He was not reduced, he said, to the condition of the cardinal of Furstemberg, and obliged to seek the protection of France. He recalled Skelton, and threw him into the Tower for his rash conduct. He solemnly disavowed D'Avaux's memorial; and protested, that no alliance subsisted between him and Lewis, but what was public and known to all the world. The States, however, still affected to appear incredulous on that head;[q] and the English, prepossessed against their sovereign, firmly believed, that he had concerted a project with Lewis for their entire subjection. Portsmouth, it was said, was to be put into the hands of that ambitious monarch: England was to be filled with French and Irish troops: And every man, who refused to embrace the Romish superstition, was by these bigotted princes devoted to certain destruction.

These suggestions were every where spread abroad, and tended to augment the discontents, of which both the fleet and army, as well as the people, betrayed every day the most evident symptoms. The fleet had begun to mutiny; because Stricland, the admiral, a Roman catholic, introduced the mass aboard his ship, and dismissed the protestant chaplain. It was with some difficulty the seamen could be appeased; and they still persisted in declaring, that they would not fight against the Dutch, whom they called friends and brethren; but would willingly give battle to the French, whom they regarded as national enemies. The king had intended to augment his army with Irish recruits, and he resolved to try the experiment on the regiment of the duke of Berwic, his natural son; But Beaumont, the lieutenant-colonel, refused to admit them; and to this opposition five captains steadily adhered. They were all

[q] That there really was no new alliance formed betwixt France and England appears both from Sunderland's apology, and from D'Avaux's negotiations, lately published: See vol. iv. p. 18. Eng. translation, 27th of September, 1687. 16th of March, 6th of May, 10th of August, 2d, 23d, and 24th of September, 5th, and 7th of October, 11th of November, 1688.

cashiered; and had not the discontents of the army on this occasion become very apparent, it was resolved to have punished those officers for mutiny.

The king made a trial of the dispositions of his army, in a manner still more undisguised. Finding opposition from all the civil and ecclesiastical orders of the kingdom, he resolved to appeal to the military, who, if unanimous, were able alone to serve all his purposes, and to enforce universal obedience. His intention was to engage all the regiments, one after another, to give their consent to the repeal of the test and penal statutes; and accordingly, the major of Litchfield's drew out the battalion before the king, and told them, that they were required either to enter into his majesty's views in these particulars, or to lay down their arms. James was surprized to find, that, two captains, and a few popish soldiers excepted, the whole battalion immediately embraced the latter part of the alternative. For some time, he remained speechless; but having recovered from his astonishment, he commanded them to take up their arms; adding with a sullen, discontented air, "That for the future, he would not do them the honour to apply for their approbation."

While the king was dismayed with these symptoms of general disaffection, he received a letter from the marquess of Albeville, his minister at the Hague, which informed him with certainty, that he was soon to look for a powerful invasion from Holland, and that pensionary Fagel had at length acknowledged, that the scope of all the Dutch naval preparations was to transport forces into England. Though James could reasonably expect no other intelligence, he was astonished at the news: He grew pale, and the letter dropped from his hand: His eyes were now opened, and he found himself on the brink of a frightful precipice, which his delusions had hitherto concealed from him. His ministers and counsellors, equally astonished, saw no resource but in a sudden and precipitate retraction of all those fatal measures, by which he had created to himself so many enemies, foreign and domestic. He paid court to the Dutch, and offered to enter into any alliance with them for common security: He replaced in all the counties the deputy-lieutenants and justices, who had been deprived of their commissions for their adherence to the test and the penal laws: He restored the charters of London, and of all the corporations: He

23d Sept.

The king retracts his measures.

CHAPTER LXXI

annulled the court of ecclesiastical commission: He took off the bishop of London's suspension: He re-instated the expelled president and fellows of Magdalen college: And he was even reduced to caress those bishops, whom he had so lately prosecuted and insulted. All these measures were regarded as symptoms of fear, not of repentance. The bishops instead of promising succour, or suggesting comfort, recapitulated to him all the instances of his maladministration, and advised him thenceforwards to follow more salutary counsel. And as intelligence arrived of a great disaster, which had befallen the Dutch fleet, it is commonly believed, that the king recalled, for some time, the concessions, which he had made to Magdalen college: A bad sign of his sincerity in his other concessions. Nay, so prevalent were his unfortunate prepossessions, that, amidst all his present distresses, he could not forbear, at the baptism of the young prince, appointing the pope to be one of the godfathers.

The report, that a supposititious child was to be imposed on the nation, had been widely spread, and greedily received, before the birth of the prince of Wales: But the king, who, without seeming to take notice of the matter, might easily have qualified that ridiculous rumour, had, from an ill-timed haughtiness, totally neglected it. He disdained, he said, to satisfy those, who could deem him capable of so base and villainous an action. Finding that the calumny gained ground, and had made deep impression on his subjects, he was now obliged to submit to the mortifying task of ascertaining the reality of the birth. Though no particular attention had been beforehand given to ensure proof, the evidence, both of the queen's pregnancy and delivery was rendered indisputable; and so much the more, as no argument or proof of any importance, nothing but popular rumour and surmize, could be thrown into the opposite scale.

Meanwhile, the prince of Orange's declaration was dispersed over the kingdom, and met with universal approbation. All the grievances of the nation were there enumerated: The dispensing and suspending power; the court of ecclesiastical commission; the filling of all offices with catholics, and the raising of a Jesuit to be privy-counsellor; the open encouragement given to popery, by building every where churches, colleges, and seminaries for that sect; the displacing of judges, if they refused to give sentence *Prince's declaration.*

according to orders received from court; the annulling of the charters of all the corporations, and the subjecting of elections to arbitrary will and pleasure; the treating of petitions, even the most modest, and from persons of the highest rank, as criminal and seditious; the committing of the whole authority of Ireland, civil and military, into the hands of papists; the assuming of an absolute power over the religion and laws of Scotland, and openly exacting in that kingdom an obedience without reserve; and the violent presumptions against the legitimacy of the prince of Wales. In order to redress all these grievances, the prince said, that he intended to come over to England with an armed force, which might protect him from the king's evil counsellors: And that his sole aim was to have a legal and free parliament assembled, who might provide for the safety and liberty of the nation, as well as examine the proofs of the prince of Wales's legitimacy. No one, he added, could entertain such hard thoughts of him as to imagine, that he had formed any other design than to procure the full and lasting settlement of religion, liberty, and property. The force, which he meant to bring with him, was totally disproportioned to any views of conquest; and it were absurd to suspect, that so many persons of high rank, both in church and state, would have given him so many solemn invitations for such a pernicious purpose. Though the English ministers, terrified with his enterprize, had pretended to redress some of the grievances complained of; there still remained the foundation of all grievances, that upon which they could in an instant be again erected, an arbitrary and despotic power in the crown. And for this usurpation there was no possible remedy, but by a full declaration of all the rights of the subject in a free parliament.

So well concerted were the prince's measures, that, in three days, above four hundred transports were hired; the army quickly fell down the rivers and canals from Nimeguen; the artillery, arms, stores, and horses, were embarked; and the prince set sail from Helvoet-Sluice, with a fleet of near five hundred vessels, and an army of above fourteen thousand men. He first encountered a storm, which drove him back: But his loss being soon repaired, the fleet put to sea under the command of admiral Herbert, and made sail with a fair wind towards the west of England. The same wind detained the king's fleet in their station near Harwich, and enabled

21st of October.

the Dutch to pass the streights of Dover without opposition. Both shores were covered with multitudes of people, who, besides admiring the grandeur of the spectacle, were held in anxious suspence by the prospect of an enterprize, the most important, which, during some ages, had been undertaken in Europe. The prince had a prosperous voyage, and landed his army safely in Torbay on the fifth of November, the anniversary of the gunpowder-treason.

The Dutch army marched first to Exeter; and the prince's declaration was there published. That whole county was so terrified with the executions, which had ensued upon Monmouth's rebellion, that no one for several days joined the prince. The bishop of Exeter in a fright fled to London, and carried to court intelligence of the invasion. As a reward of his zeal, he received the archbishopric of York, which had long been kept vacant, with an intention, as was universally believed, of bestowing it on some catholic. The first person, who joined the prince, was major Burrington; and he was quickly followed by the gentry of the counties of Devon and Somerset. Sir Edward Seymour made proposals for an association, which every one signed. By degrees, the earl of Abingdon, Mr. Russel, son of the earl of Bedford, Mr. Wharton, Godfrey, Howe came to Exeter. All England was in commotion. Lord Delamere took arms in Cheshire, the earl of Danby seized York, the earl of Bath, governor of Plymouth, declared for the prince, the earl of Devonshire made a like declaration in Derby. The nobility and gentry of Nottinghamshire embraced the same cause; and every day there appeared some effect of that universal combination, into which the nation had entered against the measures of the king. Even those who took not the field against him, were able to embarass and confound his counsels. A petition for a free parliament was signed by twenty-four bishops and peers of the greatest distinction, and was presented to the king. No one thought of opposing or resisting the invader.

General commotion.

But the most dangerous symptom was the disaffection, which from the general spirit of the nation, not from any particular reason, had creeped into the army. The officers seemed all disposed to prefer the interests of their country and of their religion to those principles of honour and fidelity, which are commonly esteemed the most sacred ties by men of that profession. Lord Colchester, son of the earl of Rivers, was the first officer that

Desertion of the army,

deserted to the prince; and he was attended by a few of his troops. Lord Lovelace made a like effort; but was intercepted by the militia under the duke of Beaufort and taken prisoner: Lord Cornbury, son of the earl of Clarendon, was more successful. He attempted to carry over three regiments of cavalry; and he actually brought a considerable part of them to the prince's quarters. Several officers of distinction informed Feversham, the general, that they could not in conscience fight against the prince of Orange.

Lord Churchill had been raised from the rank of a page, had been invested with a high command in the army, had been created a peer, and had owed his whole fortune to the king's favour: Yet even he could resolve, during the present extremity, to desert his unhappy master, who had ever reposed entire confidence in him. He carried with him the duke of Grafton, natural son of the late king, colonel Berkeley, and some troops of dragoons. This conduct was a signal sacrifice to public virtue of every duty in private life; and required, ever after, the most upright, disinterested, and public spirited behaviour to render it justifiable.

The king had arrived at Salisbury, the head quarters of his army, when he received this fatal intelligence. That prince, though a severe enemy, had ever appeared a warm, steady, and sincere friend; and he was extremely shocked with this, as with many other instances of ingratitude, to which he was now exposed. There remained none in whom he could confide. As the whole army had discovered symptoms of discontent, he concluded it full of treachery; and being deserted by those whom he had most favoured and obliged, he no longer expected, that others would hazard their lives in his service. During this distraction and perplexity, he embraced a sudden resolution of drawing off his army, and retiring towards London: A measure, which could only serve to betray his fears, and provoke farther treachery.

25th of November.

But Churchill had prepared a still more mortal blow for his distressed benefactor. His lady and he had an entire ascendant over the family of prince George of Denmark; and the time now appeared seasonable for overwhelming the unhappy king, who was already staggering with the violent shocks, which he had received. Andover was the first stage of James's retreat towards London; and there, prince George, together with the young duke of

and of prince George,

CHAPTER LXXI

Ormond,[r] Sir George Huet, and some other persons of distinction, deserted him in the night-time, and retired to the prince's camp. No sooner had this news reached London, than the princess Anne, pretending fear of the king's displeasure, withdrew herself in company with the bishop of London and lady Churchill. She fled to Nottingham; where the earl of Dorset received her with great respect, and the gentry of the county quickly formed a troop for her protection. *and of the princess Anne.*

The late king, in order to gratify the nation, had entrusted the education of his nieces entirely to protestants; and as these princesses were deemed the chief resource of the established religion after their father's defection, great care had been taken to instill into them, from their earliest infancy, the strongest prejudices against popery. During the violence too of such popular currents, as now prevailed in England, all private considerations are commonly lost in the general passion; and the more principle any person possesses, the more apt is he, on such occasions, to neglect and abandon his domestic duties. Though these causes may account for the behaviour of the princess, they had nowise prepared the king to expect so astonishing an event. He burst into tears, when the first intelligence of it was conveyed to him. Undoubtedly he foresaw in this incident the total expiration of his royal authority: But the nearer and more intimate concern of a parent laid hold of his heart; when he found himself abandoned in his uttermost distress by a child, and a virtuous child, whom he had ever regarded with the most tender affection. "God help me," cried he, in the extremity of his agony, "my own children have forsaken me!" It is indeed singular, that a prince, whose chief blame consisted in imprudences, and misguided principles, should be exposed, from religious antipathy, to such treatment as even Nero, Domitian, or the most enormous tyrants, that have disgraced the records of history, never met with from their friends and family. *King's consternation,*

So violent were the prejudices, which at this time prevailed, that this unhappy father, who had been deserted by his favourite child, was believed, upon her disappearing, to have put her to

[r] His grandfather, the first duke of Ormond, had died this year, on the 21st of July.

death: And it was fortunate, that the truth was timely discovered; otherwise the populace, even the king's guards themselves, might have been engaged, in revenge, to commence a massacre of the priests and catholics.

The king's fortune now exposed him to the contempt of his enemies; and his behaviour was not such as could gain him the esteem of his friends and adherents. Unable to resist the torrent, he preserved not presence of mind in yielding to it; but seemed in this emergence as much depressed with adversity, as he had before been vainly elated by prosperity. He called a council of all the peers and prelates who were in London; and followed their advice in issuing writs for a new parliament, and in sending Halifax, Nottingham, and Godolphin as commissioners to treat with the prince of Orange. But these were the last acts of royal authority which he exerted. He even hearkened to imprudent counsel, by which he was prompted to desert the throne, and to gratify his enemies beyond what their fondest hopes could have promised them.

The queen, observing the fury of the people, and knowing how much she was the object of general hatred, was struck with the deepest terror, and began to apprehend a parliamentary impeachment, from which, she was told, the queens of England were not exempted. The popish courtiers, and above all, the priests, were aware, that they should be the first sacrifice, and that their perpetual banishment was the smallest penalty, which they must expect from national resentment. They were, therefore, desirous of carrying the king along with them; whose presence, they knew, would still be some resource and protection to them in foreign countries, and whose restoration, if it ever happened, would again re-instate them in power and authority. The general defection of the protestants made the king regard the catholics, as his only subjects, on whose counsel he could rely; and the fatal catastrophe of his father afforded them a plausible reason for making him apprehend a like fate. The great difference of circumstances was not, during men's present distractions, sufficiently weighed. Even after the people were inflamed by a long civil war, the execution of Charles I. could not be deemed a national deed: It was perpetrated by a fanatical army, pushed on by a daring and enthusiastical leader; and the whole kingdom had ever entertained, and

CHAPTER LXXI

did still entertain, a violent abhorrence against that enormity. The situation of public affairs, therefore, no more resembled what it was forty years before, than the prince of Orange, either in birth, character, fortune, or connexions, could be supposed a parallel to Cromwel.

The emissaries of France, and among the rest, Barillon, the French ambassador, were busy about the king; and they had entertained a very false notion, which they instilled into him, that nothing would more certainly retard the public settlement, and beget universal confusion, than his deserting the kingdom. The prince of Orange had with good reason embraced a contrary opinion; and he deemed it extremely difficult to find expedients for securing the nation, so long as the king kept possession of the crown. Actuated, therefore, by this public motive, and no less, we may well presume, by private ambition, he was determined to use every expedient, which might intimidate the king, and make him quit that throne, which he himself was alone enabled to fill. He declined a personal conference with James's commissioners, and sent the earls of Clarendon and Oxford to treat with them: The terms, which he proposed, implied almost a present participation of the sovereignty: And he stopped not a moment the march of his army towards London.

The news, which the king received from all quarters, served to continue the panic, into which he was fallen, and which his enemies expected to improve to their advantage. Colonel Copel, deputy governor of Hull, made himself master of that important fortress; and threw into prison lord Langdale, the governor, a catholic; together with lord Montgomery, a nobleman of the same religion. The town of Newcastle received lord Lumley, and declared for the prince of Orange and a free parliament. The duke of Norfolk, lord lieutenant of the county of that name, engaged it in the same measure. The prince's declaration was read at Oxford by the duke of Ormond, and was received with great applause by that loyal university, who also made an offer of their plate to the prince. Every day, some person of quality or distinction, and among the rest, the duke of Somerset, went over to the enemy. A violent declaration was dispersed in the prince's name, but without his participation; in which every one was commanded to seize and punish all papists, who, contrary to law, pretended either to carry arms, or exercise any act of authority. It may not be unworthy of notice, that a merry ballad, called Lilliballero, being at this time published in derision of the papists and the Irish, it was greedily received by the people, and was sung by all ranks of men, even by the king's army, who were strongly seized with the national spirit. This incident both discovered, and served to encrease, the general discontent of the kingdom.

The contagion of mutiny and disobedience had also reached Scotland, whence the regular forces, contrary to the advice of Balcarras, the treasurer, were withdrawn, in order to re-inforce the English army. The marquess of Athole, together with viscount Tarbat, and others, finding the opportunity favourable, began to form intrigues against Perth, the chancellor; and the presbyterians and other malcontents flocked from all quarters to Edinburgh. The chancellor, apprehensive of the consequences, found it expedient to abscond; and the populace, as if that event were a signal for their insurrection, immediately rose in arms, and rifled the popish chapel in the king's palace. All the catholics, even all the zealous royalists, were obliged to conceal themselves; and the privy council, instead of their former submissive strains of address to the king, and violent edicts against their fellow subjects, now made applications to the prince of Orange, as the restorer of law and liberty.

The king every moment alarmed, more and more, by these proofs of a general disaffection, not daring to repose trust in any but those who were exposed to more danger than himself, agitated by disdain towards ingratitude, by indignation against disloyalty, impelled by his own fears and those of others, precipitately embraced the resolution of escaping into France; and he sent off beforehand the queen and the infant prince, under the conduct of count Lauzun, an old favourite of the French monarch. He himself *and flight. 12th Dec.* disappeared in the night-time, attended only by Sir Edward Hales; and made the best of his way to a ship, which waited for him near the mouth of the river. As if this measure had not been the most grateful to his enemies of any that he could adopt, he had carefully concealed his intention from all the world; and nothing could equal the surprize, which seized the city, the court, and the kingdom, upon the discovery of this strange event. Men beheld, all of a sudden, the reins of government thrown up by the hand which

CHAPTER LXXI

held them; and saw none, who had any right or even pretension, to take possession of them.

The more effectually to involve every thing in confusion, the king appointed not any one, who should, in his absence, exercise any part of the administration; he threw the great seal into the river; and he recalled all those writs, which had been issued for the election of the new parliament. It is often supposed, that the sole motive, which impelled him to this sudden desertion, was his reluctance to meet a free parliament, and his resolution not to submit to those terms, which his subjects would deem requisite for the security of their liberties and their religion. But it must be considered, that his subjects had first deserted him, and entirely lost his confidence; that he might reasonably be supposed to entertain fears for his liberty, if not for his life; and that the conditions would not probably be moderate, which the nation, sensible of his inflexible temper, enraged with the violation of their laws and the danger of their religion, and foreseeing his resentment on account of their past resistance, would, in his present circumstances, exact from him.

By this temporary dissolution of government, the populace were masters; and there was no disorder, which, during their present ferment, might not be dreaded from them. They rose in a tumult and destroyed all the mass-houses. They even attacked and rifled the houses of the Florentine envoy and Spanish ambassador, where many of the catholics had lodged their most valuable effects. Jefferies, the chancellor, who had disguised himself, in order to fly the kingdom, was discovered by them, and so abused, that he died a little after. Even the army, which should have suppressed those tumults, would, it was apprehended, serve rather to encrease the general disorder. Feversham had no sooner heard of the king's flight, than he disbanded the troops in the neighbourhood, and without either disarming or paying them, let them loose to prey upon the country.

In this extremity, the bishops and peers, who were in town, being the only remaining authority of the state (for the privy council, composed of the king's creatures, was totally disregarded) thought proper to assemble, and to interpose for the preservation of the community. They chose the marquess of Halifax speaker: They gave directions to the mayor and aldermen for keeping the peace of the city: They issued orders, which were readily obeyed, to the fleet, the army, and all the garrisons: And they made applications to the prince of Orange, whose enterprize they highly applauded, and whose success they joyfully congratulated.

The prince on his part was not wanting to the tide of success, which flowed in upon him, nor backward in assuming that authority, which the present exigency had put into his hands. Besides the general popularity, attending his cause, a new incident made his approach to London still more grateful. In the present trepidation of the people, a rumour arose, either from chance or design, that the disbanded Irish had taken arms, and had commenced an universal massacre of the protestants. This ridiculous belief was spread all over the kingdom in one day; and begat every where the deepest consternation. The alarum bells were rung; the beacons fired; men fancied that they saw at a distance the smoke of the burning cities, and heard the groans of those who were slaughtered in their neighbourhood. It is surprizing, that the catholics did not all perish, in the rage which naturally succeeds to such popular panics.

King seized at Feversham. While every one from principle, interest, or animosity, turned his back on the unhappy king, who had abandoned his own cause, the unwelcome news arrived, that he had been seized by the populace at Feversham, as he was making his escape in disguise; that he had been much abused, till he was known; but that the gentry had then interposed and protected him, though they still refused to consent to his escape. This intelligence threw all parties into confusion. The prince sent Zuylestein with orders, that the king should approach no nearer than Rochester; but the message came too late. He was already arrived in London, where the populace, moved by compassion for his unhappy fate, and actuated by their own levity, had received him with shouts and acclamations.

During the king's abode at Whitehall, little attention was payed to him by the nobility or any persons of distinction. They had, all of them, been previously disgusted on account of his blind partiality to the catholics; and they knew, that they were now become criminal in his eyes by their late public applications to the prince of Orange. He himself shewed not any symptom of spirit, nor discovered any intention of resuming the reins of government, which he had once thrown aside. His authority was now plainly

CHAPTER LXXI

expired; and as he had exercised his power, while possessed of it, with very precipitate and haughty counsels, he relinquished it by a despair, equally precipitate and pusillanimous.

Nothing remained for the now ruling powers but to deliberate how they should dispose of his person. Besides, that the prince may justly be supposed to have possessed more generosity than to think of offering violence to an unhappy monarch, so nearly related to him, he knew, that nothing would so effectually promote his own views as the king's retiring into France, a country at all times obnoxious to the English. It was determined, therefore, to push him into that measure, which, of himself, he seemed sufficiently inclined to embrace. The king having sent lord Feversham on a civil message to the prince, desiring a conference for an accommodation in order to the public settlement, that nobleman was put in arrest, under pretence of his coming without a passport: The Dutch guards were ordered to take possession of Whitehall, where James then resided, and to displace the English: And Halifax, Shrewsbury, and Delamere, brought a message from the prince, which they delivered to the king in bed after midnight, ordering him to leave his palace next morning, and to depart for Ham, a seat of the dutchess of Lauderdale's. He desired permission, which was easily granted, of retiring to Rochester, a town near the sea-coast. It was perceived, that the artifice had taken effect; and that the king, terrified with this harsh treatment, had renewed his former resolution of leaving the kingdom.

He lingered, however, some days at Rochester, under the protection of a Dutch guard, and seemed desirous of an invitation still to keep possession of the throne. He was undoubtedly sensible, that, as he had, at first, trusted too much to his people's loyalty, and in confidence of their submission, had offered the greatest violence to their principles and prejudices; so had he, at last, on finding his disappointment, gone too far in the other extreme, and had hastily supposed them destitute of all sense of duty or allegiance. But observing, that the church, the nobility, the city, the country, all concurred in neglecting him, and leaving him to his own counsels, he submitted to his melancholy fate; and being urged by earnest letters from the queen, he privately embarked on board a frigate which waited for him; and he arrived safely at Ambleteuse in Picardy, whence he hastened to St. Germains. Lewis

Second escape. 23d Dec.

received him with the highest generosity, sympathy, and regard; a conduct, which, more than his most signal victories, contributes to the honour of that great monarch.

King's character.   Thus ended the reign of a prince, whom, if we consider his personal character rather than his public conduct, we may safely pronounce more unfortunate than criminal. He had many of those qualities, which form a good citizen: Even some of those, which, had they not been swallowed up in bigotry and arbitrary principles, serve to compose a good sovereign. In domestic life, his conduct was irreproachable, and is intitled to our approbation. Severe, but open in his enmities, steady in his counsels, diligent in his schemes, brave in his enterprizes, faithful, sincere, and honourable in his dealings with all men: Such was the character with which the duke of York mounted the throne of England. In that high station, his frugality of public money was remarkable, his industry exemplary, his application to naval affairs successful, his encouragement of trade judicious, his jealousy of national honour laudable: What then was wanting to make him an excellent sovereign? A due regard and affection to the religion and constitution of his country. Had he been possessed of this essential quality, even his middling talents, aided by so many virtues, would have rendered his reign honourable and happy. When it was wanting, every excellency, which he possessed, became dangerous and pernicious to his kingdoms.

The sincerity of this prince (a virtue, on which he highly valued himself) has been much questioned in those reiterated promises, which he had made of preserving the liberties and religion of the nation. It must be confessed, that his reign was almost one continued invasion of both; yet it is known, that, to his last breath, he persisted in asserting, that he never meant to subvert the laws, or procure more than a toleration and an equality of privileges to his catholic subjects. This question can only affect the personal character of the king, not our judgment of his public conduct. Though by a stretch of candour we should admit of his sincerity in these professions, the people were equally justifiable in their resistance of him. So lofty was the idea, which he had entertained of his *legal* authority, that it left his subjects little or no right to liberty, but what was dependent on his sovereign will and pleasure. And such was his zeal for proselytism, that, whatever he might at first have intended, he plainly stopped not at toleration and equality: He confined all power, encouragement, and favour to the catholics: Converts from interest would soon have multiplied upon him: If not the greater, at least the better part of the people, he would have flattered himself, was brought over to his religion: And he would in a little time have thought it just, as well as pious, to bestow on them all the public establishments. Rigours and persecutions against heretics would speedily have followed; and thus liberty and the protestant religion would in the issue have been totally subverted; though we should not suppose, that James, in the commencement of his reign, had formally fixed a plan for that purpose. And on the whole, allowing this king to have possessed good qualities and good intentions, his conduct serves only, on that very account, as a stronger proof, how dangerous it is to allow any prince, infected with the catholic superstition, to wear the crown of these kingdoms.

After this manner, the courage and abilities of the prince of Orange, seconded by surprising fortune, had effected the deliverance of this island; and with very little effusion of blood (for only one officer of the Dutch army and a few private soldiers fell in an accidental skirmish) had dethroned a great prince, supported by a formidable fleet and a numerous army. Still the more difficult task remained, and what perhaps the prince regarded as not the least important: The obtaining for himself that crown, which had fallen from the head of his father-in-law. Some lawyers, entangled in the subtleties and forms of their profession, could think of no expedient; but that the prince should claim the crown by right of conquest; should immediately assume the title of sovereign; and should call a parliament, which, being thus legally summoned by a king in possession, could ratify whatever had been transacted before they assembled. But this measure, being destructive of the principles of liberty, the only principles on which his future throne could be established, was prudently rejected by the prince, who, finding himself possessed of the good-will of the nation, resolved to leave them entirely to their own guidance and direction. The peers and bishops, to the number of near ninety, made an address, desiring him to summon a convention by circular letters; to assume, in the mean time, the management of public affairs; and to concert measures for the security of Ireland. At the same time, they refused reading a letter, which the king had left, in order to apologize for his late desertion, by the violence which had been put upon him. This step was a sufficient indication of their intentions with regard to that unhappy monarch.

The prince seemed still unwilling to act upon an authority, which might be deemed so imperfect: He was desirous of obtaining a more express declaration of the public consent. A judicious expedient was fallen on for that purpose. All the members, who had sitten in the house of commons during any parliament of Charles II. (the only parliaments whose election was regarded as free) were invited to meet; and to them were added the mayor, aldermen, and fifty of the common council. This was regarded as the most proper representative of the people, that could be summoned during the present emergence. They unanimously voted the same address with the lords: And the prince, being thus supported by all the legal authority, which could possibly be obtained in this critical juncture, wrote circular letters to the counties and corporations of England; and his orders were universally complied with. A profound tranquillity prevailed throughout the kingdom; and the prince's administration was submitted to, as if he had succeeded in the most regular manner to the vacant throne. The fleet received his orders: The army, without murmur or opposition, allowed him to new model them: And the city supplied him with a loan of two hundred thousand pounds.

Convention summoned.

The conduct of the prince with regard to Scotland, was founded on the same prudent and moderate maxims. Finding, that there were many Scotchmen of rank at that time in London, he summoned them together, laid before them his intentions, and asked their advice in the present emergency. This assembly, consisting of thirty noblemen and about fourscore gentlemen, chose duke Hamilton president; a man, who, being of a temporizing character, was determined to pay court to the present authority. His eldest son, the earl of Arran, professed an adherence to king James; a usual policy in Scotland, where the father and son, during civil commotions, were often observed to take opposite sides; in order to secure in all events the family from attainder. Arran proposed to invite back the king upon conditions; but as he was vehemently opposed in this motion by Sir Patric Hume, and seconded by nobody, the assembly made an offer to the prince of the

1689.

7th Jan. Settlement of Scotland.

CHAPTER LXXI

present administration, which he willingly accepted. To anticipate a little in our narration; a convention, by circular letters from the prince, was summoned at Edinburgh on the twenty-second of March; where it was soon visible, that the interest of the malcontents would entirely prevail. The more zealous royalists, regarding this assembly as illegal, had forborn to appear at elections; and the other party were returned for most places. The revolution was not, in Scotland as in England, effected by a coalition of whig and tory: The former party alone had overpowered the government, and were too much enraged by the past injuries, which they had suffered, to admit of any composition with their former masters. As soon as the purpose of the convention was discovered, the earl of Balcarras and viscount Dundee, leaders of the tories, withdrew from Edinburgh; and the convention having passed a bold and decisive vote, that king James, by his mal-administration, and his abuse of power, had *forfeited* all title to the crown, they made a tender of the royal dignity to the prince and princess of Orange.

The English convention was assembled; and it immediately appeared, that the house of commons, both from the prevailing humour of the people, and from the influence of present authority, were mostly chosen from among the whig party. After thanks were unanimously given by both houses to the prince of Orange for the deliverance, which he had brought them, a less decisive vote, than that of the Scottish convention, was in a few days passed by a great majority of the commons, and sent up to the peers for their concurrence. It was contained in these words: "That king James II. having endeavoured to subvert the constitution of the kingdom, by breaking the original contract between king and people; and having, by the advice of jesuits and other wicked persons, violated the fundamental laws, and withdrawn himself out of the kingdom, has abdicated the government, and that the throne is thereby vacant." This vote, when carried to the upper house, met with great opposition; of which it is here necessary for us to explain the causes.

22d Jan.
English conven-tion meets.

The tories and the high-church party, finding themselves at once menaced with a subversion of the laws and of their religion, had zealously promoted the national revolt, and had on this occasion departed from those principles of non-resistance, of which, while the king favoured them, they had formerly made such loud professions. Their present apprehensions had prevailed over their political tenets; and the unfortunate James, who had too much trusted to those general declarations, which never will be reduced to practice, found in the issue, that both parties were secretly united against him. But no sooner was the danger past, and the general fears somewhat allayed, than party prejudices resumed, in some degree, their former authority; and the tories were abashed at that victory, which their antagonists, during the late transactions, had obtained over them. They were inclined, therefore, to steer a middle course; and, though generally determined to oppose the king's return, they resolved not to consent to dethroning him, or altering the line of succession. A regent with kingly power was the expedient, which they proposed; and a late instance in Portugal seemed to give some authority and precedent to that plan of government.

Views of the parties.

In favour of this scheme the tories urged, that, by the uniform tenor of the English laws, the title to the crown was ever regarded as sacred, and could, on no account, and by no mal-administration, be forfeited by the sovereign: That to dethrone a king and to elect his successor, was a practice quite unknown to the constitution, and had a tendency to render kingly power entirely dependent and precarious: That where the sovereign, from his tender years, from lunacy, or from other natural infirmity, was incapacitated to hold the reins of government, both the laws and former practice agreed in appointing a regent, who, during the interval, was invested with the whole power of the administration: That the inveterate and dangerous prejudices of king James had rendered him as unfit to sway the English scepter, as if he had fallen into lunacy; and it was therefore natural for the people to have recourse to the same remedy: That the election of one king was a precedent for the election of another; and the government, by that means, would either degenerate into a republic, or, what was worse, into a turbulent and seditious monarchy: That the case was still more dangerous, if there remained a prince, who claimed the crown by right of succession, and disputed, on so plausible a ground, the title of the present sovereign: That though the doctrine of non-resistance might not, in every possible circumstance, be absolutely true, yet was the belief of it very expedient; and to establish a government, which should have the contrary principle for its basis, was to lay a

CHAPTER LXXI

foundation for perpetual revolutions and convulsions: That the appointment of a regent was indeed exposed to many inconveniencies; but so long as the line of succession was preserved entire, there was still a prospect of putting an end, some time or other, to the public disorders: And that scarcely an instance occurred in history, especially in the English history, where a disputed title had not, in the issue, been attended with much greater ills, than all those, which the people had sought to shun, by departing from the lineal successor.

The leaders of the whig party, on the other hand, asserted, that, if there were any ill in the precedent, that ill would result as much from establishing a regent, as from dethroning one king, and appointing his successor; nor would the one expedient, if wantonly and rashly embraced by the people, be less the source of public convulsions than the other: That if the laws gave no express permission to depose the sovereign, neither did they authorize resisting his authority or separating the power from the title: That a regent was unknown, except where the king, by reason of his tender age or his infirmities, was incapable of a will; and in that case, his will was supposed to be involved in that of the regent: That it would be the height of absurdity to try a man for acting upon a commission, received from a prince, whom we ourselves acknowledge to be the lawful sovereign; and no jury would decide so contrary both to law and common sense, as to condemn such a pretended criminal: That even the prospect of being delivered from this monstrous inconvenience was, in the present situation of affairs, more distant than that of putting an end to a disputed succession: That allowing the young prince to be the legitimate heir, he had been carried abroad; he would be educated in principles destructive of the constitution and established religion; and he would probably leave a son, liable to the same insuperable objection: That if the whole line were cut off by law, the people would in time forget or neglect their claim; an advantage, which could not be hoped for, while the administration was conducted in their name, and while they were still acknowledged to possess the legal title: And that a nation, thus perpetually governed by regents or protectors, approached much nearer to a republic than one subject to monarchs, whose hereditary regular succession, as well as present authority, was fixed and appointed by the people.

This question was agitated with great zeal by the opposite parties in the house of peers. The chief speakers among the tories were Clarendon, Rochester, and Nottingham; among the whigs, Halifax and Danby. The question was carried for a king by two voices only, fifty-one against forty-nine. All the prelates, except two, the bishops of London and Bristol, voted for a regent. The primate, a disinterested but pusillanimous man, kept at a distance, both from the prince's court and from parliament.

The house of peers proceeded next to examine piece-meal the vote, sent up to them by the commons. They debated, "Whether there were an original contract between king and people?" and the affirmative was carried by fifty-three against forty-six; a proof that the tories were already losing ground. The next question was, "Whether king James had broken that original contract?" and after a slight opposition, the affirmative prevailed. The lords proceeded to take into consideration the word *abdicated;* and it was carried, that *deserted* was more proper. The concluding question was, "Whether king James having broken the original contract, and *deserted* the government, the throne was thereby vacant?" This question was debated with more heat and contention than any of the former; and upon a division, the tories prevailed by eleven voices, and it was carried to omit the last article, with regard to the vacancy of the throne. The vote was sent back to the commons with these amendments.

The earl of Danby had entertained the project of bestowing the crown solely upon the princess of Orange, and of admitting her as hereditary legal successor to king James: Passing by the infant prince as illegitimate or supposititious. His change of party in the last question gave the tories so considerable a majority in the number of voices.

*Free confer-
ences be-
twixt the
houses.* The commons still insisted on their own vote, and sent up reasons, why the lords should depart from their amendments. The lords were not convinced; and it was necessary to have a free conference, in order to settle this controversy. Never surely was national debate more important, or managed by more able speakers; yet is one surprised to find the topics, insisted on by both sides, so frivolous; more resembling the verbal disputes of the schools than the solid reasonings of statesmen and legislators. In public transactions of such consequence, the true motives, which produce

CHAPTER LXXI

any measure, are seldom avowed. The whigs, now the ruling party, having united with the tories, in order to bring about the revolution, had so much deference for their new allies, as not to insist, that the crown should be declared *forfeited,* on account of the king's mal-administration: Such a declaration, they thought, would imply too express a censure of the old tory principles, and too open a preference of their own. They agreed, therefore, to confound together the king's abusing his power, and his withdrawing from the kingdom; and they called the whole an *abdication;* as if he had given a virtual, though not a verbal, consent to dethroning himself. The tories took advantage of this obvious impropriety, which had been occasioned merely by the complaisance or prudence of the whigs; and they insisted upon the word *desertion,* as more significant and intelligible. It was retorted on them, that, however that expression might be justly applied to the king's withdrawing himself, it could not, with any propriety, be extended to his violation of the fundamental laws. And thus both parties, while they warped their principles from regard to their antagonists, and from prudential considerations, lost the praise of consistence and uniformity.

The managers for the lords next insisted, that, even allowing the king's abuse of power to be equivalent to an abdication, or in other words, to a civil death, it could operate no otherwise than his voluntary resignation or his natural death; and could only make way for the next successor. It was a maxim of English law, *that the throne was never vacant;* but instantly, upon the demise of one king, was filled with his legal heir, who was entitled to all the authority of his predecessor. And however young or unfit for government the successor, however unfortunate in his situation, though he were even a captive in the hands of public enemies; yet no just reason, they thought, could be assigned, why, without any default of his own, he should lose a crown, to which, by birth, he was fully intitled. The managers for the commons might have opposed this reasoning by many specious and even solid arguments. They might have said, that the great security for allegiance being merely opinion, any scheme of settlement should be adopted, in which, it was most probable, the people would acquiesce and persevere. That though, upon the natural death of a king, whose administration had been agreeable to the laws, many and great incon-

veniencies would be endured rather than exclude his lineal successor; yet the case was not the same, when the people had been
obliged, by their revolt, to dethrone a prince, whose illegal measures had, in every circumstance, violated the constitution. That
in these extraordinary revolutions, the government reverted, in
some degree, to its first principles, and the community acquired a
right of providing for the public interest by expedients, which, on
other occasions, might be deemed violent and irregular. That the
recent use of one extraordinary remedy reconciled the people to
the practice of another, and more familiarized their minds to such
licences, than if the government had run on in its usual tenor. And
that king James, having carried abroad his son, as well as withdrawn himself, had given such just provocation to the kingdom,
had voluntarily involved it in such difficulties, that the interests of
his family were justly sacrificed to the public settlement and tranquillity. Though these topics seem reasonable, they were entirely
forborne by the whig managers; both because they implied an
acknowledgment of the infant prince's legitimacy, which it was
agreed to keep in obscurity, and because they contained too express a condemnation of tory principles. They were content to
maintain the vote of the commons by shifts and evasions; and both
sides parted at last without coming to any agreement.

But it was impossible for the public to remain long in the
present situation. The perseverance, therefore, of the lower house
obliged the lords to comply; and by the desertion of some peers to
the whig party, the vote of the commons, without any alteration,
passed by a majority of fifteen in the upper house, and received the
sanction of every part of the legislature, which then subsisted.

It happens unluckily for those, who maintain an original contract between the magistrate and people, that great revolutions of
government, and new settlements of civil constitutions, are commonly conducted with such violence, tumult, and disorder, that
the public voice can scarcely ever be heard; and the opinions of the
citizens are at that time less attended to than even in the common
course of administration. The present transactions in England, it
must be confessed, are a singular exception to this observation.
The new elections had been carried on with great tranquillity and
freedom: The prince had ordered the troops to depart from all the
towns, where the voters assembled: A tumultuary petition to the

CHAPTER LXXI

two houses having been promoted, he took care, though the petition was calculated for his advantage, effectually to suppress it: He entered into no intrigues, either with the electors or the members: He kept himself in a total silence, as if he had been no wise concerned in these transactions: And so far from forming cabals with the leaders of parties, he disdained even to bestow caresses on those, whose assistance might be useful to him. This conduct was highly meritorious, and discovered great moderation and magnanimity; even though the prince unfortunately, through the whole course of his life, and on every occasion, was noted for an address so cold, dry, and distant, that it was very difficult for him, on account of any interest, to soften or familiarize it.

At length, the prince deigned to break silence, and to express, though in a private manner, his sentiments on the present situation of affairs. He called together Halifax, Shrewsbury, Danby, and a few more; and he told them, that, having been invited over to restore their liberty, he had engaged in this enterprize, and had at last happily effected his purpose. That it belonged to the parliament, now chosen and assembled with freedom, to concert measures for the public settlement; and he pretended not to interpose in their determinations. That he heard of several schemes proposed for establishing the government: Some insisted on a regent; others were desirous of bestowing the crown on the princess: It was their concern alone to chuse the plan of administration most agreeable or advantageous to them. That if they judged it proper to settle a regent, he had no objection: He only thought it incumbent on him to inform them, that he was determined not to be the regent, nor ever to engage in a scheme, which, he knew, would be exposed to such insuperable difficulties. That no man could have a juster or deeper sense of the princess's merit than he was impressed with; but he would rather remain a private person than enjoy a crown, which must depend on the will or life of another. And that they must therefore make account, if they were inclined to either of these two plans of settlement, that it would be totally out of his power to assist them in carrying it into execution: His affairs abroad were too important to be abandoned for so precarious a dignity, or even to allow him so much leisure as would be requisite to introduce order into their disjointed government.

These views of the prince were seconded by the princess herself, who, as she possessed many virtues, was a most obsequious wife to a husband, who, in the judgment of the generality of her sex, would have appeared so little attractive and amiable. All considerations were neglected, when they came in competition with what she deemed her duty to the prince. When Danby and others of her partizans wrote her an account of their schemes and proceedings, she expressed great displeasure; and even transmitted their letters to her husband, as a sacrifice to conjugal fidelity. The princess Anne also concurred in the same plan for the public settlement; and being promised an ample revenue, was content to be postponed in the succession to the crown. And as the title of her infant brother was, in the present establishment, entirely neglected, she might, on the whole, deem herself, in point of interest, a gainer by this revolution.

Settlement of the crown. The chief parties, therefore, being agreed, the convention passed a bill, in which they settled the crown on the prince and princess of Orange, the sole administration to remain in the prince: The princess of Denmark to succeed after the death of the prince and princess of Orange; her posterity after those of the princess, but before those of the prince by any other wise. The convention annexed to this settlement of the crown a declaration of rights, where all the points, which had, of late years, been disputed between the king and people, were finally determined; and the powers of royal prerogative were more narrowly circumscribed and more exactly defined, than in any former period of the English government.

Manners, arts and sciences. Thus have we seen, through the course of four reigns, a continual struggle maintained between the crown and the people: Privilege and prerogative were ever at variance: And both parties, beside the present object of dispute, had many latent claims, which, on a favourable occasion, they produced against their adversaries. Governments too steady and uniform, as they are seldom free, so are they, in the judgment of some, attended with another sensible inconvenience: They abate the active powers of men; depress courage, invention, and genius; and produce an universal lethargy in the people. Though this opinion may be just,

CHAPTER LXXI

the fluctuation and contest, it must be allowed, of the English government were, during these reigns, much too violent both for the repose and safety of the people. Foreign affairs, at that time, were either entirely neglected, or managed to pernicious purposes: And in the domestic administration there was felt a continued fever, either secret or manifest; sometimes the most furious convulsions and disorders. The revolution forms a new epoch in the constitution; and was probably attended with consequences more advantageous to the people, than barely freeing them from an exceptionable administration. By deciding many important questions in favour of liberty, and still more, by that great precedent of deposing one king, and establishing a new family, it gave such an ascendant to popular principles, as has put the nature of the English constitution beyond all controversy. And it may justly be affirmed, without any danger of exaggeration, that we, in this island, have ever since enjoyed, if not the best system of government, at least the most entire system of liberty, that ever was known amongst mankind.

To decry with such violence, as is affected by some, the whole line of Stuart; to maintain, that their administration was one continued encroachment on the *incontestible* rights of the people; is not giving due honour to that great event, which not only put a period to their hereditary succession, but made a new settlement of the whole constitution. The inconveniencies, suffered by the people under the two first reigns of that family (for in the main they were fortunate) proceeded in a great measure from the unavoidable situation of affairs; and scarcely any thing could have prevented those events, but such vigour of genius in the sovereign, attended with such good fortune, as might have enabled him entirely to overpower the liberties of his people. While the parliaments, in those reigns, were taking advantage of the necessities of the prince, and attempting every session to abolish, or circumscribe, or define, some prerogative of the crown, and innovate in the usual tenor of government: What could be expected, but that the prince would exert himself, in defending, against such inveterate enemies, an authority, which, during the most regular course of the former English government, had been exercised without dispute or controversy? And though Charles II. in 1672, may with reason be deemed the aggressor, nor is it possible to justify his conduct; yet were there some motives surely, which could engage a prince, so soft and indolent, and at the same time so judicious, to attempt such hazardous enterprizes. He felt, that public affairs had reached a situation, at which they could not possibly remain without some farther innovation. Frequent parliaments were become almost absolutely necessary to the conducting of public business; yet these assemblies were still, in the judgment of the royalists, much inferior in dignity to the sovereign, whom they seemed better calculated to counsel than controul. The crown still possessed considerable power of opposing parliaments; and had not as yet acquired the means of influencing them. Hence a continual jealousy between these parts of the legislature: Hence the inclination mutually to take advantage of each other's necessities: Hence the impossibility, under which the king lay, of finding ministers, who could at once be serviceable and faithful to him. If he followed his own choice in appointing his servants, without regard to their parliamentary interest, a refractory session was instantly to be expected: If he chose them from among the leaders of popular assemblies, they either lost their influence with the people, by adhering to the crown, or they betrayed the crown, in order to preserve their influence. Neither Hambden, whom Charles I. was willing to gain at any price; nor Shaftesbury, whom Charles II. after the popish plot, attempted to engage in his counsels, would renounce their popularity for the precarious, and, as they esteemed it, deceitful favour of the prince. The root of their authority they still thought to lie in the parliament; and as the power of that assembly was not yet uncontroulable, they still resolved to augment it, though at the expence of the royal prerogatives.

It is no wonder, that these events have long, by the representations of faction, been extremely clouded and obscured. No man has yet arisen, who has payed an entire regard to truth, and has dared to expose her, without covering or disguise, to the eyes of the prejudiced public. Even that party amongst us, which boasts of the highest regard to liberty, has not possessed sufficient liberty of thought in this particular; nor has been able to decide impartially of their own merit, compared with that of their antagonists. More noble perhaps in their ends, and highly beneficial to mankind; they must also be allowed to have often been less justifiable in the means, and in many of their enterprizes to have payed more regard to political than to moral considerations. Obliged to court the favour of the populace, they found it necessary to comply with their rage and folly; and have even, on many occasions, by propagating calumnies, and by promoting violence, served to infatuate, as well as corrupt that people, to whom they made a tender of liberty and justice. Charles I. was a tyrant, a papist, and a contriver of the Irish massacre: The church of England was relapsing fast into idolatry: Puritanism was the only true religion, and the covenant the favourite object of heavenly regard. Through these delusions the party proceeded, and, what may seem wonderful, still to the encrease of law and liberty; till they reached the imposture of the popish plot, a fiction which exceeds the ordinary bounds of vulgar credulity. But however singular these events may appear, there is really nothing altogether new in any period of modern history: And it is remarkable, that tribunitian arts, though sometimes useful in a free constitution, have usually been such as men of probity and honour could not bring themselves either to practice or approve. The other faction, which, since the revolution, has been obliged to cultivate popularity, sometimes found it necessary to employ like artifices.

The Whig party, for a course of near seventy years, has, almost without interruption, enjoyed the whole authority of government; and no honours or offices could be obtained but by their countenance and protection. But this event, which, in some particulars, has been advantageous to the state, has proved destructive to the truth of history, and has established many gross falsehoods, which it is unacountable how any civilized nation could have embraced with regard to its domestic occurrences. Compositions the most despicable, both for style and matter, have been extolled, and propagated, and read; as if they had equalled the most celebrated remains of antiquity.[s] And forgetting that a regard to liberty, though a laudable passion, ought commonly to be subordinate to a reverence for established government, the prevailing faction has celebrated only the partizans of the former, who pursued as their object the perfection of civil society, and has extolled them at the expence of their antagonists, who maintained those maxims, that are essential to its very existence. But extremes of all kinds are to

[s] Such as Rapin Thoyras, Locke, Sidney, Hoadley, &c.

be avoided; and though no one will ever please either faction by moderate opinions, it is there we are most likely to meet with truth and certainty.

We shall subjoin to this general view of the English government, some account of the state of the finances, arms, trade, manners, arts, between the restoration and revolution.

The revenue of Charles II. as settled by the long parliament, was put upon a very bad footing. It was too small, if they intended to make him independant in the common course of his administration: It was too large, and settled during too long a period, if they resolved to keep him in entire dependance. The great debts of the republic, which were thrown upon that prince; the necessity of supplying the naval and military stores, which were entirely exhausted; [t] that of repairing and furnishing his palaces: All these causes involved the king in great difficulties immediately after his restoration; and the parliament was not sufficiently liberal in supplying him. Perhaps too he had contracted some debts abroad; and his bounty to the distressed cavaliers, though it did not correspond either to their services or expectations, could not fail, in some degree, to exhaust his treasury. The extraordinary sums, granted the king during the first years, did not suffice for these extraordinary expences; and the excise and customs, the only constant revenue, amounted not to nine hundred thousand pounds a-year, and fell much short of the ordinary burthens of government. The addition of hearth-money in 1662, and of other two branches in 1669 and 1670, brought up the revenue to one million three hundred fifty-eight thousand pounds, as we learn from lord Danby's account: But the same authority informs us, that the yearly expence of government was at that time one million three hundred eighty-seven thousand seven hundred and seventy pounds, [u] without mentioning contingencies, which are always considerable, even under the most prudent administration. Those branches of revenue, granted in 1669 and 1670, expired in 1680, and were never renewed by parliament: They were computed to be above

---

[t] Lord Clarendon's speech to the parliament, Oct. 9, 1665.   [u] Ralph's History, vol. i. p. 288. We learn from that lord's Memoirs, p. 12. that the receipts of the Exchequer, during six years, from 1673 to 1679, were about eight millions two hundred thousand pounds, or one million three hundred sixty-six thousand pounds a-year. See likewise, p. 169.

two hundred thousand pounds a-year. It must be allowed, because asserted by all cotemporary authors of both parties, and even confessed by himself, that king Charles was somewhat profuse and negligent. But it is likewise certain, that a very rigid frugality was requisite to support the government under such difficulties. It is a familiar rule in all business, that every man should be payed, in proportion to the trust reposed in him, and to the power, which he enjoys; and the nation soon found reason, from Charles's dangerous connexions with France, to repent their departure from that prudential maxim. Indeed, could the parliaments in the reign of Charles I. have been induced to relinquish so far their old habits, as to grant that prince the same revenue which was voted to his successor, or had those in the reign of Charles II. conferred on him as large a revenue as was enjoyed by his brother, all the disorders in both reigns might easily have been prevented, and probably all reasonable concessions to liberty might peaceably have been obtained from both monarchs. But these assemblies, unacquainted with public business, and often actuated by faction and fanaticism, could never be made sensible, but too late and by fatal experience, of the incessant change of times and situations. The French ambassador informs his court, that Charles was very well satisfied with his share of power, could the parliament have been induced to make him tolerably easy in his revenue.[w]

If we estimate the ordinary revenue of Charles II. at one million two hundred thousand pounds a-year during his whole reign, the computation will rather exceed than fall below the true value. The convention parliament, after all the sums, which they had granted the king towards the payment of old debts, threw, the last day of their meeting, a debt upon him, amounting to one million seven hundred forty-three thousand two hundred sixty-three pounds.[x] All the extraordinary sums, which were afterwards voted him by parliament, amounted to eleven millions four hundred forty-three thousand four hundred and seven pounds; which, divided by twenty-four, the number of years which that king reigned, make four hundred seventy-six thousand eight hundred and eight pounds a-year. During that time, he had two violent wars to sustain with the Dutch; and in 1678, he made expensive prepa-

[w] Dalrymple's Appendix, p. 142.   [x] Journals, 29th of December, 1660.

rations for a war with France. In the first Dutch war, both France and Denmark were allies to the United Provinces, and the naval armaments in England were very great; so that it is impossible he could have secreted any part, at least any considerable part, of the sums, which were then voted him by parliament.

To these sums we must add about one million two hundred thousand pounds, which had been detained from the bankers on shutting up the Exchequer in 1672. The king payed six per cent. for this money during the rest of his reign.[y] It is remarkable, that, notwithstanding this violent breach of faith, the king, two years after, borrowed money at eight per cent; the same rate of interest which he had payed before that event.[z] A proof, that public credit, instead of being of so delicate a nature, as we are apt to imagine, is, in reality, so hardy and robust, that it is very difficult to destroy it.

The revenue of James was raised by the parliament to about one million eight hundred and fifty thousand pounds;[a] and his income as duke of York, being added, made the whole amount to two millions a year; a sum well proportioned to the public necessities, but enjoyed by him in too independant a manner. The national debt at the revolution amounted to one million fifty-four thousand nine hundred twenty-five pounds.[b]

The militia fell much to decay during these two reigns, partly by the policy of the kings, who had entertained a diffidence of their subjects, partly by that ill-judged law, which limited the king's power of mustering and arraying them. In the beginning, however, of Charles's reign, the militia was still deemed formidable. De Wit having proposed to the French king an invasion of England during the first Dutch war, that monarch replied, that such an attempt would be entirely fruitless, and would tend only to unite the English. In a few days, said he, after our landing, there will be fifty thousand men at least upon us.[c]

Charles in the beginning of his reign had in pay near five thousand men, of guards and garrisons. At the end of his reign he augmented this number to near eight thousand. James on Monmouth's rebellion had on foot about fifteen thousand men; and

[y] Danby's Memoirs, p. 7.   [z] Id. p. 65.   [a] Journ. 1st of March, 1689.
[b] Journ. 20th of March, 1689.   [c] D'Estrades, 20th of October, 1666.

CHAPTER LXXI

when the prince of Orange invaded him, there were no fewer than thirty thousand regular troops in England.

The English navy, during the greater part of Charles's reign, made a considerable figure, for number of ships, valour of the men, and conduct of the commanders. Even in 1678, the fleet consisted of eighty-three ships;[d] besides thirty, which were at that time on the stocks. On the king's restoration he found only sixty-three vessels of all sizes.[e] During the latter part of Charles's reign, the navy fell somewhat to decay, by reason of the narrowness of the king's revenue: But James, soon after his accession, restored it to its former power and glory; and before he left the throne, carried it much farther. The administration of the admiralty under Pepys, is still regarded as a model for order and economy. The fleet at the revolution consisted of one hundred seventy-three vessels of all sizes; and required forty-two thousand seamen to man it.[f] That king, when Duke of York, had been the first inventor of sea-signals. The military genius, during these two reigns, had not totally decayed among the young nobility. Dorset, Mulgrave, Rochester, not to mention Ossory, served on board the fleet, and were present in the most furious engagements against the Dutch.

The commerce and riches of England did never, during any period, encrease so fast as from the restoration to the revolution. The two Dutch wars, by disturbing the trade of that republic, promoted the navigation of this island; and after Charles had made a separate peace with the States, his subjects enjoyed unmolested the trade of Europe. The only disturbance, which they met with, was from a few French privateers, who infested the channel; and Charles interposed not in behalf of his subjects with sufficient spirit and vigour. The recovery or conquest of New York and the Jerseys was a considerable accession to the strength and security of the English colonies; and, together with the settlement of Pensilvania and Carolina, which was effected during that reign, extended the English empire in America. The persecutions of the dissenters, or more properly speaking, the restraints imposed upon them, contributed to augment and people these colonies. Dr. Davenant affirms,[g] that the shipping of England more than dou-

---

[d] Pepys's Memoirs, p. 4.   [e] Memoirs of English affairs, chiefly naval.
[f] Lives of the admirals, vol. ii. p. 476.   [g] Discourse on the public revenues, part ii. p. 29, 33, 36.

bled during these twenty-eight years. Several new manufactures were established; in iron, brass, silk, hats, glass, paper, &c. One Brewer, leaving the Low Countries, when they were threatened with a French conquest, brought the art of dying woollen cloth into England, and by that improvement saved the nation great sums of money. The encrease of coinage during these two reigns was ten millions two hundred sixty-one thousand pounds. A board of trade was erected in 1670; and the earl of Sandwich was made president. Charles revived and supported the charter of the East-India company; a measure whose utility is by some thought doubtful: He granted a charter to the Hudson's Bay company; a measure probably hurtful.

We learn from Sir Josiah Child,[h] that in 1688 there were on the Change more men worth 10,000 pounds than there were in 1650 worth a thousand; that 500 pounds with a daughter was, in the latter period, deemed a larger portion than 2000 in the former; that gentlewomen, in those earlier times, thought themselves well cloathed in a serge gown, which a chambermaid would, in 1688, be ashamed to be seen in; and that, besides the great encrease of rich cloaths, plate, jewels, and household furniture, coaches were in that time augmented a hundred fold.

The duke of Buckingham introduced from Venice the manufacture of glass and christal into England. Prince Rupert was also an encourager of useful arts and manufactures: He himself was the inventor of etching.

The first law for erecting turnpikes was passed in 1662: The places of the turnpikes were Wadesmill, Caxton, and Stilton: But the general and great improvement of highways took not place till the reign of George II.

In 1663, was passed the first law for allowing the exportation of foreign coin and bullion.

In 1667 was concluded the first American treaty between England and Spain: This treaty was made more general and complete in 1670. The two states then renounced all right of trading with each others colonies; and the title of England was acknowledged to all the territories in America, of which she was then possessed.

The French king, about the beginning of Charles's reign, laid

[h] Brief observations, &c.

some impositions on English commodities: And the English, partly displeased with this innovation, partly moved by their animosity against France, retaliated, by laying such restraints on the commerce with that kingdom as amounted almost to a prohibition. They formed calculations, by which they persuaded themselves, that they were losers a million and a half or near two millions a year by the French trade. But no good effects were found to result from these restraints, and in king James's reign they were taken off by parliament.

Lord Clarendon tells us, that, in 1665, when money, in consequence of a treaty, was to be remitted to the bishop of Munster, it was found, that the whole trade of England could not supply above 1000 pounds a month to Frankfort and Cologne, nor above 20,000 pounds a month to Hamburgh: These sums appear surprisingly small.[i]

At the same time that the boroughs of England were deprived of their privileges, a like attempt was made on the colonies. King James recalled the charters, by which their liberties were secured; and he sent over governors invested with absolute power. The arbitrary principles of that monarch appear in every part of his administration.

The people, during these two reigns, were, in a great measure, cured of that wild fanaticism, by which they had formerly been so much agitated. Whatever new vices they might acquire, it may be questioned, whether, by this change, they were, in the main, much losers in point of morals. By the example of Charles II. and the cavaliers, licentiousness and debauchery became prevalent in the nation. The pleasures of the table were much pursued. Love was treated more as an appetite than a passion. The one sex began to abate of the national character of chastity, without being able to inspire the other with sentiment or delicacy.

The abuses in the former age, arising from overstrained pretensions to piety, had much propagated the spirit of irreligion; and many of the ingenious men of this period lie under the imputation of deism. Besides wits and scholars by profession, Shaftesbury, Halifax, Buckingham, Mulgrave, Sunderland, Essex, Rochester, Sidney, Temple are supposed to have adopted these principles.

---

[i] Life of Clarendon, p. 237.

The same factions, which formerly distracted the nation, were revived, and exerted themselves in the most ungenerous and unmanly enterprizes against each other. King Charles being in his whole deportment a model of easy and gentleman-like behaviour, improved the politeness of the nation; as much as faction, which of all things is most destructive to that virtue, could possibly permit. His courtiers were long distinguishable in England by their obliging and agreeable manners.

Till the revolution, the liberty of the press was very imperfectly enjoyed in England, and during a very short period. The star-chamber, while that court subsisted, put effectual restraints upon printing. On the suppression of that tribunal in 1641, the long parliament, after their rupture with the king, assumed the same power with regard to the licencing of books; and this authority was continued during all the period of the republic and protectorship.[k] Two years after the restoration, an act was passed, reviving the republican ordinances. This act expired in 1679; but was revived in the first of king James. The liberty of the press did not even commence with the revolution. It was not till 1694, that the restraints were taken off; to the great displeasure of the king, and his ministers, who, seeing no where, in any government, during present or past ages, any example of such unlimited freedom, doubted much of its salutary effects, and probably thought, that no books or writings would ever so much improve the general understanding of men, as to render it safe to entrust them with an indulgence so easily abused.

In 1677, the old law for burning heretics was repealed; a prudent measure, while the nation was in continual dread of the return of popery.

Amidst the thick cloud of bigotry and ignorance, which overspread the nation, during the commonwealth and protectorship, there were a few sedate philosophers, who, in the retirement of Oxford, cultivated their reason, and established conferences for the mutual communication of their discoveries in physics and geometry. Wilkins, a clergyman, who had married Cromwel's sister, and was afterwards bishop of Chester, promoted these philosophical conversations. Immediately after the restoration, these men

[k] Scobell, i. 44, 134. ii. 88, 230.

CHAPTER LXXI

procured a patent, and having enlarged their number, were denominated the *Royal Society*. But this patent was all they obtained from the king. Though Charles was a lover of the sciences, particularly chemistry and mechanics; he animated them by his example alone, not by his bounty. His craving courtiers and mistresses, by whom he was perpetually surrounded, engrossed all his expence, and left him neither money nor attention for literary merit. His contemporary, Lewis, who fell short of the king's genius and knowledge in this particular, much exceeded him in liberality. Besides pensions conferred on learned men throughout all Europe, his academies were directed by rules and supported by salaries: A generosity which does great honour to his memory; and in the eyes of all the ingenious part of mankind, will be esteemed an atonement for many of the errors of his reign. We may be surprized, that this example should not be more followed by princes; since it is certain that that bounty, so extensive, so beneficial, and so much celebrated, cost not this monarch so great a sum as is often conferred on one useless overgrown favourite or courtier.

But though the French academy of sciences was directed, encouraged and supported by the sovereign, there arose in England some men of superior genius who were more than sufficient to cast the balance, and who drew on themselves and on their native country the regard and attention of Europe. Besides Wilkins, Wren, Wallis, eminent mathematicians, Hooke, an accurate observer by microscopes, and Sydenham, the restorer of true physic; there flourished during this period a Boyle and a Newton; men who trod, with cautious, and therefore the more secure steps, the only road, which leads to true philosophy.

Boyle improved the pneumatic engine invented by Otto Guericke, and was thereby enabled to make several new and curious experiments on the air as well as on other bodies: His chemistry is much admired by those who are acquainted with that art: His hydrostatics contain a greater mixture of reasoning and invention with experiment than any other of his works; but his reasoning is still remote from that boldness and temerity, which had led astray so many philosophers. Boyle was a great partizan of the mechanical philosophy; a theory, which, by discovering some of the secrets of nature, and allowing us to imagine the rest, is so agreeable to the natural vanity and curiosity of men. He died in 1691, aged 65.

In Newton this island may boast of having produced the greatest and rarest genius that ever arose for the ornament and instruction of the species. Cautious in admitting no principles but such as were founded on experiment; but resolute to adopt every such principle, however new or unusual: From modesty, ignorant of his superiority above the rest of mankind; and thence, less careful to accommodate his reasonings to common apprehensions: More anxious to merit than acquire fame: He was from these causes long unknown to the world; but his reputation at last broke out with a lustre, which scarcely any writer, during his own lifetime, had ever before attained. While Newton seemed to draw off the veil from some of the mysteries of nature, he shewed at the same time the imperfections of the mechanical philosophy; and thereby restored her ultimate secrets to that obscurity, in which they ever did and ever will remain. He died in 1727, aged 85.

This age was far from being so favourable to polite literature as to the sciences. Charles, though fond of wit, though possessed himself of a considerable share of it, though his taste in conversation seems to have been sound and just; served rather to corrupt than improve the poetry and eloquence of his time. When the theatres were opened at the restoration, and freedom was again given to pleasantry and ingenuity; men, after so long an abstinence, fed on these delicacies with less taste than avidity, and the coarsest and most irregular species of wit was received by the court as well as by the people. The productions, represented at that time on the stage, were such monsters of extravagance and folly; so utterly destitute of all reason or even common sense; that they would be the disgrace of English literature, had not the nation made atonement for its former admiration of them, by the total oblivion to which they are now condemned. The duke of Buckingham's Rehearsal, which exposed these wild productions, seems to be a piece of ridicule carried to excess; yet in reality the copy scarcely equals some of the absurdities, which we meet with in the originals.[l]

This severe satire, together with the good sense of the nation, corrected, after some time, the extravagancies of the fashionable

[l] The duke of Buckingham died on the 16th of April, 1688.

CHAPTER LXXI

wit; but the productions of literature still wanted much of that correctness and delicacy, which we so much admire in the ancients, and in the French writers, their judicious imitators. It was indeed during this period chiefly, that that nation left the English behind them in the productions of poetry, eloquence, history, and other branches of polite letters; and acquired a superiority, which the efforts of English writers, during the subsequent age, did more successfully contest with them. The arts and sciences were imported from Italy into this island as early as into France; and made at first more sensible advances. Spencer, Shakespeare, Bacon, Johnson, were superior to their cotemporaries, who flourished in that kingdom. Milton, Waller, Denham, Cowley, Harvey were at least equal to their cotemporaries. The reign of Charles II. which some preposterously represent as our Augustan age, retarded the progress of polite literature in this island, and it was then found that the immeasurable licentiousness, indulged or rather applauded at court, was more destructive to the refined arts, than even the cant, nonsense, and enthusiasm of the preceding period.

Most of the celebrated writers of this age remain monuments of genius, perverted by indecency and bad taste; and none more than Dryden, both by reason of the greatness of his talents and the gross abuse which he made of them. His plays, excepting a few scenes, are utterly disfigured by vice or folly or both. His translations appear too much the offspring of haste and hunger: Even his fables are ill-chosen tales, conveyed in an incorrect, though spirited versification. Yet amidst this great number of loose productions, the refuse of our language, there are found some small pieces, his Ode to St. Cecilia, the greater part of Absalom and Achitophel, and a few more, which discover so great genius, such richness of expression, such pomp and variety of numbers, that they leave us equally full of regret and indignation, on account of the inferiority or rather great absurdity of his other writings. He died in 1701, aged 69.

The very name of Rochester is offensive to modest ears; yet does his poetry discover such energy of style and such poignancy of satire, as give ground to imagine what so fine a genius, had he fallen in a more happy age, and had followed better models, was capable of producing. The ancient satyrists often used great liberties in their expressions; but their freedom no more resembles the licentiousness of Rochester, than the nakedness of an Indian does that of a common prostitute.

Wycherley was ambitious of the reputation of wit and libertinism; and he attained it: He was probably capable of reaching the fame of true comedy, and instructive ridicule. Otway had a genius finely turned to the pathetic; but he neither observes strictly the rules of the drama, nor the rules, still more essential, of propriety and decorum. By one single piece the duke of Buckingham did both great service to his age and honour to himself. The earls of Mulgrave, Dorset, and Roscommon wrote in a good taste; but their productions are either feeble or careless. The marquess of Halifax discovers a refined genius; and nothing but leisure and an inferior station seems wanting to have procured him eminence in literature.

Of all the considerable writers of this age, Sir William Temple is almost the only one, that kept himself altogether unpolluted by that inundation of vice and licentiousness, which overwhelmed the nation. The style of this author, though extremely negligent, and even infected with foreign idioms, is agreeable and interesting. That mixture of vanity which appears in his works, is rather a recommendation to them. By means of it, we enter into acquaintance with the character of the author, full of honour and humanity; and fancy that we are engaged, not in the perusal of a book, but in conversation with a companion. He died in 1698, aged 70.

Though Hudibras was published, and probably composed during the reign of Charles II. Butler may justly, as well as Milton, be thought to belong to the foregoing period. No composition abounds so much as Hudibras in strokes of just and inimitable wit; yet are there many performances, which give us great or greater entertainment on the whole perusal. The allusions in Butler are often dark and far-fetched; and though scarcely any author was ever able to express his thoughts in so few words, he often employs too many thoughts on one subject, and thereby becomes prolix after an unusual manner. It is surprizing how much erudition Butler has introduced with so good a grace into a work of pleasantry and humour: Hudibras is perhaps one of the most learned compositions, that is to be found in any language. The advantage which the royal cause received from this poem, in exposing the

CHAPTER LXXI

fanaticism and false pretences of the former parliamentary party, was prodigious. The king himself had so good a taste as to be highly pleased with the merit of the work, and had even got a great part of it by heart: Yet was he either so careless in his temper, or so little endowed with the virtue of liberality, or more properly speaking, of gratitude, that he allowed the author, a man of virtue and probity, to live in obscurity, and die in want.[m] Dryden is an instance of a negligence of the same kind. His Absalom sensibly contributed to the victory, which the tories obtained over the whigs, after the exclusion parliaments: Yet could not this merit, aided by his great genius, procure him an establishment, which might exempt him from the necessity of writing for bread. Otway, though a professed royalist, could not even procure bread by his writings; and he had the singular fate of dying literally of hunger. These incidents throw a great stain on the memory of Charles, who had discernment, loved genius, was liberal of money, but attained not the praise of true generosity.

[m] Butler died in 1680, aged 68.

NOTES TO THE
SIXTH VOLUME

NOTE [A], p. 12

The following instance of extravagance is given by Walker, in his history of Independency, part II. p. 152. About this time, there came six soldiers into the parish church of Walton upon Thames, near twilight; Mr. Faucet, the preacher there, not having till then ended his sermon. One of the soldiers had a lanthorn in his hand, and a candle burning in it, and in the other hand four candles not lighted. He desired the parishioners to stay awhile, saying he had a message from God unto them, and thereupon offered to go into the pulpit. But the people refusing to give him leave so to do, or to stay in the church, he went into the church-yard, and there told them, that he had a vision wherein he had received a command from God, to deliver his will unto them, which he was to deliver, and they to receive upon pain of damnation; consisting of five lights. (1.) "That the sabbath was abolished as unnecessary, Jewish, and merely ceremonial. And here (quoth he) I should put out the first light, but the wind is so high I cannot kindle it. (2.) That tythes are abolished as Jewish and ceremonial, a great burthen to the saints of God, and a discouragement of industry and tillage. And here I should put out my second light, &c. (3.) That ministers are abolished as antichristian, and of no longer use, now Christ himself descends into the hearts of his saints, and his spirit enlighteneth them with revelations and inspirations. And here I should put out my third light, &c. (4.) Magistrates are abolished as useless, now that Christ himself is in purity amongst us, and hath erected the kingdom of the saints upon earth. Besides they are tyrants, and oppressors of the liberty of the saints, and tye them to laws and ordinances, mere human inventions: And here I should put out my fourth light, &c. (5.) Then putting his hand into his pocket, and pulling out a little bible, he shewed it open to the people, saying, Here is a book you have in great veneration, consisting of two parts, the old and new testament: I must tell you it is abolished; it containeth beggarly rudiments, milk for babes. But now Christ is in glory amongst us, and imparts a farther measure of his spirit to his saints than this can afford. I am commanded to burn it before your face. Then putting out the candle he said; and here my fifth light is extinguished." It became a pretty common doctrine at that time, that it was unworthy of a christian man to pay rent to his fellow-creatures; and landlords were obliged to use all the penalties of law against their tenants, whose conscience was scrupulous.

NOTE [B], p. 42

When the earl of Derby was alive, he had been summoned by Ireton to surrender the isle of Man; and he returned this spirited and memorable answer. "I receiv'd your letter with indignation, and with scorn return you this answer; that I cannot but wonder whence you should gather any hopes, that I should prove like you, treacherous to my sovereign; since you cannot be ignorant of my former actions in his late majesty's service, from which principles of loyalty I am no whit departed. I scorn your proffers; I disdain your favour; I abhor your treason; and am so far from delivering up this island to your advantage, that I shall keep it to the utmost of my power to your destruction. Take this for your final answer, and forbear any farther solicitations: For if you trouble me with any more messages of this nature, I will burn the paper and hang up the bearer. This is the immutable resolution, and shall be the undoubted practice of him, who accounts it his chiefest glory to be his majesty's most loyal and obedient subject,

"DERBY."

NOTE [C], p. 44

It had been a usual policy of the presbyterian ecclesiastics to settle a chaplain in the great families, who acted as a spy upon his master, and gave them intelligence of the most private transactions and discourses of the family. A signal instance of priestly tyranny, and the subjection of the nobility! They even obliged the servants to give intelligence against their masters. Whitlocke, p. 502. The same author, p. 512. tells the following story. The synod meeting at Perth, and citing the ministers and people, who had expressed a dislike of *their heavenly government,* the men being out of the way, their wives resolved to answer for them. And on the day of appearance, 120 women with good clubs in their hands came and besieged the church, where the reverend ministers sat. They sent one of their number to treat with the females, and he threatening excommunication, they basted him for his labour, kept him prisoner, and sent a party of 60, who routed the rest of the clergy, bruised their bodies sorely, took all their baggage and 12 horses. One of the ministers, after a mile's running, taking all creatures for his foes, meeting with a soldier, fell on his knees, who knowing nothing of the matter asked the blackcoat what he meant. The female conquerors, having laid hold on the synod clerk, beat him till he forswore his office. Thirteen ministers rallied about four miles from the place, and voted that this village should never more have a synod in it, but be accursed; and that though in the years 1638 and 39, the godly women were cried up for stoning the bishops, yet now the whole sex should be esteemed wicked.

NOTE [D], p. 89

About this time an accident had almost robbed the protector of his life, and saved his enemies the trouble of all their machinations. Having got six fine Friesland coach-horses as a present from the count of Oldenburgh, he undertook for his amusement to drive them about Hyde-park; his secretary, Thurloe, being in the coach. The horses were startled and ran away: He was unable to command them or keep the box. He fell upon the pole, was dragged upon the ground for some time; a pistol, which he carried in his pocket, went off; and by that singular good fortune which ever attended him, he was taken up without any considerable hurt or bruise.

NOTE [E], p. 134

After Monk's declaration for a free parliament on the 11th of February, he could mean nothing but the king's restoration: Yet it was long before he would open himself even to the king. This declaration was within eight days after his arrival in London. Had he ever intended to have set up for himself, he would not surely have so soon abandoned a project so inviting: He would have taken some steps, which would have betrayed it. It could only have been some disappointment, some frustrated attempt, which could have made him renounce the road of private ambition. But there is not the least symptom of such intentions. The story told of Sir Anthony Ashley Cooper, by Mr. Locke, has not any appearance of truth. See lord Lansdown's Vindication, and Philips's Continuation of Baker. I shall add to what those authors have advanced, that cardinal Mazarine wished for the king's restoration; though he would not have ventured much to have procured it.

NOTE [F], p. 214

The articles were, that he had advised the king to govern by military power without parliaments, that he had affirmed the king to be a papist or popishly affected, that he had received great sums of money for procuring the Canary patent and other illegal patents, that he had advised and procured divers of his majesty's subjects to be imprisoned against law, in remote islands and garrisons, thereby to prevent their having the benefit of the law, that he had procured the customs to be farmed at under rates, that he had received great sums from the Vintners' company, for allowing them to inhance the price of wines, that he had in a short time gained a greater estate than could have been supposed to arise from the profits of his offices, that he had introduced an arbitrary government into his majesty's plantations, that he had rejected a proposal for the preservation of Nevis and St. Christopher's, which was the occasion of great losses in those parts, that when he was in his majesty's service beyond sea he held a correspondence with Cromwel and his accomplices, that he advised the sale of Dunkirk, that he had unduly altered letters patent under the king's seal, that he had unduly decided causes in council, which should have been brought before chancery, that he had issued quo warrantos against corporations with an intention of squeezing money from them, that he had taken money for passing the bill of settlement in Ireland, that he betrayed the nation in all foreign treaties, and that he was the principal adviser of dividing the fleet in June 1666.

NOTE [G], p. 237

The abstract of the report of the Brook-house committee (so that committee was called) was first published by Mr. Ralph, vol. i. p. 177. from lord Hallifax's collections, to which I refer. If we peruse their apology, which we find in the subsequent page of the same author, we shall find, that they acted with some malignity towards the king. They would take notice of no services performed before the 1st of September 1664. But all the king's preparations preceded that date, and as chancellor Clarendon told the parliament, amounted to eight hundred thousand pounds; and the computation is very probable. This sum, therefore, must be added. The committee likewise charged seven hundred thousand pounds to the king on account of the winter and summer guards, saved during two years and ten months that the war lasted. But this seems iniquitous. For though that was an usual burthen on the revenue, which was then saved; would not the diminution of the customs during the war be an equivalent to it? Besides, near three hundred and forty thousand pounds are charged for prize-money, which perhaps the king thought he ought not to account for. These sums exceed the million and a half.

NOTE [H], p. 243

Gourville has said in his memoirs, vol. ii. p. 14, 67. that Charles was never sincere in the triple alliance; and that, having entertained a violent animosity against de Wit, he endeavoured, by this artifice, to detach him from the French alliance with a view of afterwards finding an opportunity to satiate his vengeance upon him. This account, though very little honourable to the king's memory, seems probable from the events, as well as from the authority of the author.

INDEX

INDEX

INDEX

INDEX

HISTORY OF ENGLAND

INDEX

CHARLES II *(continued)*

ministry, 240. The counsels instilled into him by, 241. Is prevailed on to desert his triple alliance, and to league with France, by his sister the duchess of Orleans, 244. Is influenced also by his French mistress, the duchess of Portsmouth, *ib.* Pardons Blood for his attempt on the regalia, and promotes him, 250. Bestows a peerage and the treasurer's staff on Sir Thomas Clifford, for his expedient of shutting up the exchequer, 253. A second declaration of indulgence, 254. Suspension of the navigation act, 254. Martial law revived, *ib.* Declares war against the Dutch, 255. His reflections on the successes of Lewis in the Low Countries, 266. His demands from the States, 267. His speech to parliament, 272. His declaration of indulgence opposed by the commons, 274. Recals the declaration, 275. Prorogues the parliament, 281. Asks advice of parliament respecting making peace with the Dutch, 282. Peace concluded, *ib.* Proof of his entering into a scheme for restoring popery, 286, note. Duplicity of his conduct on this occasion, *ib.* Sir William Temple's free remonstrance to him, 289. Is unable to obtain a supply for taking off anticipations of his revenue, 295. Suppresses coffee houses by proclamation, 296. Recalls the proclamation, *ib.* His embarrassed situation at the time of the congress of Nimeguen, 302. His speech to parliament, 303. Is exhorted by parliament to guard against the growing power of France, 305. Requests supplies, and pledges his honour for the proper application of them, *ib.* Is addressed by the parliament to form an alliance with the States against France, 308. Adjourns the parliament, *ib.* Secretly signs a treaty with France, and obtains a pension from that court, on promise of his neutrality, 308. Receives the prince of Orange at Newmarket, 309. Concludes a marriage between him and the princess Mary, 310. Concerts the terms of peace with the prince, 311. Sends the terms to Paris, *ib.*, 312. His instructions to Sir William Temple, with Temple's reply, 313. Concludes an alliance with the States, to oblige France to peace, *ib.* The parliament still distrustful of him, 314. Receives a passionate address from the commons, 315. Concludes a treaty with the States to oblige Louis to an immediate evacuation of the towns in Flanders, 316. His conduct in regard to the treaty of Nimeguen, 320. His observation on the complaints made of Lauderdale's administration in Scotland, 330. Is warned of a popish plot, 333. Publishes proclamations for the discovery of the murderers of Sir Edmondbury Godfrey, 344. His speech to parliament, *ib.* Ridicules the popish plot privately, 348. Protects his queen from the accusation of Oates and Bedloe, 350. Refuses to pass the militia bill, *ib.* His private contract with Lewis, for the peace of Nimeguen, discovered by Danby's letters, in the house of commons, 351. Dissolves the parliament to screen Danby, 352. Is obliged to summon a parliament again for money, 356. Desires his brother to retire beyond sea, 358. Declares the illegitimacy of the duke of Monmouth, *ib.* Asserts the prerogative of rejecting the speaker chosen by the commons, 359. The pretension compromised, *ib.* Asserts his intention of protecting Danby against the resentment of the commons, 360. Chuses a new council by the advice of Sir William Temple, 362. A list of the new council, 363. Proposes to parliament, limitations on a popish successor to the crown, 364. Habeas corpus act passed, 366. The parliament takes advantage of his necessities, 367. Prorogues, and after dissolves the parliament, 369. The popularity of his behaviour, 377. Is prevailed on by the duke of York to deprive Monmouth of his command, and send him abroad, 378. Is strongly petitioned for a parliament, 381. His speech to the new parliament, 383. Evades passing a repeal of the thirty-fifth of Elizabeth, 398. Dissolves the parliament, and summons another to meet at Oxford, 399. His speech to the new parliament, 400. Dissolves it, 403. Persecutes the dissenters, 419. Issues a writ of *quo warranto* against the city of London, 421. Conditions on which he restored the charter, 424. Makes profit by the surrender of corporation charters, *ib.* How he escaped the Rye-house plot, 428. His motives for not sparing lord Russel, 433. Marries the lady Anne to prince George of Denmark, 442. Particulars of a

INDEX

INDEX

INDEX

COMMONS (*continued*)

demned, *ib*. Accuse the judges for their determination on Hambden's trial, *ib*. Expel monopolists and projectors, *ib*. Remarks on their proceedings, 293. Reverse the sentences of the star-chamber on Prynne and others, 295. The rapid progress of their regulations, 297. Agree to pay the Scots army, 298. Begin to attack episcopal authority, 301. Harass the clergy, 302. Vote a removal of all catholics from the army, 304. Make limited grants of tonnage and poundage, 306. Frame a bill for triennial parliaments, which is passed, 307. Pass a bill of attainder against Strafford, 320. Form a protestation, and order it to be signed by the whole nation, 322. Are offended at the king's interposition for Strafford, 323. Disband the English and Scots armies on the king's journey to Scotland, 331. Insist on the reduction of the Irish army raised by Strafford to reduce the Scots, 337. Oppose their being hired by the Spaniards, 337. Their zeal for the presbyterian discipline, 348. Credit the report of the Irish massacre being ordered by the king, 349. An account of the famous remonstrance framed by them, 351. Pass the remonstrance, and publish it without sending it up to the lords, 352. Reasoning of the parties on both sides with regard to it, *ib*. Present the remonstrance to the king on his return, 356. Pass the bill for pressing soldiers for Ireland, 358. The interposition of peers in elections declared to be a breach of privilege, *ib*. Their proceedings against the bishops, 359. Declare to the lords an intention of rejecting their authority, if opposed by them, 360. Excite apprehensions in the people, 361. Impeach the bishops, who sign a protestation, 363. Five members impeached by the king, 365. The impeached members are demanded, 366. Are demanded by the king in person, *ib*. Adjourn the house on this occasion, 367. Order a committee to sit in merchant-taylors-hall, 368. The accused members take their seats, 369. Messages between them and the king, 370. Encourage petitions from the common people, 371. Impeach the attorney-general, and prosecute their plan of the militia, 374. Form a magazine at Hull, and appoint Sir John Hotham governor, *ib*. Appoint governors of Portsmouth and the Tower, *ib*. Warn the kingdom to prepare for a defence against papists and ill-affected persons, *ib*. Appoint all the lieutenants of counties, and restore their powers, 375. Press the king by messages to pass the bill, 376. His reply, 377. Their vote on this reply, *ib*. Carry the militia bill into execution, without the king's concurrence, 379. Vote all to be traitors who assist the king, 382. Raise an army, and appoint the earl of Essex general, 383. For those transactions wherein both houses concur, see *Parliament*. Carry an impeachment of the queen up to the lords, 434. Pass the self-denying ordinance, 448. Chuse Henry Pelham speaker in the room of Lenthal, on his going to the army, 508. Their violent accusation against the king, 517. Pass a vote for bringing the king to a trial, 533. This vote being refused by the lords, they pass an ordinance for bringing him to trial by their own authority, *ib*. Vote the house of lords useless, and abolish monarchy, 546. Readmit some of the secluded members, vi. 5. Name a council to carry on the administration of government, 6. Enlarge the laws of high treason, 13. Dissolution of by Cromwel, 53. Retrospect of their proceedings, *ib*. Character of Barebone's parliament, 60. In the protector's parliament, refuse to acknowledge the house of lords summoned by him, 99. The new house of, after the final dissolution of the long parliament, meet and chuse Sir Harbottle Grimstone speaker, 138. Receive a letter from Charles II and appoint a committee to answer it, *ib*. The king proclaimed, 139. Vote presents to the king and his brothers, *ib*. Pass a vote against the indignities practised by the Dutch toward the English trade, 191. Impeach the earl of Clarendon, 213. Oblige the king to pass the act against the importation of Irish cattle, 231. Address the king for a proclamation against conventicles, 235. Obstruct the tolerating maxims of the court, *ib*. Resent the lords taking cognizance of Skinner's case, 236. As also with their altering a money bill, 248. Coventry act on what occasion passed, *ib*. Vacancies supplied by writs from the chancellor, annulled, 273. Grants to the

INDEX

Cromwel *(continued)*

independents, 443. Differences between him and the earl of Manchester, 444. His speech in parliament relative to the self-denying ordinance, 447. How he eluded the self-denying ordinance as to himself, 449. His character, 450. New models the army, 468. The fanatical spirit of the officers and soldiers, 469. Commands the right wing at the battle of Naseby, 472. His successes afterward, 476. Foments the discontents of the army, 496. Is the secret cause of the king being seized by the army, 498. His profound hypocrisy, *ib.* Is chosen general by the army, *ib.* Marches the army toward London against the parliament, 499. Retires to Reading, 504. Pays court to the king, and enters privately into treaty with him, 505. The army marches to London, 508. Remarks on his conduct between the king and parliament, 510. Suppresses the agitators, and reduces the army to obedience, 513. Calls a meeting of officers at Windsor, to settle the nation, wherein it is resolved to bring the king to a trial, 514. Prevails with the parliament to vote against all further treaty with the king, 516. Defeats Langdale and Hamilton, and marches into Scotland, 527. Sends a remonstrance to the parliament on its treating with the king, 529. Seizes the king, and confines him in Hurst-castle, *ib.* Marches the army to London, to purge the parliament, 530. His speech in the house on the ordinance for bringing the king to a trial, 533. Is appointed one of the king's judges, 534. His hypocritical conduct toward Fairfax, during the time of the king's execution, 541. His general character, and great influence in the army, vi. 5. Is named one of the council of state, 6. Procures himself to be appointed lord-lieutenant of Ireland, 11. Suppresses the agitators, 12. Arrives at Dublin, 14. Storms Tredah, and puts the garrison to the sword, 15. Storms Wexford with the same cruelty, *ib.* All Munster submits to him, 16. Takes Kilkenny, *ib.* Leaves Ireland, 28. Is declared captain-general of all the forces in England, and marches an army to Scotland, 29. Is forced to retire, and is followed by Lesley, 30. Defeats Lesley at Dunbar, *ib.* Writes polemical letters to the Scots clergy, 31. Follows Charles II into England, 34. Defeats Charles at Worcester, 35. Summons a council of officers to remonstrate to the parliament for a new election, 51. Expels the members from the house, and locks the door, 53. An account of his birth and private life, 55. Receives addresses on the dissolution of the parliament, 58. Summons a new parliament, 60. His address to it, 61, note. The parliament resigns up its authority to him, 63. Is declared protector, 64. His powers, *ib.* Makes peace with the Dutch, 67. Executes the Portugueze ambassador's brother, for assassination, 68. Summons a parliament, *ib.* His equitable regulation of elections, 69. Discontents against his administration, *ib.* The parliament disputes his authority, 70. Dissolves it, after obtaining a recognition, 71. An insurrection of royalists at Salisbury suppressed, 73. Divides England into twelve military jurisdictions, under major-generals, to suppress the royalists, *ib.* Issues letters of reprisals against France, 77. His influence over the French minister Mazarine, 78. Reflections on his foreign negociations, 79. Sends a fleet under Blake to the Mediterranean, 80. Sends a fleet under Pen and Venables to the West Indies, 81. Jamaica taken, *ib.* Sends Pen and Venables to the Tower, 82. The vigor of his foreign transactions, 85. His domestic administration, *ib.* Establishes a militia, 86. Establishes a commission of *Tryers,* to present to ecclesiastical benefices, 87. His general conduct in religious matters, *ib.* His address in procuring secret intelligence, 88. His general deportment, 89. His vein of pleasantry sometimes leads him into inconsistencies; instanced in an anecdote, 90. His plan of administration in Scotland, 91. In Ireland, 92. Endeavour to be made king, 93. Destroys the authority of the major-generals, *ib.* The crown is offered to him by parliament, 94. Is afraid to venture on it, 95. Extract from his speech on refusing it, 96, note. The motives of his refusal, 97. His protectoral authority confirmed by parliament, 98. Brings his son Richard to court, and marries his daughters, 99. Summons a new parliament in two houses, as formerly, *ib.* Dissolves it, on his house of peers not being

INDEX

INDEX

INDEX

INDEX

INDEX

INDEX

INDEX

HENRY *(continued)*
Scotland, 293. Invested with the dutchy of Normandy, *ib.* Marries Eleanor, daughter of William duke of Guienne, 294. His succession to the crown of England confirmed by Stephen, *ib.* His continental possessions at his accession, 299.

HENRY II, The first acts of his government, i. 301. Goes over to quiet his brother Geoffrey, *ib.* Punishes the incursions of the Welsh, *ib.* Visits the king of France, and contracts his infant son Henry to Margaret daughter of France, 302. His acquisitions on the continent, 303. Compounds the personal service of his Norman vassals for money, 304. His wars in France, *ib.* Accommodates his differences with Lewis by the pope's mediation, 305. Opposes the encroachments of the clergy, 306. His grateful remembrance of Theobald archbishop of Canterbury, *ib.* Creates Thomas a Becket chancellor, 307. Instance of his familiarity with him, 308. Makes him archbishop of Canterbury, 309. Provoked by his arbitrary conduct, 311. Calls an assembly of the clergy, to acknowledge a submission to the civil laws, 313. Determines to check the clerical usurpations, 314. Constitutions of Clarendon, *ib.* Applies to the pope for a legatine commission, which is rendered abortive by the pope, 317. Procures Becket to be sued for some lands, *ib.* Calls a council at Northampton, at which Becket is condemned for contempt, 318. Makes another demand on Becket, 319. Sequesters the revenues of Canterbury on Becket's flight, 323. Inhibits all appeals to the pope, *ib.* Suspends the payment of Peter's pence, 325. Endeavours at an alliance with the Emperor Frederic Barbarossa, *ib.* An accommodation prevented by the inflexibility of Becket, 326. Obtains a dispensation for the marriage of his third son Geoffrey with the heiress of Britany, *ib.* Several ineffectual attempts of reconciliation with Becket. 327. Detaches Lewis from Becket by his fair conduct, 328. Is reconciled to Becket, *ib.* Associates his son Henry with him in the regal dignity, 329. His exclamations on hearing the continuance of Becket's arbitrary behaviour, and the consequences, 332. His perplexity on the murder of Becket, 334. His submissions to the pope on the occasion, 335. Imposes a tax for the holy war, 337. Goes on an expedition to Ireland, 338. Solicits a grant of that island from Rome, 340. How prevented from the immediate execution of it, 341. Goes over to Ireland, and finds it already subdued by Strongbow and his associates, 343. This conquest improperly secured, 344. Recalled from Ireland by the menaces of the legates Albert and Theodin, to answer at the inquiry into Becket's murder, 345. His concessions to them on that occasion, *ib.* Receives absolution, 346. Review of his present flourishing situation, *ib.* Assigns portions to his sons, 347. His eldest son Henry revolts against him, 348, as do Geoffrey and Richard, at the instigation of queen Eleanor, 349. Confines his queen, *ib.* Appeals in vain to the pope against his sons, *ib.* Employs a body of Brabançons, 350. Deceived by king Lewis of France, before Vernoüil, 352. Quells the disturbances in Britany, *ib.* An ineffectual conference with Lewis, 352. His conduct in this critical situation, 353. Returns to quell the commotions in England, and does penance at Becket's tomb, 355. Raises the siege of Roüen, 357. Makes peace with his sons, *ib.* Exacts homage of William king of Scotland, taken prisoner by his forces, and of all the Scots nobles, for his ransom and crown, 358. Reforms the administration of justice in his dominions, 359. Demolishes the new erected castles of his nobility, 360. Provides for the defence of the kingdom, *ib.* Punishes the murderers of Thomas a Becket, 361. Mediates a peace between Philip, king of France, and his family, 363. His son Henry revolts again, but submits, *ib.* His grief for his son Henry's death, 364. His son Geoffrey rebels again, *ib.* Is guardian to Geoffrey's posthumous son, *ib.* Engages in a crusade, 366. Raises a tenth of moveables to carry it on, *ib.* War between him and Philip of France, occasioned by another revolt of his son Richard, *ib.* Disadvantageous peace, 369. His grief at finding John a party in Richard's revolt, *ib.* Dies, *ib.* His character, 370. Miscellaneous transactions in his reign, 371. Manners of his court, *ib.* His vig-

INDEX

INDEX

Henry VIII (*continued*)

and convocation, *ib.* Fixes his affections on the lady Catharine Howard, 275. Is influenced by the duke of Norfolk to commit Cromwel to the Tower, *ib.* Cromwel's moving letter to him, 276. Is divorced from Anne of Cleves, 277. Concludes an alliance with the emperor, 278. Marries Catharine Howard, 279. Persecutes the reformers, *ib.* Makes a progress into the north, 280. Exhorts the king of Scotland to seize the church revenues, 282. James evades a promised interview with him, 283. Is informed by Cranmer of the queen's dissolute conduct, *ib.* The queen attainted, with her associates, 284; and executed, 286. Dissolves divers colleges, hospitals, and other foundations, and seizes their revenues, *ib.* Extorts a surrender of chapter-lands from divers bishops, 287. Ireland erected into a kingdom, and added to his titles, 478, note. Mitigates the penalties of the six articles, so far as regards the marriage of priests, 287. Appoints a commission to establish a religion for the nation, *ib.* Writes and publishes his *Institution of a Christian Man,* 288. Publishes the *Erudition of a Christian Man, ib.* Prohibits the lower classes of people to read the scriptures, 289. Reviews and alters the mass-book, *ib.* Suppresses the interludes in ridicule of the former superstitions, 290. Publishes a manifesto, previous to his war with Scotland, 291. Sir Robert Bowes defeated by the Scots, 292. Battle of Solway, 293. Death of James, 294. Proposes a marriage to the Scots nobles, between prince Edward and the infant queen of Scotland, *ib.* This marriage contracted by treaty, with the earl of Arran, 296. Is disgusted with Francis, 298. Leagues with the emperor against Francis, *ib.* Obedience to his *Erudition of a Christian Man* enforced by parliament, 300. Marries Catharine Par, *ib.* Influences parliament to restore the princesses Mary and Elizabeth to their right of succession, dependent on his will, 303. His regal style settled, 304. Is released by parliament from his debts, contracted by a general loan, *ib.* Requires new loans from his people, and raises the value of specie, *ib.* Extorts a benevolence from his people, *ib.* Invades Scotland, and burns Edinburgh, 305. Concerts an invasion of France with the emperor, 306. Passes over to France, and leaves the queen regent, *ib.* Takes Boulogne, 307. Charles makes a separate war with Francis, *ib.* Returns to England, *ib.* Subsidies granted him by parliament and convocation, 310. Obtains a parliamentary grant of university revenues, which he declines, *ib.* The gross flattery of parliament to him, 311. His speech on proroguing it, *ib.* Sends the earl of Hertford with forces over to Calais, *ib.* Makes peace with France and Scotland, 312. His high encomium on the duke of Suffolk at his death, 313. Protects Cranmer against the cabals of his catholic courtiers, *ib.* The queen's tender care of him in his illness, 316. Orders her to be impeached for heresy, *ib.* Her prudent caution in evading this danger, *ib.* Abuses Wriothesely on his coming to take the queen to the Tower, 317. Commits the duke of Norfolk, and earl of Surry to the Tower, 319. Trial and execution of Surry, *ib.* Expedites the proceedings against Norfolk, 320. Orders him for execution, *ib.* Dies, *ib.* His behaviour at his death, 321. The succession, how settled by his will, *ib.* His character, *ib.* The number of parliaments summoned by him, 323. His rigorous and contradictory statutes against heresy and treason, 324. A recapitulation of his statutes, *ib.* His military laws, 325. Tonnage and poundage arbitrarily levied by him, 326. State of commerce in this reign, *ib.* His laws to restrain the decay of tillage, and throwing lands into pasturage, 330. His attention to the advancement of literature, 331. List of the regency appointed by his will, during the minority of Edward VI, 334.

Henry, prince of Wales, eldest son of James I, his death and character, v. 50.

Henry, bishop of Winchester. See *Winchester.*

Henry II of France, his character, iii. 344. His conduct toward the protestant league in Germany, *ib.* Makes an ineffectual attempt on Boulogne, 374. His treaty with England for the surrender of Boulogne, 381. Agrees to a marriage between his daughter Elizabeth and Edward VI, *ib.* Invades Germany, in favour of Maurice, elector of Saxony, 412. The emperor repulsed from Metz, 413. Montmorency defeated at St. Quintin, 453. Calais taken, *ib.* Requires the queen-

INDEX

HISTORY OF ENGLAND

INDEX

INDEX

INDEX

INDEX

INDEX

PAGET, secretary, remonstrates to lord Seymour the impropriety of caballing against his brother, the protector, iii. 359. Informs the protector of his practices, and advises him to return from Scotland, to guard against them, *ib.* Adheres to Somerset in his distress, 377. Advises Mary to the Spanish alliance, 413.

PALATINATE OF THE RHINE, See *Frederic.* The English undertake the recovery of it, v. 119. The attempt fails, *ib.* Treaty of Westphalia, vi. 75.

PALESTINE, state of, at the arrival of the crusader, Richard I of England, and Philip of France, i. 387.

PALMER, Mrs. See *Cleveland.*

PALMER, Sir Thomas, is employed by Northumberland as a spy upon Somerset, iii. 388. His accusation against Somerset, *ib.* Is apprehended for joining the party of the lady Jane Gray, 405. Is executed, 406.

PANDOLF, legate from pope Innocent III to Philip in his expedition against king John of England; his private instructions, i. 431. Proposes an interview with John, *ib.* Procures his submission to the pope, 432. Receives the resignation of his kingdom, and homage from him, *ib.* Excommunicates the earl of Albemarle and his adherents, ii. 11.

PAPACY, the seat of, how fixed in Italy, ii. 329.

PAPAL AUTHORITY, the popular sentiments of, in the reign of Edward III, ii. 278. Renounced by Henry VIII, iii. 205. See *Reformation.*

PAR, Catharine, married to Henry VIII, iii. 300. Is made regent during Henry's absence in France, 306. Her narrow escape from impeachment for heresy, 316. Her prudent evasion of this danger, *ib.* Marries lord Seymour soon after Henry's death, 359. Dies in child-bed, 360.

PARIS, massacre of the Hugonots in that city, on the eve of St. Bartholomew, iv. 163. See *France.*

PARKER, archbishop, his character, iv. 207.

PARKER, bishop of Oxford, is violently appointed president of Magdalen-hall, by James II, vi. 488.

PARLIAMENT, English, a view of, in its feudal form, i. 466. By what titles the clergy obtained seats in, *ib.* The importance of the barons in, *ib.* The commons not originally a part of, 467. Composed wholly of military tenants, *ib.* When usually assembled, 471. That summoned at Oxford in the minority of Henry III grants, in his name, a renewal and confirmation of the great charter, ii. 12. Refuses supplies to Henry, 21, 26. The spirited remonstrances of, to the king, on his demand of a supply, 30. Grants a supply on a solemn confirmation of the great charter, 32. Assembles dressed in armour, 34. That termed the *mad* one, meets at Oxford, 35. A supreme council of twenty-four chosen by, to regulate the government, *ib.* The first efforts toward sending representatives of counties to, *ib.* Regular sessions of, appointed by the council of barons, 36. A committee appointed by the council of twenty-four, of equal authority with, to act in the intervals of the sessions, 38. One called by Henry, which authorises him to resume the government, in consequence of the pope's absolution, 44. One summoned by Leicester after the battle of Lewes, which appoints a council of nine to administer government, 54. Again summoned by Leicester, and the house of commons regularly formed, 56. Approves of the ordinances of the reforming barons, after the civil wars were ended, 66. Other laws enacted in the reign of Henry III, *ib.* The first summoned by Edward I reforms the administration of justice, 75. The barons prohibited coming to, except summoned by writ, 102. Grant supplies to Edward for a French war, 114. Is awed into a confirmation of the two charters, by the earls of Norfolk and Hereford, while the king is in Flanders, 120. A summary view of the supplies granted to Edward I, 144. The banishment of Piers Gavaston demanded by Thomas earl of Lancaster, 150. Procures the government to be vested in a council of twelve, 152. Passes a sentence of forfeiture and perpetual exile against the Despencers, 162. Deposes Edward II, 171. A council of regency formed by, to act during the minority of

PARLIAMENT *(continued)*

Edward III, 183. Ratifies Mortimer's treaty with Robert Bruce, 186. Condemns Mortimer to death, 188. Assists the king in his endeavours to restore Edward Baliol in Scotland, and its advice to him, 194. Grants supplies to assist the pretensions of Edward to the crown of France, 202. Is summoned by prince Edward during his father's absence in Flanders, but no supplies obtained, 205. Remarks on the present power of, *ib.* Its conditional grants to the king, 206. Resolutions of, on his assumed title as king of France, 207. Frames an act for redress of grievances before the making the required grants, 214. Is prevailed on to repeal this act, 216. Advises the king to break the truce with Philip, and makes grants for the renewal of the war, 223. The consideration it arrived to, in the reign of Edward III, 273. Its frequent endeavours to abolish purveyance in this reign, 275. Attempts in vain to reduce the price of labour, 281. Settlement of government established by, during the minority of Richard II, 286. Is dissolved, and the increase of its authority shewn, 287. Imposes a poll-tax, and the alarming consequences of it, 289. Its peremptory deputation to the king, 296. Its undue compact with the duke of Gloucester and his party, 299. Proceedings against the ministry, 300. The irregularity of their conduct, 302. Influence of the king over, and their compliance with his measures, 303. Adjourned to Shrewsbury, 311. Grants Richard the duties on wool and leather for life, with other subsidies, *ib.* Before their dissolution vest the parliamentary authority in a committee of twelve lords and six commoners, *ib.* Names of the commissioners, *ib.* note. Heads of the accusation presented to, against king Richard, 317. Depose him, 321. Act against heresy, 328. Repealed, *ib.* The repeal suppressed by the influence of the clergy, *ib.* Confusions in, at the accession of Henry IV, 334. Opposes his attempt to exclude females from the succession, 348. Advises the king to seize the temporalities of the church, *ib.* Renews the same advice to Henry V, *ib.,* 357. Grants to Henry, after the battle of Azincour, 367, 374. Causes which contributed to increase its influence in government, 382. Appoints a new arrangement of administration during the minority of Henry VI, *ib.* Refuses supplies to the duke of Bedford, regent of France, 405. One called at St. Edmondsbury, 420. Makes the duke of York protector during pleasure, 442. Resumes all the grants to the crown since the time of Henry V, 443. That of Coventry, remarks on, 453. The title of Edward IV recognized by, 459. Attainders reversed, *ib.* Act of forfeiture and attainder passed against Henry VI and his queen, and their party, 460. Summoned, at the restoration of Henry VI, 476. New system of attainders and reversals, *ib.* Summoned by Edward on his restoration, 483. Their grants to the king toward a French war, 484. Reflections on the consistency of their proceedings, 491. One summoned by Richard III recognizes his authority, creates his son prince of Wales, and makes grants, 513. Attainders reversed on the coming in of Henry VII, iii. 9. Expedient for qualifying the king's prior attainder, 10. Entail of the crown, how managed, *ib.* Attainders of the York party, 12. Grants a supply for the assistance of the duke of Britanny, 32. Grants supplies to the king for a war with France, 39. Passes a law to indemnify all who act under the authority of the king for the time being, 50. Grants Henry another subsidy, 55. Its obsequiousness to his oppressive measures, 68. Chuses Dudley, the minister of his extortions, speaker, *ib.* Starchamber authority confirmed by, 74. The king's suit for murder limited within a year and day, 75. Benefit of clergy abridged, *ib.* Statutes against retainers, and for other salutary purposes, *ib.* Law permitting the entailment of estates to be broke, 77. Review of other laws passed by Henry VII, *ib.* The first of Henry VIII attaints Empson and Dudley, the ministers of the extortions of Henry VII, 86. Redresses some abuses in the late reign, *ib.* note. Grants supplies for a war with France, 91. Imposes a proportional poll-tax, 96. Grants of, to Henry, by the influence of cardinal Wolsey, and of Sir Thomas More, 148. Passes an act against levying annates, 195. Continues to abridge the papal authority, in the regulation

PARLIAMENT *(continued)*
of monasteries, and election of bishops, 203. The succession of the crown regulated, 204. Declares the king supreme head of the church, 206. Attaints Sir Thomas More, and bishop Fisher, *ib.* Unites England and Wales, *ib.* Passes an act of attainder against the accomplices of *the Holy Maid of Kent,* 219. The lesser monasteries suppressed by, 229. Farther progress made in the union between England and Wales, 230. The gross flattery of the speaker of the commons to the king, 240. Reason assigned for annulling the king's marriage with Anne Boleyn, *ib.* The princesses Mary and Elizabeth illegitimated, and the succession settled on the king's issue by Jane Seymour, *ib.* All authority of the bishop of Rome renounced, 241. Passes the bill of six articles, for abolishing diversity of opinions in religion, 265. Enacts that royal proclamations shall have the force of laws, 266. Yet passes a statute declaring that the king's proclamations shall not infringe the laws or customs of the realm, *ib.* Confirms the surrender of the monasteries, 268. Dissolves the order of St. John of Jerusalem, or knights of Malta, 274. Grants, with reluctance, supplies to Henry, *ib.* Instance of its servile compliance with Henry's caprices, 478. Condemns Dr. Barnes for heresy, 279. Attaints queen Catharine Howard and her associates, 285. Passes an act to secure the virtue of Henry's future wives, 286. Ireland erected into a kingdom by, 478. Ratifies the future decisions of the commissioners appointed by the king to establish a religion, 287. Prohibits the reading of the Bible to the lower classes of people, 289. Grants supplies for a French war, 299. Enacts that offences against the king's proclamations shall be judged by a council of nine, *ib.* Enforces obedience to the *Erudition of a Christian Man,* published by Henry VIII, 300. Restores the princesses Mary and Elizabeth to their right of succession, 303. The style of the king's regal title settled, *ib.* The king's debts contracted by a general loan remitted, *ib.* Another oath of the king's supremacy imposed, 304. The law of the six articles mitigated, *ib.* Grants another subsidy, 310. Bestows on the king all the university and hospital revenues, *ib.* The abject flattery bestowed on the king, 311. Henry's speech to, on proroguing it, *ib.* Attainder of the duke of Norfolk, 319. A recapitulation of the statutes passed by Henry VIII, 324. Remarks on the statute granting him the duties of tonnage and poundage, 326. One summoned by the duke of Somerset, protector, 353. The wholesome laws passed this session, *ib.* Lord Seymour condemned, 363. Celibacy recommended to the clergy, but their marriage permitted, 365. Heavy taxes laid on money and trade, 480, note. Deprives the protector of all his offices, and fines him, 379. Passes a severe act against rioters, *ib.* Interest for money declared illegal, 390. The new liturgy authorised, *ib.* Acts passed, against treason, and making provision for the poor, *ib.* The Latin mass celebrated in, at the accession of queen Mary, 410. The species of treason limited, *ib.* The queen's legitimacy established, *ib.* All Edward's statutes of religion repealed, *ib.* The duke of Norfolk's attainder reversed, 411. Is dissolved, for opposing the Spanish alliance, 414. A large sum sent over by the emperor Charles V to bribe the new one, 422. Gardiner's speech at the opening of, 423. The caution of, with respect to the pretensions of Philip, *ib.* Is dissolved, 424. A new one summoned, which reverses the attainder of cardinal Pole, 425. Implores forgiveness of the pope, for their defection from the church of Rome, 426. Its caution to prevent the resumption of church-lands, 427. Revives the sanguinary laws against heretics, *ib.* Tenths and first-fruits restored to the church, 443. Subsidies granted by a new one, 458. All sales or grants of crown-lands by the queen, for seven years to come, confirmed, *ib.* Law for regulating the militia, 463. The first law for repair of the highways by a general parish-duty, 464. The joy discovered at the accession of queen Elizabeth, iv. 4. A new one called, by whom the title of the queen is recognized, 9. The newly-erected monasteries suppressed, 10. All statutes of Edward VI concerning religion, restored, 11. The nomination of bishops given to the crown, *ib.* The mass abolished, and liturgy restored, 12. The queen's royal power over all her domin-

PARLIAMENT *(continued)*

ions strongly asserted, and the assertion of the papal authority subjected to the penalties of treason, 61. Laws against prophesying and witchcraft, 62. Supplies granted to the queen, *ib.* Elizabeth's speech at the dissolution of, 82. A new one summoned, after an interval of five years, 137. Is prohibited by the queen's order, from meddling with any matters of state, 138. Reflections on her haughty treatment of, and her declared notions of the proper objects of its attention, 144. Laws passed this session of, 146. A spirited speech of Peter Wentworth, a commoner, in favour of liberty of speech in, 178. *Petitions* the queen for church reformation, instead of proceeding on the bill introduced for that purpose, 181. Supplies granted by, to the queen, 186. Laws against popery, 187. Confirms the association for the protection of the queen, 204. Appoints a regency, in case of her violent death, 205. A severe law against Jesuits and popish priests, *ib.* Elizabeth's speech, on the applications made by the commons for farther religious reformation, 209. Ratifies the sentence against Mary, queen of Scots, and petitions for her execution, 237. Grants supplies to the queen, on the defeat of the Spanish armada, 271. Passes a severe law against recusants, 287. Votes supplies, 288. The queen's speech to, 289. Its legislative power checked by Elizabeth, 363. Tyrannical statutes passed by, 366. One summoned by James I, v. 13. Appoints commissioners at the king's desire, to treat of an union between the two kingdoms, 21. Becomes jealous of the regal prerogative in ecclesiastical affairs, 43. Buckingham lays before it an insincere account of the treaty for Spanish match, which the king and prince vouch, 112. The king's speech relative to a war with Spain, 113. An act against monopolies, 114. One summoned by Charles I on his accession, 156. Its ill-humour, owing to disgust against Buckingham, 158. Other contributing causes, *ib.* Is adjourned to Oxford on account of the plague, 161. The king lays his necessities before it, 162. Refuses supplies, *ib.* Dissolved, on the plague appearing at Oxford, 166. A second called by Charles, *ib.* A third summoned, 187. The king's threatening address to it, *ib.* The petition of right passed, 197; which is followed by a grant of supplies, 200. Is dissolved, 215. Is summoned after eleven years interval, 269. The king's pleas to procure supplies, 270. Is abruptly dissolved, 276. Meeting of the long, 285. An act for triennial parliaments, passed, 308. Attainder of Strafford, 324. Act against adjourning and proroguing the parliament without its own consent, 325. The star-chamber, and high-commission court, abolished, 328. Other arbitrary courts suppressed, 330. Adjourns, and appoints a committee of both houses to sit during the recess, 331. Appoints a committee to attend the king of Scotland, *ib.* Makes a present, with acknowledgments, to the Scottish army, which are now disbanded, 332. A day of thanksgiving appointed for the national pacification, *ib.* Applies to the earl of Essex for a guard, 335. Votes the king's interfering in a bill depending in, to be a breach of privileges, 358. Reflections on the uncertainty of parliamentary privileges, *ib.* Petitions or addresses received from divers bodies of the common people, promising to protect its privileges, 371. Is petitioned by a body of women, *ib.* The bishops' votes taken away, 373. Threatens the queen with an impeachment, *ib.* Passes the militia-bill, 375. Raises an army, and appoints the Earl of Essex general, 383. Obtains loans of the people, *ib.* Sends conditions of agreement to the king, 384. Stops all remittances of revenue to the king, 388. Their fleet intercepts supplies from the queen to the king, *ib.* Its haughty reception of the king's overtures, 391. Votes an address for a treaty after the battle of Edge-hill, 397. Its demands in the negociation at Oxford, 399. For the operations of its forces against the king; see *Essex, Waller, Fairfax, Cromwel,* &c. The military operations conducted by a committee of both houses, 411. The secret measures and despotic authority of this committee, *ib.* Applies to Scotland for assistance, 419. Sends commissioners to engage the Scots to confederate with them, 422. Receives and enforces subscriptions to the solemn league and covenant, 423. Remits money to Scotland, to raise an army, 424. Measures taken to

HISTORY OF ENGLAND

INDEX

INDEX

INDEX

HISTORY OF ENGLAND

INDEX

INDEX

INDEX

INDEX

INDEX

INDEX

INDEX

INDEX

INDEX

INDEX

INDEX

INDEX

F I N I S.